The History *of* Nations

MEXICO
CENTRAL AMERICA
AND
WEST INDIES

GHENT
EDITION

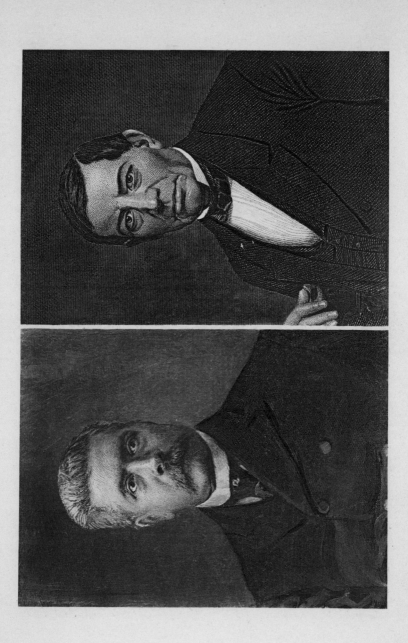

PORFIRIO DIAZ
(Born 1830. Died ————)

From a Photograph

—page 398

BENITO PABLO JUAREZ
(Born 1806. Died 1872)

From a Photograph

—page 383

THE HISTORY OF NATIONS

HENRY CABOT LODGE, Ph. D., LL. D. · EDITOR-IN-CHIEF

MEXICO
CENTRAL AMERICA

AND

WEST INDIES

EDITED FROM THE WORK OF

BRANTZ MAYER

BY FREDERICK ALBION OBER

VOLUME XXII

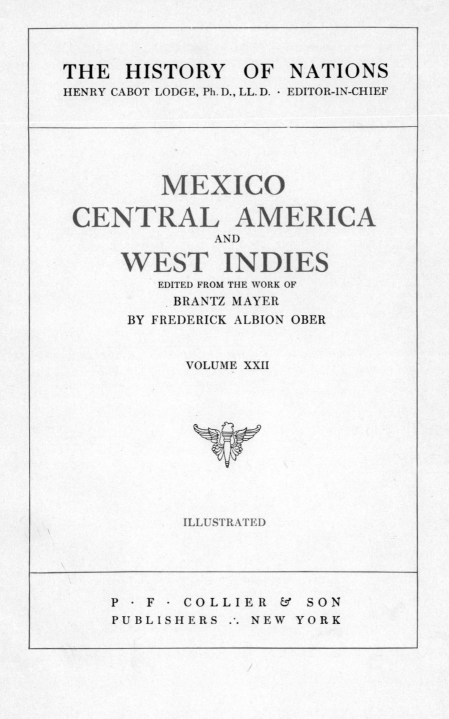

ILLUSTRATED

P · F · COLLIER & SON

PUBLISHERS ∴ NEW YORK

Designed Printed, and Bound at
The Collier Press, New York

THE HISTORY OF NATIONS

EDITOR-IN-CHIEF

HENRY CABOT LODGE, Ph.D., LL.D.

Associate Editors and Authors

ARCHIBALD HENRY SAYCE, LL.D.,
> Professor of Assyriology, Oxford University

CHRISTOPHER JOHNSTON, M.D., Ph.D.,
> Associate Professor of Oriental History and Archaeology, Johns Hopkins University

C. W. C. OMAN,
> Professor of History, Oxford University

THEODOR MOMMSEN,
> Late Professor of Ancient History, University of Berlin

ARTHUR C. HOWLAND, Ph.D.,
> Department of History, University of Pennsylvania

CHARLES MERIVALE, LL.D.,
> Late Dean of Ely, formerly Lecturer in History, Cambridge University

J. HIGGINSON CABOT, Ph.D.,
> Department of History, Wellesley College

SIR WILLIAM W. HUNTER, F.R.S.,
> Late Director-General of Statistics in India

GEORGE M. DUTCHER, Ph.D.,
> Professor of History, Wesleyan University

SIR ROBERT K. DOUGLAS,
> Professor of Chinese, King's College, London

JEREMIAH WHIPPLE JENKS, Ph.D., LL.D.
> Professor of Political Economy and Politics, Cornell University

KANICHI ASAKAWA, Ph.D.,
> Instructor in the History of Japanese Civilization, Yale University

WILFRED HAROLD MUNRO, L.H.D.,
> Professor of European History, Brown University

G. MERCER ADAM,
> Historian and Editor

FRED MORROW FLING, Ph.D.,
> Professor of European History, University of Nebraska

FRANÇOIS AUGUSTE MARIE MIGNET,
> Late Member of the French Academy

JAMES WESTFALL THOMPSON, Ph.D.,
> Department of History, University of Chicago

SAMUEL RAWSON GARDINER, LL.D.,
> Professor of Modern History, King's College, London

P. W. JOYCE, LL.D.,
> Commissioner for the Publication of the Ancient Laws of Ireland

vi

vii

NOTE

The editors of "The History of Nations" concluded their work with the chronicling of events to October, 1905, and all additions thereafter, bringing the histories to date, have been supplied by the publishers.

AUTHOR'S PREFACE

THE people of the United States have always felt a deep interest in the history and destiny of Mexico. It was not only the commercial spirit of our citizens that awakened this sentiment. In former times, when the exclusive policy of Spain closed the door of intercourse with her American colonies, the ancient history of Peru and Mexico attracted the curiosity of our students. They were eager to solve the enigma of a strange civilization which had originated in the central portions of our continent in isolated independence of all the world. They desired, moreover, to know something of those enchanted regions, which, like the fabled garden of the Hesperides, were watched and warded with such jealous vigilance; and they craved to behold those marvelous mines whose boundless wealth was poured into the lap of Spain. The valuable work of Baron Humboldt, published in the early part of the nineteenth century, stimulated this natural curiosity; and when the revolutionary spirit of Europe penetrated our continent, and the masses rose to cast off colonial bondage, we hailed with joy every effort of the patriots who fought so bravely in the war of liberation. Bound to Mexico by geographical ties, though without a common language or lineage, we were the first to welcome her and the new American sovereignties into the brotherhood of nations, and to fortify our continental alliance by embassies and treaties.

After more than twenty years of peaceful intercourse the war of 1846 broke out between Mexico and our Union. Thousands of all classes, professions, and occupations—educated and uneducated, observers and idlers—poured into the territory of the invaded republic. In the course of the conflict these sturdy adventurers traversed the central and northern regions of Mexico, scoured her coasts, possessed themselves for many months of her beautiful capital, and although they returned to their homes worn with the toils of war, none ceased to remember the delicious land amid whose sunny valleys and majestic mountains they had learned at least to admire the sublimity of nature. The returned warriors

ix

did not fail to report around their firesides the marvels they witnessed during their campaigns, and numerous works have been written to sketch the story of individual adventure, or to portray the most interesting physical features of various sections of the republic. Thus by war and literature, by ancient curiosity and political sympathy, by geographical position and commercial interest, Mexico became perhaps the most interesting portion of the world to our countrymen at that time. And I have been led to believe that the American people would not receive unfavorably a work designed to describe the entire country, to develop its resources and condition, and to sketch impartially its history from the conquest to the present day.

It has been no ordinary task to chronicle the career of a nation for more than three centuries, to unveil the colonial government of sixty-two viceroys, to follow the thread of war and politics through the mazes of revolution, and to track the rebellious spirit of intrigue amid the numerous civil outbreaks which have occurred since the downfall of Iturbide. The complete viceroyal history of Mexico is now for the first time presented to the world in the English language, while, in Spanish, no single author has ever attempted it continuously. Free from the bias of Mexican partisanship, I have endeavored to narrate events fairly, and to paint character without regard to individual men. In describing the country, its resources, geography, finances, church, agriculture, army, industrial condition, and social as well as political prospects, I have taken care to provide myself with the most recent and respectable authorities. My residence in the country and intimacy with many of its educated and intelligent patriots enabled me to gather information in which I confided, and I have endeavored to fuse the whole mass of knowledge thus laboriously procured, with my personal and, I hope, unprejudiced observation.

BRANTZ MAYER

EDITOR'S PREFACE

THIRTY years after the preceding was written, the editor of this volume followed in the footsteps of his talented predecessor. He made three journeys to Mexico and devoted three years to investigation and to writing out the results of his studies and observations, which appeared in 1883, in his " Travels in Mexico and Mexican Resources."

At that time the great railroads and other public enterprises which have conduced to Mexico's advancement were but in their inception, yet there were indubitable signs that the country was entering upon a career of progress and prosperity which would probably find few parallels in history.

Having been in the van of the modern " Mexican movement " which began with the first administration of President Porfirio Diaz, it affords him pleasure to quote a prescient paragraph from the preface in his " Travels," which events have verified:

" If, during the many months intervening between the conception of this volume and its completion, the author has wearied of his task, or has doubted its wisdom or expediency, he has constantly derived consolation from the reflection that, in helping to make Mexico better known to the world at large, he is but lending his aid to a progressive movement which is not to end until the American shall have pushed his engines to the farthest portions of that Greater South, and a trade legitimate and prosperous shall flow in those longitudinal channels which require the traversing of no broad ocean or tempestuous sea."

That " progressive movement " has not ended yet, it is a satisfaction to note, after nearly a quarter century of observation, for the United States of the North and the United States of Mexico are still together laboring in the mutually advantageous cause of an extended continental commerce. The prediction has been fulfilled —American locomotives have traversed Mexico and are already near the northern frontier of Guatemala. Once the mountains of

Central America have been overcome, nothing remains to prevent the commercial conquest of the great southern continent. And in the wake of commerce follow all the benefits of a higher civilization.

Frederick A Ober

HACKENSACK, N. J.

CONTENTS

HISTORY OF MEXICO

CONTENTS

LIST OF ILLUSTRATIONS

HISTORY OF MEXICO

HISTORY OF MEXICO

Chapter I

DISCOVERY AND EXPLORATION. 1511-1519

THERE is perhaps no page in modern history so full of dramatic incidents and useful consequences as that which records the discovery, conquest, and development of America by the Spanish and Anglo-Saxon races. The extraordinary achievements of Columbus, Cortéz, and Pizarro have resulted in the acquisition of broad lands, immense wealth, and rational liberty; and the names of these heroes are thus indissolubly connected with the physical and intellectual progress of mankind.

In the following pages we propose to write the history and depict the manners, customs, and condition of Mexico. Our narrative begins with the first movements that were made for the conquest of the country; yet we shall recount, fully and accurately, the story of those Indian princes—the splendor of whose courts, and the misery of whose tragic doom, enhance the picturesque grandeur and solemn lessons that are exhibited in the career of Hernando Cortéz.

Cuba was the second island discovered, in the West Indies; but it was not until 1511 that Diego, son of the gallant admiral, Christopher Columbus, who had hitherto maintained the seat of government in Hispaniola, resolved to occupy the adjacent Isle of Fernandina—as it was then called—amid whose virgin mountains and forests he hoped to find new mines to repair the loss of those which were rapidly failing in Hispaniola.

For the conquest of this imagined El Dorado he prepared a small armament, under the command of Diego Velasquez, an ambitious and covetous leader who, together with his lieutenant, Narvaez, soon established the Spanish authority in the island, of which he was appointed governor.

Christopher Columbus, after coasting the shores of Cuba for a great distance, had always believed that it constituted a portion of the continent, but it was soon discovered that the illustrious

admiral had been in error, and that Cuba, extensive as it appeared
to be, was, in fact, only an island.

In February, 1517, a Spanish hidalgo, Hernandez de Cordova, set sail from Cuba with three vessels toward the adjacent
Bahamas in search of slaves. He was driven by a succession of
severe storms on coasts which had hitherto been unknown to the
Spanish adventurers, and finally landed on that part of the continent
which forms the northeastern end of the peninsula of Yucatan, and
is known as Cape Catoché. Here he first discovered the evidence
of a more liberal civilization than had been hitherto known among
his adventurous countrymen in the New World. Large and solid
buildings of stone, cultivated fields, delicate fabrics of cotton and
precious metals indicated the presence of a race that had long
since emerged from the semi-barbarism of the Indian isles. The
bold but accidental explorer continued his voyage along the coast
of the peninsula until he reached the site of Campeché; and then,
after an absence of seven months and severe losses among his men,
returned to Cuba, with but half the number of his reckless companions. He brought back with him, however, numerous evidences
of the wealth and progress of the people he had fortuitously discovered on the American main; but he soon died from wounds
received at Champoton, and left to others the task of completing
the enterprise he had so auspiciously begun.

The fruits of his discoveries remained to be gathered by
Velasquez, who at once equipped four vessels and intrusted them
to the command of his nephew, Juan de Grijalva, and May 1,
1518, this new commander left the port of St. Jago de Cuba, now
commonly called Santiago de Cuba. The first land he touched on
his voyage of discovery was the Island of Cozumel, whence he
passed to the continent, glancing at the spots that had been previously visited by Cordova. So struck was he by the architecture,
the improved agriculture, the civilized tastes, the friendly character and demeanor of the inhabitants, and especially by the sight
of "large stone crosses, evidently objects of worship," that, in the
enthusiasm of the moment, he gave to the land the name of Nueva
España—or New Spain—a title which has since been extended
from the peninsula of Yucatan to even more than the entire empire
of Montezuma and the Aztecs.

Grijalva did not content himself with a mere casual visit to
the continent, but pursued his course along the coast, stopping at

the Rio de Tabasco. While at Rio de Vanderas he enjoyed the first intercourse that ever took place between the Spaniards and Mexicans. The cacique of the province sought from the strangers a full account of their distant country and the motives of their visit, in order that he might convey the intelligence to his Aztec master. Presents were interchanged, and Grijalva received, in return for his toys and tinsel, a mass of jewels, together with ornaments and vessels of gold, which satisfied the adventurers that they had reached a country whose resources would repay them for the toil of further exploration. Accordingly he dispatched to Cuba with the joyous news Pedro de Alvarado, one of his captains—a man who was destined to play a conspicuous part in the future conquest—while he, with the remainder of his companies, continued his coasting voyage to San Juan de Ulua, the Island of Sacrificios, and the northern shores, until he reached the province of Panuco; whence, after an absence of six months, he set sail for Cuba, having been the first Spanish adventurer who trod the soil of Mexico.

But his return was not hailed even with gratitude. The florid reports of Pedro de Alvarado had already inflamed the ambition and avarice of Velasquez, who, impatient of the prolonged absence of Grijalva, had dispatched a vessel under the command of Cristóval de Olid in search of his tardy officer. Nor was he content with this jealous exhibition of his temper; for, anxious to secure to himself all the glory and treasure to be derived from the boundless resources of a continent, he solicited authority from the Spanish crown to prosecute the adventures that had been so auspiciously begun; and in the meantime, after considerable deliberation, resolved to fit out another armament on a scale in some degree commensurate with the military subjugation of the country should he find himself opposed by its sovereign and people. After considerable doubt, difficulty, and delay he resolved to intrust this expedition to the command of Hernando Cortéz; "the last man," says Prescott, "to whom Velasquez—could he have foreseen the results—would have confided the enterprise."

It will not be foreign to our purpose to sketch, briefly, the previous life of a man who subsequently became so eminent in the history of both worlds. Seven years before Columbus planted the standard of Castile and Aragon in the West Indies, Hernando Cortéz was born, of noble lineage, in the town of Medellin, province of Estremadura, Spain. His infancy was frail and delicate, but his constitution strengthened as he grew, until at the age of fourteen he was placed in the venerable University of Salamanca, where his parents, who rejoiced in the extreme vivacity of his talents, designed to prepare him for the profession of law, the emoluments of which were at that period most tempting in Spain. But the restless spirit of the future conqueror was not to be manacled by the musty ritual of a tedious science whose pursuit would confine him to a quiet life. He wasted two years at the college, and, like many men who subsequently became renowned either for thought or action, was finally sent home in disgrace. Nevertheless, in the midst of his recklessness, and by the quickness of his genius, he had learned "a little store of Latin," and acquired the habit of writing good prose, or of versifying agreeably. His father, Don Martin Cortéz de Monroy, and his mother, Doña Catalina Pizarro Altamirano, seem to have been accomplished people; nor is it improbable that the greater part of their son's information was obtained under the influence of the domestic circle.

At college he was free from all restraint—giving himself up to the spirit of adventure, the pursuit of pleasure, and convivial intercourse—so that no hope was entertained of his further improvement from scholastic studies. His worthy parents were, moreover, people of limited fortune, and unable to prolong these agreeable but profitless pursuits. Accordingly when Cortéz attained the age of seventeen they yielded to his proposal to enlist under the banner of Gonsalvo of Cordova, and to devote himself, heart and soul, to the military life, which seemed most suitable for one of his wild, adventurous, and resolute disposition. It was well for Spain and for himself that the chivalric wish of Cortéz was not thwarted, and that one of the ablest soldiers produced by Castile at that period was not dwarfed by parental control into a bad lawyer or pestilent pettifogger.

The attention of Cortéz was soon directed toward the New World—the stories of whose wealth had now for upwards of twenty years been pouring into the greedy ear of Spain—and he speedily determined to embark in the armament which Nicolas de Ovando, a successor of Columbus, was fitting out for the West Indies. This design was frustrated, however, for two years longer, by an accident which occurred in one of his amours; nor did another opportunity present itself, until at the age of nineteen, in

1504, he bade adieu to Spain in a small squadron bound to the islands.

As soon as Cortéz reached Hispaniola he visited the governor, whom he had formerly known at home. Ovando was absent, but his secretary received the emigrant kindly, and assured him a liberal grant of land. "I come for gold," replied Cortéz sneeringly, "and not to toil like a peasant!" Ovando, however, was more fortunate than the secretary in prevailing upon the future conqueror to forego the lottery of adventure, for no sooner had he returned to his post than Cortéz was persuaded to accept a grant of land, a repartimiento of Indians, and the office of notary in the village of Acua. Here he seems to have dwelt until 1511, varying the routine of notarial and agricultural pursuits by an occasional adventure of an amorous character, which involved him in duels. Sometimes he took part in the military expeditions under Diego Velasquez for the suppression of Indian insurrections in the interior. This was the school in which he learned his tactics, and here did he study the native character until he joined Velasquez for the conquest of Cuba.

As soon as this famous island was reduced to Spanish authority Cortéz became high in favor with Velasquez, who had received the commission of governor. But love, intrigues, jealousy, and ambition quickly began to checker the course of his wayward life, and estranged him from the new governor, who found it difficult to satisfy the cravings of those rapacious adventurers who flocked in crowds to the New World, and in all probability clustered around Cortéz as the nucleus of discontent. It was soon resolved by these men to submit their complaints against Velasquez to the higher authorities in Hispaniola, and the daring Cortéz was fixed on as the bearer of the message in an open boat, across the eighteen intervening leagues. But the conspiracy was detected, the rash ambassador confined in chains, and only saved from hanging by the interposition of powerful friends.

Cortéz speedily contrived to relieve himself of the fetters with which he was bound, and, forcing a window, escaped from his prison to the sanctuary of a neighboring church. A few days after, however, he was seized while standing carelessly in front of the sacred edifice, and conveyed on board a vessel bound for Hispaniola, where he was to be tried. But his intrepidity and skill did not forsake him even in this strait. Ascending cautiously from the vessel's hold to the deck, he dropped into a boat, pulled ashore, and, landing on the sands, sought again the sanctuary whence he had been rudely snatched by the myrmidons of the governor.

One of the causes of his quarrel with Velasquez had been an intrigue with a beautiful woman, in whose family the governor was, perhaps, personally interested. The fickle Cortéz cruelly abandoned the fair Catalina Xuares at a most inauspicious moment of her fate, and was condemned for his conduct by all the best people in the island; but now, under the influence of penitence or policy, his feelings suddenly experienced a strange revulsion. He expressed a contrite desire to do justice to the injured woman by marriage, and thus at once obtained the favor of her family and the pardon of the governor, who, becoming permanently reconciled to Cortéz, presented him a liberal repartimiento of Indians, together with broad lands in the neighborhood of St. Jago, of which he was soon made alcalde.

The future conqueror devoted himself henceforth to his duties with remarkable assiduity. Agriculture, the introduction of cattle of the best breeds, and the revenues of a share of the mines which he wrought soon began to enrich the restless adventurer who had settled down for a while into the quiet life of a married man. His wife fulfilled her share of the cares of life with remarkable fidelity, and seems to have contented the heart even of her liege lord, who declared himself as happy with his bride as if she had been the daughter of a duchess.

At this juncture Alvarado returned with the account of the discoveries, the wealth, and the golden prospects of continental adventure, which we have already narrated. Cortéz and Velasquez were alike fired by the alluring story. The old flame of enterprise was rekindled in the breast of the wild youth of Medellin, and when the governor looked around for one who could command the projected expedition he found none, among the hosts who pressed for service, better fitted for the enterprise by personal qualities and fortune, than Hernando Cortéz, whom he named captain-general of his armada.

The high office and the important task imposed on him seem to have sobered the excitable, and heretofore fickle, mind of Cortéz. His ardent animal spirits, under the influence of a bold and lofty purpose, became the servants rather than the masters of his indomitable will, and he at once proceeded to arrange all the details of the expedition which he was to lead to Mexico. The means that he did not already possess in his own coffers he raised by mortgage, and he applied the funds thus obtained to the purchase of vessels, rations, and military stores, or to the furnishing of adequate equipments for adventurers who were too poor to provide their own outfit. It is somewhat doubtful whether Velasquez, the governor, was very liberal in his personal and pecuniary contributions to this expedition, the cost of which amounted to about twenty thousand gold ducats.[1]. It has been alleged that Cortéz was

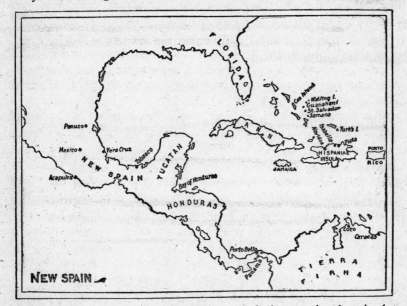

NEW SPAIN

the chief support of the adventure, and it is certain that in later years this question resulted in bitter litigation between the parties.

Six ships and three hundred followers were soon prepared for the enterprise under Cortéz, and the governor proceeded to give instructions to the leader, all of which are couched in language of unquestionable liberality.

The captain of the armada was first to seek the missing Grijalva, after which the two commanders were to unite in their quest of gold and adventure. Six Christians supposed to be lingering in captivity in Yucatan were to be sought and released. Barter

---

[1] The value of the ducat varies but little, the coin usually containing from 3.42 to 3.44 grains of fine gold, worth from $2.27 to $2.32.

and traffic, generally, with the natives were to be encouraged and carried on so as to avoid all offense against humanity or kindness. The Indians were to be Christianized—for the conversion of heathens was one of the dearest objects of the Spanish king. The aborigines, in turn, were to manifest their good will by gifts of jewels and treasure. The coasts and adjacent streams were to be surveyed, and the productions of the country, its races, civilization, and institutions, were to be noted with minute accuracy, so that a faithful report might be returned to the crown, to whose honor and the service of God it was hoped the enterprise would certainly redound.

Such was the state of things in the port of St. Jago when jealous fears began to interrupt the confidence between Velasquez and Cortéz. The counsel of friends who were companions of the governor, and his own notice of that personage's altered conduct, soon put the new captain-general of the armada on his guard. Neither his equipment nor his crew was yet complete; nevertheless he supplied his fleet with all the provisions he could hastily obtain at midnight, and, paying the provider with a massive chain which he had worn about his neck—the last available remnant, perhaps, of his fortune—he hastened with his officers on board the vessels.

November 18, 1518, he made sail for the port of Macaca, about fifteen leagues distant, and thence he proceeded to Trinidad, on the southern coast of Cuba. Here he obtained stores from the royal farms, while he recruited his forces from all classes, but especially from the returned troops and sailors of Grijalva's expedition. Pedro de Alvarado and his brothers, Cristóval de Olid, Alonzo de Avila, Juan Velasquez de Leon, Hernandez de Puerto Carrero, and Gonzalo de Sandoval united their fortunes to his, and thus identified themselves forever with the conquest of Mexico. He added considerably to his stock by the seizure of several vessels and cargoes; and prudently got rid of Diego de Ordaz, whom he regarded as a spy of the estranged Velasquez.

At Trinidad Cortéz was overtaken by orders for detention from his former friend and patron. These commands, however, were not enforced by the cautious official who received them, and Cortéz forthwith dispatched Alvarado by land to Havana, while he prepared to follow with his fleet around the coast and western part of the island. At Havana he again added to his forces, prepared arms and quilted armor as a defense against the Indian arrows, and distributed his men into eleven companies under the command of experienced officers. But before all his arrangements were completed the commander of the place, Don Pedro Barba, was ordered, by express from Velasquez, to arrest Cortéz, while the captain-general of the armada himself received a hypocritical letter from the same personage, "requesting him to delay his voyage till the governor could communicate with him in person!" Barba, however, knew that the attempt to seize the leader of such an enterprise and of such a band would be vain; while Cortéz, in reply to Velasquez, implored his Excellency to rely on his boundless devotion to the interests of his governor; but assured him, nevertheless, that he and his fleet, by divine permission, would sail on the following day!

Accordingly, February 18, 1519, the little squadron weighed anchor, with one hundred and ten mariners, sixteen horses, five hundred and fifty-three soldiers, including thirty-two crossbowmen and thirteen arquebusiers, besides two hundred Indians of the island and a few native women for menial offices. The ordnance consisted of ten heavy guns, four lighter pieces or falconets, together with a good supply of ammunition.

With this insignificant command and paltry equipment Hernado Cortéz, at the age of thirty-three, set sail for the conquest of Mexico. He invoked on his enterprise the blessing of his patron, Saint Peter, and, addressing his followers in the language of encouragement and resolution, he unfurled a velvet banner on which was emblazoned the figure of a crimson cross amid flames of blue and white, and pointed to the motto which was to be the presage of victory: "Friends, let us follow the Cross: and under this sign, if we have faith, we shall conquer!"

Chapter II

THE ARRIVAL OF CORTÉZ AMONG THE AZTECS
1519

SOON after the adventurers departed from the coast of Cuba the weather, which had been hitherto fine, suddenly changed, and one of those violent hurricanes which ravage the Indian isles during the warm season scattered and dismantled the small squadron, sweeping it far to the south of its original destination. Cortéz was the last to reach the Island of Cozumel, having been forced to linger in order to watch for the safety of one of his battered craft. But immediately on landing he was pained to learn that the impetuous Pedro de Alvarado had rashly entered the temples, despoiled them of their ornaments, and terrified the natives into promiscuous flight. He immediately devoted himself to the task of obliterating this stain on Spanish humanity by releasing two of the captives taken by Alvarado. Through an interpreter he satisfied them of the pacific purpose of his voyage, and dispatched them to their homes with valuable gifts. This humane policy appears to have succeeded with the natives, who speedily returned from the interior and commenced a brisk traffic of gold for trinkets.

The chief objection of Cortéz to the headlong destruction which Alvarado had committed in the temples seems rather to have been against the robbery than the religious motive, if such existed in the breast of his impetuous companion. We have already said that the conversion of the heathen was one of the alleged primary objects of this expedition, for the instructions of the governor of Cuba were full of zeal for the spread of Christianity; yet in the diffusion of this novel creed among the aborigines it sometimes happened that its military propagandists regarded the sword as more powerful than the sermon. The idolatrous practices of the inhabitants of Cozumel shocked the sensibility of the commander, and he set about the work of Christianization through the labors of the licentiate Juan Diaz and Bartolomé de Olmedo, the latter of whom—who remained with the army during the whole expedition—was, indeed, a mirror of zeal and charity. The discourses of these worthy priests were, however, unavailing. The Indians, who of course could not comprehend their eloquent exhortations or pious logic, refused to abandon their idols, and Cortéz resolved at once to convince them, by palpable arguments, of the inefficiency of those hideous emblems either to save themselves from destruction or to bestow blessings on the blind adorers. An order was therefore forthwith given for the immediate destruction of the Indian images; and in their place the Virgin and her Son were erected on a hastily constructed altar. Olmedo and his companion were thus the first to offer the sacrifice of the mass in New Spain, where they finally induced numbers of the aborigines to renounce idolatry and embrace the Catholic faith.

In spite of this marauding crusade against their property and creed, the Indians kindly furnished the fleet with provisions, which enabled the squadron to sail in the ensuing March. But a leak in one of the vessels compelled the adventurers to return to port—a circumstance which was regarded by many as providential—inasmuch as it was the means of restoring to his countryman a Spaniard named Aguilar, who had been wrecked on the coast of Yucatan eight years before. The long residence of this person in the country made him familiar with the language of the inhabitants of that neighborhood, and thus a valuable interpreter—one of its most pressing wants—was added to the expedition.

After the vessels were refitted Cortéz coasted the shores of Yucatan until he reached the Rio de Tabasco or Grijalva, where he encountered the first serious opposition to the Spanish arms. He had a severe conflict, in the vicinity of his landing, with a large force of the natives; but the valor of his men, the terror inspired by firearms, and the singular spectacle presented to the astonished Indians by the extraordinary appearance of cavalry soon turned the tide of victory in his favor. The subdued tribes appeased his anger by valuable gifts, and forthwith established friendly relations with their dreaded conqueror. Among the presents offered upon this occasion by the vanquished were twenty female slaves; and after one of the holy fathers had attempted, as usual, to impress the truths of Christianity upon the natives, and had closed the ceremonies of the day by a pompous procession, with all the impressive ceremonial of the Roman Church, the fleet again sailed toward the empire Cortéz was destined to penetrate and subdue.

In Passion Week of the year 1519 the squadron dropped anchor under the lee of the island or reef of San Juan de Ulua. The natives immediately boarded the vessel of the captain-general; but their language was altogether different from that of the Mayan dialects spoken in Yucatan and its immediate dependencies. In this emergency Cortéz learned that among the twenty female slaves who had been recently presented him there was one who knew the Mexican language, and, in fact, that she was an Aztec by birth. This was the celebrated Marina or Mariana, who accompanied the conqueror throughout his subsequent adventures and was so useful as a sagacious friend and discreet interpreter. Acquainted with the languages of her native land and of the Yucatecos, she found it easy to translate the idiom of the Aztecs into the Mayan dialect which Aguilar, the Spaniard, had learned during his captivity. Through this medium Cortéz was apprised that these Mexicans or Aztecs were the subjects of a powerful sovereign who ruled an empire bounded by two seas, and that his name was Montezuma.

On April 21 the captain-general landed on the sandy and desolate beach whereon is now built the modern city of Vera Cruz. Within a few days the native governor of the province arrived to greet him, and expressed great anxiety to learn whence the " fair and bearded strangers " had come? Cortéz told him that he was the subject of a mighty monarch beyond the sea who ruled over an immense empire and had kings and princes for his vassals; that, acquainted with the greatness of the Mexican emperor, his master desired to enter into communication with so great a personage, and had sent him, as an envoy, to wait on Montezuma with a present in token of his good will, and a friendly message which he must deliver in person. The Indian governor expressed surprise that there was another king as great as his master, yet assured Cortéz that as soon as he learned Montezuma's determination he would again converse with him on the subject. Teuhtle then presented the captain-general with ten loads of fine cottons, mantles of curious feather work, beautifully dyed, and baskets filled with golden ornaments. Cortéz, in turn, produced the gifts for the emperor, which were comparatively insignificant; but when the Aztec governor desired to receive the glittering helmet of one of the men it was readily given as an offering to the emperor, with the significant request that it might be returned filled with gold, which Cortéz told him was a specific remedy for a disease of the heart with which his countrymen, the Spaniards, were sorely afflicted!

During this interview between the functionaries it was noticed by the adventurers that men were eagerly employed among the Indians in sketching everything they beheld in the ranks of the strangers—for by this picture-writing the Mexican monarch was to be apprised in accurate detail of the men, horses, ships, armor, force, and weapons of this motley band of invaders.

These pictorial missives were swiftly borne by the Mexican couriers to the Aztec capital among the mountains, and, together with the oral account of the landing of Cortéz and his demand for an interview, were laid before the imperial court. It may well be imagined that the extraordinary advent of the captain-general and his squadron was productive of no small degree of excitement and even tremor among this primitive people; for not only were they unnerved by the dread which all secluded races feel for innovation, but an ancient prophecy had foretold the downfall of the empire through the instrumentality of beings, who, like these adventurers, were to " come from the rising sun." Montezuma, who was then on the throne, had been elected to that dignity in 1502 in preference to his brothers, in consequence of his superior qualifications as a soldier and a priest. His reign commenced energetically; and while he at first administered the interior affairs of his realm with justice, capacity, and moderation, his hand fell heavily on all who dared to raise their arms against his people. But as he waxed older and firmer in power, and as his empire extended, he began to exhibit those selfish traits which so often characterize men who possess for a length of time supreme power untrammeled by constitutional restraints. His court was sumptuous, and his people were grievously taxed to support its unbounded extravagance. This in some degree alienated the loyalty of his subjects, while continued oppression finally led to frequent insurrection. In addition to these internal discontents of the Aztec empire, Montezuma had met in the nominal republic of Tlascala—lying midway between the valley of Mexico and the seacoast—a brave and stubborn foe, whose civilization, unimpaired resources, and martial character enabled it to resist the combined forces of the Aztecs for upwards of two hundred years.

Such was the state of the empire when the news of Cortéz's arrival became the subject of discussion in Mexico. Some were for open or wily resistance. Others were oppressed with superstitious fears. But Montezuma, adopting a medium but fatal course, resolved without delay to send an embassy with such gifts as he imagined would impress the strangers with the idea of his magnificence and power, while at the same time he courteously commanded the adventurers to refrain from approaching his capital.

Meanwhile the Spaniards restlessly endured the scorching heats and manifold annoyances of the coast, and were amusing themselves by a paltry traffic with the Indians, whose offerings were generally of but trifling value. After the expiration of a week, however, the returned couriers and the embassy approached the camp. The time is seemingly short when we consider the difficulty of transportation through a mountain country, and recollect that the Mexicans, who were without horses, had been obliged to traverse the distance, about two hundred miles, on foot. But it is related on ample authority—so perfectly were the posts arranged among these semi-civilized people—that tidings were borne in the short period of twenty-four hours from the city to the sea, and consequently that three or four days were ample for the journey of the envoys of Montezuma, upon a matter of so much national importance.

The two Aztec nobles, accompanied by the governor of the province, Teuhtle, did not approach with empty hands the men whom they hoped to bribe if they could not intimidate. Gold, shields, helmets, cuirasses, collars, bracelets, sandals, fans, pearls, precious stones, loads of cotton cloth, extraordinary fabrics of feathers, circular plates of gold and silver as large as carriage wheels, and the Spanish helmet filled with golden grains, were all spread out as a free gift from the Emperor Montezuma to the Spaniards.

With these magnificent presents Montezuma replied, to the request of Cortéz, that it would give him pleasure to communicate with so mighty a monarch as the King of Spain, whom he respected highly, but that he could not gratify himself by according the foreign envoy a personal interview, inasmuch as the distance to his capital was great, and the toilsome journey among the mountains was beset with dangers from formidable enemies. He could do no more, therefore, than bid the strangers farewell, and request them to return to their homes over the sea with these proofs of his perfect friendship.

It may well be supposed that this naïve system of diplomacy could have but little effect on men who were bent on improving their fortunes, and whose rapacity was only stimulated by the evidences of unbounded wealth which the simple-minded king had so lavishly bestowed on them. Montezuma was the dupe of his own credulity, and only inflamed, by the very means he imagined would assuage, the avarice or ambition of his Spanish visitors. Nor was Cortéz less resolved than his companions. Accordingly he made another pacific effort, by means of additional presents and a gentle message, to change the resolution of the Indian emperor. Still the Aztec sovereign was obstinate in his refusal of a personal interview, although he sent fresh gifts by the persons who bore to the Spaniards his polite but firm and peremptory denial.

Cortéz could hardly conceal his disappointment at this second rebuff; but as the vesper bell tolled, while the ambassadors were in his presence, he threw himself on his knees with his soldiers, and, after prayer, Father Olmedo expounded to the Aztec chiefs by his interpreters the doctrines of Christianity; and, putting into their hands an image of the Virgin and Saviour, he exhorted them to abandon their hideous idolatry and to place these milder emblems of faith and hope on the altars of their bloody gods. That very night the Indians abandoned the Spanish camp and the neighborhood, leaving the adventurers without the copious supplies of food that hitherto had been bountifully furnished. Cortéz, nevertheless, was undismayed by these menacing symptoms, and exclaimed to his hardy followers: " It shall yet go hard, but we will one day pay this powerful prince a visit in his gorgeous capital! "

Chapter III

THE MARCH ON TENOCHITITLAN. 1519

CORTÉZ was not long idle after the withdrawal of the Aztec emissaries and the surly departure of the Indians, who, as we have related in the last chapter, quitted his camp and neighborhood on the same night with the ambassadors of Montezuma. He forthwith proceeded to establish a military and civil colony, of which he became captain-general and chief justice; he founded the Villa Rica de la Vera Cruz in order to secure a base on the coast for future military operation, by means of which he might be independent of Velasquez; and he formed an alliance with the Totonacs of Centoalla, whose loyalty—though they were subjects of Montezuma—was alienated from him by his merciless exactions. We shall not dwell upon the skill with which he fomented a breach between the Totonacs and the ambassadors of Montezuma, nor upon the valuable gifts and discreet dispatches he forwarded to the Emperor Charles V. in order to secure a confirmation of his proceedings. The most daring act of this period was the destruction of the squadron which had wafted him to Mexico. It was a deed of wise policy, which deliberately cut off all hope of retreat—pacified in some degree the querulous conspirators who lurked in his camp, and placed before all who were embarked in the enterprise the alternative of conquest or destruction. Only one vessel remained. Nine out of the ten were dismantled and sunk. When his men murmured for a moment and imagined themselves betrayed, he addressed them in that language of bland diplomacy which he was so well skilled to use whenever the occasion required. "As for me," said he, "I will remain here while there is one to bear me company! Let the cravens shrink from danger and go home in the single vessel that remains. Let them hasten to Cuba and relate how they deserted their commander and comrades; and there let them wait in patience till we return laden with the spoils of Mexico!"

This was an appeal that rekindled the combined enthusiasm

18

and avarice of the despondent murmurers; and the reply was a universal shout: "To Mexico! to Mexico!"

On August 16, 1519, Cortéz set out with his small army of about four hundred men, now swelled by the addition of thirteen hundred Indian warriors and a thousand porters, and accompanied by forty of the chief Totonacs as hostages and advisers. From the burning climate of the coast the army gradually ascended to the cooler regions of the *tierra templada* and *tierra fria,* encountering all degrees of temperature on the route. After a journey of three days the forces arrived at a town on one of the tablelands of the interior, whose chief magistrate confirmed the stories of the power of Montezuma. Here Cortéz tarried three days for repose, and then proceeded toward the republic of Tlascala, which lay directly in his path, and with whose inhabitants he hoped to form an alliance founded on the elements of discontent which he knew existed among these inveterate foes of the central Aztec power. But he was mistaken in his calculations. The Tlascalans were not so easily won as his allies, the Totonacs, who, dwelling in a warmer climate, had not the hardier virtues of these mountaineers. The Tlascalans entertained no favorable feeling toward Montezuma, but they nourished quite as little cordiality for men whose characters they did not know, and whose purposes they had cause to dread. A deadly hostility to the Spaniards was consequently soon manifested. Cortéz was attacked by them on the borders of their republic and fought four sharp battles with fifty thousand warriors, who maintained in all the conflicts their reputation for military skill and hardihood. At length the Tlascalans were forced to acknowledge the superiority of the invaders, whom they could not overcome either by stratagem or battle, and after the exchange of embassies and gifts they honored Cortéz with a triumphal entry into their capital. The news of these victories as well as of the alliance which ensued with the Tlascalans was soon borne to Tenochtitlan, and Montezuma began to tremble for the fate of his empire when he saw the fall of the indomitable foes who had held him so long at bay. Two embassies to Cortéz succeeded each other in vain. Presents were no longer of avail. His offer of tribute to the Spanish king was not listened to. All requests that the conqueror should not advance toward his capital were unheeded. The command of his own emperor, said Cortéz, was the only reason which could induce him to disregard the wishes of an Aztec prince, for whom he cherished the profoundest respect! Soon after another embassy came from Montezuma with magnificent gifts and an invitation to his capital, yet with a request that he would break with his new allies and approach Mexico through the friendly city of Cholula. The policy of this request on the part of Montezuma will be seen in the sequel. Cortéz, accompanied by six thousand volunteers from Tlascala, advanced toward the sacred city—the site of the most splendid temple in the empire, whose foundations yet remain in the twentieth century. The six intervening leagues were soon crossed, and he entered Cholula with his Spanish army, attended by no other Indians than those who accompanied him from Cempoalla. At first the general and his companions were treated hospitably, and the suspicions which had been instilled into his mind by the Tlascalans were lulled to sleep. However, he soon had cause to become fearful of treachery. Messengers arrived from Montezuma, and his entertainers were observed to be less gracious in their demeanor. It was noticed that several important streets had been barricaded or converted into pitfalls, while stones, missiles, and weapons were heaped on the flat roofs of houses. Besides this, Mariana had become intimate with the wife of one of the caciques, and cunningly drew from her gossiping friend the whole conspiracy that was brewing against the adventurers. Montezuma, she learned, had stationed twenty thousand Mexicans near the city, who, together with the Cholulans, were to assault the invaders in the narrow streets and avenues as they quitted the town; and thus he hoped by successful treachery to rid the land of such dangerous visitors either by slaughter in conflict, or to offer them, when made captive, upon the altars of the sacred temple in Cholula and on the Teocallis of Mexico as proper sacrifices to the bloody gods of his country.

Cortéz, however, was not to be so easily outwitted and entrapped. He, in turn, resorted to stratagem. Concentrating all his Spanish army, and concerting a signal for coöperation with his Indian allies, he suddenly fell upon the Cholulans at an unexpected moment. Three thousand of the citizens perished in the frightful massacre that ensued, and Cortéz pursued his uninterrupted way toward the fated capital of the Aztecs after this awful chastisement, which was perhaps needful to relieve him from the danger of utter annihilation in the heart of an enemy's country with so small a band of countrymen in whom he could confide.

From the plain of Cholula, now known as the fruitful vale of Puebla, the conqueror ascended the last ridge of mountains that separated him from the City of Mexico; and as he turned the edge of the Cordilleras the beautiful valley was at once revealed to him in all its indescribable loveliness. It lay at his feet, surrounded by the placid waters of Tezcoco. The sight that burst upon the Spaniards from this lofty eminence was that of the vale of Tenochtitlan, as it was called by the natives, which, in the language of Prescott, " with its picturesque assemblage of water, woodland, and cultivated plains, its shining cities and shadowy hills, was spread out like some gay and gorgeous panorama before them. In the highly rarefied atmosphere of these upper regions even remote objects have a brilliancy of coloring and a distinctness of outline which seems to annihilate distance. In the center of the great basin were beheld the lakes, occupying then a much larger portion of its surface than at present; their borders thickly studded with towns and hamlets, and in the midst, like some Indian empress with her coronal of pearls, the fair City of Mexico, with her white towers and pyramidal temples reposing, as it were, on the bosom of the waters—the fair-famed ' Venice of the Aztecs.' High over all rose the royal hill of Chapultepec, the residence of the Mexican monarchs, belted with the same grove of gigantic cypresses, which at this day fling their broad shadows over the land. In the distance, to the north, beyond the blue waters of the lake, and nearly screened by intervening foliage, was seen a shining speck, the rival capital of Tezcoco; and, still further on, the dark belt of porphyry, girdling the valley around, like a rich setting which nature had devised for the fairest of her jewels."

Cortéz easily descended with his troops by the mountain road toward the valley, and as he passed along the levels, or through the numerous villages and hamlets, he endeavored to foster and foment the ill feeling which he found secretly existing against the government of the Mexican emperor. When he had advanced somewhat into the heart of the valley he was met by an embassy of the chief lords of the Aztec court, sent to him by Montezuma, with gifts of considerable value; but he rejected a proffered bribe of " four loads of gold to the general, and one to each of his captains, with a yearly tribute to their sovereign," provided the Spanish troops would quit the country. Heedless of all menaced opposition as well as appeals to his avarice, he seems, at this

period, to have cast aside the earlier and sordid motives which
might then have been easily satisfied had his pursuit been gold
alone. The most abundant wealth was cast at his feet; but the
higher qualities of his nature were now allowed the fullest play,
and strengthened him in his resolution to risk all in the daring and
glorious project of subjecting a splendid empire to his control.
Accordingly, he advanced though Amaquemecan, a town of several
thousand inhabitants, where he was met by a nephew of the
emperor, the Lord of Tezcoco, who had been dispatched by his
vacillating uncle, at the head of a large number of influential personages, to welcome the invaders to the capital. The friendly
summons was of course not disregarded by Cortéz, who forthwith
proceeded along the most splendid and massive structure of the
New World—a gigantic causeway, five miles in length, constructed
of huge stones, which passed along the narrow strait of sand that
separated the waters of Chalco from those of Tezcoco. The lakes
were covered with boats filled with natives. Floating islands, made
of reeds and wicker-work, covered with soil, brimmed with luxuriant vegetation whose splendid fruits and odorous petals rested on
the waters. Several large towns were built on artificial foundations in the lake. And everywhere around the Spaniards beheld
the evidences of a dense population, whose edifices, agriculture,
and labors denoted a high degree of civilization and intelligence.
As the foreign warriors proceeded onward toward the city, which
rose before them with its temples, palaces, and shrines, covered
with hard stucco that glistened in the sun, they crossed a wooden
drawbridge in the causeway; and as they passed it they felt that
now, indeed, if they faltered, they were completely in the grasp
of the Mexicans, and more effectually cut off from all retreat than
they had been when the fleet was destroyed at Vera Cruz.

Near this spot they were encountered by Montezuma with his
court, who came forth in regal state to salute his future conqueror.
Surrounded by all the pagentry and splendor of an oriental monarch, he descended from the litter in which he was borne from the
city, and, leaning on the shoulders of the Lords of Tezcoco and of
Iztapalapan, his nephew and brother, he advanced toward the
Spaniards, under a canopy and over a cotton carpet, while his
prostrate subjects manifested by their abject demeanor the fear or
respect which the presence of their sovereign inspired.

" Montezuma was at this time about forty years of age. His

person was tall and slender, but not ill-made. His hair, which was black and straight, was not very long. His beard was thin; his complexion somewhat paler than is often found in his dusky, or rather copper-colored, race. His features, though serious in their expression, did not wear the look of melancholy or dejection which characterizes his portrait, and which may well have settled on them at a later period. He moved with dignity, and his whole demeanor, tempered by an expression of benignity not to have been anticipated from the reports circulated of his character, was worthy of a great prince. Such is the picture left to us of the celebrated Indian emperor in this his first interview with the white men." [1]

As this mighty prince approached Cortéz halted his men, and, advancing with a few of his principal retainers, was most courteously welcomed by Montezuma, who, adroitly concealing his chagrin, diplomatically expressed the uncommon delight he experienced at this unexpected visit of the strangers to his capital.[2] Cortéz thanked him for his friendly welcome and bounteous gifts, and hung around his neck a chain set with colored crystal. Montezuma

[1] Prescott, "Conquest of Mexico," vol. II. p. 71.

[2] "The province which constitutes the principal territory of Montezuma," says Cortéz in his letter to Charles V., "is circular, and entirely surrounded by lofty and rugged mountains, and the circumference of it is fully seventy leagues. In this plain there are two lakes which nearly occupy the whole of it, as the people use canoes for more than fifty leagues round. One of these lakes is of fresh water, and the other, which is larger, is of salt water. They are divided, on one side, by a small collection of high hills, which stand in the center of the plain, and they unite in a level strait formed between these hills and the high mountains, which strait is a gun-shot wide, and the people of the cities and other settlements which are in these lakes communicate in their canoes by water, without the necessity of going by land. And as this great salt lake ebbs and flows with the tide, as the sea does, in every flood the water flows from it into the fresh lake as impetuously as if it were a large river, and consequently at the ebb the fresh lake flows into the salt.

"This great city of Temixtitlan (meaning Tenochtitlan, Mexico), is founded in this salt lake; and from terra firma to the body of the city, the distance is two leagues on whichever side they please to enter it.

"It has four entrances, or causeways, made by the hand of man, as wide as two horsemen's lances.

"The city is as large as Seville and Cordova. The streets (I mean the principal ones) are very wide, and others very narrow; and some of the latter and all the others are one-half land and the other half water, along which the inhabitants go in their canoes; and all the streets, at given distances, are open, so that the water passes from one to the other; and in all their openings, some of which are very wide, there are very wide bridges, made of massive beams joined together and well wrought; and so wide that ten horsemen may pass abreast over many of them."—*Letters of Cortéz to Charles V.*

then opened his gates to the Spaniards and appointed his brother to conduct the general with his troops to the city.

Here he found a spacious edifice, surrounded by a wall, assigned for his future residence; and, having stationed sentinels and placed his cannon on the battlements so as to command all the important avenues to his palace, he proceeded to examine the city and to acquaint himself with the character, occupations, and temper of the people.

Chapter IV

THE SUBMISSION OF MONTEZUMA. 1519-1520

THE City of Mexico, or Tenochtitlan, was, as we have already said, encompassed by the lake of Tezcoco, over which three solid causeways formed the only approaches. This inland sea was, indeed, " an archipelago of wandering islands." The whole city was penetrated throughout its entire length by a principal street, which was intersected by numerous canals, crossed by drawbridges; and, wherever the eye could reach, long vistas of low stone buildings rose on every side among beautiful gardens or luxuriant foliage. The quadrangular palaces of the nobles whom Montezuma encouraged to reside at his court were spread over a wide extent of ground, embellished with beautiful fountains which shot their spray amid porticoes and columns of polished porphyry. The palace of Montezuma was so vast a pile that one of the conquerors alleges its terraced roof afforded ample room for thirty knights to tilt in tournament. A royal armory was filled with curious and dangerous weapons, and adorned with an ample store of military dresses, equipments, and armor. Huge granaries contained the tributary supplies which were brought to the prince by the provinces for the maintenance of the royal family, and there was an aviary in which three hundred attendants fed and reared birds of the sweetest voice or rarest plumage; while near it rose a menagerie filled with specimens of all the native beasts, together with a museum in which, with an oddity of taste unparalleled in history, there had been collected a vast number of human monsters, cripples, dwarfs, Albinos, and other freaks and caprices of nature. The royal gardens are described by eye-witnesses as spots of unsurpassed elegance, adorned with rare shrubs, medicinal plants, and ponds supplied by aqueducts and fountains, wherein amid beautiful flowers the finest fish and aquatic birds were seen forever floating in undisturbed quiet. The interior of the palace was equally attractive for its comfort and elegance. Spacious halls were covered with ceilings of odoriferous wood, while the lofty walls were hung with richly

25

tinted fabrics of cotton, the skins of animals, or feather-work wrought in mosaic imitation of birds, reptiles, insects, and flowers. Nor was the emperor alone amid the splendid wastes of his palace. A thousand women thronged these royal chambers, ministering to the tastes and passions of the elegant voluptuary. The rarest viands from far and near supplied his table, the service of which was performed by numerous attendants with utensils and equipage of the choicest material and shape. Four times daily the emperor changed his apparel, and never put on again the dress he once had worn, or defiled his lips twice with the same vessels from which he fed.

Such was the sovereign's palace and way of life, nor can we suppose that this refinement of luxury was to be found alone in the dwelling of Montezuma and his nobles. It is to be regretted that we are not more fully informed on the condition of property, wealth, and labor among the masses of this singular empire. The conquerors did not trouble themselves with acquiring accurate statistical information, nor do they seem to have counted numbers carefully, except when they had enemies to conquer or spoil to divide. In all primitive nations, however, the best idea of a people is to be attained from visiting the market-place—or rather the fair—in which it is their custom to sell or barter the products of their industry; and to this rendezvous of the Aztecs Cortéz, with the astuteness that never forsook him during his perilous enterprise, soon betook himself after his arrival in the city.

The market of Tenochtitlan was a scene of commercial activity as well as of humble thrift. It was devoted to all kinds of native traffic. In the center of the city the conqueror found a magnificent square surrounded by porticoes, in which it is alleged that sixty thousand traders were engaged in buying and selling every species of merchandise produced in the realm; jewels, goldware, toys, curious imitations of natural objects, wrought with the utmost skill of deception; weapons of copper alloyed with tin, pottery of all degrees of fineness, carved vases, bales of richly-dyed cotton; beautifully woven feather-work, wild and tame animals, grain, fish, vegetables, all the necessaries of life and all its luxuries, together with eating places and shops for the sale of medical drugs, confectionery, or stimulating drinks. It was, in fact, an immense bazaar, which at a glance gave an insight into the tastes, wants, and productive industry of the nation.

Satisfied with this inspection of the people and their talents, the next visit of the general was, doubtless, made with the double object of becoming acquainted with that class of men who in all countries so powerfully influence public opinion, while from the top of their tall temple, situated on their lofty central Teocalli or pyramid, he might with a military eye scan the general topography of the city.

This pyramidal structure, or Great Temple, as it is generally called, was perhaps rather the base of a religious structure than the religious edifice itself. We possess no accurate drawing of it among the contemporary or early relics of the conquest that have descended to us, but it is known to have been pyramidal in shape, over one hundred and twenty feet in altitude, with a base of three hundred and twenty.

It stood in a large area, surrounded by a wall eight feet high, sculptured with the figures of serpents in relief. From one end of the base of this structure a flight of steps rose to a terrace at the base of the second story of the pyramid. Around this terrace a person in ascending was obliged to pass until he came to the corner immediately above the first flight, where he encountered another set of steps, up which he passed to the second terrace, and so on, continuously, to the third and fourth terraces, until by a fifth flight he attained the summit platform of the Teocalli. These spaces or terraces at each story are represented to have been about six feet in width, so that three or four persons could easily ascend abreast. It will be perceived that in attaining the top of the edifice it was necessary to pass round it entirely four times and to ascend five stairways. Within the enclosure, built of stone and crowned with battlements, a village of five hundred houses might have been built. Its area was paved with smooth and polished stones, and the pyramid that rose in its center seems to have been constructed as well for military as religious purposes, inasmuch as its architecture made it fully capable of resistance as a citadel; and we may properly assume this opinion as a fact, from the circumstance that the enclosing walls were entered by four gates, facing the cardinal points, while over each portal was erected a military arsenal filled with immense stores of warlike equipments.

When Cortéz arrived in front of this truncated pyramid two priests and several caciques were in attendance, by order of Montezuma, to bear him in their arms to its summit. But the hardy conqueror declined this effeminate means of transportation, and marched up slowly at the head of his soldiers. "On the paved and level area at the top they found a large block of jasper, the peculiar shape of which showed it was the stone on which the bodies of the unhappy victims were stretched for sacrifice. Its convex surface, rising breast high, enabled the priest to perform more easily his diabolical task of removing the heart." Besides this, there were two sanctuaries erected on the level surface of the Teocalli; two altars, glowing with a fire that was never extinguished; and a large circular drum, which was struck only on occasions of great public concern.

Such was the Teocalli or House of God. There were other edifices, having the name of Teopan, or Places of God. Some writers allege that there were two towers erected on the great Teocalli of Tenochtitlan; but it may be safely asserted that there was at least one of these, which rose to the height of about fifty-six feet, and was divided into three stories, the lower being of stone, while the others were constructed of wrought and painted wood. In the basement of these towers were the sanctuaries, where two splendid altars had been erected to Huitzilopotchtli and Tezcatlipoca, over which the idol representatives of these divinities were placed in state.

Within the enclosure of the Teocalli there were forty other temples dedicated to various Aztec gods. Besides these there were colleges or residences and seminaries of the priests, together with a splendid house of entertainment, devoted to the accommodation of eminent strangers who visited the temple and the court. All these sumptuous ecclesiastical establishments were grouped around the pyramid, protected by the quadrangular wall, and built amid gardens and groves.

Cortéz asked leave of the emperor, who accompanied him on his visit, to enter the sanctuaries of the Aztec deities. In a spacious stuccoed saloon, roofed with carved and gilt timber, stood the gigantic idol of Huitzilopotchtli, the Mexican Mars. His countenance was harsh and menacing. In his hands he grasped a bow and golden arrows. He was girt with the folds of a serpent, formed of precious materials, while his left foot was feathered with the plumage of the humming-bird, from which he took his name. Around his throat hung suspended a massive necklace of alternate gold and silver hearts; and on the altar before him three human hearts which had recently been torn from living breasts were still quivering and bleeding, fresh from the immolated victims.

In the other chamber or sanctuary were the milder emblems of Tezcatlipoca, who " created the world and watched it with providential care." The lineaments of this idol were those of a youth, and the image, carved in black and polished stone, was adorned with disks of burnished gold and embellished with a brilliant shield. Nevertheless, the worship of this more benign deity was stained with homicide, for on its altar, in a dish of gold, the conqueror found five human hearts; and in these dens of inhumanity Bernal Diaz tells us that the " stench was more intolerable than in the slaughterhouses of Castile! "

Such is a brief summary of the observations made by the Spaniards during a week's residence in the city. They found themselves in the heart of a rich and populous empire, whose civilization, however, was, by a strange contradiction for which we shall hereafter endeavor to account, stained with the most shocking barbarity under the name of religion. The unscrupulous murder which was dignified with the associations and practice of national worship was by no means consolatory to the minds of the men who were really in the power of semi-civilized rulers and bloody priests. They discovered from their own experience that the sovereign was both fickle and feeble, and that a caprice, a hope, or a fear might suffice to make him free his country from a handful of dangerous guests by offering them as sacrifices to his gods. The Tlascalans were already looked upon with no kind feelings by their hereditary foes. A spark might kindle a fatal flame. It was a moment for bold and unscrupulous action, and it was needful to obtain some signal advantage by which the Spaniards could, at least, effect their retreat, if not insure an ultimate victory.

News just then was brought to Cortéz that four of his countrymen whom he left behind at Cempoalla had been treacherously slain by one of the tributary caciques of Montezuma; and this at once gave him a motive, or at least a pretext, for seizing the emperor himself as a hostage for the good faith of his nation. Accordingly, he visited Montezuma with a band of his most reliable followers, who charged the monarch with the treachery of his subordinates, and demanded the apprehension of the cacique to answer for the slaughter of their inoffensive countrymen. Montezuma, of course, immediately disavowed the treason and ordered the arrest of the governor; but Cortéz would not receive an apology or verbal reparation of the injury—although he professed to believe the exculpation of Montezuma himself—unless that sovereign would restore the Spaniard's confidence in his fidelity by quitting his palace and changing his residence to the quarters of the invaders.

This was, indeed, an unexpected blow. It was one of those strokes of unparalleled boldness which paralyze their victim by sheer amazement. After considerable discussion and useless appeals, the entrapped emperor tamely submitted to the surprising demand, for he saw in the resolved faces of his armed and steel-clad foes that resistance was useless, if he attempted to save his own life with the small and unprepared forces that were at hand.

For a while the most ceremonious respect was paid by the conqueror and his men to their royal prisoner, who, under strict surveillance, maintained his usual courtly pomp and performed all the functions of emperor. But Cortéz soon became his master. The will of an effeminate king was no match for the indomitable courage, effrontery, and genius of the Spanish knight. The offending cacique of Cempoalla was burned alive, either to glut his vengeance or inspire dread; and when the traitor endeavored to compromise Montezuma in his crime, fetters were placed for an hour on the limbs of the imprisoned sovereign. Every day the disgraced emperor became more and more the mere minister of Cortéz. He was forced to discountenance publicly those who murmured at his confinement, or to arrest the leading conspirators for his deliverance. He granted a province to the Castilian crown and swore allegiance to it. He collected the tribute and revenues from dependent cities or districts in the name of the Spanish king; and at last struck a blow even at his hereditary and superstitious faith by ordering the great Teocalli to be purged of its human gore and the erection of an altar on its summit, on which, before the cross and the images of the Virgin and her Son, the Christian mass might be celebrated in the presence of the Aztec multitude.

It was at this moment, when Cortéz tried the national nerve most daringly by interfering with the religious superstitions of a dissatisfied town, and when every symptom of a general rebellion was visible, that the conqueror received the startling news of the arrival on the coast of Don Pamphilo de Narvaez, with eighteen vessels and nine hundred men, who had been sent by the revengeful Velasquez to arrest Cortéz and send him in chains to St. Jago.

A more unfortunate train of circumstances can scarcely be conceived. In the midst of an enemy's capital, with a handful of men—

menaced by a numerous and outraged nation on the one hand, and with a Spanish force sent to arrest him in the name of law by authorities to whom he owed loyal respect, on the other—it is indeed difficult to imagine a situation better calculated to try the soul and task the genius of a general. But it was one of those perilous emergencies which throughout his whole career seem to have imparted additional energy rather than dismay to the heart of Cortéz, and which prove him to have been, like Nelson, a man who never knew the sensation of fear.

Nor must it be imagined that difficulty made him rash. Seldom has a hero appeared in history more perfectly free from precipitancy after he undertook his great enterprise; and in the period under consideration this is fully exhibited in the diplomacy with which he approached the hostile Spaniards on the coast who had been dispatched to dislodge and disgrace him. He resolved at once not to abandon what he had already gained in the capital; but at the same time he endeavored to tranquilize or foil Narvaez if he could not win him over to his enterprise, for it was evidently the policy of the newly arrived general to unite in a spoil which was almost ready for division rather than to incur the perils and uncertainty of another conquest.

Accordingly Cortéz addressed a letter to Narvaez requesting him not to kindle a spirit of insubordination among the natives by proclaiming his enmity. Yet this failed to affect his jealous countryman. He then desired Narvaez to receive his band as brothers in arms, and to share the treasure and fame of the conquest. But this also was rejected, while the loyal tool of Velasquez diligently applied himself to fomenting the Aztec discontent against his countrymen, and proclaimed his design of marching to Mexico to release the emperor from the grasp of his Spanish oppressor.

There was now no other opening for diplomacy, nor was delay to be longer suffered. Cortéz, therefore, leaving the mutinous capital in the hands of Pedro de Alvarado, with a band of but one hundred and fifty men to protect the treasure he had amassed, departed for the shores of the gulf with only seventy soldiers, but was joined on his way by one hundred and twenty men who had retreated from the garrison at Vera Cruz. He was not long in traversing the plains and Cordilleras toward the eastern sea; and falling suddenly on the camp of Narvaez in the dead of night, he turned the captured artillery against his foe, seized the general, received the capitulation of the army of nine hundred well-equipped men, and soon healed the factions which of course existed between the conquerors and the conquered. He had acquired the prestige which always attends extraordinary success or capacity; and men preferred the chances of splendid results under such a leader to the certainty of moderate gain under a general who did not possess his matchless genius. Thus it was that the lordly spirit and commanding talents of Cortéz enabled him to convert the very elements of disaster into the means of present strength and future success.

Chapter V

THE REVOLT AGAINST THE SPANIARDS. 1520

WHILE Cortéz was beset with the difficulties recounted in our last chapter, and engaged in overcoming Narvaez on the coast, the news reached him of an insurrection in the capital, toward which he immediately turned his steps. On approaching the city intelligence was brought that the active hostilities of the natives had been changed, for the last fortnight, into a blockade, and that the garrison had suffered dreadfully during his absence. Montezuma, too, dispatched an envoy who was instructed to impress the conqueror with the emperor's continued fidelity, and to exculpate him from all blame in the movement against Alvarado.

On June 24, 1520, Cortéz reached the capital. On all sides he saw the melancholy evidences of war. There were neither greeting crowds on the causeways nor boats on the lake; bridges were broken down; the brigantines or boats he had constructed to secure a retreat over the waters of these inland seas were destroyed; the whole population seemed to have vanished, and silence brooded over the melancholy scene.

The revolt against the lieutenant Alvarado was generally attributed to his fiery impetuosity and to the inhuman and motiveless slaughter committed by the Spanish troops under his authority during the celebration of a solemn Aztec festival, called the " incensing of Huitzilopotchtli." Six hundred victims were on that occasion slain by the Spaniards in cold blood in the neighborhood of the Great Temple; nor was a single native engaged in the mysterious rites left alive to tell the tale of the sudden and brutal assault.

Alvarado, it is true, pretended that his spies had satisfactorily proved the existence of a well-founded conspiracy which was designed to explode upon this occasion; but the evidence is not sufficient to justify the disgraceful and horrid deed that must forever tarnish his fame. It is far more probable that rapacity was the true cause of the onslaught, and that the reckless companion of the

33

conqueror who had been intrusted with brief authority during his absence miscalculated the power of his Indian foe, and confounded the warlike Mexican of the valley with the weaker soldiers dwelling in more enervating climates whom he had so rapidly overthrown in his march to the capital.

It may well be supposed that this slaughter, combined with the other causes of discontent already existing among the Aztecs, served to kindle the outraged national feeling with intense hatred of the invaders. The city rose in arms, and the Spaniards were hemmed within their defenses. Montezuma himself addressed the people from the battlements, and stayed their active assault upon the works of Alvarado; but they strictly blockaded the enemy in his castle, cut off all supplies, and entrenched themselves in hastily constructed barricades thrown up around the habitation of the Spaniards, resolved to rest behind these works until despair and famine would finally and surely throw the helpless victims into their power. Here the invaders, with scant provisions and brackish water, awaited the approach of Cortéz, who received the explanations of Alvarado with manifest disgust. "You have been false to your trust," said he; "you have done badly, indeed, and your conduct has been that of a madman!"

Yet this was not a moment to break entirely with Alvarado, whose qualities, and perhaps even his conduct, rendered him popular with a large class of the Spanish adventurers. The newly recruited forces of Cortéz gave the conqueror additional strength, for he was now at the head of no less than twelve hundred and fifty Spaniards, and eight thousand auxiliaries, chiefly Tlascalans. Yet under the untoward circumstances the increase of his forces augmented the difficulties of their support. Montezuma hastened to greet him. But the Spaniard was in no mood to trust the emperor; and as his Mexican subjects made no sign of reconciliation or submission he refused the proffered interview. "What have I," exclaimed he, haughtily, "to do with this dog of a king who suffers us to starve before his eyes!" He would receive no apology from his countrymen who sought to exculpate the sovereign, or from the mediating nobles of the court. "Go tell your master," was his reply, "to open the markets, or we will do it for him, at his cost!"

But the stern resistance of the natives was not intermitted. On the contrary, active preparations were made to assault the pile of stone buildings which formed the palace of Axayacatl, in which the

Spaniards were lodged. The furious populace rushed through every avenue toward this edifice, and encountered with wonderful nerve and endurance the ceaseless storm of iron hail which its stout defenders rained upon them from every quarter. Yet the onset of the Aztecs was almost too fierce to be borne much longer by the besieged, when the Spaniards resorted to the lingering authority of Montezuma to save them from annihilation. The pliant emperor, still their prisoner, assumed his royal robes and with the symbol of sovereignty in his hand ascended the central turret of the palace. Immediately at this royal apparition the tumult of the fight was hushed while the king addressed his subjects in the language of conciliation and rebuke. Yet the appeal was not satisfactory or effectual. " Base Aztec," shouted the chiefs; " the white men have made you a woman, fit only to weave and spin!" while a cloud of stones, spears, and arrows fell upon the monarch, who sank wounded to the ground, though the bucklers of the Spaniards were promptly interposed to shield his person from violence. He was borne to his apartments below; and, bowed to the earth by the humiliation he had suffered alike from his subjects and his foes, he would neither receive comfort nor permit his wounds to be treated by those who were skilled in surgery. He reclined in moody silence, brooding over his ancient majesty and the deep disgrace which he felt he had too long survived.

Meanwhile the war without continued to rage. The great Teocalli or mound-temple, already described, was situated at a short distance opposite the Spanish defenses; and from this elevated position, which commanded the invaders' quarters, a body of five or six hundred Mexicans began to throw their missiles into the Spanish garrison, while the natives, under the shelter of the sanctuaries, were screened from the fire of the besieged. It was necessary to dislodge this dangerous armament. An assault, under Escobar, was hastily prepared, but the hundred men who composed it were thrice repulsed, and obliged finally to retreat with considerable loss. Cortéz had been wounded and disabled in his left hand in the previous fight, but he bound his buckler to the crippled limb, and at the head of three hundred chosen men, accompanied by Alvarado, Sandoval, Ordaz, and others of his most gallant cavaliers, he sallied from the besieged palace. It was soon found that horses were useless in charging the Indians over the smooth and slippery pavements of the town and square, and accordingly Cortéz sent them back to his quarters; yet he managed to repulse the squadrons in the courtyard of the Teocalli, and to hold them in check by a file of arquebusiers. The singular architecture of this mound-temple will be recollected by the reader, and the difficulty of its ascent, by means of five stairways and four terraces, was now increased by the crowds that thronged these narrow avenues. From stair to stair, from gallery to gallery, the Spaniards fought onward and upward with resistless courage, incessantly flinging their Indian foes, by main strength, over the narrow ledges. At length they reached the level platform of the top, which was capable of containing a thousand warriors. Here, at the shrine of the Aztec war-god, was a site for the noblest contest in the empire. The area was paved with broad and level stones. Free from all impediments, it was unguarded at its edges by battlements, parapets, or any defenses which could protect the assailants from falling if they approached the sides too closely. Quarter was out of the question. The battle was hand to hand, and body to body. Combatants grappled and wrestled in deadly efforts to cast each other from the steep and sheer ledges. Indian priests ran to and fro, with streaming hair and sable garments, urging their superstitious children to the contest. Men tumbled headlong over the sides of the area, and even Cortéz himself by superior agility alone was saved from the grasp of two warriors who dragged him to the brink of the lofty pyramid and were about to dash him to the earth.

For three hours the battle raged, until every Indian combatant was either slain on the summit or hurled to the base. Forty-five of the Spaniards were killed, and nearly all wounded. A few Aztec priests, alone of all the Indian band, survived to behold the destruction of the sanctuaries which had so often been desecrated by the hideous rites and offerings of their bloody religion.

For a moment the natives were panic-struck by this masterly and victorious maneuver, while the Spaniards passed unmolested to their quarters, from which at night they again sallied to burn three hundred houses of the citizens.

Cortéz thought that these successes would naturally dismay the Mexicans, and proposed, through Mariana—his faithful interpreter, who had continued throughout his adventures the chief reliance of the Spaniards for intercourse with the Indians—that this conflict should cease at once, for the Aztecs must be convinced that a soldier who destroyed their gods, laid a part of their capital in ruins, and

CORTEZ IN THE BATTLE OF OTUMBA
Painting by M. Ramirez

—page 40

was able to inflict still more direful chastisement, was, indeed, invincible.

But the day of successful threats had passed. The force of the Aztecs was still undiminished; the bridges were destroyed; the numbers of the Spaniards were lessened; hunger and thirst were beginning to do their deadly work on the invaders; " there will be only too few of you left," said they in reply, " to satisfy the revenge of our gods."

There was no longer time for diplomacy or delay, and accordingly Cortéz resolved to quit the city as soon as practicable, and prepared the means to accomplish this desirable retreat; but on his first attempt he was unable to reach the open country through the easily defended highway of the capital or the enfilading canals and lanes. From house-tops and cross-streets innumerable Indians beset his path wherever he turned. Yet it was essential for the salvation of the Spaniards that they should evacuate the city. No other resource remained, and, desperate as it was, the conqueror persevered unflinchingly amid the more hazardous assaults of the Mexicans and all the internal discords of his own band, whom a common danger did not perfectly unite. He packed the treasure gathered during the days of prosperous adventure on his stoutest horses, and with a portable bridge, to be thrown hastily over the canals, he departed from his stronghold on the dark and rainy evening which has become memorable in history as the *noche triste,* or " melancholy night." The Mexicans were not usually alert during the darkness, and Cortéz hoped that he might steal off unperceived in this unwatchful period. But he was mistaken in his calculations. The Aztecs had become acquainted with Spanish tactics and were eager for the arrival of the moment, by day or night, when the expected victims would fall into their hands. As soon as the Spanish band had advanced a short distance along the causeway of Tlacopan the attack began by land and water; for the Indians assaulted them from their boats, with spears and arrows, or quitting their skiffs grappled with the retreating soldiers in mortal combat, and rolled them from the causeway into the waters of the lake. The bridge was wedged inextricably between the sides of a dyke, while ammunition wagons, heavy guns, bales of rich cloth, chests of gold, artillery, and the bodies of men or horses were piled in heaps on the highway or rolled into the water. Forty-six of the cavalry were cut off and four hundred and fifty of the Christians killed, while four thousand of the Indian auxiliaries perished.[1] The general's baggage, papers, and minute diary of his adventures were swallowed in the waters. The ammunition, the artillery, and every musket were lost. Meanwhile Montezuma had perished from his wounds some days before the sortie was attempted, and his body had been delivered to his subjects with suitable honors. Alvarado—Tonatiuh, the "child of the sun," as the natives delighted to call him— escaped during the *noche triste* by a miraculous leap with the aid of his lance-staff over a canal, to whose edge he had been pursued by the foe. And when Cortéz at length found himself with his thin and battered band on the heights of Tacuba, west of the city, beyond the borders of the lake, it may be said without exaggeration that nothing was left to reassure him but his indomitable heart and the faithful Indian girl whose lips, and perhaps whose counsel, had been so useful in his service.

[1] These numbers are variously stated by different authorities.—See Prescott, "Conquest of Mexico," vol. II. p. 377.

Chapter VI

THE SUCCESSES OF CORTÉZ. 1520

AFTER the disasters and fatigues of the *noche triste* the melancholy and broken band of Cortéz rested for a day at Tacuba, while the Mexicans returned to the capital, probably to bury the dead and purify their city. It is singular, yet it is certain, that they did not follow up their successes by a death-blow at the disarmed Spaniards. But this momentary paralysis of their efforts was not to be trusted, and accordingly Cortéz began to retreat eastwardly, under the guidance of the Tlascalans, by a circuitous route around the northern limits of Lake Zumpango. The flying forces and their auxiliaries were soon in a famishing condition, subsisting alone on corn or on wild cherries gathered in the forest, with occasional refreshment and support from the carcass of a horse that perished by the way. For six days these wretched fragments of the Spanish army continued their weary pilgrimage, and on the seventh reached Otumba on the way from Mexico to Tlascala. Along the whole of this march the fainting and dispirited band was ever and anon assailed by detached squadrons of the enemy, who threw stones and rolled rocks on the men as they passed beneath precipices, or assaulted them with arrows and spears. As Cortéz advanced the enemy gathered in his rear and bade him " Go on whither he should meet the vengeance due to his robbery and his crimes," for the main body of the Aztecs had meanwhile passed by an eastern route across the country and placed itself in a position to intercept the Spaniards on the plains of Otumba. As the army of the conqueror crossed the last dividing ridge that overlooked the vale of Otompan, it beheld the levels below filled, as far as eye could reach, with the spears and standards of the Aztec victors, whose forces had been augmented by levies from the territory of the neighboring Tezcoco. Cortéz presented a sorry array to be launched from the cliffs upon this sea of lances. But he was not the man to tremble or hesitate. He spread out his main body as widely as possible, and guarded the flanks by the twenty horsemen who survived the *noche triste* and the disastrous march from Tacuba. He ordered his cavalry not to cast away their lances, but to aim them constantly at the faces of the Indians, while the infantry were to thrust and not to strike with their swords. The leaders of the enemy were especially to be selected as marks, and he finally bade his men trust in God, "who would not permit them to perish by the hands of infidels." The signal was given for the charge. Spaniard and Tlascalan fought hand to hand with the foe. Long and doubtfully the battle raged on both sides, until every Spaniard was wounded. Suddenly Cortéz descried the insignia of the enemy's commanding general, and knowing that the fortunes of the day in all probability depended upon securing or slaying that personage, he commanded Sandoval, Olid; Alvarado, and Avila to follow and support him as he dashed toward the Indian chief. The Aztecs fell back as he rushed on, leaving a lane for the group of galloping cavaliers. Cortéz and his companions soon reached the fatal spot, and the conqueror, driving his lance through the Aztec leader, left him to be dispatched by Juan de Salamanca. This was the work of a moment. The death of the general struck a panic into the combined forces of Tenochtitlan and Tezcoco, and a promiscuous flight began on all sides. At sunset on July 8, 1520, the Spaniards were victors on the field of Otumba, and, gathering together in an Indian temple which they found on an eminence overlooking the plain, they offered up a *Te Deum* for their miraculous preservation as well as for the hope with which their success reinspired them.

The next day the invaders quitted their encampment on the battlefield and hastened toward the territory of their friends, the Tlascalans. The Spaniards now presented themselves to the rulers of their allies in a different guise from that worn when they first advanced toward Mexico. Fully equipped, mounted, and furnished with ammunition, they had then compelled the prompt submission of the Tlascalans, and, assuring their alliance, had conquered the Cholulans and obtained the control even of the capital and person of the Aztec emperor himself. But now they returned defeated, plundered, unarmed, poor, scarcely clad, and with the loss of a large part of those Indian allies who had acompanied the expedition. There was reason for disheartening fear in the breast of Cortéz, had it been susceptible of such an emotion. But the Lord of Tlascala reassured him, when he declared that their "cause was common against Mexico, and, come weal, come woe, they would prove loyal to the death!"

The Spaniards were glad to find a friendly palace in Tlascala in which to shelter themselves after the dreadful storms that had recently broken on their head. Yet in the quiet of their retreat, and in the excitement of their rallying blood, they began to reflect upon the past and the disheartening aspect of the future. Murmurs, which were at first confined to the barrack, at length assumed public significance, and a large body of the men, chiefly the soldiers of Narvaez, presented to Cortéz a petition which was headed by his own secretary, demanding permission to retreat to La Villa Rica de la Vera Cruz. Just at this moment, too, Cuitlahua, who mounted the throne of Mexico on the death of Montezuma, dispatched a mission to the Tlascalans, proposing to bury the hatchet and to unite in sweeping the Spaniards from the realm. The hours which were consumed by the Tlascalans in deliberating on this dread proposal were full of deep anxiety to Cortéz; for, in the present feeble condition of his Spanish force, his whole reliance consisted in adroitly playing off one part of the Indian population against another. If he lost the aid, alliance, or neutrality of the Tlascalans, his cause was lost, and all hope of reconquest, or perhaps even of retreat, was gone forever.

The promised alliance of the Mexicans was warmly and sternly supported in the debates of the Tlascalan council by some of the nobles; yet, after full and even passionate discussion, which ended in personal violence between two of the chiefs, it was unanimously resolved to reject the proposal of their hereditary foes, who had never been able to subdue them as a nation in battle, but hoped to entrap them into an alliance in the hour of common danger. These discussions, together with the positive rejection by Cortéz of the Spanish petition, seem to have allayed the anxiety of the invaders to return to Vera Cruz. With the assured friendship of the Tlascalans they could rely upon some good turn in fortune, and at length the vision of the conquest might be realized under the commander who had led them through success and defeat with equal skill.

Accordingly Cortéz did not allow his men to remain long in idle garrisons, brooding over the past or becoming moody and querulous. If he could not conquer a nation by a blow, he might perhaps subdue a tribe by a foray, while the military success or golden plunder would serve to keep alive the fire of enterprise in the breasts of his troopers. His first attack, after he had recruited the strength of his men, was on the Tepeacans, whom he speedily overthrew, and in whose chief town of Tepeaca, on the Mexican frontier, he established his headquarters in the midst of a flourishing and productive district, whence his supplies were easily gathered. Here he received an invitation from the cacique of Quauhquechollan —a town of thirty thousand inhabitants, whose chief was impatient of the Mexican yoke—to march to his relief. Olid was dispatched on this expedition; but getting entangled in disputes and frays with the Cholulans, whose people he assaulted and took prisoners, Cortéz himself assumed command of the expedition. In the assault and capture of this town Cortéz and his men obtained a rich booty. They followed up the blow by taking the strong city of Itzocan, which had also been held by a Mexican garrison; and here, too, the captors seized upon rich spoils, while the Indian auxiliaries were soon inflamed by the reports of booty, and hastened in numbers to the chief who led them to victory and plunder.

Cortéz returned to Tepeaca from these expeditions, which were not alone predatory in their character, but were calculated to pave the way for his military approach once more to the City of Mexico as soon as his schemes ripened for the conquest. The ruling idea of ultimate success never for a moment left his mind. From Tepeaca he dispatched his officers on various expeditions, and marched Sandoval against a large body of the enemy lying between his camp and Vera Cruz. These detachments defeated the Mexicans in two battles, reduced the whole country which is now known as lying between Orizaba and the western skirts of the plain of Puebla, and thus secured the communication with the seacoast. Those who are familiar with the geography of Mexico will see at a glance with what masterly generalship the dispositions of Cortéz were made to secure the success of his darling project. Nor can we fail to recognize the power of a single indomitable will over masses of Christians and Indians, in the wonderful as well as successful control which the conqueror obtained in his dealings with his countrymen as well as the natives at this period of extreme danger. When Mexico was lost after the *noche triste*, the military resources of Cortéz were really nothing, for his slender band was deprived of its most effective weapons, was broken in moral courage, and placed on an equality, as to arms, with the Indians. The successes he obtained at Otumba, Tlascala, Tepeaca, and elsewhere not only reëstablished the prestige of his genius among his countrymen, but affected even the Indians. The native cities and towns in the adjacent country appealed to him to decide in their difficulties, and his discretion and justice as an arbitrator assured him an ascendency which it is surprising that a stranger who was ignorant of their language could acquire among men who were in the semi-civilized and naturally jealous state in which he found the Aztec and Tlascalan tribes. Thus it is that, under the influence of his will and genius, "a new empire grew up in the very heart of the land, forming a counterpoise to the colossal power which had so long overshadowed it."

In the judgment of Cortéz the moment had now arrived when he was strong enough, and when it was proper, that he should attempt the reconquest of the capital. His alliance with the Tlascalans reposed upon a firm basis, and consequently he could rely upon adequate support from the Indians who would form the majority of his army. Nor were his losses of military equipments and stores unrepaired. Fortune favored him by the arrival of several vessels at Vera Cruz, from which he obtained munitions of war and additional troops. One hundred and fifty well-provided men and twenty horses were joined to his forces by these arrivals.

Before his departure, however, he dispatched a few discontented men from his camp and gave them a vessel with which they might regain their homes. He wrote an account of his adventures, moreover, to his government in Spain, and besought his sovereign to confirm his authority in the lands and over the people he might add to the Spanish crown. He addressed, also, the royal audience at San Domingo to interest its members in his cause, and when he dispatched four vessels from Vera Cruz for additional military supplies he freighted them with specimens of gold and Indian fabrics to inflame the cupidity of new adventurers.

In Tlascala he settled the question of succession in the government; constructed new arms and caused old ones to be repaired; made powder with sulphur obtained from the volcano of Popocatepetl; and, under the direction of his builder, Lopez, prepared the timber of brigantines, which he designed to carry, in pieces, and launch on the lake at the town of Tezcoco. At that port he resolved to prepare himself fully for the final attack, and this time he determined to assault the enemy's capital by water as well as by land.

Chapter VII

THE CONQUEST OF THE VALLEY. 1520-1521

AFTER a short and brilliant reign of four months Cuitlahua, the successor of Montezuma, died of smallpox, which at that period raged throughout Mexico, and he was succeeded by Guauhtemotzin, or Guatemozin, the nephew of the last two emperors. This sovereign ascended the Aztec throne in his twenty-fifth year, yet he seems to have been experienced as a soldier and firm as a patriot.

It is not to be imagined that the Aztec court was long ignorant of the doings of Cortéz. It was evident that the bold and daring Spaniard had not only been unconquered in heart and resolution, but that he even meditated a speedy return to the scene of his former successful exploits. The Mexicans felt sure that upon this occasion his advent and purposes would be altogether undisguised, and that when he again descended to the valley in which their capital nestled he would in all probability be prepared to sustain himself and his followers in any position his good fortune and strong arm might secure to him. The news, moreover, of his firm alliance with the Tlascalans and all the discontented tributaries of the Aztec throne, as well as of the reinforcements and munitions he had received from Vera Cruz, was quickly brought to the City of Mexico; and every suitable preparation was made, by strengthening the defenses, encouraging the vassals, and disciplining the troops, to protect the menaced empire from impending ruin.

Nor was Cortéz, in his turn, idle in exciting the combined forces of the Spaniards and Indians for the last effort which it was probable he could make for the success of his great enterprise. His Spanish force consisted of nearly six hundred men, forty of whom were cavalry, together with eighty arquebusiers and crossbowmen. Nine cannon of small caliber, supplied with indifferent powder, constituted his train of artillery. His army of Indian allies is estimated at the doubtless exaggerated number of over one

44

hundred thousand, armed with the *maquahuatil*, pikes, bows, arrows, and divided into battalions, each with its own banners, insignia, and commanders. His appeal to all the members of this motley array was couched in language likely to touch the passions, the bigotry, the enthusiasm, and avarice of various classes; and after once more crossing the mountains and reaching the margin of the lakes he encamped on December 31, 1520, within the venerable precincts of Tezcoco, "the place of rest."

At Tezcoco Cortéz was firmly planted on the eastern edge of the valley of Mexico, in full sight of the capital, which lay across the lake, near its western shore, at the distance of about twelve miles. Behind him toward the seacoast he commanded the country, as we have already related, while by passes through lower spurs of the mountains he might easily communicate with the valleys of which the Tlascalans and Cholulans were masters.

Fortifying himself strongly in his dwelling and in the quarters of his men in Tezcoco, he at once applied himself to the task of securing such military positions in the valley and in the neighborhood of the great causeway between the lakes as would command an outlet from the capital by land and enable him to advance across the waters of Tezcoco without the annoyance of enemies who might sally forth from strongholds on his left flank. On his right the chain of lakes, extending farther than the eye can reach, furnished the best protection he could desire. Accordingly, he first of all reduced and destroyed the ancient city of Iztapalapan—a place of fifty thousand inhabitants, distant about six leagues from the town of Tezcoco—which was built on the narrow isthmus dividing the lake of that name from the waters of Chalco. He next directed his forces against the city of Chalco, lying on the eastern extremity of the lake that bore its name, where his army was received in triumph by the peaceful citizens after the evacuation of the Mexican garrison. Such were the chief of his military and precautionary expeditions until the arrival of the materials for the boats or brigantines which Martin Lopez and his four Spanish assistant carpenters had already put together and tried on the waters of Zahuapan; and which, after a successful experiment, they had taken to pieces again and borne in fragments to Tezcoco.

Early in the spring of 1521 Cortéz intrusted his garrison at Tezcoco to Sandoval, and with three hundred and fifty Spaniards and nearly all his Indian allies departed on an expedition designed to reconnoiter the capital. He passed from his stronghold north-wardly around the head of the lakes north of Tezcoco—one of which is now called San Cristoval—and took possession of the insular town of Xaltocan. Passing thence along the western edge of the vale of Anahuac or Mexico, he reached the city of Tacuba, west of the capital, with which so many disastrous recollections were connected on his first sad exit from the imperial city. During this expedition the troops of the conqueror were almost daily en-gaged in skirmishes with the guerrilla forces of the Aztecs; yet notwithstanding their constant annoyance and stout resistance the Spaniards were invariably successful and even managed to secure some booty of trifling value. After a fortnight of rapid marching, fighting and reconnoitering, Cortéz and his men returned to Tezcoco. Here he was met by an embassy from the friendly Chalcans and pressed for a sufficient force to sustain them against the Mexicans, who dispatched the warriors of certain neighboring and loyal strongholds to annoy the inhabitants of a town which had exhibited a desire to fraternize with the invading Spaniards. In-deed, the Aztecs saw the importance of maintaining the control of a point which commanded the most important avenue to their cap-ital from the Atlantic coast. The wearied troops of Cortéz were in no state to respond to the summons of the Chalcans at that moment, for their hurried foray and incessant conflicts with the enemy had made them anxious for the repose they might justly expect in Tezcoco. Nevertheless, Cortez did not choose to rely upon his naval enterprise alone; but, conscious as he was of hold-ing the main key of the land as well as water, he dispatched with-out delay his trusty Sandoval with three hundred Spanish infantry and twenty horses to protect the town of Chalco and reduce the hostile fortifications in its vicinity. This duty he soon successfully performed. But the Aztecs renewed the assault on Chalco with a fleet of boats, and were again beaten off with the loss of a number of their nobles, who were delivered by the victors to Sandoval, whom Cortéz had sent back to support the contested town as soon as the news of the fresh attack reached him.

By this time the brigantines were nearly completed, and the canal dug by which they were to be carried to the waters of the lake, for at that time the town of Tezcoco was distant from its margin. He dared not trust these precious materials for his future success beyond the shelter of his citadel in Tezcoco, since every effort had already been made by hostile and marauding parties to destroy them; and he was therefore obliged to undergo the trouble of digging his canal, about half a league in length, in order to launch his vessels when the moment for final action arrived.

Nor was his heart uncheered by fresh arrivals from the Old World. Two hundred men, well provided with arms and ammunition, and with upwards of seventy horses—coming most probably from Hispaniola—found their way from Vera Cruz to Tezcoco and united themselves with the corps of Cortéz.

In the meantime the emperor again directed his arms against his recreant subjects of Chalco, which he seemed resolved to subdue and hold at all hazards, so as effectually to cut off the most important land approach to his capital. Envoys arrived in the Spanish camp with reports of the danger that menaced them, and earnest appeals for efficient support. This time Cortéz resolved to lead the party destined for this service, and on April 5 set out with thirty horsemen, three hundred infantry, and a large body of Tlascalans and Tezcocans, to succor a city whose neutrality, at least, it was important, as we have already shown, should eventually be secured. He seems to have effected by his personal influence in Chalco and its neighborhood what his lieutenant Sandoval had been unable to do by arms, so that he not only rendered a large number of loyal Aztecs passive, but even secured the cooperation of additional auxiliaries from among the Chalcans and the tribes that dwelt on the borders of their lake.

Cortéz was not, however, content with this demonstration against his near neighbors, but resolved, now that he was once more in the saddle, to cross the sierra that hemmed in the vale of Anahuac on the south, and to descend its southern slopes on a visit to the warmer regions that basked at their feet. Accordingly he prosecuted his southern march through large bodies of harassing skirmishers, who hung upon the rear and flanks of his troop and annoyed it with arrows and missiles, which they hurled from the crags as his men threaded the narrow defiles of the mountains. Passing through Huaxtepec and Jauhtepec, he arrived on the ninth day of his march before the strong town of Guauhnahuac, or Cuernavaca, as it it now known in the geography of Mexico. It was the capital of the Tlahuicas, and an important and wealthy tributary of the Aztecs. Here, too, he encountered hostile resistance, which he quickly overcame. His name as a successful warrior had preceded him among these more effeminate races, and the trembling lords of the territory soon submitted to his mercy.   Departing from Cuernavaca, Cortéz turned again northwards, and ascending the sierra in a new direction reëntered the valley of Anahuac or Mexico by the main route which now penetrates the southern portion of its rim.   From the summits of these mountains, where the cool air of the temperate clime sings through the limbs and tassels of hardy pines, Cortéz swooped down upon Xochimilco, or the "field of flowers," where he was again encountered by guerrillas and more formidable squadrons from the Aztec capital, which was but twelve miles distant.   Here again, after several turns in the tide of fortune, the Spaniards were triumphant and obtained a rich booty.   From Xochimilco the little band and the auxiliaries advanced among continual dangers around the western margin of the lakes, and, skirting the feet of the mountains, attained once more the town of Tacuba.

The conqueror had thus circled the valley and penetrated the adjacent southern vale in his two expeditions.   Wherever he went the strange weapons of his Spaniards, the singular appearance of his mounted men, and his uniform success served to inspire the natives with a salutary dread of his mysterious power.   He now knew perfectly the topography of the country—for he was forced to be his own engineer as well as general.   He had become acquainted with the state of the Aztec defenses as well as with the slender hold the central power of the empire retained over the tributary tribes, towns, and districts which had been so often vexed by taxation to support a voluptuous sovereign and avaricious aristocracy.   He found the sentiment of patriotic union and loyalty but feeble among the various populations he visited.   The ties of international league had everywhere been adroitly loosened by the conqueror, either through his eloquence or his weapons; and from all his careful investigations, both of character and country, he had reason to believe that the realm of Mexico was at length almost within his grasp.   The capital was now encircled with a cordon of disloyal cities.   Every place of importance had been visited, conquered, subdued, or destroyed in its moral courage or natural allegiance.   But Tacuba was too near the capital to justify him in trusting his jaded band within so dangerous a neighborhood.   Accordingly, he did not delay a day in that city, but gathering his soldiers as soon as they were refreshed he departed for Tezcoco by the northern journey around the lakes. His way was again beset with difficulties. The season of rain and storm in those lofty regions had just set in. The road was flooded, and the soldiers were forced to plow through mud in drenched garments. But as they approached their destination Sandoval came forth to meet them with companions who had freshly arrived from the West Indies; and, besides, he bore the cheering news that the brigantines were ready to be launched for the last blow at the heart of the empire.

Chapter VIII

SPANISH DEFEATS AND DISAFFECTIONS OF ALLIES
1521

THE return of Cortéz to his camp after all the toils of his arduous expedition was not hailed with unanimous delight by those who had hitherto shared his dangers and successes since the loss of the capital. There were persons in the small band of Spaniards—especially among those who had been added from the troops of Narvaez—who still brooded over the disaffection and mutinous feelings which had been manifested at Tlascala before the march to Tezcoco. They were men who eagerly flocked to the standard of the conqueror for plunder; whose hearts were incapable of appreciating the true spirit of glorious adventure in the subjugation of an empire, and who despised victories that were productive of nothing but fame.

These discontented men conspired about this period, under the lead of Antonio Villafaña, a common soldier; and it was the design of the recreant band to assassinate Sandoval, Olid, and Alvarado, together with Cortéz, and other important men who were known to be deepest in the general's councils or interests. After the death of these leaders,—with whose fall the enterprise would doubtless have perished,—a brother-in-law of Velasquez, by name Francisco Verdugo, who was altogether ignorant of the designs of the conspirators, was to be placed in command of the panic-stricken troop, which it was supposed would instantly unite under the new general.

It was the project of these wretches to assault and dispatch the conqueror and his officers while engaged in opening dispatches, which were to be suddenly presented, as if just arrived from Castile. But a day before the consummation of the treachery one of the party threw himself at the feet of Cortéz and betrayed the project, together with the information that in the possession of Villafaña would be found a paper containing the names of his associates in infamy.

Cortéz immediately summoned the leaders whose lives were

threatened, and after a brief consultation the party hastened to the quarters of Villafaña accompanied by four officers. The arch-conspirator was arrested, and the paper wrested from him as he attempted to swallow it. He was instantaneously tried by a military court—and after brief time for confession and shrift, was swung by the neck from the casement of his quarters. The prompt and striking sentence was executed before the army knew of the crime; and the scroll of names being destroyed by Cortéz, the details of the meditated treachery were forever buried in oblivion. The commander, however, knew and marked the men whose participation had been so unexpectedly revealed to him; but he stifled all discontent by letting it be understood that the only persons who suffered for the shameful crime had made no confession! He could not spare men from his thin ranks even at the demand of justice, for even the felons who sought his life were wanted in the toils and battles of his great and final enterprise.

It was on April 28, 1521, amid the solemn services of religion, and in the presence of the combined army of Spaniards and Indians, that the long-cherished project of launching the brigantines was finally accomplished. They reached the lake safely through the canal which had been dug for them from the town of Tezcoco.

The Spanish forces designed to operate in this last attack consisted of eighty-seven horse and eight hundred and eighteen infantry, of which one hundred and eighteen were arquebusiers and crossbowmen. Three large iron field-pieces and fifteen brazen falconets formed the ordnance. A plentiful supply of shot and balls, together with fifty thousand copper-headed arrows, composed the ammunition. Three hundred men were sent on board the twelve vessels which were used in the enterprise, for, unfortunately, one of the thirteen that were originally ordered to be built proved useless upon trial. The navigation of these brigantines, each one of which carried a piece of heavy cannon, was of course not difficult, for although the waters of the lake have evidently shrunken since the days of the conquest, it is not probable that it was more than three or four feet deeper than at present.[1] The distance to be traversed from Tezcoco to the capital was about twelve miles, and the subsequent service was to be rendered in the

[1] The writer sounded the lake in the channel from Mexico to Tezcoco in 1842, and did not find more than two and one-half feet in the deepest path. The Indians, at present, wade over all parts of the lake.

neighborhood of the causeways and under the protection of the walls of the city.

The Indian allies from Tlascala came up in force at the appointed time. These fifty thousand well-equipped men were led by Xicotencatl, who, as the expedition was about to set forth by land and water for the final attack, seems to have been seized with a sudden panic and deserted his standard with a number of followers. There was no hope for conquest without the alliance and loyal support of the Tlascalans. The decision of Cortéz upon the occurrence of this dastardly act of a man in whose faith he had religiously confided, although he knew he was not very friendly to the Spaniards, was prompt and terribly severe. A chosen band was directed to follow the fugitive even to the walls of Tlascala. There the deserter was arrested, brought back to Tezcoco, and hanged on a lofty gallows in the great square of that city. This man, says Prescott, " was the only Tlascalan who swerved from his loyalty to the Spaniards."

All being now prepared, Cortéz planned his attack. It will be recollected that the City of Mexico rose, like Venice, from the bosom of the placid waters, and that its communication with the mainland was kept up by the great causeways which were described in the earlier portion of this narrative. The object of the conqueror, therefore, was to shut up the capital and cut off all access to the country by an efficient blockade of the lake with his brigantines, and of the land with his infantry and cavalry. Accordingly he distributed his forces into three bodies or separate camps. The first of these, under Pedro de Alvárado, consisting of thirty horse, one hundred and sixty-eight Spanish infantry, and twenty-five thousand Tlascalans, was to command the causeway of Tacuba. The second division, of equal magnitude, under Olid, was to be posted at Cojohuacan, so as to command the causeways that led eastwardly into the city. The third equal corps of the Spanish army was intrusted to Sandoval, but its Indian force was to be drawn from native allies at Chalco. Alvarado and Olid were to proceed around the northern head of the lake of Tezcoco, while Sandoval, supported by Cortéz with the brigantines, passed around the southern portion of it, to complete the destruction of the town of Iztapalapan, which was deemed by the conqueror altogether too important a point to be left in the rear. In the latter part of May, 1521, all these cavaliers got into their assigned military positions, and it is from this period that the commencement of the siege of Mexico is dated, although Alvarado had previously had some conflicts with the people on the causeway that led to his headquarters in Tacuba, and had already destroyed the pipes that fed the water-tanks and fountains of the capital.

At length Cortéz set sail with his flotilla in order to sustain Sandoval's march to Iztapalapan.   As he passed across the lake and

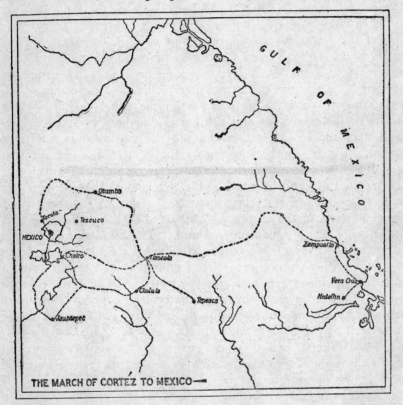

THE MARCH OF CORTÉZ TO MEXICO——

under the shadow of the "rock of the Marquis," he descried from his brigantines several hundred canoes of the Mexicans filled with soldiers and advancing rapidly over the calm lake.   There was no wind to swell his sails or give him command of his vessels' motion, and the conqueror was obliged to await the arrival of the canoes without making such disposition for action as was needful in the emergency.   But as the Indian squadron approached a breeze suddenly sprang up, and Cortéz, widening his line of battle, bore down upon the frail skiffs, overturning, crushing and sinking them by the impact of his formidable prows, while he fired to the right and left amid the discomfited flotilla. But few of these Indian boats returned to the canals of the city, and this signal victory made Cortéz the undisputed master of the lake.

The conqueror took up his headquarters at Xoloc, where the causeway of Cojohuacan met the great causeway of the south. The chief avenues to Mexico had been occupied for some time, as has been already related, but either through ignorance or singular neglect there was the third great causeway, of Tepejacac, on the north, which still afforded the means of communication with the people of the surrounding country. This had been altogether neglected. Alvarado was immediately ordered to close this outlet, and Sandoval took up his position on the dyke. Thus far the efforts of the Spaniards and auxiliaries had been confined to precautionary movements rather than to decisive assaults upon the capital. But it soon became evident that a city like Mexico might hold out long against a blockade alone. Accordingly an attack was ordered by Cortéz to be made by the two commanders at the other military points nearest their quarters. The brigantines sailed along the sides of the causeways, and aided by their enfilading fires the advance of the squadrons on land. The infantry and cavalry advanced upon the great avenue that divided the town from north to south. Their heavy guns were brought up and soon mowed a path for the musketeers and crossbowmen. The flying enemy retreated toward the great square in the center of the city, and were followed by the impetuous Spaniards and their Indian allies. The outer wall of the Great Temple itself was soon passed by the hot-blooded cavaliers, some of whom rushed up the stairs and circling corridors of the Teocalli, whence they pushed the priests over the sides of the pyramid and tore off the golden mask and jewels of the Aztec war-god. But the small band of invaders had for a moment only appalled the Mexicans, who rallied in numbers at this daring outrage, and sprang vindictively upon the sacrilegious assailants. The Spaniards and their allies fled; but the panic with which they were seized deprived their retreat of all order or security. Cortéz himself was unable to restore discipline, when suddenly a troop of Spanish horsemen dashed into the thick of the fight, and, intimidating the Indians by their superstitious fears of cavalry, they soon managed to gather and form the broken files of their Spanish and Indian army, so that soon after the hour of vespers the combined forces drew off with their artillery and ammunition to the barrack at Xoloc.

About this period the inhabitants of Xochimilco and some tribes of rude but valiant Otomies gave in their adhesion to the Spaniards. The Prince of Tezcoco, too, dispatched fifty thousand levies to the aid of Cortéz. Thus strengthened, another attack was made upon the city. Most of the injuries which had been done to the causeways in the first onslaught had been repaired, so that the gates of the capital, and finally the great square, were reached by the Spaniards with nearly as great difficulty as upon their former attempt. But this time the invaders advanced more cautiously into the heart of the city, where they fired and destroyed their ancient quarters in the old palace of Axayacatl and the edifices adjoining the royal palace on the other side of the square. These incursions into the capital were frequently repeated by Cortéz, nor were the Mexicans idle in their systematic plans to defeat the Spaniards. All communication with the country by the causeways was permanently interrupted; yet the foe stealthily, and in the night, managed to evade the vigilance of the twelve cruisers whose numbers were indeed insufficient to maintain a stringent naval blockade of so large a city as Mexico. But the success of Cortéz in all his engagements by land and water, his victorious incursions into the very heart of the city, and the general odium which was cherished against the central power of the empire by all the tributary tribes and dependent provinces, combined at this moment to aid the efforts of the conqueror in cutting off supplies from the famishing capital. The great towns and small villages in the neighborhood threw off their allegiance, and the camps of the Spanish leaders thronged with one hundred and fifty thousand auxiliaries selected from among the recreants. The Spaniards were amply supplied with food from these friendly towns, and never experienced the sufferings from famine that were soon to overtake the beleagured capital.

At length the day was fixed for a general assault upon the city by the two divisions under Alvarado and Cortéz. As usual, the battle was preceded by the celebration of mass, and the army then advanced in three divisions up the most important streets. They entered the town, cast down the barricades which had been erected to impede their progress, and with remarkable ease penetrated even

to the neighborhood of the market-place.   But the very facility of
their advance alarmed the cautious mind of Cortéz, and induced
him to believe that this slack resistance was but designed to seduce
him farther and farther within the city walls until he found himself
beyond the reach of succor or retreat.   This made him pause.   His
men, more eager for victory and plunder than anxious to secure
themselves by filling up the canals and clearing the streets of their
impediments, had rushed madly on without taking proper precaution to protect their rear, if the enemy became too hot in front.
Suddenly the horn of Guatemozin was heard from a neighboring
Teocalli, and the flying Indians, at the sacred and warning sound,
turned upon the Spaniards with all the mingled feeling of reinspired
revenge and religion.   For a while the utmost disorder prevailed in
the ranks of the invaders, Spaniards, Tlascalans, Tezcocans, and
Otomies being mixed in a common crowd of combatants.   From
the tops of houses, from converging streets, from the edges of
canals, crowds of Aztecs swarmed and poured their volleys of
javelins, arrows, and stones.   Many were driven into the lake.
Cortéz himself had nearly fallen a victim in the dreadful mêlée, and
was rescued with difficulty.   Meanwhile, Alvarado and Sandoval
had penetrated the city from the western causeway, and aided in
stemming the onslaught of the Aztecs.   For a while the combined
forces served to check the boiling tide of battle sufficiently to enable
those who were most sorely pressed to be gradually withdrawn, yet
not until sixty-two Spaniards and a multitude of allies, besides
many killed and wounded, had fallen captives and victims at the
hands of their implacable enemies.

It was yet day when the broken band withdrew from the city
and returned to the camps either on the first slopes of the hills or at
the terminations of the causeways.   But sad, indeed, was the spectacle that presented itself to their eyes as they gazed toward the city
through the clear atmosphere of those elevated regions when they
heard the drum sound from the top of the great Teocalli.   It was
the dread signal of sacrifice.   The wretched Spaniards who had
been captured in the fight were, one after another, stretched on the
stone in front of the hideous idols and their reeking hearts, torn
from their bosoms, thrown as propitiating morsels into the flames
before the deities.   The mutilated remains of the captives were
then flung down the steep sides of the pyramid, to glut the crowds
at its base with a cannibal repast.

While these repulses and dreadful misfortunes served to dispirit the Spaniards and elate the Aztecs, they were not without their signally bad effects upon the auxiliaries. Messages were sent to these insurgent bodies by the emperor. He conjured them to return to their allegiance. He showed them how bravely their outraged gods had been revenged. He spoke of the reverses that had befallen the white men in both their invasions, and warned them that a parricidal war like this could " come to no good for the people of Anahuac." Otomies, Cholulans, Tepeacans, Tezcocans, and even the loyal Tlascalans, the hereditary enemies of the Montezumas and Guatemozins, stole off secretly under the cover of night. There were, of course, exceptions in this inglorious desertion, but it seems that perhaps the majority of the tribes departed for their homes with the belief that the tide had turned against the Spanish conqueror and that it was best to escape before it was too late the scandal or danger of open treason against their lawful emperor. But amid all these disasters the heart of Cortéz remained firm and true to his purpose. He placed his artillery again in position upon the causeways, and, never wasting his ammunition, contrived to husband it carefully until the assaulting Aztecs swarmed in such numbers on the dykes that his discharges mowed them down like grass as they advanced to attack him. It was a gloomy time, requiring vigilance by day and by night—by land and by water. The brigantines were still secure. They scoured the lake continually and cut off supplies designed for the capital. The Spaniards swept the causeways with their cannon, and thus at length was the city that would not yield to storm given over to starvation.

Chapter IX

THE CAPTURE OF THE CAPITAL. 1521

THE desertion of numerous allies, which we have noticed in the last chapter, was not alone prompted by the judgment of the flying Indians, but was stimulated in a great degree by the prophecy of the Aztec priests that within eight days from the period of prediction the beleaguered city would be delivered from the Spaniards. But the sun rose on the ninth over the inexorable foes still in position on the causeways and on the lake. The news was soon sent by the allies who had remained faithful to those who had fled, and the deficient ranks were quickly restored by the numbers who flocked back to the Spanish standard as soon as they were relieved from superstitious fear.

About this time, moreover, a vessel that had been destined for Ponce de Leon in his romantic quest of Florida put into Vera Cruz with ammunition and military stores, which were soon forwarded to the valley. Thus strengthened by his renerved Indian auxiliaries and reinforced with Spanish powder and guns, Cortéz was speedily again in train to assail the capital; for he was not content to be idle except when the most serious disasters forced him to endure the slow and murderous process of subduing the city by famine.

Accordingly the conqueror resolved again to commence active hostilities. But this time he designed to permit no hazards of the moment and no personal carelessness of his officers to obstruct his entry or egress from the city. As he advanced the town was to be demolished, the canals filled up, the breaches in the dykes perfectly repaired, and as he moved onward to the north and west he determined that his path should be over a level and solid surface on which he might encounter none of the dangers that had hitherto proved so disastrous. The necessity of this course will be evident when it is recollected that all the houses were terraced with flat roofs and protecting parapets, which sheltered the assailants, while the innumerable canals bisecting the streets served as so many pitfalls for cavalry, infantry, and Indians when they became confused in the hurry of a promiscuous onset or retreat.

Meanwhile the Aztecs within the city suffered the pangs of famine. The stores that had been gathered for the siege were gone. Human bodies, roots, rats, reptiles served for a season to assuage the famished stomachs of the starving crowds, when suddenly Cortéz dispatched three Aztec nobles to Guatemozin, who were instructed to praise his defense, to assure him he had saved the honor of himself and soldiery, and to point out the utter uselessness of longer delay in submitting to inevitable fate. The message of the conqueror was weighed by the court with more favor than by the proud and spirited emperor, whose patriotic bosom burned at the disgraceful proposal of surrender. The priests turned the tide against the white men; and after two days the answer to the summons came in a warlike sortie from the city which well-nigh swept the Spanish defenders from the dykes. But cannon and musketry were too strong for mere numbers. The vessels poured in their volumes of iron hail on the flanks, and the last dread effort of defensive despair expired before the unflinching firmness of the Castilian squadrons. At length Cortéz believed that the moment for final action had arrived. He gave orders for the advance of the several corps of the army simultaneously by their several causeways; and although it pained him greatly to destroy a capital which he deemed "the gem of the world," yet he put into execution his resolve to raze the city to its foundation unless it surrendered at discretion. The number of laborers was increased daily by the hosts that flocked like vultures to the carcass of an expiring victim. The palaces, temples and dwellings were plundered, thrown down, and cast into the canals. Fresh water was entirely excluded from the city. On all sides there was fast and level land. But the Mexicans were not mere idle, contemptible spectators of their imperial city's ruin. Day after day squadrons sallied from the remains of the capital and engaged the harassed invaders. Yet the indomitable constancy of the Spaniards was not to be resisted. Cortéz and Alvarado had toiled onward toward each other from opposite sides till they met. The palace of Guatemozin fell and was burned. The district of Tlatelolco, in the north of the city, was reached, and the great market-place secured. One of the great Teocallis in this quarter was stormed, its sanctuaries burned, and the standard of Castile placed on its summit. Havoc,

death, ruin, starvation, despair, hatred were everywhere manifest.
Every hour added to the misery of the numerous and retreating
Aztecs who were pent up, as the besieging circle narrowed and
narrowed by its advances. Women remained three days and nights
up to their necks in water among the reeds. Hundreds died daily.
Others became insane from famine and thirst.

The conqueror hoped for several days that this disastrous
condition of the people would have induced the emperor to come to
terms; but, failing in this, he resolved upon a general assault. Before he resorted to this dreadful alternative, which his chivalrous
heart taught him could result only in the slaughter of men so famished, dispirited, and broken, he once more sought an interview
with the emperor. This was granted; but at the appointed time
Guatemozin did not appear. Again the appeal was renewed, and
again was Cortéz disappointed at the non-arrival of the sovereign.
Nothing then remained for him but an assault, and, as may readily
be imagined, the carnage in this combined attack of Spaniards and
confederate Indians was indescribably horrible. The long endurance of the Aztecs, their prolonged resistance and cruelty to the
Spaniards, the dreadful sacrifice of the captives during the entire
period of the siege, the memory of the first expulsion, and the speedy
hope of golden rewards nerved the arms and hearts of these ferocious men, and led them on in the work of revenge and conquest
until the sun sank and night descended on the tragic scene.

On August 13, 1521, the last appeal was made by Cortéz to the
emperor for a surrender of his capital. After the bloody scenes of
the preceding day and the increased misery of the last night, it was
not to be imagined that even insane patriotism or savage madness
could induce the sovereign to refrain from saving, at least, the
unfortunate non-combatants who still were loyal to his throne and
person. But the judgment of the conqueror was wrong. "Guatemozin would die where he was!" was the reply of the royal stoic.

Again the infuriated troops were let loose, and again were the
scenes of the day before reënacted on the bloody theater. Many
escaped in boats by the lake, but the brave or reckless Guatemozin,
who seems at the last moment to have changed his mind as to
perishing, was taken prisoner and brought, with his family, into the
presence of Cortéz. As soon as his noble figure and dignified face
were seen on the azotea or terraced roof beside the conqueror, the
battle ceased. The Indians beheld their monarch captive! And she

who had witnessed the beginning of these adventures, who had followed the fortunes of the general through all their vicissitudes—the gentle but brave Indian girl, Mariana—stood by the intrepid Cortéz to act as his interpreter in this last scene of the splendid and eventful drama.

It was on the following day that the Mexicans who still survived the slaughter and famine evacuated the city. It was a desert—but a desert covered with dead. The men who rushed in to plunder—plundered as if robbing graves. Between one and two hundred thousand people perished during the three month's siege, and their festering bodies tainted the air. The booty, though considerable, was far beneath the expectations of the conquerors; yet there was doubtless enough to reward amply the stout men-at-arms who had achieved a victory unparalleled in the annals of modern warfare.

"What I am going to say is truth, and I swear, and say Amen to it!" exclaims Bernal Diaz del Castillo, in his quaint style. "I have read of the destruction of Jerusalem, but I cannot conceive that the mortality there exceeded that of Mexico; for all the people from the distant provinces which belonged to this empire had concentrated themselves here, where they mostly died. The streets and squares, and houses, and the courts of the Tlatelolco were covered with dead bodies; we could not step without treading on them; the lake and canals were filled with them, and the stench was intolerable.

"When all those who had been able, quitted the city, we went to examine it, which was as I have described; and some poor creatures were crawling about in different stages of the most offensive disorders, the consequences of famine and improper food. There was no water; the ground had been torn up and the roots gnawed. The very trees were stripped of their bark; yet, notwithstanding they usually devoured their prisoners, no instance occurred when, amidst all the famine and starvation of this siege, they preyed upon each other.[1] The remnant of the population went, at the request of the conquered Guatemozin, to the neighboring villages until the town could be purified and the dead removed."

The capital had no sooner fallen and the ruins been searched in vain for the abundant treasures which the conquerors imagined

---

[1] This fact, as stated by Bernal Diaz, is doubted by some other writers, and seems, unfortunately, not fully sustained by authority.

were hoarded by the Aztecs, than murmurs of discontent broke forth in the Spanish camp against Cortéz for his supposed concealment of the plunder. There was a mingled sentiment of distrust both of the conqueror and Guantemozin; and at last the querulousness and taunts rose to such an offensive height that it was resolved to apply the torture to the dethroned prince in order to wrest from him the secret hiding-place of his ancestral wealth. Shameful to record, Cortéz consented to this iniquity, but it was probably owing to an avaricious and mutinous spirit in his ranks which he was unable at the moment to control. The same Indian stoicism that characterized the unfortunate prince during the war still nerved him in his hours of abject disaster. He bore the pangs without quivering or complaint and without revealing anything that could gratify the Spanish lust of gold save that vast quantities of the precious metal had been thrown into the lake—from which but little was ultimately recovered even by the most expert divers.

The news of the fall of Mexico was soon spread from sea to sea, and couriers were dispatched by distant tribes and princes to ascertain the truth of the prodigious disaster. The independent kingdom of Michoacan, lying between the vale of Anahuac or Mexico and the Pacific, was one of the first to send its envoys, and finally even its king, to the capital; and two small detachments of Spaniards returned with the new visitors, penetrating their country and passing with them even to the waters of the western ocean itself, on whose shores they planted the cross in token of rightful possession. They returned by the northern districts, and brought with them the first specimens of gold and pearls from the region now known as California.

It was not long, however, before Cortéz resolved to make his conquest available by the reconstruction of the capital that he had been forced reluctantly to mutilate and partly level during the siege. The ancient city was nearly in ruins. The massive relics of idolatry and the huge stones of which the chief palaces had been constructed were cast into the canals. The desolation was complete on the site of the ancient imperial residence. And the Indians who had served in the work of dilapidation were even compelled by their Spanish leader and his task-masters to be the principal laborers in the toil of building up a city which should surpass in splendor the ancient pride of Anahuac.

Meanwhile the sagacious mind of Cortéz was not only busy with the present duties and occupations of his men in Mexico, but began to dwell—now that the intense excitement of active war was over—upon the condition of his relations with the Spanish court and the government in the islands. He dispatched to Castile letters, presents, and the "royal fifth," together with an enormous emerald whose base was as broad as the palm of his hand. With the general's missives went a letter from his army, commending the heroic leader and beseeching its royal master to confirm Cortéz in his authority and to ratify all his proceedings. Quinoñes and Avila, the two envoys, sailed for home; but one of them, lucklessly, perished in a brawl at the Azores, while Avila, who resumed the voyage to Spain after the loss of his companion, was taken by a French privateer, who bore the spoils of the Mexicans to the court of Francis I. The letters and dispatches of Cortéz and his army, however, were saved, and Avila privately and safely forwarded them to the Spanish sovereign.

At the court of Charles V. there were, of course, numerous intrigues against the successful conqueror. The hatred of Velasquez had not been suffered to slumber in the breast of that disappointed governor, and Fonseca, Bishop of Burgos, who was chief of the colonial department, and doubtless adroitly plied and stimulated by Velasquez, managed to obtain from the churchman, Adrian, who was regent while the emperor resided in Germany, an order for the seizure of Cortéz and the sequestration of his property until the will of the court should be finally made known.

But the avaricious Velasquez, the vindictive Fonseca, and the Veedor Cristoval de Tapia, whom they employed to execute so delicate and dangerous a commission against a man who at that moment was surrounded by faithful soldiers and whose troops had been augmented by recent arrivals at Vera Cruz, reasoned with but little judgment when they planned their unjust and ungrateful measures against Cortéz. The commissioner himself seems to have soon arrived at the same conclusion, for scarcely had he landed before the danger of the enterprise and the gold of the conqueror persuaded him prudently to decline penetrating into the heart of the country as the bearer of so ungrateful a reply to the wishes of a hero whose genius and sword had given an empire, and almost a world, to Spain.

Thus at last was Cortéz for a time freed from the active hostility of the Spanish court, while he retained his authority over his conquest merely by military right and power of forcible occupation. But he did not remain idly content with what he had already done. His restless heart craved to compass the whole continent, and to discover, visit, and explore whatever lay within the reach of his small forces and of all who chose to swell them. He continually pressed his Indian visitors for information concerning the empire of the Montezumas and the adjacent territories of independent kings or tributaries. Wherever discontent lifted its head or rebellious manifestations were made he dispatched sufficient forces to whip the mutineers into contrite submission. The new capital progressed apace, and stately edifices rose on the solid land which his soldiers formed out of the fragments of ancient Mexico.

While thus engaged in his newly acquired domain, Narvaez, his old enemy, and Tapia, his more recent foe, had reached the Spanish court, where, aided by Fonseca, they once more bestirred themselves in the labor of blasting the fame of Cortéz and wresting from his grasp the splendid fruits of his valor. Luckily, however, the emperor returned about this period from eastern Europe, and from this moment the tide of intrigue seems to have been stayed, if not altogether turned. Reviled as he had hitherto been in the purlieus of the court, Cortéz was not without staunch kinsmen and warm friends who stood up valiantly in his behalf, both before councils and king. His father, Don Martin, and his friend, the Duke de Bejar, had been prominent among many in espousing the cause of the absent hero, even before the sovereign's return; and now the monarch, whose heart was not indeed ungrateful for the effectual service rendered his throne by the conqueror, and whose mind probably saw not only the justice but the policy of preserving unalienated the fidelity and services of so remarkable a personage, soon determined to look leniently upon all that was really censurable in the early deeds of Cortéz. While Charles confirmed his acts in their full extent, he moreover constituted him "Governor, Captain-General and Chief Justice of New Spain, with power to appoint to all offices, civil and military, and to order any person to leave the country whose residence there might be deemed prejudicial to the crown."

On October 15, 1522, this righteous commission was signed by Charles V. at Valladolid. A liberal salary was assigned the

1521

captain-general, his leading officers were crowned with honors and emoluments, and the troops were promised liberal grants of land. Thus the wisdom of the king and of the most respectable Spanish nobility finally crushed the mean, jealous, or avaricious spirits who had striven to defame the conqueror, while the emperor himself, with his own hand, acknowledged the services of the troops and their leader in a letter to the Spanish army in Mexico.

Among the men who felt severely the censure implied by this just and wise conduct of Charles V. was the ascetic Bishop of Burgos, Fonseca, whose influence had fallen alike upon the discoveries of Columbus and the conquests of Cortéz. He was unable to comprehend the splendid glory of the enterprises of these two heroic chieftains. Had it been his generous policy to foster them, history would have selected this son of the church as the guardian angel over the cradle of the New World; but he chose to be the shadow rather than the shining light of his era, and, whether from age or chagrin, he died in the year after this kingly rebuff from a prince whose councils he had long served.

Chapter X

THE TRIUMPH OF CORTÉZ, AND HIS LAST YEARS
1522-1547

THE royal commission of which we have spoken in the last chapter was speedily borne to New Spain, where it was joyfully received by all who had participated in the conquest or joined the original forces since that event. Men not only recognized the justice of the act, but they felt that if the harvest was rightfully due to him who had planted the seed, it was also most probable that no one could be found in Spain or the islands more capable than Cortéz of consolidating the new empire. Velasquez, the darling object of whose latter years had been to circumvent, entrap, or foil the conqueror, was sadly stricken by the defeat of his machinations. The reckless but capable soldier whom he designed to mold into the pliant tool of his avarice and glory had suddenly become his master. Wealth, renown, and even royal gratitude crowned his labors; and the disobedience, the errors, and the flagrant wrongs he was charged with while subject to gubernatorial authority were passed by in silence or forgotten in the acclamation that sounded his praise throughout Spain and Europe. Even Fonseca, the chief of the council, had been unable to thwart this darling of genius and good fortune. Velasquez himself was nothing. The great error of his life had been in breaking with Cortéz before he sailed for Mexico. He was straitened in fortune, foiled in ambition, mocked by the men whose career of dangerous adventure he had personally failed to share; and at last, disgusted with the time and its men, he retired to brood over his melancholy reverses until death soon relieved him of his earthly jealousies and annoyances.

Expeditions for conquest, and to pave the way for colonization, were sent out; a command under Sandoval to Coatzacoalcos, and another under Alvarado to the Zapotec country in the province of Oaxaca, where the famous " Tonatiuh " not only succeeded in subjugating the Indians, but found gold in such abundance that he ordered his stirrups made of it. The provinces richest in the precious metal were ascertained by means of Montezuma's tribute-books, which proved of great assistance to Cortéz.

All this was accomplished in the year 1522, during which, and for some time after, the government was in effect a military one, although there still existed the ayuntamiento, or the body of magistrates, appointed by Cortéz himself at the outset of his Mexican career, in Vera Cruz. This body had "authority over the distribution of lands to colonists, the locating and building of new cities, and the promulgation of laws for the health, order, and security of new settlers." In short, the first ayuntamiento was a very respectable body, and many of its ordinances and regulations have been observed for centuries. Justice was later dispensed by an audiencia composed of lawyers, generally five in number, these judges of the supreme court being known as oidores. Swarms of their legal brethren soon followed after from Spain, notwithstanding the entreaties of Cortéz in his dispatches to the emperor that he would keep those "pestiferous meddlers" away, who found employment as visiting and resident justices.

The first audiencia by royal appointment was created in 1528, with one Nuño de Guzman as its president, whose tyranny extended to every portion of the country, bearing particularly hard upon the poor Indians, and exemplified by the torture by fire of the native King of Michoacan, who had been one of the first to tender his allegiance.

Within two years after the conquest convents or religious houses were founded in Tlascala, Tezcoco, Mexico, and Huexotzinco by Padre Valencia, and a parochial church by the Padre Gante, who in 1529 established the college of San Juan Letran. The first body of friars, twelve barefooted Franciscans, had come out in 1523, and, received with reverence by Cortéz, became popular at once with the natives, who flocked in multitudes to hear them preach the new religion.

Four years had not entirely elapsed since the fall of Mexico when a new and splendid city rose from its ruins and attracted the eager Spaniards of all classes from the Old World and the islands. Cortéz designed this to be the continental nucleus of population. Situated on the central plateau of the realm, midway between the two seas, in a genial climate whose heat never scorched and whose cold never froze, it was indeed an alluring region to which men of all temperaments might resort with safety. Strongholds, churches, palaces were erected on the sites of the royal residences of the Aztecs and their blood-stained Teocallis. Strangers were next invited to the new capital, and in a few years the Spanish quarter contained two thousand families, while the Indian district of Tlatelolco numbered not less than thirty thousand inhabitants. The city soon assumed the air and bustle of a great mart. Tradesmen, craftsmen, and merchants thronged its streets and remaining canals.

Cortéz was not less anxious to establish, in the interior of the old Aztec empire, towns or points of rendezvous which in the course of time would grow up into important cities. These were placed with a view to the future wants of travel and trade in New Spain. Liberal grants of land were made to settlers, who were compelled to provide themselves with wives under penalty of forfeiture within eighteen months. The Indians were divided among the Spaniards by the system of repartimientos. The necessities and cupidity of the early settlers in so vast a region rendered this necessary perhaps, though it was promptly discountenanced, but never successfully suppressed, by the Spanish crown. The scene of action was too remote, the subjects too selfish, and the ministers too venal or interested to carry out with fidelity the benign ordinances of the government at home. From this apportionment of Indians, which subjected them, in fact, to a species of slavery, it is but just to the conquerors to state that the Tlascalans, upon whom the burden of the fighting had fallen, were entirely exempted at the recommendation of Cortéz.

Among all the tribes the work of conversion prospered, for the ceremonious ritual of the Aztec religion easily introduced the native worshipers to the splendid forms of the Roman Catholic. Agriculture and the mines were not neglected in the policy of Cortéz, and in fact he speedily set in motion all the machinery of civilization, which was gradually to operate upon the native population while it attracted the overflowing, industrious, or adventurous masses of his native land. Various expeditions, too, for the purpose of exploration and extension were fitted out by the Captain-General of New Spain; so that within three years after the conquest Cortéz had reduced to the Spanish sway a territory of over four hundred leagues, or twelve hundred miles, on the Atlantic coast, and of more than five hundred leagues, or fifteen hundred miles, on the Pacific.[1]

[1] Prescott, "Conquest of Mexico," vol. III. p. 274.

This sketch of a brief period after the subjugation of Mexico develops the constructive genius of Cortéz, as the preceding chapters had very fully exhibited his destructive abilities. It shows, however, that he was not liable justly to the censure which has so often been cast upon him—of being only a piratical plunderer who was seduced into the conquest by the spirit of rapine alone.

In a historical narrative which is designed to treat exclusively of Mexico, it might perhaps be considered inappropriate to relate that portion of the biography of Cortéz which is covered by his expedition to Honduras, whither he marched after he learned the defection of his lieutenant Olid, whom he had sent to that distant region with a body of Spanish soldiers to found a dependent colony. It was while on this disastrous march that the report of a conspiracy to slay the Spaniards, in which Guatemozin was implicated, reached his ears. By his orders the dethroned monarch, together with several princes and inferior nobles, was hanged. There is a difference of opinion among contemporary writers as to the guilt of Guatemozin and the Aztec nobles; but it is probable that the unfortunate prince had become a dangerous and formidable captive and that the grave was a safer prison for such a personage than the tents and bivouacs of a menaced army.

Another renowned character in this drama—the serviceable and gentle Indian girl Doña Mariana—was no longer needed and was disposed of during this expedition by marriage with Don Martin Xamarillo, to whom she brought a noble dowry of estates, which were assigned her by the conqueror in her native province, where in all likelihood she ended her romantic career. Her son by Cortéz, named after his grandfather Don Martin, became distinguished in the annals of the colony and of Spain, but in 1568 he was cruelly treated in the capital which had been won by the valor and fidelity of his parents.

From this digression in his Mexican career Cortéz was suddenly recalled by the news of disturbances in the capital, which he reached after a tempestuous and dangerous voyage. His journey from the coast to the valley was a continued scene of triumphs; and from Tezcoco, in June, 1526, he made his stately entrance into the City of Mexico amid brilliant cavalcades, decorated streets, and lakes and canals covered with the fanciful skiffs of Indians.

A month later the joy of his rapturous reception was disturbed by the announcement that the Spanish court had sent a commis-

sioner to supersede him temporarily in the government. The work
of sapping his power and influence had long been carried on at
home; and false reports, involving Cortéz in extreme dishonesty
not only to the subjects, but to the crown of Spain itself, at length
infused suspicions into the sovereign's mind. The emperor resolved to search the matter fairly to its core, and accordingly
dispatched Don Luis Ponce de Leon, a young but able nobleman,
to perform this delicate task, at the same time that he wrote with
his own hand to the conqueror, assuring him that his sole design
was not to distrust or deprive him of his honors, but to afford him
the opportunity of placing his integrity in a clear light before
the world.

De Leon and the delegate chosen on his death-bed died within
a few months, and were succeeded by Estrada, the royal treasurer,
who was hostile to Cortéz, and whose malicious mismanagement
of the investigation soon convinced even the Spanish court that
it was unjust to leave so delicate and tangled a question in his
nands. Accordingly the affair was transferred from Estrada to
a commission styled the Audiencia Real de España, and Cortéz was
commanded to hasten across the Atlantic in order to vindicate
himself from the aspersions before this august body which sat in
the midst of his countrymen.

Cortéz resolved to go at once; and, loyal to the last, rejected
all the offers that were made him to reassume the reins of power
independently of Spain. He carried with him a number of natives,
together with specimens of all the natural and artificial products of
his viceroyalty; nor did he forget a plentiful supply of gold, silver,
and jewels, with which he might maintain, in the eyes of his
luxurious countrymen, the state that was appropriate for one whose
conquests and acquisitions were so extensive. Sandoval departed
with his beloved companion in arms, but only lived to land once
more on his native land.

As he journeyed from the seaport toward Toledo the curious
crowds poured out on the wayside to behold and welcome the
hero of the New World; and from the gates of the city a gallant
crowd of cavaliers poured forth, with the Duke de Bejar and the
Count de Aguilar, to attend him to his dwelling.

The emperor received him with marked respect on the following day, and from the bountiful gifts and splendid titles which
were showered upon Cortéz before the close of 1529, it seems that

his sovereign was soon personally satisfied in his frequent and frank interviews with the conqueror that the tales he had heard from across the sea were mere calumnies unworthy his notice. The title of " Marquis of the Valley of Oaxaca " was bestowed on him. Lands in the rich province of Oaxaca and estates in the City of Mexico and other places were also ceded to him. " The princely domain thus granted him," says Prescott, " comprehended more than twenty towns and villages and twenty-three thousand vassals." The court and sovereign vied with each other in honoring and appreciating his services, and every privilege was no sooner demanded than granted, save that of again assuming the government of New Spain.

It was the policy of the Spanish court not to intrust the rule of conquered countries to the men who had subdued them. There was fancied and perhaps real danger in confiding such dearly acquired jewels to ambitious and daring adventurers who might ripen into disloyal usurpers.

Cortéz bowed submissively to the will of the emperor. He was grateful for what had been graciously conceded to his merits and services, nor was he unwilling to enjoy the luxury of careless repose after so many years of toil. His first wife—wedded, as we have related, in the islands—died a short time after she joined him in the capital after the conquest. Cortéz was yet young, nor was he ill-favored or disposed to slight the charms of the sex. A fair relative of the Aguilars and Bejars, Doña Juana Zuñiga, at this moment attracted his attention, and was soon won. Her dower of jewels, wrested from the Aztecs, and carved by their most skillful workmen, was indescribably magnificent, and after her splendid nuptials she embarked, in 1530, with the conqueror and his aged mother to return to the Indian islands, and finally to New Spain.

At Hispaniola he met an audiencia real, which was still to have jurisdiction of his case, if it ever came to trial, and at whose head was an avowed enemy of the conqueror, Nuño de Guzman. The evidence was taken upon eight scandalous charges against Cortéz, and is of so suspicious a character that it not only disgusts the general reader, but also failed in its effect upon the Spanish court by which no action was finally taken in regard to it.

Cortéz remained two months in the island before he set sail for Vera Cruz, in July, 1530; and in the meantime the Bishop of San Domingo was selected to preside over a new audiencia, inasmuch as the conduct of the late audiencia, and of Guzman especially, in relation to the Indians, had become so odiously oppressive that fears were entertained of an outbreak. The bishop and his coadjutors were men of a different stamp, who inspired the conqueror with better hopes for the future prosperity of the Indian colonies.

So jealous was the home government of the dangerous influence of Cortéz—a man so capable of establishing for himself an independent empire in the New World—that he had been inhibited from approaching the capital nearer than thirty leagues. But this did not prevent the people from approaching him. He returned to the scene of his conquest with all the personal resentments and annoyances that had been felt by individuals of old softened by the lapse of time during his prolonged absence in Spain. He came back, too, with all the prestige of his emperor's favor; and thus, both by the new honors he had won at court, and the memory of his deeds, the masses felt disposed to acknowledge, at the moment of joyous meeting, that it was alone to him they owed their possessions, their wealth, their comfort, and their importance in New Spain.

Accordingly Mexico was deserted by the courtiers, and Tezcoco, where he established his headquarters, was thronged by eager crowds who came not only to visit, but to consult, the man whose wit and wisdom were as keen as his sword, and who revisited Mexico ripened into an astute statesman.

Nevertheless, the seeming cordiality between the magistrates of the capital and the partly exiled captain-general did not long continue. Occasions arose for difference of opinion and for disputes of even a more bitter character, until at length he turned his back on the glorious valley—the scene of his noblest exploits—forever, and took up his abode in his town of Cuernavaca, which, it will be recollected, he captured from the Aztecs before the capital fell into his hands. This was a place lying in the lap of a beautiful valley, sheltered from the north winds and fronting the genial sun of the south, and here he once more returned to the cares of agriculture, introducing the sugar cane from Cuba, encouraging the cultivation of flax and hemp, and teaching the people the value of lands, cattle, and husbandry, which they had never known or fully appreciated. Gold and silver he drew from

Zacatecas and Tehuantepec; but he seems to have wisely thought that the permanent wealth and revenue of himself and his heirs would best be found in tillage.

Our limits will not permit us to dwell upon the agricultural, mineral, and commercial speculations of Cortéz, nor upon his various adventures in Mexico. It is sufficient to say that he planned several expeditions, the most important of which was unsuccessful in consequence of his necessary absence in Spain, whither he had been driven, as we have seen, to defend himself against the attacks of his enemies. Immediately, however, upon his return to Mexico, he not only sent forth various navigators to make further discoveries, but departed himself for the coast of Jalisco, which he visited in 1534 and 1535. He recovered a ship which had been seized by Nuño de Guzman, and having assembled the vessels he had commanded to be built in Tehuantepec, he embarked everything needful to found a colony. The sufferings he experienced in this expedition were extraordinarily great. His little fleet was assailed by famine and tempests, and so long was he unheard of in Mexico that at the earnest instance of his wife the viceroy Mendoza sent two vessels to search for him. He returned at length to Acapulco; but not content with his luckless efforts, he made arrangements for a new examination of the coasts, by Francisco de Ulloa, which resulted in the discovery of California, as far as the Isle de Cedros, and of all that gulf to which geographers have given the name of the "Sea of Cortéz."

His expenses in these expeditions exceeded three hundred thousand castellanos of gold, which were never returned to him by the government of Spain. Subsequently a Franciscan missionary, Fray Marcos de Naza, reported the discovery, north of Sonoma, of a rich and powerful nation called Quivara, whose capital he represented as enjoying an almost European civilization. Cortéz claimed his right to take part in or command an expedition which the viceroy Mendoza was fitting out for its conquest. But he was balked in his wishes, and was obliged to confine his future efforts for Mexico to works of beneficence in the capital.

That portion of the conqueror's life which impressed its powerful characteristics upon New Spain was now over, for although he remained long in the country, and afterward fought successfully under the emperor's banner in other lands, he was unable to win the Spanish crown to grant him authority over the empire he had subdued. He died at Castilleja de la Cuesta, near Seville, on December 2, 1547.

Cortéz provided in his will that his body should be interred in the place where he died, if that event occurred in Spain, and that within ten years his bones should be removed to New Spain and deposited in a convent of Franciscan nuns, which, under the name of La Concepcion, he ordered to be founded in Cuyoacan. Accordingly his corpse was first of all laid in the convent of San Isidro, outside the walls of Seville, whence it was carried to Mexico and deposited in the church of San Francisco, at Tezcoco, inasmuch as the convent of Cuyoacan was not yet built. Thence the ashes of the hero were carried, in 1629, to the principal chapel of the church of San Francis, in the capital; and at last were translated, on November 8, 1794, to the church of the Hospital of Jesus, which Cortéz had founded. When the revolution broke out a vindictive feeling prevailed not only against the living Spaniards, but against the dead, and men were found who invoked the people to tear these honored relics from their grave, and after burning them at San Lazaro, to scatter the hated ashes to the winds. But in the government and among the principal citizens there were many individuals who eagerly sought an opportunity to save Mexico from this disgraceful act. These persons secretly removed the monument, tablet, and remains of the conqueror from their resting place in the church of the Hospital of Jesus. Past generations deprived him, while living, of the right to rule the country he had won by his valor. Modern Mexico sought to deny his corpse even the refuge of a grave, but the ashes of Cortéz are said to be in the keeping of Señor Sebastian Aleman, the last lineal descendant of the conqueror, who, in 1903, revealed their hiding-place and expressed a desire to have them placed in the national pantheon in the City of Mexico.

Chapter XI

MEXICAN MONUMENTS AND CIVILIZATION

WHILE, according to Humboldt, "the general question of the origin of the inhabitants of a continent is beyond the limits prescribed to history," still the Aztec civilization was so unique and so highly developed as to warrant, in the opinion of the author, at least a single chapter, in addition to what has already been given incidentally to the progress of the conquest. It was in the first decade of the conquest that one of the most disgraceful destructions of paintings and manuscripts ever recorded in history took place at the instigation of the first Archbishop of Mexico, Don Juan de Zumarraga. This "Protector of the Indians" collected from every quarter, but especially from Tezcoco, where the Aztec archives were deposited, all the Indian manuscripts he could find, and causing them to be piled up in a "mountain-heap," in the market-place of Tlatelolco, he burned to ashes all these precious records, which, under the interpretation of competent natives (like the talented Ixtlilxochitl, for instance), might have relieved the early history of the Aztecs from the obscurity with which it is now clouded. Not only the hieroglyphic paintings, but every semblance of an idol, whether of gold or stone, fell before the fury of this pious iconoclast, even the great statue that once adorned the summit of the Pyramid of the Moon, miles distant from the capital. And as the soldiery imitated the example of this prelate, and eagerly emulated each other in destroying all books, charts, and papers of whatever kind which bore hieroglyphic signs whose import they had been taught to believe was as sacrilegiously symbolic and pernicious as that of the idols they had already tumbled out of Indian temples, there has ever since been a scarcity of genuine Aztec antiquities of the minor sort.

And yet it may be questioned whether these documents, had they been spared even as the curious relics of the literature or art of a semi-civilized people, would have enlightened the path of the historical student. "It has been shown," says Gallatin, "that those which have been preserved contain but a meager account of the Mexican history for the one hundred years preceding the conquest, and hardly anything that relates to prior events. The question naturally arises—from what source those writers derived their information, who have attempted to write not only the modern history of Mexico, but that of ancient times? It may without hesitation be answered that their information was traditional. The memory of important events is generally preserved and transmitted by songs and ballads, in those nations which have attained a certain degree of civilization, and have not the use of letters. Unfortunately, if we except the hymns of the great monarch of Tezcoco, which are of recent date and allude to no historical fact of an earlier epoch than his own times, no such Mexican remnants have been transmitted to us, or published. On the other hand, the recollection and oral transmission of events may have been aided by the hieroglyphics, imperfect as they were; thus, those of the significant names of a king and of a city, together with the symbol of the year, would remind the Mexicans of the history of the war of that king against that city which had been early taught him while a student in the temple."

It is thus, perhaps, that the virtuoso rather than the historical student has been the sufferer by the conflagrations of Zumarraga and the Spanish soldiers. We have unquestionably lost most of the minute events of early Aztec history. We have remained ignorant of much of the internal policy of the realm, and have been obliged to play the antiquarian in the discussion of dates and epochs whose perfect solution, even, would not cast a solitary ray of light upon the grand problem of this continent's development or population. But amid all this obscurity, ignorance, and diffuseness, it is a satisfaction to know that some valuable facts escaped the grasp of these destroyers, and that the grand historical traditions of the empire were eagerly listened to and recorded by some of the most enlightened Europeans who hastened there after the conquest of New Spain. The song, the story, and the anecdote handed down from sire to son in a nation which possessed no books, no system of writing, no letters, no alphabet— formed in reality the great chain connecting age with age, king with king, family with family; and as the gigantic bond lengthened with time, some of its links were adorned with the embellishments of fancy, while others, in the dim and distant past, became almost imperceptible. Nor were the conquerors and their successors men devoted to the antiquities of the Mexicans with the generous love of enthusiasts who delight in disclosing the means by which a people emerged from the obscurity of a tribe into the grandeur of a civilized nation. In most cases the only object they had in magnifying, or even in manifesting the real character, genius, and works of the Mexicans, is to be found in their desire to satisfy their country and the world that they had indeed conquered an empire, and not waged exterminating war against naked but wealthy savages. It was, in fact, a species of self-laudation, and it has therefore not been without at least a slight degree of incredulity that we read the glowing early accounts of the palaces, the state, and the power of the Mexican emperors. The graphic works of Stephens on Yucatan and Central America, and, since his time, of other explorers, seem, however, to open new authorities upon this vast problem of civilization. Architecture never lies. It is one of the most massive records which require too much labor in order to record a falsehood. The men who could build the edifices of Uxmal, Palenque, Copan, and Chichen-Itza were far removed from the aboriginal condition of nomadic tribes. Taste and luxury had been long grafted on the mere wants of the natives. They had learned not only to build for protection against weather, but for permanent homes whose internal arrangements should afford them comfort, and whose external appearance should gratify the public taste. Order, symmetry, elegance, beauty of ornament, gracefulness of symbolic imagery, had all combined to exhibit the external manifestations which are always seen among people who are not only anxious to gratify others as well as themselves, but to vie with each other in the exhibition of individual tastes. Here, however, as in Egypt, the architectural remains are chiefly of temples, tombs, and palaces. The worship of God, the safety of the body after death, and the permanent idea of loyal obedience to authority are symbolized by the temple, tomb, and the rock-built palace. The masses, who felt they had no constant abiding-place on earth, did not in all probability build for themselves those substantial and beautifully embellished homes under whose influence modern civilization has so far exceeded the barren humanism of the valley of the Nile. It was useless, they deemed, to enshrine in marble, while living, the miserable spirit that, after death, might crawl in a crocodile or burrow in a hog.

Christianity alone has made the dwelling paramount to the tomb and the palace.

We cannot leave the early history of Spanish occupation without naturally casting our eye over the empire which it was the destiny of Cortéz to conquer. Of its geographical boundaries we know but little. The dominions of the original Axtecs covered but a small part of the territory comprehended in modern Mexico; and although they were enlarged during the empire, they did not even then extend beyond the eighteenth degree and the twenty-first on the Atlantic or Gulf of Mexico, and beyond the fourteenth and nineteenth degree, including a narrow slip on the Pacific.

The seat and center of the Mexican empire was in the valley of Mexico, in a temperate climate, whose genial mildness is gained by its elevation of over seven thousand feet above the level of the sea. On the eastern or western borders of the lake of Tezcoco, facing each other, stood the ancient cities of Tenochtitlan or Mexico, and of Tezcoco. These were the capitals of the two most famous, flourishing, and civilized states of Anahuac, the sources of whose population and progress are veiled in the general mystery that overhangs the early history of the continent.

The general and best received tradition that we possess upon the subject declares that the original inhabitants of this beautiful valley came from the north; and that perhaps the earliest as well as the most conspicuous in the legends were the Toltecs, who moved to the south before the end of the seventh century, and settled at Tollan or Tula, north of the Mexican valley, where extensive architectural remains were yet to be found at the period of the conquest. This spot seems to have gradually become the parent hive of civilization and advancement; but after four centuries, during which they extended their sway over the whole of Anahuac, the Toltecs are alleged to have wasted away by famine, disease, and the slow desolation of unsuccessful wars. This occurred about the year 1051, as the Indian tradition relates, and the few who escaped the ravages of death departed for those more southern regions now known as Yucatan and Guatemala, in which are perhaps found the present remains of their civilization displayed in the temples, edifices, and tombs of Palenque and Uxmal. During the next century these valleys and mountains were nearly desolate and bare of population, until a rude and altogether uncivilized tribe, known as the Chichimecas, came from Amaqueme-

can, in the north, and settled in villages among the ruins of their
Toltec predecessors. After eight years, six other Indian tribes,
called Nahuatlacs, arrived, and announced the approach of another
band from the north, known as the Aztecs, who soon afterward
entered Anahuac. About this period the Acolhuans, who are said
to have emigrated from Teoacolhucan, near the original territories of the Chichimecas, advanced into the valley and speedily
allied themselves with their ancient neighbors. These tribes appear to have been the founders of the Tezcocan government and
nation which was once assailed successfully by the Tepanecs, but
was finally delivered from thraldom by the signal bravery and
talents of the Prince Nezahualcoyotl, who was heir of the crown,
supported by his Mexican allies.

The chief concern, however, in groping a way through the
tangled labyrinth of tradition is to ascertain the story of the
Aztecs, whose advent has been already announced. It was about
the year 1160 that they departed from Aztlan, the original seat
of their tribe, on their journey of southern emigration. Their
pilgrimage seems to have been interrupted by numerous halts and
delays, both on their route through the northern regions now
comprehended in the modern republic of Mexico, as well as in
different parts of the Mexican valley which was subsequently to
become their home and capital. At length, in 1325, they descried
an eagle resting on a cactus which sprang from the crevice of a
rock in the lake of Tezcoco, and grasping in his talons a writhing
serpent. This had been designated by the Aztec oracles as the site
of the home in which the tribe should rest after its long and weary
migration; and accordingly the city of Tenochtitlan was founded
upon the sacred spot, and like another Venice rose from the bosom
of the placid waters.

It was nearly a hundred years after the founding of the city,
and in the beginning of the fifteenth century, that the Tepanecs
attacked the Tezcocan monarchy. The Tezcocans and the Aztecs
or Mexicans united to put down the power of the spoiler, and as a
recompense for the important services of the allies the supreme
dominion of the territory of the royal house of Tezcoco was transferred to the Aztecs. The Tezcocan sovereigns thus became, in a
measure, mediatized princes of the Mexican throne; and the two
states, together with the neighboring small kingdom of Tlacopan
south of the lake of Chalco, formed an offensive and defensive

league which was sustained with unwavering fidelity through all the wars and assaults which ensued during the succeeding century. The bold leaguers united in that spirit of plunder and conquest which characterizes a martial people as soon as they are surrounded by the necessaries, comforts, and elegances of life in their own country, and whenever the increase of population begins to require a vent through which it may expand those energies that would destroy the state by rebellions or civil war, if pent up within the narrow limits of so small a realm as the valley of Mexico. Accordingly we find that the sway of this small tribe, which had but just nestled among the reeds, rocks, and marshes of the lake was quickly spread beyond the mountain barrier that hemmed in the valley. Like the Hollanders, they became great by the very wretchedness of their site and the vigilant industry enforced. The Aztec arms were triumphant throughout all the plains that swept downward toward the Atlantic, and even maintained dominion on the shores of the Pacific, and penetrated, under the bloody Ahuitzotl, the remotest corners of Guatemala and Nicaragua.

Such was the extent of Aztec power at the beginning of the sixteenth century, at the period of the Spanish incursion. The Aztecs, as is very well known, were not the only Indians inhabiting the Mexican tableland, for, according to the learned Mexican, Orozco y Berra, there are eleven distinct language families in Mexico, comprehending thirty-five idioms and eighty-five dialects, or a total of one hundred and twenty, still spoken within this relatively restricted territory between the Atlantic and Pacific, south of the conterminous border-line with the United States. All these languages belong, with the single exception of the Otomi, which is monosyllabic, to the polysynthetic order of speech, in common with all, or nearly all, the aboriginal idioms of North America.

"The culture of the aborigines occupying Mexico and Central America," says the ethnologist, Professor Thomas Wilson, of Washington, "was of a totally different character from that in the other regions of North America. They were sedentary, agricultural, religious, and highly ceremonial; they built immense monuments of the most enduring character, the outside of the stone walls of some of which were decorated in a high order of art, resembling more the great Certosa of Pavia than any other monument in Europe. The Teocalli, or mounds of ceremony or sacrifice, were immense. The manufacture and use of stone images and idols were extensive and surprising to the last degree. Their working of jade, and the extensive use thereof, surpasses that of any other locality in prehistoric times. Their pottery excites our wonder and admiration; some specimens for their beauty, their elegance of form and fineness of decoration; other specimens, of idols or images, are astonishing on account of the precision of their manufacture and the difficulty of its accomplishment by hand."

In order to gain an intelligible view of the inhabitants of ancient Mexico it should be remembered that there were tribes to the north, south, east, and west of the Aztecs hardly inferior to them in civilization, such, for example, as the Tarascos of Michoacan, whose capital, on the shore of Lake Patzcuaro, was Tzintzun-tzan, the House of the Humming-bird. The Tarascan empire was contemporary with the Aztec, and in time of war its soldiers bore three hundred standards of heron-plumes into battle, their priests marching ahead with their war-gods on their backs, and their caciques with silver shields and quivers of tiger-skin filled with arrows. This empire fell at the advent of the Spaniards.

We have seen, in following Cortéz from the coast of Mexico to its capital, that he was received by the Totonacs,—whose capital was Cempoalla,—people of culture whose ancestors have the credit of constructing, not only the wonderful Pyramid of Papantla, yet standing in the State of Vera Cruz, in its *tierra caliente,* but the equally wonderful pyramids of the Sun and the Moon, at San Juan Teotihuacan, near which Cortéz and the Aztecs fought the great and decisive battle of Otumba.

The barbarous Chichimecas, and perhaps the Otomies, are represented to-day by the Apaches, who have been mainly removed from Mexico through the energetic coöperation of the United States Government with Mexicans in combating them for many years. Some of the Otomies yet live in a region to the north of the valley of Mexico, and claim to be descendants of the most ancient people of that country. There are about five hundred thousand of them, mainly nomadic, and speaking an archaic, monosyllabic language.

We have already glanced at the Tezcocans, neighbors and coequals with the Aztecs, whose literature and traditions have been to some extent preserved through the efforts of Ixtlilxochitl, a descendant of the royal line of Tezcoco and a contemporary of the early colonists.

South of the Aztec region dwelt the Miztecs, Zapotecs, and Mixes, people in many respects as great in achievement as their northern congeners. The Mixtecs are a hardy people who for a long time resisted the Aztec invasions, but who were partially conquered about the middle of the fifteenth century. Speaking a nearly related idiom are the Zapotecs, the center of whose country is Oaxaca, near the site of which city Montezuma held a garrison. Traces of this occupation may be found in the speech of the present people, which is Aztec, though entirely surrounded by Zapotecs.

There were two great centers of civilization at the time of the Spanish conquest, namely in the valley of Mexico and in Yucatan—judging by the remains still existing of monumental structures. The dwellers of Yucatan were the Mayas, still represented in that territory in large numbers. To the remote ancestors of the Mayas are ascribed the erection of such wonderful temples and cities as those of Chichen-Itza, Tulum, Uxmal, Aké, Labná, and which, to the number of more than sixty distinct groups, have been discovered in Yucatan. Nearly related to these structures in similarities of architectural adornment is the great ruined city of Palenque, in which was discovered the wonderful "cross," one portion of which is in the museum at the City of Mexico and another in the keeping of the Smithsonian Institution at Washington. Over the border-line in Guatemala are still other ruined cities evidently the work of the same people, who are supposed to have been the semi-mythical Toltecs of antiquity. The Toltec culture is supposed to be evidenced in these structures of Yucatan, Palenque, Guatemala, and Copan in Honduras; though nothing may ever be discovered settling the question of their origin positively. Until fifty years ago the only work in these ruined cities was that of Stephens and Catherwood, while Mayas of Yucatan had been exploited by the authors of long-ago, Landa and Cogolludo.

Within the past twenty years a great work has been carried on among the ruins of Mexico and Central America, chiefly by archæologists sent out by museums and antiquarian societies in the United States. The names of Charnay, Le Plongeon, Thompson, Salisbury of Worcester, and Putnam of Cambridge, Massachusetts, occur in this connection, as having contributed, either by great efforts in the field or by intelligent coöperation with funds and experience, to the exploitation of these ruins.

There is a distinct difference between the ruined structures of the *tierra caliente,* as in Papantla, Yucatan, Guatemala, Copan, and Palenque, and those of the great Mexican plateau. The "hot-country" ruins are those of vast stone structures mainly, with a solidity of architectural design and a wealth of ornamentation lacking in those of the tableland. In the far north, for example, in the borderland of Sonora and Chihuahua, are found the adobé ruins of the Casas Grandes, resembling the communal dwellings still in use by the Pueblo peoples of New Mexico and Arizona. In Tula, north of the City of Mexico, the structures were of stone and adobé, as also were the pyramids of Teotihuacan; but at Xochicalco, on or near the western verge of the tableland, there are splendid examples of the finest work in sculptured stone. The great temple-pyramid of Cholula is of adobé brick, but was probably faced with stone in ancient times. Southward still further stand the magnificent ruins of Mitla, in the Zapotec country, which are apparently connecting links in the two styles of architecture, the stone and the adobé.

Space forbids a detailed description of these wonderful structures scattered throughout Mexico, since great volumes have been written upon them alone, without even exhausting the subject. It may be mentioned in passing, however, that increasing attention has been given to the subject of Mexico's archæology in the past twenty years, and much has been discovered which, half a century ago, was unknown.

Within a few years Mexico has awakened to the great value of its archæological material, and the government has conducted extensive explorations under the supervision of the director of the Mexican Museum.

No longer ago than in 1900 a section of the famous "Wall of Serpents," which formerly surrounded the Aztec Teocalli, was uncovered and its ornamentation of gigantic serpents' heads brought to view. The largest of these heads were about a meter in length and half a meter in breadth, with open mouths showing two large fangs in each. They fully bear out the descriptions given by the conquerors of their horrid appearance, being hideous beyond belief.

Another interesting object revealed by the excavations in the great square of Mexico was a slab known as the Aztec "Rock of

Famine," which was set up by the Mexicans to commemorate the return of abundance, after they had been brought near to starvation, about the year 1454.

Human skulls and bones of various description, as well as numerous small bells of brass (the old "cascabels" of the Spaniards) were found near a tower, which was also uncovered, and is supposed to have pertained to the chapel of the god of the air. Without going to the length of enumerating all the valuable objects of antiquity recently brought to light, it may be said that more has been done in recent years toward revealing the buried treasures of ancient Mexico than in centuries preceding.

It is perhaps altogether impossible to judge, at this remote day, of the absolute degree of civilization enjoyed at the period of the conquest by the inhabitants not only of the valley of Mexico and Tezcoco, but also of Oaxaca, Tlascala, Michoacan, Yucatan, and their various dependencies. In studying this subject carefully, even in the classical pages of Prescott and in the laborious criticisms of Gallatin, we find ourselves frequently bewildered in the labyrinth of historical details and picturesque legends which have been carefully gathered and grouped to form a romantic picture of the Aztec nation. Yet facts enough have survived, not only the wreck of the conquest, but also the comparative stagnation of the viceroyalty, to satisfy us that there was a large class of people, at least in the capitals and their vicinity, whose tastes, habits, and social principles were nearly equal to the civilization of the Old World at that time. There were strange inconsistencies in the principles and conduct of the Mexicans, and strange blendings of softness and brutality, for the savage was as yet but rudely grafted on the citizen and the wandering or predatory habits of a tribe were scarcely tamed by the needful restraints of municipal law.

It is probable that the Aztec refinement existed chiefly in the city of Tenochtitlan or Mexico; or that the capital of the empire, like the capital of France, absorbed the greater share of the genius and cultivation of the whole country.

The Aztec government was a monarchy, but the right to the throne did not fall by the accident of descent upon a lineal relative of the last king, whose age would have entitled him, by European rule, to the royal succession. The brothers of the deceased prince, or his nephews, if he had no nearer kin, were the individuals from

THE CATHEDRAL OF MEXICO

Showing the Aztec Calendar Stone imbedded near the base of the left-hand tower

From a Photograph

—page 95

whom the new sovereign was chosen by four nobles who had been selected as electors by their own aristocratic body during the preceding reign. These electors, together with the two royal allies of Tezcoco and Tlacopan, who were united in the college as merely honorary personages, decided the question as to the candidate, whose warlike and intellectual qualities were always closely scanned by these severe judges.

The elevation of the new monarch to the throne was pompous, yet, republican and just as was the rite of selection, the ceremony of coronation was not performed until the new king had procured, by conquest in war, a crowd of victims to grace his assumption of the crown with their sacrifice at the altar. The palaces of these princes and their nobles were of the most sumptuous character, according to the description that has been left us by the conquerors themselves.

The royal state and style of these people may be best described in the artless language of Bernal Diaz del Castillo, a soldier of the conquest, whose simple narrative, though sometimes colored with the superstitions of his age, is one of the most valuable and veritable relics of that great event that has been handed down to posterity.

In describing the entrance of the Spaniards into the city, Diaz declares, with characteristic energy, that the whole of what he saw on that occasion appeared to him as if he had beheld it but yesterday, and he fervently exclaims: " Glory be to our Lord Jesus Christ, who gave us courage to venture on such dangers and brought us safely through them! "

The Spaniards, as we have already said in a preceding chapter, were lodged and entertained at the expense of Montezuma, who welcomed them as his guests, and unwisely attempted to convince them of his power by exhibiting his wealth and state. Two hundred of his nobility stood as guards in his ante-chamber.

" Of these," says Diaz, " only certain persons could speak to him, and when they entered they took off their rich mantles and put on others of less ornament, but clean. They advanced toward his apartment barefooted, their eyes fixed on the ground and making three inclinations of the body as they approached him. In addressing the king they said, ' Lord—my lord—great lord!' When they had finished he dismissed them with a few words, and they retired with their faces toward him and their eyes fixed on the ground. I also observed that when great men came from a distance about business, they entered his palace barefooted, and in plain habit; and also that they did not come in by the gate directly, but took a circuit in going toward it.

"His cooks had upward of thirty different ways of dressing meats, and they had earthen vessels so contrived as to keep them constantly hot. For the table of Montezuma himself, above three hundred dishes were dressed, and for his guards above a thousand. Before dinner Montezuma would sometimes go out and inspect the preparations, and his officers would point out to him which were the best, and explain of what birds and flesh they were composed; and of those he would eat. But this was more for amusement than anything else.

"Montezuma was seated on a low throne or chair, at a table proportioned to the height of his seat. The table was covered with white cloths and napkins, and four beautiful women presented him with water for his hands, in vessels which they call xicales, with other vessels under them, like plates, to catch the water. They also presented him with towels.

"Then two other women brought small cakes of bread, and, when the king began to eat, a large screen of gilded wood was placed before him, so that during that period people should not behold him. The women having retired to a little distance, four ancient lords stood by the throne, to whom Montezuma from time to time spoke or addressed questions, and as a mark of particular favor gave to each of them a plate of that which he was eating. I was told that these old lords, who were his near relations, were also counselors and judges. The plates which Montezuma presented to them they received with high respect, eating what was on them without taking their eyes off the ground. He was served in earthenware of Cholula, red and black. While the king was at the table no one of his guards in the vicinity of his apartment dared, for their lives, make any noise. Fruit of all kinds produced in the country was laid before him; he ate very little; but from time to time a liquor prepared from cocoa, and of a stimulative quality, as we were told, was presented to him in golden cups. We could not, at that time, see whether he drank it or not; but I observed a number of jars, above fifty, brought in, filled with foaming chocolate, of which he took some that the women presented him.

" After he had dined they presented to him three little canes, highly ornamented, containing liquid-amber, mixed with an herb they call tobacco; and when he had sufficiently viewed and heard the singers, dancers, and buffoons, he took a little of the smoke of one of these canes, and then laid himself down to sleep.

" The meal of the monarch ended, all his guards and domestics sat down to dinner; and, as near as I could judge, above a thousand plates of those eatables that I have mentioned were laid before them, with vessels of foaming chocolate and fruit in immense quantity. For his women and various inferior servants his establishment was of a prodigious expense; and we were astonished, amid such a profusion, at the vast regularity that prevailed.

" His major domo kept the accounts of Montezuma's rents in books which occupied an entire house.

" Montezuma had two buildings filled with every kind of arms, richly ornamented with gold and jewels; such as shields, large and small clubs like two-handed swords, and lances much larger than ours, with blades six feet in length, so strong that if they fix in a shield they do not break; and sharp enough to use as razors.

" There was also an immense quantity of bows and arrows, and darts, together with slings, and shields which roll up into a small compass and in action are let fall, and thereby cover the whole body. He had also much defensive armor of quilted cotton, ornamented with feathers in different devices, and casques for the head, made of wood and bone, with plumes of feathers, and many other articles too tedious to mention." [1]

Besides this sumptuous residence in the city, the emperor is supposed to have had others at Chapultepec, Tezcoco, and elsewhere.

If the sovereign lived thus in state befitting the ruler of such an empire, it may be supposed that his courtiers were not less sumptuous in their style of domestic arrangements. The great body of the nobles and caciques possessed extensive estates, the tenures of which were chiefly of a military character; and upon these large possessions, surrounded by warlike natives and numerous slaves, they lived, doubtless, like many of the independent, powerful chieftains in Europe who in the Middle Ages maintained their feudal splendor both in private life and in active service whenever summoned by their sovereigns to give aid in war.

The power of the emperor over the laws of the country as well

[1] Bernal Diaz del Castillo, " History of the Conquest of Mexico."

as over the lives of the people was perfectly despotic. There were supreme judges in the chief towns, appointed by the emperor, who possessed final jurisdiction in civil and criminal causes; and there were, besides, minor courts in each province, as well as subordinate officers, who performed the duty of police officers or spies over the families that were assigned to their vigilance. Records were kept in these courts of the decisions of the judges; and the laws of the realm were likewise perpetuated and made certain, in the same hieroglyphic or picture-writing. "The great crimes against society," says Prescott, "were all made capital—even the murder of a slave was punished with death. Adulterers, as among the Jews, were stoned to death. Thieving, according to the degree of the offense, was punished with slavery or death. It was a capital offense to remove the boundaries of another's lands; to alter the established measures; and for a guardian not to be able to give a good account of his ward's property. Prodigals who squandered their patrimony were punished in like manner. Intemperance was visited with the severest penalties, as if they had foreseen in it the consuming canker of their own as well as of the other Indian races in later times. It was punished in the young with death, and in older persons with loss of rank and confiscation of property.

"The rites of marriage were celebrated with as much formality as in any Christian country; and the institution was held in such reverence that a tribunal was established for the sole purpose of determining questions in regard to it. Divorces could not be obtained until authorized by a sentence of this court after a patient hearing of the parties." [2]

Slavery seems to have always prevailed in Mexico. The captives taken in war were devoted to the gods under the sacrificial knife; but criminals, public debtors, extreme paupers, persons who willingly resigned their freedom, and children who were sold by their parents, were allowed to be held in bondage and to be transferred from hand to hand, but only in cases in which their masters were compelled by poverty to part with them.

A nation over which the god of war presided and whose king was selected mainly for his abilities as a chieftain, naturally guarded and surrounded itself with a well-devised military system. Religion and war were blended in the imperial ritual. Montezuma himself had been a priest before he ascended the throne. This dogma of the Aztec policy originated, perhaps, in the necessity of

[2] Prescott, "Conquest of Mexico," vol. I. p. 35.

keeping up a constant military spirit among a people whose instincts were probably civilized, but whose geographical position exposed them, in the beginning, to the attacks of unquiet and annoying tribes. The captives were sacrificed to the bloody deity in all likelihood because it was necessary to free the country from dangerous Indians who could neither be imprisoned, for they were too numerous, nor allowed to return to their tribes, because they would speedily renew the attack on their Aztec liberators.

Accordingly we find that the Mexican armies were properly officered, divided, supported, and garrisoned throughout the empire; that there were military orders of merit; that the dresses of the leaders, and even of some of the regiments, were gaudily picturesque; that their arms were excellent and that the soldier who died in combat was considered by his superstitious countrymen as passing at once to "the region of ineffable bliss in the bright mansions of the sun." Nor were these military establishments left to the caprice of petty officers for their judicial system. They possessed a set of recorded laws which were as sure and severe as the civil or criminal code of the empire; and, finally, when the Aztec soldier became too old to fight, or was disabled in the national wars, he was provided for in admirable hospitals which were established in all the principal cities of the realm.

But all this expensive machinery of state and royalty was not supported without ample revenues from the people. There was a currency of different values regulated by trade, which consisted of quills filled with gold dust; of pieces of tin cut in the form of a T; of balls of cotton, and bags of cacao containing a specified number of grains. The greater part of Aztec trade was, nevertheless, carried on by barter; and thus we find that the large taxes which were derived by Montezuma from the crown lands, agriculture, manufactures, and the labors or occupations of the people generally were paid in "cotton dresses and mantles of featherwork; ornamented armor; vases of gold; gold dust, bands and bracelets; crystal, gilt and varnished jars and goblets; bells, arms and utensils of copper; reams of paper; grain; fruits, copal, amber, cochineal, cacao, wild animals, birds, timber, lime, mats," and a general medley in which the luxuries and necessaries of life were strangely mixed. It is not a little singular that silver, which since the conquest has become the leading staple export of Mexico, is not mentioned in the royal inventories which escaped destruction.

The Mexican mythology was a barbarous compound of spiritualism and idolatry. The Aztecs believed in and relied on a supreme God whom they called Teotl, " God," or Ipalnemoani—" he by whom we live," and Tloque Nahuaque,—" he who has all in himself "; while their counter-spirit or demon, who was ever the enemy and seducer of their race, bore the inauspicious title of Tlaleatecolototl, or the " Rational Owl." The dark, nocturnal deeds of this ominous bird probably indicated its greater fitness for the typification of wickedness than of wisdom, of which the Greeks had flatteringly made it the symbol, as the pet of Minerva. These supreme spiritual essences were surrounded by a numerous court of satellites or lesser deities, who were perhaps the ministerial agents by which the behests of Teotl were performed. There was Huitzilopotchtli, the god of war, and Teoyaomiqui, his spouse, whose tender duties were confined to conducting the souls of warriors who perished in defense of their homes and shrines into the " house of the sun," which was the Aztec heaven.

Texcatlipoca was the shining mirror, the god of providence, the soul of the world, creator of heaven and earth, and master of all things. Ometcuctli and Omecihuatl, a god and goddess presiding over newborn children and reigning in Paradise, benignantly granted the wishes of mortals. Cihuacohuatl, or woman-serpent, was regarded as the mother of human beings. Tonatricli and Meztli were deifications of the sun and moon. Quetzalcoatl and Tlaloc were deities of the air and of water, while Xiuhteuctli was the god of fire to whom the first morsel and the first draught at table were always devoted by the Aztecs. Mictlanteuctli and Joalteuctli were the gods of hell and night, while the generous goddess of the earth and grain who was worshiped by the Totonacos as an Indian Ceres, enjoyed the more euphonious title of Centeotl. Huitzilopotchtli or Mexitli, the god of war, was an especial favorite with the Aztecs, for it was this divinity, according to their legends, who had led them from the north and protected them during their long journey until they settled in the valley of Mexico. Nor did he desert them during the rise and progress of their nation. Addicted as they were to war, this deity was always invoked before battle and was recompensed for the victories he bestowed upon his favorite people by bloody hecatombs of captives taken from the enemies of the empire.

If the Mexicans had their gods, so also had they their

final abodes of blessedness and misery. Soldiers who were slain in conflict for their country or who perished in captivity, and the spirits of women who died in childbirth, went at once to the "house of the sun" to enjoy a life of eternal pleasure. At dawn they hailed the rising orb with song and dances, and attended him to the meridian and his setting with music and festivity. The Aztecs believed that after some years spent amid these pleasures, the beatified spirits of the departed were changed into clouds or birds of beautiful plumage, though they had power to ascend again whenever they pleased to the heaven they had left. There was another place called Tlalocan, the dwelling-place of Tlaloc, the deity of water, which was also an Aztec elysium. It was the spirit-home of those who were drowned or struck by lightning, of children sacrified in honor of Tlaloc, and of those who died of dropsy, tumors, or similar diseases. Last of all was Mictlan, a gloomy hell of perfect darkness, in which incessant night, unilluminated by the twinkling of a single ray, was the only punishment, and the probable type of annihilation.

The reader who has accompanied us from the beginning of this volume and perused the history of the Spanish conquest has doubtless become somewhat familiar with the great square of ancient Tenochtitlan, its Teocalli, or pyramidal temple, and the bloody rites that were celebrated upon it by the Aztec priests and princes. It served as a place of sacrifice, not only for the Indian victims of war, but streamed with the blood of the unfortunate Spaniards who fell into the power of the Mexicans when Cortéz was driven from the city.

This Teocalli is said to have been completed in the year 1486, during the reign of the eighth sovereign of Tenochtitlan or Mexico, and occupied that portion of the present city upon which the cathedral stands and which is occupied by some of the adjacent streets and buildings.

The Mexican theology indulged in two kinds of sacrifice, one of which was an ordinary offering of a common victim, while the other, or gladiatorial sacrifice, was only used for captives of extraordinary courage and bravery.

When we recollect the fact that the Aztec tribe was an intruder into the valley of Anahuac, and that it laid the foundations of its capital in the midst of enemies, we are not surprised that so **hardy a race from the northern hive was both warlike** in its habits

and sanguinary in its religion.   With a beautiful land around it on
all sides, level, fruitful, but incapable of easy defense, it was forced
to quit the solid earth and to build its stronghold in the waters of
the lake.   We can conceive no other reason for the selection of such
a site.   The eagle may have been seen on a rock amid the water
devouring the serpent; but we do not believe that this emblem of
the will of heaven, in guiding the wanderers to their refuge in the
lake of Tezcoco, was known to more than the leaders of the tribe
until it became necessary to control the band by the interposition of
a miracle.   Something more was needed than mere argument to
plant a capital in the water, and thus, we doubt not that the singular
omen, in which the modern arms of Mexico have originated, was
contrived or invented by the priests or chiefs of the unsettled
Aztecs.

Surrounded by enemies, with nothing that they could strictly
call their own save the frail retreat among the reeds and rushes of
their mimic Venice, it undoubtedly became necessary for the
Aztecs to keep no captives taken in war.   Their gardens, like their
towns, were constructed upon the chinampas, or floating beds of
earth and wicker work which were anchored in the lake.   They
could not venture at any distance from its margin to cultivate the
fields.   When they sallied from their city they usually left it for
the battlefield; and when they returned it is probable that it seemed
to them not only a propitiation of their gods, but a mercy to the
victims, to sacrifice their numerous captives, who if retained in
idleness as prisoners would exact too large a body for their custody,
or, if allowed to go at large, might rise against their victor, and
in either case would soon consume the slender stores they were enabled to raise by their scant horticulture.   In examining the history
of the Aztecs and noticing the mixture of civilization which
adorned their public and private life, and the barbarism which
characterized their merciless religion, we have been convinced that
the Aztec rite of sacrifice originated in the infancy of the state
in a national necessity, and at length, under the influence of super-
stition and policy, grew into an ordinance of faith and worship.

The common sacrifice offered in the Aztec temples was performed by a chief priest and six assistants.   The principal flamen,
habited in a red scapulary fringed with cotton and crowned with a
circlet of green and yellow plumes, assumed, for the occasion, the
name of the deity to whom the offering was made.   His acolytes

—clad in white robes embroidered with black, their hands covered with leathern thongs, their foreheads filleted with parti-colored papers, and their bodies dyed perfectly black—prepared the victim for the altar, and having dressed him in the insignia of the deity to whom he was to be sacrificed, bore him through the town begging alms for the temple. He was then carried to the summit of the Teocalli, where four priests extended him across the curving sur- face of an arched stone placed on the sacrificial stone, while another held his head firmly beneath a yoke. The chief priest, the topiltzin or sacrificer, then stretched the breast of the victim tightly by bending his body back as far as possible, and, seizing the obsidian knife of sacrifice, cut a deep gash across the region of the cap- tive's heart. The extreme tension of the flesh and muscles at once yielded beneath the blade, and the heart of the victim lay palpitating in the bloody gap. The sacrificer immediately thrust his hand into the wound, and, tearing out the quivering vital, threw it at the feet of the idol, inserted it with a golden spoon into its mouth, or, after offering it to the deity, consumed it in fire and preserved the sacred ashes with the greatest reverence. When these horrid rites were finished in the temple the victim's body was thrown from the top of the Teocalli, whence it was borne to the dwelling of the individual who offered the sacrifice, where it was eaten by himself and his friends, or was devoted to feed the beasts in the royal menagerie.

Numerous cruel sacrifices were practiced by the Indians of Mexico, and especially among the Quauhtitlans, who every four years slew eight slaves or captives in a manner almost too brutal for description. Sometimes the Aztecs contented themselves with other and more significant oblations; and flowers, fruits, bread, meat, copal, gums, quails, and rabbits were offered on the altars of their gods. The priests, no doubt, approved these gifts far more than the tough flesh of captives or slaves!

The gladiatorial sacrifice was reserved, as we have already said, for noble and courageous captives. According to Clavigero, a circular mass, three feet high, resembling a mill-stone, was placed within the area of the Great Temple upon a raised terrace about eight feet from the wall. The captive was bound to this stone by one foot, and was armed with a sword or maquahuitl and shield. In this position, and thus accoutered, he was attacked by a Mexican soldier or officer, who was better prepared with weapons for the deadly encounter. If the prisoner was conquered he was immediately borne to the altar of common sacrifice. If he overcame six assailants he was rewarded with life and liberty, and permitted once more to return to his native land with the spoils that had been taken from him in war. Clavigero supposes that for many years twenty thousand victims were offered on the Mexican teocallis in the "common sacrifice"; and in the consecration of the great temple sixty thousand persons were slain in order to baptize the pyramid with their blood.

The largest collection of Mexican antiquities, including most of the minor idols, and also many examples of the famous picture-writing, as well as the feather shield of Montezuma, an authentic portrait of Cortéz, and portraits of all the viceroys, is contained in the National Museum in the City of Mexico. Its history, translated from the annals of the museum itself, is as follows:

To that pious furor which had animated the first Archbishop of Mexico, Zumarraga, the conquistadores and the missionaries (who destroyed all the ancient writings and Aztec monuments that fell in their way, considering them as invincible obstacles to the abolishment of idolatry among the subjugated Indians) there succeeded a more enlightened epoch, in which was seen what an irreparable loss the New World had met with. Some of the kings of Spain undertook to repair by every means possible the evil caused by ignorance and fanaticism, and at different times ordered to be collected all the documents that would serve to illustrate the history of America, and appointed chroniclers who were charged with writing it out. The viceroys of Mexico followed this impulse, and commenced to collect and deposit in the archives of the viceroyalty what they thought might be of interest. Particular mention should be made of the great collection made by the Chevalier Boturini, which he called his historical Indian museum, an invaluable collection of maps, hieroglyphs on skin and cloth of agave, as well as manuscripts written posterior to the conquest. This valuable treasure was practically confiscated by the colonial government and disappeared little by little, until to-day the museum possesses only a small portion of the original. It was probably on this account that all documents relating to Mexican antiquities were ordered to be delivered into the care of the Royal University. One of the viceroys, Count Revillagigedo, ordered that the antiquities found at the time of leveling the ground for the Plaza

Mayor, in 1790, should be deposited in the university for special study—with the exception of the Calendar Stone, which was asked of him by a commission of the cathedral, and set up against the western wall of that edifice. In this manner a gathering point was formed in the university for the historic documents and archæological remains of Mexico. In November, 1822, the national government established in the same edifice a conservatory of antiquities and cabinet of natural history; in 1831 both establishments were reconstructed under the name of the National Museum, which, in 1865, the Archduke Maximilian removed to quarters in the National Palace, formerly occupied by the mint. At the organization of the national government, in 1867, a sum of five hundred dollars per month was voted for the expenses of this establishment.

A valuable feature of this institution is the publication of its " Annals," with descriptions of historic objects in the museum, and of all the antiquities pertaining to Mexico. The first of these " Anales del Museo Nacional de Mexico" appeared in 1877, and they have since been published with regularity.

The articles in these " Anales" by native writers, such as Barcena, Orozco y Berra, Cubas, Sanchez, and Mendoza, are valuable contributions to Mexico's ethnology and archæology and are eagerly read. The museum is now well equipped for the work of exploration and publication, and in charge of an eminent Mexican of ability. Valuable antiquities have been found during the past twenty years, and, through the indefatigable exertions of Mexican and North American scientists, some light has been shed upon that obscure subject, the Aztec civilization.

The Aztec Calendar Stone, another monument of Mexican antiquity, was found in December, 1790, buried underground in the great square of the capital. Like the idol image of Teoyaomiqui and the sacrificial stone, it is carved from a mass of basalt, and is eleven feet eight inches in diameter, the depth of its circular edge being about seven and a half inches from the fractured square of rock out of which it was originally cut. It is supposed, from the fact that it was found beneath the pavement of the present plaza, that it was part of the fixtures of the great Teocalli of Tenochtitlan, or that it was placed in some of the adjoining edifices or palaces surrounding the temple. It is now walled into the west side of the cathedral, and is a remarkable specimen of the talent of the Indians for sculpture, at the same time that its huge mass, together with those of the sacrificial stone and the idol Teoyaomiqui, denote the skill of their inventors in the movement of immense weights without the aid of horses.

The Aztecs calculated their civil year by the solar; they divided it into eighteen months of twenty days each, and added five complimentary days, as in Egypt, to make up the complete number of three hundred and sixty-five. After the last of these months the five nemontemi or "useless days" were intercalated, and, belonging to no particular month, were regarded as unlucky by the superstitious natives. Their week consisted of five days, the last of which was the market day; and a month was composed of four of these weeks. As the tropical year is composed of about six hours more than three hundred and sixty-five days, they lost a day every fourth year, which they supplied, not at the termination of that period, but at the expiration of their cycle of fifty-two years, when they intercalated the twelve days and a half that were lost. Thus it was found, at the period of the Spanish conquest, that their computation of time corresponded with the European, as calculated by the most accurate astronomers.

At the end of the Aztec or Toltec cycle of fifty-two years—for it is not accurately ascertained to which of the tribes the astronomical science of Tenochtitlan is to be attributed,—these primitive children of the New World believed that the world was in danger of instant destruction. Accordingly its termination became one of their most serious and awful epochs, and they anxiously awaited the moment when the sun would be blotted out from the heavens and the globe itself once more resolved unto chaos. As the cycle ended in the winter, the season of the year, with its drearier sky and colder air in the lofty regions of the valley, added to the gloom that fell upon the hearts of the people. On the last day of the fifty-two years all the fires in temples and dwellings were extinguished, and the natives devoted themselves to fasting and prayer. They destroyed alike their valuable and worthless wares, rent their garments, put out their lights, and hid themselves for a while in solitude.

At dark, on the last dread evening—as soon as the sun had set, as they imagined, forever—a sad and solemn procession of priests and people marched forth from the city to a neighboring hill, to rekindle the "New Fire." This mournful march was

called the "procession of the gods," and was supposed to be their
final departure from their temples and altars.

As soon as the melancholy array reached the summit of the
hill it reposed in fearful anxiety until the Pleiades reached the
zenith in the sky, whereupon the priests immediately began the
sacrifice of a human victim, whose breast was covered with a
wooden shield, which the chief flamen kindled by friction. When
the sufferer received the fatal stab from the sacrificial knife of
obsidian, the machine was set in motion on his bosom until the
blaze had kindled. The anxious crowd stood round with fear and
trembling. Silence reigned over nature and man. Not a word
was uttered among the countless multitude that thronged the hill-
sides and plains while the priest performed his direful duty to the
gods. At length, as the first sparks gleamed faintly from the
whirling instrument, low sobs and ejaculations were whispered
among the eager masses. As the sparks kindled into a blaze, and
the blaze into a flame, and the flaming shield and victim were cast
together on a pile of combustibles which burst at once into the
brightness of a conflagration, the air was rent with the joyous
shouts of the relieved and panic-stricken Indians. Far and wide
over the dusky crowds beamed the blaze like a star of promise.
Myriads of upturned faces greeted it from hills, mountains, temples, terraces, teocallis, housetops, and city walls; and the prostrate
multitudes hailed the emblem of light, life, and fruition as a blessed
omen of the restored favor of their gods and the preservation of
the race for another cycle. At regular intervals Indian couriers
held aloft brands of resinous wood, by which they transmitted the
"New Fire" from hand to hand, from village to village, and
town to town, throughout the Aztec empire. Light was radiated
from the imperial or ecclesiastical center of the realm. In every
temple and dwelling it was rekindled from the sacred source; and
when the sun rose again on the following morning the solemn
procession of priests, princes, and subjects which had taken up its
march from the capital on the preceding night, with solemn steps
returned once more to the abandoned capital, and restoring the
gods to their altars, abandoned themselves to joy and festivity in
token of gratitude and relief from impending doom.[2]

[2] For details, see the "Calendario Azteco," by A. Chavero, Mexico, 1876.
Also, "The Mexican Calendar Stone," by Philipp J. J. Valentini; Proceedings
of the American Antiquarian Society, Worcester, Mass., October, 1878.

Chapter XII

CONDITION UNDER THE COLONIAL SYSTEM
1521-1530

AS soon as the Spaniards had plundered the wealth accumulated by the Incas and the Aztecs in the semi-civilized empires of Mexico and Peru, they turned their attention to the government of the colonies which they saw springing up as if by enchantment. The allurements of gold and the enticements of a prolific soil, under delicious skies, had not yet ceased to inflame the ardent national fancy of Spain, so that an eager emigration escaped by every route to America. An almost regal and absolute power was vested by special grants from the king in the persons who were dispatched from his court to found the first governments in the New World. But this authority was so abused by some of the ministerial agents that Charles V. took an early occasion to curb their power and diminish their original privileges. The Indians who had been divided with the lands among the conquerors by the slavish system of repartimientos were declared to be the king's subjects. In 1537 the Pope issued a decree declaring the aborigines to be "really and truly men"—"*ipsos veros homines*"—who were capable of receiving the Christian faith.

The sovereign was ever regarded from the first as the direct fountain of all authority throughout Spanish America. All his provinces were governed as colonies and his word was their supreme law. In 1511 Ferdinand created a new governmental department for the control of his American subjects, denominated the Council of the Indies, but it was not fully organized until the reign of Charles V. in 1524. *The Recopilación de las leyes de las Indias* declared that this council should have supreme jurisdiction over all the Western Indies pertaining to the Spanish crown which had been discovered at that period, or which might thereafter be discovered; that this jurisdiction should extend over all their interests and affairs; and, moreover, that the council, with the roya. assent, should make all laws and ordinances necessary for the welfare of those provinces. This Council of the Indies consisted of a president, who was the king, four secretaries, and twenty-two counselors, and the members were usually chosen from among those who had either been viceroys or held high stations abroad. It appointed all the officers employed in America in compliance with the nomination of the crown, and everyone was responsible to it for his conduct. As soon as this political and legislative machine was created it began its scheme of law-making for the colonies; not, however, upon principles of national right, but according to such dictates of expediency or profit as might accrue to the Spaniards. From time to time they were apprised of the wants of the colonists, but far separated as they were from the subject of their legislation, they naturally committed many errors in regard to a people with whom they had not the sympathy of a common country and common social or industrial interests. They legislated either for abstractions or with the selfish view of working the colonies for the advantage of the Spanish crown rather than for the gradual development of American capabilities. The mines of the continent first attracted the attention of Spain, and the prevailing principle of the scheme adopted in regard to them was that the mother country should produce the necessaries or luxuries of life for her colonial vassals, while they recompensed their parent with a bountiful revenue of gold and silver.

The bungling, blind, and often corrupt legislation of the Council of the Indies soon filled its records with masses of contradictory and useless laws, so that although there were many beneficient acts, designed especially for the comfort of the Indians, the administration of so confused a system became almost incompatible with justice. If the source of law was vicious its administration was not less impure. The principal courts of justice were the audiencias reales, or royal audiences. In addition to the president—who was the viceroy, or captain-general—the audiencia or court was composed of a regent, three judges, two fiscales or attorneys (one for civil and the other for criminal cases), a reporter, and an alguazil, or constable. The members of these courts were appointed by the king himself, and, being almost without exception natives of old Spain, they possessed but few sympathies for the colonists.

After the royal audiences came the cabildos, whose members, consisting of regidores and other persons appointed by the king,

and of two alcaldes annually elected by the regidores from among
the people, constituted a municipal body in almost every town or
village of importance.   These cabildos had no legislative jurisdiction, but superintended the execution of the laws within their districts and regulated all minor local matters.   The office of regidor
was a regular matter of bargain and sale; and, as the regidores
subsequently elected the alcaldes, it will be seen that this admitted
of great corruption and tended to augment the direct oppression
of the masses subjected to their jurisdiction.   It was an instrument
to increase the wealth and strengthen the tyrannical power of the
rulers.

These ill-regulated audiencias and cabildos were in themselves capable of destroying all principles of just harmony, and
were sufficient to corrupt the laws both in their enactment and
administration.   But all men were not equal before these tribunals.
A system of fueros or privileges opposed innumerable obstacles.
These were the privileges of corporate bodies and of the professions; of the clergy, called public or common; and of the monks,
canons, inquisitions, colleges, and universities; the privileges of
persons employed in the royal revenue service; the general privileges of the military, which were extended also to the militia, and
the especial privileges of the marines, of engineers, and of the artillery.   An individual enjoying any of these privileges was elevated
above the civil authority, and, whether as plaintiff or defendant, was
subject only to the chief of the body to which he belonged, both in
civil and criminal cases.   So great a number of jurisdictions created an inextricable labyrinth which, by keeping up a ceaseless conflict between the chiefs in regard to the extent of their powers,
stimulated each one to sustain his own authority at all hazards,
and with such resoluteness as to employ even force to gain his
purpose.   Bribery, intrigue, delay, denial of justice, outrage, and
ruin were the natural results of such a system of complicated irre-
sponsibility; and consequently it is not singular to find even now in
Mexico and South America large masses of people who are utterly
ignorant of the true principles upon which justice should be administered or laws enacted for its immaculate protection.   The
manifesto of independence issued by the Buenos Ayrean Congress
in 1816 declares that all public offices belong exclusively to the
Spaniards; and although the Americans were equally entitled to
them by the laws, they were appointed only in rare instances, and

even then not without satiating the cupidity of the court by enormous sums of money. Of one hundred and seventy viceroys who governed on this continent but four were Americans; and of six hundred and ten captains-general and governors, all but fourteen were natives of old Spain! Thus it is evident that not only were the Spanish laws bad in their origin, but the administrative system under which they operated denied natives of America in almost all cases the possibility of self-government.

The evil schemes of Spain did not stop, however, with the enactment of laws or their administration. The precious metals had originally tempted her, as we have already seen, and she did not fail to build up a commercial system which was at once to bind the colonists forever to the mines, while it enriched and excited her industry at home in arts, manufactures, agriculture, and navigation. As the Atlantic rolled between the Old World and the New, America was excluded from all easy or direct means of intercourse with other states of Europe, especially at a period when the naval power of Spain was important and frequent wars made the navigation of foreign merchantmen or smugglers somewhat dangerous in the face of her cruisers. Spain therefore interdicted all commercial intercourse between her colonies and the rest of the world, tnus maintaining a strict monopoly of trade in her own hands. All imports and exports were conveyed in Spanish bottoms, nor was any vessel permitted to sail for Vera Cruz or Porto Bello, her only two authorized American ports, except from Seville, until the year 1720, when the trade was removed to Cadiz as a more convenient outlet. It was not until the War of the Succession that the trade of Peru was opened, and even then only to the French. By the Peace of Utrecht, in 1713, Great Britain, with the asiento, or contract for the supply of slaves, obtained a direct participation in the American trade, by virtue of a permission granted her to send a vessel of five hundred tons annually to the fair at Porto Bello. This privilege ceased with the partial hostilities in 1737, but Spain found herself compelled, on the restoration of peace in 1739, to make some provision for meeting the additional demand which the comparatively free communication with Europe had created. Licenses were granted, with this view, to vessels called register-ships, which were chartered during the intervals between the usual periods for the departure of the galleons. In 1764 a further improvement was made by the establishment of monthly packets to Havana, Porto Rico, and Buenos Ayres, which were allowed to carry out half cargoes of goods. This was followed in 1774 by the removal of the interdict upon the intercourse of the colonies with each other; and this again, in 1778, under what is termed a decree of free trade, by which seven of the principal ports of the peninsula were allowed to carry on a direct intercourse with Buenos Ayres and the South Sea. Up to the period when these civilized modifications of the original interdict were made, the colonists were forbidden to trade either with foreigners or with each other's states, under any pretext whatever. The penalty of disobedience and detection was death.

Having thus enacted that the sole vehicle of colonial commerce should be Spanish, the next effort of the paternal government was to make the things it conveyed Spanish also. As an adjunct in this system of imposition, the laws of the Indies prohibited the manufacture or cultivation, in the colonies, of all those articles which could be manufactured or produced in Spain. Factories were therefore inhibited, and foreign articles were permitted to enter the viceroyalties direct from Spain alone, where they were, of course, subjected to duty previous to reëxportation. But these foreign products were not allowed to be imported in unstinted quantities. Spain fixed both the amount and the price, so that by extorting, ultimately, from the purchaser, the government was a gainer in charges, profits, and duties, while the merchants of Cadiz and Seville, who enjoyed the monopoly of trade, were enabled to affix any valuation they pleased to their commodities. The ingenuity of the Spaniards in contriving methods to exact the utmost farthing from their submissive colonists is not a little remarkable. "They took advantage of the wants of the settlers, and were at one time sparing in their supplies, so that the price might be enhanced, while at another they sent goods of poor quality, at a rate much above their value, because it was known they must be purchased. It was a standing practice to dispatch European commodities in such small quantities as to quicken the competition of purchasers and command an exorbitant profit. In the most flourishing period of the trade of Seville the whole amount of shipping employed was less than twenty-eight thousand tons, and many of the vessels made no more than annual voyages. The evident motive on the part of the crown for limiting the supply was that the same amount of revenue could be more easily levied, and collected with more certainty as well as dispatch, on a small than on a large amount of goods." [1]

While the commerce of Spain was thus burdened by enormous impositions, the colonies were of course cramped in all their energies. There could be no independent action of trade, manufacture, or even agriculture, under such a system.

America, under the tropics and in the temperate regions, abounding in a prolific soil, was not allowed to cultivate the grape or the olive, while even some kinds of provisions which could easily have been produced there were imported from Spain.

Such were some of the selfish and unnatural means by which the Council of the Indies—whose laws have been styled by some writers beneficent—sought to drain America of her wealth, while they created a market for Spain. This was the external code of oppression; but the internal system of this continent, which was justified and enacted by the same council, was not less odious. Taxation without representation or self-government was the foundation of the American Revolution; yet the patient colonies of Spain were forced to bear it from the beginning of their career, so that the idea of freedom, either of opinion or of impost, never entered the minds of an American creole.

Duties, taxes, and tithes were the vexatious instruments of royal plunder. The alcabala, an impost upon all purchases and sales, including even the smallest transactions, was perhaps the most burdensome. " Every species of merchandise, whenever it passed from one owner to another, was subject to a new tax; and merchants, shopkeepers, and small dealers were obliged to report the amount of their purchases and sales under oath." From the acquisition of an estate to the simple sale of butter, eggs, or vegetables in market all contracts and persons were subject to this tax, except travelers, clergymen and paupers. Independently of the destruction of trade, which must always ensue from such a system, the reader will at once observe the temptations to vice opened by it. The natural spirit of gain tempts a dealer to cheat an oppressive government by every means in his power. It is therefore not wonderful to find the country filled with contrabandists, and the towns with dishonest tradesmen. Men who defraud in acts will lie in words, nor will they hesitate to conceal their infamy under the sanction of an oath. Thus was it that the oppressive taxation of Spain became the direct instrument of popular corruption, and by

[1] *North American Review*, vol. XIX. p. 117.

extending imposts to the minutest ramifications of society it made
the people smugglers, cheats, and perjurers. In addition to the
alcabala, there were transit duties through the country, under
which, it has been alleged, that European articles were sometimes
taxed thirty times before they reached their consumer. The king
had his royal fifth of all the gold and silver, and his monopolies
of tobacco, salt, and gunpowder. He often openly vended the
colonial offices, both civil and ecclesiastical. He stamped paper
and derived a revenue from its sale, and affixed a poll tax on every
Indian.

Inasmuch as the Indians formed the great bulk of Hispano-
American population, the king, of course, soon after the discovery
directed his attention to their capabilities for labor. By a system of
repartimientos they were divided among the conquerors and made
vassals of the landholders, although kept distinct from the negroes
afterward imported from Africa. Although the Emperor Charles
V. enacted a number of mild laws for the amelioration of their
fate, their condition seems, nevertheless, to have been very little
improved, according to our personal observation, even to the
present day. The capitation tax levied on every Indian varied in
different parts of Spanish America, from four to fifteen dollars,
according to the ability of the Indians. They were likewise
doomed to labor on the public works, as well as to cultivate the soil
for the general benefit of the country, while by the imposition
of the mita they were forced to toil in the mines under a rigorous
and debasing system which the world believed altogether unequaled in mineral districts until the British parliamentary reports
in years past disclosed the fact that even in England men and
women are sometimes degraded into beasts of burden in the
mines whose galleries traverse in every direction the bowels of
that proud kingdom. Toils and suffering were the natural conditions of the poor Indian in America after the conquest, and it
might have been supposed that the plain dictates of humanity
would make the Spaniards content with the labor of their serfs,
without attempting afterward to rob them of the wages of such
ignominious labor. But even in this Spanish ingenuity and
avarice were not to be foiled, for the corregidores in the towns
and villages, to whom were granted the minor monopolies of
almost all the necessaries of life, made this a pretext of obliging
the Indians to purchase what they required at the prices they chose

to affix to their goods.   Monopoly was the order of the day in the sixteenth and seventeenth centuries.   Its oppressions extended through all ranks, and its grasping advantages were eagerly seized by every magistrate from the alguazil to the viceroy.   The people groaned, but paid the burdensome exaction, while the relentless officer, hardened by the contemplation of misery and the constant commission of legalized robbery, only became more watchful, sagacious, and grinding in proportion as he discovered how much the down-trodden masses could bear.   Benevolent viceroys and liberal kings frequently interposed to prevent the continuance of these unjust acts, but they were unable to cope with the numerous officials who performed all the minor ministerial duties throughout the colony.   These inferior agents in a new and partially unorganized country had every advantage in their favor over the central authorities in the capital.   The poorer Spaniards and the Indian serfs had no means of making their complaints heard in the palace. There was no press or public opinion to give voice to the sorrows of the masses, and personal fear often silenced the few who might have reached the ear of merciful and just rulers.   At court the rich, powerful, and influential miners or landholders always discovered pliant tools who were ready by intrigue and corruption to smother the cry of discontent, or to account plausibly for the murmurs which upon extraordinary occasions burst through all restraints until they reached either the audiencia or the representative of the sovereign.   These slender excuses may in some degree account for and palliate the maladministration of Spanish America from the middle of the sixteenth to the beginning of the nineteenth century.

Chapter XIII

ANTONIO DE MENDOZA, FIRST VICEROY OF NEW SPAIN. 1530-1551

IN the year 1530 the accusations received in Spain against Nuño de Guzman and the oidores Matinezo and Delgadillo, who at that period ruled in Mexico under royal authority, were not only so frequent, but of so terrible a character, that Charles V. resolved to adopt some means of remedying the evils of his transatlantic subjects. He was about to depart from Spain, however, for Flanders, and charged the empress to adopt the necessary measures for this purpose during his absence. This enlightened personation of sovereignty, the direct representative of the national and rich an appendage of the Spanish crown by inferior officials alone, wisely determined to establish a viceroyalty in New Spain. It was a measure which seemed to place the two worlds in more loyal affinity. The vice king, it was supposed, would be the impersonation of sovereignty, the direct representative of the national head, and would always form an independent and truthful channel of information. His position set him eminently above the crowd of adventurers who were tempted to the shores of America, and, removable at the royal pleasure as well as selected from among those Spanish nobles whose fidelity to the crown was unquestionable, there was but little danger that even the most ambitious subjects would ever be tempted to alienate from the emperor the affection and services either of emigrants or natives.

The empress, in fulfilling the wishes of her august spouse, at first fixed her eyes upon the Count de Oropesa and on the Marshal de Fromesta as persons well fitted to undertake the difficult charge of founding the Mexican viceroyalty. But these individuals upon various pretexts declined the mission, which was next tendered to Don Manuel Benavides, whose exorbitant demands for money and authority finally induced the sovereign to withdraw her nomination. Finally she resolved to dispatch Don Antonio de Mendoza, Count de Tendilla, one of her chamberlains, who requested only

106

sufficient time to regulate his private affairs before he joyfully set forth for his viceroyalty of New Spain. In the meantime, however, in order not to lose a moment in remedying the disorders on the other side of the Atlantic, the empress created a new audiencia, at the head of which was Don Sebastian Ramirez de Fuenleal, Bishop of San Domingo, and whose members were the Licenciados Vasco de Quiroga, Alonso Maldonado, Francisco Cainos, and Juan de Salmeron. The appointment of the bishop was well justified by his subsequent career of integrity, beneficence, and wisdom; while Vasco de Quiroga has left in Michoacan, and, indeed, in all Mexico, a venerated name, whose renown is not forgotten, in private life and the legends of the country, to the present day.

In 1535 Mendoza arrived in Mexico with letters for the audiencia, and was received with all the pomp and splendor becoming the representative of royalty. His instructions were couched in the most liberal terms, for, after all, it was chiefly on the personal integrity and discretion of a viceroy that the Spanish sovereigns were obliged to rely for the sure foundation of their American empire.

Of the desire of the emperor and empress to act their parts justly and honestly in the opening of this splendid drama in America there can be no doubt. Their true policy was to develop, not to destroy; and they at once perceived that in the New World they no longer dealt with those organized classes of civilized society which, in Europe, yield either instinctively to the feeling of loyalty or are easily coerced into obedience to the laws.

Mendoza was commanded, in the first place, to direct his attention to the condition of public worship; to the punishment of clergymen who scandalized their calling; to the conversion and good treatment of the Indian population, and to the erection of a mint in which silver should be coined according to laws made upon this subject by Ferdinand and Isabella. All the wealth which was found in Indian tombs or temples was to be sought out and devoted to the royal treasury. It was forbidden, under heavy penalties, to sell arms to negroes or Indians, and the latter were, moreover, denied the privilege of learning to work in those more difficult or elegant branches of labor which might interfere with the sale of Spanish imported productions.

During the following year Mendoza received dispatches from the emperor in which, after bestowing encomiums for the manifestations of good government which the viceroy had already given, he was directed to pay particular attention to the Indians; and, together with these missives, came a summary of the laws which the Council of the Indies had formed for the welfare of the natives. These benevolent intentions, not only of the sovereign but of the Spanish people also, were made known to the Indians and their caciques, upon an occasion of festivity, by a clergyman who was versed in their language, and in a similar way they were disseminated throughout the whole viceroyalty.

This year was, moreover, memorable in Mexican annals as that in which the first book, entitled " *La Escala de San Juan Climaca,*" was published in Mexico, in the establishment of Juan Pablos, having been printed at a press brought to the country by the viceroy, Mendoza. Nor was 1536 alone signalized by the first literary issue of the new kingdom; for the first money came at this time from the Mexican mint. According to Torquemada two hundred thousand dollars were coined in copper; but the emission of a circulation medium in this base metal was so distasteful to the Mexicans that it became necessary for the viceroy to use stringent means in order to compel its reception for the ordinary purposes of trade.

Between the years 1536 and 1540 the history of the Mexican viceroyalty was uneventful, save in the gradual progressive efforts made not only by Mendoza, but by the emperor himself, in endeavoring to model and consolidate the Spanish empire in America. Schools were established, hospitals were erected, the protection of the Indians, under the apostolic labors of Las Casas, was honestly fostered, and every effort appears to have been zealously made to give permanent and domestic character to the population which found its way rapidly into New Spain. In 1541 the copper coin, of which we have already spoken as being distasteful to the Mexicans, suddenly disappeared altogether from circulation, and it was discovered that the natives had either buried or thrown it into the lake as utterly worthless. The viceroy endeavored to remedy the evil and dispel the popular prejudice by coining cuartillas of silver; but these, from their extreme smallness and the constant risk of loss, were equally unacceptable to the people, who either collected large quantities and melted them into bars, or cast them contemptuously into the water as they had before done with the despised copper.

It was not until about the year 1542 that we perceive in the viceroyal history any attempts upon the part of the Indians to make formidable assaults against the Spaniards, whose oppressive and grinding system of repartimientos was undoubtedly beginning to be felt. At this period the Indians of Jalisco rose in arms, and symptoms of discontent were observed to prevail also among the Tarascos and Tlascalans, who even manifested an intention of uniting with the rebellious natives of the north. Mendoza was not an idle spectator of these movements, but resolved to go forth in person at the head of his troops to put down the insurgents. Accordingly he called on the Tlascalans, Cholulans, Huexotzinques, Tezcocans, and other bands or tribes for support, and permitted the caciques to use horses and the same arms that were borne by the Spaniards. This concession seems to have greatly pleased the natives of the country, though it was unsatisfactory to some of their foreign masters.

In the meanwhile the coasts of America on the west, and the shores of California especially, were examined by the Portuguese Juan Rodriguez Cabrillo as far north as near the forty-first degree of latitude, while another expedition was dispatched to the Spice Islands, under the charge of Ruy Lopez de Villalobos.

The viceroy was, moreover, busy with the preparation of his army designed to march upon Jalisco, and on October 8, 1542, departed from Mexico with a force of 50,000 Indians, 300 cavalry, and 150 Spanish infantry. Passing through Michoacan, where he was detained for some time, he at length reached the scene of the insurrection in Jalisco; but before he attacked the rebels he proclaimed through the ecclesiastics who accompanied him his earnest wish to accommodate difficulties, and even graciously to pardon all who would lay down their arms and return to their allegiance. He ordered that no prisoners should be made except of such as were needed to transport the baggage and equipments of his troops, and in every possible way he manifested a humane desire to soften the asperities and disasters of the unequal warfare. But the rebellious Indians were unwilling to listen to terms. "We are lords of all these lands," said they, heroically, in reply, "and we wish to die in their defense!"

Various actions ensued between the Spaniards, their allies, and the insurgents, until at length Mendoza obtained such decided advantages over his opponents that they gave up the contest, threw down their arms, and enabled the viceroy to return to his capital with the assurance that the revolted territory was entirely and permanently pacified. His conduct to the Indians after his successes was characterized by all the suavity of a noble soul. He took no revenge for this assault upon the Spanish authority, and seems to have continually endeavored to win the natives to their allegiance by kindness rather than compulsion.

These outbreaks among the Indians were of course not unknown in Spain, where they occasioned no trifling fear for the integrity and ultimate dominion of New Spain. The natural disposition of the emperor toward the aborigines was, as we have said, kind and gentle; but he perceived that the causes of these Indian discontents might be attributed not so much, perhaps, to a patriotic desire to recover their violated rights over the country, as to the cruelty they endured at the hands of bold and reckless adventurers who had emigrated to New Spain and converted the inoffensive children of the country into slaves. Accordingly the emperor convened a council composed of eminent persons in Spain, to consider the condition of his American subjects. This council undertook the commission in a proper spirit, and adopted a liberal system toward the aborigines as well as toward the proprietors of estates in the islands and on the main, which in time would have fostered the industry and secured the ultimate prosperity of all classes. There were to be no slaves made in the future wars of these countries, the system of repartimientos was to be abandoned, and the Indians were not, as a class, to be solely devoted to ignoble tasks. The widest publicity was given to these humane intentions in Spain. The Visitador of Hispaniola, or San Domingo, Miguel Diaz de Armendariz, was directed to see their strict fulfillment in the islands, and Francisco Tello de Sandoval was commissioned to cross the Atlantic to Mexico, with full powers and instructions from the emperor, to enforce their obedience in New Spain.

In February, 1544, this functionary disembarked at St. Juan de Ulua, and a month afterwards arrived in the capital. No sooner did he appear in Mexico than the object of his mission became gradually noised about among the proprietors and planters whose wealth depended chiefly upon the preservation of their estates and Indians in the servile condition in which they were before the assemblage of the emperor's council in Spain during the previous year. Every effort was therefore made by these persons and their satellites to prevent the execution of the royal will. Appeals were addressed to Sandoval, invoking him to remain silent. He was cautioned not to interfere with a state of society upon which the property of the realm depended. The ruin of many families, the general destruction of property, and the complete revolution of the American system were painted in glowing colors by these men who pretended to regard the just decrees of the emperor as mere " innovations " upon the established laws of New Spain.

But Sandoval was firm, and he was stoutly sustained in his honorable loyalty to his sovereign and Christianity by the countenance of the viceroy, Mendoza. Accordingly the imperial decrees were promulgated throughout New Spain, and resulted in seditious movements among the disaffected proprietors, which became so formidable that the peace of the country was seriously endangered. In this dilemma,—feeling, probably, that the great mass of the people was the only bulwark of the government against the Indians, and that it was needful to conciliate so powerful a body,—permission was granted by the authorities to appoint certain representatives as a commission to lay the cause before the emperor himself. Accordingly two delegates were dispatched to Spain, together with the provincials of San Francisco, San Domingo and San Agustin, and other Spaniards of wealth and influence in the colony.

In the following year Sandoval, who had somewhat relaxed his authority, took upon himself the dangerous task of absolutely enforcing the orders of the emperor with some degree of strictness, notwithstanding the visit of the representatives of the discontented Mexicans to Spain. He displaced several oidores and other officers who disgraced their trusts, and deprived various proprietors of their repartimientos, or portions of Indians who had been abused by the cruel exercise of authority. But in the meantime the agents had not ceased to labor at the court in Spain. Money, influence, falsehood, and intrigue were freely used to sustain the system of masked slavery among the subjugated natives, and at last a royal cedula was procured commanding the revocation of the humane decrees and ordering the division of the royal domain among the conquerors.

The Indians of course followed the fate of the soil; and thus by chicanery and baleful influence the gentle efforts of the better portion of Spanish society were rendered entirely nugatory. The news of this decree spread joy among the Mexican landed proprietors. The chains of slavery were riveted upon the natives. The principle of compulsory labor was firmly established, and even to this day the Indian of Mexico remains virtually the bondsman he was doomed to become in the sixteenth century.

Between the years 1540 and 1542 an expedition was undertaken for the subjugation of an important nation which it was alleged existed far to the north of Mexico. A Franciscan missionary, Marcos de Naza, reported that he had discovered, north of Sonora, a rich and powerful people inhabiting a realm known as Quivara, or the seven cities, whose capital, Cibola, was quite as civilized as a European city. After the report had reached and been considered in Spain, it was determined to send an armed force to this region in order to explore, and if possible to reduce the Quivarans to the Spanish yoke. Mendoza had designed to intrust this expedition to Pedro de Alvarado, after having refused Cortéz permission to lead the adventurers—a task which he had demanded as his right. But when all the troops were enlisted, Alvarado had not yet reached Mexico from Guatemala, and accordingly the viceroy dispatched Vasquez de Coronado at the head of the enterprise. At the same time he fitted out another expedition, with two ships, under the orders of Francisco Alarcon, who was to make a reconnoissance of the coast as far as the thirty-sixth degree, and after having frequently visited the shores he was in that latitude to meet the forces sent by land.

Coronado set forth from Culiacan, with 350 Spaniards and 800 Indians, and, after reaching the source of the Gila, passed the mountains to the Rio del Norte. He wintered twice in the region now called New Mexico, explored it thoroughly from north to south, and then, striking off to the northeast, crossed the mountains and wandered eastward as far north as the fortieth degree of latitude, but he unfortunately found neither Quivara nor gold. A few wretched ruins of Indian villages were all the discoveries made by these hardy pioneers, and thus the enchanted kingdom eluded the grasp of Spain forever. The troop of strangers and Indians soon became disorganized and disbanded; nor was Alarcon more successful by sea than Coronado by land. His vessels explored the shores of the Pacific carefully, but they found no wealthy cities to plunder, nor could the sailors hear of any from the Indians with whom they held intercourse.

In 1546 a desolating pestilence swept over the land, destroying, according to some writers, eight hundred thousand Indians, and, according to others, five-sixths of the whole population. It lasted for about six months; and at this period a projected insurrection among the black slaves and the Tenochan and Tlatelolcan Indians was detected through a negro. This menaced outbreak was soon crushed by Mendoza, who seized and promptly executed the ring-leaders.

A portion of the Visitador Sandoval's orders related to the convocation of the Mexican bishops with a view to the spiritual welfare of the natives, and the prelates were accordingly all summoned to the capital, with the exception of the virtuous Las Casas, whose humane efforts in behalf of the Indians and whose efforts to free them from the slavery of the repartimientos had subjected him to the mortal hatred of the planters. The council of ecclesiastics met; but it is probable that their efforts were quite as ineffectual as the humane decrees of the emperor, and that even in the church itself there may have been persons who were willing to tolerate the involuntary servitude of the natives rather than forego the practical and beneficial enjoyment of estates which were beginning to fall into the possession of convents and monastaries on the death of pious penitents.

Meanwhile the population of New Spain increased considerably, especially toward the west. It was soon perceived by Mendoza that a single audiencia was no longer sufficient for so extended a country. He therefore recommended the appointment of another, in Compostella de la Nueva Gallacia, and in 1547 the emperor ordered two letrados for the administration of justice in that quarter. The ultimate reduction of the province of Vera-Paz was likewise accomplished at this period. The benignant name of "True Peace" was bestowed on this territory from the fact that the inhabitants yielded gracefully and speedily to the persuasive influence and spiritual conquest of the Dominican monks, and that not a single soldier was needed to teach them the religion of Christ at the point of the sword.

During the two or three following years there was but little to disturb the quietness of the colony, save in brief and easily suppressed outbreaks among the Indians. Royal lands were divided among poor and meritorious Spaniards; property which was found to be valueless in the neighborhood of cities was allowed to be exchanged for mountain tracts, in which the eager adventurers supposed they might discover mineral wealth; and the valuable mines of Tasco, Zultepec, and Temascaltepec, together with others, probably well known to the ancient Mexicans, were once more thrown open and diligently worked.

The wise administration of the Mexican viceroyalty by Mendoza had been often acknowledged by the emperor. He found in this distinguished person a man qualified by nature to deal with the elements of a new society when they were in their wildest moments of confusion and before they had become organized into the order and system of a regular state. Mendoza, by nature firm, amiable, and just, seems nevertheless to have been a person who knew when it was necessary in a new country to bend before the storm of popular opinion in order to avoid the destruction, not only of his own influence, but perhaps of society, civilization, and the Spanish authorities themselves. In the midst of all the fiery and unregulated spirit of a colony like Mexico, he sustained the dignity of his office unimpaired, and by command, diplomacy, management, and probably sometimes by intrigue, he appears to have insured obedience to the laws even when they were distasteful to the masses. He was successful upon all occasions except in the enforcement of the complete emancipation of the Indians; but it may be questioned whether he did not deem it needful, in the infancy of the viceroyalty at least, to subject the Indians to labors which his countrymen were either too few in number or too little acclimated in Mexico to perform successfully. History must at least do him the justice to record the fact that his administration was tempered with mercy, for even the Indians revered him as a man who was their signal protector against wanton inhumanity.

While these events occurred in Mexico, Pizarro had subjugated Peru, and added it to the Spanish crown. But there, as in Mexico, an able man was needed to organize the fragmentary society which was in the utmost disorder after the conquest. No one appeared to the emperor better fitted for the task than the viceroy whose administration had been so successful in Mexico. Accordingly in 1550 the viceroyalty of Peru was offered to him, and its acceptance urged by the emperor at a moment when a revolt against the Spaniards occurred among the Zapotecas, instigated by their old men and chiefs, who, availing themselves of an ancient prophecy relative to the return of Quetzalcoatl, assured the youths and warriors of their tribe that the predicted period had arrived and that, under the protection of their restored deity, their chains would be broken. In this, as in all other endeavors to preserve order, the efforts of Mendoza were successful. He appeased the Indians, accepted the proffered task of governing Peru, and, after meeting and conferring with his successor, Velasco, in Cholula, departed from Mexico for the scene of his new labors on the distant shores of the Pacific.

Chapter XIV

VELASCO AND PERALTA. 1551-1568

THE new viceroy, Don Luis de Velasco, arrived in Mexico without especial orders changing the character of the government. He was selected by the emperor as a person deemed eminently fitted to sustain the judicious policy of his predecessor, and it is probable that he had secret commands from the court to attempt once more the amelioration of the Indian population. There is no doubt that Charles V. was sincere in his wish to protect the natives; and if he yielded at all to the demands of the owners of repartimientos, it was probably with the hope that a better opportunity of sustaining his humane desires would occur as soon as the conquerors or their followers were glutted by the rich harvests they might reap during the early years of the settlement.

Accordingly we find as soon as Velasco had been received in Mexico with all suitable ceremony and honor that, notwithstanding the continued opposition of the proprietors and planters, he proclaimed his determination to carry out the orders that had been given to Mendoza so far as they tended to relieve the Indians from the personal labors, tributes, and severe service in the mines with which they had been burdened by the conquerors. This, as was expected, created extraordinary discontent. The cupidity of the sovereign and of his representative were appealed to. It was alleged that not only would the Spanish emigrants suffer for the want of laborers, but that the royal treasury would soon be emptied of the taxes and income which thus far had regularly flowed into it. But Don Luis was firm in his resolution, and declared that "the liberty of the Indians was of more importance than all the mines in the world, and that the revenues they yielded to the Spanish crown were not of such a character that all divine and human laws should be sacrificed in order to obtain them."

In 1553 the attention of the viceroy was especially directed to the subject of education, for the population had so greatly increased in the few years of stable government that unless the best means of instructing the growing generation were speedily adopted it was probable that New Spain would lose many of the descendants of those families which it was the policy of the crown to establish permanently in America. The University of Mexico was therefore consecrated and opened in this year, and in 1555 Paul IV. bestowed upon it the same privileges and rights as were enjoyed by that of Salamanca in Spain.

But this was a sad year for the City of Mexico in other respects. The first inundation since the conquest occurred in 1553, and for three days the capital was under water and the communication kept up in boats and canoes. Every effort was made by the viceroy to prevent the recurrence of the evil, by the erection of a dike to dam up the waters of the lake; and it is related by contemporary historians that he even wrought with his own hands at the gigantic work, during the first day, in order to show a good example to the citizens who were called on to contribute their personal labor for their future protection from such a disaster.

There were few outbreaks among the Indians during this viceroyalty, yet there were troublesome persons among the original tribes of the Chichimecas,—some bands of whom were not yet entirely subjected to the Spanish government,—who contrived to keep up a guerrilla warfare which interrupted the free circulation of the Spaniards through the plains and mountain passes of the Bajio. These were in all probability mere predatory attacks, but as it was impossible for the viceroy to spare sufficient numbers of faithful soldiers for the purpose of scouring the hiding places and fastnesses of these robber bands, he resolved to found a number of villages composed of natives and foreigners, and to place in them, permanently, sufficient numbers of troops to protect the adjacent country roads and to form the nucleus of towns, which in the course of time would grow to importance. Such was the origin, by military colonization, of San Felipe Yztlahuaca and of San Miguel el Grande, now known as Allende, from the hero of that name, to whom it gave birth. It was the constant policy of the emperor to extend the avenues of industry for his emigrant subjects by such a system of security and protection, and accordingly Don Francisco Ibarra was dispatched to the interior with orders to explore the northern and western regions, but on no account to use arms against the natives except in case of the utmost urgency. Ibarra traversed a wide and nearly unknown region, discovered rich mines of gold and silver, and colonized many places of considerable importance in the subsequent development of Mexico, and, among them, the city of Durango, which is now the capital of the State of that name.

The abdication of Charles V. was unofficially announced in Mexico in 1556, but it was not until June 6 of the following year that his successor, Philip II., was proclaimed in the capital of New Spain. The policy of the old emperor was not changed by the accession of the new king; nor does the monarch appear to have influenced in any particular manner the destiny of Mexico during the continuance of Velasco's government, except by the fitting out, at his special command, under the order of his viceroy, of an expedition for the conquest of Florida, which proved disastrous to all concerned in it. Crowds flocked in the year 1558 to the standard raised for this adventure, which it was supposed would result in gratifying the Spanish thirst for gold. In the following year the few who remained of the untoward enterprise returned with their commanders to Havana and thence to New Spain.

Thus far Velasco's administration had been successful in preserving the peace in Mexico, in opening the resources of the country in mines, agriculture, and pastoral affairs, and in alleviating the condition of the Indians by gradual restraints on his countrymen. His power was unlimited, but he had in no instance abused it or countenanced its abuse in others. Anxious not to rely exclusively upon his own resources, but to take council from the best authorities in cases of difficulty or doubt, he invariably consulted the audiencia in all emergencies. But just and loyal as had been his official conduct, it had not saved him from creating enemies; and these, unfortunately, were not only found among the rich oppressors whose shameless conduct he strove to punish, but even among the members of the audiencia itself. These men combined secretly to undermine the influence of the viceroy, and dispatched commissioners to Spain, who represented to the king that the health of his representative was in a failing state, and that it was extremely needful he should be sustained by a council whose duty it was to direct him upon all questions of public interest. The intriguers were successful in their appeal, and a decree soon arrived in New Spain announcing that the viceroy should thenceforth do nothing without the previous sanction of the audiencia. This order of the king immediately put the power into the hands of individuals whose object was rather to acquire sudden wealth than to govern a new and semi-civilized nation justly, or to enact laws which would develop the resources of the country. The viceroy had been impartial. He held the balance between the Indian laborer and the Spanish extortioner. His office and emoluments placed him at that period high above the ordinary temptations of avarice. But the audiencia, composed of several persons whose position was far inferior to the viceroy's, was accessible to intrigue and corruption, and the unfortunate Indians soon found to their cost that the royal limitation on Velasco's power had lost them a friend and staunch supporter. The audiencia and the viceroy were soon surrounded by parties who advocated their different causes with zeal, but the loyal viceroy did not murmur in the discharge of his duty, and faithfully followed the order of the king to submit his judgment to the council. Still all were not so patient as Velasco. Counter statements were sent by skillful advocates to Spain, and Velasco himself required an examination to be made into his official conduct.

Accordingly Philip II. appointed a certain licenciado, Valderrama, as visitador of New Spain, who arrived in 1563, and immediately began the discharge of his functions by a course of exaction, especially from the Indians, which neither the appeals nor the arguments of the viceroy could induce him to abandon. The arrival of this harsh and cruel personage was indeed sad for Mexico, and in the country's history he still retains the name of " *El Molestador de los Indios.*"

Fortunately for Velasco an escape from the double tyranny of the audiencia and of Valderrama was opened to him in an expedition to the Philippine Islands, which the king had ordered him to colonize. But while he was engaged in organizing his forces and preparing for the voyage, his health suddenly gave way, and on July 31, 1564, he expired, amid the general grief of all the worthier classes of Mexico, and especially of the Indians whom he had befriended. Death silenced the murmurs of the intriguers. When the beneficent viceroy could no longer interfere with the selfish interests of the multitude, crowds flocked around his bier to honor his harmless remains.

On the death of Don Luis de Velasco the reins of government remained in the hands of the royal audiencia in conformity with the order of Philip II. Francisco de Zeinos, Pedro de Villalobos, and Geronimo de Orozoco were then the oidores; while Valderrama, whose visit occurred during the government of Don Luis de Velasco, as we have already narrated, had departed for Spain. In 1564 the expedition which was planned and prepared under the last viceroy sailed for the Philippine Islands, and founded the celebrated city of Manila, which has since played so distinguished a part in the history of oriental commerce.

The year 1566 was an important one, at least in the social history of Mexico, for it was fraught with danger to the son and representative of the illustrious conqueror. The Marques del Valle,

Spanish territories.
Portuguese "
SPANISH AND PORTUGUESE EMPIRES
XVITH CENTURY

heir of Hernando Cortéz, had been for some time established in the capital, where he formed the nucleus of a noble circle, and was admired by all classes for the splendor with which he maintained the honor of his house. His palace was constantly filled with the flower of Mexican aristocracy, and among the knightly train of gallant men few were more distinguished for gentle bearing and personal accomplishment than Alonso de Avila and his brother Gil Gonzalez. The Marques del Valle distinguished the former by his special attentions, and this, together with the imprudent conduct or expressions of Alonso, made him suspected by persons who simulated an extraordinary zeal for the Spanish monarchy, while in fact their chief object was to ingratiate themselves with men of power or influence in order to further their private interests.

On June 30, 1566, the dean of the cathedral, Don Juan Chico de Molina, baptized in that sacred edifice the twin daughters of the Marques del Valle, whose sponsors were Don Lucas de Castilla and Doña Juana de Sosa. The festivities of the gallant marques upon this occasion of family rejoicing were, as usual among the rich in Spanish countries, attended with the utmost magnificence; and in order to present a picture of the manners of the period we shall describe the scene as it is related by those who witnessed it.

It was a day of general rejoicing and festivity in the City of Mexico. From the palace of the marques to the door of the cathedral a passage was formed under lofty and splendid canopies composed of the richest stuffs. A salute of artillery announced the entry of the twins into the church, and it was repeated at their departure. At the moment when the rites of religion were completed and the infants were borne back to their home through the covered way, the spectators in the plaza were amused by a chivalric tournament between twelve knights in complete steel. Other rare and costly diversions succeeded in an artificial grove which the marques had caused to be erected in the plazuela, or lesser square, intervening between his palace and the cathedral. Nor were these amusements designed alone for persons of his own rank, for the masses of the people were also summoned to partake of his bountiful hospitality. At the doors of his princely dwelling tables were sumptuously spread with roasted oxen, all kinds of wild fowl and numberless delicacies, while two casks of white and red wine— then esteemed in Mexico the most luxurious rarities—were set flowing for the people.

At night Alonso de Avila, the intimate companion of the marques, entertained the chief personages of Mexico with a splendid ball, during which there was a performance or symbolical masque representing the reception of Hernando Cortéz by the Emperor Montezuma. Alonso, splendidly attired, sustained the part of the Mexican sovereign. During one of the evolutions of the spectacle Avila threw around the neck of the young marques a collar of intermingled flowers and jewels, similar to the one with which his father had been adorned by Montezuma; and at the conclusion of the scene he placed on the heads of the marques and his wife a coronet of laurel, with the exclamation, " How well these crowns befit your noble brows ! "

These simple diversions of a family festival were doubtless altogether innocent, and certainly not designed to prefigure an intention upon the part of the marques and his friends to usurp the government of the New World. But it is probable that he had unwisely made enemies of men in power who were either ridiculously suspicious or eagerly sought for any pretext, no matter how silly, to lay violent hands upon the son of Cortéz. It is probable, too, that the prestige, the moral power, of the great conqueror's name had not yet ceased to operate in Mexico; and in those days when individuals were not dainty in ridding themselves of dangerous intruders, it is not unlikely that it was the policy of the audiencia and its coadjutors to drive the gallant marques from scenes which in the course of time might tempt his ambition. The extreme popularity of such a man was not to be tolerated.

However, the domestic festival, symbolical as it was deemed by some of a desire to foreshadow the destiny of the son of Cortéz, was allowed to pass over. The oidores and their spies, meditating in secret over the crowning of Cortéz and his wife by Avila, and the remarkable words by which the graceful act was accompanied, resolved to embrace the first opportunity to detect what they declared was a conspiracy to wrest the dominion of New Spain from Philip II.

When men are anxious to commit a crime, a pretext or an occasion is not generally long wanting to accomplish the wicked design. Accordingly we find that on August 13, the anniversary of the capture of the capital, the alleged conspiracy was to break out. A national procession in honor of the day was to pass along the street of San Francisco and to return through that which now bears the name of Tacuba. Certain armed bands, convened under the pretext of military display, were to be stationed in the way, while from a small turret in which he had concealed himself Don Martin Cortéz, the son of the conqueror by the Indian girl Mariana, was to sally forth and seize the royal standard, and, being immediately joined by the armed bands, was forthwith to proclaim the Marques del Valle, king of Mexico, and to slay the oidores as well as all who should offer the least resistance.

Such was the story which the authorities had heard or feigned to have heard through their trusty spies. Nearly a month before the dreaded day, however, the audiencia assembled, and requested the presence of the Marques del Valle, under the pretext that dispatches had been received from the King of Spain which by his special order were only to be opened in presence of the son of Cortéz. The marques, who imagined no evil, immediately responded to the call of the oidores, and the moment he entered the hall the doors were guarded by armed men. Cortéz was ordered to seat himself on a common stool, while one of the functionaries announced to him that he was a prisoner, in the name of the king. " For what? " eagerly demanded the marques. " As a traitor to his majesty! " was the foul reply. " You lie! " exclaimed Cortéz, springing from his seat, and grasping the hilt of his dagger; " I am no traitor to my king—nor are there traitors among any of my lineage! "

The natural excitement of the loyal nobleman subsided after a moment's reflection. He had been entrapped into the hands of the audiencia, and finding himself completely, though unjustly, in their power, he at once resolved to offer no childish opposition, when resistance would be so utterly useless. With the manly dignity of a chivalrous Spaniard he immediately yielded up his weapons and was taken prisoner to the apartments that had been prepared for him. His half brother, Don Martin, was also apprehended, and orders were sent to the city of Tezcoco for the seizure of Don Luis Cortéz, who resided there as justice or governor. In Mexico Alonso de Avila and his brother Gil Gonzalez, with many other distinguished men, were incarcerated, and the papers of all the prisoners were, of course, seized and eagerly scrutinized by the satellites who hoped to find in them a confirmation of the imaginary conspiracy.

Among the documents of Alonso de Avila a large number of love letters were found; but neither in his papers nor in those of his brother, or of the many victims of these foul suspicions who languished in prison, did they discover a single line to justify their arrest. Nevertheless, Don Alonso and his brother Don Gil Gonzalez were singled out as victims and doomed to death. The authorities dared not, probably, strike at a person so illustrious and so popular as the Marques del Valle; but they resolved to justify in the public eye their inquisitorial investigation by the sacrifice of someone. The public would believe that there was in reality a crime when the scaffold reeked with blood; and, besides, the blow would fall heaviest on the family of Cortéz when it struck the cherished companions of his home and heart.

On August 7, at seven in the evening, Alonso and Gil Gonzalez were led forth to the place of execution in front of the Casa de Cabildo. Their heads were struck off and stuck on spears on the roof of the edifice, whence they were finally taken, at the earnest remonstrance of the ayuntamiento, and buried with the bodies of the victims in the church of San Agustin. Every effort had been made to save the lives of these truly innocent young men. But although the principal persons in the viceroyalty united in the appeal for mercy, if not for justice, the inexorable oidores carried out their remorseless and bloody decree. It is even asserted that these cruel men would not have hesitated to inflict capital punishment upon the marques himself had not the new viceroy, Don Gaston de Peralta, Marques de Falces, arrived at San Juan de Ulua, on September 17, 1566.

As soon as this personage reached Mexico he began to inquire into the outrage. He was quickly satisfied that the whole proceeding was founded in malice. The oidores were removed, and others being placed in their posts, the viceroy dispatched a missive to the court of Spain containing his views and comments upon the conduct of the late officials. But the document was sent by a man who was secretly a warm friend of the brutal oidores, and to save them from the condign punishment they deserved he withheld it from the king.

Yet these functionaries, still fearing that their crime would be finally punished, not only treacherously intercepted the dispatch of the viceroy, but also took the speediest opportunity to send to the king accusations against Don Gaston himself, in which they charged him with negligence in his examination of the conspiracy, with treasonable alliance with the Marques del Valle, and with a design to usurp the government of New Spain. They founded their allegations upon the false oaths of several deponents, who alleged that the viceroy had already prepared and held at his orders thirty thousand armed men. This base imposture, as ridiculous as it was false, originated in an act of Peralta which was altogether innocent. Being a man of fine taste, and determining that the viceroyal residence should be worthy the abode of his sovereign's representative, he caused the palace to be refitted, and among the adornments of the various saloons he ordered a large painting to be placed on the walls of one of the chambers in which a battle was represented containing an immense number of combatants. This was the army which the witnesses upon their oaths represented to the king as having been raised and commanded by the viceroy! It can scarcely be supposed possible that the audiencia of Mexico would have resorted to such flimsy means to cover their infamy. It seems incredible that such mingled cruelty and childishness could ever have proceeded from men who were deputed to govern the greatest colony of Spain. Yet such is the unquestionable fact, and it indicates at once the character of the age and of the men who managed through the intrigues of court to crawl to eminence and power which they only used to gratify vindictive selfishness or to glut their inordinate avarice.

Philip II. could not at first believe the accusations of the oidores against the family of Cortéz and the distinguished nobleman whom he had sent to represent him in Mexico. He resolved, therefore, to wait the dispatches of the viceroy. But the oidores had been too watchful to allow those documents to reach the court of Spain; and Philip therefore, construing the silence of Don Gaston de Peralta into a tacit confession of his guilt, sent the Licenciados Jaraba, Muñoz, and Carillo to New Spain, as jueces pesquisidores, with letters for the viceroy commanding him to yield up the government and to return to Spain in order to account for his conduct.

These men immediately departed on their mission and arrived safely in America without accident, save in the death of Jaraba. As soon as they reached Mexico they presented their dispatches to the viceroy, and Muñoz took possession of the government of New Spain. The worthy and noble Marques de Falces was naturally stunned by so unprecedented and unexpected a proceeding; but, satisfied of the justice of his cause as well as of the purity of his conduct, he left the capital and retired to the castle of San Juan de Ulua, leaving the reins of power in the hands of Muñoz, whose tyrannical conduct soon destroyed all the confidence which hitherto had always existed, at least between the audiencia and the people of the metropolis. It was probably before this time that the Marques del Valle was released, and deeming the new empire which his father had given to Spain no safe resting place for his descendants he departed for the Spanish court. The viceroy himself had fallen a victim to deception and intrigue.

It seems to have been one of the weaknesses of Philip II.'s character to have but little confidence in men. With such examples as we have just seen, it may nevertheless have been an evidence of his wisdom that he did not rely upon the courtiers who usually surround a king. He had doubted in reality the actual guilt of the Marques de Falces, and was therefore not surprised when he learned the truth upon these weighty matters in the year 1568. The government of Muñoz, his visitador, was, moreover, represented to him as cruel and bloody. The conduct of the previous audiencia had been humane when compared with the acting governor's. The prisons which already existed in Mexico were not adequate to contain his victims, and he built others darker and damper yet.

Don Martin Cortéz, the half brother of the Marques del Valle, who remained in the metropolis as the attorney and representative of his kinsman, was seized and put to torture for no crime save that the blood of the conqueror flowed in his veins and that he had enjoyed friendly relations with the suspected conspirators. Torture, it was imagined, would wring from him a confession which might justify the oidores. The situation of New Spain could not, indeed, be worse than it was, for no man felt safe in the midst of such unrestrained power and relentless cruelty; and we may be permitted to believe that outraged humanity would soon have risen to vindicate itself against such brutes and to wrest the fruits of the conquest from a government that sent forth such wicked satellites. Even the audiencia itself—the moving cause of this new and bad government—began to tremble when it experienced the humiliating contempt with which it was invariably treated by the monster Muñoz.

But all these acts of maladministration were more safely reported to the Spanish court by the nobles and oidores of Mexico than the dispatches of the unfortunate Marques de Falces. Philip eagerly responded to the demand for the removal of Muñoz. He dispatched the oidores Villanueva and Vasco de Puga to Mexico, with orders to Muñoz to give up the government in three hours after he received the royal dispatch, and to return immediately to Spain for judgment of his conduct. The envoys lost no time in reaching their destination, where they found that Muñoz had retired to the convent of San Domingo, probably as a sanctuary, in order to pass Holy Week. But the impatient emissaries, responding to the joyful impatience of the people, immediately followed him to his retreat, and after waiting a considerable time in the ante-chamber, and being at last most haughtily received by Muñoz, who scarcely saluted them with a nod, Villanueva drew from his breast the royal cedula, and commanded his secretary to read it in a loud voice.

For a while the foiled visitador sat silent, moody, and thoughtful, scarcely believing the reality of what he heard. After a pause, in which all parties preserved silence, he rose and declared his willingness to yield to the king's command; and this brutal chief, who but a few hours before believed himself a sovereign in Mexico, was indebted to the charity of some citizens for a carriage in which he traveled to Vera Cruz. Here a fleet was waiting to transport him to Spain. The late viceroy, the Marques de Falces, departed in a ship of the same squadron, and upon his arrival at the court soon found means to justify himself entirely in the eyes of his sovereign. But it went harder with Muñoz. He vainly tried his skill at exculpation with the king. Philip seems to have despised him too much to enter into discussion upon the merits of the accusations. The facts were too flagrant. The king returned him his sword, declining to hear any argument in his justification. "I sent you to the Indies to govern, not to destroy!" said Philip, as he departed from his presence; and that very night the visitador suddenly expired!

Whether he died of mortification or violence is one of those state secrets which, like many others of a similar character, the chronicles of Spain do not reveal.

Don Martin Cortéz and his family took refuge in Spain, where his case was fully examined; and while the investigation lasted, from 1567 to 1574, his estates in Mexico were confiscated. He was finally declared innocent of all the charges; but his valuable property had been seriously injured and wasted by the officers of the crown to whom it was intrusted during the long period of sequestration.

Chapter XV

THE GROWTH OF COMMERCE
1568-1590

THE salutary lesson received by the audiencia in the events which occurred in the metropolis during these years induced its members to conduct themselves with less arrogance during the short time they held supreme power after the departure of the visitadores. In October of 1568 a new viceroy, the fourth of New Spain, Don Martin Enriquez de Almanza, arrived at Vera Cruz, whence he reached the capital on November 5, after having routed the English whom he found in possession of the Isle of Sacrificios.

Don Martin immediately perceived, upon assuming the reins of government, that it was necessary to calm the public mind in the metropolis, which from recent occurrences now began to regard all men in authority with jealousy and distrust. He let the people understand, therefore, from the first that he did not design to countenance any proceedings similar to those which had lately almost disorganized and revolutionized the colony. An occasion soon presented itself in which his prudence and discretion were required to adjust a serious dispute concerning the Franciscan monks, and in which the people sympathized with the brotherhood and their supposed rights. Any act of rigor or harshness would have kindled the flame of sedition, but the mild diplomacy of the viceroy sufficed to calm the litigants and to restore perfect peace to the capital.

But the attention of Don Martin was soon to be drawn from the capital toward the frontiers of his government, where he found that the troublesome bands of wandering Chichimecas had been busy in their old work of robbery and spoliation while the audiencia was engaged in its intrigues and corruption in the City of Mexico. The impunity with which these martial vagabonds had been allowed to proceed increased their daring, and the evils they inflicted on the country were becoming continually greater. Not satisfied with having dispatched the chief alcalde of the hostile region with the militia to punish the rebels, he joined the forces of that officer, and succeeded after great slaughter in compelling the Indians to quit the soil they had hitherto ravaged. It should be recorded, in justice to the viceroy, that he ordered the Indian children who fell into the hands of his soldiery to be spared, and at the end of the campaign brought them all to the metropolis, where he distributed them among rich families so that they might receive a Christian education. In order to save the region from further devastation he established therein a colony, to which he gave the name of San Felipe, perhaps in honor of his king, as he bestowed upon it the title of " city."

Such was the condition of things when Pedro Moya de Contreras arrived in Mexico as inquisitor, having been sent by Philip to establish the tribunal of the faith in that capital. The Spanish king feared that the doctrines of the Reformation, which were then rife in Europe, might find friends among his transatlantic subjects, and he resolved to give them, as a guardian of their consciences, this sad and dreadful present. In 1572 Doctor Pedro Sanchez, a Jesuit, with various brethren of the same order, came to the City of Mexico and founded a college in certain edifices which were ceded to them for that purpose by Alonso Villaseca. The brethren of the holy office, or inquisition, meanwhile organized for future operations, and settled under the wings of the church of San Domingo.

It was at this period, also, that Don Martin established the alcabala; and although the merchants opposed the measure, which was entirely new to them, and alleged that it was a mortal blow to their business, they were unable to force the viceroy to retract his measure. His determination was founded on the fact that trade had now become established on a firm and robust basis, and that it could well bear without injury an impost of this character.

In the years 1574 and 1575 there were serious discussions between the temporal and spiritual powers of Mexico, growing out of a royal order that no prelate should be admitted in the country unless he bore a suitable license from the Council of the Indies. In 1576 Mexico was again visited by a frightful pestilence, which spread rapidly, and carried off large numbers of victims. The whole of New Spain was ravaged by it, and neither care nor medical science seems to have had the least effect either in curing or in relieving the sufferers. The symptoms of this malady were a violent pain in the head, which was succeeded by a burning fever, under which the patient sank. None survived the seventh day, and it is reported that nearly two millions perished under the dreadful scourge. The malady abated at the close of the rainy season, and disappeared entirely at the beginning of 1577.

In the two succeeding years Don Martin commanded that the usual annual tribute should not be collected from the Indians. This measure was designed to alleviate the lot of these suffering subjects of the king and to testify the paternal regard which he cherished for a race that served him and his subjects so beneficially in the mines. It was in the mineral districts that the Indians were in reality the greatest sufferers and laborers in New Spain. Their toil was incessant. Their task-masters gave them no respite in the bowels of the earth, for they wrought as if they designed to scrape every vein and artery of the colony's soil. Silver and labor were calculated with exactness, and no limit to the Indian's industry was prescribed save that which was imposed by his capacity for work and his power of endurance. The viceroy, seeking to alleviate this, introduced a milder system, as far as he was able, among the leading miners of the colony. He insisted upon permitting the Indians regular repose, and he forbade their entire confinement within the mines, but commanded that they should be allowed time to breathe the fresh air on the surface of the earth, and suffered to attend to their own domestic labors, or to toil on public works for a competent recompense.

The government of Don Martin had thus far been unusually calm, but his last moments in Mexico were to be disturbed by a quarrel with a Franciscan monk, named Rivera, who had called at the palace to see the viceroy on a matter of business for his convent, and had been forced to wait a considerable time without being finally honored with an audience. The petulant friar regarded this as a slight upon the brotherhood, and shortly afterward, while preaching in the cathedral, declared, with a sneering and offensive purpose against the viceroy, that " in the palace all became equal, and that no difference was made between ecclesiastics and secular folks! "

The viceroy could not permit so flagrant a breach of decorum and so dangerous a taunt in a popular appeal to rest unrebuked. He, therefore, demanded the punishment of the public critic and the audiencia ordered Rivera to depart forthwith for Spain. But the haughty monk in order to avoid the disgrace of expulsion united the whole body of his fraternity in the quarrel, and singing the psalm, "*In exitu Israel de Ægipto*," they departed from the city by the road leading to Vera Cruz. The viceroy seems to have been moved by this act of the brotherhood, and immediately wrote to Rivera in soothing terms requesting him to return to Mexico, where justice should be done him. The Franciscan returned, but soon after received a royal order to depart for Spain.

In 1580 the abundant rain again caused an inundation of the capital, and Don Martin Enriquez was about to engage in the construction of the celebrated canal of Huehuetoca when he was removed to the viceroyalty of Peru.

As successor of Almanza, Don Lorenzo Xuares, Conde de la Coruña, was appointed by the king, and made his triumphal entry into the City of Mexico on the evening of October 4, 1580. The gay and affable character of this personage at once attracted the people and the colonial court; and in consequence of the rapidly increasing population, wealth, and luxury of New Spain, as well as from the unreserved demeanor of the viceroy, it was supposed that a golden age had arrived in the history of Mexico, which would forever signalize the administration of Xuares.

Perhaps the viceroy was too lenient and amiable for the task that had been imposed on him in America. The epoch of speculation and adventure had not yet passed by, and of course the corruption which ever follows in their train required still to be closely watched and quickly checked. To this duty Xuares did not immediately address himself, and the result was that the oidores, the alcaldes, and all who administered justice at once put themselves up to auction and sold their services, their favors, or their decisions to the highest bidder. Disorder reigned in every department in the year following the arrival of Xuares; and even the royal revenues, which hitherto had generally remained sacred, were squandered or secreted by the persons to whose care and fidelity their collection was intrusted. The limitations which we have already seen were placed upon a viceroy's power in the time of Velasco, now tied the hands of Xuares. He could not dismiss or even suspend the defrauders of the revenue or the public wretches who prostituted their official power for gold. Nor was he, probably, unwilling to be deprived of a dangerous right which would have placed him in direct hostility to the army of speculators and jobbers. And yet it was necessary for the preservation of the colony that these evils should be quickly abated. In this political strait, concealing his intentions from the viceroyal court, he applied to Philip to send a visitador with ample powers to readjust the disorganized realm.

The commerce of New Spain had augmented astonishingly within a few years. Vera Cruz and Acapulco had become splendid emporiums of wealth and trade. The East and the West poured their people into Mexico through these cities, and in the capital some of the most distinguished merchants of Europe, Asia, and Africa met every year, midway between Spain and China, to transact business and exchange opinions upon the growing facilities of an extended commerce. Peru and Mexico furnished the precious metals which were always so greedily demanded by the East. In 1581 Philip II., in view of this state of things in his colony, issued a royal order for the establishment in Mexico for a Mercantile Tribunal de Consulado, though it was not in fact actually put in effective operation until the year 1593, under the administration of the second Velasco. In the midsummer of 1582 the viceroy expired, probably of mingled anxiety and old age; and it was well for Mexico that he passed so rapidly from a stage in whose delicate drama his years and his abilities altogether unfitted him to play so conspicuous a part.

Upon the death of Xuares the audiencia immediately assumed the direction of the state; but the members of this august tribunal were altogether ignorant of the demand made by the late viceroy for a visitador until Don Pedro de Contreras, Archbishop of Mexico, placed in their hands the dispatch from Philip, naming him for this important service.

The archbishop was a man well known in Mexico. Cold, austere, rigid in his demeanor and principles, he was the very man to be chosen for the dangerous duty of contending with a band of rich, proud, and unscrupulous officials. His sacred character as arch-prelate of Mexico was of no little use in such an exigency, for it gave him spiritual as well as temporal power over masses which might sometimes be swayed by their conscientious dread of the church, even when they could not be controlled by the arm of law. Besides this, he was the first inquisitor of Mexico, and in the dreaded mysteries of the holy office there was an overwhelm-

ADMIRAL DRAKE'S SQUADRON INTERCEPTING THE MEXICAN GALLEON DESTINED FOR THE PHILIPPINES AND
LADEN WITH A MOST PRECIOUS CARGO

Painting by Hans Bohrdt

—page 135

ing power before which the most daring offenders would not venture to rebel or intrigue.

It may be well imagined that the unexpected appearance of so formidable an ecclesiastic upon the scene, armed with the sword as well as the cross, was well calculated to awe the profligate officials. The members of the audiencia trembled when they read the royal order, for the archbishop knew them well, and had been long cognizant, not only of their own maladministration, but of the irregularities they countenanced in others.

Don Pedro immediately undertook the discharge of his office and in a few days heard a great number of complaints against various individuals; but as he did not design proceeding with revengeful severity against even the most culpable, he resolved to report his proceedings to the king, and in the meanwhile to retain in office all persons who performed their duties faithfully, while he put an end to the most flagrant abuses.

As soon as Philip II. heard, in 1584, of the death of Mendoza, he added the title and powers of viceroy to those already possessed by the archbishop, and, with his commission as royal representative, he sent him additional authority which had never been enjoyed by any of his predecessors. He was thus empowered to remove at will all persons from public employment, and even to expel ministers and oidores, as well as to visit with severe punishments all who deserved them. Under this ample discretion the viceroy removed some of the oidores, suspended others, hanged certain royal officers who had disgraced their trusts, and brought the tribunals of justice into perfect order. The king had proposed to bring the dispersed Indians into towns and villages so as to control them more effectually, but the viceroy, after consulting the priests who were best acquainted with that population, deemed it best to defer the execution of the royal order until he laid the objections to it before Philip.[1] In 1585 a seminary for the Indians was established, in which they were taught to read, write, and comprehend the rudiments of the Catholic faith. This institution was under the charge of the Jesuits, whose zeal for education has been celebrated in the history of all countries into which this powerful order of the priesthood has penetrated. A provincial council of American bishops

---

[1] The Indians alluded to in this passage were vaguely designated as Chichimecas, Otomies, and Mexican. They probably inhabited a tract of country lying northwest of the kingdom of Michoacan.

Hist. Nat.

was, moreover, convened this year in Mexico under the auspices of Contreras.

Nor was the viceroy eager only to correct the civil and religious abuses of the country without attending to the fiscal advantages which he knew the king was always eager to secure from his colonies. In testimony of his zeal he dispatched at this period a rich fleet for Spain. It bore 3,300,000 ducats in coined silver, and 1100 marks in gold, together with a variety of other valuable products, all of which arrived safely in port.

The power of this vigorous ruler as viceroy continued, however, but for a single year. He was the scourge of officials in all classes, while the good men of the colony prayed heartily for the continuance of his authority; but it is probable that his rigor had excited against him the talents for intrigue which we have heretofore seen were sometimes so actively and successfully employed both in Mexico and Spain. In October of 1585 his successor arrived in the capital.

This successor was Don Alvaro Enrique de Zuñiga, Marques de Villa Manrique. The arrival of the Marques de Villa Manrique was not designed to interfere with the functions of the archbishop and former viceroy Contreras as visitador, who was solicited to continue his plenary examination into the abuses of government in New Spain, and to clear the country of all malefactors before he retired once more to the cloisters. Accordingly Don Pedro remained in Mexico some time discharging his duties, and it is probably owing to his presence that the first year of the new viceroy passed off in perfect peace. But in the succeeding year, in which the archbishop departed for Spain, his troubles began by a serious discussion with the Franciscans, Agustins, and Dominicans, in which the monks at last appealed from the viceroy to the king. Before Contreras, the visitador, left Mexico he had managed to change all the judges composing the tribunals of the colony. The men he selected in their stead were all personally known to him or were appointed upon the recommendation of persons whose integrity and capacity for judgment were unquestionable.

This remarkable man died soon after his arrival in Madrid, where he had been appointed president of the Council of the Indies. Like all reformers, he went to his grave poor; but when the king learned his indigence he took upon himself the costs of sepulture, and laid his colonial representative and bishop in the tomb in a manner befitting one who had exercised so great and beneficial an influence in the temporary reform of the New World.

In 1587 the viceroy Zuñiga dispatched a large amount of treasure to Spain. Enormous sums were drained annually from the colonies for the royal metropolis; but in this year the fleet from Vera Cruz sailed with 1156 marks of gold, in addition to an immense amount of coined silver and merchandise of great value. These sums passed safely to the hands of the court; but such was not the case with all the precious freights that left the American coasts, for at this period the shores of the continent on both oceans began to swarm with pirates. The subjects of various European nations, but especially the English, were most active in enterprises which, in those days, were probably regarded more as privateering than as the bandit expeditions they have since been considered not only in morals but in law. In the year before, Cavendish had taken in the Pacific a Spanish ship which was bound from Manila to Acapulco with a rich cargo of wares from China; and in this year it was known that Drake, another noted adventurer, after making himself celebrated by the capture of San Agustin, in Florida, had sailed for the Pacific ocean, whose rich coasts, as well as the oriental traders, formed a tempting booty for the buccaneers who then infested these seas.

As soon as the viceroy heard of this piratical sailor's approach to the western boundary of his colony, he commanded the troops in Guadalajara to embark at Acapulco, under the orders of Doctor Palacios, in all the vessels which were then in port, and to scour the shores of America until the British marauder was captured. But upon the commander's arrival at Acapulco he was informed that the freebooter had already abandoned the west coast after sacking several towns, and that he had not been seen or heard of anywhere for a long period. Drake meanwhile was in concealment among the distant and unfrequented coves of California, in such a situation, however, that he could easily intercept the galleon which passed every year from the Philippines to Mexico laden with goods and metals of considerable value. In due time he pounced upon his unsuspecting prey, and, carrying her into a bay near the Cape of San Lucas, plundered her valuable cargo and set fire to the deserted hull. The news of this mishap soon reached the ears of Palacios, who of course immediately set sail after the corsair. But Drake was already far on his way to a spot of safety in which he and his companions might enjoy the fruits of their piratical adventure.

This successful attack upon a vessel of so much importance to the colony—for only one was annually permitted to cross the Pacific—greatly troubled the people who depended upon its arrival for their yearly supply of oriental wares. But as soon as the general calm was gradually restored, an internal trouble arose which was well-nigh proving of serious import to the viceroyalty. Zuñiga does not seem to have been contented with the jurisdiction which had hitherto been conceded to the viceroy, but, being anxious to extend his authority over certain towns and villages under the control of the audiencia of Guadalajara, he demanded of that body the surrender of their dominion. The audiencia, however, was jealous of its rights, and would not yield to the viceroy, who was equally pertinacious. The dispute ran high between the parties. Threats were used when diplomacy failed, and at length the disputants reached, but did not pass, the verge of civil war, for on both sides they seem to have ordered out troops, who fortunately never actually engaged in combat.

This ill-judged act of the viceroy was fatal to his power. Letters and petitions were forthwith dispatched to Madrid requiring and begging the removal of a man whose rashness was near producing a civil war. This was a charge not to be disregarded by the king, and accordingly we find that a successor to Zuñiga was immediately named, and that the Bishop of Tlascala was appointed visitador to examine the conduct of the deposed viceroy.

On January 17, 1590, this prelate, who seems to have been originally inimical to Zuñiga, and who should therefore have disdained the office of his judge, ordered him to depart from Mexico. All the property of the late viceroy—even the linen of his wife—was sequestrated; the most harassing annoyances were constantly inflicted upon him, and after six years, poor and worn down by unceasing trials, he returned to Spain, where the influence of his friends at court procured the restoration of his property.

Chapter XVI

THE EXPLORATION OF THE CALIFORNIAS
1590-1607

LUIS DE VELASCO, Count de Santiago, was the son of the second viceroy of New Spain, and during the administration of his father, as well as for some years afterward, had resided in Mexico, where he filled several offices, and especially that of corregidor of Cempoalla. He was not on friendly terms with the last viceroy, Zuñiga, for he had suddenly quitted New Spain in the same vessel that brought his predecessor to America. Upon his arrival at the Spanish court he was sent as ambassador to Florence, and, the exaggerated news of the supposed civil war in Mexico having been received just as he returned from his mission, Philip determined to send him back to New Spain. This decision was no doubt founded upon Velasco's intimate acquaintance with Mexico and its people, with whom his interests had been so long bound up that he might almost be regarded as a native of the country.

On January 25, 1590, Velasco entered the capital with more pomp and rejoicing than had ever attended the advent of previous viceroys, for the Mexicans looked upon him as a countryman. As soon as he was seated in power his first acts demonstrated his good sense and mature judgment. His wish was to develop the country, to make not only its mineral and agricultural resources available to Spain, but to open the channels through which labor could obtain its best rewards. He therefore ordered the manufactories of coarse stuffs and cloths which had been established by Mendoza to be once more opened, after the long period in which the Spanish mercantile influence had kept them shut. This naturally produced an excitement among the interested foreign traders, but the viceroy firmly maintained his determination to punish severely anyone who should oppose his decree.

In 1591 the troublesome Chichimecas again manifested a desire to attack the Spaniards. They were congregated in strongly armed bands in the neighborhood of Zacatecas, and menaced the Spanish population living in the vicinity of the rich mines. Travelers could not pass through the country without a military escort. Strong garrisons had been placed by the government on the frontiers, and merciless war declared against them, but all was unavailing to stop their marauding expeditions among the whites. In this year, however, they sent commissioners to treat with the Spaniards in Mexico, and after confessing that they were tired of a war which they found useless, they consented to abstain from further molestation of the district provided the viceroy would agree to furnish them with a sufficiency of meat for their support. Velasco of course consented to this demand of the cattle stealers, and, moreover, obtained their consent to the admission among them of a body of Tlascalans who would instruct them in a civil and Christian mode of life. Four hundred families of these faithful friends of the Spaniards were selected for this colony; and, together with some Franciscan friars, they settled in four bodies so as to form an equal number of colonies. One of these settlements was made on the side of a rich mineral hill and took the name of San Luis Potosi, the second formed San Miguel Mesqitic, the third San Andres, and the fourth Colotlan. Such was the origin of these towns, in which the two tribes lived for many years in perfect harmony, but without intermingling or losing their individuality.

Another attempt was also made, as had been done previously, to gather the dispersed bands of Mexican and Otomi Indians into villages and settlements, where they would gradually become accustomed to civilized life. Velasco, like his predecessor Contreras, consulted with the curas and the people who were best acquainted with the temper of these races, and learned that they still opposed humane efforts for civilization, preferring the vagabond life they had so long led and which had now become necessary and natural. Nevertheless he thought it his duty to try the experiment. But the first Otomi who was reduced to the necessity of abandoning his nomadic habits and building for himself a regular habitation, not only destroyed his wife and children, but terminated his own existence by hanging. The viceroy then suspended his operations and reported the untoward result, together with the opinion of his advisers, to the court of Spain.

Velasco, ever anxious not only for the amelioration of the condition of the Indians, but for the embellishment of the capital which was now growing into considerable importance, caused the Alameda of Mexico to be laid out and planted in 1593, for the recreation of the citizens. This magnificent grove, with its beautifully shaded avenues and walks, embellished by fountains and filled with everything that can give repose or comfort to the fatigued people who are anxious to steal off awhile from the toil and bustle of a large city, still exists in Mexico as an evidence of the taste and liberality of the viceroy.

In 1594 Philip II. finding himself straitened for means to carry on the European wars in which he was engaged, recurred to the unfortunate and unjust system of forced loans to increase his revenue. He did not confine himself in this odious compulsory tax to the Old World, which was most concerned in the result of his wars, but instructed Velasco to impose a tribute of four reales, or fifty cents upon Indians, in addition to the sum they already paid his majesty. Velasco reluctantly undertook the unwelcome task; but anxious to lighten the burden upon the natives as much as possible, and at the same time to foster the raising of poultry and cattle among these people, he compounded the whole tax of a dollar, which they were obliged to pay, for seven reales, or eighty-seven and a half cents, and one fowl, which at that time was valued at a single real, or twelve and a half cents. This, it will be perceived, was amiably designed by the viceroy, but became immediately the subject of gross abuse. The Indians are slowly moved either to new modes of cultivation or to new objects of care, even of the most domestic and useful character. Instead of devoting themselves to the raising of poultry with the industrious thrift that would have saved one-eighth of their taxation, or twelve and a half per cent., they allowed the time to pass without providing the required bird in their homesteads, so that when the tax gatherer arrived they were forced to buy the fowl instead of selling it. This of course raised the price, and the consequence was that the Indian was obliged often to pay two or three reales more than the original amount of the whole taxation of one dollar! It is related that one of the oidores who had taken eight hundred fowls reserved two hundred for the consumption of his house, and through an agent sold the rest at three reales, or thirty-seven and a half cents each, by which he contrived to make a profit of two hundred per cent. Various efforts were made to remedy this shameful abuse or to revoke the decree, but the system was found to be too profitable among the officials to be abandoned without a severe struggle. We are unable to discover that the viceroy in this instance used his authority to restore the Indians to their original rights.

In 1595 it was determined to colonize the supposed kingdom of Quivara, which now received the name of New Mexico, but before the expedition could set forth under the command of Juan de Oñate, Velasco received a dispatch informing him that he had been named viceroy of Peru, and that his successor, Don Gaspar de Zuñiga Acebedo, Count of Monterey, would soon appear in the colonial metropolis.

The Count of Monterey, the ninth viceroy of New Spain, arrived at San Juan de Ulua on September 18, 1595, and on November 5 entered the capital. At first he exhibited a cold and apathetic temper, and appeared to take but little interest in the affairs of the government; but it is supposed that, being a prudent and cautious man, he was in no haste to undertake the direction of affairs while he was altogether unacquainted both with the temper of the people and the nature of their institutions. An early measure, however, of his administration deserves to be recorded and remembered. He found the Indians still suffering and complaining under the odious fowl tax created by his predecessor for the protection of domestic industry, but which had been perverted for the selfish and avaricious purposes of the receivers. He immediately abolished this impost, and diminished the whole amount of taxation upon the Indians.

In consequence of the loss of the galleon from the Philippines, which we have related, the king ordered an expedition under the command of General Sebastian Viscaino to examine and scour the coasts of the Californias, where it was alleged the precious metals, and, especially, the most valuable pearls, would be found in abundance. Viscaino recruited a large number of followers in Mexico for this enterprise, and set sail with three vessels, in 1596, from Acapulco. The adventurers coasted the territory for a considerable time without finding a suitable location in which they might settle advantageously, until at length they disembarked in the port of La Paz, whence, however, they soon departed for want of provisions and supplies of every kind.

Meanwhile the Count of Monterey examined into the state of the expedition to New Mexico, which he found had been projected and partly prepared by his predecessor. He made some changes in the plan agreed on between Velasco and Oñate, and in order to exhibit his good will to the latter personage he joined with him in the enterprise his relation, Vicente Saldivar, who had gathered a number of emigrants for these remote and northern regions. People were tempted to abandon their homes by the reports of extraordinary mineral wealth which was to be obtained in these unexplored portions of New Spain; and accordingly, when the standard of the expedition was raised in the great square of the capital, crowds of men with their families flocked around it to enlist for the hazardous and toilsome service.

The first news received from the emigrant colonists, when they reached Caxco, two hundred leagues from the capital, was disastrous. Quarrels had originated among the adventurers, who asserted that the terms of the expedition had not been complied with faithfully. As soon as the viceroy heard of the discontent he dispatched Don Lope de Ulloa as a pacificator to the inflamed band, which was quickly reduced to harmony and persuaded to continue its journey to the promised land. At length the weary emigrants reached the boasted El Dorado; but finding the reports of mineral wealth altogether exaggerated, and, doubting the advantage of residing with their families permanently in such distant outposts, many of them retraced their way southward to regions that were more densely populated.

In 1598 another effort was resolved on to gather the dispersed and refractory vagabond Indians who wandered about the territory under the name of Mexicans and Otomies. While they maintained their perfectly nomadic state it was evident that they were useless either as productive laborers for the Spaniards or as objects of taxation for the sovereign. It was a wise policy, therefore, to attempt what was philanthropically called their civilization; but upon this occasion, as upon all the others that preceded it, the failure was signal. Commissioners and notaries were selected and large salaries paid these officials to insure their faithful services in congregating the dispersed natives. But the government agents, who well knew the difficulty if not the absolute impossibility of achieving the desired object, amused themselves by receiving and spending the liberal salaries disbursed by the government, while the Indians still continued as uncontrolled as ever. The Count of Monterey was nevertheless obstinately bent on the prosecution of this favorite policy of the king, and squandered upon these vile ministerial agents upward of two hundred thousand dollars without producing the least beneficial result. In the following viceroy's reign he was sentenced to pay the government this large sum as having been unwisely spent; but was finally absolved from its discharge by the court to which he appealed from the decision of his successor.

In the beginning of 1599 the news was received in Mexico of the death of Philip II. and of the accession of Philip III. This event was perhaps the most remarkable in the annals of the colony during the last year of the sixteenth century, except that the town of Monterey in New Leon was founded, and that a change was made by the viceroy of the port of Vera Cruz, from its former sickly site at La Antigua, to one which has since become equally unhealthful.

The first three years of the seventeenth century were chiefly characterized by renewed viceroyal efforts among the Indians. The project of congregating the nomadic natives was abandoned, and various attempts were made to break up the system of repartimientos, which had been, as we have seen, the established policy of the colony, if not of the king, ever since the conquest. If the Indians were abandoned to their own free will, it was supposed that their habits were naturally so thriftless that they would become burdensome instead of beneficial to the Spanish colonists, and ultimately might resolve themselves into mere wanderers like the Otomies and their vagabond companions. Yet it was acknowledged that their involuntary servitude, and the disastrous train of impositions it entailed, were unchristian and unjust. There was a dilemma, in fact, between idleness and tyranny; but the viceroy conceived it his duty to endeavor once more with an honest zeal to sustain the humane policy of freedom which was recommended, not only by the sovereign, but by the religious orders who were supposed to know the natives best. Various projects were adopted to harmonize their freedom with a necessary degree of labor, in order to insure them wages and support, while they were preserved together in organized societies. After the repartimientos were abrogated, the Indians were compelled to assemble on every Sabbath in the public squares of the villages and towns, where they made their contracts of service by the day. The viceroy himself, anxious to prevent fraud, assisted personally in the reunions at the plazas or squares of San Juan and Santiago. But it was all in vain. The proprietors, landowners, and agents were opposed to the scheme. Brokers interposed, and, after hiring the Indians at moderate rates in contracts made with themselves, sublet them to others on higher terms. And at last it is alleged that the unfortunate natives, seeing the bad operation of the viceroy's kind intentions in their behalf, and finding their condition less happy when they had to take care of themselves than when they were taken care of, appealed to the Count of Monterey to restore the old system of repartimientos, under which they were at least spared the trouble of seeking for task-masters and support. Indolent by nature, creatures of habit, and living in a country whose bosom afforded them spontaneously most of the luxuries required by such a class, they submitted to what in fact was the greatest evil of their lot, because it relieved them of the trouble of individual effort!

In 1602 Philip III. ordered another expedition for the colonization and exploration of the Californias. It departed in three ships and a bark from Acapulco, on May 5, under the command of Viscanio. Torribio Gomez Corban was the admiral of the little fleet, and Antonio Flores, pilot. From the day of its departure it was driven by severe gales, but at length the port of Monterey was reached by the weary crews, who continued along the coast until they arrived at Cape Blanco de San Sabastian, somewhat beyond Cape Mendozino. There the voyagers were sorely attacked with scurvy, which thinned their numbers to such an extent that, of the whole, only six were able to do duty. With this scant equipment of men the vessels reached Mazatlan, where the crews recruited their health; and, passing thence to Acapulco, the expedition once more landed in the midst of civilization and hastened back to the capital to give a bad report of the country which has since become the El Dorado of the world.

The Count of Monterey was transferred to the viceroyalty of Peru in 1603, and left the capital amid the general grief of a society whose cordial esteem he seems to have won and retained during his whole administration.

The advent of his successor, Don Juan de Mendoza y Luna, Marques de Montesclaros, to the viceroyalty of New Spain was distinguished by an unusual degree of tranquillity throughout the colony. During the preceding administrations most of the subjects of internal discontent were set at rest, and the aborigines who had been subjected to the yoke were now becoming accus-

tomed to bear it. In 1604 the abundant rains in the valley
of Mexico during the month of August caused an inundation
which greatly alarmed the population. The city and adjacent
country were laid under water, and such was the general distress that the marques solicited the opinions of skillful persons
in regard to the canal of Huehuetoca, which had heretofore been
spoken of as the only means of freeing the capital from destruction
by the swollen flood of the lakes. The reports made to him, however, represented the enterprise as one of immense labor and
expense, as well as requiring a great length of time for its completion. He therefore abandoned the project for the present, and
merely repaired the albarrada or dyke which Velasco had already
constructed. In addition to this precautionary measure he caused
the calzadas, or raised turnpikes, of Guadalupe and San Cristoval
to be constructed, which, while they led to the open country beyond
the city, served also as additional barriers against the waters.
After the completion of these highways, he next directed his attention to those of San Antonio and Chapultepec, which were quickly
finished, and merited the name of " Roman works," for the massive
strength and durability of their construction. Various other useful
municipal works, such as aqueducts and sewers, engaged the notice
of the viceroy until 1607; and after the proclamation of the Prince
of Asturias (Philip IV.) by order of the king he was ordered to
pass from Mexico to Peru, where he was charged with the duties
of the viceroyalty.

Chapter XVII

THE CANAL OF HUEHUETOCA. 1607-1896

DON LUIS VELASCO, the second Count de Santiago and the first Marques de Salinas, had been seven years viceroy of Peru since he left the government of Mexico, when he was summoned once more to rule a country of which he felt himself almost a native. He was tired of public life, and being advanced in years would gladly have devoted the rest of his existence to the care of his family and the management of his valuable estates in the colony. But he could not refuse the nomination of the king, and at the age of seventy once more found himself at the head of affairs in New Spain.

The government of this excellent nobleman has been signalized in history by the erection of the magnificent public work designed for the drainage of the valley. The results of Velasco's labors were permanent, and as his work, or at least a large portion of it, remains to the present day, and serves to secure the capital from the floods with which it is constantly menaced, we shall describe the whole of this magnificent enterprise at present, though our description will carry us, chronologically, out of the period under consideration, and lead us from the seventeenth to the nineteenth century.

The valley of Mexico is a great basin, which, although 7500 feet above the level of the sea, and of course subject to constant and rapid evaporation, is yet exceedingly humid for so elevated a region. No stream except the small arroyo or rivulet of Tequisquiac issues from the valley, while the rivers Papalotla, Tezcoco, Teotihuacan, Guadalupe, Pachuca, and Guautitlan pour into it and form the five lakes of Chalco, Xochimilco, Tezcoco, San Cristoval, and Zumpango. "These lakes rise by stages as they approach the northern extremity of the valley; the waters of Tezcoco being in their ordinary state four Mexican varas and eight inches lower than the waters of the lake of San Cristoval, which again are six varas lower than the waters of the lake Zumpango, which forms the northernmost link of this dangerous chain. The level of Mexico in 1803 was exactly one vara, one foot, and one inch above that of the lake of Tezcoco, and consequently was nine varas and five inches lower than that of the lake of Zumpango; a disproportion the effects of which have been more severely felt because the lake of Zumpango receives the tributary streams of the River Guautitlan, whose volume is more considerable than that of all the other rivers which enter the valley combined.

" In the inundations to which this peculiarity in the formation of the valley of Mexico has given rise a similar succession of events has been always observed. The lake of Zumpango, swollen by the rapid increase of the River Guautitlan during the rainy season, forms a junction with that of San Cristoval, and the waters of the two combined burst the dykes which separate them from the lake of Tezcoco. The waters of this last again, raised suddenly more than a vara above their usual level, and prevented from extending themselves to the east and southeast by the rapid rise of the ground in that direction, rush back toward the capital and fill the streets which approach nearest to their own level. This was the case in the years 1553, 1580, 1604, and 1607, in each of which years the capital was entirely under water, and the dykes which had been constructed for its protection destroyed."

Such is a topographical sketch of the country accurately given by a careful writer [1]; and to protect an important region so constantly menaced with inundation the viceroy now addressed himself. Accordingly he commissioned the engineer, Enrique Martinez, in 1607 to attempt the drainage of the lake of Zumpango by the stupendous canal known under the name of the Desague de Huehuetoca.

" The plan of Martinez appears to have embraced two distinct objects, the first of which extended to the lakes of Tezcoco and San Cristoval, while the second was confined to the lake of Zumpango, whose superfluous waters were to be carried into the valley of Tula by a subterraneous canal, into which the River Guautitlan was likewise compelled to flow. The second of these projects only was approved by the government; and the line of the canal having been traced by Martinez between the cerro or hill of Sincoque and the hill of Nochistongo to the northwest of Huehuetoca, where the mountains that surrounded the valley are less elevated than in any other spot, the great subterraneous gallery of Nochistongo was

[1] Ward, " Mexico in 1827," vol II. p. 282 ff.

commenced on November 28, 1607. Fifteen thousand Indians were employed in this work, and as a number of air-shafts were sunk, in order to enable them to work upon the different points at once, in eleven months a tunnel of six thousand six hundred meters in length, three meters five in breadth and four meters two in height, was concluded.

"From the northern extremity of this tunnel, called la boca de San Gregorio, an open cut of eight thousand six hundred meters conducted the waters to the salto or fall of the River Tula, where, quitting the valley of Mexico, they precipitate themselves into that of Tula from a natural terrace of twenty Mexican varas in height and take their course toward the bar of Tampico, where they enter the Gulf of Mexico. An enterprise of such magnitude could hardly be free from defects, and Martinez soon discovered that the unbaked bricks of which the interior of the tunnel was composed were unable to resist the action of water, which, being confined within narrow limits, was at times impelled through the tunnel with irresistible violence. A facing of wood proved equally ineffectual, and masonry was at last resorted to; but even this, though successful for a time, did not answer permanently, because the engineer, instead of an elliptical arch, constructed nothing but a sort of vault, the sides of which rested upon a foundation of no solidity. The consequence was that the walls were gradually undermined by the water, and that the vault itself in many parts fell in.

"This accident rendered the government indifferent to the fate of the gallery, which was neglected, and finally abandoned in the year 1623, when a Dutch engineer, named Adrian Boot, induced the viceroy to resume the old system of dyke and embankments, and to give orders for closing the tunnel of Nochistongo. A sudden rise in the lake of Tezcoco caused these orders to be revoked, and Martinez was again allowed to proceed with his works, which he continued until June 20, 1629, when an event took place the real causes of which have never been ascertained.

"The rainy season having set in with unusual violence, Martinez, either desirous to convince the inhabitants of the capital of the utility of his gallery, or fearful, as he himself stated, that the fruits of his labor would be destroyed by the entrance of too great a volume of water, closed the mouth of the tunnel without communicating to anyone his intention to do so. The effect was instantaneous; and in one night the whole town of Mexico was laid under water, with the exception of the great square and one of the suburbs. In all the other streets the water rose upwards of three feet, and during five years, from 1629 to 1634, canoes formed the only medium of communication between them. The foundations of many of the principal houses were destroyed, trade was paralyzed, the lower classes reduced to the lowest state of misery, and orders were actually given by the court of Madrid to abandon the town and build a new capital in the elevated plains between Tacuba and Tacubaya, to which the waters of the lakes, even before the conquest, had never been known to extend.

"The necessity of this measure was obviated by a succession of earthquakes in the dry year of 1634, when the valley was cracked and rent in various directions, and the waters gradually disappeared; a miracle for which due credit should be given to the Virgin of Guadalupe, by whose powerful intercession it is said to have been effected.

"Martinez, who had been thrown into confinement in 1629, was released upon the termination of the evils which his imprudence was said to have occasioned, and was again placed by a new viceroy, the Marques de Cerralvo, at the head of the works by which similar visitations were to be averted in future. Under his superintendence the great dyke or calzada of San Cristoval was put in order,[2] by which the lake of that name is divided from that of Tezcoco. This gigantic work, which consists of two distinct masses, the first, one league, and the second, one thousand five hundred varas in length, is ten varas in width or thickness throughout, and from three and a half to four varas in height. It is composed entirely of stone, with buttresses of solid masonry on both sides, and three sluices by which in any emergency a communication between the lakes can be effected and regulated at the same time. The whole was concluded, like the gallery of Nochistongo, in eleven months, although as many years would now be required for such an undertaking. But in those days the sacrifice of life, and particularly of Indian life, in public works was not regarded. Many thousands of the natives perished before the desague was completed; and to their loss, as well as to the hardships endured by the survivors, may be ascribed the horror with which the name of Huehuetoca is pronounced by their descendants.

[2] The calzada of San Cristoval was originally erected, according to good authority, in the year 1605.

The "*Guia General Descriptiva de la República Mexicana*"[3] divides the work undertaken for the proper drainage of the valley of Mexico into four epochs. In the year 1449, during the rule of Montezuma, the first dams connecting Tenochtitlan (Mexico) with Tepeyac (Guadalupe) and Xochimilco were constructed. During the colonial empire (1553) a curved dam was built to replace those destroyed by Cortéz during the war, others being built in 1604 and 1708. During the republican régime President Comonfort, in 1856, invited the competition of experts, both native and foreign, whose plans for the drainage works should fulfill certain conditions, among them being the stipulation that the waste waters be always used for irrigation purposes. Of the seven projects presented, that of engineer Francisco Garay was selected, and the work has lately been finished in accordance with his plans. The delay in the completion of the work was due to several disturbances in the country, until, in 1885, President Díaz approved an appropriation of $400,000 a year for the continuance of the work until it should be finished, which was successfully effected in 1896 at a cost of $13,000,000. The work on the main canal, which necessitated the removal of 10,215,000 cubic meters of earth, kept 3000 men and 5 dredging machines constantly employed. During the progress of the work upheavals of the soft bed of the canal occurred several times, thus rendering it necessary to commence the work anew. The canal starts at a point east of the city about on a level with the lake of Tezcoco, 1.30 meters below the mean level of Mexico, crosses the River Guadalupe by means of an aqueduct 50 centimeters above the mean level of the river, extends for a distance of 48 kilometers, penetrating deeper and deeper into the earth until it enters a tunnel 10 kilometers in length, constructed at a slight incline and furnished with vent holes to a depth of 94 meters.

The valley of Mexico has undergone a great modification with the opening of the main canal. The waters, which formerly emptied into the small lakes, and owing to the configuration of the land had no natural outlets, thus constituting at times centers of infectious diseases, are now drained into the lake of Tezcoco and can be controlled at will, either allowed to flow out when too abundant, or retained for irrigation purposes in case of need. As the valley is situated within the torrid zone, its climate might nat-

[3] Compiled by J. Figueroa Domenech-Araluce, publisher, Mexico, 1899.

turally be expected to be exceedingly hot, but as its altitude above
sea level is 2280 meters, the mean temperature is that of the temperate zone. During the summer the maximum temperature is
reached at two o'clock in the afternoon in the months of April and
May, and does not exceed 26° C. (78.80° F.), while the lowest
temperature in the morning during the same months is about
10° C. (50° F.), the mean temperature being from 18° to 19° C.
(64° to 66° F.). During the winter the minimum temperature
recorded in the mornings of November, December, and January
is about 2° C. (35° F.), while the maximum experienced during
the same months is from 19° to 20° C. (66° to 68° F.), the mean
temperature being, therefore, about 12° C. (53.60° F.). As indicated by these figures, the mornings are cool and pleasant all
the year and the afternoons temperate. There are only two seasons—the dry season from October to March, and the rainy season
from April to September. The rainfall throughout the year is not
very heavy, but as it is all utilized in the valley for irrigation purposes, it equals in its effect a much larger quantity. The winds
blow from the northeast, but are never so strong as to become
hurricanes.

In the year 1609 a large number of negroes rebelled against
the Spaniards. It seems that the blacks in the neighborhood of
Cordova, who were in fact slaves on many of the haciendas or plantations, having been treated in an inhuman manner by their owners,
rose against them in great force, and gathering together in the
adjacent mountains menaced their tyrannical taskmasters with
death and their property with ruin. Velasco sent one hundred
soldiers, one hundred volunteers, one hundred Indian archers,
together with two hundred Spaniards and Mestizos, to attack
them in their fastnesses. Several skirmishes took place between
the slaves and these forces, and at length the negroes yielded to
the Spaniards, craving their pardon, inasmuch as their "insurrection was not against the king," and promising that they would
no longer afford a refuge to the blacks who absconded from the
plantations. Velasco at once granted their request, and permitted
them to settle in the town of San Lorenzo.

In 1610 and 1611 there were but few important incidents in
the history of New Spain, which was now gradually forming itself
into a regularly organized state, free from all those violent internal
commotions which nations, like men, are forced to undergo in their

infancy. The viceroy still endeavored to ameliorate the condition of the Indians, and dispatched a mission to Japan in order to extend the oriental commerce of Spain. The true policy of Castile would have been, instead of crushing Mexico by colonial restrictions, to have raised her gradually into a gigantic state, which, situated in the center of America, on the narrowest part of the continent between the two oceans, and holding in her veins the precious metals in exhaustless quantities, might reasonably have been expected to grasp and hold the commerce of the East and of Europe, for such would seem the natural destiny of Mexico if we examine her geographical features carefully.

Velasco was now well-stricken in years and required repose. His master, appreciating his faithful services and his unquestionable loyalty, added to his already well-earned titles that of Marques de Salinas, and creating him president of the Council of the Indies recalled him to Spain, where he could pass in quiet the evening of his days, while he was also enabled to impart the results of his vast American experience to the king and court.

Velasco, as an especial mark of royal favor, was desired to retain his power as viceroy until the moment of embarkation for Spain, and then to depose it in favor of the monk Garcia Guerra, who had been the worthy prior of a Dominican convent at Burgos in Spain until he was nominated to the archepiscopal see of Mexico. His government was brief and altogether eventless. He became viceroy on June 17, 1611, and died on February 22, in the following year, of a wound he received in falling as he descended from his coach.

Upon his death the audiencia of course took possession of the government during the interregnum; and, as it seems that this body of men was always doomed to celebrate its authority by acts of folly or cruelty, we find that soon after its accession to power the city was alarmed by the news of another outbreak among the negroes. The people were panic-stricken. A terrible noise had been heard in the streets of the metropolis during the night, and although it was proved that the disturbance was entirely caused by the entrance during the darkness of a large drove of hogs, the audiencia determined nevertheless to appease public opinion by the execution of twenty-nine male negroes and four negro women! Their withered and fetid bodies were left to hang on the gallows, tainting the air and shocking the eyes of every passer, until the neighborhood could no longer bear the sickly stench and imperiously demanded their removal.

The Marques de Guadalcazar, Don Diego Fernandez de Cordova, entered upon the viceroyalty on October 28, 1612, and his government passed in quiet, engaged in the mere ordinary discharge of executive duties during the first four years, subsequent to which an Indian insurrection of a formidable character broke out in one of the departments, under a chief who styled himself " Son of the Sun and God of Heaven and Earth." This assault was fatal to every Spaniard within reach of the infuriated natives, who broke into the churches, murdered the whites seeking sanctuary at their altars, and spared not even the ecclesiastics, who in all times have so zealously proved themselves to be the defenders of their race. Don Gaspar Alvear, Governor of Durango, assembled a large force as soon as the viceroy informed him of the insurrection, and marched against the savages. After three months of fighting, executions, and diplomacy, this functionary succeeded in suffocating the rebellion; but he was probably more indebted for the final reconciliation of the Indians to the persuasive talents of the Jesuits who accompanied the expedition than to the arms of his soldiers.

The remaining years of this viceroyalty are only signalized by the founding of the city of Cordova, whose neighborhood is renowned for the excellent tobacco and coffee it produces, and for the construction of the beautiful aqueduct of San Cosmé, which brings the sweet waters of Santa Fé to the capital. This monument to the intelligence and memory of Guadalcazar was completed in 1620; and in March, 1621, the viceroy was removed to the government of Peru.

Chapter XVIII

THE RISING AGAINST GELVES. 1621-1624

UPON the removal of the Marques de Guadalcazar, and until September 21, 1621, the audencia again ruled in Mexico, without any interruption, however, upon this occasion, of the public peace. The six months of the interregnum might, indeed, have been altogether forgotten in the history of the country had not the audiencia been obliged to announce the reception of a royal cedula from Philip IV., communicating the news of his father's death and commanding a national mourning for his memory. In September a new viceroy arrived in the capital, and immediately caused the royal order to be carried into effect and allegiance to be sworn solemnly to Philip IV. as king and lord of Old and New Spain.

The Marques de Gelves was selected by the sovereign as fourteenth viceroy of New Spain, for the reputation he bore in the home country as a lover of justice and order, qualities which would insure his utility in a country whose quietness, during several of the last viceroyal reigns, had indicated either a very good or a very bad government, which it was impossible for the king to examine personally. Accordingly Gelves took the reins with a firm hand. He found many of the departments of government in a bad condition, and is said to have reformed certain abuses which were gradually undermining the political and social structure of the colony. In these duties the first two years of his viceroyalty passed away quietly; but Gelves, though an excellent magistrate so far as the internal police of the country is concerned, was nevertheless a selfish and avaricious person, and seems to have resolved that his fortune should prosper by his government of New Spain.

The incidents which we are about to relate are stated on the authority of Father Gage, an English friar who visited Mexico in 1625, and whose pictures of the manners of the people correspond so well with our personal knowledge of them at present that we are scarcely at liberty to question his fidelity as a historian.

In the year 1624 Mexico was for a time in a state of great distraction, and well-nigh revolted from the Spanish throne. The passion for acquiring fortune, which had manifested itself somewhat in other viceroys, seemed in Gelves unbounded. He resolved to achieve his end by a bold stroke; and in 1623, having determined to monopolize the staff of life among the Indians and creoles, he dispatched one of the wealthiest Mexicans, Don Pedro de Mexia, to buy up corn in all the provinces at the rate of fourteen reales, the sum fixed by law at which the corn was sold in times of famine. The farmers, who of course knew nothing of Mexia's plan, readily disposed of their corn, with which the artful purveyor filled his storehouses all over the country. After the remnant of the crop was brought to market and sold, men began to compare notes, and suddenly discovered that corn was nowhere to be procured save from the granaries of Mexia. "The poor began to murmur, the rich began to complain; and the tariff of fourteen reales was demanded from the viceroy." But he, the secret accomplice of Mexia, decided that as the crops had been plentiful during the year, it could not be regarded as one of scarcity according to the evident intention of the law, so that it would be unfair to reduce the price of grain to that of famine. And thus the people, balked in their effort to obtain justice from their ruler, though suffering from extreme imposition, resolved to bear the oppression rather than resort to violence for redress.

After awhile, however, the intimacy between Gelves and Mexia became more apparent as the confederates supposed they had less cause for concealment, and the poor again besought the viceroy for justice and the legal tariff. But the temptation was too great for the avaricious representative of the king. He again denied their petition; and then as a last hope they resorted to a higher power, which in such conflicts with their rulers had usually been successful.

In those days Don Alonzo de la Serna, a man of lofty character and intrepid spirit, was Archbishop of Mexico, and perceiving the avaricious trick of the viceroy and his agent, threw himself on the popular side and promptly excommunicated Mexia. But the sturdy merchant, protected by viceroyal authority, was not to be conquered by so immaterial a thing as a prelate's curse placarded on the door of a cathedral. He remained quietly ensconced in his house, dispatched orders to his agents, and even raised the price of his extravagant bread-stuffs. For a moment, perhaps, De la Serna was confounded by this rebellious son of the church, yet the act convinced him, if indeed he entertained any doubt on the subject, that Mexia was backed by the viceroy, and consequently that any further attempts would bring him in direct conflict with the government. Nevertheless, a man like him was not to be easily alarmed or forced to retreat so quickly. The church, supreme in spiritual power, would never yield, especially in a matter of popular and vital concern, and the archbishop therefore determined to adopt the severest method at once, and by an order of *cessato divinis,* to stop immediately all religious worship throughout the colony. This was a direful interdict, the potency of which can only be imagined by those who have lived in Catholic countries whose piety is not periodically regulated upon the principle of a seven-day clock, but where worship is celebrated from hour to hour in the churches. The doors of chapels, cathedrals, and religious buildings were firmly closed. A death-like silence prevailed over the land. No familiar bells sounded for matins or vespers. The people, usually warned by them of their hours of labor or repose, had now no means of measuring time. The priests went from house to house lamenting the grievous affliction with which the country was visited and sympathizing cordially with the people. The church mourned for the unnatural pains her rebellious son had brought upon her patient children. But still the contumacious Mexia sold his corn and exacted his price!

At length, however, popular discontent became so clamorous that even among this orderly and enduring people the life of the viceroy's agent was no longer safe. He retreated therefore from his own dwelling to the palace, which was strongly guarded, and demanded protection from Gelves. The viceroy admitted him and took issue with the archbishop. He immediately sent orders to the priests and curates of the several parishes, to cause the orders of interdict and excommunication to be torn from the church walls, and all the chapels to be thrown open for service. But the resolute clergy, firm in their adherence to the prelate, would receive no command from the viceroy. Finding the churches still closed, and the people still more clamorous and angry, Gelves commanded De la Serna to revoke his censures; but the archbishop answered that what he had done was but an act of divine justice against a cruel oppressor of the poor, whose cries had moved him to compassion, and that the offender's contempt for his excommunication had deserved the rigor of both of his censures, neither of which he would recall until Don Pedro de Mexia submitted himself reverently to the church, received public absolution, and threw up the unconscionable monopoly wherewith he had wronged the commonwealth. "But," says the chronicle of the day, "the viceroy, not brooking the saucy answer of a churchman, nor permitting him to imitate the spirit of the holy Ambrose against the Emperor Theodosius," forthwith sent orders to arrest De la Serna, and to carry him to Vera Cruz, where he was to be confined in the castle of San Juan de Ulua until he could be dispatched to Spain. The Archbishop, however, followed by a long train of his prebends, priests, and curates, immediately retired from the capital to the neighboring village of Guadalupe, but left a sentence of excommunication on the cathedral door against the viceroy himself! This was too much for the haughty representative of the Spanish king to bear without resentment, and left no means open for conciliation between church and state. Gelves could as little yield now as De la Serna could before, and of course nothing remained for him but to lay violent hands on the prelate wherever he might be found. His well-paid soldiers were still faithfully devoted to the viceroy, and he forthwith committed the archbishop's arrest to a reckless and unscrupulous officer named Tirol. As soon as he had selected a band of armed men upon whose courage and obedience he could rely, this person hastened to the village of Guadalupe. In the meantime the archbishop was apprised of his coming and prepared to meet him. He summoned his faithful clergy to attend in the sanctuary of the church, clad in their sacred vestments. For the first time, after many a long and weary day, the ears of the people were saluted by the sound of bells calling them to the house of God. Abandoning their business, some of them immediately filled the square, eagerly demanding by what blessed interposition they had been relieved from the fearful interdict, while others thronged the doors and crowded the aisles of the long forsaken chapel. The candles on the altar were lighted, the choir struck up a solemn hymn for the church, and then, advancing along the aisle in gorgeous procession, De la Serna and his priestly train took up their position in front of the tabernacle, where, crowned with his miter, his crozier in one hand and the holy sacrament in the other, this brave prelate awaited the forces which had been sent to seize him. It is difficult to say if De la Serna de-

signed by so imposing a spectacle to strike awe into the mind of the
sacrilegious soldier, or whether he thought it his duty to be arrested,
if he must be, at that altar he had sworn to serve. It is probable,
however, from his exalted character and courage that the latter was
the true motive of his act, and, if so, he met his fate nobly in the
cause of justice and religion.

Tirol was not long in traversing the distance between Mexico
and Guadalupe. As soon as he arrived he entered the church
accompanied by his officers, and seemed appalled by the gorgeous
and dramatic display round the shrine. Not a whisper was heard
in the edifice as the crowd slowly parted to make way for the
soldiers, who advanced along the aisle and humbly knelt for a moment at the altar in prayer. This done, Tirol approached De la
Serna, and with " fair and courteous words " required him to lay
down the sacrament, to quit the sanctuary, and to listen to the
orders issued in the royal name. The archbishop abruptly refused
to comply, and answered that " as the viceroy was excommunicated he regarded him as beyond the pale of the church and in no
way empowered to command in Mexico "; he therefore ordered
the soldiers, as they valued the peace of their souls, to desist from
infringing the privileges of the church by the exercise of secular
power within its limits, and he finally declared that he would
on no account depart from the altar unless torn from it with the
sacrament. Upon this Tirol arose and read the order for his
arrest, describing him as a " traitor to the king, a disturber of the
peace, and a mover of sedition in the commonwealth."

De la Serna smiled contemptuously at the officer as he finished,
and taunted him with the viceroy's miserable attempt to cast upon
the church the odium of sedition, when his creature Mexia was, in
fact, the shameless offender. He conjured Tirol not to violate
the sanctuary to which he had retreated, lest his hand should be
withered like that of Jeroboam, who stretched forth an arm against
the prophet of the Lord at the altar!

Tirol seems to have been a man upon whose nerves such appeals
had but little effect. He was a blunt soldier, who received the
orders of his superiors and performed them to the letter. He had
been ordered to arrest the archbishop wherever he found him, and
he left the ecclesiastical scandal to be settled by those who sent
him. Beckoning to a recreant priest who had been tampered with
and brought along for the purpose, he commanded him in the king's

name to wrest the sacrament from the prelate's hand. The clergy-man, immediately mounting the steps of the altar, obeyed the orders, and the desecrated bishop at once threw off his pontifical robes and yielded to civil power. The cowardly Mexicans made no attempt to protect their intrepid friend, who, as he left the sanctuary, paused for a moment and stretched his hands in benediction over the recreants. Then bidding an affectionate farewell to his clergy, whom he called to witness how zealously he had striven to preserve the church from outrage as well as the poor from plunder, he departed as a prisoner for Vera Cruz, whence he was dispatched to Spain in a vessel expressly equipped for his conveyance.

For a while the people were alarmed at this high-handed move-ment against the archbishop, but when the momentary effect had passed away and they began to reflect on the disgrace of the church as well as the loss of their protector, they vented their displeasure openly against Mexia and the viceroy. The temper of the masses was at once noticed by the clergy, who were still faithful to their persecuted bishop, nor did they hesitate to fan the flame of discon-tent among the suffering Indians, Mestizos, and Creoles, who omitted no occasion to express their hatred of the Spaniards, and especially of Tirol, who had been the viceroy's tool in De la Serna's arrest. A fortnight elapsed after the occurrences we have just de-tailed, and that daring officer had already delivered his prisoner at Vera Cruz and returned to Mexico. Popular clamor at once became loud against him; whenever he appeared in public he was assailed with curses and stones, until at last an enraged mob at-tacked him in his carriage with such violence that it was alone owing to the swiftness of the mules, lashed by the affrighted pos-tilion, that he escaped into the viceroyal palace, whose gates were immediately barred against his pursuers. Meantime the news had spread over town that this "Judas," "this excommunicated dog," had taken refuge with Gelves, and the neighboring market-place became suddenly filled with an infuriated mob, numbering nearly seven thousand Indians, negroes, and mulattoes, who rushed toward the palace with the evident intention of attacking it. See-ing this outbreak from a window, the viceroy sent a message to the assailants desiring them to retire, and declaring that Tirol had escaped by a postern. But the blood of the people was up, and not to be calmed by excuses. At this juncture several priests entered the crowd, and a certain Salazar was especially zealous in exciting the multitude to summary revenge. The pangs of hunger were for a moment forgotten in the more bitter excitement of religious outrage. By this time the mob obtained whatever arms were nearest at hand. Poles, pikes, pistols, guns, halberds, and stones were brought to the ground, and fierce onsets were made on every accessible point of the palace. Neither the judges nor the police came forward to aid in staying the riot and protecting Gelves. "Let the youngsters alone," exclaimed the observers, "they will soon find out both Mexia and Tirol, as well as their patron, and the wrongs of the people will be quickly redressed!" A portion of the mob drew off to an adjacent prison, whose doors were soon forced and the convicts released.

At length things became alarming to the besieged inmates of the palace, for they seemed to be entirely deserted by the respectable citizens and police. Thereupon the viceroy ascended to the azotéa or flat roof of the palace with his guard and retainers, and, displaying the royal standard, caused a trumpet to be sounded calling the people to uphold the king's authority. But the reply to his summons was still in an unrelenting tone: *"Viva el Rey! Muera el mal gobierno; mueran los dos comulgados!"* "Long live the king! but down with the wicked government, and death to the excommunicated wretches!" These shouts, yelled forth by the dense and surging mob, were followed by volleys discharged at the persons on the azotéa, who for three hours returned the shots and skirmished with the insurgents. Stones, also, were hurled from the parapet upon the crowd, but it is related in the chronicles of the time that not a single piece of ordnance was discharged upon the people, "for the viceroy in those days had none for the defense of his palace or person, neither had that great city any for its strength and security."

So passed the noon and evening of that disastrous day; but at nightfall the baffled mob that had been unable to make any impression with their feeble weapons upon the massive walls of the palace, brought pitch and inflammable materials, with which they fired the gates of the viceroyal palace. The bright flames of these combustibles sent up their light in the still evening air, and far and wide over the town spread the news that the beautiful city was about to be destroyed. Frightened from their retreats, the judges and chief citizens who had influence with the people rushed to the plaza, and by their urgent entreaties efforts were made to extinguish the fire. But the palace gates had already fallen, and over their smoldering ruins the infuriated assailants rushed into the edifice to commence the work of destruction. The magistrates, however, who had never taken part against the people in their quarrels, soon appeared upon the field, and by loud entreaties stopped the pillage. It was soon discovered that Mexia and Tirol had escaped by a postern, while the conquered viceroy, disguised as a friar, stole through the crowd to the Franciscan cloister, where for many a day he lay concealed in the sanctuary which his rapacious spirit had denied to the venerable De la Serna.

So ended this base attempt of a Spanish nobleman and representative of royalty in America to enrich himself by plundering the docile Mexicans. The fate of Mexia and Tirol is unknown. But Spanish injustice toward the colonies was strongly marked by the reception of the viceroy and the archbishop on their return from Madrid. Gelves, it is true, was recalled, but, after being graciously welcomed at court, was made "master of the royal horse," while the noble-hearted De la Serna was degraded from his Mexican archprelacy and banished to the petty bishopric of Zamora in Castile!

Chapter XIX

THE INDIAN REBELLIONS. 1624-1696

UPON the violent expulsion of the viceroy Gelves by the popular outbreak, narrated in the last chapter, the government of New Spain fell once more into the hands of the audiencia during the interregnum. This body immediately adopted suitable measures to terminate the disaffection. The people were calmed by the deposition of one they deemed an unjust ruler; but for a long time it was found necessary to keep on foot in the capital large bands of armed men in order to restrain those troublesome persons who are always ready to avail themselves of any pretext for tumultuary attacks either against property or upon people who are disposed to maintain the supremacy of law and order.

As soon as Philip IV. was apprised of the disturbances in his transatlantic colony, he trembled for the security of Spanish power in that distant realm, and immediately dispatched Don Martin Carillo, Inquisitor of Valladolid, with unlimited power to examine into the riots of the capital and to punish the guilty participants in a signal and summary manner. It is not our purpose, at present, to discuss the propriety of sending from Spain special judges in the character of visitadors or inquisitors whenever crimes were committed by eminent individuals in the colony, or by large bodies of people, which required the infliction of decided punishment. But it may be regarded as one of the characteristic features of the age, and as demonstrative of the peculiar temper of the king, that an inquisitor was selected upon this occasion for so delicate and dangerous a duty. It is true that the church, through the late archbishop, was concerned in this painful affair; but it little accords with the ideas of our age to believe it necessary that a subject of such public concern as the insurrection against an unjust and odious viceroy should be confined to the walls of an inquisition or conducted by one of its leading functionaries alone. Had the investigation been intrusted exclusively to a civil and not an ecclesiastical judge, it is very questionable whether he should have been sent from Spain for this purpose alone. Being a foreigner, at least so far as the colony was concerned, he could have scarcely any knowledge of or sympathy with the colonists. Extreme impartiality may have been insured by this fact; yet as the visitador or inquisitor departed as soon as his special function ceased, he was never responsible for his decrees to that wholesome public opinion which visits the conduct of a judge with praise or condemnation during his lifetime when he permanently resides in a country, and is always the safest guardian of the liberty of the citizen.

It seems, however, that the inquisitor administered his office fairly and even leniently in this case, for his judgments fell chiefly on the thieves who stole the personal effects of the viceroy during the sacking of the palace. The principal movers in the insurrection had absented themselves from the capital, and prudently remained in concealment until the visitador terminated his examinations, inflicted his punishments upon the culprits he convicted, and crossed the sea to report his proceedings at court.

Carillo had been accompanied to New Spain by a new viceroy, Don Roderigo Pacheco Osorio, Marques de Cerralvo, who arrived in the capital on November 3, 1624, and assumed the government. He left the examination of the insurrection entirely in the hands of the inquisitor and directed his attention to the public affairs of the colony. These he found peaceful, except that a Dutch squadron, under the command of the Prince of Nassau, attacked Acapulco, and the feeble city and garrison readily surrendered without resistance. The fleet held the city, however, only for a few days, and set sail for other enterprises. This assault upon an important port alarmed the viceroy, who at once sent orders to have the town immediately surrounded with a wall, and suitable forts and bastions erected which would guard it in all subsequent attacks. These fortifications were hardly commenced when another Dutch fleet appeared before the town. But this time the visit was not of a hostile nature—it was an exhausted fleet demanding water and provisions, after receiving which it resumed its track for the East Indies. While the Spaniards were thus succoring and sustaining their enemies, the Dutch, a dreadful famine scourged Sinaloa and neighboring provinces, carrying off upwards of eight thousand Indians.

During the long reign of Philip IV. Spain was frequently at war with England, Holland, and France; and the Dutch, who inflicted dreadful ravages on the American coasts, secured immense spoil from the Spaniards. In 1628 Pedro Hein, a Hollander of great distinction, placed a squadron in the gulf on the coasts of Florida to intercept the fleet of New Spain. The resistance made by the Spaniards was feeble, and, their vessels being captured by the Dutch, the commerce of Mexico experienced a severe blow from which it was long in recovering.

The remaining years of this viceroyalty were consumed in matters of mere local detail and domestic government, and in fact we know but little of it, save that the severe inundations of 1629 caused the authorities to use their utmost efforts in prosecuting the work of the desague, as we have already seen in the general account given of that gigantic enterprise. In 1635 this viceroy's reign terminated and he was followed by the Marques de Cadereita, the sixteenth viceroy of New Spain.

The five years of this personage's government were unmarked by any events of consequence in the colony; except that in the last of them, 1640, he dispatched an expedition to the north, where he founded, in New Leon, the town of Cadereita, which the emigrants named in honor of their viceroy.

The Duke of Escalona succeeded the Marques de Cadereita, and arrived in Mexico on June 28, 1640, together with the venerable Palafox, who came in the character of visitador to inquire into the administration of the last viceroy, whose reputation, like that of other chief magistrates in New Spain, had suffered considerably in the hands of his enemies. While this functionary proceeded with his disagreeable task against a man who was no longer in power, the duke in compliance with the king's command ordered the governor of Sinaloa, Don Luis Cestinos, accompanied by two Jesuits, to visit the Californias and examine their coasts and the neighboring isles in search of the wealth in pearls and precious metals with which they were reputed to be filled. The reports of the explorers were altogether satisfactory both as to the character of the natives and of the riches of the waters as well as of the mines, though they represented the soil as extremely sterile. The gold of California was reserved for another age.

Ever since the conquest the instruction of Indians in Christian doctrine had been confided exclusively to the regular clergy of the Roman Catholic Church. The secular priests were thus entirely deprived of the privilege of mingling their cares with their monastic brethren, who in the course of time began to regard this as an absolute, indefeasible right whose enjoyment they were unwilling to forego, especially as the *obvenciones,* or tributes of the Indian converts, formed no small item of corporate wealth in their respective orders. The Indians were in fact lawful tributaries, not only of the whole church, in the estimation of these friars, but of the special sect or brotherhood which happened to obtain the first hold on a tribe or nation by its missionary residence among its people. Palafox requested the Duke of Escalona to deprive the monkish orders of this monopoly; a desire to which the viceroy at once acceded, inasmuch as he was anxious to serve the bishop in all matters pertaining to his religious functions.

The kindly feeling of the viceroy does not appear to have been appreciated or sincerely responded to by Palafox. This personage was removed in 1642 to the archiepiscopal see of Mexico, and under the pretext of installation in his new office and opening his tribunals he visited the capital with the actual design of occupying the viceroyal throne to which he had been appointed! This was a sudden and altogether unexpected blow to the worthy duke, who was so unceremoniously supplanted. No one seems to have whispered to him even a suspicion of the approaching calamity, until the crafty Palafox assembled the oidores at midnight on the eve of Pentecost, and read to them the royal dispatches containing his commission. His conduct to the jovial-hearted duke was not only insincere but unmannerly, for immediately after the assumption of his power at dead of night he commanded a strong guard to surround the palace at dawn, and required the oidor Lugo to read the royal cedula to the duke even before he left his bed. The deposed viceroy immediately departed for the convent at Churubusco, outside the city walls on the road to San Agustin de las Cuevas. All his property was sequestrated, and his money and jewels were secured within the treasury.

The reader will naturally seek for an explanation of this political enigma, or base intrigue, and its solution is again eminently characteristic of the reign in which it occurred. It will be remembered that the Duke of Braganza had been declared King of Portugal, which kingdom had separated itself from the Spanish domination, causing no small degree of animosity among the Castilians against the Portuguese, and all who favored them. The Duke of Escalona, unfortunately, was related to the house of Braganza,

and the credulous Philip, having heard that his viceroy exhibited
some evidences of attachment to the Portuguese, resolved to supersede him by Palafox. Besides this, the duke committed the
impolitic act of appointing a Portuguese to the post of castellan of
St. Juan de Ulua; and upon a certain occasion, when two horses
had been presented to him by Don Pedro de Castilla and Don
Cristobal de Portugal, he, unluckily, remarked that he liked best
the horse that was offered by Portugal! It is difficult to believe
that such trifles would affect the destiny of empires when they were
discussed by grave statesmen and monarchs; but such was the
miserable reign of Philip IV.; the most disastrous, indeed, in the
annals of Spain, except that of Roderic the Goth. Folly like this
may justly be attributed to the imbecile king who witnessed the
Catalan insurrection, the loss of Rousillon, Conflans, a part of
Cordaña, Jamaica, and, above all, of Portugal; and who, moreover, recognized the independence of the Seven United Provinces.

The administration of Palafox, Bishop of Puebla, as viceroy
was of but short duration. He occupied the colonial throne but
five months, yet during that brief space he did something that
signalized his name both honorably and disgracefully. He seems
to have been ridiculously bent upon the sacrifice of all the interesting monuments which were still preserved from the period of the
conquest as memorials of the art and idolatry of the Aztecs. These
he collected from all quarters and destroyed. He was evidently
no friend of the friars, but sought to build up and strengthen the
secular clergy, whose free circulation in the world brought them
directly under the eyes of society, and whose order made them
dependent upon that society, and not upon a corporation, for maintenance. During his short reign he manifested kindness for the
Indians, caused justice to be promptly administered, and even suspended certain worthy oidores who did not work as quickly and
decide as promptly as he thought they ought to; he regulated
the ordinances of the audiencia, prepared the statutes of the university, raised a large body of militia to be in readiness in case of
an attack from the Portuguese, visited the colleges under his secular jurisdiction, and finally, in proof of his disinterestedness, refused the salary of viceroy and visitador.

Philip IV. seems to have been more anxious to use Palafox
as an instrument to remove the Duke of Escalona than to em-
power him for any length of time with viceroyal authority;

for no sooner did he suppose that the duke was displaced quietly
without leaving the government in the hands of the audiencia,
than he appointed the Conde de Salvatierra as his representative.   This nobleman reached his government on November 23,
1642, and Palafox immediately retired from his office, still preserving, however, the functions of visitador.   At the conclusion of this
year the duke departed from Churubusco for San Martin, in order
to prepare for his voyage home; and in 1643 this ill-used personage
left New Spain, having previously fortified himself with numerous
certificates of his loyalty to the Spanish crown, all of which he
used so skillfully in vindication before the vacillating and imbecile
king that he was not only exculpated entirely, but offered once more
the viceroyalty from which he had been so rudely thrust.   The
duke promptly rejected the proposed restoration, but accepted the
viceroyalty of Sicily.   Before he departed for the seat of government he gave the king many wise councils as to his American colonies, but especially advised him to colonize the Californias.   Don
Pedro Portal de Casañete was commissioned by Philip for this
purpose.

In 1664 there were already in Mexico twelve convents of nuns,
and nearly as many monasteries, which, by the unwise but pious
zeal of wealthy persons, were becoming rich, and aggregating
to themselves a large amount of urban and rural property.   Besides this, the dependents upon these convents, both males and
females, were largely increasing; all of which so greatly prejudiced
not only property, but population, that the ayuntamiento or city
council solicited the king not to permit the establishment in future
of similar foundations, and to prohibit the acquisition of real estate
by monasteries, inasmuch as the time might come when these establishments would be the only proprietors.

Meanwhile Casañete arrived in Mexico on his way to the
shores of the Pacific.   Salvatierra received him kindly and made
proper efforts to equip him for the enterprise.   The chiefs and
governors of the interior were ordered to aid him in every way;
but just as he was about to sail two of his vessels were burned,
whereupon his soldiers dispersed, while the families of his colonists
withdrew, in hope of being again soon summoned to embark.

The civil government of Salvatierra passed in quietness; but
the domineering spirit of Palafox did not allow the church to
remain at peace with the state.   In 1647 this lordly churchman en-

gaged in warm discussion with the Jesuits and other orders. Palafox persevered in his rancorous controversy as long as he remained in America, and even after his return to Europe pursued his quarrel at the court of Rome. At the close of this year Salvatierra was removed to the viceroyalty of Peru.

The rule of Torres y Rueda, who succeeded, was brief and eventless. It extended from March 13, 1648, to April 22, 1649, when the bishop-governor died, and was sumptuously interred in the church of San Agustin in the City of Mexico.

The audiencia ruled in New Spain until July 3, 1650, when Don Luis Enriquez de Guzman, Count de Alvadeliste and twenty-first viceroy of New Spain, arrived in the capital. This nobleman had been, in fact, appointed by the king immediately upon the transfer of the Conde de Salvatierra to Peru; but inasmuch as he could not immediately cross the Atlantic, the Bishop of Yucatan had been directed to assume his functions *ad interim.* Alvadeliste, a man of amiable character and gentle manners, soon won the good opinion of the Spanish colonists and creoles. But if he was to experience but little trouble from his countrymen and their descendants, he was not to escape a vexatious outbreak among the northern Indians, who had remained quiet for so long that it was supposed they were finally and successfully subjected to the Spanish yoke.

The viceroy had not been long installed when he received news of a rebellion against the Spaniards by the Tarahumares, who inhabited portions of Chihuahua and Sinaloa, and who had hitherto yielded implicitly to the gentle and persuasive voice of the evangelical teachers dwelling among them. The portion of this tribe inhabiting Sinaloa commenced the assault, but the immediate cause of the rebellion is not known. We are not aware whether they experienced a severe local government at the hands of the Spaniards, whether they were tired of the presence of the children of the Peninsula, or whether they feared that the priestly rule was only another means of subjecting them more easily to the crown of Castile. Perhaps all these causes influenced the rebellion. Already in 1648 the chief of the nation had compromised three other tribes in the meditated outbreak; but lacking the concerted action of the Tepehuanes and other bands, upon whose aid they confidently counted, they resolved to attack alone the village of San Francisco de Borja, whose garrison and village they slaughtered and burned. San Francisco was the settlement which supplied the local missions with provisions, and its loss was consequently irreparable to that portion of the country.

As soon as the chief judge of Parral heard of this sanguinary onslaught he hastily gathered the neighboring farmers, herdsmen, and merchants, and hastened into the wilderness against the insurgents, who fled when they had destroyed the great depot of the Spaniards. The troops, hardy as they were on these distant frontiers, were not calculated for the rough warfare of woodsmen, and after some insignificant and unsuccessful skirmishes with the marauders the new levies retired hastily to their homes.

Fajardo, governor of Nueva Biscaya, soon heard of the rebellion and of the ineffectual efforts to suppress it. He was satisfied that no time was to be lost in crushing it, and accordingly marched with Juan Barraza to the seat of war with an adequate force: The Indians had meanwhile left their villages and betaken themselves to the mountains, woods, and fastnesses. Fajardo immediately burned their abandoned habitations and desolated their cultivated fields; and when the Indians, who were now satisfied of their impotence, demanded peace, he granted it on condition that the four insurgent chiefs of the rebellion should be surrendered for punishment. The natives in reply brought him the head of one of their leaders, together with his wife and child; soon after another head was delivered to him, and in a few days the other two leaders surrendered.

This for a while calmed the country; but in order to confirm the peace and friendship which seemed to be now tolerably well established, a mission was founded in the valley of Papigochi, in which the chief population of the Tarahumares resided. The reverend Jesuit, Father Bendin, was charged with the duty of establishing this benignant government of the church, and in a short time it appeared that he had succeeded in civilizing the Indians and in converting them to the Christian faith. There were, nevertheless, discontented men among the tribes, whose incautious acts occasionally gave warning of the animosity which still lingered in the breasts of the Indians. The most prudent of the Spaniards warned the governor of Nueva Biscaya to beware a sudden or personal attack. But this personage treated the advice with contempt, and felt certain that the country was substantially pacified. Nevertheless, while things wore this aspect of seeming calm, three chiefs or caciques who had embraced the Catholic faith prepared the elements for a new rebellion, and on June 5, 1649, at daybreak, they attacked the dwelling of the missionaries, set fire to its combustible materials, and, surrounding the blazing house in numbers, awaited the moment when the unsuspecting inmates attempted to escape. The venerable Bendin and his companions were quickly aroused, but no sooner did they rush from the flames than they were cruelly slain by the Indians. The church was then sacked. The valuables were secured and carried off by the murderous robbers, but all the images and religious emblems were sacrilegiously destroyed before the Indians fled to the country.

Fajardo once more dispatched Juan Barraza, with three hundred Spanish soldiers and some Indians, against the rebel Tarahumares. But the tribe had in its intercourse with the foreigners acquired some little knowledge of the art of war, and consequently did not await the expected attack in the open or level fields, where the Spanish cavalry could act powerfully against them. They retired, accordingly, to a rocky pass, flanked by two streams, which they fortified at all points with stone walls and other formidable impediments. Here they rested in security until the Spanish forces approached them; nor did they even then abandon their defensive warfare. Barraza, finding the Indians thus skillfully entrenched behind barriers and ready to repel his attack, was unable after numerous efforts to dislodge them from their position. Indeed, he appears to have suffered serious losses in his vain assaults; so that instead of routing the natives entirely, he found it necessary to withdraw his troops, who were greatly weakened by losses, while the daring insurgents continually received auxiliary reinforcements. In this untoward state of affairs Barraza resolved to make his escape during the night from such dangerous quarters, and, ordering his Indian allies to light the usual watchfires and keep up the ordinary bustle of a camp, he silently but gradually withdrew all his Spanish and native forces, so that at daybreak the Tarahumares found the country cleared of their foes.

As soon as Fajardo heard of the forced retreat of Barraza he determined to take the management of the campaign in his own hands. But his military efforts were as unsuccessful as those of his unfortunate captain. The rainy season came on before he could make a successful lodgment in the heart of the enemy's country, and his march was impeded by floods which destroyed the roads and rendered the streams impassable. Accordingly he retired to Parral, where he received orders from the viceroy to establish a garrison in Papigochi.

The Spaniards found that their cruelty in the first campaign against these untamed savages had inflamed their minds against the viceroyal troops. They attempted, therefore, to use once more the language of persuasion, and, offering the insurgents a perfect amnesty for the past, prevailed upon the old inhabitants of the vale of Papigochi to return to their former residences, where, however, they did not long remain faithful to their promised allegiance. The new garrison was established, as had been commanded by the viceroy; but in 1652 the relentless tribes, again seizing an unguarded moment, burned the barracks and destroyed in the flames a number of Spaniards, two Franciscan monks, and a Jesuit priest. The soldiery of Barraza and the governor retired from the doomed spot amid showers of Indian arrows.

In 1653 the war was resumed. The whole country was aroused and armed against these hitherto invincible bands. Other Indian tribes were subdued by the Spanish forces, and their arms were then once more turned upon the Tarahumares at a moment when the Indian chiefs were distant from the field. But the absence of the leaders neither dismayed nor disconcerted these relentless warriors. The Spaniards were again forced to retire, and the viceroy caused an extensive enlistment to be undertaken and large sums appropriated to crush or pacify the audacious bands. Before the final issue and subjugation, however, the Count de Alvadeliste received the king's command to pass from Mexico to the government of Peru, and, awaiting only the arrival of his successor, he sailed from Acapulco for his new viceroyalty.

This successor, the Duke of Albuquerque, who had married Doña Juana, daughter of the former viceroy, the Marques de Cadereita, arrived in Mexico on August 16, 1654. His accession was signalized by unusually splendid ceremonies in the capital, and the new viceroy immediately devoted himself to the improvement of Mexico, as well as to the internal administration of affairs. He zealously promoted the public works of the country; labored diligently to finish the cathedral; devoted himself in hours of leisure to the promotion of literature and the fine arts; regulated the studies in the university; and caused the country to be scoured for the apprehension of robbers and vagabonds who infested and rendered insecure all the highways of the colony. Great numbers of these wretches were soon seized and hanged after summary trials.

In 1656, the British forces having been successful against Jamaica, the Mexicans were apprehensive that their arms would next be turned against New Spain, and accordingly Albuquerque fitted out an armada to operate against the enemy among the islands before they could reach the coast of his viceroyalty. This well-designed expedition failed, and most of the soldiers who engaged in it perished. The duke, unsuccessful in war, next turned his attention to the gradual and peaceful extension, northward, of the colonial emigration; and, distributing a large portion of the territory of New Mexico among a hundred families, he founded the city of Albuquerque and established in it several Franciscan missions as the nucleus of future population.

The year 1659 was signalized in Mexico by one of those dramas which occasionally took place in all countries into which the institution of the inquisition was introduced, and fifty human victims were burned alive by order of the audiencia. It must be remembered that this was the first occurrence of the kind, and, either from curiosity or from a superior sense of duty, the dreadful pageant was not only witnessed by an immense crowd of eager spectators, but was even presided over by the viceroy himself. In 1660 the duke narrowly escaped death by the hands of an assassin. While on his knees at prayer in a chapel of the cathedral the murderer—a youthful soldier seventeen years old—stole behind him, and was in the act of striking the fatal blow when he was arrested. In less than twelve hours he had gone to account for the meditated crime.

Albuquerque appears to have been popular, useful, and intelligent, though, from his portrait which is preserved in the gallery of the viceroys in Mexico, we would have imagined him to be a gross sensualist, resembling more the usual pictorial representations of Sancho Panza than one who was calculated to wield the destinies of an empire. Nevertheless the expression of public sorrow was unfeigned and loud among all classes when he departed for Spain in the year 1660.

The successor of the Duke of Albuquerque entered Mexico on September 16, 1660. Don Juan de Leyva y de la Cerda, the twenty-third viceroy of New Spain, approached the colony with the best wishes and resolutions to advance its prosperity and glory. His earliest efforts were directed to the pacification of the Tara- humares, whose insurrection was still entirely unquelled, and whose successes were alarmingly disastrous in New Mexico, whither they advanced in the course of their savage warfare. With the same liberal spirit that characterized his predecessor, he continued to be the zealous friend of those remote frontier colonists, and in a short time formed twenty-four villages. It was doubtless his plan to subdue and pacify the north by an armed occupation.

In 1661 and 1662 the despotic conduct of the Spaniards to the Indians stirred up sedition in the south as well as at the north. The natives of Tehuantepec were at this period moved to rebel- lion with the hope of securing their personal liberty, even if they could not reconquer their national independence. Spanish forces were immediately marched to crush the insurrection, but the soft children of the south were not as firmly pertinacious in resistance as their sturdier brothers of the northern frontier. More accessible to the gentle voices and power of the clergy, they yielded to the persuasive eloquence of Bishop Ildefonzo Davalos, who, animated by honest and humane zeal for the children of the forest, went among the incensed tribes, and by kindness secured the submission which arms could not compel at the north. For this voluntary and valuable service the sovereign conferred on him the miter of Mexico, which in the year 1664 was renounced by Osorio Escobar.

The only other event of note during this viceroyalty was an attempt at colonization and pearl fishing on the coasts of Cali- fornia by Bernal Piñaredo, who seems rather to have disturbed than to have benefited the sparse settlers on those distant shores. He was coldly received on his return by the viceroy, who formally accused him to the court for misconduct during the expedition.

Don Juan de Leyva sailed for Spain in 1664, and soon after died, afflicted by severe family distresses, and especially by the misconduct of his son and heir.

The reign of Don Diego Osorio Escobar y Llamas, Bishop of Puebla, and twenty-fourth viceroy of New Spain, was remarkable for nothing except its extraordinarily brief duration. The bishop entered upon his duties on June 29, and resigned them in favor of his successor in the following October.

Don Sebastian de Toledo, Marques de Mancera, was the

twenty-fifth viceroy and New Spain enjoyed profound internal peace when Don Sebastian arrived in the capital on October 15, 1664. But the calm of the political world does not seem to have extended to the terrestrial, for about this period occurred one of the few eruptions of the famous mountain of Popocatepetl—the majestic volcano which lies on the eastern edge of the valley, and is the most conspicuous object from all parts of the upper table-lands of Mexico. For four days it poured forth showers of stones from its crater and then suddenly subsided into quietness.

In the beginning of 1666 a royal cedula was received from the queen apprising her faithful subjects of her husband's death, and that during the minority of Charles II. the government would be carried on by her. The loss of Jamaica during the last reign was irreparable for Spain. The possession of so important an island by the British enabled the enemies of Castile to find a lurking place in the neighborhood of her richest colonies from which the pirates and privateers could readily issue for the capture of Spanish commerce or wealth. The armada of the Marques de Cadareita was useless against the small armed craft which not only possessed great advantages in swiftness of sailing, but were able also to escape from the enemies' pursuit or guns in the shallows along the coast into which the larger vessels dared not follow them. But the general war in Europe which had troubled the peace of the Old World for so many years had now drawn to a close, and a peace was once more for a while reëstablished. The ambitious desires of the Europeans were now, however, turned toward America, and with eager and envious glances at the possessions of the Spaniards. The narrow, protective system of Spain had, as we have related in our introductory chapter, closed the colonial ports against all vessels and cargoes that were not Spanish. This of course was the origin of an extensive system of contraband, which had doubtless done much to corrupt the character of the masses, while it created a class of bold, daring, and reckless men, whose representatives may still be found even at this day in the ports of Mexico and South America. This contraband trade not only affected the personal character of the people, but naturally injured the commerce and impaired the revenues of New Spain. Accordingly the ministers in Madrid negotiated a treaty with Charles II. of England, by which the sovereigns of the two nations pledged themselves not to permit their subjects to trade in their colonies. Notwithstanding the treaty, however, Governor Lynch, of Jamaica, still allowed the equipment of privateers and smugglers in his island, where they were furnished with the necessary papers; but the king removed him as soon as he was apprised of the fact, and replaced the conniving official by a more discreet and conscientious governor. Nevertheless the privateers and pirates still continued their voyages, believing that this act of the British Government was not intended in good faith to suppress their adventures, but simply to show Spain that in England treaties were regarded as religiously binding upon the state and the people. They did not imagine that the new governor would finally enforce the stringent laws against them. But this personage permitted the outlaws to finish their voyages without interference on the high seas, and the moment some of them landed they were hanged, as an example to all who were still willing to set laws and treaties at defiance.

In 1670 the prolonged Tarahumaric war was brought to a close by Nicholas Barraza. An Indian girl pointed out the place in which the majority of the warriors might be surprised; and, all the passes being speedily seized and guarded, three hundred captives fell into the victors' hands. In 1673 the viceroy departed for Spain, after an unusually long and quiet reign of eight years.

The nomination to the viceroyalty of the distinguished nobleman, Don Pedro Nuño Colon de Portugal, Duke of Veraguas, a descendant of the discoverer of America, was unquestionably designed merely as a compliment to the memory of a man whose genius had given a new world to Castile. He was so far advanced in life that it was scarcely presumed he would be able to withstand the hardships of the voyage or reach the Mexican metropolis. And such, indeed, was the result of his toilsome journey. His baton of office, assumed on December 8, 1673, fell from his decrepit hand on the 13th of the same month. So sure was the Spanish court that the viceroy would not long survive his arrival, that it had already appointed his successor, and sent a sealed dispatch with the commission, which was to be opened in the event of Don Pedro's death. It thus happened that the funeral of one viceroy was presided over by his successor, and the august ceremonial was doubtless more solemn from the fact that this successor was Rivera, who at that time was the Archbishop of Mexico.

The Duke of Veraguas, as we have seen, enjoyed none of his viceroyal honors save those which crowned his entrance into the capital; and as soon as his remains were temporarily interred in the cathedral, Fray Payo Enrique de Rivera assumed the reins of government.

This excellent prelate had fulfilled the functions of his bishopric for nine years in Guatemala so satisfactorily to the masses that his elevation to supreme power in Mexico was hailed as a national blessing. He devoted himself from the first diligently to the adornment of the capital and the just and impartial administration of public affairs. He improved the roads and entrances into the city, and, by his moderation, justice, and mildness, united with liberality and economy, raised the reputation of his government to such a degree of popular favor that in the annals of New Spain it is referred to as a model public administration.

In 1677, by the orders of the queen regent, Rivera dispatched a colony to California; and in the following year Charles II., who had attained his majority, signified his gratitude to the viceroy for his paternal government of New Spain, as well as for the care he had shown not only for the social, artistical, and political improvement of the nation committed to his charge, but for the honest collection of the royal income, which in those days was a matter of no small moment or interest to the Spanish kings. But in 1680 the viceroy's health began to fail, and Charles II., who still desired to preserve and secure the invaluable services of so excellent a personage to his country, nominated him bishop of Cuenca, and created him president of the Council of the Indies. For viceroy of New Spain Don Tomas Antonio Manrique de la Cerda, Marques de la Laguna, was selected.

The Archbishop Rivera when he left the viceroyal chair handed to his successor the letter he had just received from the north, imparting the sad news of a general rising of the Indians in New Mexico against the Spaniards. The aborigines of that region, who then amounted to about twenty-five thousand residing in twenty-four villages, had entered into combination with the wilder tribes thronging the broad plains of the north and the recesses of the neighboring mountains, and had suddenly descended in great force upon the unfortunate Spaniards scattered through the country. The secret of the conspiracy was well kept until the final moment of rupture. The spirit of discontent and the bond of Indian union were fostered and strengthened silently, steadily, and gradually throughout a territory one hundred and twenty-five leagues in extent without the revelation of the fact to any of the foreigners in the region. Nor did the strangers dream of impending danger until August 10, when at the same moment the various villages of Indians took arms against the Spaniards, and, slaughtering all who were not under the immediate protection of garrisons, even wreaked their vengeance upon twenty-one Franciscan monks who had labored for the improvement of their social condition as well as for their conversion to Christianity.

Having successfully assaulted all the outposts of this remote government of New Spain, the Indians next directed their arms against the capital, Santa Fé, which was the seat of government and the residence of the wealthiest and most distinguished inhabitants of the north. But the garrison was warned in time by a few natives who still remained faithful to their foreign task-masters, and was thus enabled to muster its forces and to put its arms in order, so as to receive the meditated assault. The Spanish soldiers allowed the rebellious conspirators to approach their defenses until they were sure of their aim, and then, discharging their pieces upon the impetuous masses, covered the fields with dead and wounded. But the brave Indians were too excited, resolved, and numerous to be stayed or repulsed by the feeble garrison. New auxiliaries took the places of the slaughtered ranks. On all sides the country was dark with crowds of dusky warriors whose shouts and war-whoops continually rent the air. Clouds of arrows and showers of stones were discharged on the heads of the beleagured townsmen. No man dared show himself beyond the covering of houses and parapets, and thus for ten days the Indian siege was unintermitted for a single moment around the walls of Santa Fé. At the expiration of this period the provisions as well as the munitions of the Spaniards were expended, and the wretched inhabitants, who could no longer endure the stench from the carcasses of the slain which lay in putrefying heaps around their town, resolved to evacuate the untenable place. Accordingly under cover of the night they contrived to elude the besiegers' vigilance, and, quitting the town by secret and lonely paths, they fled to Paso del Norte, whence they dispatched messengers to the viceroy with the news of their misfortune. The day after this precipitate retreat the Indians, who were altogether unaware of the Spaniards' departure, expected a renewal of the combat. But the town was silent. Advancing cautiously from house to house and street to street, they saw that Santa Fé was in reality deserted; and, content with having driven their oppressors from the country, they expended their wrath upon the town by destroying and burning the buildings. The cause of this rising was the bad conduct of the Spaniards to the Indians and the desire of these wilder northern tribes to regain their natural rights.

In the commencement of 1681 the viceroy began to fear that this rebellion, which seemed so deeply rooted and so well organized, would spread throughout the neighboring provinces, and accordingly dispatched various squadrons of soldiers to New Mexico, and ordered levies to join them as they marched to the north toward El Paso del Norte, which was the present refuge of the expelled and flying government. In this place all the requisite preparations for a campaign were diligently prepared, and thence the troops departed in quest of the headstrong rebels. But all their pains and efforts were fruitless. The object of the Indians seems to have been accomplished in driving off the Spaniards and destroying their settlements. The wild children of the soil and of the forest neither desired the possession of their goods nor waged war in order to enjoy the estates they had been forced to till. It was a simple effort to recover once more the wild liberty of which they had been deprived and to overthrow the masked slavery to which the more enervated races of the south submitted tamely, under the controlling presence of ampler forces. They contented themselves, therefore, with destroying towns, plantations, farms, and villages, and, flying to the fastnesses of the mountain forests, either kept out of reach of the military bands that traversed the country or descended in force upon detached parties. The Spaniards were thus denied all opportunity to make a successful military demonstration against the Indians, and, after waiting a season in fruitless efforts to subdue the natives, they retired to El Paso, leaving the country still in the possession of their foes, who would neither fight nor come to terms, although an unconditional pardon and a future security of rights were freely promised.

The unsuccessful expedition of the previous year induced the viceroy in 1682 to adopt other means for the reduction of the refractory Indians to obedience. That vast region was not to be lost, nor were the few inhabitants who still continued to reside on its frontiers to be abandoned to the mercy of savages. The Mar-

ques de la Laguna therefore resolved to recolonize Santa Fé,
and accordingly dispatched three hundred families of Spaniards
and mulattoes, among whom he divided the land by caballerians.
Besides this, he augmented the garrison in all the forts and strongholds scattered throughout the territory, so that agriculture and
trade, grouped under the guns of his soldiery, might once more
lift up their heads in that remote region in spite of Indian hostility.
This measure was of great service in controlling the natives elsewhere.   The Indians in the neighboring provinces had begun to
exhibit a strong desire to imitate the example of the New Mexican
bands, and in all probability were only prevented by this stringent
measure of the viceroy from freeing themselves from the Spanish yoke.

The administration of the Marques de la Laguna was an unfortunate one for his peace, if not for his fame.   The expedition
which he dispatched in 1683 to California under Don Isidor
Otondo, and in which were Jesuits, among whom was the celebrated
Father Kino, returned from that country three years afterward
after a fruitless voyage and exploration of the coasts.   Nor was the
eastern coast of New Spain more grateful for the cares of the
viceroy.   Vera Cruz, the chief port of the realm, was at this time
warmly besieged and finally sacked by the English pirate Nicholas
Agramont, who was drawn thither by a mulatto, Lorencellio, after
taking refuge in Jamaica for a crime that he had committed in
New Spain.   On May 17 Vera Cruz surrendered to the robbers,
who possessed themselves of property to the amount of seven
millions of dollars, which was awaiting the arrival in the harbor
of the fleet that was to carry it to Spain.   The chief portion of the
inhabitants took sanctuary in the churches, where they remained
pent up for a length of time; but the pirates contrived to seize
a large number of clergymen, monks, and women, whom they
forced to bear the spoils of the city to their vessels, and afterward
treated with the greatest inhumanity.

The coasts of Mexico were at this period sorely harrassed with
the piratical vessels of France and England.   The wealth of the
New World, inadequately protected by Spanish cruisers in its
transit to Europe, was a tempting prize to the bold nautical adventurers of the north of Europe, and the advantages of the Spanish
colonies were thus reaped by nations who were freed from the
expenses of colonial possessions.   There are perhaps still many

families in these countries whose fortunes were founded upon the robbery of Castilian galleons.

The twenty-ninth viceroy of New Spain was the Conde de Monclova, surnamed "Brazo de Plata," from the fact that he supplied with a silver arm the member he had lost in battle. He arrived in Mexico on November 30, 1686, and immediately devoted himself to the improvement of the capital, the completion of the canal which was to free the city from inundations, and the protection of the northern provinces and the coasts of the gulf against the menaced settlements of the French. He dispatched several Spanish men-of-war and launches to scour the harbors and inlets of the eastern shores as far as Florida in order to dislodge the intruders, and, having obtained control over the Indians of Coahuila, he established a strong garrison and founded a colonial settlement, called the town of Monclova, with a hundred and fifty families, in which there were two hundred and seventy men capable of bearing arms against the French whom he expected to encounter in that quarter.

The Conde de Monclova contemplated various plans for the consolidation and advancement of New Spain, but before two years had expired he was relieved from the government and transferred to the viceroyalty of Peru.

The Conde de Galve was the next incumbent and entered upon his viceroyalty September 17, 1688. Even before the departure of his predecessor for Peru he learned that the fears of that functionary had been realized by the discovery of attempts by the French to found settlements in New Spain. The governor of Coahuila in the course of his explorations in the wilderness found a fort which had been commenced, and the remains of a large number of dead Frenchmen, who had no doubt been engaged in the erection of the stronghold when they fell under the blows and arrows of the savages.

Besides this intrusion in the north, from which the Spaniards were, nevertheless, somewhat protected by the Indians, who hated the French quite as much as they did the subjects of Spain, the viceroy heard, moreover, that the Tarahumare and Tepehuane tribes had united with other wild bands of the northwest and were in open rebellion. Forces were immediately dispatched against the insurgents, but they fared no better than the Spanish troops had done in previous years in New Mexico. The love of liberty, or the desire of entire freedom from labor, was in this case, as in the former, the sole cause of the insurrection. When the blow was struck, the Indians fled to their fastnesses, and when the regular soldiery arrived on the field to fight them according to the regular laws of war, the children of the forest were, as usual, nowhere to be found. Nor is it likely that the rebellion would have been easily suppressed, or improbable that those provinces would have been lost had not the Jesuits, who enjoyed considerable influence over the insurgent tribes, devoted themselves, forthwith, to calming the excited bands. Among the foremost of these clerical benefactors of Spain was the noble Milanese Jesuit, Salvatierra, whose authority over the Indians was perhaps paramount to all others, and whose successful zeal was acknowledged by a grateful letter from the viceroy. This worthy priest had been one of the ablest missionaries among these warlike tribes. He won their love and confidence while endeavoring to diffuse Christianity among them, and the power he obtained through his humanity and unvary, ing goodness was now the means of once more subjecting the revolted Indians to the Spaniards. The cross achieved a victory which they refused to the sword.

In 1690 another effort was made to populate California, in virtue of new orders received from Charles; and while the preparations were making to carry the royal will into effect, the viceroy commanded the governor of Coahuila to place a garrison at San Bernardo, where the French attempted to build their fort. Orders were also sent about the same time by Galve to extend the Spanish power northward, and in 1691 the province of Asinais, or Texas, as it was called by the Spaniards, was settled by some emigrants, and visited by fourteen Franciscan monks, who were anxious to devote themselves to the conversion of the Indians. A garrison and a mission were established at that time in Texas, but in consequence, not only of an extraordinary drought which occurred two or three years after, destroying the crops and the cattle, but also of a sudden rebellion among the natives against the Spaniards, who desired to subject them to the same ignoble toils that were patiently endured by the southern tribes, nearly all the posts and missions were immediately abandoned.

The year 1690 was signalized in the annals of New Spain by an attack and successful onslaught, made by the orders of the viceroy, with creole troops upon the Island of Hispaniola, which was occupied by the French. Six ships of the line and a frigate, with 2700 soldiers, sailed from the port of Vera Cruz upon this warlike mission; and after fighting a decisive battle and destroying the settlements upon parts of the island, but without attacking the more thickly peopled and better defended districts of the west, they returned to New Spain with a multitude of prisoners and some booty.

But the rejoicings to which these victories gave rise were of short duration. The early frosts of 1691 had injured the crops, and the country was menaced with famine. On June 9, in this year, the rain fell in torrents and, accompanied as it was by hail, destroyed the grain that was cultivated not only around the capital, but also in many of the best agricultural districts. The roads became impassable, and many parts of the City of Mexico were inundated by floods from the lake, which continued to lie in the low level streets until the end of the year. Every effort was made by the authorities to supply the people with corn,—the staff of life among the lower classes,—and commissaries were even dispatched to the provinces to purchase grain which might be stored and sold to the masses at reasonable prices. But the suspicious multitude did not justly regard this provident and humane act. They imagined that the viceroy and his friends designed to profit by the scarcity of food and to enrich themselves by the misery of the country. Accordingly loud murmurs of discontent arose among the lower classes in the capital, and on June 8, 1692, the excited mob rushed suddenly to the palace of the viceroy, and, setting fire not only to it but to the Casa de Cabildo and the adjacent buildings, destroyed that splendid edifice, together with most of the archives, records, and historical documents which had been preserved since the settlement of the country. A diligent search was made for the authors of this atrocious calamity, and eight persons were tried, convicted, and executed for the crime. The wretched incendiaries were found among the dregs of the people. Many of their accomplices were also found guilty and punished with stripes, and the viceroy took measures to drive the hordes of skulking Indians who had been chiefly active in the mob from their haunts in the city, as well as to deprive them of the intoxicating drinks, and especially their favorite pulque, in which they were habituated to indulge. The crop of 1693 in some degree repaired the losses of previous years, and in the ensuing calm the Conde de Galve commenced the rebuilding of the viceroyal palace.

The property destroyed in the conflagration in June, 1692, amounted in value to at least three million of dollars.

In this year the viceroy, who was anxious for the protection of the northern shores of the gulf, and desirous to guard the territory of Florida from the invasion or settlement of the northern nations of Europe, fitted out an expedition of expert engineers to Pensacola, who designed and laid the foundations of the fortifications of this important port. Three years afterward, before the termination of his command in New Spain, Galve had the satisfaction to dispatch from Vera Cruz the colony and garrison which were to occupy and defend this stronghold.

In 1694 the capital and the adjacent province were once more afflicted with scarcity, and to this was added the scourge of an epidemic that carried thousands to the grave. In the following year a dreadful earthquake shook the City of Mexico on the night of August 24, and at seven o'clock of the following morning. But amid all these afflictions, which were regarded by multitudes as specially sent by the hand of God to punish the people for their sins, the authorities managed to preserve order throughout the country, and in 1695 sent large reinforcements for the expedition which the English and Spaniards united in fitting out against the French who still maintained their hold on the Island of Hispaniola. This adventure was perfectly successful. The combined forces assaulted the Gauls with extraordinary energy, and bore off eighty-one cannons as trophies of their victorious descent. The checkered administration of the Conde de Galve was thus satisfactorily terminated, and he returned to Spain after eight years of government, renowned for the equity and prudence of his administration during a period of unusual peril.

Chapter XX

DON JUAN DE ORTEGA MONTAÑEZ, Bishop of Michoacan, was the next viceroy of New Spain. Scarcely had Galve departed and the new episcopal viceroy assumed the reins of government, on February 27, 1696, when news reached Mexico that a French squadron was lying in wait near Havana to seize the galleons which were to leave Vera Cruz in the spring for Spain. The fleet was accordingly ordered to delay its departure until the summer, while masses were said and prayers addressed to the miraculous image of the Virgin of Remedios to protect the vessels and their treasure from disaster. The failure of the fleet to sail at the appointed day seems to have caused the French squadron to depart for Europe after waiting a considerable time to effect their piratical enterprise; and in the end all the galleons save one reached the harbor of Cadiz, where the duties alone on their precious freights amounted to $412,000.

At this period the settlement of the Californias, which was always a favorite project among the Mexicans, began again to be agitated. The coasts had been constantly visited by adventurers engaged in the pearl fishery, but these persons, whose manners were not conciliatory and whose purposes were altogether selfish, did not contribute to strengthen the ties between the Spaniards and the natives. Indeed, the Indians continually complained of the fisherman's ill-usage, and were unwilling to enter either into trade or friendship with so wild a class of unsettled visitors. The colonial efforts previously made had failed in consequence of the scarcity of supplies, nor could sufficient forces be spared to compel the submission of the large and savage tribes that dwelt in those remote regions. Accordingly when the worthy Father Salvatierra, moved by the descriptions of Father Kino, prayed the audiencia to intrust the reduction of the Californias to the care of the Jesuits, who would undertake it without supplies from the royal treasury, that body and the episcopal viceroy consented to the proposed spiritual conquest, and imposed on the holy father no other condi-

tions except that the effort should be made without cost to Spain and
that the territory subdued should be taken possession of in the
name of Charles II. Besides this concession to the Jesuits, the
viceroy and audiencia granted to Salvatierra and Kino the right
to levy troops and name commanders for their protection in the
wilderness. A few days after the conclusion of this contract with
the zealous missionaries, the government of Montañez was terminated by the arrival of his successor, the Conde de Montezuma.

This viceroy arrived in Mexico on December 18, 1696. Early
in the ensuing January the annual galleon from the Philippine
Islands reached the port of Acapulco, and this year the advent of
the vessel laden with oriental products seems to have been the
motive for the assemblage of people, not only from all parts of Mexico, but even from Peru, at a fair, at which nearly two millions of
dollars were spent by inhabitants of the latter viceroyalty in merchandise from China. Hardly had the festivities of this universal
concourse ended when a violent earthquake shook the soil of New
Spain, and extended from the west coast to the interior beyond
the capital, in which the inhabitants were suffering from scarcity,
and beginning already to exhibit symptoms of discontent, as they
had done five years before, against the supreme authorities, who
they always accused of criminally withholding grain or maintaining its exorbitant price whenever the seasons were inauspicious.
But the Conde de Montezuma was on his guard, and immediately
took means to control the Indians and lower classes who inhabited
the suburbs of the capital. In the meanwhile he caused large quantities of corn to be sent to Mexico from the provinces, and, as long
as the scarcity continued and until it was ascertained that the new
crop would be abundant, he ordered grain to be served out carefully
to those who were really in want or unable to supply themselves at
the prices of the day.

In 1698 the joyful news of the peace concluded in the preceding year between France, Spain, Holland, and England reached
Mexico, and gave rise to unusual rejoicings among the people.
Commerce, which had suffered greatly from the war, recovered its
wonted activity. The two following years passed over New Spain
uneventfully; but the beginning of the eighteenth century was signalized by a matter which not only affected the politics of Europe,
but might have interfered essentially with the loyalty and prosperity
of the New World.

In 1701 the monarchy of Spain passed from the house of Austria to that of Bourbon. The history of this transition of the crown, and of the conflicts to which it gave rise not only in Spain but throughout Europe, is well known. Yet America does not appear to have been shaken in its fidelity, amid all the convulsions of the parent state. Patient, submissive, and obedient to the authorities sent them from across the sea, the people of Mexico were as willing to receive a sovereign of a new race as to hail the advent in their capital of a new viceroy. Accordingly the inhabitants immediately manifested their fealty to the successor named by Charles II., a fact which afforded no small degree of consolation to Philip V. during all the vicissitudes of his fortune. It is even related that this monarch thought at one period of taking refuge among his American subjects and thus relieving himself of the quarrels and conflicts by which he was surrounded and assailed in Europe.

The public mourning and funeral obsequies for the late sovereign were celebrated in Mexico with great pomp according to a precise ritual which was sent from the Spanish court, and, while the people were thinking of the festivities which were to signalize Philip's accession to the throne, the Conde de Montezuma returned to Spain after four years of uneventful rule.

For the second time Don Juan de Ortega Montañez was viceroy. The brief period of one year, during which he again exercised his functions in Mexico, is chiefly, and perhaps only, memorable for the additional efforts made by the worthy Jesuits in California to subdue and settle that distant province. The colonists and clergymen who had already gone thither complained incessantly of their sufferings in consequence of the sterility of the coasts. But Salvatierra remained firm in his resolution to spread the power of Spain and of his church among the wild tribes at the feet of the western sierra along the Pacific coast. His labors and those of his diligent coadjutors were slow but incessant. Trusting confidently in Providence, they maintained their post at the Presidio of Loreto, and gathered around them by their persuasive eloquence and gentle demeanor large numbers of natives, until the success of their teachings threatened them with starvation in consequence of the abundance of their converts, all of whom relied upon the fathers for maintenance as soon as they abandoned their savage life. Yet there was no other means of attaching the Indians to the Spanish Government. The authorities in Mexico had refused and continued obstinate in their denial of men or money to conquer or hold the country; so that, after various efforts to obtain the aid of the government, the pious mendicants resolved to return again to their remote missions with no other reliance than honest zeal and the support of God. At this juncture Philip V. and a number of influential people in the capital volunteered to aid the cause of Christianity and Spain by supplies which would ensure the final success of the Jesuits.

The Duke of Albuquerque assumed the government of Mexico in 1702 and soon perceived that more than ordinary care was necessary to consolidate a loyal alliance between the throne and its American possessions during the dangerous period in which portions of Spain in the Old World were armed and aroused against the lawful authorities of the land. Accordingly the new viceroy immediately strengthened the military arm of the colony, and extended the government of provinces and the custody of his strongholds and fastnesses to Spaniards upon whose fidelity he could implicitly rely. Without these precautions he perhaps justly feared that notwithstanding the loyalty manifested in New Spain upon the accession of Philip, the insubordination of certain parts of the Spanish monarchy at home might serve as a bad example to the American colonists, and finally result in a civil war that would drench the land with blood. Besides this, the foreign fleets and pirates were again beginning to swarm along the coasts, lying in wait for the treasure which was annually dispatched to Spain; but to meet and control these adventurers the careful duke increased the squadron of Barlovento, with instructions to watch the coast incessantly and to lose no opportunity to make prizes of the enemy's vessels.

Peace was thus preserved in New Spain both on land and water, while the Jesuits of California still continued their efforts, unaided by the government, whose resources were drained for the wars of the Old World. Thus after eight years of a strong but pacific reign, during which he saved New Spain from imitating the disgraceful dissensions of the parent state, the Duke of Albuquerque resigned his government into the hands of the Duke of Linares.

The Duke of Linares entered Mexico in 1710. The first years of his administration were uneventful, nor was his whole government distinguished, in fact, by any matter which will make the thirty-fifth viceroyalty particularly memorable in the history of New Spain.[1]

In 1712 Philip V. found himself master of nearly the whole of Spain, and, being naturally anxious to end the war with honor, his emissaries improved every opportunity to withdraw members of the combined powers from a contest which threatened to be interminable. Accordingly he approached the English with the temptations of trade, and through his ambassadors who were assisting at the Congress of Utrecht he proposed that Queen Anne should withdraw from the contest if he granted her subjects the right to establish trading houses in his ports on the Main and in the islands for the purpose of supplying the colonies with African slaves. A similar contract had been made ten years before with the French, and was about to expire on May 1.

Anne, who was wearied of the war and glad to escape from its expense and danger, was not loath to accept the proffered terms; and the treaty known by the name of " El Asiento," which was put in force in Vera Cruz and other Spanish ports, resulted most beneficially to the English. They filled the markets with negroes, and at the same time continued to reap profit from the goods they smuggled into the colonies, notwithstanding the treaty forbade the introduction of British merchandise to the detriment of Spanish manufactures. This combined inhumane and illicit trade continued for a considerable time, until the authorities were obliged to menace the officers of customs with death if they connived any longer at the secret and scandalous introduction of British wares.

In 1714 a brief famine and severe epidemic again ravaged the colony. In this year, too, the Indians of Texas once more manifested a desire to submit themselves to Spain and to embrace the Christian faith. Orders were therefore given to garrison that northern province, and the Franciscan monks were again commanded to return to their missions among the Ansinais. At the same time a new colony was founded in Nuevo Leon, forty leagues southeast from Monterey, which in honor of the viceroy received the name of San Felipe de Linares. At the close of this year, 1715,

---

[1] The year 1711 is remarkable in the annals of the valley of Mexico for a snowstorm, which is only known to have occurred again on the Feast of the Purification of the Virgin in 1767. In August of 1711 there was an awful earthquake, which shattered the city and destroyed many of its strongest houses.

the garrisons of Texas were already completed and the Franciscan friars busy in their mission of inducing the savages to abandon their nomadic habits for the quieter life of villagers. This was always the most successful effort of the Spaniards in controlling the restless wanderers and hunters of the wilderness. It was the first step in the modified civilization that usually ended in a mere knowledge of the formula of prayers, and in the more substantial return of the labor of the Indians, which was in reality nothing but slavery.

The year 1716 was the last of the reign of the Duke of Linares, who in the month of August resigned his post to the Duke of Arion.

Scarcely had the Duke of Arion taken charge of the viceroyal government when he received an express from Texas, dispatched by Domingo Ramon, who was captain of the Spaniards in the province, informing the authorities of the famine which prevailed throughout his command, and demanding supplies, without which he would be obliged to abandon his post and take refuge with his soldiers in Coahuila. The new viceroy saw at once the importance of preserving this province as an outpost and frontier against the French, who had already begun their settlements in Louisiana, and accordingly he commanded the governor of Coahuila to send provisions and troops to Texas, together with mechanics who should teach the useful arts to the Indians.

While these occurrences took place in the north of Mexico, war was once more declared between Spain and France without any apparent motive save the hatred which the Duke of Orleans, the regent during the minority of Louis XV., entertained for the Cardinal Alberoni, who was prime minister of Spain and had intrigued to dispossess him of his regency. The news of this war reached New Spain, and on May 19, 1719, the French attacked Pensacola and received the capitulation of the governor, who was unprepared, either with men or provisions, to resist the invaders. In the following month the garrison and missionaries of Texas returned hastily to Coahuila and apprised the viceroy of their flight for safety. But that functionary saw at once the necessity of strengthening the frontier. Levies were therefore immediately made. Munitions were dispatched to the north. And five hundred men, divided into eight companies, marched forthwith to reëstablish the garrisons and missions under the command of the Marques San Miguel de Aguayo, the new governor of Florida and Texas.

It may not be uninteresting or unprofitable to state in this place some of the efforts at positive settlement in Texas which were made by the Spaniards during the first quarter of the eighteenth century. Alarcon, the governor, early in 1718 crossed the Medina with a large number of soldiers, settlers, and mechanics and founded the town of Bejar, with the fortress of San Antonio, and the mission of San Antonio Valero. Thence he pushed on to the country of the Cenis Indians, where, having strengthened the missionary force, he crossed the River Adayes, which he called the Rio de San Francisco de Sabinas, or the Sabine, and began the foundation of a fortress within a short distance of the French fort, at Natchitoches, named by him the Presidio de San Miguel Arcangel de Linares de Adayes. These establishments were reinforced during the next year, and another stronghold was erected on the Oreoquisas, probably the San Jacinto, emptying into Galveston Bay, west of the mouth of Trinity.

The French, who were not unobservant of these Spanish acts of occupation in a country they claimed by virtue of La Salle's discovery and possession in 1684, immediately began to establish counter settlements on the Mississippi and in the valley of the Red River. When Alarcon was removed from the government of Texas he was succeeded by the Marques de Aguayo, who made expeditions through the country in 1721 and 1722, during which he considerably increased the Spanish establishments, and after this period no attempt was ever made by the French to occupy any spot southwest of Natchitoches.

Notwithstanding the hostilities between France and Spain and the eager watchfulness of the fleets and privateers of the former nations, the galleons of New Spain reached Cadiz in 1721 with a freight of eleven millions of dollars! The years 1722 and 1723 were signalized by some outbreaks among the Indians which were successfully quelled by the colonial troops, and in October the Duke of Arion, who had controlled New Spain for six years, was succeeded by the Marques de Casa-Fuerte, a general of artillery. He entered Mexico amid the applauses of the people, not only because he was a creole or native of America, but for the love that was borne him by Philip V., who well knew the services for which the crown was indebted to so brave a warrior.

In recording these brief memorials of the viceroys of Mexico it has been our purpose rather to mention the principal public events that signalized their reigns and developed or protected the nation committed to their charge than to trace the intrigues or exhibit the misconduct of those functionaries and their courtiers. We have abstained from noticing many of the corrupt practices which crept into the administration of Mexico. But in sketching the

EARLY SETTLEMENTS IN TEXAS

viceroyalty of the Marques de Casa-Fuerte, who succeeded the Duke of Arion, we cannot justly avoid observing the marked and moral change he wrought in the government of the country, and the diligence with which this brave and trusty soldier labored to purify the corrupt court of New Spain. Other viceroys had endeavored zealously to aid the progress of the colony. They had planted towns, villages, and garrisons throughout the interior. They had sought to develop the mining districts and to foster agricultural interests. But almost all of them were more or less tainted with avarice, and willingly fell into the habits of the age, which countenaced the traffic in office or permitted the reception of liberal " gratifications " whenever an advantage was to be derived by an individual from his transactions with the government.

In the time of Casa-Fuerte there was no path to the palace but that which was open to all. Merit was the test of employment and reward. He forbade the members of his family to receive gifts or to become intercessors for office-seekers, and in all branches of public affairs he introduced wholesome reforms which were carefully maintained during the whole of his long and virtuous administration.

In 1724 Philip V. suddenly and unexpectedly, for his American subjects, resolved to abdicate the crown of Spain and raise his son Louis I. to the throne. Scarcely had the news reached Mexico, and the inhabitants prepared themselves to celebrate the accession of the prince, when they learned that he was already dead, and that his father, fearing to seat the minor Ferdinand in the place of h·s lost son, had again resumed the scepter. The Marques de Casa-Fuerte instantly proclaimed the fact to the people, whose loyalty to the old sovereign continued unabated; and during the unusually long and successful government of this viceroy the greatest cordiality and confidence was maintained between himself and his royal master.

Casa-Fuerte dispatched a colony of emigrants from the Canary Isles to Texas, and, establishing a town for their occupation, he modestly refused the proffered honor of bestowing upon it his name, but caused it to be called San Fernando, in honor of the heir of the Spanish crown. Nor did he neglect commerce while he attended to a discreet colonization in the north which might encounter and stay the southern progress of the English and the French. In 1731 the oriental trade of New Spain had become exceedingly important. The galleons that regularly passed across the Pacific from the East Indies, and arrived every year in America about Christmas, had enjoyed almost a monopoly of the Indian trade in consequence of the wars which continually existed during that century and filled the northern and southern Atlantic with pirates and vessels of war. The Pacific, however, was comparatively free from these dangers, and the galleons were allowed to go and come with but little interruption. The American creoles in reality preferred the manufactures of China to those of Europe, for the fabrics of silk and cotton especially, which were sent to Mexico from Asia, had been sold at half the price demanded for similar articles produced in Spain. The galleon of 1731, which discharged its cargo in Acapulco, bore a freight of unusual value, whence we may estimate the Mexican commerce of that age. The duties collected upon this oriental merchandise exceeded $170,000, exhibiting an extraordinary increase of Eastern trade with Mexico compared with thirty-five years before, when the impost collected on similar commerce in 1697 amounted to but $80,000. The anxiety to preserve the mercantile importance of Cadiz and to prevent the ruin of the Old World's commerce interposed many difficulties in the trade between the East Indies and New Spain; but the influence of Spanish houses in Manila still secured the annual galleon, and the thrifty merchants stowed the vessels with nearly double the freight that was carried by similar ships on ordinary voyages. Acapulco thus became the emporium of an important trade, and its streets were crowded with merchants and strangers from all parts of Mexico, in spite of the dangerous diseases with which they were almost sure to be attacked while visiting the western coast.

The year 1734 was a sad one for New Spain. The Marques de Casa-Fuerte, who governed the country for twelve years most successfully, and had served the crown for fifty-nine, departed this life at the age of seventy-seven. He was a native of Lima, and, like a true creole, seems to have had the good of America constantly at heart. Philip V. fully appreciated his meritorious services, and, had the viceroy lived, would doubtless have continued him longer in the government of Mexico. The counselors of the king often hinted to their sovereign that it was time to remove the Mexican viceroy; but the only reply they received from Philip was "Long live Casa-Fuerte!" The courtiers answered that they hoped he might, indeed, live long, but that oppressed with years and toils he was no longer able to endure the burdens of so arduous a government. "As long as Casa-Fuerte lives," answered the king, "his talents and virtues will give him all the vigor required for a good minister."

Impartial posterity has confirmed the sensibility and judgment of the king. During the reign of Casa-Fuerte the capital of New Spain was adorned with many of its most sumptuous and elegant edifices. The royal mint and custom house were built under his orders. All the garrisons throughout the viceroyalty were visited, examined, and reported. He was liberal with alms for the poor, and even left a sum to be distributed twice a year for food among the prisoners. He endowed an asylum for orphans, expended a large part of his fortune in charitable works, and is still known in the traditionary history of the country as the "Great Governor of New Spain." His cherished remains were interred with great pomp, and are still preserved in the church of the Franciscans of San Cosmé and Damian.

Chapter XXI

DEVELOPMENT OF INTERNAL RESOURCES. 1734-1794

THE thirty-eighth viceroy of New Spain was the Archbishop of Mexico, Don Juan Antonio de Vizarron y Eguiarreta. This viceroy, who governed New Spain from the year 1734 to 1740, passed an uneventful reign so far as the internal peace and order of the colony were concerned. War was declared during this period between France and Spain, but Mexico escaped from all its desolating consequences, and nothing appears to have disturbed the quiet of colonial life but a severe epidemic, which is said to have resembled the yellow fever, and carried off many thousands of the inhabitants, especially in the northeastern section of the territory. The viceroy was naturally solicitous to follow the example of his predecessors in preventing the encroachments of the French on the northern indefinite boundaries of New Spain, and took measures to support the feeble garrisons and colonies which were the only representatives of Spanish rights and power in that remote quarter.

On August 17 he was succeeded by Don Pedro Castro Figueroa Salazar, Duke de la Conquista. The new viceroy reached the capital and learned from the governor of New Mexico that the French had actually visited that region of the colonial possessions, yet, finding the soil and country unsuited to their purposes, had returned again to their own villages and settlements. At the same time the English, under the command of Oglethorpe, bombarded the town and fort of San Agustin in Florida, but the brave defense made by the Spaniards obliged them to raise the siege and depart.

In 1741 the sky of New Spain was obscured by the approaching clouds of war, for Admiral Vernon, who had inflicted great damages upon the commerce of the Indies, captured Porto Bello and occupied the forts of Cartagena. New Spain was thus in constant dread of the arrival of a formidable enemy upon her own coasts, and the Duke de la Conquista, anxious for the fate of Vera Cruz, hastily levied an adequate force for the protection of the shore along the gulf, and resolved to visit it personally in order to hasten the works which were requisite to resist the English. He departed for the eastern districts of New Spain upon the warlike mission, but in the midst of his labors was suddenly seized by a severe illness which obliged him to return to the capital, where he died on August 22. His body was interred with great pomp, amid the lamentations of the Mexicans, for in the brief period of his government he had manifested talents of the highest order and exhibited the deepest interest in the welfare and progress of the country committed to his charge. His noble title of " Duke of Conquest " was bravely won on the battlefield of Bitonto, and although it is said that Philip slighted him during the year of his viceroyalty, yet it is certain that he was repaid by the admiration of the Mexican people for the lost favor of his king. Upon his death the audencia took charge of the government and continued in power until the following November without any serious disturbance from the enemy. Anson, the English admiral, with his vessels, was in the Pacific, and waited anxiously in the neighborhood of Acapulco to make a prize of the galleon which was to sail for the East Indies laden with a rich cargo of silver to purchase oriental fabrics. But the inhabitants of Acapulco and the audencia were on their guard, and the vessel and treasure of New Spain escaped the grasp of the famous adventurer.

The Count de Fuen-Clara assumed the viceroyal baton on November 3, 1742. His term of four years was passed without any events of remarkable importance for New Spain save the capture, by Anson, of one of the East Indian galleons with a freight of $1,313,000 in coined silver and 4,470 marks of the same precious metal, besides a quantity of the most valuable products of Mexico.

This period of the viceroyalty must necessarily be uninteresting and eventless. The wars of the Old World were confined to the continent and to the sea. Mexico, locked up amid her mountains, was not easily assailed by enemies who could spare no large armies from the contests at home for enterprises in so distant a country. Besides, it was easier to grasp the harvest on the ocean that had been gathered on the land. England contented herself, therefore, with harassing and pilfering the commerce of Castile, while Mexico devoted all her energies to the development of her internal resources of mineral and agricultural wealth. Emigrants poured into the country. The waste lands were filling up. North, south, east and west the country was occupied by industrious settlers and zealous curates, who were engaged in the cultivation of the soil and the spiritual subjection of the Indians. The spirit as well as the dangers of the conquest were past, and Mexico assumed in the history of the age the position of a quiet, growing nation, equally distant from the romantic or adventurous era of early settlement when danger and difficulty surrounded the Spaniards, and from the lethean stagnation into which she fell in future years under Spanish misrule.

The Conde de Revilla-Gigedo, the first of that name who was viceroy of Mexico, reached the capital on July 9, 1746, and on the 12th of the same month his master, Philip V., died, leaving Ferdinand VI. as his successor. Throughout the reign of this nobleman the colony prospered rapidly, and his services in increasing the royal revenues were so signally successful that he was retained in power for nine years. Mexico had become a large and beautiful city. The mining districts were extraordinarily prolific, and no year of his government yielded less than eleven millions of dollars; the whole sum that passed through the national mint during his term being $114,231,000 of the precious metals! The population of the capital amounted to 50,000 families composed of Spaniards, Europeans, and creoles, 40,000 mestizos, mulattoes, negroes, and 8000 Indians, who inhabited the suburbs. This population annually consumed at least 2,000,000 arobas of flour, about 160,000 fanegas of corn, 300,000 sheep, 15,500 beeves, and about 25,000 swine. In this account the consumption of many religious establishments is not included, as they were privately supplied from their estates, nor can we count the numerous and valuable presents which were sent by residents of the country to their friends in the capital.

It has been already said that this viceroy augmented largely the income of Spain. The taxes of the capital, accounted for by the consulado, were collected yearly, and amounted to $333,333, while those of the whole viceroyalty reached $718,375. The income from pulque alone, the favorite drink of the masses, was $172,000, while other imposts swelled the gross income in proportion.

The collection of tributes was not effected invariably in the same manner throughout the territory of New Spain. In Mexico the administrador general imposed this task on the justices whose duty it was to watch over the Indians. The aborigines in the capital were divided into two sections, one comprising the Tenochas of San Juan, and the other the Tlatelolcos of Santiago, both of which had their governors and other police officers, according to Spanish custom. The first of these bands, dwelling on the north and east of the capital, was in the olden time the most powerful and noble, and at that period numbered 5900 families. The other division, existing on the west and south, was reduced to 2500 families. In the several provinces of the viceroyalty the Indian tributes were collected through the intervention of 149 chief alcaldes who governed them, and who, before they took possession of their offices, were required to give security for the tribute taxed within their jurisdiction. The frontier provinces of this vast territory, inhabited only by garrisons and a few scattered colonists, were exempt from this odious charge. In all the various sections of the nation, however, the Indians were accurately enumerated. Two natives were taxed together, in order to facilitate the collection by making both responsible, and every four months from this united pair six reales were collected, making in all eighteen in the course of the year. This gross tax of $2.25 was divided as follows: eight reales were taxed as tribute; four for the royal service; four and a half as commutation for a half fanega of corn which was due to the royal granary; half a real for the royal hospital, in which the Indians were lodged when ill; another half real for the costs of their lawsuits; and, finally, the remaining half real for the construction of cathedrals.

In 1748 the Count Revilla-Gigedo, in conformity to the orders of the king, and after consultation in general meeting with the officers of various tribunals, determined to lay the foundation of a grand colony in the north, under the guidance of Colonel José Escandon, who was forthwith appointed governor. This decree, together with an account of the privileges and lands which would be granted to colonists, was extensively published, and in a few years a multitude of families and single emigrants founded eleven villages of Spaniards and mulattoes between Alta-Mira and Camargo. The Indians who were gathered in this neighborhood composed four missions; and although it was found impossible to clear the harbor of Santander, or to render it capable of receiving vessels of deep draft, the government was nevertheless enabled to found several flourishing villages which were vigilant in the protection of the coast against pirates.

In 1749 the crops were lost in many of the provinces, where the early frost blighted the fields of corn and fruit. The crowded capital and its neighborhood, fortunately, did not experience the want of food, which in other regions of the tierra adentro, or interior, amounted to absolute famine. The people believed that the frown of Heaven was upon the land, for to this calamity repeated earthquakes were added, and the whole region, from the volcano of Colima to far beyond Gaudalajara, was violently shaken and rent, causing the death of many persons and the ruin of large and valuable villages.

In 1750 Mexico was still free from scarcity, and even able, not only to support its own population, but to feed the numerous strangers who fled to it from the unfruitful districts. Yet in the cities and villages of the north and west, where the crops had been again lost, want and famine prevailed as in the previous year. From Guanajuato, a city rich in mines, to Zacatecas the scarcity of food was excessive, and the enormous sum of twenty-five dollars was demanded and paid for a fanega, or bushel, of corn. Neither man nor beast had wherewith to support life, and for a while the labors in the mines of this rich region were suspended. The unfortunate people left their towns in crowds to subsist on roots and berries which they found in the forests. Many of them removed to other parts of the country, and, as it was at this period that the rich veins of silver at Bolaños were discovered, some of the poor emigrants found work and food in a district whose sudden mineral importance induced the merchants to supply it liberally with provisions. The end of the year, however, was fortunately crowned with abundant crops.

In 1755, after founding the Presidio of Horcasitas, in Sonora, designed to restrain the incursions of the Apaches into that province, the Count Revilla-Gigedo was recalled at his own request from the Mexican viceroyalty in order that he might devote himself to the management of his private property, which had increased enormously during his government. In the history of Mexican viceroys this nobleman is celebrated as a speculative and industrious trader. There was no kind of commercial enterprise or profitable traffic in which he did not personally engage. His palace degenerated into an exchange, frequented by all kinds of adventurers, while gaming tables were openly spread out to catch the doubloons of the viceroyal courtiers. The speculations and profits of Revilla-Gigedo enabled him to found estates for his sons in Spain, and he was regarded throughout Europe as the richest vassal of Ferdinand VI. His son, who subsequently became a Mexican viceroy, and was the second bearing the family title, labored to blot out the stain which the trading propensities of his father had cast upon his name. He was a model of propriety in every respect; but, while he made no open display of anxiety to enrich himself corruptly through official influence or position, he nevertheless exhibited the avaricious traits of his father in requiring from his butler each night an exact account of every cent that was spent during the day and every dish that was prepared in his kitchen.

Notwithstanding the notorious and corrupting habits of the first count, that personage contrived to exercise an extraordinary influence or control over the masses in Mexico. The people feared and respected him; and upon a certain occasion when they were roused in the capital and gathered in menacing mobs, this resolute viceroy, whose wild and savage aspect aided the authority of his determined address, rode into the midst of the turbulent assemblage without a soldier in attendance and immediately dispersed the revolutionists by the mere authority of his presence and command.

The government of the Marques de las Amarillas, the forty-second viceroy, commenced on November 10, 1755. He immediately devoted himself to the task of reforming many of the abuses which had doubtless crept into the administration of public affairs during the reign of his trafficking predecessor. Valuable mineral deposits were discovered in New Leon, whose veins were found so rich and tempting that crowds of miners from Zacatecas and Guanajuato flocked to the prolific region. Great works were commenced to facilitate the working of the drifts, but the wealth, which had so suddenly appeared on the scene as if by magic, vanished amid the interminable quarrels and lawsuits of the parties. Many of the foremost adventurers who imagined themselves masters of incalculable riches were finally forced to quit their discoveries on foot without a dollar to supply themselves with food.

In 1759 a general mourning was proclaimed in Mexico for the Queen of Spain, Maria Barbara of Portugal, who was speedily followed to the tomb by her husband, Ferdinand VI. His brother, Charles III., ascended the throne, and while the mingled ceremonies of sorrow and festivity for the dead and living were being performed in Mexico, the worthy viceroy was suddenly struck with apoplexy, which his physicians thought might be alleviated by his residence in the healthful and lower regions of Cuernavaca. But neither the change of level nor temperature improved the condition of the viceroy, who died of this malady on January 5, 1760, in the beautiful city to which he had retreated. He was a remarkable contrast to his predecessor in many respects, and although he had been viceroy for five years, it is stated, as a singular fact in the annals of Mexico, that he left his widow poor and altogether unprovided for. But his virtuous conduct as an efficient minister of the crown had won the confidence and respect of the Mexicans, who were anxious to succor those whom he left dependent upon the favor of the crown. The liberality of the Archbishop Rubio y Salinas, however, supplied all the wants of the gentle marquesa, who was thus enabled to maintain a suitable state until her return to the court of Spain, where the merits of her husband as a Spanish soldier in the Italian wars doubtless procured her a proper pension for life.

As the death of the Marques de las Amarillas was sudden and unexpected, the King of Spain had not supplied the government with the usual *pliego de mortaja,* or mortuary dispatch, which was generally sent from Madrid whenever the health of a viceroy was feeble, so as to supply his place by an immediate successor in the event of death. The audiencia, of course, became the depository of executive power during the interregnum, and its dean, Don Francisco Echavarri, directed public affairs under its sanction until the arrival of the viceroy, *ad interim,* from Havana. This viceroy, Don Francisco de Cagigal, employed himself merely in the adornment of the capital and the general police of the colony. He was engaged in some improvements in the great square of Mexico when his successor arrived; but he left the capital with the hearty regrets of the townsmen, for his intelligence and affability during his brief tenure had won their confidence and induced them to expect the best results had his reign been prolonged.

From 1760 to 1766 Don Joaquim de Monserrat, Marques de Cruillas was viceroy. In 1761, soon after the entrance of the Marques de Cruillas into Mexico, the ceremony of proclaiming the accession of Charles III. to the throne was observed with great pomp by the viceroy, the nobles, and the municipality. But the period of rejoicing was very short, for news soon reached Mexico that war was again declared between Spain and England—a fact which was previously concealed, in consequence of the interception of dispatches that had been sent to Havana. Don Juan de Prado was the governor of that important point, and he, as well as the viceroy of Mexico, had consequently been unable to make suitable preparations for the attacks of the British on the West Indian and American possessions of Spain.

In the meantime an English squadron, which had recruited its forces and supplied itself with provisions in Jamaica, disembarked its troops without resistance on June 6, two leagues east of the Moro Castle. The Havanese fought bravely with various success against the invaders until July 30, when the Spaniards, satisfied that all further defense was vain and rash, surrendered the Moro Castle to the foe. On August 13 the town also capitulated, private property and the rights of religion being preserved intact. By this conquest the English obtained nine ships of the line, four frigates, and all the smaller vessels belonging to the sovereign and his subjects which were in the port; while $4,600,000 belonging to the king, and found in the city, swelled the booty of the fortunate invaders.

While this was passing in Havana it was falsely reported in Mexico that the British, being unsuccessful in their attacks on Cuba, had raised the siege and were about to leave the islands for the Spanish Main. The important port of Vera Cruz and its defenses were of course not to be neglected under such circumstances. This incorrect rumor was, however, soon rectified by the authentic news of the capture of the Moro Castle and of the city of Havana. The Marquis de Cruillas immediately ordered all the militia to be raised in the provinces, even six hundred miles from the eastern coast, and to march forthwith to Vera Cruz. That city and its castle were at once placed in the best possible condition of defense; but the unacclimated troops from the high and healthy regions of the interior who had been brought suddenly to the sickly sea shore of the *tierra caliente* suffered so much from malaria that the viceroy was obliged to withdraw them to Jalapa and Perote.

While Mexico was thus in a state of alarm in 1763, and while the government was troubled in consequence of the arrest of a clergyman who had been seized as a British spy, the joyful news arrived that peace had again been negotiated between France and Spain and England.

Pestilence as well as war appears to have menaced Mexico at this epoch. The smallpox broke out in the capital and carried off ten thousand persons. Besides this, another malady, which is described by the writers of the period as similar to that which had ravaged the country 107 years before, and which terminated by an

unceasing flow of blood from the nostrils, filled the hospitals of the
capital with its victims. From Mexico this frightful and contagious
malady passed to the interior, where immense numbers, unable to
obtain medical advice, medicine, or attendance, were carried to
the grave.

The general administration of the viceroyalty by the Marques
de Cruillas was unsatisfactory both to the crown and the people of
New Spain. The best historians of the period are not definite in
their charges of misconduct against this nobleman, but his demeanor as an executive officer required the appointment of a visitador in order to examine and remedy his abuse of power. The
person charged with this important task, Don José Galvez, was
endowed with unlimited authority entirely independent of the viceroy, and he executed his office with severity. He arrested high
officers of the government and deprived them of their employments.
His extraordinary talents and remarkable industry enabled him to
comprehend at once, and search into, all the tribunals and governmental posts of this vast kingdom. In Vera Cruz he removed the
royal accountants from their offices. In Puebla and in Mexico he
turned out the superintendents of customs, and throughout the
country all who were employed in public civil stations feared from
day to day that they would either be suspended or deposed. While
Galvez attended thus to the faithful discharge of duty by the officers
of the crown, he labored also to increase the royal revenue. Until
that period the cultivation of tobacco had been free, but Galvez determined to control it, as in Spain, and made its preparation and
sale a monopoly for the government. Gladly as his other alterations
and reforms were received by the people, this interference with one
of their cherished luxuries was well-nigh the cause of serious difficulties. In the city of Cordova and in many neighboring places
some of the wealthiest and most influential colonists depended for
their fortunes and income upon the unrestrained production and
manufacture of this article. Thousands of the poorer classes were
engaged in its preparation for market, while in all the cities, towns,
and villages there were multitudes who lived by selling it to the
people. Every man, and perhaps every woman, in Mexico used
tobacco, and consequently this project of the visitador gave reasonable cause for dissatisfaction to the whole of New Spain. Nevertheless, the firmness of Galvez, the good temper of the Mexicans,
and their habitual submission to authority overcame all difficulties.

The inhabitants of Cordova were not deprived of all control over the cultivation of tobacco, and were simply obliged to sell it to the officers of the king at a definite price, while these personages were ordered to continue supplying the families of the poor with materials for the manufacture of cigars; and by this device the public treasury was enabled to derive an important revenue from an article of universal consumption. Thus the visitador appears to have employed his authority in the reform of the colony and the augmentation of the royal revenue, without much attention to the actual viceroy, who was displaced in 1766. The fiscal or attorney general of the audiencia of Manila, Don José Aréché, was ordered officially to examine into the executive conduct of the Marques de Cruillas, who had retired from the City of Mexico to Cholula, and although it had been universally the custom to permit other viceroys to answer the charges made against them by attorney, this favor was denied to the marques, who was subjected to much inconvenience and suffering during the long trial that ensued.

The Marques de Croix, who succeeded in 1766, was a native of the city of Lille in Flanders, and, born of an illustrious family, had obtained his military renown by a service of fifty years in the command of Ceuta, Santa-Maria, and the captaincy general of Galicia. He entered Mexico as viceroy on August 25, 1766.

For many years past in the Old World and in the New there had been a silent but increasing fear of the Jesuits. It was known that in America their missionary zeal among the Indians in the remotest provinces was unequaled. The winning manners of the cultivated gentlemen who composed this powerful order in the Catholic Church gave them a proper and natural influence with the children of the forest, whom they had withdrawn from idolatry and partially civilized. But the worthy Jesuits did not confine their zealous labors to the wilderness. Members of the order, all of whom were responsible and implicitly obedient to their great central power, were spread throughout the world, and were found in courts and camps as well as in the lonely mission house of the frontier or in the wigwam of the Indian. They had become rich as well as powerful, for while they taught Christianity they did not despise the wealth of the world. Whatever may have been their personal humility, their love for the progressive power and dignity of the order was never permitted for a moment to sleep. A body stimulated by such a combined political and ecclesiastical passion, all of whose movements might be controlled by a single central despotic will, may now be kept in subjection in the Old World, where the civil and military police is ever alert in support of the national authorities. But at that epoch of transition in America, whose vast regions were filled with credulous and ignorant aborigines, and thinly sprinkled with intelligent, educated and loyal Europeans, it was deemed dangerous to leave the superstitious Indians to become the prey, rather than the flock, the instruments, rather than the acolytes, of such insidious shepherds. These fears had seized the mind of Charles III., who dreaded a divided dominion in America, with the venerable fathers. We do not believe that there was just cause for the royal alarm. We do not suppose that the Jesuits, whose members, it is true, were composed of the subjects of all the Catholic powers of Europe, ever meditated political supremacy in Spanish America or designed to interfere with the rights of Charles or his successors. But the various orders of the Roman Church, the various congregations, and convents of priests and friars, were unfortunately not free from that jealous rivalry which distinguishes the career of laymen in all the other walks of life.

It may be that some of the pious brethren whose education, manners, position, wealth, or power was not equal to the influence, social rank, and control of the Jesuits, had perhaps been anxious to drive this respectable order from America. It may be that the king and his council were willing to embrace any pretext to rid his colonial possessions of the Jesuits. But certain it is that on June 25, before the dawn of day, at the same hour throughout the whole of New Spain, the decree for their expulsion was promulgated by order of Charles. The king was so anxious upon this subject that he wrote with his own hand to the viceroy of Mexico soliciting his best services in the fulfillment of the royal will. When the question was discussed in the privy council of the sovereign a chart of both Americas was spread upon the table, the distances between the colleges of the Jesuits accurately calculated, and the time required for the passage of couriers carefully estimated, so that the blow might fall simultaneously upon the order. The invasion of Havana by the English and its successful capture induced the king to supply his American possessions with better troops and more skillful commanders than had been hitherto sent to the colonies. Thus there **were various veteran** Spanish regiments in Mexico capable of re-

straining any outbreaks of the people in favor of the outraged
fathers who had won their respect and loyal obedience.

At the appointed hour the order of Charles was enforced.
The Jesuits were shut up in their colleges, and all avenues to these
retreats of learning and piety were filled with troops. The fathers
were dispatched from Mexico for Vera Cruz on June 28, surrounded by soldiers. They halted awhile in the town of Guadalupe, where the Visitador Galvez, who governed the expedition,
permitted them to enter once more into the national sanctuary, where
amid the weeping crowds of Mexicans they poured forth their last
and fervent vows for the happiness of a people who idolized them.
Their entrance into Jalapa was a triumph. Windows, balconies,
streets, and housetops were filled with people whose demeanor
manifested what was passing in their hearts, but who were restrained by massive ranks of surrounding soldiery from all demonstration in behalf of the banished priests. In Vera Cruz some
silent but respectful tokens of veneration were bestowed upon the
fathers, several of whom died in that pestilential city before the
vessels were ready to transport them beyond the sea. Nor did
their sufferings cease with their departure from New Spain. Their
voyage was long, tempestuous, and disastrous, and after their
arrival in Spain, under strict guardianship, they were again embarked for Italy, where they were finally settled with a slender
support in Rome, Bologna, Ferrara, and other cities, in which they
honored the country whence they had been driven by literary labors
and charitable works. The names of Abade, Alegre, Clavigero,
Landibares, Maneyro, Cavo, Lacunza, and Marques sufficiently
attest the historical merit of these Mexican Jesuits who were victims of the suspicious Charles. For a long time the Mexican mind
was sorely vexed by the oppressive act against this favorite order.
But the Visitador Galvez imposed absolute silence upon the people,
telling them in insulting language that it was their " sole duty to
obey," and that they must " speak neither for nor against the
royal order, which had been passed for motives reserved alone for
the sovereign's conscience ! "

Thus all expression of public sentiment as well as of amiable
feeling at this daring act against the worthiest and most benevolent
clergymen of Mexico was effectually stifled. If the act of Henry
VIII. in England was unjust and cruel, it was matched both in
boldness and wickedness by the despotic decree of the unrelenting

Charles of Spain.   Nor can the latter sovereign claim the merit of
having substituted virtue for vice, as the British king pretended he
had done in the suppression of the monasteries. Henry swept priest
and friar from his kingdom with the same blow; but the trimming
Charles banished the intellectual Jesuit while he saved and screened
the monk.

The pretext of Charles III. for his outrageous conduct was
found in an insurrection which occurred on the evening of Palm
Sunday, 1766, and gave up the capital of Spain for forty-eight
hours to a lawless mob.   It was doubtless the result of a preconcerted plan to get rid of an obnoxious minister; and as soon as it
was known that this personage had been exiled the rioters instantly
surrendered their arms, made friends with the soldiers, and departed to their homes.   In fact, it was a political intrigue which the
king and his minister charged on some of the Spanish grandees
and on the Jesuits.   But as the former were too powerful to be
assailed by the king, his wrath was vented on the fathers of the
Order of Jesus, whose lives at this time were not only innocent, but
meritorious.

"Some years preceding, on a charge as destitute of foundation, they had been expelled from Portugal," says Dunham.   "In
1764 their inveterate foe, the Duc de Choiseul, minister of Louis
XV., had driven them from France; and in Spain their possessions
were regarded with an avaricious eye by some of the needy
courtiers. To effect their downfall the French minister eagerly
joined with the advocates of plunder; and intrigues were adopted
which must cover their authors with everlasting infamy. Not
only was the public alarm carefully excited by a report of pretended plots, and the public indignation by slanderous representations of their persons and principles; but, in the name of the
chiefs of the order, letters were forged, which involved the most
monstrous doctrines and the most criminal designs. A pretended
circular from the general of the order at Rome to the provincial,
calling on him to join with the insurgents; the deposition of
perjured witnesses to prove that the recent commotion was chiefly
the work of the body, deeply alarmed Charles, and drew him into
the views of the French cabinet."

Spain was thus made a tool of France in an act of gross injustice, not only to the reverend sufferers, but to the people over whose
spiritual and intellectual wants they had so beneficially watched.

From this digression to the mingled politics of Mexico and Europe we shall now return to the appropriate scene of our brief annals. The capture of so important a port as Havana, and the inadequate protection of the coast along the Main, obliged the government to think seriously about the increase and discipline of domestic troops, and especially to improve the condition of the coast defense. These fears were surely not groundless. The possessions of Great Britain north of Mexico on the continent were growing rapidly in size and importance, and from the provinces which now form the United States the viceroy imagined England might easily dispatch sufficient troops without being obliged to transport reinforcements from Europe. Accordingly suitable preparations were made to receive the enemy should he venture to descend suddenly on the Spanish Main. The veteran regiments of Savoy and Flanders were sent to the colony in June, 1768, and the Marshal de Rubi was charged with the disposition of the army. From that period it may be said that Mexico assumed the military aspect which it has continuously worn to the present time.

Besides the increase and improvement of the troops of the line, the government's attention was directed toward the fortification of the ports and interior passes. The Castle of San Juan de Ulua was repaired at a cost of $1,500,000. The small Island of Anton Lizardo was protected by military works at an expense of $1,200,000. A splendid battery was sent from Spain for the castle, and the inefficient guns of Acapulco were dispatched to the Philippine Islands to be recast and sent back to America. In the interior of the country in the midst of the plain of Perote the Castle of San Carlos was built in the most substantial and scientific manner; and although this fortress seems useless, placed as it is in the center of a broad and easily traversed prairie, yet at the time of its construction it was designed as an *entre depot* between the capital and the coast in which the royal property might always be safely kept until the moment of exportation, instead of being exposed to the danger of a sudden seizure by the enemy in the port of Vera Cruz.

Such were some of the leading acts and occurrences in New Spain during the viceroyalty of the Marques de Croix. His general administration of affairs is characterized by justice. He lived in harmony with the rigid Visitador Galvez, and although the gossips of the day declared he was too fond of wine, yet on his return to Spain he was named captain-general of the army and treated most kindly by the king.

Bucareli, lieutenant general of the Spanish army, and forty-sixth viceroy of New Spain, reached Vera Cruz from Havana on August 23, 1771, and took possession on the 2d of the following month. During his administration the military character of the colony was still carefully fostered, while the domestic interests of the people were studied and every effort made to establish the public works and national institutions upon a firm basis. The new mint and the Monte de Piadad are monuments of this epoch. Commerce flourished in those days in Mexico. The fleet under the command of Don Luis de Cordova departed for Cadiz on November 30, 1773, with $26,000,255, exclusive of a quantity of cacao, cochineal and twenty-two marks of fine gold, and the fleet of 1744 was freighted with $26,457,000.

Nor was the accumulation of wealth derived at that time from the golden placeres of Cieneguilla in Sonora less remarkable. From January 1, 1773, to November 17 of the year following there were accounted for, in the royal office at Alamos, 4832 marks of gold, the royal duties on which, of tithe and señorage, amounted to $72,348. The custom house of Mexico, according to the accounts of the consulado, produced in 1772 $687,041, the duty on pulque alone being $244,530.

In 1776 Bucareli endeavored to liberate trade from many of the odious restrictions which had been cast around it by old commercial usages and by the restrictive policy of Spain. The consulado of Mexico complained to Bucareli of the suffering it endured by the monopoly which had hitherto been enjoyed by the merchants of Cadiz, and through the viceroy solicited the court to be permitted to remit its funds to Spain and to bring back the return freights in vessels on its own account. Bucareli supported this demand with his influence, and may be said to have given the first impulse to free-trade. Meanwhile the mineral resources of Mexico were not neglected. During the seven years of Bucareli's reign the yield of the mines had every year been greater than at any period since the conquest. During his viceroyalty $127,-396,000 in gold and silver were coined. Laborde, in Zacatecas, and Terreros in Pachuca, had undertaken extensive works at the great and rich mine of Quebradilla and in the splendid vein of Vizcayna. Other mines were most successfully wrought by their proprietors. From 1770 to the end of 1778 Don Antonio Obregon presented to the royal officers, in order to be taxed, 4692 bars of silver, the royal income from which amounted to $648,972. The same individual had, moreover, presented to the same personages 53,088 castellanos of gold, which paid $13,871 in duties. In order to work his metals Obregon had been furnished to that date 1839 quintals of quicksilver, for which he paid $159,241.

In June, 1778, the mineral deposits of Hostotipaquillo, in the province of Guadalajara, now Jalisco, were discovered, and promised the most extraordinary returns of wealth. In the following year the valuable mines of Catorce were accidentally found by a soldier while searching for a lost horse. All these discoveries and beneficial labors induced Bucareli to recommend the mineral interests of New Spain particularly to the sovereign, and various persons were charged to explore the country for the discovery of quicksilver mines, which it was alleged existed in Mexico. The extraction of quicksilver from American mines had hitherto been prohibited by Spain, but the fear of wars, which might prevent its importation from abroad and consequently destroy the increasing mineral industry of the nation, induced the court to send Don Raphael Heling and Don Antonio Posada, with several subordinates who formerly wrought in the mines of Almaden, to examine the deposits at Talchapa and others in the neighborhood of Ajuchitlan, in October, 1778, under the direction of Padre Alzate. But this reconnoisance proved unavailing at that time, inasmuch as the explorers found no veins or deposits which repaid the cost and labor of working.

At this epoch the Spanish government began to manifest a desire to propagate information in its American possessions. There is a gleam of intellectual dawn seen in a royal order of Charles, in 1776, commanding educated ecclesiastics to devote themselves to the study of Mexican antiquities, mineralogy, metallurgy, geology, and fossils. This decree was directed to the clergy because his majesty, perhaps justly, supposed that they were the only persons who possessed any knowledge of natural sciences, while the rest of his American subjects were in the most profound ignorance.

Archbishop Lorenzano published in Mexico in 1770 his annotated edition of the letters of Cortéz, which is a well-printed work, adorned with coarse engravings, a few maps, and the curious fac-simile pictures of the tributes paid to the Emperor Montezuma. But the jealous monks of the inquisition kept a vigilant watch over the issues of the press, and we find that in those days the commercial house of Prado and Freyre was forced to crave a license from the court empowering them to ship two boxes of types to be used in the printing of the calendar!

The administration of Bucareli was not disturbed by insurrections among the creoles and Spaniards, for he was a just ruler and the people respected his orders, even when they were apparently injurious to their interests. The viceroy adorned their capital, built aqueducts, improved roads, and facilitated intercourse between the various parts of the country; but the Indians of the north in the province of Chihuahua harassed the colonists dwelling near the outposts during nearly all the period of his government. These warlike, nomadic tribes have been the scourge of the frontier provinces since the foundation of the first outpost settlement. They are wild hunters, and appear to have no feeling in common with those southern bands who were subdued by the mingled influences of the sword and of the cross into tame agriculturists. Bucareli attacked and conquered parties of these wandering warriors, but every year fresh numbers descended upon the scattered pioneers along the frontier, so that the labor of recolonization and fighting was annually repeated. Toward the close of his administration De Croix, who succeeded Hugo Oconor in the command along the northern line, established a chain of well-appointed presidios, or garrisons, which in some degree restrained the inroads of these barbarians.

Bucareli died, after a short illness, on April 9, 1779, and his remains were deposited in the church of Guadalupe in front of the sacred and protecting image of the Virgin who watches, according to the legend, over the destinies of Mexico.

In consequence of the death of Bucareli the audiencia assumed the government of New Spain until the appointment of his successor, and in the meanwhile, on May 18, 1779, Charles III. solemnly declared war against England. The misunderstanding which gave rise to the revolutionary outbreak in the English colonies of North America was beginning to attract the notice of Europe. France saw in the quarrel between the Americans and the British an opportunity to humiliate her dangerous foe; and, although Spain had no interest in such a contest, the minister of Charles, Florida

Blanca, persuaded his master to unite with France in behalf of the revolted colonies. Spain in this instance, as in the expulsion of the Jesuits, was doubtless submissive to the will of the French court, and willingly embraced an occasion to humble the pride or destroy the power of a haughty nation whose fleets and piratical cruisers had so long preyed upon the wealthy commerce of her American possessions. The Spanish minister probably did not dream of the dangerous neighbor whose creation he was aiding north of the Gulf of Mexico. It is not likely that he imagined republicanism would be soon and firmly established in the British united colonies of America, and that the infectious love of freedom would spread beyond the wastes of Texas and the deserts of California to the plateaus and plains of Mexico and Peru. The policy was at once blind and revengeful. If it was produced by the intrigue of France, the old hereditary foe and rival of England, it was still less pardonable, for a fault or a crime when perpetrated originally and boldly by a nation sometimes rises almost into glory, if successful; but a second-hand iniquity, conceived in jealousy and vindictiveness, is as mean as it is short-sighted. England had no friends at that epoch. Her previous conduct had been so selfishly grasping that all Europe rejoiced when her colonial power was broken by the American Revolution. Portugal, Holland, Russia, Morocco, and Austria all secretly favored the course of Spain and France, and the most discreet politicians of Europe believed that the condition of Great Britain was hopeless.

The declaration of this impolitic war was finally made in Mexico on August 12, 1779, before the arrival of Don Martin de Mayorga, the new viceroy, who did not reach the capital till the 23d of the same month. The Mexicans were not as well acquainted with the politics of the world as the Spanish cabinet, and did not appreciate all the delicate and diplomatic motives which actuated Charles III. They regarded a war with England as a direct invitation to the British to ravage their coasts and harass their trade; and accordingly, as soon as the direful news was announced, prayers were offered in all the churches for the successful issue of the contest. Nor did war alone strike the Mexicans with panic; for in this same period the smallpox broke out in the capital, and in the ensuing months in the space of sixty-seven days no less than 8821 persons were hurried by it to the grave. It was a sad season of pestilence and anxiety. The streets were filled with

dead bodies, while the temples were crowded with the diseased and
the healthy who rushed promiscuously to the holy images in order
to implore divine aid and compassion. This indiscriminate mixture
of all classes and conditions, this stupid reunion of the sound and
the sick, whose superstitions led them to the altar instead of the
hospital, soon spread the contagion far and wide, until all New
Spain suffered from its desolating ravages and scarcely a person
was found unmarked by its frightful ravages.

An expedition had been ordered during the viceroyalty of
Bucareli to explore portions of the Pacific adjacent to the Mexican
coast, and in February of 1779 it reached a point $55°$ $17'$ north.
It continued its voyage until July 1, when it took possession of the
land at $60°$ $13'$, in the name of Charles III. It then proceeded
onwards, in sight of the coast, and on August 1 arrived at a group
of islands at $59°$ $8'$, upon one of which the explorers landed and
named the spot "Nuestra Señora de Regla."

About this period the Spanish Government detached General
Solano and a part of his squadron, with orders for America, to
aid in the military enterprises designed against Florida, in which
Mexico was to take a significant part. This commander was to
coöperate with Don Bernardo de Galvez, and both these personages, in the years 1779, 1780, and 1781, making common cause
with the French against the English, carried the war actively up
the Mississippi and into various portions of Florida. The remaining period of Mayorga's viceroyalty was chiefly occupied with
preparations in the neighborhood of Vera Cruz against an assault
from the British, and in suppressing, by the aid of the alcalde,
Urizar, a trifling revolt among the Indians of Izucar. An unfortunate disagreement arose between Mayorga and the Spanish
minister, Galvez, and he was finally, after many insults from the
count, displaced in order to make room for Don Matias Galvez.
The unfortunate viceroy departed for Spain, but never reached his
native land. He died in sight of Cadiz, and his wife was indemni-
fied for the ill-treatment of her husband by the contemptible gift
of twenty thousand dollars.

Mayorga was the victim apparently of an ill-disposed minister, who controlled the pliant mind of Charles. The viceroy in
reality had discharged his duties as lieutenant of the king with
singular fidelity. All branches of art and industry in Mexico
received his fostering care, but he had enemies who sought his

disgrace at court, and they were finally successful in their shameful efforts.

Don Matias Galvez hastened rapidly from Guatemala and took possession of the viceroyalty in 1783. He soon exhibited his generous character and his ardent desire to improve and embellish the beautiful capital. The academy of fine arts was one of his especial favorites, and he insisted that Charles should not only endow it with nine thousand dollars, but should render it an effective establishment by the introduction of the best models for the students. Galvez directed his attention, also, to the police of Mexico and its prisons; he required the streets to be leveled and paved, prohibited the raising of recruits for Manila, and solicited from the king authority to reconstruct the magnificent palace of Chapultepec on the well-known and beautiful hill of that name which lies about two miles west of the capital, still girt with its ancient cypresses.

It was during the brief reign of this personage that the political *Gazette* of Mexico was established, and the exclusive privilege of its publication granted to Manuel Valdez. On November 3 Don Matias died, after a brief illness, unusually lamented by the people, from amid whose masses he had risen to supreme power in the most important colony of Spain.

As the death of this officer was sudden and unexpected, no mortuary dispatch had been sent from Spain announcing his successor, and accordingly the audiencia assumed the reigns of government until the arrival of the new viceroy.

The Count Galvez, son of the last viceroy, Don Matias, took charge of the government on June 17, 1785, but enjoyed as brief a reign as his respected father. Hardly had he attained power when a great scarcity of food was experienced among the people of New Spain in consequence of an extraordinarily unfavorable season. The excellent disposition of the new officer was shown in his incessant and liberal efforts to relieve the public distress in all parts of the country afflicted by misery. Meetings were held and committees appointed under his auspices, composed of the most distinguished Spanish and native subjects to aid in this beneficent labor; and over four hundred thousand dollars were given by the Archbishop of Mexico and the bishops of Puebla and Michoacan to encourage agriculture as well as to relieve the most pressing wants of the people. In order to afford employment to the indigent, at the same time that he permanently improved and beautified the capital and the country generally, the viceroy either commenced or continued a number of important public works, among which were the national roads and the magnificent palace of Chapultepec, the favorite retreat of his father. This splendid architectural combination of fortress and palace was a costly luxury to the Spanish Government, for the documents of the period declare that up to the month of January, 1787, $123,077 had been expended in its construction. Nor was the ministry well pleased with so lavish an outlay upon this royal domain. Placed on a solitary hill at a short distance from the capital, and built evidently for the double purpose of defense and dwelling, it created a fear in the minds of some sensitive persons that its design might not be altogether so peaceful as was pretended. An ambitious viceroy, surrounded by troops whose attachment and firmness could be relied on, might easily convert the palace into a citadel; and it was noted that Galvez had upon various occasions played the demagogue among the military men who surrounded him in the capital. All these fears were, however, idle. If the count in reality entertained any ambitious projects, or desired to put himself at the head of an American kingdom independent of Spain, these hopes were soon and sadly blighted by his early death. He expired on November 30, 1786, in the archiepiscopal palace of Tacubaya. His funeral ceremonies were conducted by the archbishop, and his honored remains interred in the church of San Fernando.

The audiencia real assumed the government of Mexico, inasmuch as the Spanish ministry had provided no successor in the event of the count's death. Its power continued until the following February, during which period no event of note occurred in New Spain, save the destruction by fire of valuable mining property at Bolaños, and a violent hurricane at Acapulco, accompanied by earthquakes, which swept the sea over the coast and caused great losses to the farmers and herdsmen who dwelt on the neighboring lowlands.

But on February 25, 1787, Nuñez de Haro, Archbishop of Mexico, was appointed viceroy, *ad interim,* of New Spain. The selection of this eminent prelate was perhaps one of those strokes of policy by which the Spanish ministry strove to reconcile and connect the ecclesiastical and civil unity of the American empire.

The sway of the archbishop, complimentary as it was to himself and to the church, was exceedingly brief, for he was superseded by Flores in the same year. New Spain was undisturbed during his government; and no event is worthy of historical record in these brief annals of the country, save the effort that was made to prohibit the repartimiento or subdivision of the Indians among the agriculturists and miners by the sub-delegados, who had succeeded the alcaldes mayores in the performance of this odious task. The conduct of the latter personages had been extremely cruel to the natives. They either used their power to oppress the Indians or had trafficked in the dispensation of justice by allowing the sufferers to purchase exemption from punishment; and it is related that in certain alcaldais mayors in Oaxaca, the alcaldes had enriched themselves to the extent of more than two hundred thousand dollars by these brutal exactions. Inhumanity like this was severely denounced to the king by the Bishop Ortigoza, who merited, according to Revilla-Gigedo, the title of the Saint Paul of his day, and the eloquent prelate complained in behalf of his beloved Indians as vehemently as Las Casas at an earlier period, of this loathsome oppression. But interest has overcome the appeals of mercy in almost all instances since the foundation of the American empire. The Spaniards required laborers. The ignorant and unarmed Indians of the south and of the tablelands were docile or unorganized, and although the Spanish court and Council of the Indies seconded the viceroy's zeal in attempting to suppress the cruelty of the planters and miners, the unfortunate aborigines only experienced occasional brief intervals of respite in the system of forced labor to which they were devoted by their legal taskmasters.

Don Manuel Flores received the reins of government from the hands of the archbishop on May 16, 1787, but his power over the finances of the nation was taken from him and given to Fernando Mangino, with the title of Superintendente Sub-delegado de Hacienda. Flores was thus left in possession solely of the civil administration generally, and of the military organization of the viceroyalty. Being satisfied that the ordinary militia system of New Spain was inadequate for national protection during war, he immediately devoted himself to the forced levy and equipment of three regiments of infantry, named "Puebla," "Mexico" and "New Spain." The command of these forces was given to the

most distinguished and noble young men of Mexico; and as the
minister Galvez died, and Mangino was about this period transferred to the Council of the Indies, the superintendence of the
finances of Mexico was appropriately restored again to the viceroyal government.

The northern part of Mexico in 1788 and for many previous
years had been constantly ravaged by the wild Indian tribes that
ranged across the whole frontier from the western limits of Sonora
to the Gulf of Mexico. Immense sums were squandered in the
support of garrisons or the maintenance of numerous officers
whose duty it was to hold these barbarians in check. But their
efforts had been vain. The fine agricultural districts of Chihuahua,
New Leon, New Mexico, and even in parts of Texas had attracted
large numbers of adventurous pioneers into that remote region;
yet no sooner did their fields begin to flourish and their flocks or
herds to increase than these savages descended upon the scattered
settlers and carried off their produce and their families. Whenever the arms of New Spain obtained a signal victory over one of
these marauding bands, the Indians would talk of peace and even
consent to bind themselves by treaties. But these compacts were
immediately broken as soon as they found the country beginning
to flourish again or the military power in the least degree relaxed.

Flores appears to have understood the condition of the northern frontier and the temper of the Indians. He did not believe
that treaties, concessions, or kindness would suffice to protect the
Spanish pioneers, and yet he was satisfied that it was necessary to
sustain the settlements in that quarter in order to prevent the
southern progress of European adventurers who were eager to
seize the wild and debatable lands lying on both sides of the Rio
Grande. Accordingly he proposed to the Spanish court to carry
on a war of most inexorable character against the Apaches, Lipans,
and Mesclaros. He characterized in his dispatches all the Indian
tribes dwelling or wandering between the Presidio of the Bay of
Espiritu Santo, in the province of Texas, to beyond Santa Ger-
trudis del Altar, in Sonora,—the two opposite points of the dangerous frontier line,—as Apaches or their hostile colleagues; and
he resolved to fight them without quarter, truce, or mercy until
they surrendered unconditionally to the power of Spain.

The history of these provinces later shows the wisdom of this
advice in regard to a band of savages whose habits are peculiarly

warlike and whose robber traits have made them equally dangerous to all classes of settlers in the lonely districts of the Rio Grande or of the Gila and Colorado of the west. His secretary, Bonilla, who had fought bravely in the northern provinces, and was practically acquainted with warfare among these barbarians, seconded the mature opinion of the viceroy. The plan was successful for the time, and the frontier enjoyed a degree of peace while the military power was sustained throughout the line of presidios. Flores enforced his system rigidly during his viceroyalty. He equipped the expeditions liberally, promoted the officers who distinguished themselves, rewarded the bravest soldiers, and dispatched a choice regiment of dragoons to Durango, whose officers formed in that city the nucleus of its future civilization.

Nor was this viceroy stinted in his efforts to improve the capital and protect the growing arts and sciences of the colony. He labored to establish a botanical garden, under the auspices of Don Martin Sesé; but the perfect realization of this beneficial and useful project was reserved for his successor, the Count Revilla-Gigedo.

The mining interests, too, were prospering, and improvements on the ancient Spanish system were sought to be introduced through the instrumentality of eleven German miners whose services had been engaged by the home government in Dresden through its envoy, Don Luis Orcis. These personages presented themselves in New Spain with the pompous title of practical professors of mineralogy, but they were altogether unskilled in the actual working of mines, and unable to render those of Mexico more productive. The only benefit derived from this mineralogical mission was the establishment of a course of chemical lectures in the seminary of mines under the direction of Lewis Leinder, who set up the first laboratory in Mexico.

On December 23, 1788, the minister of the Indies apprised the viceroy of the death of Charles III., which had occurred in the middle of that month. Funeral ceremonies were celebrated with great pomp in Mexico in honor of the defunct monarch, and on February 22, 1789, the resignation of the viceroyalty by Flores—who desired heartily to retire from public life—was graciously accepted by the Spanish court, and his successor named, in the person of the second Count Revilla-Gigedo.

This distinguished nobleman, who was the fifty-second viceroy and whose name figures so favorably in the annals of Mexico, reached Guadalupe on October 16, 1789, and on the following day entered the capital with all the pompous ceremonies usual in New Spain upon the advent of a new ruler. In the following month the new sovereign Charles IV. was proclaimed, and the viceroy at once set about the regulation of the municipal police of his capital, which seems to have been somewhat relaxed since the days of his dreaded and avaricious father. Assassinations of the most scandalous and daring character had recently warned the viceroy of the insecurity of life and property even in the midst of his guards. But Revilla-Gigedo possessed some of the sterner qualities that distinguished his parent, and never rested until the guilty parties were discovered and brought to prompt and signal justice. The capital soon exhibited a different aspect under his just and rigorous government. He did not trust alone to the reports of his agents in order to satisfy his mind in regard to the wants of Mexico, for he visited every quarter of the city personally, and often descended unexpectedly upon his officers when they least expected a visit from such a personage. The poor as well as the rich received his paternal notice. He inquired into their wants and studied their interests. One of his most beneficent schemes was the erection of a Monte Pio for their relief, yet the sum he destined for this object was withheld by the court and used for the payment of royal debts. Agriculture, horticulture, and botany were especially fostered by this enlightened nobleman. He carried out the project of his predecessor by founding the botanical garden, and liberally rewarded and encouraged the pupils of this establishment, for he rightly deemed the rich vegetable resources of Mexico quite as worthy of national attention as the mines which had hitherto absorbed the public interest. Literature, too, did not escape his fostering care, as far as the jealous rules of the inquisition and of royal policy permitted its liberal encouragement by a viceroy. He found the streets of the capital and its suburbs badly paved and kept, and he rigidly enforced all the police regulations which were necessary for their purity and safety. As he knew that one of the best means of developing and binding together the provinces of the empire was the construction of substantial and secure roads, he proposed that the highways to Vera Cruz, Acapulco, Meztitlan de la Sierra, and Toluca should be reconstructed in the most enduring manner. But the Junta Superior de Hacienda opposed the measure, and the count was obliged to expend from his own purse the requisite sums for the most important repairs. He established weekly posts between the capitals of the intendencies; regulated and restricted the cutting of timber in the adjacent mountains; established a professorship of anatomy in the Hospital de Naturales; destroyed the provincial militia system and formed regular corps out of the best veterans found in the ranks. Knowing the difficulty with which the poor or uninfluential reached the ear of their Mexican governors, he placed a locked case in one of the halls of his palace into which all persons were at liberty to throw their memorials designed for the viceroy's scrutiny. It was in reality a secret mode of espionage, but it brought to the count's knowledge many an important fact which he would never have learned through the ordinary channels of the court. Without this secret chest, whose key was never out of his possession, Revilla-Gigedo with all his personal industry might never have comprehended the actual condition of Mexico, or have adopted the numerous measures for its improvement which distinguished his reign.

Besides this provident measure for the internal safety and progressive comfort of New Spain, the count directed his attention to the western coast of America, upon which he believed the future interests of Spain would materially rely. The settlement of the Californias had engaged the attention of many preceding viceroys, as we have already related, and their coasts had been explored and missionary settlements made wherever the indentures of the sea shore indicated the utility of such enterprises. But the count foresaw that the day would come when the commercial enterprises of European nations, and especially of the English, would render this portion of the Mexican realm an invaluable acquisition. Accordingly he dispatched an expedition to the Californias to secure the possessions of Spain in that quarter; and has left for posterity an invaluable summary or recopilación of all the enterprises of discovery made by the Spaniards in that portion of the west coast of America. This document—more useful to the antiquarian than the politician—may be found in the third volume of " *Los Tres Siglos de Mejico*," a work which was commenced by the Jesuit Father Cavo, and continued to the year 1821, by Don Carlos Maria Bustamante. Revilla-Gigedo recommended the Spanish court to avoid all useless parade or expense, but resolutely to prevent the approach of the English or of any other foreign power to their possessions in California, and promptly to occupy the port of Bodega, and even the shores of the Columbia River, if it was deemed necessary. He advised the minister, moreover, to fortify these two points; to garrison strongly San Francisco, Monterey, San Diego and Loreto; to change the department of San Blas to Acapulco; and to guard the fondos piadosos of the missions, as well as the salt works of Zapotillo, by which the treasury would be partly relieved of the ecclesiastical expenses of California, while the needful marine force was suitably supported. These safeguards were believed by the viceroy sufficient to confine the enterprising English to the regions in which they might traffic for peltries without being tempted into the dominions of Spain, at the same time that they served as safeguards against all illicit or contraband commerce.[1]

We have thus endeavored to describe rather than to narrate historically the principal events that occurred in the reign of the second Count Revilla-Gigedo, all of which have characterized him as a just, liberal, and far-seeing ruler. In the account of his father's reign we have already noticed some of this viceroy's meritorious qualities; but we shall now break the ordinary tenor of these brief annals by inserting a few anecdotes which are still traditionally current in the country whose administration he so honestly conducted.

The count was accustomed to make nightly rounds in the city in order to assure himself that its regulations for quiet and security were carried into effect. On one occasion, it is related that, in passing through a street which he had ordered to be paved, he suddenly stopped and dispatched a messenger to the director of the work, requiring his instant presence. The usual phrase with which he wound up such commands was " *le espero aqui,*"—" I await him here,"—which had the effect of producing an extraordinary degree of celerity in those who received the command. On this occasion the officer, who was enjoying his midnight repose, sprang from his bed on receiving the startling summons, and rushed, half dressed, to learn the purport of what he presumed to be an important business. He found the viceroy standing stiff and composed on the sidewalk. When the panting officer had paid his obeisance to his master, " I regret to have disturbed you, señor," said the latter, " in order to call your attention to the state of your

---

[1] During the administration of the second Count Revilla-Gigedo the sum of $109,704,417 was coined in gold and silver in Mexico.

pavement. You will observe that this flagstone is not perfectly even," touching with his toe one which rose about half an inch above the rest of the sidewalk. " I had the misfortune to strike my foot against it this evening, and I fear that some others may be as unlucky as myself unless the fault be immediately remedied. You will attend to it, sir, and report to me to-morrow morning!" With these words he continued his round, leaving the officer in a state of stupefaction; but it is asserted that the pavements of Mexico for the rest of his excellency's government were unexceptionable.

Another anecdote of this kind places his peculiarity of temper in a still stronger light. In perambulating the city one pleasant evening about sunset, he found that the street in which he was walking terminated abruptly against a mass of wretched tenements, apparently the lurking places of vice and beggary. He inquired how it happened that the highway was carried no farther, or why these hovels were allowed to exist; but the only information he could gain was that such had always been the case, and that none of the authorities considered themselves bound to remedy the evil. Revilla-Gigedo sent immediately to the corregidor. " Tell him that I await him here," he concluded, in a tone that had the effect of bringing that functionary at once to the spot, and he received orders to open, without delay, a broad and straight avenue through the quarter as far as the barrier of the city. It must be finished —was the imperious command—that very night, so as to allow the viceroy to drive through it on his way to mass the next morning. With this the count turned on his heel, and the corregidor was left to reflect upon his disagreeable predicament.

The fear of losing his office, or perhaps worse consequences, stimulated his energy. No time was to be wasted. All his subordinate officers were instantly summoned, and laborers were collected from all parts of the city. The very buildings that were to be removed sent forth crowds of leperos willing for a few reales to aid in destroying the walls which had once harbored them. A hundred torches shed their radiance over the scene. All night long the shouts of the workmen, the noise of pickax and crowbar, the crash of falling roofs, and the rumbling of carts kept the city in a fever of excitement. Precisely at sunrise the state carriage with the viceroy, his family and suite left the palace and rattled over the pavements in the direction from which the noise had proceeded. At length the new street opened before them, a thousand workmen in double file fell back on either side and made the air resound with *vivas* as they passed. Through clouds of dust and dirt, over the unpaved earth, strewn with fragments of stone and plaster, the coach and train swept onward, till at the junction of the new street with the road leading to the suburbs the corregidor, hat in hand, with a smile of conscious desert, stepped forward to receive his excellency and to listen to the commendation bestowed on the prompt and skillful execution of his commands!

Should anyone doubt the truth of this story, let him be aware that the Calle de Revilla-Gigedo still remains in Mexico to attest its verity. These anecdotes impart some idea of the authority exercised by the viceroys, which was certainly far more arbitrary and personal than that of their sovereign in his Spanish dominions.

Chapter XXII

THE EFFECT OF EUROPEAN WARS ON COLONIAL DEVELOPMENT. 1794-1809

CONTRASTING unfavorably with the illustrious Revilla-Gigedo is the next viceroy, the Marques Branciforte, who reached Mexico July 11, 1794. Partaking of the avaricious qualities of the first Count Revilla-Gigedo, he seems to have possessed but few of the latter's virtues, and probably accepted the viceroyalty of New Spain with no purpose but that of plunder.

Scarcely had he begun to reign when his rapacity was signally exhibited. It is said that his first essay in extortion was the sale of the sub-delegation of Villa-Alta to a certain Don Francisco Ruiz de Conejares, for the sum of forty thousand dollars, and the bestowal of the office of apoderado on the Count de Contramina, the offices of whose subordinates were bought and sold in the political market like ordinary merchandise.

At this epoch the warlike hostility to France was excessive, and orders had been received to exercise the strictest vigilance over the subjects of that nation who resided in Mexico. Their number, however, was small, for Spanish America was almost as closely sealed as China against the entrance of strangers. Nevertheless Branciforte encouraged a most disgraceful persecution against these unfortunate persons, by arresting them on the slightest pretexts, throwing them into prison, and seizing their possessions. He found in his assessor general, Don Pedro Jacinto Valenzuela, and in his criminal prosecutor, Francisco Xavier de Borbon, fitting instruments to carry out his inexorable determinations. Upon one occasion he even demanded of the Sala de Audiencia that certain Frenchmen, after execution, should have their tongues impaled upon iron spikes at the city gates because they had spoken slightingly of the virtue of the queen, Maria Louisa! Fortunately, however, for the wretched culprits, the Sala was composed of virtuous magistrates, who refused to sanction the cruel demand, and the victims were only despoiled of their valuable property. These acts, it may well be supposed, covered the name of Branciforte with infamy.

On October 7, 1796, war was declared by Spain against England, in consequence of which the viceroy immediately distributed the colonial army, consisting of not less than eight thousand men, in Orizaba, Cordova, Jalapa, and Perote; and in the beginning of the following year he left the capital, to command the forces from his headquarters near the eastern coast. This circumstance enabled him to leave, with an air of triumph, a city in which he was profoundly hated. The people manifested their contempt of so despicable an extortioner and flatterer of royalty not only by words, but by caricatures. When the sovereign sent him the order of the Golden Fleece, they depicted Branciforte with a collar of the noble order, but in lieu of the lamb, which terminates the insignia, they placed the figure of a cat. At his departure the civil and financial government of the capital was entrusted to the regency of the audiencia, while its military affairs were conducted by the Brigadier Davalos. In Orizaba the conduct of Branciforte was that of an absolute monarch. All his troops were placed under the best discipline, but none of them were permitted to descend to Vera Cruz; yet scarcely had he been established in this new military command, when it was known that Don Miguel José de Azanza was named as his viceroyal successor. Nevertheless Branciforte continued in control, with the same domineering demeanor as in the first days of his government, relying for justification and defense in Spain upon the support of his relative, Manuel de Godoy. In Orizaba he was surrounded by flatterers and his court was a scene of disgraceful orgies; yet the day of his fall was at hand. The ship *Monarch* anchored at Vera Cruz on May 17, 1798, and on the 31st of the same month Azanza, the new viceroy who reached America in her, received the viceroyal baton from Branciforte. That supercilious peculator departed from New Spain with five millions of dollars, a large portion of which was his private property, in the vessel that had brought his successor, and arrived at Ferol, after a narrow escape from the English in the waters of Cadiz. But he returned to Spain loaded with wealth and curses, for never had the Mexicans complained so bitterly against any Spaniard who was commissioned to rule them. The respectable and wealthy inhabitants of the colony were loudest in their denunciations of the "Italian adventurer" who enriched himself at the expense of their unfortunate country, nor was his conduct less hateful because he had been the immediate successor of so just and upright a viceroy as Revilla-Gigedo.

Azanza, who, as we have related, assumed the viceroyalty in May, 1798, was exceedingly well received in Mexico. His worthy character was already known to the people, and almost any new viceroy would have been hailed as a deliverer from the odious administration of Branciforte. Azanza was urbane toward all classes, and his discreet conversation at once secured the respect and confidence of the colonists. Besides this, the early measures of his administration were exceedingly wise. He dissolved the various military encampments established and maintained at enormous cost by his predecessor in the neighborhood of the eastern coasts. This heavy charge on the treasury was distasteful to the people, while so large an assemblage of colonial troops necessarily withdrew multitudes from agricultural and commercial pursuits, and greatly interfered with the business of New Spain. Anxious, however, to protect the important post of Vera Cruz, the viceroy formed a less numerous encampment in its neighborhood; but the greater portion of its officers and men perished in that unhealthful climate.

The war with England was not altogether disadvantageous to Mexico, for although the royal order of November 18, 1797, was repeated on April 20, 1799, by which a commerce in neutral vessels had been permitted with the colony's ports, yet, as the seas were filled with enemy's cruisers, the Spanish trade in national vessels was narrowed chiefly to exports from the mother country. This course of commerce resulted in retaining the specie of Mexico within her territory, for the precious metals had hitherto been the principal article of export to Spain in return for merchandise dispatched from Cadiz. The internal trade of Mexico was accordingly fostered and beneficially sustained by the continuance of its large annual metallic products within the viceroyalty until peace permitted their safe transmission abroad. The beneficial retention of silver and gold in the country was not only manifested in the activity of domestic trade, but also in the improvement of its towns and cities and in the encouragement of manufactures of silk, cotton, and wool. In Oaxaca, Guadalaxara, Valladolid, Puebla, Cuautitlan, San Juan, Teotihuacan, Cempoalla, Metepec, Ixtlahuaca, and Tulancingo the number of looms increased rapidly between 1796 and 1800. In Oaxaca thirty were added; in San Juan Teotihuacan thirty-three; in Queretaro thirty-four hundred persons were employed; while, in the town of Cadereita there existed more than two hundred looms, giving employment to more than five hundred individuals.

In attending wisely and justly to the civil administration of New Spain and in fostering the internal trade and industry, Azanza bestirred himself while the war continued. There were but few actions between the combatants, but as the contest between the nations sealed the ports in a great degree, Mexico was made chiefly dependent on herself for the first time since her national existence. The politics and intrigues of the Old World thus acquainted the colony with her resources and taught her the value of independence.

Azanza's administration was for a while disturbed by a threatened outbreak among the lower classes, whose chief conspirators assembled in an obscure house in the capital, and designed at a suitable moment rising in great numbers and murdering without discrimination all the wealthiest or most distinguished Spaniards. This treasonable project was discovered to the viceroy, who went in person with a guard to the quarters of the leaguers and arrested them on the spot. They were speedily brought to trial, but the cause hung in the courts until after the departure of Azanza, when powerful and touching intercessions were made with his successor to save the lives of the culprits. The project of a pardon was maturely considered by the proper authorities, and it was resolved not to execute the guilty chiefs, inasmuch as it was believed that their appearance upon a scaffold would be the signal for a general revolt of the people against the dominion of the parent country. The sounds of the approaching storm were already heard in the distance, and justice yielded to policy.

Azanza, with all his excellent qualities as a governor in America, did not give satisfaction to the court at home. There is no doubt of the value of his administration in Mexico, and it is therefore difficult to account for his loss of favor, except upon the ground of intrigue and corruption which were rife in Madrid. The reign of Charles IV. and the administration of Godoy, the " Prince of Peace " are celebrated in history as the least respectable in modern Spanish annals. While the royal favorite controlled the king's councils, favoritism and intrigue ruled the day. Among other legends of the time, it is asserted by Bustamante, in his continuation of Cavo's " *Los Tres Siglos de Mejico,*" that the Mexican viceroyalty was almost put up at auction in Madrid, and offered for eighty thousand dollars to the secretary Bonilla. In consequence of this personage's inability to procure the requisite sum, it was conferred, through another bargain and sale, upon Don Felix Berenguer de Marquina, an obscure officer who was unknown to the king either personally or as a meritorious servant of the crown and people.

The Mexican author to whom we have just referred characterizes Azanza as the wisest, most politic, and amiable viceroy ever sent by Spain to rule over his beautiful country.

The next viceroy, Don Felix Berenguer de Marquina, took charge on April 30, 1800, after a sudden and mysterious arrival in New Spain, having passed through the enemy's squadron and been taken prisoner. It was inconceivable to the Mexicans why the vice-admiral of Jamaica deemed it proper to release a Spanish officer who came to America on a warlike mission; yet it is now known that in November, of 1800, the king ordered forty thousand dollars to be paid the viceroy to reimburse the extraordinary expenses of his voyage!

The government of this personage was not remarkable in the development of the colony. The war with England still continued, but it was of a mild character, and vessels constantly passed between the belligerents with flags of truce, through whose intervention the Mexicans were permitted to purchase in Jamaica the paper, quicksilver, and other European commodities which the British cruisers had captured from Spanish ships in the Gulf of Mexico.

In 1801 an Indian named Mariano, of Tepic in Jalisco, son of the governor of the village of Tlascala in that department, attempted to excite a revolution among the people of his class by means of an anonymous circular which proclaimed him king. Measures were immediately taken to suppress this outbreak, and numbers of the natives were apprehended and carried to Guadalajara. The fears of Marquina were greatly excited by this paltry rebellion, which he imagined, or feigned to believe, a widespread conspiracy excited by the North Americans and designed to overthrow the Spanish power. The viceroy accordingly detailed his services in exaggerated terms to the home government, and it is probably owing to the eulogium passed by him upon the conduct of Abascal, president of Guadalajara, that this personage was made viceroy of Buenos Ayres, and afterward honored with the government of Peru and created Marques de la Concordia.

A definitive treaty of peace was concluded between the principal European and American belligerents in 1802, and soon after, Marquina, who was offended by some slights received from the Spanish ministry, resigned an office for the performance of whose manifold duties and intricate labors he manifested no ability save that of a good disposition. He was probably better fitted to govern a village of fifty inhabitants than the vast and important empire of New Spain.

On the morning of January 4, 1803, Don José Iturrigaray reached Guadalupe near Mexico, where he received the staff of viceroyalty from his predecessor and was welcomed by the audiencia, tribunals, and nobility of the capital.

The revolution in the British provinces of North America had been successful, and they had consolidated themselves into nationality under the title of United States. France followed in the footsteps of liberty, and, overthrowing the rotten throne of the Bourbons, was the first European state to give an impulse to freedom in the Old World. The whole western part of that continent was more or less agitated by the throes of the moral and political volcano whose fiery eruption was soon to cover Europe with destruction. In the midst of this epoch of convulsive change Spain alone exhibited the aspect of passive insignificance, for the king, queen and "Prince of Peace," still conducted the government of that great nation, and their corrupt rule has become a proverb of imbecility and contempt. Godoy, the misnamed "Prince of Peace," was the virtual ruler of the nation. His administration was at once selfish, depraved, and silly. The favorite of the king, and the alleged paramour of the queen, he controlled both whenever it was necessary, while the colonies, as well as the parent state, naturally experienced all the evil consequences of his debauched government. Bad as had been the management of affairs in America during the reign of the long series of viceroys who commanded on the continent, it became even worse while Godoy swayed Charles IV. through the influence of his dissolute queen. Most of the serious and exciting annoyances which afterwards festered and broke out in the Mexican Revolution owe their origin to this epoch of Spanish misrule.

Iturrigaray was exceedingly well received in Mexico, where his reputation as an eminent servant of the crown preceded him. Shortly after his arrival he undertook a journey to the interior, in order to examine personally into the condition of the mining districts; and after his return to the capital he devoted himself to the ordinary routine of colonial administration until it became necessary, in consequence of the breaking out of the war between Spain and England, to adopt measures for the protection of his viceroyalty. In consequence of this rupture Iturrigaray received orders from the court to put the country in a state of complete defense, and accordingly he gathered in haste the troops of Mexico, Puebla, Perote, Jalapa, and Vera Cruz, and, descending several times to the latter place, personally inspected all the encampments and garrisons along the route. Besides this, he made a rapid military reconnoissance of the country along the coast and the chief highways to the interior. The road from Vera Cruz to Mexico was constructed in the best manner under his orders, and the celebrated bridge called El Puente del Rey, now known as El Puente Nacional, was finally completed.

These preparations were designed not only to guard New Spain from the invasions of the English, but also from a dreaded attack by the people of the United States. This fear seems to have been fostered by the Marques de Casa Irujo, who was Spanish envoy in Washington at this epoch, and informed the government that the menaced expedition against Mexico would throw twenty thousand men upon her shores. Nor was the attention of Iturrigaray diverted from the enterprise which was projected by Don Francisco Miranda to secure the independence of Caraccas; and although the scheme failed, it appears to have aroused the whole of Spanish America to assert and maintain its rights.

It was during the government of this viceroy that the celebrated Baron Humboldt visited Mexico,—by permission of the patriotic minister, D'Urquijo,—authorized by the home government to examine its dominions and their archives, and to receive from the colonial authorities all the information they possessed in regard to America. He was the first writer who developed the resources or described the condition of the Spanish portion of the American continent, which until that time had been studiously veiled from the examination of all strangers who were likely to reveal their knowledge to the world.

In 1806 the news of the destruction of the combined fleets in the waters of Cadiz became known in Mexico, and the resident Spaniards, exhibiting a lively sympathy with the mother country in this sad affliction, collected upwards of thirty thousand dollars for the widows of their brave companions who had fallen in action. Meanwhile the war in Europe was not only destroying the subjects of the desperate belligerents, but was rapidly consuming their national substance. In this state of things America was called upon to contribute for the maintenance of a bloody struggle in which she had no interest save that of loyal dependence. Taxes, duties, and exactions of all sorts were laid upon the Mexicans, and under this dread infliction the domestic and foreign trade languished, notwithstanding the extraordinary yield of the mines, which, in 1805, sent upwards of twenty millions into circulation. Of all the royal interferences with Mexican interests and capital, none seems to have been more vexatiously unpopular than the decree for the consolidation of the capitals of obras pias, or, charitable and pious revenues, which was issued by the court; and Iturrigaray, as the executive officer employed in this consolidation, drew upon himself the general odium of all the best classes in the colony.

Charles IV. fell before the revolutionary storm in Europe, and signed his abdication on August 9, 1808, in favor of his son Ferdinand VII. But the weak and irresolute monarch soon protested against this abdication, alleging that the act had been extorted from him by threats against his life; and while the supreme council of Spain was examining into the validity of Charles's renunciation, and Ferdinand was treating his father's protest with contempt, Napoleon, who had steadily advanced to supreme power after the success of the French Revolution, took prompt advantage of the dissensions in the Peninsula, and, making himself master of it, seated his brother Joseph on the Spanish throne. As soon as Joseph was firmly placed in power Ferdinand congratulated him upon his elevation, and ordered all his Spanish and colonial subjects to recognize the upstart king. But the servility of Ferdinand to the ascending star of European power did not meet with obedience from the people of Mexico, who, resolving to continue loyal to their legitimate sovereign, forthwith proclaimed Ferdinand VII. throughout New Spain. The conduct of the colonists was secretly approved by the dissembling monarch, although he ratified a decree of the Council of the Indies commanding the Mexicans to obey Joseph. The natives of the Peninsula dwelling in New Spain were nearly all opposed to the Bourbons and faithful to the French propagandists, while the creoles, or American natives, denounced the adherents of Joseph and burned the proclamation which declared him to be their king. The orders received at this period by Iturrigaray from Ferdinand, Joseph, and the Council of the Indies were of course all in conflict with each other; and, in order to relieve himself from the political dilemma in which he was placed by these mixed commands, Iturrigaray determined to summon a Junta of Notable Persons, similar to that of Seville, which was to be composed of the viceroy, the Archbishop of Mexico, and representatives from the army, the nobility, the principal citizens, and the ayuntamiento of the capital. But inasmuch as this plan of concord leaned in favor of the people, by proposing to place the creoles of America upon an equality with the natives of Spain, the old hatred or jealousy between the races was at once aroused. The Europeans who composed the partisans of France, headed by Don Gabriel Yermo, a rich Spaniard and proprietor of some of the finest sugar estates in the valley of Cuernavaca, at once resolved to frustrate the viceroy's design. Arming themselves hastily, they proceeded on the night of September 15, 1808, to his palace, where they arrested Iturrigaray and, accusing him of heresy and treason, sent him as prisoner to Spain. This revolutionary act was openly countenanced by the audiencia, the oidores, Aguirre and Bataller, and the body of Spanish traders. For three years, until released by an act of amnesty in 1811, Iturrigaray continued in close confinement; and although he was not regarded favorably by all classes of Mexicans, this outrage against his person by the Spanish emigrants seems to have produced a partial reaction in his favor among the loyal natives.

Iturrigaray's successor was Field Marshal Don Pedro Garibay, who, though more than eighty years of age, in 1808 was honored with the viceroyalty of New Spain. He had passed the greater portion of his life in Mexico, and rose from the humble grade of lieutenant of provincial militia to the highest post in the colony. He was familiar with the habits and feelings of the people, was generally esteemed for the moderation with which he conducted himself in office, and was altogether the most endurable viceroy who could have been imposed upon the Mexicans at that revolutionary period.

During the government of the preceding viceroy the troubles which began, as we have seen, in the Old World had extended to the New, and we shall therefore group the history of the war that resulted in Mexican independence under the titles of the last viceroys who were empowered by Peninsular authorities to stay, if they could not entirely control, the progress of American liberty.

Chapter XXIII

SPREAD OF THE REVOLT AGAINST FOREIGN DOMINATION. 1809-1815

THE pictures presented in the introductory chapter to the viceroyal history and in the subsequent detailed narrative of that epoch will suffice, we presume, to convince our readers that they need not penetrate deeply for the true causes of misery and misrule in Spanish America. The decadence of Spain as well as the unhappiness of nearly all her ancient colonies may be fairly attributed to the same source of national ruin—bad, unnatural government. A distinguished statesman of our country has remarked that "the European alliance of emperors and kings assumed, as the foundation of human society, the doctrine of unalienable allegiance, while our doctrine was founded on the principle of unalienable right."[1] This mistaken European view, or rather assumption of royal prerogative and correlative human duties, was the baleful origin of colonial misrule. The house of Austria did not govern Spain as wisely as its predecessors. The Spain that Philip I. received and the Spain of those who followed him present a sad contrast. As the conquest of America had not been conceived, although it was declared to be, in a beneficent spirit, the sovereigns continued the system of plunder with which it was begun. Its results are known. The Americans were their subjects, bound to them by "unalienable allegiance"; vassals, serfs, creatures whose human rights in effect were nothing when compared to the monarch's will. This doctrine at once converted the southern portions of the American continent into a soulless machine, which the king had a right to use as he pleased, and especially as he deemed most beneficial for his domestic realm. The consequence was that in concurrence with the Council of the Indies he established, as we have seen, an entirely artificial system, which contradicted nature and utterly thwarted both physical and intellectual development..

[1] John Quincy Adams's letter to Anderson, minister to Columbia, May 27, 1823.

The Indians and creoles of Mexico and Peru, ignorant and stupid as they were believed to be by Spain, had nevertheless sense enough to understand and feel the wretchedness of their condition. They cherished in their hearts an intense hatred for their foreign masters. There was no positive or merely natural enmity of races in this, but rather a suppressed desire to avenge their wrongs.

When the French seized Spain, the colonies in America were for a period forced to rely upon themselves for temporary government. They did not at once desire to adopt republican institutions, but rather adhered to monarchy, provided they could free themselves from bad rulers and vicious laws. This especially was the case in Mexico. Her war against the mother country originated in a loyal desire to be completely independent of France. The news of the departure of Ferdinand VII. for Bayonne, and the alleged perfidy of Napoleon in that city, excited an enthusiasm among the Mexicans for the legitimate king, and created a mortal hatred against the conqueror of Europe. All classes of original Mexican society seem to have been united in these sentiments. Subscriptions were freely opened, and in a few months seven millions were collected to aid their Peninsular friends who were fighting for religion, king, and nationality. The idea did not strike any Mexican that it was a proper time to free his native land entirely from colonial thraldom.[2] But after a short time the people began to reflect. The prestige of Spanish power, to which we have alluded heretofore, was destroyed. A French king sat upon the Spanish throne. The wand of the enchanter, with which he had spellbound America across the wide Atlantic, was broken. The treasured memory of oppression, conquest, bad government and misery was suddenly refreshed, and it is not surprising to find that when the popular rising finally took place it manifested its bitterness in an universal outcry against the Spaniards.

After the occurrences at Bayonne, emissaries from King Joseph Bonaparte spread themselves over the continent to prepare the people for the ratification and permanence of the French government. These political propagandists were charged, as we have stated, with orders from Ferdinand VII. and the Council of the Indies to transfer the allegiance of America to France.[3] It may be imagined that this would have gratified the masses in America,

[2] Zavala, "Historia," vol. I. p. 38.
[3] Robinson's "History of the Mexican Revolution," p. 10.

who perhaps had heard that the French were the unquestionable patrons of " liberty and equality." But the exact reverse was the case among the creoles, while the Spaniards in America received the emissaries with welcome and bowed down submissively to the orders they brought. Blinded for centuries to all ideas of government save those of regal character, the Mexicans had no notion of rule or ruler except their traditional Spanish king. They clung to him, therefore, with confidence, for they felt the necessity of some paramount authority, as political self-control was as yet an utter impossibility.

A secret union among leading men was therefore formed in 1810, which contemplated a general rising throughout the provinces, but the plot was detected at the moment when it was ripe for development. This conspiracy was based upon a desire to overthrow the Spaniards. " They felt," says Ward, " that the question was not now one between themselves as subjects, but between themselves and their fellow-subjects, the European Spaniards, as to which should possess the right of representing the absent king " as guardians and preservers of the rights of Ferdinand. The Europeans claimed this privilege exclusively, with customary insolence. " The ayuntamiento of Mexico was told by the audiencia that it possessed no authority except over the leperos "— or mob of the capital; and it was a favorite maxim of the oidor Battaller that " while a Manchego mule or a Castilian cobbler remained in the Peninsula he had a right to govern."

In those times a certain country curate by name Miguel Hidalgo y Costilla dwelt in the Indian village of Dolores, adjacent to the town of San Miguel el Grande, lying in the province of Guanajuato. One of the conspirators, being about to die, sent for his priest, and, confessing the plot, revealed also the names of his accomplices. The curate Hidalgo was one of the chiefs of this revolutionary band, and the viceroy Venegas, hoping to crush the league in its bud, dispatched orders for his arrest and imprisonment as soon as the confession of the dead conspirator was disclosed to him. Hidalgo's colleagues were also included in this order, but some of the secret friends of the insurgents learned what was occurring at court and appraised the patriot-priest of his imminent danger. The news first reached Don Ignacio Allende, who commanded a small body of the king's troops in San Miguel, and who hastened with the disastrous tidings to his friend at Dolores. Con-

cealment and flight were now equally unavailing.   The troops of
Allende were speedily won to the cause of their captain, while the
Indians of Dolores rushed to defend their beloved pastor.   As
they marched from their village to San Miguel and thence to
Zelaya, the natives, armed with clubs, slings, staves, and missiles,
thronged to their ranks from every mountain and valley.   The
wretched equipment of the insurgents shows their degraded condition as well as the passionate fervor with which they blindly
rushed upon the enemies of their race. Hidalgo put on his military
coat over the cassock, and, perhaps unwisely, threw himself at the
head of a revolution, which rallied at the cry of " Death to the
Gachupines." [4]

The result of this onslaught was dreadful.   Wherever the
rebellious army passed Spaniards and uncomplying creoles they
were indiscriminately slaughtered, and though many of the latter
were originally combined with the conspirators and eagerly longed
for the emancipation of their country, they were dismayed by the
atrocities of the wild insurgents.   As the rebel chief, armed with
the sword and cross, pressed onward, immense numbers of Indians
flocked to his banner, so that when he left Zelaya a fierce and undisciplined mob of twenty thousand hailed him as undisputed commander. At the head of this predatory band he descended upon the
noble city of Guanajuato, in the heart of the wealthiest mining
district of Mexico.   The Spaniards and some of the creoles resolved upon a stout resistance, shut themselves up in the city and
refused the humane terms offered by Hidalgo upon condition of
surrender.   This rash rejection led to an immediate attack and
victory.   When the city fell it was too late for the insurgent priest
to stay the savage fury of his troops.   The Spaniards and their
adherents were promiscuously slaughtered by the troops, and for
three days the sacking of the city continued, until, wearied with
conquest, the rebels at length stopped the plunder of the town.
Immense treasures hoarded in this place for many years were the
fruits of this atrocious victory which terrified the Mexican authorities and convinced them that the volcanic nature of the people had
been fully roused, and that safety existed alone in uncompromising
resistance.

[4] This term has been variously interpreted; it is supposed to be an ancient
Indian word significant of contempt. It is applied by the natives to the
European Spaniards or their full-blooded descendants. See Robinson's " His-
tory of the Mexican Revolution," p. 15.

The original rebellion was thus thrown from the hands of the creoles into those of the Indians. A war of races was about to break out; and although there were not among the insurgents more than a thousand muskets, yet the mere numerical force of such an infuriate crowd was sufficient to dismay the staunchest. The viceroy Venegas and the church therefore speedily combined to hurl their weapons against the rebels. While the former issued proclamations or decrees and dispatched troops under the command of Truxillo to check Hidalgo, who was advancing on the capital, the latter declared all the rebels to be heretics, and excommunicated them in a body.

But the arms of the Spanish chiefs and the anathemas of the Roman Church were unequal to the task of resistance. Hidalgo was attacked by Truxillo at Las Cruces, about eight leagues from the capital, where the Indian army overwhelmed the Spanish general and drove him back to Mexico, with the loss of his artillery. In this action we find it difficult to apportion, with justice, the ferocity between the combatants, for Truxillo boasted in this dispatch that he had defended the defile with the "obstinacy of Leonidas," and had even "fired upon the bearers of a flag of truce which Hidalgo sent him."

The insurgents followed up their success at Las Cruces by pursuing the foe until they arrived at the hacienda of Quaximalpa, within fifteen miles of the City of Mexico. But here a fatal distrust of his powers seems first to have seized the warrior priest. Venegas, it is said, contrived to introduce secret emissaries into his camp, who impressed Hidalgo and his officers with the belief that the capital was abundantly prepared for defense, and that an assault upon the disciplined troops of Spain by a disordered multitude without firearms would only terminate in the rout and destruction of all his forces. In fact, he seems to have been panic-stricken, and to have felt unable to control the revolutionary tempest he had raised. Accordingly, in an evil moment for his cause, he commenced a retreat, after having remained several days in sight of the beautiful City of Mexico, upon which he might easily have swept down from the mountain like an eagle to his prey.

It is related by the historians of these wars that in spite of all Venegas's boasted valor and assurance, he was not a little dismayed by the approach of Hidalgo. The people shared his alarm, and would probably have yielded at once to the insurgents, whose imposing forces were crowding into the valley. But in this strait the viceroy had recourse to the well-known superstitions of the people in order to allay their fears. He caused the celebrated image of the Virgin of Remedios to be brought from the mountain village, where it was generally kept in a chapel, to the cathedral, with great pomp and ceremony. Thither he proceeded, in full uniform, to pay his respects to the figure, and after imploring the Virgin to take the government into her own hands, he terminated his appeal by laying his baton of command at her feet.

It is now that we first encounter in Mexican history the name of Don Felix Maria Calleja, a name that is coupled with all that is shameless, bloody, and atrocious in modern warfare. Calleja was placed at the head of a well-appointed creole army of ten thousand men and a train of artillery, and with these disciplined forces, which he had been for some time concentrating, he was ordered to pursue Hidalgo.[6] The armies met at Aculco, and the Indians in their first encounter with a body of regulars exhibited an enthusiastic bravery that nearly defies belief. They were almost as completely ignorant of the use or power of firearms as their Aztec ancestors three hundred years before. They threw themselves upon the serried ranks of infantry with clubs and staves. Rushing up to the mouths of the cannon they drove their sombreros or hats of straw into the muzzles. Order, command, or discipline was entirely unknown to them. Their effort was simply to overwhelm by superiority of numbers. But the cool phalanx of creoles stood firm, until the Indian disorder became so great, and their strength so exhausted by repeated yet fruitless efforts, that the regulars commenced the work of slaughter with impunity. Calleja boasts that Hidalgo lost " ten thousand men, of whom five thousand were put to the sword." It seems, however, that he was unable to capture or disband the remaining insurgents, for Hidalgo retreated to Guanajuato, and then fell back on Guadalaxara, leaving in the former city a guard under his friend Allende.

Calleja next attacked the rebel forces at the hacienda of Marfil, and having defeated Allende, who defended himself bravely, rushed onward toward the city of Guanajuato. This place he

---

[5] Ward, "Mexico in 1827," vol. I. p. 169.

[6] The creoles, although unfriendly to the Spaniards and ready to rebel against them, were nevertheless willing to aid them against the Indians, whom they more reasonably regarded, under the circumstances, as the more dangerous of the two classes.

entered as conqueror. "The sacrifice of the prisoners of Marfil," says Robinson, "was not sufficient to satiate his vindictive spirit. He glutted his vengeance on the defenseless population of Guanajuato. Men, women, and children were driven by his orders into the great square; and fourteen thousand of these wretches, it is alleged, were butchered in a most barbarous manner. Their throats were cut. The principal fountain of the city literally overflowed with blood. But far from concealing these savage acts, Calleja in his account of the conflict exults in the honor of communicating the intelligence that he had purged the city of its rebellious population. The only apology offered for the sacrifice was that it would have wasted too much powder to have shot them, and therefore on the principle of economy he cut their throats. Thus was this unfortunate city, in a single campaign, made the victim of both loyalists and insurgents.

Hidalgo and his division were soon joined by Allende, and although they suffered all the disasters of a bad retreat as well as of Spanish victories, he still numbered about eighty thousand under his banners. He awaited Calleja at Guadalaxara, which he had surrounded with fortifications and armed with cannon, dragged by the Indians over mountain districts from the port of San Blas on the Pacific; but it is painful to record the fact that in this city Hidalgo was guilty of great cruelties to all the Europeans. Ward relates that between seven and eight hundred victims fell beneath the assassin's blade. A letter, produced on Hidalgo's trial, written to one of his lieutenants, charges the officer to seize as many Spaniards as he possibly can, and moreover directs him, if he has any reason to suspect his prisoners of entertaining seditious or restless ideas, to bury them at once in oblivion by putting such persons to death in some secret and solitary place, where their fate may remain forever unknown! As the cruelty of Old Spain to the Mexicans had well-nigh driven them to despair, such savage assassinations in turn drove the Spaniards to revenge, or at least furnished them with an excuse for their horrible atrocities.

Calleja, intent on the pursuit of his Indian prey, was not long in following Hidalgo. The insurgent chief endeavored to excite the ardor of his troops, while he preserved some show of discipline in their ranks; and, thus prepared, he gave battle to the Spaniards, at the bridge of Calderon, on January 17, 1811. At first Hidalgo was successful, but the rebels were no match for the royal troops kept in reserve by Calleja. With these he made a fierce charge upon the Indians, and sweeping through their broken masses he " pursued and massacred them by thousands."

Calleja was not a person either to conciliate or to pause in victory. He believed that rebellion could only be rooted out by utter destruction of the insurgents and their seed. Accordingly orders were issued to " exterminate the inhabitants of every town or village that showed symptoms of adherence to the rebels," while from the pulpit new denunciations were fulminated against all who opposed the royal authority. The insurgent chiefs fled, and reached Saltillo with about four thousand men. There it was resolved to leave Rayon in command, while Hidalgo, Allende, Aldama, and Absolo endeavored to reach the United States with an escort for the purpose of purchasing munitions of war with the treasure they had saved from the sacking of Guanajuato. But these fierce and vindictive soldiers were destined to end their lives by treachery. Hidalgo's associate rebel, Ignacio Elizondo, hoping to make his peace with the government by betraying so rich a prize, delivered them up to the authorities on March 21, 1811, at Acatila de Bajan. Hidalgo was taken to Chihuahua, and, after being degraded from holy orders, was shot on July 27, while Calleja was rewarded for his victories with the title of Conde de Calderon, won by his brilliant charge at the bridge near Guanajuato.[7]

Such is an outline of the warfare between the Sylla and Marius of this continent, and of some of the most prominent events in the origin of that revolution which finally resulted in the Mexican independence.

After Hidalgo's death the country was for a considerable time involved in a guerrilla warfare which extended throughout the whole territory of Mexico to the *provincias internas* of the north. Rayon assumed command of the fragments of Hidalgo's forces at Saltillo and retired to Zacatecas, but he had no command, or indeed authority, except over his own men. The whole country was in ferment. The valley of Mexico was full of eager partisans, who lassoed the sentinels even at the gates of the town; yet in all the chief cities the viceroy's authority was still acknowledged.

[7] Hidalgo's head was cut off and sent as a present to the city of Guanajuato, where it was exposed upon a pike on the roof of the Granaditas Castle. To-day that pike is considered as a most sacred relic, and in front of the castle, now used as a prison, stands a bronze statue of the patriot priest.

Men of reflection immediately saw that the cause of liberation would be lost if, amid all these elements of boiling discontent, there was no unity of opinion and action. The materials of success were ample throughout the nation, but they required organization under men in whose judgment and bravery the insurgent masses could rely.

Such were the opinions of Rayon and his friends who, in May, 1811, occupied Zitacuaro, when on the 10th of the following September they assembled a junta, or central government, composed of five members chosen by a large body of the most respectable landed proprietors in the neighborhood, in conjunction with the ayuntamiento and inhabitants of the town.

The doctrines of this junta were liberal, but they maintained a close intimacy with Spain, and even admitted the people's willingness to receive Ferdinand VII. as sovereign of Mexico, provided he abandoned his European possessions for New Spain. When Morelos joined the junta he disapproved this last concession to the royalists, though it was chiefly defended by Rayon as an expedient measure when dealing with people over whom the name of king still exercised the greatest influence. This junta was finally merged in the congress of Chilpanzingo. Its manifesto, directed to the viceroy in March, 1812, is worthy of remembrance, as it contains the several doctrines of the revolution admirably expressed by its author, Dr. Cos. He paints in forcible language the misery created by the fifteen months of civil war, and the small reliance that Spain could place on creole troops, whose sympathies at present, and whose efforts in the end, would all be thrown into the scale of their country. He assumes as fundamental principles that America and Spain are naturally equal; that America has as much right to her Cortes as Spain has to hers; that the existing rulers in the Peninsula have no just authority over Mexico as long as their sovereign is a captive, and, finally, he proposes that if " the Europeans will consent to give up the offices they hold and allow the assemblage of a general congress, their persons and property shall be religiously respected, their salaries paid, and the same privileges granted them as to native Mexicans, who, on their side, will acknowledge Ferdinand as the legitimate sovereign, and assist the Peninsula with their treasure, while they will at all times regard the Spaniards as fellow-subjects of the same great empire."

The alternative of war was presented to the viceroy together with these moderate demands, but he was only requested to abate the personal cruelties that had hitherto been committed, and to save the towns and villages from sacking or destruction by fire. Yet the insane Venegas would listen to no terms with the rebels, and caused the manifesto to be burned in the great square by the common executioner. The principles of the document, however, had been spread abroad among the people, and the flames of the hangman could no longer destroy the liberal doctrines which were deeply sown in the hearts of the people.

The distinguished revolutionary chief, Morelos, a clergyman, now appears prominently upon the stage. He had been commissioned by Hidalgo as captain-general of the provinces on the southwest coast in 1810, and departed for his government with as sorry an army as the troop of Falstaff. His escort consisted of a few servants from his curacy, armed with six muskets and some old lances. But he gathered forces as he advanced. The Galeanas joined him with their adherents and swelled his numbers to near a thousand. They advanced to Acapulco, and having captured it with abundant booty, the insurgents soon found their ranks joined by numerous important persons, and among them the Cura Matamoros and the Bravos, whose names have ever since been prominently connected with the history and development of Mexico.

The year 1811 was passed in a series of petty engagements, but in January, 1812, the insurgents penetrated within twenty-five leagues of the capital, where Galeana and Bravo took the town of Tasco.

Morelos was victorious in several other actions in the same and succeeding months, and pushed his advance guards into the valley of Mexico, where he occupied Chalco and San Agustin de las Cuevas, about twelve miles from the metropolis. Morelos finally resolved to make his stand at Cuautla, in the *tierra caliente,* on the other side of the mountain ranges which hem in the valley, and to this place the viceroy Venegas dispatched Calleja, who was summoned from the north and west, where, as may readily be imagined, so fiery a spirit had not been idle or innocent since the defeat of Hidalgo.

On January 1, 1812, Calleja reached Zitacuaro, whence the alarmed junta fled to Sultepec. The insatiate Spaniard took the town, decimated the inhabitants, razed the walls to the ground, and burned the dwellings, sparing only the churches and convents. After this dreadful revenge upon a settlement which had committed no crime but in harboring the junta, he made a triumphal entrance into Mexico, and on February 14, after a quarrel with the viceroy, and a solemn *Te Deum,* he departed toward Morelos, who was shut up in Cuautla de Amilpas.

On the 19th Calleja attacked the town, but was forced to retreat. He then regularly besieged the place and its insurgent visitors for more than two months and a half. In this period the troops on both sides were not unoccupied. Various skirmishes took place, but without signal results of importance to either party. Morelos strove to prolong the siege until the rainy season set in, when he felt confident that Calleja would be forced to withdraw his troops, who could not endure the combined heat and moisture of the *tierra caliente* during the summer months. Calleja, on the other hand, supposed that by sealing the town hermetically, and cutting off all supplies, its inhabitants and troops would soon be forced to surrender. Nor did he act unwisely for the success of his master. Famine prevailed in the besieged garrison. Corn was almost the only food. A cat sold for six dollars, a lizard for two, and rats and other vermin for one. But Morelos still continued firm, hoping by procrastination and endurance to preserve the constancy of his men until the month of June, when the country is generally deluged with rain and rendered insalubrious to all who dwell habitually in colder regions or are unacclimated in the lower valleys and tablelands of Mexico. His hopes, however, were not destined to be realized, for upon consultation it was found absolutely necessary to risk a general engagement or to abandon the town. The general engagement was considered injudicious in the present condition of his troops, so that no alternative remained but that of retreat. This was safely effected on the night of May 2, 1812, notwithstanding the whole army of the insurgents was obliged to pass between the enemy's batteries. After quitting the town, the forces were ordered to disperse, so as to avoid forming any concentrated point of attack for the pursuing Spaniards, and to reunite as soon as possible at Izucar, which was held by Don Miguel Bravo. Calleja entered the abandoned town cautiously after the departure of the besieged, but the cruel revenge he took on the innocent inhabitants and harmless edifices is indelibly imprinted in Mexican history as one of the darkest stains on the character of a soldier whose memory deserves the execration of civilized men.

From Izucar, Morelos entered Tehuacan triumphantly, whence he passed to Orizaba, where he captured artillery, vast quantities of tobacco, and a large amount of treasure. But he was not allowed to rest long in peace. The regular forces pursued his partisan warriors; and we next hear of him at Oaxaca, where he took possession of the town after a brief resistance. It was at this place that Guadalupe Victoria, afterwards president of the republic, performed a feat which merits special remembrance as an act of extraordinary heroism and daring in the face of an enemy. The town was moated and the single drawbridge suspended, so as to cut off the approach of the insurgents. There were no boats to cross the stagnant water, and the insurgents, as they approached, were dismayed by the difficulty of reaching a town which seemed almost in their grasp. At this moment Guadalupe Victoria sprang into the moat, swam across the strait in sight of the soldiers in the town, who seem to have been paralyzed by his signal courage, and cut the ropes that suspended the drawbridge, which, immediately falling over the moat, allowed the soldiers of Morelos a free entrance into the city.

Here Morelos rested for some time undisturbed by the Spaniards. He conquered the whole of the province with the exception of Acapulco, to which he laid siege in February, 1813, but it did not lower its flag until the following August. The control of a whole province, and the victories of Bravo and Matamoros elsewhere in 1812 and 1813, considerably increased the importance and influence of Morelos, who now devoted himself to the assemblage of a national congress at Chilpanzingo, composed of the original junta of Zitacuaro, the deputies elected by the province of Oaxaca, and others selected by them as representatives of the provinces which were in the royalists' hands. On November 13, 1813, this body published a declaration of the absolute independence of Mexico.[8]

[8] We must mention an event characteristic of Bravo, which occurred during this period. Bravo took Palmar by storm, after a resistance of three days. Three hundred prisoners fell into his hands, who were placed at his disposal by Morelos. Bravo immediately offered them to the viceroy Venegas in exchange for his father, Don Leonardo Bravo, who had been sentenced to death in the capital. The offer was rejected, and Don Leonardo ordered to immediate execution. But the son at once commanded the prisoners to be liberated, saying that he "wished to put it out of his power to avenge his parent's death, lest, in the first moments of grief the temptation should prove irresistible."—Ward, vol. I. p. 204.

This was the period at which the star of the great leader, Morelos, culminated. Bravo was still occasionally successful, and the commander-in-chief, concentrating his forces at Chilpanzingo, prepared an expedition against the province of Valladolid. He departed on November 8, 1813, and, marching across a hitherto untraversed country of a hundred leagues, he reached this point about Christmas. But here he found a large force under Llano and Colonel Iturbide, who was still a loyalist, drawn up to encounter him. He attacked the enemy rashly with his jaded troops, and on the following day was routed, with the loss of his best regiments and all his artillery.

At Puruaran, Iturbide again assailed Morelos successfully, and Matamoros was taken prisoner. Efforts were made to save the life of this eminent soldier, yet Don Felix Maria Calleja, who had succeeded Venegas as viceroy in 1813, was too cruelly ungenerous to spare so daring a rebel. He was shot, and his death was avenged by the slaughter of all the prisoners who were in the hands of the insurgents.

For a while Morelos struggled bravely against adversity, his character and resources rising with every new danger, difficulty, or loss. But the die was cast. Oaxaca was recaptured by the royalists on March 28, 1814. Miguel Bravo died at Puebla on the scaffold, Galeana fell in battle, and the congress was driven from Chilpanzingo to the forest of Apatzingo, where, on October 22, 1814, it enacted the constitution which bears the name of its wild birthplace.

From this temporary refuge the insurgents resolved to cross the country by rapid marches to Tehuacan in the province of Puebla, where Mier y Teran had gathered a considerable force, which Morelos imagined would become the nucleus of an overwhelming army as soon as he joined them. But his hopes were not destined to be realized. He had advanced as far as Tesmaluca when the Indians of the village betrayed his slender forces to General Concha, who fell upon them on November 5, 1815, in the narrow gorge of a mountain road. The assault was from the rear, so that Morelos, ordering Nocalas Bravo to hasten his march with the main body of the army as an escort for the ill-starred congress, resolved to fight the royalists until he placed the national legislature out of danger. "My life," said he, "is of little consequence, provided congress be saved; my race was run when I saw an independent government established!"

The brave soldier-priest, with fifty men, maintained the pass against Concha until only one trooper was left beside him. So furious was his personal bearing during this mortal conflict, that the royalists feared to advance until he was bereft of all support. When finally captured, he was stripped, chained, treated with the most shameless cruelty, and carried back to Tesmaluca. Concha, however, was less cruel than his men. He received the rebel chief politely, and dispatched him to the capital for trial. Crowds of eager citizens flocked to see the celebrated partisan warrior who had so long held the Spanish forces at bay. But his doom was sealed; and on December 22, 1815, Concha removed him to the hospital of San Cristoval. After dining with the general, and thanking him for his kindness, he walked to the rear of the building, where, kneeling down, he bound a handkerchief over his eyes and, uttering the simple ejaculation, "Lord, if I have done well, Thou knowest it; if ill, to Thy infinite mercy I commend my soul," he gave the fatal signal to the soldiers who were drawn up to shoot him.

Chapter XXIV

THE SUCCESS OF THE POPULAR CAUSE. 1815-1824

WITH the death of Morelos the hopes of the insurgents were crushed and their efforts paralyzed. This extraordinary man, so fertile in resources, and blending in himself the mingled power of priest and general, had secured the confidence of the masses, who found among his officers none upon whom they could rely with perfect reliance. Besides this, the congress which had been conducted safely to Tehuacan by Bravo, was summarily dissolved by General Teran, who considered it an " inconvenient appendage of a camp." We cannot but regard this act of the general's as unwise at a moment when the insurgents lost such a commander as Morelos. By the dissolution of the congress the nation abandoned another point of reunion; and from that moment the cause began to fail in all parts of the country.

The constitution sanctioned by the Cortes in 1812 had meanwhile been proclaimed in Mexico, on September 29 of that year; and while the people felt somewhat freer under it, they were enabled by the liberty of the press, which lasted sixty-six days, to expend their newborn patriotism on paper instead of in battles. These popular excitements served to sustain the spirits of the people, notwithstanding the losses of the army; so that when Apodaca assumed the reins of the viceroyalty in 1816 the country was still republican at heart, though all the insurgent generals were either captured or hidden in the wilderness, while their disbanded forces in most instances had accepted the indulto, or pardon, proffered for their return to allegiance.

The remaining officers of Morelos spread themselves over the country, as there was no longer any center of action, and each of them, occupying a different district, managed for a while to support revolutionary fervor throughout the neighborhood. Guerrero occupied the west coast, where he maintained himself until the year 1821, when he joined Iturbide. Rayon commanded in the vicinity of Tlalpujahua, where he successively maintained two fortified camps on the Cerro del Gallo, and on Coporo. Teran held the district of Tehuacan, in Puebla. Bravo was a wanderer throughout the country. The Bajio was tyrannized over by the Padre Torres, while Guadalupe Victoria occupied the important province of Vera Cruz.

The chief spite of the royalists, who hunted these republican heroes among the forests and mountain fastnesses of Mexico, as the Covenanters had been hunted in Scotland, seems to have fallen upon the last named of these patriot generals. Victoria's haunt was chiefly in the passes near the Puente del Rey, now the Puente Nacional, or national bridge, on the road leading from the port of Vera Cruz to the capital. He was prepared to act either with a large force of guerrillas, or with a simple bodyguard; and, knowing the country perfectly, he was enabled to descend from his fastnesses among the rocks and thus to cut off almost entirely all communication between the coast and the metropolis. At length superior forces were sent to pursue him with relentless fury. His men gradually deserted when the villages that formerly supplied them with food refused further contributions. Efforts were made to seduce him from his principles and to ensure his loyalty. But he refused the rank and rewards offered by the viceroy as the price of his submission. At length he found himself alone in his resistance, in the midst of countrymen who, if they would no longer fight under his banner, were too faithful to betray him. Yet he would not abandon the cause, but, taking his sword and a small stock of raiment, departed for the mountains, where he wandered for thirty months, living on the fruits of the forest and gnawing the bones of dead animals found in their recesses. Nor did he emerge from this impenetrable concealment until two faithful Indians, whom he had known in prosperous days, sought him out with great difficulty, and, communicating the joyous intelligence of the revolution of 1821, brought him back once more to their villages, where he was received with enthusiastic reverence as a patriot raised from the dead. When discovered by the Indians he was worn to a skeleton, covered with hair, and clad in a tattered wrapper; but amid all his distress and losses he had preserved and treasured his loyalty to the cause of liberty and his untarnished sword!

Meanwhile another actor in this revolutionary army had appeared upon the stage. This was Xavier Mina, a guerrilla chief of old Spain, who fled from his country in consequence of the unfortunate effort to organize an outbreak in favor of the Cortes, at

Pampeluna, after the dissolution of that assembly by the king. He landed on the coast of Mexico at Soto la Marina with a brave band of foreigners, chiefly North Americans, on April 15, 1817. His forces amounted to only 359 men, including officers, of whom 51 deserted before he marched into the interior. Leaving 100 of these soldiers at Soto la Marina under the command of Major Sarda, he attempted with the remainder to join the independents in the heart of the country.

Mina pressed onwards successfully, defeating several royalist parties, until he reached Sombrero, whence he sallied forth upon numerous expeditions, one of which was against the fortified hacienda or plantation of the Marques de Jaral, a creole nobleman, from which the inhabitants and the owner fled at his approach. His troops sacked this wealthy establishment, and Mina transferred to the public chest one hundred and forty thousand dollars, found concealed in the house. This nobleman, it is true, had given in his adhesion to the royal cause and fortified his dwelling against the insurgents who hitherto refrained from attacking him. Nevertheless, the unprovoked blow of an independent leader against a native of the country, and especially against a man whose extensive farming operations concentrated the interests of so large a laboring class, was not calculated to inspire confidence in Mina among the masses of the people.

While the guerrilla chief was thus pursuing his way successfully in the heart of the country, and receiving occasional reinforcements from the natives, the garrison he left at Soto la Marina fell into the hands of Spanish levies, two thousand of whom surrounded the slender band. Notwithstanding the inequality of forces between the assailants and the besieged, the royalists were unable to take the place by storm; but after repeated repulses General Arredondo proposed terms, which were accepted by Major Sarda, the independent commander. It is scarcely necessary to say that this condition was not fulfilled by the Spaniards, who sent the capitulated garrison in irons, by a circuitous journey, to the Castle of San Juan de Ulua at Vera Cruz, whence some of the unfortunate wretches were marched into the interior, while others were dispatched across the sea to the dungeons of Cadiz, Melilla, and Ceuta. This was a severe blow to Mina, who nevertheless was unparalyzed by it, but continued active in the vicinity of Sombrero, to which he retreated after an ill-judged attempt upon the town of Leon, where the number of his troops was considerably diminished. Sombrero was invested soon after by a force of 3540 soldiers under Don Pascual Liñan, who had been appointed field marshal by Apodaca, and dispatched to the Bajio. This siege was ultimately successful on the part of the royalists. The fresh supplies promised to Mina did not arrive. Colonel Young, his second in command, died in repulsing an assault; and upon the garrison's attempting to evacuate the town, under Colonel Bradburn, on the night of August 19, the enemy fell upon the independents with such vigor that but fifty of Mina's whole corps escaped. " No quarter," says Ward, "was given in the field, and the unfortunate wretches, who had been left in the hospital wounded, were by Liñan's orders carried or dragged along the ground from their beds to the square where they were stripped and shot!"

Mina as a last resort threw himself into the fort of Los Remedios, a natural fortification on the lofty mountain chain rising out of the plains of the Bajio between Silao and Benjamo, separated from the rest by precipices and deep ravines.

Liñan's army sat down before Remedios on August 27. Mina left the town so as to assail the army from without by his guerrillas, while the garrison kept the main body engaged with the fort. During this period he formed the project of attacking the town of Guanajuato, which, in fact, he accomplished; yet after his troops had penetrated the heart of the city their courage failed and they retreated before the loyalists, who rallied after the panic created by the unexpected assault at nightfall. On retreating from Guanajuato our partisan warrior took the road to the Rancho del Venadito, where he designed passing the night in order to consult upon his future plans with his friend, Mariano Herrera. Here he was detected by a friar, who apprised Orrantia of the brave Mina's presence, and on the morning of October 27 he was seized and conveyed to Irapuato. On November 11, 1817, in the twenty-eighth year of his age, he was shot, by order of Apodaca, on a rock in sight of Los Remedios.

At the end of December the ammunition of the insurgents in this stronghold was entirely exhausted, and its evacuation was resolved on. This was attempted on January 1, 1818, but, with the exception of Padre Torres, the commander, and twelve of Mina's division, few or none of the daring fugitives escaped. The wretched inmates of the fort, the women, and garrison hospitals of

wounded were cut down, bayoneted, and burned.   On March 6 the
fort of Jauxilla, the insurgents' last stronghold in the central parts
of the country, fell, while toward the middle of the year all the
revolutionary chiefs were dislodged and without commands, except Guerrero, who still maintained himself on the right bank
of the River Zacatula, near Colima, on the Pacific.   But even he
was cut off from communication with the interior, and was altogether without hope of assistance from without.   The heart of
the nation and the east coast—which was of most importance so far
as the reception of auxiliaries by the independents was concerned
—were thus in complete possession of the royalists; so that the
viceroy declared in his dispatches to Spain that "he would be
answerable for the safety of Mexico without a single additional
soldier being sent out to reinforce the armies that were in the
field."

But the viceroy Apodaca, confident as he was of the defeat of
the insurrection, did not know the people with whom he dealt as
well as his predecessor, Calleja,[1] who, with all his cruelty, seems
to have enjoyed sagacious intervals in which he comprehended
perfectly the deep-seated causes of the revolutionary feeling in
Mexico, even if he was indisposed to sympathize with them or to
permit their manifestation by the people.   In fact, the revolution
was not quelled.   It slept, for want of a leader; but at last he
appeared in the person of Agustin de Iturbide, a native Mexican
whose military career in the loyalist cause had been not only brilliant, but eminently useful, for it was in consequence of the two
severe blows inflicted by him upon the insurgents in the actions of
Valladolid and Puruaran that the great army of Morelos was
routed and destroyed.

In 1820 Apodaca, who was no friend of the constitution, and
who suffered a diminution of power by its operation, was well-
disposed to put it down by force and to proclaim once more the
absolute authority of the king.   The elective privileges which the
constitution secured to the people, together with the principles of
freedom which those elections were calculated to foster among
the masses, were considered by the viceroy as dangerous in a
country so recently the theater of revolution.   The insurrection
was regarded by him as ended forever.   He despised, perhaps, the

[1] See Calleja's confidential letter to the Spanish minister of war, with a
private report on the Mexican Revolution. Ward, vol. I. p. 509—Appendix.

few distinguished persons who yet quietly manifested their preference for liberalism; and, like all men of despotic character and
confident of power, he undervalued the popular masses, among
whom there is ever to be found common sense, true appreciation
of natural rights, and firmness to vindicate them whenever they
are confident of the leaders who are to control their destiny when
embarked upon the stormy sea of rebellion.

Apodaca, in pursuit of his project to restore absolutism on the
continent, fixed his eyes upon the gallant Iturbide, whose polished
manners, captivating address, elegant person, ambitious spirit, and
renowned military services signalized him as a person likely to
play a distinguished part in the restoration of a supreme power
whose first favors would probably be showered upon the successful
soldier of a crusade against constitutional freedom.

Accordingly the viceroy offered Iturbide the command of a
force upon the west coast, at the head of which he was to proclaim
the reëstablishment of the king's absolute authority. The command was accepted; but Iturbide, who had been for four years
unemployed, had in this interval of repose reflected well upon the
condition of Mexico, and was satisfied that if the creoles could be
induced to coöperate with the independents, the Spanish yoke
might be cast off. There were only eleven Spanish expeditionary
regiments in the whole of Mexico, and although there were upwards
of seventy thousand old Spaniards in the different provinces who
supported these soldiers, they could not effectually oppose the
seven veteran and seventeen provincial regiments of natives, aided
by the masses of people who had signified their attachment to
liberalism.

Instead, therefore, of allying himself with the cause of a
falling monarchy, whose reliance must chiefly be confined to succors
from across the ocean, Iturbide resolved to abandon the viceroy
and his criminal project against the constitution, and to throw himself with his forces upon the popular cause of the country. It was
a bold but successful move.

On February 2, 1821, he was at the small town of Iguala, on
the road to Acapulco; and on that day, at his headquarters, he
proclaimed the celebrated Plan of Iguala, the several principles of
which are: " Independence, the maintenance of Roman Catholic-
ity, and Union; " whence his forces obtained the name of the
" Army of the Three Guaranties."

As this is probably one of the most important state papers in the history of Mexico, and is often referred to without being fully understood, we shall present it to the reader entire:

PLAN OF IGUALA.

ARTICLE 1.—The Mexican nation is independent of the Spanish nation, and of every other, even on its own continent.

ART. 2.—Its religion shall be the Catholic, which all its inhabitants profess.

ART. 3.—They shall all be united, without any distinction between Americans and Europeans.

ART. 4.—The government shall be a constitutional monarchy.

ART. 5.—A junta shall be named, consisting of individuals who enjoy the highest reputation in different parties which have shown themselves.

ART. 6.—This junta shall be under the presidency of his excellency the Conde del Venadito, the present viceroy of Mexico.

ART. 7.—It shall govern in the name of the nation, according to the laws now in force, and its principal business will be to convoke, according to such rules as it shall deem expedient, a congress for the formation of a constitution more suitable to the country.

ART. 8.—His Majesty Ferdinand VII. shall be invited to the throne of the empire, and in case of his refusal, the Infantes Don Carlos and Don Francisco De Paula.

ART. 9.—Should his Majesty Ferdinand VII. and his august brothers decline the invitation, the nation is at liberty to invite to the imperial throne any member of reigning families whom it may choose to select.

ART. 10.—The formation of the constitution by the congress, and the oath of the emperor to observe it, must precede his entry into the country.

ART. 11.—The distinction of castes is abolished, which was made by the Spanish law, excluding them from the rights of citizenship. All the inhabitants are citizens, and equal, and the door of advancement is open to virtue and merit.

ART. 12.—An army shall be formed for the support of religion, independence, and union, guaranteeing these three principles, and therefore shall be called the army of the three guaranties.

ART. 13.—It shall solemnly swear to defend the fundamental basis of this plan.

ART. 14.—It shall strictly observe the military ordinances now in force.

ART. 15.—There shall be no other promotions than those which are due to seniority, or which are necessary for the good of the service.

ART. 16.—The army shall be considered as of the line.

ART. 17.—The old partisans of independence who shall adhere to this plan shall be considered as individuals of this army.

ART. 18.—The patriots and peasants who shall adhere to it hereafter shall be considered as provincial militiamen.

ART. 19.—The secular and regular priests shall be continued in the state which they now are.

ART. 20.—All the public functionaries, civil, ecclesiastical, political, and military, who adhere to the cause of independence shall be continued in their offices, without any distinction between Americans and Europeans.

ART. 21.—Those functionaries, of whatever degree and condition who dissent from the cause of independence, shall be divested of their offices, and shall quit the territory without taking with them their families and effects.

ART. 22.—The military commandants shall regulate themselves according to the general instructions in conformity with this plan, which shall be transmitted to them.

ART. 23.—No accused person shall be condemned capitally by the military commandants. Those accused of treason against the nation, which is the next greatest crime after that of treason to the Divine Ruler, shall be conveyed to the fortress of Barbaras, where they shall remain until congress shall resolve on the punishment that ought to be inflicted on them.

ART. 24.—It being indispensable to the country that this plan should be carried into effect, inasmuch as the welfare of that country is its object, every individual of the army shall maintain it, to the shedding (if it be necessary) of the last drop of his blood.

Town of Iguala, February 24, 1821.

It will be seen by the Plan of Iguala that Mexico was designed to become an independent sovereignty under Ferdinand VII. or, in the event of his refusal, under the Infantes Don Carlos and

Don Francisco de Paula. Iturbide was still a royalist, not a republican; and it is very doubtful whether he would ever have assented to popular authority, even had his life been spared to witness the final development of the revolution. It is probable that his penetrating mind distinguished between popular hatred of unjust restraint and the genuine capacity of a nation for liberty, nor is it unlikely that he found among his countrymen but few of those self-controlling, self-sacrificing, and progressive elements which constitute the only foundation upon which a republic can be securely founded. His ambition had not yet been fully developed by success, and it cannot be imagined that he had already fixed his heart upon the imperial throne.

When the Plan of Iguala was proclaimed, the entire army of the future emperor, consisted of only eight hundred men, all of whom took the oath of fidelity to the project, though many deserted when they found the country was not immediately unanimous in its approval.

In the capital the viceroy appears to have been paralyzed by the sudden and unexpected movement of his officer. He paused, hesitated, failed to act, and was deposed by the Europeans, who treated him as they had Iturrigaray in 1808. Don Francisco de Novella, an artillery officer, was installed temporarily in his stead, but the appointment created a dissension among the people in the capital and the country, and this so completely prostrated the action of the central authorities, who might have crushed the revolution by a blow, that Iturbide was enabled to prosecute his designs throughout the most important parts of the interior of the country without the slightest resistance.

He seized a million of dollars on their way to the west coast, and joined Guerrero, who still held out on the River Zacatula with the last remnant of the old revolutionary forces. Guerrero gave in his adhesion to Iturbide as soon as he ascertained that it was the general's design to make Mexico independent, though in all likelihood he disapproved the other features of the plan. Guerrero's act was of the greatest national importance. It rallied all the veteran fighters and friends of Morelos and the Bravos. Almost all of the former leaders and their dispersed bands came forth at the cry of "independence," under the banner of Iturbide. Victoria even for a while befriended the rising hero; but he had fought for a liberal government, and did not long continue on amicable terms with one who could not control his truly independent spirit. The clergy as well as the people signified their intention to support the gallant insurgent; and in fact the whole country, from Vera Cruz to Acapulco, with the exception of the capital, was soon open in its adhesion to him and his army.

Iturbide was now in full authority, and while preparing to march on the City of Mexico, in which the viceroy *ad interim* was shut up, he learned that Don Juan O'Donoju had arrived at San Juan de Ulua to fill the place of Apodaca as viceroy. Proposals were immediately sent by the general to this new functionary, and in an interview with him at Cordova Iturbide proposed the adoption of the Plan of Iguala by treaty, as the only project by which the Spaniards in Mexico could be saved from the fury of the people and the sovereignty of the colony preserved for Ferdinand.

We shall not pause to inquire whether the viceroy was justified or even empowered to compromise the rights of Spain by such a compact. O'Donoju, though under the safeguard of a truce, was in truth a helpless man as soon as he touched the soil of Mexico, for no portions of it were actually under the Spanish authority except the castle of San Juan de Ulua and the capital, whose garrisons were chiefly composed of European levies. Humanity, perhaps, ultimately controlled his decision, and in the name of his master he recognized the independence of Mexico and yielded the metropolis to the "army of the three guaranties," which entered it peacefully on September 27, 1821. A provisional junta of thirty-six persons immediately elected a regency of five, of which Iturbide was president, and at the same time he was created generalissimo, lord high admiral, and assigned a yearly stipend of $120,000.

On February 24, 1822, the first Mexican congress, or cortes, met; but it contained within it the germ of all the future discontents which since that day have harassed and nearly ruined Mexico. Scarcely had this body met when three parties manifested their bitter animosities and personal ambitions. The Bourbonists adhered loyally to the Plan of Iguala, a constitutional monarchy and the sovereignty of Ferdinand. The Republicans discarded the plan as a device that had served its day, and insisted upon a central or federal republic; and, last of all, the partisans of the successful soldier still clung to all of the plan save the clause which gave the throne to a Bourbon prince, for at heart they desired to place

Iturbide himself upon it, and thus to cut off their country forever
from all connection with Europe.

As soon as O'Donoju's treaty of Cordova reached Spain, it
was nullified by the Cortes, and the Bourbon party in Mexico of
course fell with it.   The Republicans and Iturbidists alone remained on the field to contend for the prize, and after congress
had disgraced itself by incessant bickerings over the army and the
public funds, a certain Pio Marcha, first sergeant of the first regiment of infantry, gathered a band of leperos before the palace of
Iturbide on the night of May 18, 1822, and proclaimed him emperor, with the title of Agustin I.   A show of resistance was
made by Iturbide against the proffered crown, but it is likely that
it was in reality as faint as his joy was unbounded at the sudden elevation from a barrack room to the imperial palace.   Congress of course approved the decision of the mob and army.   The
provinces sanctioned the acts of their representatives, and Iturbide
ascended the throne.

But his reign was brief.   Rapid success, love of power, impatience of restraint,—all of which are characteristic of the Spanish
soldier,—made him strain the bonds of constitutional right.   His
struggles for control were incessant.   "He demanded," says
Ward, "a veto upon all articles of the constitution then under discussion, and the right of appointing and removing at pleasure the
members of the supreme tribunal of justice.   He recommended
also the establishment of a military tribunal in the capital, with
powers but little inferior to those exercised by the Spanish commandants during the revolution; and when these proposals were
firmly rejected, he arrested, on the night of August 26, 1822, fourteen of the deputies who had advocated during the discussion
principles but little in unison with the views of the government."

This high-handed measure and the openly manifested displeasure of congress produced so complete a rupture between the
emperor and the popular representatives that it was impossible to
conduct public affairs with any concert of action.   Accordingly
Iturbide dissolved the assembly, and on October 30, 1822, created
an instituent junta of forty-five persons selected by himself from
among the most pliant members of the recent congress.   This ir-
regularly formed body was intolerable to the people, while the
expelled deputies, who had returned to their respective districts, soon
spread the spirit of discontent and proclaimed the American

usurper to be as dangerous to the welfare of the country as had
been the European despot.

In November General Garza headed a revolt in the northern
provinces.   Santa Anna, then governor of Vera Cruz, declared
against the emperor.   General Echavari, sent by Iturbide to crush
the future president of Mexico, resolved not to stem the torrent of
public opinion, and joined the general he had been commissioned
to capture.   Guadalupe Victoria, driven to his fastnesses by the
emperor, who was unable to win the incorruptible patriot, descended once more from the mountain forests, where he had been
concealed, and joined the battalions of Santa Anna.   And on February 1, 1823, a convention, called the " Act of Casa-Mata," was
signed, by which the reëstablishment of the national representative assembly was pledged.

The country was soon in arms.   The Marques Vibanco, Generals Guerrero, Bravo, and Negrete, in various sections of the
nation, proclaimed their adhesion to the popular movement; and
on March 8, 1823, Iturbide, finding that the day was lost, offered
his abdication to such members of the old congress as he was able
to assemble hastily in the metropolis.   The abdication was, however, twice refused on the ground that congress, by accepting it,
would necessarily sanction the legality of his right to wear the
crown; nevertheless, that body permitted his departure from
Mexico, after endowing him liberally with an income of twenty-
five thousand dollars a year, besides providing a vessel to bear him
and his family to Leghorn in Italy.

Victoria, Bravo, and Negrete entered the capital on March
27, and were chosen by the old congress, which quickly reassem-
bled, as a triumvirate to exercise supreme executive powers until
the new congress assembled in the following August.   In October,
1824, this body finally sanctioned the federal constitution, which,
after various revolutions, overthrows, and reforms, was readopted
in the year 1847.

On July 14, 1824, a vessel under British colors was perceived
on the Mexican coast near the mouth of the Santander.   On the
next day a Polish gentleman came on shore from the ship, and,
announcing himself as Charles de Beneski, visited General Felix la
Garza, commandant of the district of Soto la Marina.   He professed to visit that remote district with a friend for the purpose of
purchasing land from the government on which they designed

establishing a colony. Garza gave them leave to enter the country for this purpose, but suspicions were soon aroused against the singular visitors, and they were arrested. As soon as the friend of the Pole was stripped of his disguise, the Emperor Iturbide stood in front of Garza, whom he had disgraced for his participation in the revolt during his brief reign.

La Garza immediately secured the prisoner and sent him to Padilla, where he delivered him to the authorities of Tamaulipas. The state legislature being in session, promptly resolved, in the excess of patriotic zeal, to execute a decree of the congress passed in the preceding April, by condemning the royal exile to death. Short time was given Iturbide to arrange his affairs. He was allowed no appeal to the general government. He confessed to a priest on the evening of July 19, and was led to the place of execution, where he fell, pierced with four balls, two of which took effect in his brain and two in his heart.

Thus perished the hero who, suddenly, unexpectedly, and effectually, crushed the power of Spain in North America. It is not fair to judge him by the standards that are generally applied to the life of a distinguished civilian, or even of a successful soldier, in countries where the habits and education of the people fit them for duties requiring forbearance, patience, or high intellectual culture. Iturbide was, according to all reliable accounts, a refined gentleman; yet he was tyrannical and sometimes cruel, for it is recorded in his own handwriting, that on Good Friday, 1814, " in honor of the day, he had just ordered three hundred excommunicated wretches to be shot! " His early life was passed in the saddle and the barrack room; nor had he much leisure to pursue the studies of a statesman, even if his mind had been capable of resolving all their mysteries. His temper was not calculated for the liberal debates of a free senate. He was better fitted to discipline an army than to guide a nation. Educated in a school in which subordination is a necessity, and where unquestioning obedience is exacted, he was unable to appreciate the rights of deliberative assemblies. He felt, perhaps, that in the disorganized condition of his country it was needful to control the people by force in order to save the remnant of civilization from complete anarchy. But he wanted conciliatory manners to seduce the congress into obedience to his behests, and he therefore unfortunately and unwisely played the military despot when he should have acted the part of a quiet diplomatist. Finding himself, in two years, emperor of Mexico, after being at the commencement of that period nothing more than commander of a regiment, it may be pardoned if he was bewildered by the rapidity of his rise, and if the air he breathed in his extraordinary ascent was too ethereal for a man of so excitable a temperament.

In every aspect of his character we must regard him as one altogether inadequate to shape the destiny of a nation emerging from the blood and smoke of two revolutions—a nation whose political tendencies toward absolute freedom were at that time naturally the positive reverse of his own.

Death sealed the lips of men who might have clamored for him in the course of a few years, when the insubordinate spirit that was soon manifested needed as bold an arm as that of Iturbide in his best days to check or guide it. Public opinion was decidedly opposed to his sudden and cruel slaughter. Mexicans candidly acknowledged that their country's independence was owing to him; and while they admitted that Garza's zeal for the emperor's execution might have been lawful, they believed that revenge for his former disgrace, rather than patriotism, induced the rash and ruthless soldier to hasten the death of the noble victim whom fortune had thrown in his lonely path.

Chapter XXV

STRUGGLES OF THE POLITICAL PARTIES. 1824-1843

WE must pause a moment over the past history of Mexico, for the portion we now approach has few of the elements either of union or patriotism which characterized the early struggles for national independence. The revolutionary war had merited and received the commendation of freemen throughout the world. The prolonged struggle exhibited powers of endurance, an unceasing resolution, and a determination to throw off European thraldom which won the respect of those northern powers in America which were most concerned in securing to themselves a republican neighborhood. But as soon as the domination of Spain was crushed the domestic quarrels of Mexico began, and we have already shown that in the three parties formed in the first congress were to be found the germs of all the feuds that have since vexed the republic or impeded its successful progress toward national grandeur. After the country had been so long a battlefield, it was perhaps difficult immediately to accustom the people to civil rule or to free them from the baleful influence which military glory is apt to throw round individuals who render important services to their country in war. Even in the United States, where the ballot-box instead of the bayonet has always controlled elections, and where loyalty to the constitution would blast the effort of ambitious men to place a conqueror in power by any other means than that of peaceful election, we constantly find how difficult it is to screen the people's eyes from the bewildering glare of military glory. What then could be expected from a country in which the self-relying, self-ruling, civil idea never existed at any period of its previous history? The revolution of the North American colonies was not designed to obtain liberty, for they were already free; but it was excited and successfully pursued in order to prevent the burdensome and aggressive impositions of England, which would have curtailed that freedom, and reduced the states to colonial dependence as well as royal or ministerial dictation. Mexico, on the contrary, had never been free. Spain regarded the country as a mine which was to be diligently wrought, and the masses of the people as acclimated serfs whose services were the legitimate perquisites of a court and aristocracy beyond the sea. There had been, among the kings and viceroys who controlled the destinies of New Spain, men who were swayed by just and amiable views of colonial government; but the majority considered Mexico as a speculation rather than an infant colony whose progressive destiny it was their duty to foster with all the care and wisdom of Christian magistrates. The minor officials of the viceroyal government misruled and peculated. They were all men of the hour, and even the viceroys themselves regarded their governments on the American continent as rewards for services in Europe, enabling them to secure fortunes with which they returned to the Castilian court, forgetful of the Indian miner and agriculturist from whose sweat their wealth was coined. The Spaniard never identified himself with Mexico. His home was on the other side of the Atlantic. Few of the best class formed permanent establishments in the viceroyalty; and all of them were too much interested in maintaining both the state of society and the castes which had been created by the conquerors to spend a thought upon the amelioration of the people. We do not desire to blacken by our commentary the fame of a great nation like that of Spain; yet this dreary but true portrait of national selfishness has been so often verified by all the colonial historians of America, and especially by Pazo and Zavala in their admirable historical sketches of Castilian misrule, that we deem it fair to introduce these palliations of Mexican misconduct since the revolution.

The people of New Spain were poor and uneducated; the aristocracy was rich, supercilious, and almost equally illiterate. It was a society without a middle ground, in which gold stood out in broad relief against rags. Was such a state of barbaric semi-civilization entitled or fitted to emerge at once into republicanism? Was it to be imagined that men who had always been controlled, could learn immediately to control themselves? Was it to be believed that the military personages, whose ambition is as proverbial as it is natural, would voluntarily surrender the power they possessed over the masses and retire to the obscurity and poverty of private life when they could enjoy the wealth and influence of political control so long as they maintained their rank in the army? This would have been too much to expect from the self-denial of creole chiefs; nor is it surprising to behold the people themselves looking toward these very men as proper persons to consolidate or shape the government they had established. It was the most natural thing conceivable to find Iturbide, Guerrero, Bustamante, Negrete, Bravo, Santa Anna, Paredes, and the whole host of revolutionary heroes succeeding each other in power, either constitutionally or by violence. The people knew no others. The military idea, military success, a name won in action, and repeated from lip to lip until the traditionary sound became a household word among the herdsmen, rancheros, vaqueros, and Indians—these were the sources of Mexican renown or popularity, and the appropriate objects of political reward and confidence. What individual among the four or five millions of Indians knew anything of the statesmen of their country who had never mixed in the revolutionary war or in the domestic brawls constantly occurring? There were no gazettes to spread their fame or merit, and even if there had been the people were unable to buy or peruse them. Among the mixed breeds and lower classes of creoles an equal degree of ignorance prevailed; and thus from the first epoch of independence the people ceased to be a true republican tribunal in Mexico, while the city was surrendered as the battlefield of all the political aspirants who had won reputations in the camp which were to serve them for other purposes in the capital. By this means the army rose to immediate significance and became the general arbiter in all political controversies. Nor was the church—that other overshadowing influence in all countries in which religion and the state are combined—a silent spectator in the division of national power. The Roman hierarchy, a large landholder, had much at stake in Mexico besides the mere authority which so powerful a body is always anxious to maintain over the consciences of the multitude. The church was thus a political element of great strength; and, combined with the army, created and sustained an important party, which has been untiring in its efforts to support centralism as the true political principle of Mexican government.

On October 4, 1824, a federal constitution, framed partly upon the model of the constitution of the United States, with some grafts from the Spanish constitution, was adopted by congress; and by it the territory comprehended in the old viceroyalty of New Spain, the captaincy-general of Yucatan, the commandancies of the eastern and western Internal Provinces, Upper and Lower California, with the lands and isles adjacent to both seas, were placed under the protection of this organic law. The religion of the Mexican nation was declared to be, in perpetuity, the Catholic Apostolic Roman; and the nation pledged its protection, at the same time prohibiting the exercise of any other!

Previous, however, to these constitutional enactments the country had not been entirely quiet, for as early as January of this year General Echavari, who occupied the state of Puebla, raised the standard of revolt against the triumvirate. This seditious movement was soon suppressed by the staunch old warrior, Guerrero, who seized and bore the insurgent chief to the capital as a prisoner. Another insurrection occurred not long after in Cuernavaca, which was also quelled by Guerrero. Both of these outbreaks were caused by the centralists, who strove to put down by violence the popular desire for the federal system. Instead of destroying the favorite charter, however, they only served to cement the sections who sustained liberal doctrines in the different provinces or states of the nation, and finally aided materially in enforcing the adoption of the federal system.

Another insurrection occurred in the City of Mexico, growing out of the old and national animosity between the creoles and the European Spaniards. The expulsion of the latter from all public employments was demanded by the creoles of the capital, backed by the garrison commanded by Colonels Lobato and Staboli. The revolt was suppressed at the moment, but it was deemed advisable to conciliate feeling in regard to the unfortunate foreigners; and accordingly changes were made in the departments, in which the offices were given to native Mexicans, while the Spaniards were allowed a pension for life of one-third of their pay. At this period, moreover, the supreme executive power was altered, and Nicholas Bravo, Vicente Guerrero, and Miguel Dominguez were appointed to control public affairs until a president was elected under the new constitution.

Early in 1825 the general congress assembled in the City of Mexico. Guadalupe Victoria was declared president, and Nicolas Bravo vice-president. The national finances were recruited by a loan from England, and a legislative effort was made to narrow the influence of the priesthood, according to the just limits it should occupy in a republic.

All Spanish America had been in a ferment for several years, and the power of Castile was forever broken on the continent. Peru, as well as Mexico, had cast off the bonds of dependence, for the brilliant battle of Ayacucho rescued the republican banner from the danger with which for a while it was menaced. The European forces had never been really formidable, except for their superior discipline and control under royalist leaders, but they were now driven out of the heart of the continent, while the few pertinacious troops and generals who still remained were confined to the coasts of Mexico, Peru, and Chile, where they clung to the fortress of San Juan de Ulua, the castle of Callao, and the strongholds of Chiloe.

Victoria was sworn into office on April 15, 1825. Several foreign nations had already recognized the independence of Mexico, or soon hastened to do so; for all were eager to grasp a share of the commerce and mines which they imagined had been so profitable to Spain. The British especially, who had become holders of Mexican bonds, were particularly desirous to open commercial intercourse and to guard it by international treaties.

In the winter of 1826 it was discovered, by the discussions in congress of projects for their suppression, that the party leaders, fearing an open attempt to conduct their unconstitutional machinations, had sought the concealment of masonic institutions in which they might foster their antagonistic schemes. The rival lodges were designated as Escocesses and Yorkinos, the former numbering among its members the vice-president, Nicolas Bravo, Gomez Pedraza, and José Montayno, while the Yorkinos boasted of Generals Victoria, Santa Anna, Guerrero, Lorenzo de Zavala, and Bustamante.

The adherents of the Escocesses were said to be in favor of a limited monarchy with a Spanish prince at its head; but the Yorkinos maintained the supremacy of the constitution and declared themselves hostile to all movements of a central character. The latter party was by far the most numerous. The intelligent liberals of all classes sustained it; yet its leaders had to contend with the dignitaries of the church, the opulent agriculturists, landholders and miners, and many of the high officers of the army whose names had been identified with the early struggles of the independents against the Spaniards.

These party discussions, mainly excited by the personal ambitions of the disputants, which were carried on not only openly in congress, but secretly in the lodges, absorbed for a long time the entire attention of the selfish but intelligent persons who should have forgotten themselves in the holy purpose of consolidating the free and republican principles of the constitution of 1824. The result of this personal warfare was soon exhibited in the total neglect of popular interests, so far as they were to be fostered or advanced by the action of congress. The states, however, were in some degree free from these internecine contests, for the boldest of the various leaders, and the most ambitious aspirants for power, had left the provinces to settle their quarrels in the capital. This was fortunate for the country, inasmuch as the states were in some measure recompensed by their own care of the various domestic industrial interests for the neglect they suffered at the hands of national legislators.

At the close of 1827 Colonel José Montayno, a member of the Escocesses, proclaimed in Otumba the plan which in the history of Mexican pronunciamientos, or revolts, is known by the name of this leader. Another attempt of a similar character had been previously made against the federative system and in favor of centralism by Padre Arénas; but both of these outbreaks were not considered dangerous, until Bravo denounced President Victoria for his union with the Yorkinos, and, taking arms against the government, joined the rebels in Tulancingo, where he declared himself in favor of the central plan of Montayno. The country was aroused. The insurgents appeared in great strength. The army exhibited decided symptoms of favor toward the revolted party, and the church strengthened the elements of discontent by its influence with the people. Such was the revolutionary state of Mexico when the patriot Guerrero was once more summoned by the executive to use his energetic efforts in quelling the insurrection. Nor was he unsuccessful in his loyal endeavors to support the constitution. As soon as he marched against the insurgents they dispersed throughout the country; so that without bloodshed he was enabled to crush the revolt and save the nation from the civil war. Thus, amid the embittered quarrels of parties who had actually designed to transfer their contests from congress and lodges to the field of battle, terminated the administration of Guadalupe Victoria, the first president of Mexico. His successor, Gomez Pedraza, the candidate of the Escocesses, was elected by a majority of but two votes over his competitor, Guerrero, the representative of the liberal Yorkinos.

These internal discontents of Mexico began to inspire the Spanish court with hope that its estranged colony would be induced, or perhaps easily compelled, after a short time to return to its allegiance; and accordingly it was soon understood in Mexico, even during Victoria's administration, that active efforts were making in Cuba to raise an adequate force for another attempt upon the republic. This for a moment restrained the fraternal hands raised against each other within the limits of Mexico, and forced all parties to unite against the common danger from abroad. Suitable measures were taken to guard the coasts where an attack was most imminent, and it was the good fortune of the government to secure the services of Commodore Porter, a distinguished officer of the United States Navy, who commanded the Mexican squadron most effectively for the protection of the shores along the Gulf of Mexico, and took a number of Spanish vessels, even in the ports of Cuba, some of which were laden with large and costly cargoes.

The success of the centralist Pedraza over the federalist Guerrero—a man whose name and reputation were scarcely less dear to the genuine republicans than that of Guadalupe Victoria— was not calculated to heal the animosities of the two factions, especially as the scant majority of two votes had placed the Escoces partisan in the presidential chair. The defeated candidate and his incensed companions of the liberal lodge did not exhibit upon this occasion that loyal obedience to constitutional law which should have taught them that the first duty of a republican is to conceal his mortification at a political defeat and to bow reverentially to the lawful decision of a majority. It is a subject of deep regret that the first bold and successful attack upon the organic law of Mexico was made by the federalists. They may have deemed it their duty to prevent their unreliable competitors from controlling the destinies of Mexico even for a moment under the sanction of the constitution; but there can be no doubt that they should have waited until acts, instead of suspicions or fears, entitled them to exercise their right of impeachment under the constitution. In an unregulated, military nation such as Mexico was at that period men do not pause for the slow operations of law when there is a personal or a party quarrel in question. The hot blood of the impetuous,

tropical region combines with the active intellectual temperament
of the people, and laws and constitutions are equally disregarded
under the impulse of passion or interest. Such was the case in the
present juncture. The Yorkinos had been outvoted lawfully, according to the solemn record of congress, yet they resolved not to
submit; and accordingly Lorenzo de Zavala, the grand master of
their lodge, and Antonio Lopez de Santa Anna, who was then a
professed federalist, in conjunction with the defeated candidate,
Guerrero, and Generals Montezuma and Lobato, determined to
prevent Pedraza from occupying the chair of state. Santa Anna,
who now appeared prominently on the stage, was the chief agitator
in the scheme, and being in garrison at Jalapa, in the autumn of
1828 pronounced against the chief magistrate-elect, and denounced
his nomination as " illegal, fraudulent, and unconstitutional." The
movement was popular, for the people were in fact friendly to
Guerrero. The prejudices of the native or creole party against
the Spaniards and their supposed defenders, the Escocesses, were
studiously fomented in the capital; and, December 4, the pronunciamiento of the Acordada, in the capital, seconded the sedition
of Santa Anna in the provinces. By this time the arch-conspirator
in this drama had reached the metropolis and labored to control
the elements of disorder which were at hand to support his favorite
Guerrero. The defenseless Spaniards were relentlessly assailed by
the infuriate mob which was let loose upon them by the insurgent
chiefs. Guerrero was in the field in person at the head of the
Yorkinos. The Parian in the capital and the dwellings of many
of the noted Escocesses were attacked and pillaged, and for some
time the city was given up to anarchy and bloodshed. Pedraza,
who still fulfilled the functions of minister of war while awaiting
his inauguration, fled from the official post, which he abandoned to
his rival, Santa Anna; and on January 1, 1829, congress, reversing
its former act, declared Guerrero to have been duly elected president of the republic! General Bustamante was chosen vice-president, and the government again resumed its operation under the
federal system of 1824.

Violent as was the conduct of the pretended liberals in overthrowing their rivals, the Escocesses, and firmly as it may be
supposed such a band was cemented in opposition to the machina-
tion of a bold monarchical party, we nevertheless find that
treason existed in the hearts of the conspirators against the

patriot-hero whom they had used in their usurpation of the presidency. Scarcely had Guerrero been seated in the chair of state when it became known that there was a conspiracy to displace him. He had been induced by the condition of the country and by the bad advice of his enemies to assume the authority of dictator. This power, he alleged, was exercised only for the suppression of the intriguing Escocesses; but its continued exercise served as a pretext, at least, for the vice-president, General Bustamante, to place himself at the head of a republican division and pronounce against the president he had so recently contributed to place in power. The executive commanded Santa Anna to advance against the assailants; but this chief at first feebly opposed the insurgents, and finally, fraternizing with Bustamante, marched on the capital, whence they drove Guerrero and his partisans to Valladolid in Michoacan. Here the dethroned dictator organized a government, while the usurping vice-president, Bustamante, assumed the reins in the capital. In Michoacan, Guerrero, who was well known and loved for his revolutionary enterprises in the west of Mexico, found no difficulty in recruiting a force with which he hoped to regain his executive post. Congress was divided in opinion between the rival factions of the liberalists, and the republic was shaken by the continual strife, until Bustamante dispatched a powerful division against Guerrero, which defeated and dispersed his army. This was the conclusion of that successful warrior's career. He was a good soldier, but a miserable statesman. His private character and natural disposition are represented by those who knew him best to have been irreproachable; yet he was fitted alone for the early struggles of Mexico in the field, and was so ignorant of the administrative functions needed in his country at such a period that it is not surprising to find he had been used as a tool and cast aside when the service for which his intriguing coadjutors required him was performed. His historical popularity and character rendered him available for a reckless party in overthrowing a constitutional election; and even when beaten by the new usurper, and with scarcely the shadow of a party in the nation, it was still feared that his ancient usefulness in the wars of independence might render him again the nucleus of political discontent. Accordingly the pursuit of Guerrero was not abandoned when his army fled. The west coast was watched by the myrmidons of the usurpers, and the war-worn hero was finally betrayed on board a vessel by a spy, where he was arrested for bearing arms against the government of which he was the real head, according to the solemn decision of congress. In February, 1831, a court-martial, ordered by General Montezuma, tried him for this pretended crime. His sentence was of course known as soon as his judges were named; and thus another chief of the revolutionary war was rewarded by death for his patriotic services. We cannot regard this act of Bustamante and Santa Anna except as a deliberate murder, for which they richly deserve the condemnation of impartial history, even if they had no other crimes to answer for at the bar of God and their country.

While these internal contests were agitating the heart of Mexico an expedition had been fitted out at Havana composed of four thousand troops commanded by Barradas, designed to invade the lost colony and restore it to the Spanish crown. The accounts given of this force and its condition when landed at Tampico vary according to the partisans by whom they are written; but there is reason to believe that the Spanish troops were so weakened by disease and losses in the summer of 1830, that when Santa Anna and a French officer, Colonel Woll, attacked them in the month of September, they fell an easy prey into the hands of the Mexicans. Santa Anna, however, with his usual talent for such composition, magnified the defeat into a magnificent conquest. He was hailed as the victor who broke the last link between Spain and her viceroyalty. Pompous bulletins and dispatches were published in the papers, and the commander-in-chief returned to the capital covered with honors, as the savior of the republic.

There is an anecdote connected with the final expulsion of the Spaniards from Mexico which deserves to be recorded, as it exhibits a fact which superstitious persons might conceive to be the avenging decree of retributive providence. Doña Isabel Montezuma, the eldest daughter of the unfortunate emperor, had been married to his successor on the Aztec throne, and after his wretched death was united to various distinguished Spaniards, the last of whom was Juan Andrade, ancestor of the Andrade Montezumas and Counts of Miravalle. General Miguel Barragan, who afterward became president *ad interim* of Mexico, and to whom the castle of San Juan de Ulua was surrendered by the European forces, was married to Manuela Trebuesta y Casasola, daughter of the last Count of Miravalle, and it is thus a singular coincidence that the husband of a lady who was the legitimate descendant of

Montezuma should have been destined to receive the keys of the last stronghold on which the Spanish banner floated!

By intrigue and victories Santa Anna had acquired so much popular renown throughout the country and with the army that he found the time was arriving when he might safely avail himself of his old and recent services against Iturbide and Barradas. Under the influence of his machinations Bustamante began to fail in popular estimation. He was spoken of as a tyrant; his administration was characterized as inauspicious; and the public mind was gradually prepared for an outbreak in 1832. Santa Anna, who had, in fact placed and sustained Bustamante in power, was in reality the instigator of this revolt. The ambitious chief first of all issued his pronunciamiento against the ministry of the president, and then shortly after against that functionary himself. But Bustamante, a man of nerve and capacity, was not to be destroyed as easily as his victim, Guerrero. He threw himself at the head of his loyal troops, and encountering the rebels at Tolomi routed them completely. Santa Anna therefore retired to Vera Cruz, and, strengthening his forces from some of the other states, declared himself in favor of the restoration of the constitutional president, Pedraza, whom he had previously driven out of Mexico. As Bustamante advanced toward the coast his army melted away. The country was opposed to him. He was wise enough to perceive that his usurped power was lost; and prudently entered into a pacific convention with Santa Anna at Zavaleta in December, 1832. The successful insurgent immediately dispatched a vessel for the banished Pedraza and brought him back to the capital to serve out the remaining three months of his unexpired administration!

The object of Santa Anna in restoring Pedraza was not to sustain any one of the old parties, which had now become strangely mingled and confused by the factions or ambitions of all the leaders. His main design was to secure the services and influence of the centralists, so far as they were yet available, in controlling his election to the presidency, upon which he had fixed his heart. On May 16, 1833, he reached the goal of his ambition.

The congress of 1834 was unquestionably federal republican in its character, and Santa Anna seemed to be perfectly in accord with his vice-presidential compeer, Gomez Farias. But the church party, warned by a bill introduced into congress the previous year by Zavala, by which he aimed a blow at the temporalities of the spiritual lords, did not remain a contented spectator while the power reposed in the hands of federal partisans. However, it was soon found that the centralists were stronger represented in a body hitherto regarded as altogether republican. It is charged in Mexico that bribery was freely resorted to; and, when the solicitations became sufficiently powerful, even the inflexible patriotism of Santa Anna yielded, though the vice-president, Farias, remained incorruptible.

On May 13, 1834, the president suddenly and unwarrantably dissolved congress, and maintained his arbitrary decree and power by the army, which was entirely at his service. In the following year Gomez Farias was deposed from the vice-presidency by the venal congress, and Barragan raised to the vacant post. The militia was disarmed, and central forces strengthened, and the people placed entirely at the mercy of the executive and his minions, who completed the destruction of the constitution of 1824 by blotting it from the statute book of Mexico.

Puebla, Jalisco, Oaxaca, parts of Mexico, Zacatecas, and Texas revolted against this assumption of the centralists, though they were finally not able to maintain absolutely their free stand against the dictator. Zacatecas and Texas alone presented a formidable aspect to Santa Anna, who was nevertheless too strong and skillful for the ill-regulated forces of the former state. The victorious troops entered the rebellious capital with savage fury; and, after committing the most disgusting acts of brutality and violence against all classes and sexes, they disarmed the citizens entirely and placed a military governor over the province. In Coahuila and Texas symptoms of discontent were far more important, for the federalists met at Monclova, and, after electing Agustin Viesca governor, defied the opposite faction by which a military officer had been assigned to perform the executive duties of the state. General Cos, however, soon dispersed the legislature by violence and imprisoned the governor and his companions, whom he arrested as they were hastening to cross the Rio Grande. These evil doings were regarded sorrowfully but sternly by the North Americans who had flocked to Texas under the sanctions and assurances of the federal constitution, and they resolved not to countenance the usurpation of their unquestionable rights.

Such was the state of affairs in the Mexican Republic when the Plan of Toluca was issued, by which the federal constitution was absolutely abolished, and the principles of a consolidated central government fully announced. Previous to this, however, a pronunciamiento had been made by a certain Escalada at Morelia, in favor of the fueros, or especial privileges and rights of the church and army. This outbreak was of course central in its character, while another ferment in Cuautla had been productive of Santa Anna's nomination as dictator, an office which he promptly refused to accept.

The Plan of Toluca was unquestionably favored by Santa Anna, who had gone over to the centralists. It was a scheme designed to test national feeling and to prepare the people for the overthrow of state governments. The supreme power was vested by it in the executive and national congress, and the states were changed into departments under the command of military governors, who were responsible for their trust to the chief national authorities instead of the people. Such was the central constitution of 1836.

It is quite probable that Santa Anna's prudent care of himself and his popularity, as well as his military patriotism, induced him to leave the government in the hands of the vice-president, Barragan, while the new constitution was under discussion, and to lead the Mexican troops personally against the revolted Texans, who had never desisted from open hostility to the central usurpations. On April 21, 1836, the president and his army were completely routed by General Houston and the Texans; and, instead of returning to the metropolis crowned with glory, as he had done from the capture of Barradas, Santa Anna owed his life to the generosity of the Texas insurgents, whose companions in arms had recently been butchered by his orders at Goliad and San Antonio de Bejar.[1]

During Santa Anna's absence Vice-President Barragan filled the executive office up to the time of his death, when he was succeeded by Coro, until the return from France of Bustamante, who had been elected president under the new central constitution of 1836. In the following year Santa Anna was sent back to Mexico in a vessel of the United States government. But he was a disgraced man in the nation's eyes. He returned to his hacienda of Manga de Clavo, and, burying himself for a while in obscurity,

[1] See General Waddy Thompson's "Recollections of Mexico," p. 69, for Santa Anna's wretched vindication of these sanguinary deeds.

was screened from the open manifestation of popular odium. Here he lurked until the brilliant attempt was made to disenthral his country by Mexia in 1838. Demanding once more the privilege of leading the army, he was intrusted with its command, and, encountering the defender of federation in the neighborhood of Puebla, he gave him battle immediately. Mexia lost the day; and, with brief time for shrift or communication with his family, he was condemned by a drum-head court-martial and shot upon the field of battle. This was a severe doom, but the personal animosity between the commanders was equally unrelenting, for when the sentence was announced to the brave but rash Mexia, he promptly and firmly declared that Santa Anna was right to execute him on the spot, inasmuch as he would not have granted the usurper half the time that elapsed since his capture, had it been his destiny to prove victorious!

Soon after the accession of Bustamante there had been clamors in favor of federation and Gomez Farias, who was at that period imprisoned; but these trifling outbreaks were merely local and easily suppressed by Pedraza and Rodriguez.

In the winter of 1838, however, Mexico was more severely threatened from abroad than she had recently been by her internal discords. It was at this time that a French fleet appeared at Vera Cruz, under the orders of Admiral Baudin, to demand satisfaction for injuries to French subjects and unsettled pecuniary claims which had been long and unavailingly subjects of diplomacy. Distracted for years by internal broils that paralyzed the industry of the country ever since the outbreak of the revolution, Mexico was in no condition to respond promptly to demands for money. But national pride forbade the idea of surrendering without a blow. The military resources of the country and of the castle of San Juan de Ulua were accordingly mustered with due celerity, and the assailed department of Vera Cruz intrusted to the defense of Santa Anna, whose fame had been somewhat refreshed by his victory over Mexia. Meanwhile the French fleet kept up a stringent blockade of Vera Cruz, and still more crippled the commercial revenues of Mexico by cutting off the greater part of its most valuable trade. Finding, however, that neither the blockade nor additional diplomacy would induce the stubborn government to accede to terms which the Mexicans knew would finally be forced on them, the French squadron attacked the city with forces landed from the vessels, while they assailed the redoubtable castle with three frigates, a corvette and two bomb vessels, whence, during an action of six hours, they threw 302 shells, 177 paixhan, and 7771 solid shot. The assaults upon the town were not so successful as those on the castle, where the explosion of a magazine forced the Mexicans to surrender. The troops that had been landed were not numerous enough to hold the advantages they gained; and it was in gallantly repulsing a storming party at the gates of the city that Santa Anna lost a leg by a parting shot from a small piece of ordnance as the French retreated on the quay to their boats.

The capture of the castle, however, placed the city at the mercy of the French, and the Mexicans were soon induced to enter into satisfactory stipulations for the adjustment of all debts and difficulties.

In 1839 General Canales fomented a revolt in some of the northeastern departments. The proposal of this insurgent was to form a republican confederation of Coahuila, Tamaulipas, and Durango, which three states or departments, he designed, should adopt for themselves the federal constitution of 1824, and, assuming the title of the independent "Republic of the Rio Grande," should pledge themselves to coöperate with Texas against Bustamante and the centralists. An alliance was entered into with Texas to that effect, and an expedition of united Texans and Republicans of the Rio Grande was set on foot to occupy Coahuila; but at the appearance of General Arista in the field early in 1840, and after an action in which the combined forces were defeated, Canales left the discomfited Texans to seek safety by hastening back to their own territory.

The administration of Bustamante was sorely tried by foreign and domestic broils, for, while Texas and the Republic of the Rio Grande were assailing him in the north the federalists attacked him in the capital and the Yucatecos revolted in the south. This last outbreak was not quelled so easily as the rebellion in the north; nor was it, in fact, until long afterward, during another administration, that the people of the peninsula were again induced to return to their allegiance. Bustamante seems to have vexed the Yucatecos by unwise interference in the commercial and industrial interests of the country. The revolt was temporarily successful. On March 31, 1841, a constitution was proclaimed in Yucatan, which erected it into a free and sovereign state, and exempted the people from many burdens that had been imposed by both the federal constitution of 1824 and the central one of 1836.

The discontent with Bustamante's administration, arising chiefly from a consumption duty of fifteen per cent. which had been imposed by congress, was now well spread throughout the republic. The pronunciamiento of Urrea on July 15, 1840, at the palace of Mexico was mainly an effort of the federalists to put down violently the constitution of 1836; and although the insurgents had possession at one period of the person of the president, yet the revolt was easily suppressed by Valencia and his faithful troops in the capital.

But a year later the revolutionary spirit had ripened into readiness for successful action. We have reason to believe that the most extensive combinations were made by active agents in all parts of Mexico to insure the downfall of Bustamante and the elevation of Santa Anna. Accordingly in August, 1841, a pronunciamiento of General Paredes, in Guadalajara, was speedily responded to by Valencia and Lombardini in the capital and by Santa Anna himself at Vera Cruz. But the outbreak was not confined merely to proclamations or the adhesion of military garrisons, for a large body of troops and citizens continued loyal to the president and resolved to sustain the government in the capital. This fierce fidelity to the constitution on the one hand and bitter hostility to the chief magistrate on the other resulted in one of the most sanguinary conflicts that had taken place in Mexico since the early days of independence. For a whole month the contest was carried on with balls and grape shot in the streets of Mexico, while the rebels, who held the citadel outside the city, finished the shameless drama by throwing a shower of bombs into the metropolis, shattering the houses, and involving innocent and guilty, citizens, strangers, combatants, and non-combatants, in a common fate. This cowardly assault under the orders of Valencia was made solely with the view of forcing the citizens who were unconcerned in the quarrel between the factions into insisting upon the surrender of Mexico, in order to save their town and families from destruction. There was a faint show of military maneuvers in the fields adjoining the city; but the troops on both sides shrank from battle when they were removed from the protecting shelter of walls and houses. At length the intervention of Mexican citizens who were most interested in the cessation of hostilities produced an arrangement between the belligerents at Estanzuela near the capital, and finally the Plan of Tacubaya was agreed on by the chiefs as a substitute for the constitution of 1836. By the seventh article of this document Santa Anna was effectually invested with dictatorial powers until a new constitution was formed.

The Plan of Tacubaya provided that a congress should be convened in 1842 to form a new constitution, and in June a body of patriotic citizens chosen by the people assembled for that purpose in the metropolis. Santa Anna opened the session with a speech in which he announced his predilection for a strong central government, but he professed perfect willingness to yield to whatever might be the decision of congress. Nevertheless, in December of the same year, after the assembly had made two efforts to form a constitution suitable to the country and the cabinet, President Santa Anna, in spite of his professed submission to the national will expressed through the representatives, suddenly and unauthorizedly dissolved the congress. It was a daring act, but Santa Anna knew that he could rely upon his troops, his officers, and the mercantile classes for support. The capital wanted quietness for a while, and the interests of trade as well as the army united in confidence in the strong will of one who was disposed to maintain order by force.

After congress had been dissolved by Santa Anna there was of course no further necessity of an appeal to the people. The nation had spoken, but its voice was disregarded. Nothing therefore remained save to allow the dictator himself to frame the organic laws; and for this purpose he appointed a junta of notables, who proclaimed, on June 13, 1843, an instrument which never took the name of a constitution, but bore the mongrel title of "Bases of the Political Organization of the Mexican Republic." It is essentially central in its provisions, and while it is as restrictive upon the subject of religion as the two former fundamental systems, it is even less popular in its general provisions than the constitution of 1836.

Chapter XXVI

OUTBREAK OF THE WAR WITH UNITED STATES
1843-1846

AFTER the foundation of the new system in 1843, the country continued quiet for a while, and when the Mexican congress met, in January, 1844, propositions were made by the executive department to carry out Santa Anna's favorite project of reconquering Texas. It is probable that there was not much sincerity in the president's desire to march his troops into a territory the recollection of which must have been at least distasteful to him. There is more reason to believe that the large sum which it was necessary to appropriate for the expenses of the campaign—the management of which would belong to the administration—was the real object he had in view. Four millions were granted for the reconquest, but when Santa Anna demanded ten millions more while the first grant was still uncollected, the members refused to sustain the president's demand. The congressmen were convinced of that chieftain's rapacity, and resolved to afford him no further opportunity to plunder the people under the guise of patriotism.

Santa Anna's sagacious knowledge of his countrymen immediately apprised him of approaching danger, and having obtained permission from congress to retire to his estate at Manga de Clavo, near Vera Cruz, he departed from the capital, leaving his friend General Canalizo as president *ad interim*. Hardly had he reached his plantation in the midst of friends and faithful troops when a revolt burst out in Jalisco, Aguas Calientes, Zacatecas, Sinaloa, and Sonora against his government, headed by General Paredes. Santa Anna rapidly crossed the country to suppress the rebellion, but as he disobeyed the constitutional compact by taking actual command of the army while he was president, without the previous assent of congress, he became amenable to law for this violation of his oath. He was soon at enmity with the rebels and with the constitutional congress, and thus a threefold contest was carried on, chiefly through correspondence, until January 4, 1845, when Santa Anna finally fell. He fled from the insurgents and constitutional authorities toward the eastern coast, but, being captured at the village of Jico, was conducted to Perote, where he remained imprisoned under a charge and examination for treason, until an amnesty for the late political factionists permitted him to depart, May 29, 1845, with his family for Havana.

Upon Santa Anna's ejection from the executive chair the president of the council of government became under the laws of the country provisional president of the republic. This person was General José Joaquim de Herrera, during whose administration the controversies rose which resulted in the war between Mexico and the United States.

The thread of policy and action in both countries is so closely interwoven during this pernicious contest that the history of the war becomes in reality the history of Mexico for the epoch. We are therefore compelled to narrate succinctly the circumstances that led to that lamentable issue.

The first impresario, or contractor, for the colonization of Texas was Moses Austin, a native citizen of the United States, who, as soon as the treaty of limits between Spain and the United States was concluded in 1819, conceived the project of establishing a settlement in that region. Accordingly in 1821 he obtained from the commandant general of the Provincias Internas permission to introduce three hundred foreign families. In 1823 a national colonization law was approved by the Mexican emperor, Iturbide, during his brief reign, and on February 18 Stephen F. Austin, who accepted the contract upon his father's death, in carrying out the project, was authorized to proceed with the founding of the colony. After the emperor's fall this decree was confirmed by the first executive council in conformity to the express will of congress.

In 1824 the federal constitution of Mexico was, as we have narrated, adopted by the republican representatives upon principles analogous to those of the constitution of the United States; and by a decree of May 7 Texas and Coahuila were united in a State. In this year another general colonization law was enacted by congress, and foreigners were invited to the new domain by a special State colonization law of Coahuila and Texas.

Under these local laws and constitutional guaranties large numbers of foreigners flocked to this portion of Mexico, opened farms, founded towns and villages, reoccupied old Spanish settlements, introduced improvements in agriculture and manufactures, drove off the Indians, and formed, in fact, the nucleus of an enterprising and progressive population. But there were jealousies between the race that invited the colonists and the colonists who accepted the invitation. The central power in the distant capital did not estimate at their just value the independence of the remote pioneers or the State-right sovereignty to which they had been accustomed in their former home in the United States. Mexico was convulsed by revolutions, but the lonely residents of Texas paid no attention to the turmoils of the factionists. At length, however, direct acts of interference upon the part of the national government, not only by its ministerial agents, but by its legislature, excited the mingled alarm and indignation of the colonists, who imagined that in sheltering themselves under a republic they were protected as amply as they would have been under the constitution of the North American Union. In this they were disappointed; for in 1830 an arbitrary enactment—based no doubt upon a jealous dread of the growing value and size of a colony which formed a link between the United States and Mexico, stretching from Louisiana to Tamaulipas on the south—prohibited entirely the future immigration of American settlers into Coahuila and Texas. To enforce this decree and to watch the loyalty of the actual inhabitants, military posts composed of rude and ignorant Mexican soldiers were sprinkled over the country. And at last the people of Texas found themselves entirely under military control.

This suited neither the principles nor tastes of the colonists, who, in 1832, took arms against this warlike interference with their municipal liberty, and after capturing the fort at Velasco, reduced to submission the garrisons at Anahuac and Nacogdoches. The separate State constitution which had been promised Texas in 1824 was never sanctioned by the Mexican congress, though the colonists prepared the charter and were duly qualified for admission. But the crisis arrived when the centralists of 1835 overthrew the federal constitution of 1824. Several Mexican States rose independently against the despotic act. Zacatecas fought bravely for her rights, and saw her people basely slain by the myrmidons of Santa Anna. The legislature of Coahuila and Texas was dispersed by the military; and at last the whole republic, save the pertinacious North Americans, yielded to the armed power of the resolute oppressor.

The alarmed settlers gathered together as quickly as they could and resolved to stand by their federative rights under the charter whose guaranties allured them into Mexico. Meetings were held in all the settlements, and a union was formed by means of correspondence. Arms were next resorted to, and the Texans were victorious at Gonzales, Goliad, Bejar, Concepcion, Lepantitlan, San Patricio, and San Antonio. In November they met in consultation, and in an able, resolute, and dignified paper declared that they had only taken up arms in defense of the constitution of 1824; that their object was to continue loyal to the confederacy if laws were made for the guardianship of their political rights, and that they offered their lives and arms in aid of other members of the republic who would rightfully rise against the military despotism.

But the other States, in which there was no infusion of North Americans or Europeans, refused to second this hardy handful of pioneers. Mexico will not do justice, in any of her commentaries on the Texan war, to the motives of the colonists. Charging them with an original and long-meditated design to rob the republic of one of its most valuable provinces, she forgets entirely, or glosses over, the military acts of Santa Anna's invading army in March, 1836, at the Alamo and Goliad, which converted resistance into revenge. After those disgraceful scenes of carnage peace was no longer possible. Santa Anna imagined, no doubt, that he would terrify the settlers into submission if he could not drive them from the soil. But he mistook both their fortitude and their force; and after the fierce encounter at San Jacinto, on April 21, 1836, with Houston and his army, the power of Mexico over the insurgent State was effectually and forever broken.

After Santa Anna had been taken prisoner by the Texans in this fatal encounter, and was released and sent home through the United States in order to fulfill his promise to secure the recognition of Texan independence, the colonists diligently began the work of creating for themselves a distinct nationality, for they failed in all their early attempts to incorporate themselves with the United States during the administrations of Jackson and Van Buren. These presidents were scrupulous and faithful guardians of national honor, while they respected the Mexican right of reconquest. Their natural sympathies were of course yielded to Texas, but their executive duties, the faith of treaties, and the sanctions of international law forbade their acceding to the proposed union. Texas accordingly established a national government, elected her officers, regu-

lated her trade, formed her army and navy, maintained her frontier
secure from assault, and was recognized as, *de facto,* an independent sovereignty by the United States, England, France, and Belgium. But these efforts of the infant republic did not end in mere
preparations for a separate political existence and future commercial wealth. The rich soil of the lowlands among the numerous
rivers that veined the whole region soon attracted large accessions
of immigrants, and the trade of Texas began to assume significance
in the markets of the world.

Meanwhile Mexico busied herself at home in revolutions, or
in gathering funds and creating armies destined, as the authorities
professed, to reconquer the lost province. Yet all these military
and financial efforts were never rendered available in the field, and
in reality no adequate force ever marched toward the frontier. The
men and money raised through the services and contributions of
credulous citizens were actually designed to figure in the domestic
drama of political power in the capital. No hostilities of any significance occurred between the revolutionists and the Mexicans
after 1836, for we cannot regard the Texan expedition to Santa Fé,
or the Mexican assault upon the town of Mier, as belligerent acts
deserving consideration as grave efforts made to assert or secure
national rights.

Such was the condition of things from 1836 until 1844, during
the whole of which period Texas exhibited to the world a far better
aspect of well regulated sovereignty than Mexico herself. On
April 12 of that year, more than seven years after Texas had established her independence, a treaty was concluded by President Tyler
with the representatives of Texas for the annexation of that republic
to the United States. In March, 1845, Congress passed a joint
resolution annexing Texas to the Union upon certain reasonable
conditions, which were acceded to by that nation, whose convention
erected a suitable State constitution, with which it became finally a
member of the Union. In the meantime the envoys of France
and England had opened negotiations for the recognition of Texan
independence, which terminated successfully; but when they announced their triumph, on May 20, 1845, Texas had already
been annexed conditionally to the United States by the Act of
Congress.

The joint resolution of annexation passed by Congress was
protested against by General Almonte, the Mexican minister at

that period in Washington, as an act of aggression, "the most unjust which can be found in the annals of modern history," and designed to despoil a friendly nation of a considerable portion of her territory. He announced, in consequence, the termination of his mission, and demanded his passports to leave the country. In Mexico soon after a bitter and badly conducted correspondence took place between the minister of foreign affairs and Shannon, the United States envoy. And thus within a brief period these two nations found themselves unrepresented in each other's capital and on the eve of a serious dispute.

But the government of the United States—still sincerely anxious to preserve peace, or at least willing to try every effort to soothe the irritated Mexicans and keep the discussion in the cabinet rather than transfer it to the battlefield—determined to use the kindly efforts of its consul, who still remained in the capital, to seek an opportunity for the renewal of friendly intercourse. This officer was accordingly directed to visit the minister of foreign affairs and ascertain from the Mexican Government whether it would receive an envoy from the United States invested with full power to adjust all the questions in dispute between the two governments. The invitation was received with apparent good will, and in October, 1845, the Mexican Government agreed to receive one, commissioned with full powers to settle the dispute in a peaceful, reasonable, and honorable manner.

As soon as this intelligence reached the United States John Slidell was dispatched as envoy extraordinary and minister plenipotentiary on the supposed mission of peace; but when he reached Vera Cruz in November he found the aspect of affairs changed. The government of Herrera, with which the consul's arrangement had been made, was tottering. General Paredes, a leader popular with the people and the army, availing himself of the general animosity against Texas and the alleged desire of Herrera's cabinet to make peace with the United States, had determined to overthrow the constitutional government. There is scarcely a doubt that Herrera and his ministers were originally sincere in their desire to settle the international difficulty, and to maintain the spirit of the contract they had made. But the internal danger with which they were menaced by the army and its daring demagogue induced them to prevaricate as soon as Slidell presented his credentials for reception. All their pretexts were in reality frivolous, when we consider the serious results which were to flow from their enunciation. The principal argument against the reception of the minister was that his commission constituted him a regular envoy, and that he was not confined to the discussion of the Texan question alone. Such a mission, the authorities alleged, placed the countries at once diplomatically upon an equal and ordinary footing of peace, and their objection therefore, if it had any force at all, was to the fact that the United States exhibited through the credentials of its envoy the strongest evidence that one nation can give to another of perfect amity! There were, in truth, no questions in dispute, except boundary and indemnity; for Texas as a sovereignty acknowledged not only by the acts of the United States and of European powers, but in consequence of her own maintenance of perfect nationality and independence, had a right to annex herself to the United States. The consent of Mexico to acknowledge her independence in 1845, under certain conditions, effectually proved this fact beyond dispute.

While the correspondence between Slidell and the Mexican ministry was going on Paredes continued his hostile demonstrations, and on December 30, 1845, President Herrera, who anxiously desired to avoid bloodshed, resigned the executive chair to him without a struggle. Feeble as was the hope of success with the new authorities, the United States, still anxious to close the contest peacefully, directed Slidell to renew the proposal for his reception to Paredes. These instructions he executed on March 1, 1846, but his request was refused by the Mexican minister of foreign affairs on the 12th of that month, and the minister was forthwith obliged to return from his unsuccessful mission.

All the public documents and addresses of Paredes made during the early movements of his revolution and administration breathe the deadliest animosity to the United States. He invokes the god of battles and calls the world to witness the valor of Mexican arms. The revolution which raised him to power was declared to be sanctioned by the people, who were impatient for another war in which they might avenge the aggressions of a government that sought to prostrate them. Preparations were made for a Texan campaign. Loans were raised, and large bodies of troops were moved to the frontiers. General Arista, suspected of kindness to the United States, was superseded in the north by General Ampudia, who arrived at Matamoros on April 11, 1846, with 200 cavalry, followed by 2000 men, to be united with the large body of soldiery already in Matamoros.

These military demonstrations denoted the unquestionable design and will of Paredes, who had acquired supreme power by a revolution founded upon the solemn pledge of hostility against the United States and reconquest of Texas. His military life in Mexico made him a despot. He had no confidence in the ability of his fellow-citizens to govern themselves. He believed republicanism a Utopian dream of his visionary countrymen. Free discussion through the press was prohibited during his short rule, and his satellites advocated the establishment of a throne to be occupied by a European prince. These circumstances induced the United States to believe that any counter-revolution in Mexico which might destroy the ambitious and unpatriotic project of Paredes would promote the cause of peace, and accordingly it saw with pleasure the prospect of a new outbreak which might result in the downfall and total destruction of its greatest enemy on the soil of the sister republic.

While Slidell was negotiating and, in consequence of the anticipated failure of his effort to be received—as was clearly indicated by the conduct of the Mexican Government upon his arrival in the capital—General Taylor, who had been stationed at Corpus Christi, in Texas, since the fall of 1845, with a body of regular troops, was directed, on January 13, 1846, to move his men to the mouth of the Rio Grande. He accordingly left his encampment on March 8, and on the 25th reached Point Isabel, having encountered no serious opposition on the way. The march to the Rio Grande has been made the subject of complaint by politicians in Mexico and the United States, who believed that the territory lying between that river and the Nueces was not the property of Texas. But inasmuch as Mexico still continued vehemently to assert her political right over the whole of Texas, the occupation of any part of its soil south of the Sabine by American troops was in that aspect of the case quite as much an infringement of Mexican sovereignty as the march of the troops from the Nueces to the Rio Grande.

As it is important that the reader should understand the original title to Louisiana, under which the boundary of the Rio Grande was claimed first of all for that State, and subsequently for Texas, we shall relate its history in a summary manner.

Louisiana had been the property of France, and by a secret contract between that country and Spain in 1762, as well as by treaties between France, Spain, and England in the following year, the French dominion was extinguished on the continent of America. In consequence of the treaty between the Union and England in 1783 the Mississippi became the western boundary of the United States, from its source to the thirty-first degree of north latitude, and thence, on the same parallel, to the St. Mary's. France, it will be remembered, had always claimed dominion in Louisiana to the Rio Bravo del Norte, or Rio Grande, by virtue:

First. Of the discovery of the Mississippi from near its source to the ocean.

Second. Of the possession taken and establishment made by La Salle at the Bay of Saint Bernard, west of the River Trinity and Colorado, by authority of Louis XIV. in 1635—notwithstanding the subsequent destruction of the colony.

Third. Of the charter of Louis XIV. to Crozat in 1712.

Fourth. Of the historical authority of Du Pratz, Champigny, and the Comte de Vergennes.

Fifth. Of the authority of De Lisle's map, and of the map published in 1762 by Don Thomas Lopez, geographer to the King of Spain, as well as of various other maps, atlases, and geographical authorities.

By an article of the secret Treaty of San Ildefonso in October, 1800, Spain retroceded Louisiana to France, but this treaty was not promulgated until the beginning of 1802. The paragraph of cession is as follows: "His Catholic Majesty engages to retrocede to the French Republic, six months after the full and entire execution of the conditions and stipulations above recited relative to his Royal Highness, the Duke of Parma, the colony and province of Louisiana, with the same extent that it already has in the hands of Spain, and that it had when France possessed it, and such as it should be after the treaties passed subsequently between Spain and other powers." In 1803 Bonaparte, the first consul of the French Republic, ceded Louisiana to the United States as fully and in the same manner at it had been retroceded to France by Spain under the Treaty of San Ildefonso; and by virtue of this same grant Madison, Monroe, Adams, Clay, Van Buren, Jackson, and Polk contended that the original limit of the new State had been the Rio Grande. However, by the third article of the treaty of 1819 between Spain and the United States, all pretensions to extend the territory of Louisiana toward Mexico on the Rio Grande were abandoned by adopting the River Sabine as the boundary in that quarter.

The Mexican authorities upon this subject are either silent or doubtful. No light is to be gathered from the geographical researches of Humboldt, whose elucidations of New Spain are in many respects the fullest and most satisfactory. In the year 1835 Stephen Austin published a map of Texas, representing the Nueces as the western confine, and in 1836 General Almonte, the former minister from Mexico to the United States, published a memoir upon Texas in which, while describing the Texan department of Bejar, he says, " that notwithstanding it has been hitherto believed that the Rio de las Nueces is the dividing line of Coahuila and Texas, inasmuch as it is always thus represented on maps, I am informed by the government of the State that geographers have been in error upon this subject; and that the true line should commence at the mouth of the River Aransaso, and follow it to its source; thence it should continue by a straight line until it strikes the junction of the Rivers Medina and San Antonio, and then, pursuing the east bank of the Medina to its headwaters, it should terminate on the confines of Chihuahua." [1]

The true origin of the Mexican War was not this march of Taylor and his troops from the Nueces to the Rio Grande through the debatable land. The American and Mexican troops were brought face to face by the act, and hostilities were the natural result after the exciting annoyances upon the part of the Mexican Government which followed the union of Texas with the United States. Besides this, General Paredes, the usurping president, had already declared in Mexico, on April 18, 1846, in a letter addressed to the commanding officer on the northern frontier, that he supposed him at the head of a valiant army on the theater of action; and that it was indispensable to commence hostilities, the Mexicans themselves taking the initiative!

We believe that the United States and its rulers earnestly desired honorable peace, though they did not shun the alternative of war. It was impossible to permit a conterminous neighbor who owed them large sums of money, and was hostile to the newly adopted State, to select unopposed her mode and moment of attack.

[1] *"Memorias para la Historia de la Guerra de Tejas,"* vol. II. p. 543.

Mexico would neither resign her pretensions upon Texas, negotiate, receive a minister, nor remain at peace. She would neither declare war nor cultivate friendship, and the result was that when the armies approached each other but little time was lost in resorting to the cannon and the sword.

As soon as General Taylor reached the Rio Grande he left a command at the mouth of the river, and, taking post opposite Matamoros, erected a fort, the guns of which bore directly upon the city. The Mexicans, whose artillery might have been brought to play upon the works from the opposite side of the river, made no hostile demonstration against the left bank for some time, nor did they interrupt the construction of the fort. Reinforcements, however, were constantly arriving in the city. Ampudia and Arista were there. Interviews were held between the Mexican authorities and American officers, in which the latter were ordered to retire from the soil it was alleged they were usurping. But as this was a diplomatic, and not a military, question, General Taylor resolved to continue in position, though his forces were perhaps inadequate to contend with the augmenting numbers of the foe. He examined the country thoroughly by his scouting parties and pushed his reconnoissances on the left bank from Point Isabel to some distance beyond his encampment opposite Matamoros. While engaged in this service some of his officers and men were captured or killed by the ranchero cavalry of the enemy, and on April 24 Captain Thornton, who had been sent to observe the country above the encampment with sixty-three dragoons, fell into an ambuscade, out of which they endeavored to cut their way, but were forced to surrender with a loss of sixteen killed and wounded. This was the first blood spilled in actual conflict.

Meanwhile in the United States the news of Taylor's supposed danger, greatly exaggerated by rumor, was spread far and wide. An actual war had perhaps not been seriously apprehended. Taylor had been expressly commanded to refrain from aggression. It was supposed that the mere presence of the troops on the frontier would preserve Texas from invasion, and that negotiations would ultimately terminate the dispute. This is the only ground upon which we can reasonably account for the apparent carelessness of the government in not placing a force upon the Rio Grande adequate to encounter all the opposing array. Congress was in session when the news reached Washington. The president immediately announced the fact, and on May 13, 1846, ten millions of dollars were appropriated to carry on the war, and fifty thousand volunteers were ordered to be raised. An "Army of the West" was directed to be formed under command of Kearny, at Fort Leavenworth on the Missouri, which was to cross the country to the Pacific, after capturing New Mexico. An "Army of the Center," under General Wool, was to assemble at San Antonio de Bejar, whence it was to march upon the Coahuila and Chihuahua, and while the middle portion and the west of Mexico were penetrated by these officers, it was designed that Taylor should make war on the northern and eastern States of the Mexican Republic. In addition to these orders to the army, the naval forces, under Commodores Stockton and Sloat in the Pacific and Commodore Conner in the Gulf of Mexico, were commanded to coöperate with the land forces, to harass the enemy, and to aid with all their power in the subjugation and capture of Mexican property and territory.

Immediately after Thornton's surrender General Taylor, availing himself of authority with which he had been invested to call upon the governors of Louisiana and Texas for military aid, demanded four regiments of volunteers from each State, for the country in the neighborhood of the Rio Grande was alive with belligerent Mexicans. He then visited the fortifications opposite Matamoros, and, finding the garrison but scantily supplied with provisions, hastened back to Point Isabel with a formidable escort, and obtaining the requisite rations, commenced his march back to Matamoros and the fort on May 7. But in the interval General Arista had crossed the Rio Grande with his forces, and on the 8th Taylor encountered him, drawn up in battle array at Palo Alto and ready to dispute his passage along the road. A sharp engagement ensued between the two armies from two o'clock in the afternoon until nearly dark, when the Mexicans withdrew from the action for the night. The total American force in this affair, according to official reports, was 2228, while that of Mexico, according to the admission of the officers, amounted to 6000 regulars, with a large and probably undisciplined force drawn at random from the country.

The night of the 8th was passed with some anxiety in the American camp, for the fierce conflict of the day induced many prudent officers to believe it best either to return to Point Isabel or await reinforcements before again giving battle to the enemy. General Taylor heard and weighed the opinions of his most reliable officers, but after due reflection determined to advance. The condition of the fort opposite Matamoros demanded his urgent aid. The moral effect of a retreat would be great at the commencement of a war, both on Mexico and on the United States troops; and moreover he had perfect confidence in the disciplined regulars who sustained so nobly the brunt of the first battle.

Accordingly the troops were advanced early on the 9th, for they found at daydawn that the Mexicans had abandoned Palo Alto for a stronger position nearer the center of action and interest at Matamoros. After advancing cautiously, in readiness for immediate battle, they came up with the Mexicans in the Resaca de la Palma, or, as it is properly called, La Resaca del Guerrero—the " Ravine of the Warrior "—which afforded them a natural defense against an approach along the road. The ravine curved across the highway and was flanked by masses of prickly plants, aloes, and undergrowth matted into impenetrable thickets, known in Mexico as " chapparal." The action was begun by the infantry in skirmishes with the foe, and after the center of the position on the road had been severely harassed and damaged by the flying artillery, a gallant charge of the dragoons broke the Mexican lines and opened a pathway to Matamoros. The engagement lasted a short time after this combined movement of artillery and cavalry, but before nightfall the enemy was in full flight to the river and the garrison at the fort joyously relieved. In the interval this position had been bombarded and cannonaded by the Mexicans from the opposite side of the river, and its commanding officer slain. In memory of his valiant defense the place has been honored with the name of Fort Brown.

After General Taylor had occupied Matamoros on May 18— and he was only prevented from capturing it and all the Mexican forces and ammunition on the night of the 9th by the want of a pontoon train, which he had vainly demanded—he established his base-line for future operations in the interior along the Rio Grande, extending several hundred miles near that stream. His task of organizing, accepting, or rejecting the multitudes of recruits who flocked to his standard was not only oppressive, but difficult, for he found it hard to disappoint the patriotic fervor of hundreds who were anxious to engage in the war. The quartermaster's department, too, was one of incessant toil and anxiety; because, called unexpectedly and for the first time into active service in the field, it was comparatively unprepared to answer the multitude of requisitions that were daily made upon it by the government, the general officers, and the recruits. The whole material of a campaign was to be rapidly created. Money was to be raised, steamers bought, ships chartered, wagons built and transported, levies brought to the field of action, and munitions of war and provisions distributed over the whole vast territory which it was designed to occupy! While these things were going on the whole country was aroused and most eager for action.

Nor was the United States inattentive to the internal politics of Mexico. It perceived at once that there was no hope of effecting a peace with the administration of Paredes, whose bitter hostility was of course not mitigated by the first successes of the American arms. Santa Anna, it will be recollected, had left Mexico after the amnesty in 1845, and it was known there was open hostility between him and Paredes, who had contributed so greatly to his downfall. Information was moreover received from reliable sources in Washington that a desire prevailed in the republic to recall the banished chief and to seat him once more in the presidential chair; and at the same time there was cause to believe that if he again obtained supreme power he would not be averse to accommodate matters upon a satisfactory basis between the countries. Orders were accordingly issued to Commodore Conner, who commanded the squadron in the Gulf of Mexico, to offer no impediment if Santa Anna approached the coast with a design of entering Mexico. The exiled president was duly apprised of these facts, and, when the revolution actually occurred in his favor in the following summer and his rival fell from power, he availed himself of the order to pass the lines of the blockading squadron at Vera Cruz.

After General Taylor had completely made his preparations to advance into the interior along his base on the Rio Grande, he moved forward gradually, capturing and garrisoning all the important posts along the river. At length the main body of the army, under Worth and Taylor, reached the neighborhood of Monterey, the capital of the State of New Leon, situated at the foot of the Sierra Madre on a plain, but in a position which would enable it to make a stout resistance, especially as it was understood that the Mexican army had gathered itself up in this stronghold, which was the key of the northern provinces and on the main highway to the interior, in order to strike a deathblow at the invaders. On September 5 the divisions concentrated at Marin, and on the 9th they advanced to the Walnut Springs, which afterward became for so long a period the headquarters of the gallant "Army of Occupation."

Reconnoissances of the adjacent country were immediately made, and it was resolved to attack the city by a bold movement toward its southern side that would cut off its communication through the gap in the mountains by which the road led to Saltillo. Accordingly General Worth was detached on this difficult but honorable service with a strong and reliable corps, and, after excessive toil, hard fighting, and wonderful endurance upon the part of his men, the desired object was successfully gained. An unfinished and fortified edifice called the Bishop's Palace, on the summit of a steep hill, was stormed and taken, and thus an important vantage ground commanding the city by a plunging shot was secured.

Meanwhile General Taylor, seeking to withdraw or distract the enemy from his designs on the southern and western sides of the city, made a movement under General Butler, of Kentucky, upon its northern front. What was probably designed only as a feint soon became a severe and deadly conflict. The men, especially the volunteers, eager to flesh their swords in the first conflict with which the war indulged them, rushed into the city, which seems to have been amply prepared in that quarter with barricades, forts, loopholes, and every means of defense suitable for the narrow streets and flat-roofed and parapeted houses of a Spanish town. After the first deadly onset there was, of course, no intention or desire to abandon the conflict, fatal as its prosecution might ultimately become. On they fought from street to street, and house to house, and yard to yard, until night closed over the dying and the dead. On the second day a different system of approach was adopted. Instead of risking life in the street, which was raked from end to end by artillery or rendered untenable by the hidden marksmen who shot from behind the walls of the housetops, the forces were thrown into the dwellings, and breaking onward through walls and enclosures, gradually mined their way toward the plaza or great square of Monterey.

Thus both divisions under the eyes of Worth, Butler, and Taylor successfully performed their assigned tasks, until it became evident to the Mexicans that their town must fall, and that if finally

ANTONIO LOPEZ DE SANTA ANNA
(Born 1795. Died 1876)
From a contemporaneous lithograph

ZACHARY TAYLOR
(Born 1784. Died 1850)
From a daguerreotype

taken by the sword it would be given up to utter destruction and pillage. A capitulation was therefore proposed by Ampudia, who stipulated for the withdrawal of his forces and an armistice. The United States force was in no condition to seize, hold, and support a large body of prisoners of war, nor was it prepared immediately to follow up the victory by penetrating the interior. General Taylor, who was resolved not to shed a single drop of needless blood in the campaign, granted the terms; and thus this strong position, garrisoned by nearly 10,000 troops, sustained by more than forty pieces of artillery, yielded to an army of 7000, unsupported by a battering train, which won the day by hard fighting alone. The attack began on September 21, continued during the two following days, and the garrison capitulated on the 24th. This capitulation and armistice was assented to by General Taylor after mature consultation and the approval of his principal officers. The Mexicans informed him that Paredes had been deposed, that Santa Anna was in power, and that peace would soon be made; but the home authorities, eager for fresh victories, or pandering to public and political taste, did not approve and confirm an act for which General Taylor has neverthless received, as he truly merits, the just applause of impartial history.

Chapter XXVII

OCCUPANCY OF NEW MEXICO AND CALIFORNIA
1846-1847

GENERAL WOOL, who had been for a long period inspector-general of the United States army, was intrusted with the difficult task of examining the recruits in the West, and set forth on his journey after receiving his orders on May 29, 1846. He traversed the States of Ohio, Indiana, Illinois, Kentucky, Tennessee, and Mississippi, and in somewhat less than two months had journeyed three thousand miles and mustered 12,000 men into service.

Nearly 9000 of these recruits were sent to Taylor on the Rio Grande, while those who were destined for the "Army of the Center" rendezvoused at Bejar, in Texas. At this place their commander, Wool, joined them, and commenced the rigid system of discipline, under accomplished officers, which made his division a model in the army. He marched from Bejar with 500 regulars and 2450 volunteers, on September 20, and passed onward through Presidio, Nava, and across the sierra of San José and Santa Rosa, and the Rivers Alamos, Sabine, and Del Norte, until he reached Monclova. He had been directed to advance to Chihuahua, but as this place was in a great measure controlled by the States of New Leon and Coahuila, which were in the possession of the United States, he desisted from pursuing his march thither, and, after communicating with General Taylor and learning of the fall of Monterey, he pushed on to the fertile region of Parras and thence to the headquarters of General Taylor, in the month of December, as soon as he was apprised of the danger which menaced him at that period.

It was part of the United States Government's original plan to reduce New Mexico and California—a task which was imposed upon Colonel Kearny, a hardy frontier fighter long used to Indian character and Indian warfare, who, upon being honored with the command, was raised to the rank of brigadier general. This officer moved from Fort Leavenworth on June 30 toward

Santa Fé, the capital of New Mexico, with an army of 1600 men, and after an unresisted march of 873 miles he reached his destination on August 18. Possession of the place was given without a blow, and it is probable that the discreet Armijo yielded to the advice of American counselors in his capital in surrendering without bloodshed to the forces. Kearny had been authorized to organize and muster into service a battalion of emigrants to Oregon and California, who eagerly availed themselves of this favorable military opportunity to reach their distant abodes on the shores of the Pacific. After organizing the new government of Santa Fé, forming a new code of organic laws, and satisfying himself of the stability of affairs in that quarter, Kearny departed on his mission to California. But he had not gone far when he was met by an express with information of the fall of that portion of Mexico, and immediately sent back the main body of his men, continuing his route through the wilderness with the escort of one hundred dragoons alone. In September of this year a regiment of New York volunteer infantry had been dispatched thither also by sea, under the command of Colonel Stevenson.

There is evidence in existence that shortly before the commencement of this war it had been contemplated to place a large portion of the most valuable districts of California indirectly under British protection by grants to a Catholic clergyman named Mac-Namara, who projected a colony of his countrymen in those regions. He excited the Mexicans to accede to his proposal by appeals to their religious prejudices against the Protestants of the north, who, he alleged, would seize the jewel unless California was settled by his countrymen, whose creed would naturally unite them with the people and institutions of Mexico. The government of Mexico granted three thousand square leagues in the rich valley of San Joaquin, embracing San Francisco, Monterey, and Santa Barbara, to this behest of the foreign priest; but his patent could not be perfected until the governor of California sanctioned his permanent tenure of the land.

In November, 1845, Lieutenant Gillespie was dispatched from Washington with verbal instructions to Captain Frémont, who had been pursuing his scientific examinations of California, and had been inhospitably ordered by the authorities to quit the country. Early in March of 1846 the bold explorer was within the boundaries of Oregon, where he was found, in the following May, by Gillespie, who delivered him his verbal orders and a letter of credence from the secretary of state.

In consequence of this message Frémont abandoned his camp in the forest, surrounded by hostile Indians, and moved south to the valley of the Sacramento, where he was at once hailed by the American settlers, who, together with the foreigners generally, had received orders from the Mexican General Castro to leave California. Frémont's small band immediately formed the nucleus of a revolutionary troop, which gathered in numbers as it advanced south, and, abstaining guardedly from acts which might disgust the people, they injured no individuals and violated no private property. On June 14 Sonoma was taken possession of, and was garrisoned by a small force, under Ide, who issued a proclamation inviting all to come to his camp and aid in forming a republican government. Coure and Fowler, two young Americans, were murdered about this period in the neighborhood, and others were taken prisoners under Padilla. But the belligerents were pursued to San Raphael by Captain Ford, where they were conquered by the Americans; and on June 25 Frémont, who heard that Castro was approaching with 200 men, joined the camp at Sonoma. Thus far everything had been conducted with justice and liberality by the Americans. They studiously avoided disorderly conduct or captures, and invariably promised payment for the supplies that were taken for the support of the troopers. The Californians were in reality gratified by the prospect of American success in their territory, for they believed that it would secure a stable and progressive government, under which that beautiful region would be gradually developed.

On July 5 the Californian Americans declared their independence, and, organizing a battalion, of which Frémont was the chief, they raised the standard of the Bear and Star.

Frémont, at the head of his new battalion, moved his camp to Sutter's Fort on the Sacramento, and while he was preparing in July to follow General Castro to Santa Clara, he received the joyful news that Commodore Sloat had raised the American flag on the 7th of the month at Monterey, and that war actually existed between Mexico and the United States. The Californian Americans of course immediately abandoned their revolution for the national war, and substituted the American ensign for the grisly emblem under which they designed conquering the territory.

On July 8 Commodore Montgomery took possession of San Francisco, and soon after Frémont joined Commodore Sloat at Monterey. Sloat, who had in reality acted upon the faith of Frémont's operations in the north, knowing that Gillespie had been sent to him as a special messenger, and having heard while at Mazatlan of the warlike movements on the Rio Grande, was rather fearful that he had been precipitate in his conduct; but he resolved to maintain what he had done, and accordingly, when Admiral Sir George Seymour arrived in the *Collingwood* at Monterey on July 6 the grants to the Irish clergyman were not completed, and the American flag was already floating on every important post in the north of California. Seymour took MacNamara on board his ship, and thus the hopes of the British partisans were effectually blighted when the admiral and his passenger sailed from the coast.

Commodore Stockton arrived at Monterey during this summer and Sloat returned to the United States, leaving the commodore in command. Frémont and Gillespie, who were at the head of the forces on shore, determined to act under the orders of the naval commander, and Stockton immediately prepared for a military movement against the city of Los Angeles, where, he learned, General Castro and the civil governor, Pico, had assembled 600 men. Frémont and the commodore, embarking their forces at Monterey, sailed for San Pedro and San Diego, where, landing their troops, they united and took possession of Los Angeles on August 13. The public buildings, archives, and property fell into their possession without bloodshed, for Castro, the commanding general, fled at their approach. Stockton issued a proclamation announcing these facts to the people on August 17, and, having instituted a government, directed elections and required an oath of allegiance from the military. He appointed Frémont military commandant and Gillespie secretary. On August 28 he reported these proceedings to the government at Washington by the messenger who was met by General Kearny, as we have already related, on his way from Santa Fé to the Pacific. Carson, the courier, apprised the general of the conquest of California, and was obliged by him to return as his guide, while a new messenger was dispatched toward the East with the missives, escorted by the residue of the troop which was deemed useless for further military efforts on the shores of the Pacific.

But before Kearny reached his destination a change had come

over affairs in California. Castro returned to the charge in September with a large Mexican force headed by General Flores, and, the town of Los Angeles and the surrounding country having revolted, expelled the American garrison. Four hundred marines who landed from the *Savannah* under Captain Mervine were repulsed, while the garrison of Santa Barbara, under Lieutenant Talbott, had retired before a large body of Californians and Mexicans. Frémont, immediately resolving to increase his battalion, raised 428 men, chiefly from the emigrants who moved this year to California. He mounted his troopers on horses procured in the vicinity of San Francisco and Sutter's Fort, and marched secretly but quickly to San Luis Obispo, where he surprised and captured Don Jesus Pico, the commandant of that military post. Pico, having been found in arms, had broken his parole, given during the early pacification, and a court-martial sentenced him to be shot; but Frémont, still pursuing his humane policy toward the Californians, pardoned the popular and influential chieftain, who from that hour was his firm friend throughout the subsequent troubles.

On Christmas Day of 1846, amid storm and rain, in which a hundred horses and mules perished, Frémont and his brave battalion passed the mountain of Santa Barbara. Skirting the coast through the long maritime pass at Punto Gordo—protected on one flank by one of the vessels of the navy and assailed on the other by fierce bands of mounted Californians—they moved onward until they reached the plain of Couenga, where the enemy was drawn up with a force equal to their own. Frémont summoned the hostile troops to surrender, and after their consent to a parley, went to them, with Don Jesus Pico and arranged the terms of the capitulation, by which they bound themselves to deliver their arms to the soldiers and to conform at home to the laws of the United States, though no Californians should be compelled to take an oath of allegiance to the United States until the war was ended and the treaty either exonerated them or changed their nationality.

Meanwhile General Kearny, on his westward march from Santa Fé, had reached a place called Warner's Rancho, thirty-three miles from San Diego, where a captured Californian mail for Sonoma apprised him that the southern part of the territory was wrested from the United States troops. The letters exulted, but it was supposed that, as usual in Mexico, they exaggerated the misfortunes of the Americans. Kearny's small troop was much enfeebled by the long and fatiguing journey it had made from Santa Fé amid great privations. From Warner's Rancho the commander communicated with Stockton by means of a neutral Englishman, and on December 5 was joined by Gillespie, who informed him that a mounted Californian force under Andres Pico was prepared to dispute his passage toward the coast. On the 6th the Americans left the rancho, resolving to come suddenly upon the enemy, and confident that the usual success of the troops would attend the exploit; but the fresh forces of this hardy and brave Californian band, composed perhaps of some of the most expert horsemen in that region, were far more than a match for the toil-worn troopers of Kearny. Eighteen of Kearny's men were killed in this action at San Pascual and thirteen wounded. For several days the camp of the Americans was besieged by the fierce and hardy children of the soil. The provisions of the beleagured band were scant, and it was almost entirely deprived of water. Its position was in every respect most disastrous, and in all probability it would have perished from famine or fallen an easy prey to the Mexicans had not the resolute Kit Carson, accompanied by Lieutenant Beale and an Indian, volunteered to pass the dangerous lines of the enemy to seek assistance at San Diego. These heroic men performed their perilous duty, and Lieutenant Grey, with 180 soldiers and marines, reached and relieved his anxious countrymen on December 10, bringing them in two days to the American camp at San Diego.

As soon as the band had recruited its strength, Kearny naturally became anxious to engage in active service. He had been sent to California, according to the language of his instructions, to conquer and govern it; but he found Commodore Stockton already in the position of governor, with an ample naval force at his orders, while the broken remnant of the dragoons who accompanied him from Santa Fé was altogether incompetent to subdue the revolted territory. By himself therefore he was altogether inadequate for any successful military move. Stockton, quite as anxious as Kearny to engage in active hostilities, was desirous to accompany the general as his aid; but Kearny declined the service, and in turn volunteered to become the aid of Stockton. The commodore, less accustomed, perhaps, to military etiquette than to prompt and useful action at a moment of difficulty, resolved at once to end the game of idle compliments, and accepted the offer of General Kearny; but before they departed Stockton agreed that he might command the expedition in a position subordinate to him as commander-in-chief.

On December 29, with 60 volunteers, 400 marines, 6 heavy pieces of artillery, 11 heavy wagons, and 57 dragoons composing the remains of General Kearny's troop, they marched toward the north, and on January 7 found themselves near the River San Gabrielle, the passage of which the enemy, with superior numbers under General Flores, was prepared to dispute. It was a contest between American sailors and soldiers and California horsemen, for the whole Mexican troop was mounted; yet the Americans were successful and crossed the river. This action occurred about nine miles from Los Angeles, and the Americans pushed on six miles farther, till they reached the Mesa, a level prairie, where Flores again attacked them and was beaten off. Retreating thence to Couenga, the Californians, refusing to submit to Stockton and Kearny, capitulated, as we have already declared, to Colonel Frémont, who had been raised to this rank by the government. On the morning of January 10, 1847, the Americans took final possession of Los Angeles. Soon after this a government was established for California which was to continue until the close of the war, or until the government or the population of the region changed it.

Chapter XXVIII

GENERAL SCOTT TAKES COMMAND IN MEXICO
1846-1847

WE return from the theater of these military operations on the shores of the Pacific to the valley of the Rio Grande and the headquarters of General Taylor. The armistice at Monterey had ceased by the order of the government, and the American commander, leaving Generals Worth and Butler at Monterey and Saltillo, which had been seized, hastened with a sufficient body of troops to the Gulf of Mexico for the purpose of occupying Tampico, the capital of the State of Tamaulipas. But he did not advance farther than Victoria when he found that Tampico had surrendered to Commodore Conner on November 14.

In the meanwhile the political aspect of Mexico was changed under the rule of Santa Anna, who had returned to power, though he had not realized the hopes of the Americans by acceding to an honorable peace. A secret movement that was made by an agent sent into the country proved altogether unsuccessful, for the people were aroused against the United States, and would listen willingly to no advances for accommodation. Santa Anna cautiously noted the national feeling, and being altogether unable to control or modify it—although he studiously refrained from committing himself prior to his return to the capital—he resolved to place himself at the head of the popular movement in defense of the northern frontier. Accordingly in December, 1846, he had already assembled a large force, amounting to 20,000 men, at San Luis Potosi, the capital of the State of that name south of Monterey, on the direct road to the heart of the internal provinces and nearly midway between the Gulf and the Pacific.

The news of this hostile gathering, which was evidently designed to assail the Army of Occupation, soon reached the officers who had been left in command at headquarters during Taylor's absence; and, in consequence of a dispatch sent by express to General Wool at Parras for reinforcements, that officer immediately put his whole column in motion, and after marching one hundred and twenty miles in four days found himself at Agua Nueva, within twenty-one miles of Saltillo. Thus sustained, the officers in command awaited with anxiety the movements of the Mexican chief and the return of General Taylor.

But in the meantime the administration at Washington, seeing the inutility of continuing the attacks upon the more northern outposts of Mexico—which it was nevertheless resolved to hold as indemnifying hostages, inasmuch as they were contiguous to United States soil and boundaries—determined to strike a blow at the vitals of Mexico by seizing her principal eastern port and proceeding thence to the capital. For this purpose General Scott, who had been set aside at the commencement of the war in consequence of a rupture between himself and the War Department while arranging the details of the campaign, was once more summoned into the field and appointed commander-in-chief of the American army in Mexico. Up to this period, November, 1846, large recruits of regulars and volunteers had flocked to the standard of Taylor and were stationed at various posts in the valley of the Rio Grande, under the command of Generals Butler, Worth, Patterson, Quitman, and Pillow. But the project of a descent upon Vera Cruz, which was warmly advocated by General Scott, made it necessary to detach a considerable portion of these levies, and of their most efficient and best-drilled members. Taylor and his subordinate commanders were thus placed in a merely defensive position, and that too at a moment when they were threatened in front by the best army that had been assembled for many a year in Mexico.

It is probable that the government of the United States at the moment it planned this expedition to Vera Cruz and the capital was not fully apprised of the able and efficient arrangements of Santa Anna, or imagined that he would immediately quit San Luis Potosi in order to defend the eastern access to the capital, inasmuch as it was not probable that Taylor would venture to penetrate the country with impaired forces, which, in a strictly military point of view, were not more than adequate for garrison service along an extended base of three hundred miles. But as the sequel showed, they neither estimated properly the time that would be consumed in concentrating the forces and preparing the means for their transportation to Vera Cruz, nor judged correctly of the military skill of Santa Anna, who naturally preferred to crush the weak northern foe with his overwhelming force than to encounter the strong battalions of veterans who were to be led against him on the east by the most brilliant captain of the country.

The enterprise of General Scott was one of extraordinary magnitude and responsibility. With his usual foresight he determined that he would not advance until the expedition was perfectly complete in every essential of certain success. Nothing was permitted to disturb his equanimity or patient resolution in carrying out the scheme as he thought best. He weighed all the dangers and all the difficulties of the adventure, and placed no reliance upon the supposed weakness of the enemy. This was the true, soldier-like view of the splendid project; and if at the time men were found inconsiderate enough to blame him for procrastinating dalliance, the glorious result of his enterprise repaid him for all the petty sneers and misconceptions with which his discretion was undervalued by the carpet knights at home. There is but one point upon which we feel justified in disagreeing with his plan of campaign. He should not have weakened the command of General Taylor in the face of Santa Anna's army. It was almost an invitation to that chief for an attack upon the valley of the Rio Grande; and had the Army of Occupation been effectually destroyed at Buena Vista, scarcely an American would have remained throughout the long line of Taylor's base to tell the tale of cruelties perpetrated by the flushed and vengeful victors.

While events were maturing and preparations making in the valley of the Rio Grande and the Island of Lobos, we shall direct our attention again for a short time to the central regions of the north of Mexico in the neighborhood of Santa Fé.

A considerable force of Missourians had been organized under the command of Colonel Doniphan and marched to New Mexico, whence it was designed to dispatch him toward Chihuahua. Soon after General Kearny's departure from Santa Fé for California, Colonel Price, who was subsequently raised to the rank of general, reached that post with his western recruits and took command, while Doniphan was directed by order from Kearny, dated near La Joya, to advance with his regiment against the Navajo Indians, who had threatened with war the New Mexicans, now under United States protection. He performed this service successfully; and on November 22, 1846, made a treaty with the chiefs, binding them to live in amity with the Spaniards and Americans. Reassembling all his troops at Val Verde, he commenced his march to the south in the middle of December, and after incredible difficulties and great sufferings from inadequate supplies and equipments he reached Chihuahua, fighting on the march two successful actions against the Mexicans at Bracito and Sacramento. Having

THE MEXICAN WAR

completely routed the enemy in the latter contest, Chihuahua fell into his power. Here he tarried, recruiting his toil-worn band, for six weeks, and as the spring opened pushed onward to the south until he reached the headquarters of Taylor, whence he returned with his regiment to the United States. His army marched five thousand miles during the campaign, and its adventures form one of the most romantic episodes in the war with Mexico.

While Doniphan was advancing southward, the command of

Price was well-nigh destroyed in New Mexico and the wild region intervening between its borders and the frontiers of the United States. A conspiracy had been secretly organized among the Mexican and half-breed population, to rise against the Americans. On January 19, 1847, massacres occurred simultaneously at Taos, Arroyo Hondo, Rio Colorado, and Mora. At Taos Governor Charles Bent, one of the oldest and most experienced residents in that region, was cruelly slain, and a great deal of valuable property destroyed by the merciless foe. Price received intelligence of this onslaught on the 20th, and rapidly calling in his outposts, marched with a hastily gathered band of about 350 men against the enemy, whom he met, attacked, and overawed on the 24th at Cañada. Reinforced by Captain Burgwin from Albuquerque, he again advanced against the insurgents, and on the 28th defeated a Mexican force estimated at 1500 at the pass of El Embudo. Passing thence over the Taos Mountain through deep snows in midwinter, the resolute commander pursued his way unmolested through the deserted settlement which had been recently ravaged by the rebels, nor did he encounter another force until he came upon the enemy at Pueblo, when he stormed the fortified position and gained the day, but with the loss of the gallant Burgwin and other valuable officers. Mora was reduced again to subjection early in February by Captain Morin, and in all these rapid but successful actions it is estimated that nearly 300 Mexicans paid the forfeit of their lives for the cruel conspiracy and its fatal results.

From this moment the tenure of the United States possessions in New Mexico was no longer considered secure. The troops in that district were not the best disciplined or most docile in the army, and to the dangers of another sudden outbreak among the treacherous Mexicans was added the fear of a sudden rising among the Indian tribes, who were naturally anxious to find any pretext or chance for ridding the country of a foe whom they feared far more as a permanent neighbor than the comparatively feeble half-breeds and Mexicans.

In December of 1846 Lieutenant Richie, who bore dispatches to Taylor apprising him of the meditated attack upon Vera Cruz, was seized and slain by the Mexicans while on his way to the headquarters, and thus Santa Anna became possessed of the plan of the proposed campaign. The Army of Occupation had been sadly impaired by the abstraction of its best material for future action on the southern line under the commander-in-chief. But General Taylor resolved at once to face the danger stoutly and to manifest no symptom of unsoldierlike querulousness under the injustice he experienced from the government. Nevertheless—prudent in all things, and foreseeing the danger of his command, of the lower country, and the *morale* of the whole army in the event of his defeat—he exposed the error of the War Department in his dispatches to the adjutant general and secretary, so that history, if not arms, might eventually do justice to his discretion and fortitude.

The note of preparation preceded for some time the actual advent of Santa Anna from San Luis Potosi, and all was bustle in the American encampments, which were spread from Monterey to Agua Nueva beyond Saltillo, in order to give him the best possible reception under the circumstances. Wool was encamped with a force at Agua Nueva, in advance on the road from Saltillo to San Luis, about thirteen miles from the pass of Angostura, where the road lies through a mountain gorge defended on one side by a small tableland near the acclivities of the steep sierra and cut with the channels of rough barrancas or ravines worn by the waters as they descend from the summits, and on the other by an extensive network of deep and impassable gullies which drained the slopes of the western spurs.

This spot was decided upon as the battle ground in the event of an attack, and the encampment at Agua Nueva in front of it was kept up as an extreme outpost, whence the scouts might be sent forth to watch the approach of Santa Anna.

On February 21 the positive advance of that chief was announced. The camp was immediately broken up, and all the forces rapidly concentrated in the gorge of Angostura. The troops did not amount to more than 4690 efficient men, and they had reason to believe that Santa Anna commanded nearly five times that number, and was greatly superior in cavalry, a part of which had been sent by secret paths through the mountains to the rear of the American position, so as to cut off the retreat in the event of failure in the battle.

The great object of Taylor in selecting his ground and forming his plan of battle was to make his small army equal, as nearly as possible, to that of Santa Anna by narrowing the front of attack nd thus concentrating his force upon any point through which he Mexicans might seek to break. In other words, it was his lesign to dam up the strait of Angostura with a living mass, and o leave no portion of the unbroken ground on the narrow table- and undefended by infantry and artillery. The battle ground that iad been selected was admirably calculated for this purpose, and iis foresight was justified by the result. It was not necessary for Taylor to capture or annihilate his enemy, for he was victor, if vith but a single regiment he kept the valley closed against the Mexicans. The center of the American line was the main road, n which was placed a battery of eight pieces, reduced during the iction to five, supported by bodies of infantry. On the right of he stream which swept along the edge of the western mountains vas a single regiment and some cavalry, with two guns, which it vas supposed would be sufficient, with the aid of the tangled gulleys, to arrest the Mexicans in that quarter. On the left of he stream, where the ravines were fewer and the plain between hem wider, stood two regiments of infantry, suitably furnished vith artillery, and extending from the central battery on the road o the base of the eastern mountains on whose skirts an adequate force of cavalry and riflemen was posted.

In order to break this array Santa Anna divided his army into three attacking columns, each of which nearly doubled the whole of Taylor's force. One of these was opposed to the battery of eight guns in order to force the road, and the other two were lesigned to outflank the American position by penetrating or turn- ing the squadrons stationed at the base of the mountains.

On the afternoon of February 22 the attack began by a skir- mishing attempt of the Mexicans to pass to the rear of the Ameri- can left wing; but as they climbed the mountain in their endeavor to outflank in that quarter, they were opposed by the infantry and riflemen, who disputed successfully every inch of ground, until night closed and obliged the Mexicans to retire. General Taylor, fearing an attack from the cavalry upon Saltillo, immediately de- parted with a suitable escort to provide for its safety, and left General Wool to command during his absence.

After daydawn on the 23d Santa Anna again commenced the battle by an attack upon the left wing, and for a while was withstood, until a portion of the American forces, after a brave defense, mistaking an order to retire for an order to retreat, became suddenly panic-stricken and fled from the field. At this moment Taylor returned from Saltillo and found the whole left of the position broken, while the enemy was pouring his masses of infantry and cavalry along the base of the eastern mountains toward the rear.

Meanwhile the battery in the road had repulsed the Mexican column sent against it, and spared three of its guns for service on the upper plain. The regiment on the right of the stream had been brought over to the left bank with its cannon, and was now in position with two other regiments, facing the mountains, between which and this force was a gap through whose opening the Mexicans steadily advanced under a dreadful fire. Nearly all the artillery had been concentrated at the same place, while in other parts of the field and nearer to the hacienda of Buena Vista, in the American rear, were bodies of cavalry engaged in conflict with the advancing foe.

As Taylor approached this disastrous scene he met the fugitives, and speedily made his dispositions to stop the carnage. With a regiment from Mississippi he restrained a charge of Mexican cavalry and ordered all the artillery, save four guns, to the rear to drive back the exulting Mexicans. This maneuver was perfectly successful, and so dreadfully was the enemy cut up by the new attack that Santa Anna availed himself of a ruse, by a flag of truce, in order to suspend the action while he withdrew his men.

The transfer of so large a portion of Taylor's most efficient troops to the rear of his original line had greatly weakened his front in the best positions, where the inequalities of ground sustained his feeble numbers. Santa Anna was not unmindful of the advantage he had gained by these untoward events, and prepared all his best reserves, which were now brought for the first time into action, for another attack. Taylor had with him three regiments and four pieces of artillery. His front was rather toward the mountain than the open pass, while his back was toward the road along the stream. On his right was the whole Mexican army; on his left, far off in the rear, were the troops that had repulsed and cut up the Mexican column; and the great effort, upon whose success all depended, was to bring these dispersed squadrons again into action while he maintained the position against the assault of the fresh reserves. As Santa Anna advanced with his inspirited columns he was met by regiments of infantry, which stood firm, until overwhelmed by numbers and driven into a ravine they were cruelly slaughtered. After the American infantry had been overcome, the last hope was in the artillery, and with this the Mexican advance was effectually stopped and the battle won.

The whole day had been spent in fighting, and when night came the field was covered with dead. It was an anxious season for the battered troops, and while all were solicitous for the event of a contest which it was supposed would be renewed on the morrow, the greatest efforts were made not only to inspirit the troops who had borne the brunt of two days' battle, but to bring up reinforcements of artillery and cavalry that had been stationed between Saltillo and Monterey. At daydawn, however, on February 24, the enemy was found to have retreated, and Buena Vista was won.

This wonderful battle saved the north of Mexico and the valley of the Rio Grande, for Miñon and Urrea were already in the rear with regular troops and bands of rancheros ready to cut up the flying army and descend upon the slender garrisons. Urrea captured a valuable wagon train at Ramos in the neighborhood of Monterey. From February 22 to 26 he continually threatened the weakened outposts, and from that period until March 7 inflicted severe injuries upon trains and convoys from the Gulf. In the meantime Santa Anna retreated to San Luis Potosi with the fragments of his fine army, and not long after General Taylor retired from a field of service in which he was no longer permitted to advance, or required except for garrison duty.

In the months of October and November, 1846, Tabasco and Tampico had yielded to the American navy; the former after a severe attack conducted by Commodore Matthew C. Perry, and the latter without bloodshed.

Chapter XXIX

AFFAIRS IN THE CAPITAL. 1846-1847

WHEN General Antonio Lopez de Santa Anna landed from the steamer *Arab,* after having been permitted to pass the line of the blockading fleet at Vera Cruz, he was received by only a few friends. His reception was in fact not a public one, nor marked by enthusiasm.

By the revolution which overthrew Paredes General Salas came into the exercise of the chief executive authority, and as soon as Santa Anna arrived he dispatched three high officers to welcome him, among whom was Valentin Gomez Farias, a renowned leader of the federalist party—in former days a bitter foe of the exiled chief. Santa Anna in his communications with the revolutionists from Cuba had confessed his political mistake in former years in advocating the central system. "The love of provincial liberty," said he, in a letter to a friend dated in Havana on March 8, 1846, "being firmly rooted in the minds of all, and the democratic principle preponderating everywhere, nothing can be established in a solid manner in the country which does not conform to these tendencies, nor can we without them attain either order, peace, prosperity, or respectability among foreign nations.

"To draw everything to the center, and thus to give unity of action to the republic, as I at one time deemed best, is no longer possible; nay, more, I say it is dangerous; it is contrary to the object I proposed to myself in the unitarian system, because we thereby expose ourselves to the separation of the northern departments which are most clamorous for freedom of internal administration. . . . I therefore urge you to use all your influence to reconcile the liberals, communicating with Señor Farias and his friends, in order to induce them to come to an understanding with us. . . . I will in future support the claims of the masses, leaving the people entirely at liberty to organize their system of government and to regulate their offices in a manner that may please them best."

These declarations, and the knowledge of Santa Anna's sagacity and influence with the masses, had probably induced Farias to adhere to the project of his recall which was embraced in the movements of the revolutionists. And accordingly we find that upon his landing, Santa Anna published a long manifesto to the people, which he concludes by recommending that, until they proclaim a new constitution, the federal constitution of 1824 be readopted for the internal administration of the country.

Salas, who had previously ordered the governors of the departments to be guided solely by the commands of Santa Anna, immediately issued a bando nacional, or edict, countersigned by the acting secretary of state, Monasterio, which embodied the views of the returned exile, and proclaimed the constitution of 1824, in accordance with his recommendation.

General Salas, who exercised supreme command from August 7 to 20, professed to have done as little as possible of his own will, and only what was urgently demanded by the necessity of the case. He boasted, however, that he had effected what he could "to aid the brave men who, in Monterey, have determined to die rather than succumb to the invasion and perfidiousness of the Americans." In his communications to Santa Anna he urged him to hasten to Mexico as soon as possible to assume his powers, and the Mexican gazettes commended him for refusing to accept the pay of president while discharging the functions of his office.

On August 15 Salas issued a proclamation, in which he announced to his countrymen that a new insult had been offered to them, and that another act of baseness had been perpetrated by the Americans. He alluded to the Californias, which, he said, " the Americans have now seized by the strong hand, after having villainously robbed us of Texas." He announced that the expedition which had been so long preparing would set forth in two days for the recovery of the country, and that measures would be taken to arrange the differences existing between the people of the Californias and the various preceding central administrations. In conclusion, he appealed eloquently to the Californians to second with their best exertions the attempt which would be made to drive out the Americans, and to unite their rich and fertile territories forever to the republic.

During the administration of this chief various proclamations were issued to arouse the people to take part in the war by enlisting and by contributing their means. Efforts were also made to organize the local militia, but with little effect.

Santa Anna, in his reply to Salas on August 20, accepts the trust which is formally devolved upon him, and approves of the acts of the latter, especially in sending forward all the troops to Monterey, New Mexico, and California, and in summoning a congress for December 6. These, he says, are the first two wants of the nation—the formation of a constitution for the country and the purification of the soil of the country from foreign invaders. These ends gained, he will gladly lay down his power. "My functions will cease," he says, "when I have established the nation in its rights; when I see its destinies controlled by its legitimate representatives, and when I may be able, by the blessing of Heaven, to lay at the feet of the national representatives laurels plucked on the banks of the Sabine—all of which must be due to the force and the will of the Mexican people."

Santa Anna at length quitted his hacienda, where he had doubtless been waiting for the opportune moment to arrive when he could best exhibit himself to the inhabitants of the capital and profit by their highest enthusiasm, pushed to an extreme by alternate hopes and fears. On September 14, 1846, he reached Ayotla, a small town distant twenty-five miles from the City of Mexico. Here he received a communication from Almonte, the secretary of war *ad interim,* proposing to him the supreme executive power, or dictatorship. This offer was made on the part of the provisional government.

Santa Anna immediately replied in the following strain to the missive of his partisan:

GENERAL SANTA ANNA, Commander-in-chief of the Liberating Army, to General Almonte, Minister of War of the Republic of Mexico:

AYOTLA, 1 o'clock A. M., September 14, 1846.

SIR: I have received your favor of this date, acknowledging a decree issued by the supreme government of the nation, embracing a programme of the proceedings adopted to regulate a due celebration of the reëstablishment of the constitution of 1824, the assumption by myself of the supreme executive power, and the anniversary of the glorious *grito* of Dolores.

My satisfaction is extreme to observe the enthusiasm with which preparations are made to celebrate the two great blessings which have fallen upon this nation—her independence and her liberty; and I am penetrated with the deepest gratitude to find that my arrival at the capital will be made to contribute to the solemnities of so great an occasion. In furtherance of this object I shall make my entrée into that city to-morrow at midday, and desire, in contributing my share to the national jubilee, to observe such a course as may best accord with my duties to my country—beloved of my heart—and with the respect due to the will of the sovereign people.

I have been called by the voice of my fellow-citizens to exercise the office of commander-in-chief of the army of the republic. I was far from my native land when intelligence of this renewed confidence, and of these new obligations imposed upon me by my country, was brought to me, and I saw that the imminent dangers which surrounded her on all sides formed the chief motive for calling me to the head of the army. I now see a terrible contest with a perfidious and daring enemy impending over her, in which the Mexican Republic must reconquer the insignia of her glory and a fortunate issue, if victorious, or disappear from the face of the earth, if so unfortunate as to be defeated. I also see a treacherous faction raising its head from her bosom, which, in calling up a form of government detested by the united nation, provokes a preferable submission to foreign dominion; and I behold at last, that after much vacillation, that nation is resolved to establish her right to act for herself and to arrange such a form of government as best suits her wishes.

All this I have observed, and turned a listening ear to the cry of my desolate country, satisfied that she really needed my weak services at so important a period. Hence I have come, without hesitation or delay, to place myself in subjection to her will; and, desirous to be perfectly understood upon reaching my native soil, I gave a full and public expression of my sentiments and principles. The reception which they met convinced me that I had not deceived myself, and I am now the more confirmed in them, not from having given them more consideration, but because they have found a general echo in the hearts of my fellow-citizens.

Your excellency will at once perceive how great an error I should commit in assuming the supreme magistracy, when my duty calls me to the field, to fight against the enemies of the republic. I should disgrace myself, if, when called to the point of danger, I should spring to that of power! Neither my loyalty nor my honor requires the abandonment of interests so dear to me. The single motive of my heart is to offer my compatriots the sacrifice of that blood which yet runs in my veins. I wish them to know that I consecrate myself entirely to their service, as a soldier ought to do, and am only desirous further to be permitted to point out the course by which Mexico may attain the rank to which her destinies call her.

In marching against the enemy, and declining to accept power, I give a proof of the sincerity of my sentiments; leaving the nation her own mistress, at liberty to dispose of herself as she sees fit. The elections for members of a congress to form the constitution which the people wish to adopt are proceeding. That congress will now soon convene, and while I shall be engaged in the conflict in armed defense of her independence, the nation will place such safeguards around her liberties as may best suit herself.

If I should permit myself for a single moment to take the reins of government, the sincerity of my promises would be rendered questionable, and no confidence could be placed in them.

I am resolved that they shall not be falsified, for in their redemption I behold the general good, as well as my honor as a Mexican and a soldier. I cannot abandon this position. The existing government has pursued a course with which the nation has shown itself content, and I have no desire to subvert it by taking its place. I feel abundant pleasure in remaining where I am, and flatter myself that the nation will applaud my choice. I shall joyfully accept such tasks as she shall continue to impose upon me; and while she is engaged in promoting the objects of civilization, I will brave every danger in supporting its benefits, even at the cost of my existence.

Will your excellency have the goodness to tender to the supreme government my sincere thanks for their kindness? I will personally repeat them to-morrow, for which purpose I propose to call at the palace. I shall there embrace my friends, and, hastily pressing them to my heart, bid them a tender farewell and set out to the scene of war, to lend my aid to serve my country, or to perish among its ruins.

I beg to repeat to your excellency assurances of my continued and especial esteem.

ANTONIO LOPEZ DE SANTA ANNA.

On September 15 Santa Anna arrived at the capital amid enthusiastic rejoicings. The people seemed to behold in him their savior, and were almost frantic with joy. The testimonies of attachment to his person were unbounded, and the next day the most vigorous measures, so far as declarations go, were adopted by the provisional government.

A levy of 30,000 men to recruit the army was ordered. Requisitions were forthwith transmitted to all the principal places in the republic for their respective quotas of men. Puebla and all the towns within a circuit of fifty or sixty leagues of the metropolis are stated to have complied with the requisition for troops with the greatest alacrity. To facilitate the arming and equipping of this large body, the government ordered that duties on all munitions of war should cease to be levied until further notice.

Santa Anna was thus once more in the capital and effectually at the head of power; but he remained only a short time to attend to political matters, and, dreading doubtless to assume openly the management of the government or to trust himself away from the protection of the military, he hastened to surround his person with the army; as commander-in-chief he effectually controlled all the departments of the government.

In order to perceive distinctly the perilous position of Santa Anna, we must understand the state of parties in Mexico. The revolution which placed him in power was brought about by a union of the federalists with his partisans. Santa Anna of course retained an influence over his adherents after arriving in Mexico; but the federalists were divided into two parties—the Puros and Moderados, or, Democrats and Conservatives. The dissensions in these sections enabled Santa Anna in a degree to hold the balance between them. Salas, the acting executive, was a Conservative, and Gomez Farias, president of the council of government, was a

Democrat. Intrigue after intrigue occurred in the cabinet and elsewhere among the ultras to supplant Salas, and several resignations gave evidence of the ill-feeling and dissensions between the ministers. Cortina and Pacheco, both Conservatives, resigned, and so did Rejon and Farias. The national guard intimated its discontent with the condition of things very manifestly, and the new cabinet was filled with old enemies of Santa Anna. Meanwhile Almonte, the ablest man in the country, retained the ministry of war.

About this time the State of San Luis Potosi pronounced against the presidency of General Salas, demanding that General Santa Anna should assume the executive functions, or that someone should be named by him. As a precaution against the apprehended attempts upon his life, Salas retired on October 25 from the capital to Tacubaya. The greater part of the permanent garrison of the capital took up its quarters in the same place. Santa Anna was probably determined that General Salas should not obtain too absolute an ascendency. Report said that Salas was honest enough to attempt to carry into effect all the guaranties of the revolution of Jalisco and the citadel, and that his policy did not suit the chief; but Santa Anna professed to act in the utmost harmony with him.

This outbreak against the provisional government of General Salas was soon suppressed, and Santa Anna remained in command of the army at San Luis Potosi, but without making any attack upon the forces on the Rio Grande after the defeat of Ampudia at Monterey or endeavoring to prevent the subsequent capture of Victoria and Tampico.

On December 23 congress voted, by States, for provisional president and vice-president. Each State had one vote in this election, determined by the majority of its deputies. Twenty-two States voted, including the Federal District of Mexico, and two territories. Santa Anna's opponent, Francisco Elorriega, was the choice of nine States, and Gomez Farias was elected vice-president. The day before the election the members of the cabinet threw up their portfolios; and in the midst of his evident political unpopularity with the politicians, Santa Anna seems to have been left by the authorities at San Luis Potosi with an army destitute of efficient arms, of military knowledge, and of the means of support. Santa Anna accepted the provisional presidency.

Meanwhile the American army had been advancing steadily since the battles of Resaca de la Palma and Palo Alto on May 8 and 9, 1846. California had fallen, and New Mexico had been subjugated. Tampico was also taken, and Taylor had pushed his victorious army to Saltillo. Santa Anna stood at bay in San Luis Potosi, for he was not yet prepared to fight, and popular opinion would not permit him to negotiate. In this forlorn condition he resorted to the usual occupation of the Mexican Government when in distress, and issued dispatch after dispatch to stimulate congress, the cabinet, and the people in the lingering war.

Nor was the government of the United States meanwhile inattentive to this position of affairs in Mexico or indisposed to afford the government an opportunity to reconcile the difficulties by negotiation. Two distinct efforts were made by Buchanan, the secretary of state, in the summer of 1846, and in January, 1847; but both proved abortive, and hostilities were continued.

At length, when Santa Anna perceived the enfeebled condition of General Taylor and believed that Scott would be for a long time hindered from effecting his attack upon Vera Cruz, he marched to Buena Vista and experienced the sad reverse which we have already recounted. As soon as the battle was over the wily and discomfited chief immediately began to repair the losses of his arms by the eloquence and adroitness of his pen. In a long account of the battle he treats the affair as almost a victory, and leaves the public mind of Mexico in doubt as to whether he had been beaten or victorious. The few trophies taken in the saddest moments of the action were sent in triumph to the interior and paraded as the *spoilio opima* in San Luis and the City of Mexico. The public men of the country knew that Angostura had in reality been lost, and Miñon, who was seriously assailed in the press by Santa Anna for not coöperating at the critical moment, published a reply in which he treated Santa Anna in the plainest terms, and denounced as false the general's statement that his troops were famishing for food on February 24, and that his failure to destroy Taylor's army was only owing to this important fact! This system of mutual denunciation and recrimination was quite common in Mexico whenever a defeat was to be accounted for or thrown on the shoulders of an individual who was not in reality answerable for it.

When Santa Anna returned to San Luis Potosi he entered

that city with not one-half the army that accompanied him on his departure to the north. It was, moreover, worn out and disorganized by the long and painful march over the bleak desert, and had entirely lost its habit of discipline. Such was the condition of things at San Luis in the month of March, when Santa Anna found himself compelled to organize another force to resist the enemy on the east; but while his attention was diligently directed to this subject the sad news reached him that Mexico was not only assailed from without, but that her capital was torn by internal dissensions.

The peace between the president and the vice-president, Don Valentin Gomez Farias, had been cemented by the good offices of mutual friends, though it is not likely that any very ardent friendship could have sprung up suddenly between men whose politics had always been so widely variant. Nor was there less difference between the moral than the political character of these personages. Santa Anna, the selfish, arrogant military chieftain —a man of unquestionable genius and talent for command—had passed his life in spreading his sails to catch the popular breeze, and by his alliances with the two most powerful elements of Mexican society, the army and the church, had always contrived to sustain his eminent political position, or recover it when it was temporarily lost. Such was the case in his return to power after the invasion of the French, in the attack upon whom he fortunately lost a limb, which became a constant capital upon which to trade in the corrupt but sentimental market of popular favor. Valentin Gomez Farias, on the contrary, was a pure, straightforward, uncompromising patriot, always alive to the true progressive interests of the Mexican nation, and satisfied that these could only be secured by the successful imitation of the federal system of the United States, together with the destruction of the large standing army and the release of the large church properties from the incubus of mortmain.

There was much discontent in Mexico with the election of these two personages to the presidency and vice-presidency. Reflecting men thought the union unnatural, and although the desperate times required desperate remedies, there was something so incongruous in the political alliance between Farias and Santa Anna that little good could be expected to issue from it. The church party was alarmed for its wealth, and the moderate party was frightened by the habitual despotism of Santa Anna. The latter personage was in fact regarded with more favor at the moment by all classes than Farias, because the country had reason to believe him a man of action, and familiar in times of danger and distress with all its resources of men and money; and as he was entirely occupied with the organization and management of the army at San Luis, the opposition party directed all its blows against the administration of the vice-presidency.

A few days after the installation of the new government the agitation of the mortmain question was commenced in congress. The Puro party, united with the executive, made every effort to destroy the power of the clergy by undermining the foundation of its wealth, while the Moderados became the supporters of the ecclesiastics, under the lead of Don Mariano Otero.

At length the law was passed, but it was not a frank and decided act, destroying at once the privileges of the clergy and declaring their possessions to be the property of the republic. In fact it was a mere decree for the seizure of ecclesiastical incomes, which threatened the non-complying with heavy fines if they did not pay over to the civil authorities the revenues which had formerly been collected by the stewards of convents and monks.

This act, comparatively mild as it was, and temporary as it might have been considered, did not satisfy the clergy, even in this moment of national peril. They resorted to the spiritual weapons which they reserved for extreme occasions. They fulminated excommunications, and warned against the certainty of punishment hereafter for the crime that had been committed by placing an impious hand upon wealth which they asserted belonged to God alone. This conduct of the religious orders had its desired effect not only among the people, but among the officers of government, for the chief clerk of the finance department, Hurci, refused to sign the law, and it was some time before a suitable person could be found to put the law in operation. Santa Anna adroitly kept himself aloof from the controversy, and wrote from San Luis that he merely desired support for the army, and that in other questions, especially those touching the clergy, he had no desire to enter, but would limit himself to the recommendation that neither the canons nor the collegiate establishment of Guadalupe should be molested, inasmuch as he entertained the greatest friendship for the one and the most reverential devotion for the other.

But the executive, fixed in its intention to liberate the property held in mortmain, took every means to carry the law into effect, and experienced the utmost resistance from the incumbents.

This rigorous conduct of the executive, and the opposition it encountered from the Moderados, fomented by that powerful spiritual class which has so long guided the conscience of the masses, gave rise at this period to the outbreak in the capital which is known as the revolution of the Polkos. It began on February 22, 1847, in Mexico, while Santa Anna was firing the first guns at Angostura; and its great object was to drive Farias from executive power. The forces on both sides amounted to 6000 men, and were divided between the Polkos and the partisans of the government. Funds were found to support both factions, and from that time to March 21 the City of Mexico was converted into a battlefield. On the morning of that day Santa Anna, who had already dispatched a portion of his broken army toward the coast, and who had been approached on his journey from the capital by emissaries from both factions, arrived at Guadalupe, and immediately the contest ceased. The stewards of the convents refused to expend more money for the support of their partisans, and the treasury of the government was closed against its adherents. The personal influence of Santa Anna thus put an end to a disgraceful rebellion which threatened the nationality of Mexico within, while a foreign enemy was preparing to attack its most vital parts from the Gulf.

The conflict of arms was over, but the partisans of the clergy did not intermit their efforts to get rid of the obnoxious vice-president; and at length they effected pacifically what they had been unable to do by force.

They brought in a bill declaring that "the vice-presidency of the republic, created by the decree of December 21, 1846, should be suppressed." The debate upon this was of the most animated nature, the friends and enemies of Farias showing equal vehemence in sustaining their views. On March 31 the vote was taken, and the proposition carried by a vote of thirty-eight to thirty-five.

The following day a decree was passed embodying the above proposition and others:

1. Permission is granted to the actual President of the republic to take command in person of the forces which the government may place under his command to resist the foreign enemy.

2. The vice-presidency of the republic, established by the law of December 21, last, is suppressed.

3. The place of the provisional President shall be filled by a substitute, named by congress according to the terms of the law just cited.

4. If in this election the vote of the deputations should be tied, in place of determining the choice by lot, congress shall decide, voting by person.

5. The functions of the substitute shall cease when the provisional President shall return to the exercise of power.

6. On May 15 next the legislatures of the States shall proceed to the election of a President of the republic, according to the form prescribed by the constitution of 1824, and with no other difference save voting for one individual only.

7. The same legislatures shall at once transmit to the sovereign congress the result of the election in a certified dispatch.

This decree having been passed, it was at once signified to congress through a minister that Santa Anna was desirous of assuming the command of the army immediately and marching to the east to provide for the national defense. Congress went at once into permanent session in order to choose a substitute for the president. The election resulted in the choice of Pedro Anaya. He received sixty votes and General Almonte eleven, voting by persons, and eighteen votes against three, counting by deputations. The result being promulgated, permission was granted that Anaya should at once take the oath of office. This was on April 1, and on the 2d Anaya entered upon his duties. He dispensed with the usual visits of congratulation and ceremony on account of the pressure of public business, and Santa Anna left the capital for the army in the afternoon of the same day.

Chapter XXX

THE ADVANCE TO THE CAPITAL. 1847

THE extraordinary genius of Santa Anna and the influence he possessed over his countrymen were perhaps never more powerfully manifested than in the manner in which amid all these disasters he maintained his reputation and popularity, and gathered a new army to defend the eastern frontier of Mexico. But while he was engaged in the interior we must return to the scene of General Scott's operations on the coast. The small Island of Lobos, about 125 miles from Vera Cruz, had been selected for the rendezvous of the several corps which were to compose the American invading army; and the magnitude of the enterprise may be estimated from the fact that 163 vessels were employed as transports. On March 7 Scott embarked his troops in the squadron under Commodore Conner, and on the 9th landed the army upon the coast below the Island of Sacrificios without the loss of a man and without opposition from the neighboring city of Vera Cruz, which he summoned in vain to surrender. Having planted his batteries and placed them under the command of Colonel Bankhead, as chief of artillery, he commenced a vigorous bombardment of the city on the 18th, aided afloat and on shore by the guns of the fleet, which had been transferred from Commodore Conner to the command of Commodore Perry. The town was thus invested by land and water, and although the Mexican castle, city walls, and forts were but poorly garrisoned and provided, they held out bravely during the terrible siege, which nearly converted Vera Cruz into a slaughter-house. On the morning of the 26th, when no hope remained for the Mexicans, General Landero, the commander, made overtures for a capitulation, which being satisfactorily arranged, the principal commercial port and the most renowned fortress in Mexico were surrendered, together with 400 guns, 5000 stand of arms, and as many prisoners, who were released on parole.

General Scott had endeavored to mitigate the dangers of this

terrific attack upon Vera Cruz by the employment of such a force
as would honorably satisfy the inefficient garrison of the town and
castle that it was in truth unable to cope with the American forces.
He delayed opening his batteries to allow the escape of non-combatants; he refrained, moreover, from storming the town, a mode
of assault in which multitudes would have fallen on both sides in
the indiscriminate slaughter which always occurs when an enemy's
town is invaded in hot blood and with a reckless spirit of conquest
and carnage.   Yet, weak and badly provided as was the garrison
of both strongholds, the walls of the city, its batteries, and its
guardian castle held out for sixteen days, during which time it is
estimated that the besieging forces threw into the town about 6000
shot and shells, weighing upward of 463,000 pounds.   On the side
of the Mexicans the slaughter was exceedingly great.   Nearly a
thousand fell victims during the siege; and among the slain numerous unfortunate citizens, women, and children were found to
have perished by the bombs or paixhan shot, which destroyed the
public and private edifices and ruined many important portions of
the city.

When this new disaster was reported in the capital and among
the highlands of Mexico, it spread consternation among the more
secluded masses, who now began to believe that the heart of the
country was seriously menaced.   They had doubtless trusted to the
traditionary proverbial strength of San Juan de Ulua, and believed
that the danger of disease and storm on the coast would serve to
protect Vera Cruz from the attack of unacclimated strangers during
a season of hurricanes.   Indeed, it was fortunate that the invaders
were landed from the transports and men-of-war as early as they
were in March, for almost immediately afterward, and during
the siege, one of the most violent " northers " that ever ravaged
these shores raged incessantly, destroying many of the vessels
whose warlike freight of men and munitions had been so recently
disembarked.

But if the people were ignorant of the true condition and
strength of Vera Cruz or its castles, such was not the case with the
military men and national authorities.   They had made but little
effort to guard it against Scott, of whose designed attack they had
been long apprised, and they were probably prevented from doing
so chiefly by the plans of Santa Anna, who supposed that Taylor
would fall an easy prey to the large Mexican forces in the field

at Buena Vista, especially as the American army had been weakened
by the abstraction of its regulars for the operations at Vera Cruz.
Victorious at Buena Vista, he could have hastened by forced
marches to attack the invaders on the eastern coast, and under
the dismay of his anticipated victory in the north he unquestionably imagined that they too would have fallen at once into his
grasp. Besides these military miscalculations, Mexico was so
embarrassed in its pecuniary affairs and disorganized in its central
civil government that the proper directing power in the capital,
warned as it was, had neither men nor means at hand to dispose
along the coast of the Gulf or to station at points in its neighborhood whence they might quickly be thrown into positions which
were menaced.

It was at this juncture that Santa Anna's voice was again
heard in the council and the field. At the conclusion of the last
chapter we left him hastening to the new scene of action; and
when he announced the capitulation of the vaunted castle and
seaport of the republic, he declared in his proclamation that although " chance might decree the fall of the capital of the Aztec
empire under the power of the proud American host, yet the
nation shall not perish." " I swear," continues he, " that if my
wishes are seconded by a sincere and unanimous effort, Mexico
shall triumph! A thousand times fortunate for the nation will the
fall of Vera Cruz prove, if the disaster shall awaken in Mexican
bosoms the dignified enthusiasm and generous ardor of true patriotism!" This was the tone of appeal and encouragement in
which he rallied the credulous and vain masses, the disheartened
country, the dispersed troops of the north, and reanimated the
broken fragments of the army which still continued in the field.

Meanwhile General Scott placed Vera Cruz under the command of General Worth, opened the port to the long abandoned
commerce which had languished during the blockade, established
a moderate tariff, and together with the forces of the navy took
possession of the ports of Alvarado and Tlacotlalpam on the south,
and directed the future capture of Tuspan on the north of Vera
Cruz. All his arrangements being completed, and these captures
made and projected, he marched a large portion of his 12,000
victorious troops toward the capital.

When the road to the interior leaves Vera Cruz it runs for a
mile or two along the low, sandy, sea-beaten shore, and then

strikes off nearly at a right angle in a gap among the sand-hills toward the west. For many miles it winds slowly and heavily through the deep and shifting soil, until, as the traveler approaches the River Antigua, the country begins to rise and fall by gentle elevations like the first heavy swells of the ocean. Passing this river at Puente Nacional over the noble and renowned bridge of that name, the aspect of the territory becomes suddenly changed. The nearer elevations are steeper and more frequent, the road firmer and more rocky, while in the western distance the high slopes of the sierras rise rapidly in bold and wooded masses. All the features of nature are still strictly tropical, and wherever a scant and thriftless cultivation has displaced the thick vines, the rich flowers, and the dense foliage of the forest, indolent natives may be seen idling about their cane-built huts or lazily performing only the most necessary duties of life. Further on, at Plan del Rio, the geological features of the coast assume another aspect. Here the road again crosses a small streamlet, and then suddenly strikes boldly into the side of the mountain which is to be ascended. About seven leagues from Jalapa the edge of one of the tablelands of the Cordilleras sweeps down from the west abruptly into this pass of the River Plan. On both sides of this precipitous elevation the mountains tower majestically. The road winds slowly and roughly along the scant sides which have been notched to receive it. When the summit of the pass is attained one side of the road is found to be overlooked by the Hill of the Telegraph, while on the other side the streamlet runs in an immensely deep and rugged ravine several hundred feet below the level of the tableland. Between the road and the river many ridges of the neighboring hills unite and plunge downward into the impassable abyss. At the foot of the Hill of the Telegraph rises another eminence known as that of Atalaya, which is hemmed in by other wooded heights rising from below, and forming in front of the position a boundary of rocks and forests beyond which the sight cannot penetrate.

When Don Manuel Robles left Vera Cruz after its fall he was desired by General Canalizo to examine the site of Cerro Gordo. After a full reconnoissance it was his opinion that it afforded a favorable spot in which the invaders might be at least injured or checked, but that it was not the proper point to dispute their passage to the capital by a decisive victory. The most favorable position for resistance he believed to be at Corral Falso.

These views, however, did not accord with the opinions of the commander-in-chief, who, when the ground was explored under his own eye, resolved to fortify it for the reception of the Americans. The brigades of General Pinzon and Ranjel, the companies of Jalapa and Coatepec, commanded by Mata, and the veterans of the division of Angostura arrived also about this period, and their last sections reached the ground on April 12. Meanwhile all was activity in the work of hasty fortification. Robles constructed a parapet at the edge of the three hills, but failing to obtain all requisite materials for such a work, his erection merely served to mark the line of the Mexican operations and to form a breastwork whence the artillery and infantry might command the ground over which, as the defenders supposed, the Americans would be obliged to advance. Colonel Cano had already cut off the access by the road at the point where it turned on the right slope of the Telegraph by placing a heavy battery. He also formed a covered way leading to the positions on the right, while General Alcorta constructed a circular work on the summit of the eminence and established within it a battery of four guns. In the center of this the national flag was hoisted, and off to the left nothing was seen but thick, thorny dells and barrancas, which were regarded by Santa Anna as impassable.

Such was the Mexican line of defenses extending on the brink of these precipices for nearly a mile, and throughout it the commander-in-chief hastened to distribute his forces. The extreme right was placed under the command of General Pinzon, the next position under the naval captain, Buenaventura Aranjo, the next under Colonel Badillo, the next under General Jarero, the next post, at the road, under General La Vega, and finally the extreme left, at the Telegraph, under Generals Vazquez and Uraga and Colonel Palacios. The forces thus in position, according to the Mexican account, amounted to 3372 men, with 52 pieces of ordnance of various caliber. The remainder of the army, with the exception of the cavalry, which remained at Corral Falso until the 15th, was encamped on the sides of the road at the rancheria of Cerro Gordo, situated in the rear of the position. In this neighborhood was placed the reserve, composed of the 1st, 2d, 3d, and 4th Light Infantry, comprising 1700 men; and the 1st and 11th Regiments of the Line, with 780 men, together with their artillery. It is said that the army was badly provided with food and suffered greatly from the climate and the innumerable insects which infest the region.

As Scott advanced against this position the dangers of his enterprise became manifest, and he caused a series of bold reconnoissances to be made by Lieutenant Beauregard and Captain Lee, of the Engineers. He found that the deep rock ravine of the river protected the right flank of the Mexican position, while abrupt and seemingly impassable mountains and ridges covered the left. Between these points for nearly two miles a succession of fortified summits bristled with every kind of available defense, while the top of Cerro Gordo commanded the road on a gentle slope, like a glacis, for nearly a mile. An attack in front, therefore, would have been fatal to the American army, and Scott resolved, accordingly, to cut a road to the right of his position so as to turn the left flank of the Mexicans. To cover his flank movements, on April 17 he ordered General Twiggs to advance against the fort on the steep ascent in front and slightly to the left of the Cerro. Colonel Harney, with the rifles and some detachments of infantry and artillery, carried this position under a heavy fire and, having secured it, elevated a large gun to the summit of the eminence and made a demonstration against a strong fort in the rear. Early on April 18 the columns moved to the general attack. General Pillow's brigade assaulted the right of the Mexican entrenchments, and, although compelled to retire, produced a powerful impression on that part of the enemy's line. General Twiggs's division stormed the vital part of Cerro Gordo, pierced the center, gained command of the fortifications and cut them off from support, while Colonel Riley's brigade of infantry rushed on against the main body of the foe, turned the guns of their own fort against them, and compelled the panic-stricken crowd to fly in utter confusion. Shields's brigade meanwhile assaulted the left, and carrying the rear battery aided materially in completing the rout of the enemy. The whole American force in action and reserve was 8500. About 3000 prisoners, 4000 to 5000 stand of arms, and 43 pieces of artillery fell into Scott's hands. In the two days of conflict the American loss amounted to 33 officers and 398 men, of whom 63 were killed. The Mexican loss was computed at 1000 at least, while among the prisoners no less than 280 officers and 5 generals were included. Santa Anna, with General Ampudia, who was in the action, escaped with difficulty, and the commander-in-chief, accompanied by a few friends and a small escort, finally reached Orizaba in safety, after encountering numerous dangers amid the mountains and lonely paths through which he was obliged to pass.

This very decisive victory opened the path for the American army to the highlands of the upper plateau of Mexico, and accordingly the forces immediately pushed on to Jalapa and Peroté, both of which places were abandoned by the Mexicans without firing a gun. General Worth took possession of Peroté on April 22, and received from Colonel Velasquez, who had been left in charge of the fortress or castle of San Carlos de Peroté by his retreating countrymen, 54 guns and mortars of iron and bronze, 11,065 cannonballs, 14,300 bombs and hand grenades, and 500 muskets. On capturing the post he learned that the rout at Cerro Gordo had been complete. Fully 3000 cavalry passed the stronghold of Peroté in deplorable plight, while not more than 2000 disarmed and famishing infantry had returned toward their homes in the central regions of Mexico. From Peroté Worth advanced toward Puebla on the direct road to the capital.

Thus was Mexico again reduced to extreme distress by the loss of two important battles, the destruction of her third army raised for this war, and the capture of her most valuable artillery and munitions. But the national spirit of resistance was not subdued. If the government could no longer restrain the invaders by organized armies, it resolved to imitate the example of the mother country during Napoleon's invasion, and to rouse the people to the formation of guerrilla bands under daring and reckless officers. Bold as was this effort of patriotic despair, and cruelly successful as it subsequently proved against individuals or detached parties of the Americans, it could effect nothing material against the great body of the consolidated army. Meanwhile the master spirit of the nation—Santa Anna—had not been idle in the midst of his disheartening reverses. In little more than two weeks he gathered nearly 3000 men from the fragments of his broken army and marched to Puebla, where he received notice of Worth's advance from Peroté. Sallying forth immediately with his force, he attacked the American general at Amozoque, but, finding himself unable to check his career, returned with a loss of nearly 90 killed and wounded. On May 22 Puebla yielded submissively to General Worth, and Santa Anna retreated in the direction of the national capital, halting at San Martin Tesmalucan, and again at Ayotla, about twenty miles from Mexico. Here he learned that the city was in double fear of the immediate assault of the victorious Americans and of his supposed intention to defend it within its own walls, a project which the people believed would only result, in the present disastrous condition of affairs, in the slaughter of its citizens and ruin of their property. The commander-in-chief halted therefore at Ayotla, and playing dexterously on the hopes and fears of the people in a long dispatch addressed to the minister of war, he at length received the presidential and popular sanction of his return to Mexico.

In truth, the nation at large had no one but Santa Anna at that moment of utter despair in whose prestige and talents—in spite of all his misfortunes and defeats—it could rely for even the hope of escape from destruction, if not of ultimate victory.

While the Mexican nation had been thus sorely vexed by intestinal commotions and foreign invasion, an extraordinary constituent congress—*Congreso Extraordinario Constituyente*—had been summoned and met in the capital, chiefly to revise the constitution, or the " Bases of Political Organization," of 1843, which had been superseded by the temporary adoption of the federal constitution of 1824, according to the edict issued by Salas under the direction of Santa Anna soon after that personage's return from exile. This extraordinary congress readopted the old federal constitution of 1824 without altering its terms, principles, or phraseology, and made such slight changes as were deemed needful by an *Acta Constitutiva y de Reformas,* containing thirty articles, which was sanctioned on May 18, and proclaimed on the 21st by Santa Anna, who had reassumed the presidency. By this approval of the federal system the executive entirely abandoned the central policy for which he had so long contended, but which, as we have seen, he no longer believed, or feigned to believe, suitable for the nation.

Notwithstanding this submission to popular will and apparent desire to deprive the central government of its most despotic prerogatives, the conduct of Santa Anna did not save him entirely from the machinations of his rivals or of intriguers. Much discontent was expressed publicly and privately, and the president accordingly tendered his resignation to congress, intimating a desire to hasten into private life! This strategic resignation was followed by the retirement of General Rincon and General Bravo,

who commanded the troops in the city. Acts of such vital significance upon the part of the ablest men in the republic in an hour of
exceeding danger at once recalled congress and the people to their
senses; and if they were designed, as they probably were, merely
to throw the anarchists on their own resources and to show them
their inefficiency at such an epoch, they seem to have produced the
desired effect, for they placed Santa Anna and his partisans more
firmly in power. Congress refused to accept his resignation. Unfortunate as he had been, it perhaps saw in him the only commander
who was capable in the exigency of controlling the Mexican elements of resistance to the invaders, and he was thus enabled to
form his plans, to collect men, means and munitions, and to commence the system of fortifications around the capital. " War to
the knife " was still the rallying cry of the nation. The congressional resolutions which had been passed on April 20, immediately
after the battle of Cerro Gordo, proclaimed " every individual a
traitor, let him be private person or public functionary, who should
enter into treaties with the United States! " Parties in the capital
were nevertheless not unanimous upon this subject. There were
wise men and patriots who foresaw the issue, and counseled the
leaders to come to honorable terms before the capital was assaulted.
Others craved the continuance of the war with the hope that its
disasters would destroy the individuals who conducted it to an
unfortunate issue, and among these they saw that Santa Anna
was finally pledged to abide that issue for weal or woe. Nor were
politicians wanting in the republic who honestly looked to the
prolongation of the conflict as an undoubted blessing to Mexico,
believing that it would ultimately result in the complete subjugation
of the whole country by American arms and its final annexation to
that union.

In June a coalition was formed at Lagos by deputies from
Jalisco, San Luis Potosi, Zacatecas, Mexico, and Querétaro, in
which these States combined for mutual defense; but, while they
opposed peace, they resolved to act independently of the general
government. Many other parts of the republic looked on the scene
with apathy. There was no longer a revenue from foreign commerce. The products of the mines were smuggled from the west
coast in British vessels. Disorder and uncertainty prevailed everywhere in regard to the collection of the national income from internal resources. Individuals, and not States, corporations, or

municipalities, were now to be relied on for support; and as the most important parts of the nation on the north and east were virtually in the enemy's hands, the whole effort of the frail authorities was confined to the protection of the capital. In the midst of all this complication of confusion Santa Anna found that the election for president, which was held by the States on May 15, had resulted unfavorably to his pretensions, and by an adroit movement he prevailed on congress to postpone the counting of the votes from June 15 until January of the following year! All who opposed his schemes of defense or resistance were disposed of by banishment, persecution, or imprisonment, nor did he fail to establish so severe a censorship of the press that in July it is believed but one paper was allowed to be issued in the capital, and that one, of course, entirely under his control. Throwing himself, like a true military demagogue, publicly, if not at heart, at the head of popular feeling in regard to the war with the United States, he adopted every measure and availed himself of every resource in his power to place the city in a state of defense and to fan the flame of resistance. In the meanwhile the guerrilla forces organized on the eastern coast, chiefly under a recreant clergyman named Jarauta, harassed every American train and detachment on its way to the interior, and rendered the country insecure, until a fearful war of extermination was adopted by American garrisons on the line.

The government of the United States had during the whole of this unfortunate contest availed itself of every supposed suitable occasion to sound Mexico in relation to peace. In July, 1846, and in January, 1847, overtures were made to the national authorities, and rejected; and again, early in the spring of 1847, as soon as the news of the defeat at Cerro Gordo reached Washington Nicholas P. Trist was dispatched by the president upon a mission which it was hoped would result in the restoration of international amity. The commissioner reached Vera Cruz while the American army was advancing toward the interior, but it was not until the forces reached Puebla and General Scott had established his headquarters in that capital that he was enabled, through the intervention of the British minister, to communicate with the Mexican Government. The stringent terms of the decree to which we have already alluded, of course, prevented Santa Anna, powerful as he was, from entertaining the proposals in the existing state of the public mind, and accordingly he referred the subject to congress, a quorum of whose members was with difficulty organized. On July 13 seventy-four assembled, and voted to strip themselves of the responsibility by a resolution that it was the executive's duty to receive ministers and to make treaties of peace and alliance, and that their functions were confined to the approval or disapproval of those treaties or alliances when submitted in due form under the constitution. But Santa Anna, still adhering to the letter of the mandatory decree passed after the battle of Cerro Gordo in April, alleged his legal incapaciy to treat, and recommended the repeal of the order, inasmuch as the American commissioner's letter was courteous, and the dignity of Mexico required the return of a suitable reply. Before the appeal could reach congress its members had dispersed, foreseeing probably the delicacy, if not danger, of the dilemma in which they were about to be placed. Without a constitutional tribunal to relieve him from his position, the president finally referred the matter to a council of general officers of the army. This body, however, was quite as timorous as congress had been, and dismissed the project by declaring that " it was inexpedient to enter into negotiations for peace until another opportunity had been afforded Mexico to retrieve her fortunes in the field."

These were the negotiations that met the public eye and are reported in the military and diplomatic dispatches of the day; but there was a secret correspondence, also, which denotes either the duplicity or strategy of Santa Anna, and must be faithfully recorded. It seems that the Mexican president, about the time that the public answer was proclaimed, sent private communications to the American headquarters at Puebla, intimating that if a million of dollars were placed at his disposal, to be paid upon the conclusion of a treaty of peace, and ten thousand dollars were paid forthwith, he would appoint commissioners to negotiate! The proposal was received and discussed by General Scott, Trist, and the leading officers, and being agreed to, though not unanimously, the ten thousand dollars were disbursed from the secret service money which Scott had at his disposal, and communications were opened in cipher, the key of which had been sent from Mexico. Intimations soon reached Puebla from Santa Anna that it would be also necessary for the American army to advance and threaten the capital; and, finally, another message was received, urging

Scott to penetrate the valley and carry one of the outworks of the Mexican line of defenses, in order to enable him to negotiate! [1]

The sincerity of these proposals from the Mexican president is very questionable, and we are still in doubt whether he designed merely to procrastinate and feel the temper of the Americans, or whether he was in reality angling for the splendid bribe of a million, which he might appropriate privately, in the event of playing successfully upon the feelings or fears of the masses. The attempt, however, proved abortive, and although both General Scott and Trist deemed it proper to entertain the proposal, the commander-in-chief never for a moment delayed his military preparations for an advance with all the force he could gather. Thus were the last efforts of the American authorities in Mexico and Washington repulsed in the same demagogic spirit that hastened the rupture between the nations in the spring of 1846, and nothing remained but to try again whether the sword was mightier than the pen.

The American forces, as we have stated, had concentrated at Puebla on the main road to the City of Mexico, but their numbers had been thinned by desertion, disease, and the return of many volunteers whose term of service was over, or nearly completed. Meanwhile the Mexican army was increased by the arrival of General Valencia from San Luis with 5000 troops and 36 pieces of artillery, and General Alvarez, with his Pinto Indians from the south and southwest, all of which, added to the regiments in the city and its immediate vicinity, swelled the numbers of the Mexican combatants to at least 25,000 or 30,000. It was discovered that General Taylor would not advance toward the south, and consequently the presence of Valencia's men was of more importance at the point where the vital blow would probably be struck.

While the events we have related were occurring in the interior, Commodore Perry had swept down the coast and captured Tabasco, which, however, owing to its unhealthfulness, was not long retained by the Americans. But every other important port in the Gulf, from the Rio Grande to Yucatan, was occupied, while an active blockade was maintained before those in the Pacific. Colonel Bankhead subsequently occupied Orizaba and seized a large quantity of valuable public property. It had been

[1] *Cf.* Major Ripley's account in " History of the War with Mexico," p. 148 *et seq.*

the desire of the American authorities from the earliest period of the war to draw a large portion of the means for its support from Mexico, but the commanding generals, finding the system not only annoying to themselves, but exasperating to the people and difficult of accomplishment, refrained from the exercise of a right which invaders have generally used in other countries. The officers accordingly paid for the supplies obtained from the natives. Nor did they confine this principle of action to the operations of the military authorities alone while acting for the army at large, but wherever it was possible restrained that spirit of private plunder and destruction which too commonly characterizes the common soldier when flushed with victory over a weak but opulent foe. When the ports of Mexico had fallen into the hands of the Americans and the blockade was raised, they were at once opened to the trade of all nations upon the payment of duties more moderate than those which had been collected by Mexico. The revenues thus levied in the form of a military contribution from Mexican citizens upon articles they consumed was devoted to the use of the American army and navy. It was, in effect, the seizure of Mexican commercial duties and their application to necessary purposes, and thus far only was the nation compelled to contribute toward the expense of the war it had provoked.

Early in August General Scott had been reinforced by the arrival of new regiments at Puebla, and on the 7th of that month he resolved to march upon the capital. Leaving a competent garrison in that city under the command of Colonel Childs, and a large number of sick and enfeebled men in the hospitals, he departed with about 10,000 eager soldiers toward the renowned valley of Mexico.

In the same month, 328 years before, Hernando Cortéz and his slender military train departed from the eastern coasts of Mexico on the splendid errand of Indian conquest. After fighting two battles with the Tlascalans, who then dwelt in the neighborhood of Puebla, and with the Cholulans, whose solitary pyramid— a grand and solemn monument of the past—still rises majestically from the beautiful plain, Scott slowly toiled across the steeps of the grand volcanic sierra which divides the valleys and hems in the plain of Mexico. Patiently winding up its wooded sides and passing the forests of its summit, the same grand panoramic scene lay spread out in sunshine at the feet of the American general that three centuries before had greeted the eager and longing eyes of the greatest Castilian soldier who ever trod the shores of America.

In order to comprehend the military movements which ended the drama of the Mexican War, it will be necessary for us to describe the topography of the valley with some minuteness, although it is not designed to recount in detail all the events and personal heroism of the battles that ensued. This would require infinitely more room than we can afford, and we are accordingly spared the discussion of many circumstances which concern the merits, the opinions, and the acts of various commanders.

Looking downward toward the west from the shoulders of the lofty elevations which border the feet of the volcano of Popocatepetl, the spectator beholds a remarkable and perfect basin, enclosed on every side by mountains whose height varies from two hundred to ten thousand feet from its bottom. The form of this basin may be considered nearly circular, the diameter being about fifty miles. As the eye descends to the levels below, it beholds every variety of scenery. Ten extinct volcanoes rear their ancient cones and craters in the southern part of the valley, multitudes of lesser hills and elevations break the evenness of the plain, while, interspersed among its 830 square miles of arable land and along the shores of its six lakes of Chalco, Xochimilco, Tezcoco, San Cristoval, Xaltocan, and Zumpango, stretching across the valley from north to south, are seen the white walls of ten populous cities and towns. In front of the observer, about forty miles to the west, is the capital of the republic, while the main road thither descends rapidly from the last mountain slopes, at the Venta de Cordova, until it is lost in the plain on the margin of Lake Chalco near the hacienda of Buena Vista. From there to the town of Ayotla it sweeps along the plain between a moderate elevation on the north and the lake of Chalco on the south.

On August 11 General Scott, after crossing the mountains, concentrated his forces in the valley. General Twiggs encamped with his division in advance, on the direct road, at Ayotla, near the northern shore of Lake Chalco; General Quitman was stationed with his troops a short distance in the rear; General Worth occupied the town of Chalco on the western shore of its lake, while General Pillow brought up the rear by an encampment near Worth.

This position of the army commanded four routes to the capital whose capture was the coveted prize. The first of these, as well as the shortest and most direct, was the main post road which reaches the city by the gate or garita of San Lazaro on the east. After passing Ayotla this road winds round the foot of an extinct volcanic hill for five miles, when it approaches the sedgy shores and marshes of Lake Tezcoco on the north, thence it passes over a causeway built across an arm of Tezcoco for two miles, and by another causeway of seven miles finally strikes the city. The road is good, level, perfectly open and comfortable for ordinary traveling, but the narrow land between the lakes of Chalco and Tezcoco, compressed still more by broken hills and rocks, admits the most perfect military defense. At the end of the first causeway over the arm of Tezcoco which we have just described is the abrupt oblong volcanic hill styled El Peñon, 450 feet above the level of the lake, its top accessible in the direction of Ayotla at only one point, and surrounded by water except on the west toward Mexico. It is a natural fortress; yet Santa Anna had not neglected to add to its original strength, and to seize it as the eastern key to his defenses. Three lines of works were thrown up, at the base, at the brow, and on the summit of the eminence. The works at the base, completely encircling El Peñon, consisted of a ditch fifteen feet wide, four and a half feet deep, and a parapet fifteen feet thick, whose slope was raised eight and a half feet above the bottom of the ditch. Ample breastworks formed the other two lines of the bristling tiara. In addition to this, the causeway across the arm of Tezcoco, immediately in front, had been cut and was defended by a battery of two guns, while the fire from all the works, mounting about sixty pieces, swept the whole length of the causeway.

The second road to the capital was by Mexicalzingo. After leaving Ayotla the highway continues along the main post road for six or seven miles and then deflects southwardly toward the village of Santa Maria, whence it pursues its way westwardly toward Istapalapan, but just before reaching Mexicalzingo it crosses a marsh, formed by the waters of Lake Xochimilco, on a causeway nearly a mile long. This approach, dangerous as it was by its natural impediments, was also protected by extensive field works which made it almost as perilous for assault as the Peñon.

The third route lay through Tezcoco. Leaving Chalco and the hacienda of Buena Vista, it strikes off from the main route directly north, and passing through the town of Tezcoco it sweeps westwardly around the shores of the lake of that name until it crosses the stone dyke of San Cristoval, near the lake and town of that name; thence, by a road leading almost directly south for fifteen miles, through the sacred town of Guadalupe Hidalgo, it enters the capital. It is an agreeable route through a beautiful country, yet extremely circuitous, though free from all natural or artificial obstacles, until it reaches Santiago Zacualco, within two miles of Guadalupe. But at the period of Scott's invasion of the valley General Valencia, with the troops that were afterward convened at Contreras, was stationed at Tezcoco, either for the purpose of observation or to induce an attack in that quarter, and thus to draw the forces into a snare on the northern route, or to fall on the rear of the American commander if he attacked El Peñon or advanced by the way of Mexicalzingo. At Santiago Zacualco, west of the lake and on the route, formidable works were thrown up to defend the entire space between the western shore of Lake Tezcoco and the mountains; while on the road to Querétaro, at the mountain pass north of Tenepantla, other defenses were erected, so as to screen the country on all sides of the group of hills which lies west of the lakes of Tezcoco and San Cristoval and north of the town of Guadalupe Hidalgo.

The fourth and last advance to the city was that which turned to the south from the hacienda of Buena Vista, and, passing by the town of Chalco, led along the narrow land intervening between the shores of Lake Chalco and the first steeps of the mountains forming the southern rim of the valley, until it fell at right angles, at Tlalpam or San Agustin de las Cuevas, into the main road from the City of Mexico toward the southern States of the republic.

All these routes were boldly reconnoitered by the brave engineers accompanying the American army, and, where they could not extend their personal observations, the officers obtained from the people of the country information upon which subsequent events proved that they were justified in relying. From the knowledge thus gained as to the route south of the lake of Chalco, they were induced to believe, although it was rough, untraveled, difficult, and narrowly hemmed in between the lake and the mountains, yet that the long and narrow defile which was open to resistance at many points was not sufficiently obstructed or fortified to prevent a passage. All the routes on the lower lands, it should also be remembered, were liable to increased difficulties from the deluging rains prevailing at this season on the highlands of Mexico, and which sometimes convert the highways and their borders for many leagues into almost impassable lagoons.

The description of the various routes to the capital has necessarily acquainted the reader with the important Mexican defenses on the north, the east, and the northeast of the capital, both by military works hastily thrown up after Santa Anna's retreat from Cerro Gordo, and by the encampment of large bodies of soldiery. We thus already know a part of the external line of defenses at El Peñon, Mexicalzingo, Tezcoco, Santiago Zacualco, and the pass north of Tenepantla. But in addition to these there are others that must be noticed on the south and west of the capital, which it should always be recollected is situated in the lap of the valley, but near the western edge of the gigantic rim of mountains.

Along the Chalco route there were no more fortifications, but west of lakes Chalco and Xochimilco a line of entrenchments had been commenced, connecting the fortified hacienda, or massive stone plantation house of San Antonio, about six miles south of the city, with the town of Mexicalzingo. West of this hacienda, the Pedregal, a vast broken field of lava, spread out along the edge of the main road, and skirting it to San Agustin, extended high upon the mountain slopes still further west near San Angel and Contreras, whose neighboring fields were cut into deep ravines and barrancas by the wash from the declivities. The Pedregal was a most formidable obstacle in the march or maneuvers of an army. But few levels of arable land were found among its rocky wastes. It admitted the passage of troops at but few points, and was entirely impracticable for cavalry or artillery, except by a single mule-path. North of San Angel and the edge of the Pedregal, at the distance of about four miles, rose the solitary hill and castle of Chapultepec, which had been amply prepared for defense; and still further north on the same line frowned the stern ridges of the sierra, cut by barrancas and profound dells, until the ring of the outer series of military works was thus finally united at the pass beyond Tenepantla. But inside of this formidable barrier of outworks, nearer the city, another line of fortifications had been prepared to dispute the American march. The first, and perhaps the most important of these, was at Churubusco, a scattered village lying midway between San Agustin and the City of Mexico, directly on the road at a spot where the stream or rivulet of Churubusco runs eastwardly from a point on the road from San Angel to the capital toward the lake of Xochimilco. The sides of the water course were planted with the prickly maguey, and one of the most western buildings in the village was a strong, massive stone convent, whose walls had been cut for musketry, and whose parapets, azotéas, or flat roofs, and windows all afforded suitable positions for soldiery. Large quantities of ammunition were stored within the edifice. The enclosure of the church and convent was defended by about 2000 men and mounted seven guns, while toward the east was a beautiful, solid, and scientifically constructed *tête de pont* which covered the bridge over the stream by which the road led to the capital. In this work three heavy guns were mounted, while the neighborhood is said to have swarmed with troops.

We have already mentioned the garita or gate of San Lazaro, which was the entrance to the city by the main road from the east, passing the hill and fortification of El Peñon. This garita was strengthened by strong works on the road, with platforms and embrasures for heavy cannon, which would have swept the path, while the marches on the south were protected by redoubts and lunettes extending to the garita or entrance of La Candelaria on the canal from Xochimilco. North of San Lazaro strong works hemmed in the city to the garita of Peralvillo, and connected with defenses and fortified houses reaching to the garita of Santiago. Other advanced works were begun in that quarter, while the ground in front of the main line was cut into *troux de loups*.

On the west of the city are the garitas of San Cosmé and Belen. "Works had been commenced to connect that of San Cosmé, the most northerly of the two, with that of Santiago, and the nature of the country and of the buildings formed obstructions to any advance between San Cosmé and Belen. Belen was defended principally by the citadel of Mexico, a square bastioned work with wet ditches, immediately inside the garita. Barricades had also been commenced; but the great obstacle to an entrance by either garita was presented in the rock and castle of Chapultepec, two miles southwest of the city. From this hill two aqueducts extended to the capital, the one, northeast, in a direct line to Belen, and the other, north, to the suburb of San Cosmé, where, turning at right angles, it continued onward and entered at the Garita. The roads from the west ran along the sides of the aqueducts. Two roads enter the city from the south between the garita of San Antonio and Belen, one at Belen and the other at the garita of El

Niño Perdido; neither of these roads have branches to the Acapulco road south of the Pedregal and the hacienda of San Antonio, and therefore had been left comparatively unfortified." [2]

These defenses, overlooked by the lofty sierras and the barrancas which broke their feet, hemmed in the capital, and the Mexicans readily imagined that they could not be turned by an army marching from the east, so as to reach the city on the west, except by a tedious circuit which would allow them time to complete their protective works in that quarter. The east had claimed their chief and most natural attention, and thus the south and the west became unquestionably their weakest points.

Such were the Mexican lines, natural and artificial, around the capital in the valley in the middle of August, 1847, and such was the position of the American troops in front of them. The Mexicans numbered then, with all their levies, probably more than 30,000 fighting men, while the Americans did not count more than 10,000 —under arms at all points. The invaders had prepared as well as circumstances admitted, and their *materiel* for assault or siege had been gathered carefully and transported slowly into the interior, through the country intervening between Vera Cruz and Puebla, every train being usually attacked by guerrillas, and fighting its way boldly through the most dangerous passes.

The equipments of the Mexicans, except the weapons saved from the wreck of former battles, had been chiefly prepared at the cannon foundries and powder factories of the country, and it is quite amazing to notice how completely a great exigency brought forth the latent energies of the people, teaching them what they might ordinarily effect if guided by a spirit of industry and progress. Under the most disheartening depression, but fired by the stimulus of despair, by an overpowering sense of patriotic duty, and by religious enthusiasm which had been excited by the crusading address of the clergy of San Luis Potosi, issued in the month of April, they manifested in their last moments a degree of zeal, calmness, and foresight that will forever redound to their credit on the page of history.

The Mexican preparations for defense were not, of course, as completely known to the Americans as we now describe them. Through spies, scouts, and reconnoissances of engineers, some of the exterior, and even of the interior, lines were ascertained with

[2] Major Ripley, "History of the War with Mexico," vol. II. p. 182.

tolerable accuracy; but sufficient was known to satisfy General
Scott that of all the approaching routes to the capital, that which
led along the southern shores of Lake Chalco was the only one he
ought to adopt.[3]

Accordingly on August 15 the movement was commenced in the
reverse order from that in which the army had entered the valley
from Puebla.   Worth's division passing Pillow's, led the advance,
Pillow and Quitman followed, while Twiggs's brought up the rear.
Scott took his position with Pillow, so as to communicate easily
with all parts of the army.   Water transportation to some extent
had been obtained by General Worth at Chalco by the seizure of
market boats which plied between that place and the capital.
When Twiggs moved he was assailed by Alvarez and his Pintos,
but soon drove them off, while the advance columns, after passing
San Gregorio, were frequently assailed by the enemy's light troops
in their front, and harassed and impeded by ditches that had been
hastily cut across the road or by rocks rolled down from the mountains.   These obstacles necessarily consumed time, but the simple-
minded Indians of the neighborhood, who had just been compelled
by the Mexicans to throw the impediments in the Americans' way,
were perhaps more easily induced to aid in clearing the path for the
invaders than their ancestors had been in the days of Cortéz.   On
the afternoon of the 17th Worth, with the advance, reached San
Agustin, at the foot of the mountains and at the intersection of the
southern road from Mexico to Cuernavaca and Acapulco—a point
whose topography we have already described; and on the 18th the
rear division entered the town.

As soon as Santa Anna discovered Scott's advance by the
Chalco route, and that the attack on Mexico would be made from
the south instead of the east, he at once perceived that it was useless
to attack the American rear while passing the defiles between the
lake and the mountains even if he could possibly come up with it,
and consequently that it was best for him to quit his headquarters
at El Peñon, while he also recalled General Valencia with the most
of the troops at Tezcoco and at Mexicalzingo, which were no
longer menaced by the foe.   Santa Anna himself established his

---

[3] General Scott had set his heart, even at Puebla, on the Chalco route, but
he resolved not to be obstinate, if, on a closer examination of the ground, a
better route was presented.   The last information of his spies and officers, in
the valley, satisfied him as to the propriety of advancing by Chalco.

quarters at the fortified hacienda of San Antonio, and ordered
Valencia to march his whole division, cavalry, infantry, and artillery, to the town of San Angel and Coyoacan, so as to cover the
whole west and center of the valley in front of Mexico.

In order to understand the ensuing military movements it will
be proper for the reader to study the map of the valley and acquaint
himself fully with the relative position of both parties.   The plans

of both generals-in-chief were well made; but the blunders and
obstinacy of the Mexican second in command disconcerted Santa
Anna's desired combination, and ultimately opened the ground to
the American advance with more ease than was anticipated.

We will sketch rapidly the military value of the arena upon
which the combatants stood, on August 18, 1847.

Let us imagine ourselves beside General Scott, standing on one
of the elevations above the town of San Agustin de las Cuevas, at

the base of the southern mountain barrier of the valley, and looking northward toward the capital. Directly in front, leading to the
city, is the main road, the left or western side of which, even from
the gate of San Agustin to the hacienda of San Antonio, and thence
westwardly to San Angel, forms, together with the bases of the
southern and western mountains about St. Geronimo and Contreras, a vast basin ten or twelve square miles in extent, covered
with the Pedregal or the field of broken lava which we have already
mentioned. This mass of jagged volcanic matter, we must remember, was at that time barely passable with difficulty for infantry, and altogether impassable for cavalry or artillery, save by a
single mule path. North, beyond the fortified hacienda and headquarters of Santa Anna at San Antonio, the country opened. A
line of field works, the lake of Xochimilco, a few cultivated farms,
and vast flooded meadows were on its right to the east, but from
the hacienda a road branches off to the west, leading around the
northern edge of the Pedregal, or lava field, through Coyoacan and
San Angel, whence it deflects southwardly to Contreras. The main
road, however, continues onward northwardly from the hacienda
of San Antonio until it crosses the Churubusco River at the strong
fortification we have described. Beyond Churubusco the highway
leads straight to the gate of San Antonio Abad, whence a work had
been thrown northwestwardly toward the citadel. The City of
Mexico, built on the bed of an ancient lake, was on a perfect level,
nor were there any commanding or protecting elevations of importance around it within two or three miles, and the first of these beyond this limit were chiefly on the north and west.

Thus General Santa Anna in front on the main road to the
city at the massive fortified hacienda of San Antonio blocked up
the highway in that direction, protected on his right by the barrier
of the Pedregal; and by the lake of Xochimilco, the field works,
and the flooded country on his left. General Valencia had been
placed by him with his troops at San Angel on the western edge
of the valley, and at the village of Coyoacan, a little further east in
the lap of the valley on roads communicating easily with his position at San Antonio, while they commanded the approaches to the
city by the circuitous path of the Pedregal around the edge of the
valley from San Agustin de las Cuevas through Contreras or Padierna. Valencia and Santa Anna were consequently within supporting distance of each other; and in their rear, in front of the

city, were the fortifications of Churubusco. General Scott, with the whole American army, was therefore apparently hemmed in between the lakes and the Pedregal on his flanks, the Mexican fortifications and army in front, and the steep mountains toward Cuernavaca in his rear. He was obliged, accordingly, either to retreat by the defiles through which he had advanced from Chalco—to climb the steeps behind him and pass them to the *tierra caliente*—to force the position in front at the hacienda of San Antonio, or to burst the barrier of the Pedregal on his left, and, sweeping round the rim of the valley, to advance toward the capital through the village of San Angel. Such were some of the dangers and difficulties that menaced Scott on his arrival at San Agustin. He was in the heart of the enemy's country, in front of a capital aroused by pride, patriotism, and despair, and possessing all the advantages of an accurate knowledge of the ground on which it stood or by which it was surrounded. Scott, on the other hand, like the mariner in storm on a lee shore, was obliged to feel his way along the dangerous coast with the lead, and could not advance with that perfect confidence which is ever the surest harbinger of success.

The reconnoissances of the American engineers which had been pushed boldly in front on the main road to the north by the hacienda of San Antonio soon disclosed the difficulty in that direction. But among the mass of information which the American general received at Puebla his engineers learned that there was a pathway through this Pedregal whose route had been indicated by the spies with sufficient distinctness and certainty to justify a hope that he might be able to render it practicable for his whole army, and thus enable him to turn the right flank of the Mexicans' strongest positions. There is no doubt, as subsequent events demonstrated, that the ground in the neighborhood of Contreras, where the road descends from the mountains and barrancas toward San Angel, was of great importance to the Mexicans in the defense of the various modes of access to the city, and it is unquestionable that a strong post should have been placed in that quarter to cripple the American advance. It is stated by Mexican writers that General Mendoza, with two members of his topographical corps, had reconnoitered this route and pass and pronounced it "absolutely indefensible." It is probable, therefore, that no general action involving the fortunes of a division or of a large mass of the Mexican army should have been risked among the ravines between the mountains and the Pedregal near Contreras; yet we do not believe that it should have been left by Santa Anna without a force capable of making a staunch resistance.

We are now acquainted with the ground and with the positions of the two armies. Scott's plan was to force a passage by either or both of the two adits to the levels of the valley in front of the city, while Santa Anna's, according to his manifesto dated subsequently on August 23, was to have made a concerted retrograde movement with his troops and to have staked the fortunes of the capital on a great battle in which all his fresh, enthusiastic, and unharmed troops would have been brought into a general action against the comparatively small American army, upon an open ground where he would have had full opportunity to use and maneuver infantry, cavalry, and artillery.

But this plan was disconcerted at first, and probably destroyed, both in its *materiel* and *morale,* by the gross disobedience of General Valencia, who forgot as a soldier that there can never be two commanders in the field. Valencia, apparently resolving to seize the first opportunity to attack the Americans in spite of the reported untenable character of the ground about Padierna or Contreras, left his quarters at Coyoacan and San Angel, and advanced, without consulting his commander, to Contreras, upon whose heights he threw up an entrenched camp! As soon as Santa Anna learned this fact he ordered the vain and reckless officer to retire, but finding him obstinately resolute in his insubordination, the commander-in-chief suffered him, in direct opposition to his own opinion, to remain and to charge himself with the whole responsibility of the consequences. Thus if Scott advanced upon the main road he would meet only Santa Anna in front, and the efficiency of Valencia's force on his left flank would be comparatively destroyed. If he conquered Valencia, however, at Contreras, after passing the Pedregal, he would rout a whole division of the veterans of the north—the remnants of San Luis and Angostura—while the remainder of the army, composed of recent levies and raw troops disciplined for the occasion, would in all likelihood fall an easy prey to the eager Americans.

The reconnoissances of the American army were now completed both toward San Antonio over the main northern road and toward Padierna or Contreras over the southern and southwestern edge of the Pedregal. That brave and accomplished engineer,

Captain Robert E. Lee, had done the work on the American left across the fields of broken lava, and being convinced that a road could be opened, if needed, for the whole army and its trains, Scott resolved forthwith to advance.

On August 19 General Pillow's division was commanded to open the way, and, advancing carefully, bravely, and laboriously over the worst portion of the pass—cutting its road as it moved onward—it arrived about one o'clock in the afternoon at a point amid the ravines and barrancas near Padierna or Contreras where the new road could only be continued under the direct fire of twenty-two pieces of Mexican artillery, most of which were of large caliber. These guns were in a strongly entrenched camp, surrounded by every advantage of ground and by large bodies of infantry and cavalry, reinforced from the city, over an excellent road beyond the volcanic field. Pillow's and Twiggs's force, with all its officers on foot, picking a way along the Mexican front and extending toward the road from the city and the enemy's left, advanced to dislodge the foe. Captain Magruder's field battery of twelve and six-pounders, and Lieutenant Callender's battery of mountain howitzers and rockets, were also pushed forward with great difficulty within range of the Mexican fortifications, and thus a stationary battle raged until night fell drearily on the combatants amid a cold rain which descended in torrents. Wet, chilled, hungry, and sleepless, both armies passed a weary time of watching until early the next morning, when a movement was made by the Americans which resulted in a total rout of Valencia's forces. Firing at a long distance against an entrenched camp was worse than useless on such a ground, and although General Smith's and Colonel Riley's brigades, supported by Generals Pierce's and Cadwallader's, had been under a heavy fire of artillery and musketry for more than three hours along the almost impassable ravine in front and to the left of the Mexican camp, yet so little had been effected in destroying the position that the main reliance for success was correctly judged to be in an assault at close quarters. The plan had been arranged in the night by Brigadier General Persifer F. Smith, and was sanctioned by General Scott, to whom it was communicated through the indefatigable diligence of Captain Lee, of the Engineers.

At 3 o'clock A. M. of August 20 the movement commenced on the rear of the enemy's camp, led by Colonel Riley and followed successively by Cadwallader's and Smith's brigades, the whole force being commanded by General Smith.

The march was rendered tedious by rain, mud, and darkness; but about sunrise Riley reached an elevation behind the Mexicans, whence he threw his men upon the works, and, storming the entrenchments, planted his flag upon them in seventeen minutes. Meanwhile Cadwallader brought on the general assault by crossing the deep ravine in front and pouring into the work and upon the fugitives frequent volleys of destructive musketry. Smith's own brigade under the temporary command of Major Dimick discovered opposite and outside the work a long line of Mexican cavalry drawn up in support, and by a charge against the flank routed the horse completely, while General Shields held masses of cavalry, supported by artillery, in check below him, and captured multitudes who fled from above.

It was a rapid and brilliant feat of arms. Scott, the skillful and experienced general of the field, doubts in his dispatch whether a more brilliant or decisive victory is to be found on record when the disparity of numbers, the nature of the ground, the artificial defenses, and the fact that the Americans accomplished their end without artillery or cavalry are duly and honestly considered. All his forces did not number more than 4500 rank and file, while the Mexicans maintained at least 6000 on the field, and double that number in reserve under Santa Anna, who had advanced to support, but probably seeing that it was not a spot for his theory of a general action, and that an American force intervened, declined aiding his disobedient officer. The Mexicans lost about 700 killed, 813 prisoners, including 4 generals among 88 officers. Twenty-two pieces of brass ordnance, thousands of small arms and accouterments, many colors and standards, large stores of ammunition, seven hundred pack mules, and numbers of horses fell into the hands of the victors.

The rage of Santa Anna against Valencia knew no bounds. He ordered him to be shot wherever found; but the defeated chief fled precipitately toward the west beyond the mountains, and for a long time lay in concealment until the storm of private and public indignation had passed. The effect of this battle, resulting in the loss of the veterans of the north, was disastrous not only in the city, but to the *morale* of the remaining troops of the main division under Santa Anna. It certainly demonstrated the importance of

Padierna or Contreras as a military point of defense; but it unquestionably proved that the works designed to maintain it should have been differently planned and placed at a much earlier day after mature deliberation by skillful engineers. The hasty decision and work of Valencia, made without preconcert or sanction of the general-in-chief, and in total violation of his order of battle, followed by the complete destruction of the entire division of the northern army, could only result in final disaster.

While the battle of Contreras was raging early in the day, brigades from Worth's and Quitman's divisions had been advanced to support the combatants; but before they arrived on the field the post was captured, and they were accordingly ordered to return to their late positions. Worth, advanced from San Agustin in front of San Antonio, was now in better position, for a road to the rear of the hacienda had been opened by forcing the pass of Contreras. Moving from Contreras or Padierna through San Angel and Coyoacan, Pillow's and Twiggs's divisions would speedily be able to attack it from the north, while Worth, advancing from the south, might unquestionably force the position. Accordingly while Pillow and Twiggs were advanced, General Scott reached Coyoacan, about two miles, by a cross road in the rear of the hacienda of San Antonio. From Coyoacan he dispatched Pillow to attack the rear of San Antonio, while a reconnoissance was made of Churubusco, on the main road, and an attack of the place ordered to be effected by Twiggs with one of his brigades and Captain Taylor's field battery.

General Pierce was next dispatched under the guidance of Captain Lee by a road to the left, to attack the enemy's right and rear in order to favor the movement on the convent of Churubusco and cut off retreat to the capital. And finally Shields, with the New York and South Carolina volunteers, was ordered to follow Pierce and to command the left wing. The battle now raged from the right to the left of the whole line. All the movements had been made with the greatest rapidity and enthusiasm. Not a moment was lost in pressing the victory after the fall of Contreras. Shouting Americans and rallying Mexicans were spread over every field. Everyone was employed; and in truth there was ample work to do, for even the commander-in-chief was left without a reserve or an escort and had to advance for safety close in Twiggs's rear.

Meanwhile, about an hour earlier, Worth by a skillful and dar-

ing movement upon the enemy's front and right at the hacienda
of San Antonio had turned and forced that formidable point, whose
garrison no doubt was panic-struck by the victory of Contreras.
The enterprise was nobly achieved. Colonel Clarke's brigade, conducted by the engineers Mason and Hardcastle, found a practicable
path through the Pedregal west of the road, and by a wide sweep
came out upon the main causeway to the capital. At this point the
3000 men of the Mexican garrison at San Antonio were met in
retreat, and cut by Clarke in their very center, one portion being
driven off toward Dolores on the right, and the other upon Churubusco in the direct line of the active operations of the Americans.
While this brave feat of out-flanking was performed, Colonel Garland, Major Galt, Colonel Belton, and Lieutenant Colonel Duncan
advanced to the front attack of San Antonio, and rushing rapidly
on the flying enemy, took one general prisoner and seized a large
quantity of public property, ammunition, and the five deserted guns.

Thus fell the two main keys to the valley, and thus did all the
divisions of the American army at length reach the open and comparatively unobstructed plains of the valley.

Worth soon reunited his division on the main straight road to
the capital, and was joined by General Pillow, who, advancing from
Coyoacan to attack the rear of San Antonio, as we have already related, soon perceived that the hacienda had fallen, and immediately
turned to the left through a broken country of swamps and ditches,
in order to share in the attack on Churubusco. And here, it was
felt on all sides, that the last stand must be made by Mexico in
front of her capital.

The hamlet or scattered houses of Churubusco formed a strong
military position on the borders of the stream which crosses the
highway, and, besides the fortified and massive convent of San
Pablo, it was guarded by a *tête de pont* with regular bastions and
curtains at the head of a bridge over which the road passes from
the hacienda of San Antonio to the city. The stream was a defense, the nature of the adjacent country was a defense, and here
the fragments of the Mexican army, cavalry, artillery, and infantry,
had been collected from every quarter—panic-stricken, it is true—
yet apparently resolved to contest the passage of the last outwork
of importance in front of the garita of San Antonio Abad.

When Worth and Pillow reached this point Twiggs had already been some time hotly engaged in attacking the embattled

convent.   The two advancing generals immediately began to maneuver closely upon the *tête de pont,* which was about 450 yards
east of the convent, where Twiggs still earnestly plied the enemy.
Various brigades and regiments under Cadwallader, Lieutenant
Colonel Smith, Garland, Clark, Major White, and Lieutenant
Colonel Scott continued to press onward toward the *tête de pont,*
until by gradual encroachments under a tremendous fire they attained a position which enabled them to assault and carry the formidable work by the bayonet.   But the convent still held out.
Twenty minutes after the *tête de pont* had been taken, and after a
desperate battle of two hours and a half, that stronghold threw
out the white flag.   Yet it is probable that even then the conflict
would not have ended had not the Third Infantry under Captains
Alexander and J. M. Smith, and Lieutenant O. L. Shepherd cleared
the way by fire and the bayonet to enter the work.

While this gallant task was being performed in front of the
Mexican defenses, Generals Pierce and Shields had been engaged
on the left in turning the Mexicans' works so as to prevent the escape of the garrisons and to oppose the extension of numerous corps
from the rear upon and around the left.   By a winding march of a
mile around to the right, this division, under the command of
Shields, found itself on the edge of an open, wet meadow near
the main road to the capital, in the presence of nearly 4000 of the
Mexicans' infantry, a little in the rear of Churubusco.   Shields
posted his right at a strong edifice, and extended his left wing
parallel to the road, to outflank the enemy toward the capital.   But
the Mexicans extended their right more rapidly, and were supported by several regiments of cavalry, on better ground.   Shields
accordingly concentrated his division about a hamlet and attacked
in front.   The battle was long and bravely sustained with varied
success, but finally resulted in crowning with victory the zeal and
courage of the American commander and his gallant troops.
Shields took 380 prisoners, including officers; while at Churubusco
7 field pieces, some ammunition, 1 standard, 3 generals, and 1261
prisoners, including other officers, were the fruits of the sharply
contested victory.

This was the last conquest on that day of conquests.   As soon
as the *tête de pont* fell Worth's and Pillow's divisions rushed onward by the highway toward the city, which now rose in full
sight before them at the distance of four miles.   Bounding onward,

flushed and exultant, they encountered Shields's division, now also victorious, and all combined in the headlong pursuit of the flying foe.   At length the columns parted, and a small part of Harney's cavalry, led by Captain Kearney of the First Dragoons, dashed to the front and charged the retreating Mexicans up to the very gates of the city.

Thus terminated the first series of American victories in the valley of Mexico.

Chapter XXXI

THE ARMISTICE BEFORE THE CAPITAL. 1847

IT was late in the day when the battles ended.   One army was wearied with fighting and victory; the other equally oppressed by labor and defeat.   The conquered Mexicans fled to their eastern defenses or took refuge within the gates of their city.   There was for the moment utter disorganization among the discomfited, while the jaded band of a few thousand invaders had to be rallied and reformed in their ranks and regiments after the desperate conflicts of the day over so wide a field.   It surely was not a proper moment for an unconcentrated army, almost cut off from support, three hundred miles in the interior of an enemy's country, and altogether ignorant of the localities of a great capital containing nearly two hundred thousand inhabitants, to rush madly at nightfall into the midst of that city.   Mexico, too, was not an ordinary town with wide thoroughfares and houses like those in which the invaders had been accustomed to dwell.   Spanish houses are almost castles in architectural strength and plan, while from their level and embattled roofs a mob, when aroused by the spirit of revenge or despair, may do the service of a disciplined army. Nor was it known whether the metropolis had been defended by works along its streets—by barricades, impediments, and batteries —among which the entangled assailants might be butchered with impunity in the narrow passages during the darkness and before they could concentrate upon any central or commanding spot.   Repose and daylight were required before a prudent general would venture to risk the lives of his men and the success of his whole mission upon such a die.

Accordingly the army was halted; the dispersed recalled, the wounded succored, the dead prepared for burial, and the tired troops ordered to bivouac on the ground they had wrested from the enemy.

Meanwhile the greatest consternation prevailed within the city.   When Santa Anna reached the palace he hastily assembled

the ministers of state and other eminent citizens, and, after reviewing the disasters of the day and their causes, he proclaimed the indispensable necessity of recurring to a truce in order to take a long
respite.   There was a difference of opinion upon this subject; but
it was finally agreed that a suspension of arms should be negotiated
through the Spanish minister and the British consul general.
Pacheco, the minister of foreign relations, accordingly addressed
Mackintosh and Bermudez de Castro, entreating them to effect
this desired result.   During the night the British consul general
visited the American camp, and was naturally anxious to spare
the effusion of blood and the assault by an army on a city in
which his country had so deep an interest.   On the morning of
August 21, when General Scott was about to take up battering or
assaulting positions, to authorize him to summon the capital to surrender or to sign an armistice with a pledge to enter at once into
negotiations for peace, he was met by General Mora y Villamil and
Señor Arrangoiz, with proposals for an armistice in order to bury
the dead, but without reference to a treaty.   Scott had already determined to offer the alternative of assault or armistice and treaty
to the Mexican Government, and this resolution had been long
cherished by him.   Accordingly he at once rejected the Mexican
proposal, and, without summoning the city to surrender, dispatched a note to Santa Anna, expressing his willingness to sign,
on reasonable terms, a short armistice in order that the American
commissioner and the Mexican Government might amicably and
honorably settle the international differences and thus close an
unnatural war in which too much blood had already been shed.
This frank proposal, coming generously from the victorious chief,
was promptly accepted.   Commissioners were appointed by the
commanders of the two armies on the 22d; the armistice was
signed on the 23d, and ratifications exchanged in the 24th; and thus
the dispute was for a while transferred once more from the camp to
the council chamber.   On the morning of the 21st the American
army was posted in the different villages in the vicinity.   Worth's
division occupied Tacubaya, Pillow's Mixcoac, Twiggs's San Angel,
while Quitman's remained still at San Agustin, where it had served
during the battles of the 19th and 20th in protecting the rear and
the trains of the army.   Tacubaya became the residence of General Scott, and the headquarters of the commander-in-chief were
established in the bishop's palace.

There are critics and politicians who are never satisfied with results, and, while their prophecies are usually dated after the events which they claim to have foreseen, they unfortunately find too much favor with the mass of readers who are not in the habit of ascertaining precisely what was known and what was not known at the period of the occurrences which they seek to condemn. General Scott has fallen under the heavy censure of these writers for offering the armistice and avoiding the immediate capture of the capital, the practicability of which they now consider as demonstrated. We propose to examine this question, but we believe that the practicability or impracticability of that event does not become one of the primary or even early elements of the discussion.

If we understand the spirit of this age correctly, we must believe that mankind, purified by the progressive blessings of Christianity and modern civilization, desires the mitigation rather than the increase of the evils of war. It does not seek merely to avert danger or disaster from the forces of one party in the strife, but strives to produce peace with as little harm as possible to all who are engaged in warfare. It is not the mission of a soldier to kill because his profession is that of arms. It is ever the imperative duty of a commander to stop the flow of blood as soon as he perceives the slightest chance of peace; and if his honorable efforts fail entirely, through the folly or obstinacy of the foe, he will be more fully justified in the subsequent and stringent measures of coercion.

The Mexican masses, mistaking vanity for true national pride, had hitherto persevered in resisting every effort to settle the international difficulties. Diplomacy with such a nation was extremely delicate. If symptoms of leniency were exhibited she became presumptuous; if hostilities were pushed to the extreme, she grew doggedly obstinate. On August 21 her capital was in Scott's power. His victorious army was at her gates. Two terrible battles had been fought, and the combatants on both sides had shown courage, skill, and endurance. The Mexican army was routed, but not entirely dispersed or destroyed. At this moment it doubtless occurred to General Scott, and to all who were calm spectators of the scene, that before the last and fatal move was made it was his duty to allow Mexico to save her point of honor by negotiating, ere the city was entered, and while she could yet proclaim to her citizens and the world that her capital had never been seized by the enemy. This assuaged national vanity and preserved the last vantage ground upon which the nation might stand with pride, if not with perfect confidence. It still left something to the conquered people which was not necessary or valuable to the conquerors.

There are other matters, unquestionably, that weighed much in the very responsible deliberations of General Scott. If the army entered the city triumphantly, or took it by assault, the frail elements of government still lingering at that period of disorganization would either fly or be utterly destroyed. All who were in power, in that nation of jealous politicians and wily intriguers, would be eager to shun the last responsibility. If Santa Anna should be utterly beaten, the disgrace would blot out the last traces of his remaining prestige. If so fatal a disaster occurred, as subsequent events proved, the Americans would be most unfortunately situated in relation to peace, for there would be no government to negotiate with! Santa Anna's government was the only constitutional one that had existed in Mexico for a long period, and with such a legalized national authority peace must be concluded. It was not the duty of the United States to destroy a government and with the fragments reconstruct another with which it might treat. If a revolutionary or provisional authority existed, what prospect could there be of enduring pacification? What guaranty could be held in a treaty celebrated with a military despot, a temporary chief, or a sudden usurper, that such a treaty could be maintained before the nation? What constitutional or legal right would an American general or commissioner have to enter into such a compact? Was it not, therefore, Scott's duty to act with such tender caution as not to endanger the fate of the only man who might still keep himself at the head of his rallied people?

Besides these political considerations there are others, of a military character, that will commend themselves to the prudent and the just. The unacclimated American army had marched from Puebla to the valley of Mexico during the rainy season, in a tropical zone, when the earth is saturated with water and no one travels who can avoid exposure. The men were forced to undergo the hardships of such a campaign, to make roads, to travel over broken ground, to wade marshes, to bivouac on the camp soil with scarce a shelter from the storm, to march day and night, and finally, without an interval of repose, to fight two of the sharpest actions of the war. The seven or eight thousand survivors of these actions—many of whom were new levies—demanded care and zealous husbanding for future events. They were distant from the coast and cut off from support or immediate succor. The enemy's present or prospective weakness was not to be relied on. Wisdom required that what was in the rear should be thought of as well as what was in advance.

May it not then be justly said that it was a proper moment for a heroic general to pause, in front of a national capital containing two hundred thousand people, and to allow the civil arm to assume for a moment of trial the place of the military? Like a truly brave man, he despised the *éclat* of entering the capital as Cortéz had done on nearly the same day of the same month, 326 years before. Like a wise man, he considered the history and condition of the enemy instead of his personal glory, and laid aside the false ambition of a soldier to exhibit the forbearance of a Christian statesman.[1]

The American commissioner unquestionably entered upon the negotiations in good faith, and it is probable that Santa Anna was personally quite as well disposed for peace. He, however, had a delicate game to play with the politicians of his own country, and was obliged to study carefully the attitude of parties as well as the momentary strength of his friends and enemies. Well acquainted as he was with the value of men and the intrigues of the time, he would have been mad not to guard against the risk of ruin, and accordingly his first efforts were directed rather toward obtaining the ultimatum of the United States than to pledging his own government in any project which might prove either presently unpopular or destroy his future influence. The instructions, therefore, that were given to the Mexican commissioners were couched in such extreme terms that much could be yielded before there was a likelihood of approaching the American demands. In the meanwhile, as negotiations progressed, Mexico obtained time to rally her soldiers, to appease those who were discontented with the proposed peace, and to adjure the project if it should be found either inadmissible or impossible of accomplishment without loss of popularity.

[1] It will be remembered that even Cortéz had paused in the precincts of the ancient capital of the Aztecs in order to give them a chance of escape before striking the fatal blow. It is a little remarkable also, that the dates of Scott's and Cortéz's victories coincide so closely. Cortéz's victory was on August 13, 1521, Scott's on August 20, 1847. The date of Cortéz's achievement is given according to the old style, but if we add ten days to bring it up to new style, it will be corrected to August 23!

For several days consultations took place between Trist and the commissioners, but it was soon found that the American pretensions in regard to the position of Texas, the boundary of the Rio Grande, and the cession of New Mexico and Upper California were of such a character that the Mexicans would not yield to them at the present moment. The popular feeling, stimulated by the rivals of Santa Anna, his enemies, and the demagogues, was entirely opposed to the surrender of territory. Sensible as the president was that the true national interests demanded instantaneous peace, he was dissuaded by his confidential advisers from presenting a counter *projét,* which would have resulted in a treaty. Congress, moreover, had virtually dissolved by the precipitate departure of most of its members after the battles of the 20th.

All the party leaders labored diligently at this crisis, but none of them with cordiality for Santa Anna, in whose negotiations of a successful peace with the United States they either foresaw or feared the permanent consolidation of his power. The Puros, or Democrats, still clung to their admiration of the constitution of the United States; to their opposition to the standing army; to their desire for modifying the power and position of the church and its ministers, and to their united hostility against the president. They were loud in their exhortations to continue the war, while Olaguibel, one of their ablest men and most devoted lover of American institutions, issued a strong manifesto against the projected treaty. This was the party which, it is asserted, in fact desired the prolongation of the war until the destroyed nationality of Mexico took refuge from domestic intrigues, misgovernment, and anarchy in annexation to the United States.

The Monarquistas, who still adhered to the church and the army, proclaimed their belief in the total failure of the republican system. Revolutions and incessant turmoils, according to their opinions, could only be suppressed by the strong arm of power, and in their ranks had again appeared General Mariano Paredes y Arrellaga, who, returning from exile, landed in disguise at Vera Cruz, and passing secretly through the American lines, proceeded to Mexico to continue his machinations against Santa Anna, whom he cordially hated.

The Moderados formed a middle party equally opposed to the ultraisms of monarchy and democracy. They counted among their number many of the purest and wisest men in the republic, and although they were not as inimical to the United States as the Monarquistas, or as many of the Puros pretended to be, yet they cordially desired or hoped to preserve the nationality and progressive republicanism of Mexico. In this junto Santa Anna found a few partisans who adhered to him more from policy than principle, for all classes had learned to distrust a person who played so many parts in the national drama of intrigue, war, and government. As a party, they were doubtless unwilling to risk their strength and prospects upon a peace which might be made under his auspices.

In this crisis the president had no elements of strength still firmly attached to him but the army, whose favor, amid all his reverses, he generally contrived to retain or to win. But that army was now much disorganized, and the national finances were so low that he was scarcely able to maintain it from day to day. The mob, composed of the lower classes, and the leperos, knowing nothing of the principles of the war, and heedless of its consequences—plied moreover by the demagogues of all the parties—shouted loudly for its continuance, and thus the president was finally forced to yield to the external pressure and to be governed by an impulse which he was either too timid or too weak to control.

The armistice provided that the Americans should receive supplies from the city, and that no additional fortifications should be undertaken during its continuance; nevertheless the American trains were assailed by the populace of the city, and it is alleged that Santa Anna disregarded the provision forbidding fortifications. When it became evident to the American commissioner and General Scott that the Mexicans were merely trifling and temporizing, that the prolongation of the armistice would be advantageous to the enemy, without affording any correspondent benefits to them, and when their supplies had been increased so as to afford ample support for the army during the anticipated attack on the city, it was promptly resolved to renew the appeal to arms. Accordingly on September 6 General Scott addressed Santa Anna, calling his attention to the infractions of the compact, and declaring that unless satisfaction was made for the breaches of faith before noon of the following day he would consider the armistice terminated from that hour. Santa Anna returned an answer of false recriminations, and threw off the mask. He asserted his willingness to rely on arms; he issued a bombastic appeal to the people, in which he announced that the demands of the Americans would have converted the nation into a colony of their Union. He improved upon the pretended patriotic zeal of all the parties—Puros, Moderados, Monarquistas, and Mob—who had proclaimed themselves in favor of the war. Instead of opposing or arguing the question, he caught the war strain of the hour and sent it forth to the multitude in trumpet tones. He was determined not to be hedged or entrapped by those who intrigued to destroy him, and resolved that if he must fall, his opponents should share the political disaster. Nor was he alone in his electioneering gasconade, for General Herrera—a man who had been notoriously the advocate of peace, both before and since the rupture—addressed the clergy and the people, craving their aid by prayer, money, fire, and sword, to exterminate the invaders! All classes were thus placed in a false and uncandid position.

Chapter XXXII

THE FALL OF THE CAPITAL. 1847-1848

AT the termination of the armistice the position of the American forces was greatly changed from what it had been on the morning of August 20. The occupation of San Agustin had been followed by that of Contreras, San Angel, Coyoacan, and Churubusco in the course of that day, and on the next Mixcoac and Tacubaya were taken possession of. Thus the whole southern and southwestern portion of the valley, in front of Mexico, were now held by the Americans; and this disposition of their forces, commanding most of the principal approaches to the capital, enabled them for the first time to select their point of attack.

In reconnoitering the chief outworks of the Mexicans by which he was still opposed, General Scott found that there were several of great importance. Directly north of his headquarters at Tacubaya, and distant about a mile, arose the lofty, isolated hill of Chapultepec, surmounted by its massive edifice, half castle, half palace, crowned with cannon. This point, it was known, had been strongly fortified to maintain the road leading from Tacubaya to the garita of San Cosmé on the west of the city. Westwardly, beyond the hill of Chapultepec, whose southern side and feet are surrounded by a dense grove of cypresses, and on a rising ground within the military works designed to strengthen the castle, was the Molino del Rey, or King's Mill, which was represented to be a cannon foundry to which large quantities of church bells had been sent to be cast into guns. Still further west, but near the Molino or Mill, was the fortified Casa Mata, containing a large deposit of powder.

These, together with the strong citadel lying near the garita of Belen in the southwestern corner of the city, were the principal external defenses still remaining beyond the immediate limits of the capital. The city itself stands on a slight swell between Lake Tezcoco and the western edge of the valley, and throughout its greater extent is girdled by a ditch or navigable canal extremely difficult to bridge in the face of an enemy, which served the Mexicans not only as a military defense, but for drainage, and protection of their customs. Each of the eight strong city gates was protected by works of various character and merit. Outside and within the cross fires of these gates there were other obstacles scarcely less formidable toward the south. The main approaches to the city across the flat lands of the basin are raised on causeways flanked by wide and deep ditches designed for their protection and drainage. These causeways, as well as the minor cross-roads, which are similarly built, were cut in many places and had their bridges destroyed so as to impede the Americans' advance and to form an entangling network, while the adjacent meadows were in this rainy season either filled with water in many places or liable to be immediately flooded by a tropical storm.

With these fields for his theater of action, and these defenses still in front of him, it was an important and responsible question whether General Scott should attack Mexico on the west or on the south.

There can be hardly a doubt that the capture of the hill and castle of Chapultepec, before assaulting the city, was imperatively demanded by good generalship. If the capital were taken first, the Mexicans instead of retreating toward Guadalupe and the north, when attacked from the south, would of course retire to the avoided stronghold of Chapultepec; and if the American forces were subsequently obliged to leave the city in order to take the fortress, its sick, wounded, and thinned regiments would be left to the mercy of the mob and the leperos. Chapultepec would thus become the nucleus and garrison of the whole Mexican army, and the Americans might be compelled to fight two battles at the same time—one in the city and the other at the castle. But, by capturing the castle first and seizing the road northward beyond it, they possessed all the most important outworks in the lap of the valley and cut off the retreat of the Mexicans from the city either to the west, to the castle, or toward the rear in the valley. They obtained, moreover, absolute command of two of the most important entrances to the capital, inasmuch as from the eastern foot of the hill of Chapultepec two causeways, and aqueducts raised on lofty arches, diverged northeastwardly and eastwardly toward the city. The northernmost of these entered Mexico by the garita of San Cosmé, while the other reached it by that of Belen near the citadel.

In attacking Chapultepec it was important to consider the value of the Molino del Rey or King's Mill, and Casa Mata, both of which lie on rising ground within the works designed to protect Chapultepec. The Molino del Rey bears the relation of a very strong western outwork both to the castle of Chapultepec and its approaches by the inclined plain which serves to ascend its summit. As the Molino del Rey is commanded and defended by the castle, so it reciprocally commands and defends the only good approach to the latter.[1] As long as the Molino was held by the Mexicans it would of course form an important stronghold easily reached from the city around the rear of Chapultepec; so that if Scott attacked the castle and hill from the south, where the road that ascends it commenced, he would be in danger of an attack on his left flank from the Mexicans in the defenses at Molino and Casa Mata.

If the King's Mill fell, the result to the enemy would be that, in addition to the loss of an important outwork and the consequent weakening of the main work, its occupants or defenders would be driven from a high position above the roads and fields into the low grounds at the base of Chapultepec, which were completely commanded from the Molino, and thus the Mexicans would be unable to prevent the American siege-pieces from taking up the most favorable position for battering the castle. It was important, therefore, not only that the foundry should be destroyed, but, in a strategetic view, it was almost indispensable in relation to future operations that the position should be taken. It is undeniable, as following events showed, that the Mexicans regarded it as one of their formidable military points. The capture of Chapultepec and the destruction of the post at Molino del Rey were accordingly determined on as preliminary to the final assault upon the city.

As soon as the armistice was terminated bold reconnoissances were made by the engineers in the direction of Chapultepec and the Molino and Casa Mata. On September 7 Santa Anna's answer to Scott's dispatch was received, and on the same day the commander-in-chief and General Worth examined the formidable dispositions near and around the castle-crowned hill. The Mexican array was found to consist of an extended line of cavalry and infantry, sustained by a field battery of four guns, either occupying directly or supporting a system of defenses collateral to the castle and summit; but as the lines were skillfully masked a very inadequate idea of the extent of the forces was

[1] See Lieutenant Smith's "Memoir," *ut antea,* p. 8.

obtained. Captain Mason's reconnoissance on the morning of the same day represented the enemy's left as resting on and occupying the group of strong stone buildings at the Molino adjacent to the grove at the foot of Chapultepec and directly under the castle's guns. The right of his line rested on the Casa Mata, at the foot of the ridge sloping gradually to the plain below from the heights above Tacubaya; while midway between these buildings were the field battery and infantry forces disposed on either side to support it. This reconnoissance indicated that the center was the weak point of the position, and that its left flank was the strongest. In the Mill or Molino on the left was the brigade of General Leon, reinforced by the brigade of General Rangel; in the Casa Mata on the right was the brigade of General Perez; and on the intermediate ground was the brigade of General Ramirez, with several pieces of artillery. The Mexican reserve was composed of the First and Third Light, stationed in the groves of Chapultepec, while the cavalry, consisting of 4000 men, rested at the hacienda of Morales, not very far from the field. Such was the arrangement of the Mexican forces made by Santa Anna in person on September 7, though it has been alleged by Mexican writers that it was somewhat changed during the following night. The wily chief had not allowed the time to pass during the negotiation between Trist and the commissioners in political discussion alone. Regarding the failure of the treaty as most probable, he had striven to strengthen once more the military arm of his nation, and the first result of this effort was demonstrated in his disposition of troops at El Molino del Rey. The Americans' attack upon Chapultepec, as commanding the nearest and most important access to the city, had been foreseen by him as soon as the armistice ended, and as a military man he well knew that the isolated hill and castle could not be protected by the defenders within its walls alone or by troops stationed either immediately at its base or on the sloping road along its sides.

General Scott's plan of assault upon the city seems now to have been matured, though it required several days for full development according to the reconnoissances of his engineers. He designed to make the main assault on the west and not on the south of the city. Possessing himself suddenly of the Molino del Rey and the adjacent grounds, he was to retire after the capture without carrying Chapultepec, the key of the roads to the western garitas of San Cosmé and Belen. The immediate capture of Chapultepec would have been a signal to Santa Anna to throw his whole force into the western defense of the city; but by retiring, after the fall of the Molino, and by playing off skillfully on the south of the city in the direction of the garita of San Antonio Abad, Scott would effectually divert the attention of the Mexicans to that quarter and thus induce them to weaken the western defenses and strengthen the southern. At length at the proper moment, by a rapid inversion of his forces from the south to the west, he intended to storm the castle-crowned hill, and thence rush along the causeways to the capital before the enemy could recover his position.

In pursuance of this plan an attack upon El Molino del Rey and La Casa Mata was the first great work to be accomplished, and as soon as Santa Anna's reply closing the armistice was received on the 7th the advance toward that place was ordered for the following morning. This important work was intrusted to General Worth, whose division was reinforced by three squadrons of dragoons, one command of 270 mounted riflemen under Major Sumner, 3 field-pieces under Captain Drum, 2 twenty-four pounders under Captain Huger, and Cadwallader's brigade, 784 strong. The reconnoissances had been completed; at three o'clock in the morning of September 8 the several columns were put in motion on as many different routes, and when the gray dawn enabled them to be seen they were as accurately posted as if in midday for review. Colonel Duncan was charged with the general disposition of the artillery, while the cavalry were under Major Sumner.

At the first glimmer of day Huger's powerful guns saluted the walls of El Molino and continued to play in that quarter until this point of the Mexican line became sensibly shaken. At that moment the assaulting party, commanded by Wright of the Eighth Infantry, dashed forward to assault the center. Musketry and canister were showered upon them by the aroused enemy, but on they rushed, driving infantry and artillerists at the point of the bayonet, capturing the field pieces and training them on the flying foe, until the Mexicans, perceiving that they had been assailed by a mere handful of men, suddenly rallied and reformed. In an instant the reassured and gallant foe opened upon the Americans a terrific fire of musketry, striking down eleven out of the fourteen officers who composed the command, and for the time staggering the staunch assail-

ants. But this paralysis continued for an instant only. A light
battalion which had been held to cover Huger's battery, commanded
by Captain E. Kirby Smith, rushed forward to support, and exe-
cuting its bloody task amid horrible carnage, finally succeeded in
carrying the line and ocupying it with troops. In the meanwhile Garland's brigade, sustained by Drum's artillery, assaulted
the enemy's left near the Molino, and after an obstinate contest drove
him from his position under the protecting guns of Chapultepec.
Drum's section and Huger's battering guns advanced to the enemy's
position, and his captured pieces were now opened on the retreating
force. While these efforts were successfully making on the Mexican center and left, Duncan's battery blazed on the right, and Colonel
Mackintosh was ordered to assault that point. The advance of his
brigade soon brought it between the enemy and Duncan's guns,
and their fire was of course discontinued. Onward sternly and
steadily moved the troops toward the Casa Mata, which, as it was
approached, proved to be a massive stonework surrounded with
bastioned entrenchments and deep ditches, whence a deadly fire
was delivered and kept up without intermission upon the advancing
troops until they reached the very slope of the parapet surrounding
the citadel. The havoc was dreadful. A large proportion of the
command was either killed or wounded; but still the ceaseless fire
from the Casa Mata continued its deadly work, until the maimed
and broken band of gallant assailants was withdrawn to the left of
Duncan's battery, where its remnants rallied. Duncan and Sumner
had meanwhile been hotly engaged in repelling a charge of Mexican
cavalry on the left, and having just completed the work the brave
colonel found his countrymen retired from before the Casa Mata
and the field again open for his terrible weapons. Directing them
at once upon the fatal fort, he battered the Mexicans from its walls,
and as they fled from its protecting enclosure he continued to play
upon the fugitives as relentlessly as they had recently done upon
Mackintosh and his doomed brigade.

The Mexicans were now driven from the field at every point.
La Casa Mata was blown up by the conquerors. Captured ammunition and cannon molds in El Molino were destroyed. And the
Americans, according to Scott's order previous to the battle,
returned to Tacubaya, with 3 of the enemy's guns (a fourth being
spiked and useless), 800 prisoners, including 52 commissioned officers, and a large quantity of small arms, with gun and musket

ammunition. On this day 3251 Americans had driven four times
their number from a selected field; but they had paid a large and
noble tribute to death for the victory. Nine officers were included
in the 116 of the killed, and 49 officers in the 665 of the wounded.
The Mexicans suffered greatly in wounded and slain, while the
gallant General Leon and Colonel Balderas fell fighting bravely on
the field of battle.

The battle was over by nine o'clock in the morning. The
Americans, after collecting their dead and wounded, retired from
the bloody field, but they were not allowed to mourn over their
painful losses. They had suffered severely, yet the battle had been
most disastrous to the Mexicans. The fine commands of Generals
Perez and Leon and of Colonel Balderas were broken up, the position, once destroyed, could not serve for a second defense, and the
morale of the soldiers had suffered. The Mexicans were beginning
to believe that mere formidable masses, if not directed by skillful
chiefs, were in truth but harmless things, and not to be relied on
very confidently for national defense. The new levies, the old regular army, and the volunteers of the city had all been repeatedly
beaten in the valley both before and since the armistice. Nevertheless Santa Anna, in spite of all these defeats and disasters at the
Molino and Casa Mata, caused the bells of the city to be merrily
rung for a victory, and sent forth proclamations by extraordinary
couriers in every direction announcing the triumph of Mexican valor
and arms!

On the morning of the 11th Scott proceeded to carry out the
remainder of his projected capture of the capital. His troops had
been already for some time hovering around the southern gates,
and he now surveyed them, closely covered by General Pillow's
division and Riley's brigade of Twiggs's command, and then ordered Quitman from Coyoacan to join Pillow by daylight before
the southern gates. By night, however, the two generals with their
commands were to pass the two intervening miles between their
position and Tacubaya, where they would unite with Worth's division, while General Twiggs was left, with Riley, Captain Taylor,
and Steptoe, in front of the gates to maneuver, threaten, or make
false attacks so as to occupy and deceive the enemy. General
Smith's brigade was halted in supporting distance at San Angel,
in the rear, till the morning of the 13th, so as to support the general
depot at Mixcoac. This stratagem against the south was admirably

executed throughout the 12th and until the afternoon of the 13th, when it was too late for Santa Anna to recover from his delusion.

In the meanwhile preparations had been duly made for the operations on the west by the capture of Chapultepec. Heavy batteries were established and the bombardment and cannonade under Captain Huger were commenced early on the morning of the 12th. Pillow and Quitman had been in position, as ordered, since early on the night of the 11th, and Worth was now commanded to hold his division in reserve near the foundry to support Pillow, while Smith was summoned to sustain Quitman. Twiggs still continued to inform with his guns that held the Mexicans on the defensive in that quarter and kept Santa Anna in constant anxiety. Scott's positions and strategy perfectly disconcerted him. One moment on the south, the next at Tacubaya, then reconnoitering the south again, and at last concentrating his forces so that they might be easily moved northward to Chapultepec or southward to the gate of San Antonio Abad. These movements rendered him constantly sensible of every hour's importance, yet he would not agree with the veteran Bravo, who commanded Chapultepec and was convinced that the hill and castle would be the points assailed. During the whole of the 12th the American pieces, strengthened by the captured guns, poured an incessant shower of shot into the fortress until nightfall, when the assailants slept upon their arms, to be in position for an early renewal on the 13th.

At half-past five in the morning the American guns recommenced upon Chapultepec; but still Santa Anna clung to the southern gates, while Scott was silently preparing for the final assault according to a preconcerted signal. About eight o'clock, judging that the missiles had done the work, the heavy batteries suddenly ceased firing, and instantaneously Pillow's division rushed forward from the conquered Molino del Rey, and overbearing all obstacles and rapidly clambering up the steep acclivities, raised their scaling ladders and poured over the walls.[2]

[2] The importance of the previous capture of El Molino del Rey was proved in this assault upon Chapultepec, for Pillow's division started from this very Mill, from within the enemy's works, and found itself on an equality with the foe up to the very moment of scaling the walls at the crest of the mount, whereas the other assaulting column under Quitman, taking the only remaining road to the castle, a causeway leading from Tacubaya, was successfully held at bay by the outworks defending this road at the base of the hill until after the castle was taken and the opposing force was taken in rear by troops passing

Quitman, supported by Generals Shields and Smith, was meanwhile advancing rapidly toward the southeast of the works over a causeway with cuts and batteries defended by an army strongly posted outside the works toward the east. But nothing could resist the impulse of the storming division, though staunchly opposed and long held at bay, and while it rushed to complete the work, the New York, South Carolina, and Pennsylvania volunteers, under Shields, crossed the meadows in front amid a heavy fire, and entered the outer enclosure of Chapultepec in time to join the enterprise from the west. The castle was now possessed at every point. The onslaught had been so rapid and resistless that the Mexicans stood appalled as the human tide foamed and burst over their battlements. Men who had been stationed to fire the mines either fled or were shot down. Officers fell at their posts, and the brave old Bravo, fighting to the last, was taken prisoner, with a thousand combatants.

Santa Anna was at last undeceived. He detached at once the greater portion of his troops from near the garita of San Antonio Abad; but it was too late—the key to the roads of San Cosmé and Belen had fallen. The advance works were weak, and the routed troops of Chapultepec fled rapidly along the causeways and over the meadows. Still as they retreated they fought courageously, and as the Americans approached the walls the fresh troops in the neighborhood poured their volleys from behind parapets, windows, and steeples. Nevertheless, Santa Anna dared not withdraw all his forces in the presence of Twiggs's threatening division on the south.

Meanwhile Worth had seized the causeway and aqueduct of San Cosmé, while Quitman advanced by the other toward the garita of Belen. The double roads on each side of these aqueducts which rested on open arches spanning massive pillars afforded fine points for attack and defense. Both the American generals were prompt in pursuing the retreating foe, while Scott, who had ascended the battlements of Chapultepec and beheld the field spread out beneath him like a map, hastened onward all the stragglers and detachments to join the flushed victors in the final assault.

Worth speedily reached the street of San Cosmé and became

through and around Chapultepec. Had El Molino still been held by the Mexicans, the siege pieces would not have been allowed to play uninterruptedly, nor would the assaulting parties been able to take position or attack with impunity. See Lieutenant Smith's "Memoir," *ut antea* p. 8.

engaged in desperate conflict with the enemy from the houses and defenses. Ordering forward Cadwallader's brigade with mountain howitzers, preceded by skirmishers and pioneers with pick-axes and crowbars to force windows and doors and to burrow through the walls, he rapidly attained an equality of position with the enemy; and by eight o'clock in the evening, after carrying two batteries in this suburb, he planted a heavy mortar and piece of artillery from which he might throw shot and shells into the city during the night. Having posted guards and sentinels and sheltered his weary men, he at length found himself with no obstacle but the gate of San Cosmé between his gallant band and the great square of Mexico.

The pursuit by Quitman on the road to the gate of Belen had been equally hot and successful. Scott originally designed that this general should only maneuver and threaten the point so as to favor Worth's more dangerous enterprise by San Cosmé. But the brave and impetuous Quitman, seconded by the eager spirits of his division, longing for the distinction of which they had been hitherto deprived, heeded neither the external defenses nor the more dangerous power of the neighboring citadel. Onward he pressed his men under flank and direct fires, seized an intermediate battery of two guns, carried the gate of Belen, and thus before two o'clock was the first to enter the city and maintain his position with a loss proportionate to the steady firmness of his desperate assault. After nightfall he added several new defenses to the point he had won so gloriously, and sheltering his men as well as he was able, awaited the return of daylight under the guns of the formidable and unsubdued citadel.

So ended the battles of September 13, 1847, and so, in fact, ended the great contests of the war. Santa Anna had been again "disconcerted" in his plan of battle by Scott, as he had previously been thwarted by Valencia's disobedience and willfulness. Scott would not attack the south of the city, where he expected him, and consequently the American chief conquered the point where he had not expected him!

When darkness fell upon the city a council of disheartened officers assembled in the Mexican citadel. After the customary crimination and recrimination had been exhausted between Santa Anna and other officers, it was acknowledged that the time had come to decide upon future movements. Beaten in every battle, they now saw one American general already within the city gate, while another was preparing to enter on the following morning, and kept the city sleepless by the loud discharges of his heavy cannon or bursting bombs as they fell in the center of the capital. General Carrera believed the demoralization of his army complete. Lombardini, Alcorta, and Perez coincided in his opinion, and Santa Anna at length closed the panic-stricken council by declaring that Mexico must be evacuated during the night, and by naming Lombardini general-in-chief and General Perez second in command. Between eight and nine o'clock Señor Trigueros called at the citadel with his coach and bore away the luckless military president to the sacred town of Guadalupe Hidalgo, three miles north of the capital.

The retreat of the Mexican army began at midnight, and not long after a deputation from the ayuntamiento, or city council, waited upon General Scott with the information that the federal government and troops had fled from the capital. The haggard visitors demanded terms of capitulation in favor of the church, the citizens, and the municipal authorities. Scott refused the ill-timed request, and promising no terms that were not self-imposed, sent word to Quitman and Worth to advance as soon as possible on the following morning, and, guarding carefully against treachery, to occupy the city's strongest and most commanding points. Worth was halted at the Alameda, a few squares west of the Plaza, but Quitman was allowed the honor of advancing to the great square, and hoisting the American flag on the national palace. At nine o'clock the commander-in-chief, attended by his brilliant staff, rode into the vast area in front of the venerable cathedral and palace amid the shouts of the exulting army to whose triumphs his prudence and genius had so greatly contributed. It was a proud moment for Scott, and he might well have flushed with excitement as he ascended the palace stairs and sat down in the saloon which had been occupied by so many viceroys, ministers, presidents, and generals, to write the brief order announcing his occupation of the capital of Mexico. Yet the elation was but momentary. The cares of conquest were now exchanged for those of preservation. He was allowed no interval of repose from anxiety. His last victories had entirely disorganized the republic. There was no longer a national government, a competent municipal authority, or even a police force which could be relied on to regulate the fallen city. Having accomplished the work of destruction, the responsibility of reconstruction was now imposed upon him; and first among his duties was the task of providing for the safety and subordination of that slender band which had been so suddenly forced into a vast and turbulent capital.[3]

Scarcely had the divisions of the American army, after the enthusiastic expression of their joy, begun to disperse from the great square of Mexico in search of quarters when the populace commenced firing upon them from within the deep embrasures of the windows and from behind the parapet walls of the house-tops. This dastardly assault by the mob of a surrendered city lasted for two days, until it was terminated by the vigorous military measures of General Scott. Yet it is due to the Mexicans to state that this horrible scheme of assassination was not countenanced by the better classes, but that the base outbreak was altogether owing to the liberation of about two thousand convicts by the flying government on the previous night. These miscreants, the scum and outcasts of Mexico—its common thieves, assassins, and notorious vagrants—banded with nearly an equal number of the disorganized army, had already thronged the palace when Quitman arrived with his division, and it was only by the active exertion of

---

[3] We shall record as very interesting historical facts the numbers with which General Scott achieved his victories in the valley.

FORCES.

He left Puebla with............................ 10,738 rank and file.
At Contreras and Churubusco there were........ 8,497 engaged.
At El Molino del Rey and La Casa Mata........ 3,251 "
On September 12 and 13, at Chapultepec, etc.... 7,180 "
Final attack on city, after deducting killed,
　　wounded, garrison of Mixcoac and Chapul-
　　tepec 6,000

LOSSES.

At Contreras and Churubusco...... 137 killed. 877 wounded. 38 missing.
At El Molino, etc.................. 116 " 665 " 18 "
September 12, 13, and 14.......... 130 " 703 " 29 "

Grand total of losses, 2703.

"On the other hand," says Scott in his dispatch September 18, 1847, "this small force has beaten on the same occasions, in view of the capital, the whole Mexican army, composed at the beginning of thirty odd thousand men, posted always in chosen positions, behind entrenchments or more formidable defenses of nature and art; killed or wounded more than 7000 officers and men, taken 3730 prisoners, one-seventh officers, including 13 general, of whom three had been presidents of this republic: captured more than 20 colors and standards, 75 pieces of ordnance, besides 57 wall pieces, 20,000 small arms, and an immense quantity of shot, shells and powder."—See Ex. Doc. No. 1 Senate, 30th Congress, 1st Session, p. 384.

Watson's marines that the vagrant crowd was driven from the edifice.

General Quitman was immediately appointed civil and military governor of the conquered capital, and discharged his duties under the martial law proclaimed by Scott on September 7. The general order of the commander-in-chief breathes the loftiest spirit of self-respect, honor, and national consideration. He points out clearly the crimes commonly incident to the occupation of subdued cities, and gives warning of the severity with which their perpetrators will be punished. He protects the administration of justice among the Mexicans in the courts of the country. He places the city, its churches, worship, convents, monasteries, inhabitants, and property under the special safeguard of the faith and honor of the American army. And finally, instead of demanding, according to the custom of many generals in the Old World, a splendid ransom from the opulent city, he imposed upon it a trifling contribution of $150,000 — $20,000 of which he devoted to extra comforts for the sick and wounded, $90,000 to purchase blankets and shoes for gratuitous distribution among the common soldiers, while but $40,000 were reserved for the military chest. This act of clemency and consideration is in beautiful contrast with the last malignant spitefulness of the conquered army, whose commander, unable to overthrow the invaders in fair combat, had released at midnight the desperadoes from his prisons, with the hope that assassination might do the work which military skill and honorable valor had been unable to effect.

Meanwhile Santa Anna dispatched a circular from the town of Guadalupe recounting to the governors of the different States the loss of the capital, and on the 16th he issued a decree requiring congress to assemble at Querétaro, which was designated as the future seat of government. As president and politician he at once saw that he could do nothing more without compromising himself still further. Resigning, therefore, the executive chair in favor of his constitutional successor, Señor Peña-y-Peña, Chief Justice of the Supreme Court, he dispatched General Herrera with 4000 troops to Querétaro, and departed to assail the Americans in Puebla. On the 18th he evacuated Guadalupe, and took the road to the eastward, with 2000 cavalry commanded by General Alvarez. He knew that communication with the American base of operations in that quarter was seriously interrupted if not entirely cut off, and he vainly hoped to recover his military prestige by some brilliant feat of arms over detached or unequal squadrons.

When Scott marched into the valley of Mexico Puebla was left in charge of Colonel Childs, with 400 efficient men and nearly 1800 in his hospitals. The watchful commander and his small band preserved order until the false news of Mexican success at Molino del Rey was received. But at that moment the masses, joined by about 3000 troops under General Rea, a brave and accomplished Spaniard, rose upon and besieged the slender garrison. On the 22d Santa Anna arrived and, increasing the assailants to nearly 8000, made the most vigorous efforts during the six following days and nights to dislodge the Americans from the position they had seized.

About the middle of the month Brigadier General Lane left Vera Cruz with a fresh command, and at Jalapa joined the forces of Major Lally, who, with nearly 1000 men and a large and valuable train, had fought his way thither against Jarauta and his guerrilleros at San Juan, Paso de Ovejas, Puente Nacional, Plan del Rio, Cerro Gordo, and Los Animas. As soon as the news of Puebla's danger reached these commanders they marched to support the besieged band, while Santa Anna, believing that Rea could either conquer or hold Childs in check until his return, departed in quest of the advancing columns of Lane and Lally, who were reported to have convoyed from the coast an immense amount of treasure. The combined lust of glory and gold perhaps stimulated this last effort of the failing chief. Rea continued the siege of Puebla bravely. Santa Anna, advancing eastward, and apparently confident of success, established his headquarters at Huamantla; but while maneuvering his troops to attack the approaching columns Lane fell upon him suddenly on October 9, and after a sharp action remained victor on the field. On the next day General Lane continued his march to Puebla, and, entering it on October 13, drove the Mexicans from all their positions and effectually relieved the pressed but pertinacious commander of the beleagured Americans.

It was now the turn of those who had been so long assailed to become assailants. Rea retired to Atlixco, about twenty-five miles from Puebla, but the inexorable Lane immediately followed in his steps, and, reaching the retreat at sunset on the 19th, by a bright moonlight cannonaded the town from the overlooking heights.

After an hour's incessant labor Atlixco surrendered, the enemy fled, and thus was destroyed a nest in which many a guerrillero party had been fitted out for the annoyance or destruction of Americans.

Mexico possesses a wonderful facility in the creation of armies or in the aggregation of men under the name of soldiers. Wherever a standard is raised it is quickly surrounded by the idlers, the thriftless, and the improvident, who are willing at least to be supported, if not munificently recompensed, for the task of bearing arms. At this period, and notwithstanding all the recent disgraceful and disheartening defeats, a large corps had already been gathered in different parts of the republic. The recruits were, however, divided into small, undisciplined, and consequently inefficient bodies. It was reported that Lombardini and Reyes were in Querétaro with 1000 men; Santa Anna's command, now turned over to General Rincon by order of President Peña-y-Peña, consisted of 4000; in Tabasco and Chiapas there were 2000; Urrea, Carrabajal, and Canales commanded 2000; Filisola was at San Luis Potosi with 3000; Peña y Barrangan had 2000 at Toluca; 1000 were in Oaxaca, while nearly 3000 guerrilleros harassed the road between Puebla and Vera Cruz, and rendered it impassable after the victories in the valley. The conflict was now almost given up to these miscreants, under Padre Jarauta and Zenobio, for in the eastern districts General Lane with his ardent partisans held Rincon, Alvarez, and Rea in complete check.

These guerrilla bands had inflicted such injury upon the Americans that it became necessary to destroy them at all hazards. This severe task was accomplished by Colonel Hughes and Major John R. Kenly, who commanded at Jalapa, and by General Patterson, whose division of 4000 new levies was shortly to be reinforced by General Butler with several thousand more. Patterson garrisoned the National Bridge in the midst of these bandits' haunts, and having executed, at Jalapa, two paroled Mexican officers captured in one of the marauding corps, and refused the surrender of Jarauta, he drove that recreant priest from the neighborhood into the valley of Mexico, in which Lane pursued and destroyed his reorganized band.

While these scattered military events were occurring, Peña-y-Peña, as president of the republic, had endeavored, both at Toluca and at Querétaro, to combine once more the elements of a congress and a government. He summoned, moreover, the governors of

States to convene and consult upon the condition of affairs; he suspended Santa Anna; ordered Paredes into nominal arrest at Tololopan; directed a court-martial upon Valencia for his conduct at Contreras; attempted to reform the army, and in all his acts seems to have been animated by a sincere spirit of national reorganization and peace. Nevertheless, among the deputies who were assembled the same quarrels that disgraced former sessions again arose between the Puros, the Moderados, the Monarquistas, and Santannistas, or friends of Santa Anna, who now formed themselves into a zealous party, notwithstanding the disgraceful downfall of their leader. These contests were continued until early in November, when a quorum of the members reached Querétaro and elected Anaya, the former president substitute, to serve until the month of January, to which period the counting of votes for the presidency had been postponed, as we have already stated, by the intrigues of Santa Anna. Anaya's election was a triumph of the Moderados.

Congress broke up after a few days' session, having provided for the assemblage of a new one on January 1, 1848; but unfortunately most of the leaders did not depart from Querétaro, which was henceforth for many months converted into a political battle-field for the benefit or disgrace of the military partisans. The Puros, led by Gomez Farias, were joined by the disaffected officers of the army ready for revolution, pronunciamientos, or anything that might prolong the war with the same ultimate views that animated them during the armistice in August. But Peña-y-Peña and Anaya were firm, discreet, and consistent in their resistance. The assembled governors of States resolved to support the president, his opinions, and acts with their influence and means, while the mass of substantial citizens and men of property throughout the republic joined in an earnest expression of anxiety for peace. Guanajuato, San Luis Potosi, and Jalisco, under the lead of Santannistas and Puros, who mutually hated each other, alone continued hostile to a treaty.

Trist soon after the capture of Mexico had sounded Peña-y-Peña in relation to the renewal of negotiations; but it was not until the end of October that the prudent president thought himself justified in expressing, through his minister, Don Luis de la Rosa, a simple but ardent wish for the cessation of war. When Anaya assumed the presidency a few days afterward, Peña-y-Peña did not disdain to enter his cabinet as minister, and on November 22 offered the American envoy the appointment of commissioners. But in the meanwhile the government in Washington, believing that the continuance of Trist in Mexico was useless, and probably discontented with his conduct, had recalled him from the theater of action. The American commissioner hastened, therefore, to decline the negotiation and apprised the Mexicans of his position. But mature reflection upon the political state of Mexico as well as upon the real desires of his government and people, induced Trist to change his views, and accordingly he notified the Mexican cabinet that in spite of his recall he would assume the responsibility of a final effort to close the war. Good judgment at the moment and subsequent events fully justified the envoy's diplomatic resolve. Commissioners were at once appointed to meet him, and negotiations were speedily commenced in a spirit of sincerity and peace. General Scott, nevertheless, though equally anxious to terminate the conflict, did not for a moment intermit his military vigilance. The capital and the captured towns were still as strictly governed, the growing army was organized for future operations, and a general order was issued demanding a large contribution from each of the States for the support of the army. This military decree, moreover, reformed and essentially changed the duties, taxation, and collections of the nation; it indicated the intention of the United States to spread its troops all over the land; and while it reasserted the supremacy of law, and the purity of its administration, it announced instant death by sentence of a drumhead court-martial to all who engaged in irregular war. This decree satisfied reflecting Mexicans, who noticed the steady earnestness and increase of the army, that their nationality was seriously endangered, and greatly aided, as doubtless it was designed to do, in stimulating the action of the cabinet and commissioners.

Thus closed the eventful year of 1847. On January 1, 1848, only thirty deputies of the new congress appeared in their places; and on the 8th—the day for the decision of the presidency—as there was still no quorum in attendance, and Anaya's term had expired, he promptly resigned his power to his minister of foreign affairs, Peña-y-Peña, who reassumed the executive chair, as he formerly had done, by virtue of his constitutional right as chief justice. Anaya at once came into his cabinet as minister of war, while De la Rosa took the portfolio of foreign relations. All these persons were still sincere coadjutors in the work of peace.

The destiny of Santa Anna was drawing to a close. Huamantla had been perhaps his last battlefield in Mexico. About the middle of January General Lane received information of the lurking-place of the chieftain, who now, with scarcely the shadow of his ancient power or influence, was concealed at Tehuacan in the neighborhood of Puebla. The astute intriguer's admission into the republic had once been considered a master-stroke of American policy; but his death, capture, or expulsion was now equally desired by those who had watched him more closely and knew him better. Lane accordingly, with a band of about 350 mounted men, undertook the delicate task of seizing Santa Anna, and had he not received timely warning, notwithstanding the secrecy of the American's movements, it is scarcely probable that he would have quitted his retreat alive. Among the corps of partisan warriors who went in search of the fugitive there were many Texans who still smarted under the memory of the dreary march from Santa Fé in 1841, the decimation at Mier, the cruelties of Goliad and the Alamo, and the imprisonments in Mexico, Puebla, or Peroté in 1842. But when Lane and his troopers reached Tehuacan the game had escaped, though his lair was still warm. All the personal effects left behind in his rapid flight were plundered, with the exception of his wife's wardrobe, which, with a rough though chivalrous gallantry, was sent to the beautiful but ill-matched lady. A picked military escort, personally attached and doubtless well paid, still attended him. But beyond this he had no military command, and as a soldier and politician his power in Mexico had departed.

Having sought by public letters to throw, as usual, the disgrace of his defeats at Belen and Chapultepec upon General Terres and the revolutionary hero Bravo, he aroused the united hatred of these men and the disgust of their numerous friends. Public opinion openly condemned him everywhere. After Lane's assault he took refuge in Oaxaca; but the people of that region were qually inimical and significantly desired his departure. Thus, broken in fame and character, deprived of a party, personal influence, patronage, and present use of his wealth, the foiled warrior-president stood for a moment at bay. But his resolution was soon taken. From Cascatlan he wrote to the minister of war on February 1, demanding passports, and at the same time he intimated to the American commander-in-chief his willingness to leave an ungrateful republic and to " seek an asylum on a foreign soil where he might pass his last days in that tranquillity which he could never find in the land of his birth." The desired passports were granted. He was assured that neither Mexicans nor Americans would molest his departure; and, moving leisurely toward the eastern coast with his family, he was met near his hacienda of Encero by a select guard, detailed by Colonel Hughes and Major Kenly, and escorted with his long train of troopers, domestics, treasure, and luggage to La Antigua, where he embarked on April 5, 1848, on board a Spanish brig bound to Jamaica. One year and eight months before, returning from exile, he had landed from the steamer *Arab* in the same neighborhood to regenerate his country!

But before his departure from Mexico Santa Anna had been doomed to see the peace concluded. The complete failure of the Mexicans in all their battles, notwithstanding the courage with which they individually fought at Churubusco, Chapultepec, and Molino del Rey, impressed the nation deeply with the conviction of its inability to cope in arms with the United States. The discomfiture of Paredes, the want of pecuniary resources, the disorganization of the country, the growing strength of the Americans, who were pouring into the capital under Patterson, Butler, and Marshall, and the utter failure of the arch-intriguer—all contributed to strengthen the arm of the executive and to authorize both the negotiation of a treaty and the arrangement of an armistice until the two governments should ratify the terms of peace. Nicholas P. Trist, Don Luis G. Cuevas, Don Bernardo Couto, and Don Miguel Atristain signed the treaty thus consummated on February 2, 1848, at the town of Guadalupe Hidalgo. Its chief terms were: 1st, the reëstablishment of peace; 2d, the boundary which confirmed the southern line of Texas and ceded New Mexico and Upper California; 3d, the payment of fifteen millions by the United States, in consideration of the extension of its boundaries; 4th, the payment by the United States of all the claims of its citizens against the Mexican Republic to the extent of three and a quarter millions, so as to discharge Mexico forever from all responsibility; 5th, a compact to restrain the incursions and misconduct of the Indians on the northern frontier. The compact contained, in all, thirty-three articles and a secret article prolonging the period of ratification in Washington beyond the four months from its date as stipulated in the original instrument.

This important treaty, which we believe history will justly

characterize as one of the most liberal ever assented to by the
conquerors of so great a country, was dispatched immediately by
an intelligent courier to Washington, and notwithstanding the irreg-
ularity of its negotiation after Trist's recall, was at once sent
to the Senate by President Polk. In that illustrious body of statesmen it was fully debated, and after mature consideration ratified,
with but slight change, on March 10. Senator Sevier and Attor-
ney-General Clifford resigned their posts and were sent as plenipotentiaries to Mexico to secure its passage by the Mexican congress.

Meanwhile the last action of the war was fought and won on
March 16, in ignorance of the armistice, by General Price at Santa
Cruz de Rosales, near Chihuahua; and the diplomatic and military
career of two distinguished men, Trist and Scott, was abruptly
closed on the theater of their brilliant achievements. Scott, the
victor of so many splendid fields, was suspended from the command of the army he had led to glory, and General William O.
Butler was ordered to replace him. Hot dissensions had occurred
between the commander-in-chief, Worth, Pillow, and other meritorious officers, and although the United States might well have
avoided a scandalous rupture at such a moment in any enemy's
capital, a court of inquiry was nevertheless convened to discuss the
battles and the men who had achieved the victories!

While the court of inquiry pursued its investigations in the
capital, and the United States Senate was engaged in ratifying
the treaty, President Peña-y-Peña and his cabinet still labored
zealously to assemble a congress at Querétaro. The Mexican
president resolved, if necessary to obtain a quorum, to exclude
New Mexico, California, and Yucatan from representation; the
first two being in possession of the United States and the latter in
revolt. The disturbance in Yucatan which had been for some time
fermenting broke out fiercely in July, 1847, and became in fact a
long-continued war of castes. The Indian peones and rancheros,
under their leaders Pat and Chi, carried fire and sword among the
thinly-scattered whites, until relief was afforded them by Commodore Perry, the Havanese, the English of Jamaica, and some
enlisted corps of American volunteers returning from the war.
About Tuspan and Tampico on the east coast, in the interior State
of Guanajuato, and on the northern frontiers of Sonora, Durango,
and San Luis the wild Indians and the semi-civilized Indian laborers were rebellious and extremely annoying to the lonely settlers.

There were symptoms everywhere, not only of national disorganiza-tion, but almost of national dissolution. Yet difficult as was the position of the government amid all these foreign and domestic dangers, every member strove loyally to sustain the nation and its character until the return of the ratified treaty. Money was con-tributed freely by the friends of peace, who sought a renewal of trade and desired to see the labors of the mines and of agriculture again pursuing their wonted channels. The clergy, too, who feared national ruin, annexation, or complete conquest, bestowed a portion of their treasures; and thus the members of congress were supplied with means to assemble at the seat of government.

On May 25 a brilliant cortége of American cavalry was seen winding along the hills toward Querétaro as the escort of the American commissioners, who were welcomed to the seat of govern-ment by the national authorities, and entertained sumptuously in an edifice set apart for their accommodation. The town was wild with rejoicing. Those who had been so recently regarded as bitter foes were hailed with all the ardor of ancient and uninterrupted friendship. No one would have imagined that war had ever been waged between the soldiers of the north and south who now shared the same barracks and pledged each other in their social cups. If the drama was prepared for the occasion by the government it was certainly well played, and unquestionably diverted the minds of the turbulent and dangerous classes of the capital at a moment when good feeling was most needed.

Congress was in session when the commissioners arrived, and on the same day the Senate ratified the treaty, which, after a stormy debate, had been previously sanctioned by the Chamber of Deputies. On May 30 the ratifications were finally exchanged, and, the first installment of indemnity being paid in the City of Mexico, the troops evacuated the country in the most orderly manner during the following summer.

It cannot be denied that the Mexican Government, whose tenure of power was so frail, almost trembled at the sudden with-drawal of the forces and the full restoration of a power for which, as patriots, they naturally craved. The sudden relaxation of a firm and dreaded military authority in the capital, amid all those classes of intriguing politicians, soldiers, and demagogues who had so long disturbed the nation's peace before Scott's capture of Mexico, naturally alarmed the president and cabinet, who possessed no reliable army to replace the departing Americans. But the three millions received opportunely for indemnity were no doubt judiciously used by the authorities, while the men of property and opulent merchants leagued zealously with the municipal authorities to preserve order until national reorganization might begin. One of the first steps in this scheme was the election by congress of General Herrera, a hero of revolutionary fame, as constitutional president, and of Peña-y-Peña as Chief Justice of the Supreme Court. These and other conciliatory but firm acts gave peace at least for the moment to the heart of the nation, but beyond the capital all the bonds of the federal union were totally relaxed. Scarcely had the national government been reinstalled in the City of Mexico when General Mariano Paredes y Arrillaga unfurled the standard of rebellion in Guanajuato, under the pretext of opposing the treaty. The administration, possessing only the skeleton of an army, did not halt to consider the smallness of its resources, but promptly placed all its disposable men under the command of Anastasio Bustamante, who, with Miñon, Cortazar, and Lombardini, not only put down the revolution of Paredes, but by their influence and admirable conduct imposed order and inspired renewed hopes for the future wherever they appeared. In the same way the strong arm of power was honestly used to destroy faction wherever it dared to lift its turbulent head, and the national guard of the Federal District faithfully performed its duty in this patriotic task. Paredes disappeared after his fall in Guanajuato, and remained in concealment or obscurity until his death.

Chapter XXXIII

FOREIGN INTERVENTION AND THE EMPIRE UNDER MAXIMILIAN. 1848-1867

WE find Mexico to-day a federated republic consisting of twenty-seven States, three Territories, and one Federal District, each State " with a right to manage its own local affairs, but the whole number bound together in one body politic by fundamental and constitutional laws." The country has been at peace with all the world for many years. For a very brief period after the departure of the American army from its capital in 1848 the distracted republic was quiet, perforce, except for the prowling bands of guerrillas which, deprived of foreign prey, turned upon their countrymen and for years set all laws at defiance.

President Herrera, who was elected by congress in 1848, was the first executive to take peaceful possession of power within the memory of any person then in politics. His administration on the whole was economical and tolerant, and was continued in its main features by General Mariano Arista, who succeeded him in 1851.

In accordance with the terms of a treaty negotiated December 30, 1853, the government of the United States paid Mexico ten millions of dollars for that portion of New Mexico and Arizona now included in the " Gadsden Purchase," and comprising an area of 45,535 square miles. Together with what had been paid at the conclusion of the war, this made twenty-five million dollars received by Mexico from the country that had conquered her, and presented substantial evidence of the good feeling that then prevailed.

That same year the arch-pronunciador, Santa Anna, returned from exile, and was received by certain classes with open arms. His prestige was sufficient to attract a multitude of followers; but his decrees of December, 1853, which in effect declared himself a perpetual dictator, aroused the opposition of the Liberals, who started a counter-rebellion against an arbitrary and centralized government such as Santa Anna would establish. The noted leaders of this movement were Generals Alvarez and Comonfort, who drove Santa Anna from the capital and from the country and took possession, Alvarez being elected president. He made Comonfort his minister of war, but soon resigned the presidency in his favor, to which he was constitutionally elected by the people's votes in 1857. This was the year in which was adopted the famous " Constitution of 1857," under which, with its various amendments, the Republic of Mexico is governed to-day.

It will be seen that Comonfort occupied the presidential chair at a most critical period of the republic's history, for the constitution of 1857 was a vastly different instrument from that declared by the first national congress in 1812. The since celebrated "Law of Juarez" "abolished the whole system of class-legislation, suppressed the military and ecclesiastical fueros—those privileged and special tribunals and charters of the army and the clergy—and established for the first time in Mexico's history the equality of all citizens before the law." Elected to office as a Liberal, yet Comonfort gave government aid to General Zuloaga, who, commanding a brigade in the army, "pronounced" in favor of the church party and against the constitution. In January, 1858, Zuloaga proclaimed the "Plan of Tacubaya," by which the fueros were to be restored, the press again subjected to church censorship, and an "irresponsible central dictatorship established looking, if possible, to the restoration of monarchic principles. The constitution of 1857 implied a complete reconstruction of society in all the domain of government, of religious institutions, and of the entire fabric of civil, social, and educational life." It was the outcome of more than thirty years of almost continuous war. "From 1824—when the first really national congress met and the first constitution was proclaimed—to 1853 the country had been rent by a succession of conflicts, in which the distinctive principles of the two great parties were ever uppermost. The power of the church was wielded with indefatigable energy to baffle the Republicans and stay the progress of constitutional freedom. But its march was irresistible."

The church at that time possessed, it is said, two-thirds of the nation's wealth; but when, in 1846, at a critical period in the war, it had been asked for a loan of fourteen millions—and at a moment, too, when the very life of the nation was threatened by a foreign foe —it had not only refused, but drove Gomez Farias, who had suggested this loan, from power in disgrace. But in the person of

Benito Juarez, upon whom devolved the presidency after the ignominious flight of Comonfort, the church had quite a different man
to deal with. Juarez was born in 1806, a Zapotec Indian, belonging to a race that had never been conquered. He was thus a true
Mexican, and, as his subsequent career gave proof, the very man to
bring Mexico out of the labyrinth into which she had been led and
where she seemed inextricably, hopelessly, lost. In Guanajuato,
whither he had been driven by the army of the church, Juarez and
the faithful members of his cabinet undertook to organize the government on the basis of the constitution of 1857. But though the
president of the people, he had against him then the almost invincible powers of the army and the church. He and his cabinet were
captured, but rescued by a patriot leader and sent to Colima, on
the west coast of Mexico, whence they finally reached Vera Cruz,
on the east coast, by crossing the Isthmus of Panama and via New
Orleans. Aiding Juarez in the "Three Years' War of Reform,"
which existed from 1858 to and through 1861, were such generals
as Doblado, Degollado, Arteaga, Ortega, and Zaragoza, who
fought in defense of the constitution; while against it and in favor
of the church were Osollo, Robles, Marquez, Miramon, and Zuloaga. This insane, fratricidal strife went on for years; but in December, 1860, the decisive battle of Calpulalpam was fought, through
the victory of which, gained by the Liberals, Juarez finally entered
the capital of Mexico and took possession of the government.

Elected constitutional president in 1860, Juarez was properly
the nation's head; but even after the defeat of the church's army
he could not at once minister to the needs of his long-suffering
people. Peace might have ensued had time been granted the distracted country; but a new element of disturbance now entered into
the scheme of government. Absolutely impoverished as well as
exhausted, the government was forced to resort to most extraordinary measures in order to raise funds, and so a law was passed,
on July 17, 1861, suspending payment of interest on all debts,
internal and foreign, for two years from that date. "With the
funds thus obtained from the nation's revenues, temporarily diverted
to the relief of the country, it was hoped that all armed opposition
could be put down, internal peace preserved, and the government
finally established."

But this scheme was fatal to the success of the Liberal cause,
then on the eve of its ultimate reward, for it gave the enemies of

Mexico, its foreign enemies, an opportunity to intervene in its internal affairs.

It was not the first time Mexico had made herself conspicuous in the eyes of the world, for during more than forty years she had been convulsed with feuds and strife, having in that period passed through thirty-six different forms of government under seventy-three rulers of various stripe.

"For a few years past," wrote Corwin, the United States minister to Mexico, "the condition of this country has been so unsettled as to raise the question, on both sides the Atlantic, whether the time has not come when some foreign power ought, in the general interests of society, to intervene to establish a protectorate or some other form of government here, and guarantee its continuance."

And yet, when in October, 1861, a tripartite alliance was entered into between Spain, France, and England for intervention, with the act of the Juarez government as a pretext, and the government of the United States was tardily invited to join in demanding redress, Corwin wrote: "I cannot find in this republic any men, of any party, better qualified in my judgment for the task than those now in power! . . . Her late suspension, leading to the cessation of diplomatic relations with England and France [for the French and British ministers had demanded their passports] may, perhaps, have been imprudent. She could not pay her debts, however, and maintain her government; and perhaps it was as well to say she would not pay for two years, as to promise to pay and submit herself to the mortification of constantly asking further time. She is impoverished to the last degree, by forty years of civil war."

The total amount of Mexico's foreign indebtedness at that time was about $86,000,000, of which nearly four-fifths was to the British and less than $10,000,000 to the French. Yet, after English and Spanish troops had been landed at Vera Cruz, a treaty was effected under which Spain and England retreated from their humiliating position, though the French troops persisted in marching into the interior, reaching Orizaba without opposition, but suffering defeat at Puebla, on May 5, 1862.

The "glorious Fifth of May"—the *Cinco de Mayo*—has been called the Mexican Fourth of July, for it has ever since been annually celebrated as the anniversary of the most decisive victory ever won by Mexican troops over a foreign foe. General Zaragoza was in command of the Mexican patriots; later on other generals came to the front, such as Porfirio Diaz, the savior of the south; Negretti, and Escobedo, fighting desperately in the north.[1]

It should not be overlooked, in reviewing the events connected with the intervention, that from the very first the United States held and maintained a most friendly attitude toward the government of Mexico, even going to the length of offering to negotiate a loan for its relief rather than permit anything detrimental to its autonomy. The maintenance of friendly relations has become the traditional policy between *Los Estados Unidos del Norte* and *Los Estados de Mexico;* but the friendship begun at the close of the Mexican War, incited by the mutual admiration of worthy foes and cemented by the generosity of the United States on several occasions, has never been more conspicuously exemplified than in this instance. Invited by the European Powers to join them in demanding redress, the United States, through Seward, the secretary of state, made reply as follows: " . . . It is true, as the high contracting parties assume, that the United Staes have, on their part, claims to urge against Mexico. Upon due consideration, however, the President is of opinion that it would be inexpedient to seek satisfaction of their claims at this time through an act of accession to the convention. Among the reasons for this decision are, first, that the United States, so far as it is practicable, prefer to adhere to a traditional policy, recommended to them by their first President and confirmed by a happy experience, which forbids them from making close alliances with foreign nations; second, Mexico being a neighbor of the United States on this continent, and possessing a system of government similar to our own in many of its important features, the United States habitually cherish a decided good will toward that republic, and a lively interest in its security, prosperity, and welfare. Animated by these sentiments, the United States do not feel inclined to resort to forcible remedies for their claims at the present moment, when

[1] Mexico has two national holidays, the *Cinco de Mayo*, or Fifth of May, the anniversary of the defeat of the French at Puebla, May 5, 1862, by Mexican troops under General Zaragoza. The second national holiday, the first in order of importance and in its history, falls due on September 15, and is the anniversary of the " *Grito de Dolores*," the war-cry of the warrior-priest, Hidalgo, who gave the watchword, " *Independencia*," on September 15, 1810. This is the true "Independence Day," and as such is annually celebrated with great *éclat* throughout the country.

the government is deeply disturbed by factions within and war with foreign nations. And, of course, the same sentiments render them still more disinclined to allied war against Mexico than to war to be urged against her by themselves alone.

" The undersigned is further authorized to state to the plenipotentiaries, for the information of Spain, France, and Great Britain, that the United States are so earnestly anxious for the safety and welfare of the Republic of Mexico that they have already empowered their minister residing there to enter into a treaty with the Mexican Republic, conceding to it some material aid and advantage, which it is to be hoped may enable that republic to satisfy the just claims and demands of the said sovereigns, and so avert the war which these sovereigns have agreed among each other to levy against Mexico."[2]

It should be remembered that at the time of this friendly offer from the United States that country was itself plunged into a civil war which promised to tax its utmost energies and resources. In fact, there is every reason for assuming that the emperor of France, Napoleon III., took account of the conditions prevailing in the United States at this time, as well also as those in Mexico, and regarded the moment as opportune for the establishing of French dominion.

The governments of England, France, and Spain had offered mediation to Mexico, proposing to guarantee the Liberals the establishment of social reforms such as they desired; and to the Conservatives, or church party, the maintenance of political principles in accord with their wishes. As these foreign powers were disposed to recognize the church party as the *de facto* government of Mexico, which steadily invited mediation, the Mexican people as persistently refused any form of intervention in their home affairs. It was acknowledged that they had thus far afforded the Powers an excuse for interposing under the pretext that the domestic dissensions would be interminable; but the Mexican commonalty still had faith in themselves, and they showed their confidence in Juarez and his cabinet by reëlecting him constitutional president for another term. This was in 1861, and the offer of mediation was made in March of that year. In October the tripartite alliance was entered into, and in December Spanish troops were

[2] From "Diplomatic Correspondence, Mexican Affairs," 1862, page 189 *et seq.*

landed at Vera Cruz. Mexican diplomacy, however, brought about an armistice, followed by the treaty for the future regulation of commerce between Mexico and the great Powers of Europe, by which the English and Spanish withdrew their troops from Mexican soil.

But the French persisted in their intention to force themselves upon a people unwilling to receive them and distrustful of their motives. The French force already in Mexico was strongly reinforced, and in May, 1863, General Forey, in command, advanced upon Puebla and took it, in spite of a determined resistance. Allying with the reactionary party, their forces augmented by the soldiers faithful to the church, the French marched upon the City of Mexico, of which they gained possession on the last of May, the Juarez government retreating northward toward San Luis Potosi. Subsequently these faithful adherents of the constitution, to defend which they had been elected by the people, were driven from one place to another, ever fleeing northward toward the frontier of the United States, which was their final refuge.

Against Puebla General Forey had brought a force of 26,000 men, and by the time the army under his command had arrived before the capital its augmentation by disaffected Mexicans of the Reactionists was such as to make it actually overwhelming. At all events, though the Mexican soldiers commanded by General Porfirio Diaz (who has since appeared in various rôles from that of the pronunciador to president of the republic) would have made a brave defense, it was finally resolved, in order to deliver the city from the horrors of a bombardment, to withdraw the government, which was accordingly removed to San Luis Potosi. The capital was occupied by Forey on June 10, 1863, and on the 16th he issued a decree declaring for the formation of a provisional government. Thirty-five Mexican citizens were named as constituting a "Junta Superior de Gobierno," who chose, as a substitute for the republican congress, 215 persons as an "Assembly of Notables," who were to decide the form of government to be adopted. The junta also named three eminent citizens as a provisional triumvirate, consisting of Almonte, who had figured as president of the Conservatives; the Centralist, ex-President Salas, and Archbishop Labastida. The people of the capital, with their natural tendency to satire, baptized this triumvirate as the "mariposa de San Juan," composed, as they said, of an Indian, a dotard, and a saint, denoting thus the pronounced racial type of Almonte, the decrepitude of Salas (who was president as far back as 1846), and the sanctity of the archbishop.

In brief, the French commander-in-chief dictated the appointment of the junta, the junta elected the notables, and the notables created the triumvirs as the supreme executives pending the establishment of a definitive government. This proceeding reminds one of the equally farcical doings of Hernando Cortéz, when, at La Villa Rica de la Vera Cruz in 1519, he nominated the magistrates to whom he resigned his command, in order to be immediately reappointed captain-general and chief justice of the first colony in New Spain.

The Assembly of Notables first met as a body on July 8, 1863, and three days later issued their " Decree " embodying the declaration that the Mexican " nation " adopts (first) for its form of government a limited, hereditary monarchy, with a Catholic prince at its head; second, " the Sovereign will take the title, Emperor of Mexico "; third, " the Imperial Crown of Mexico is hereby offered to his Imperial Highness, Prince Ferdinand Maximilian, Archduke of Austria, for him and his descendants."

The reception of this declaration by the people was not of the most cordial character, for most of them had hardly become reconciled to the invasion of Mexico by a foreign power, let alone the unnatural union between the invaders and the Conservatives. There still remained the fixed idea that, despite their numerous failures to set up a stable republican government, the time had not arrived for inviting intervention by a foreign power, backed by an army, and in union with the church. The popular indignation was great, for the soil of Mexico was still moist with the blood of her sons, slaughtered while defending her honor from assault by the very army which backed with its bayonets the Decree of the Notables, by which a ruler was invited from across the ocean to govern a land presumably unable to govern itself.

Still, provided a foreign prince were chosen, the Archduke Maximilian might be considered the least objectionable of any. He was the brother of Austria's emperor and a descendant of Charles V., the first sovereign of Mexico after the conquest; thus it was hoped that through the prestige of his birth and an alliance with a powerful nation, the contending factions would be united, or at least blinded, by the brilliancy of his name. Personally, also,

MAXIMILIAN GOING TO EXECUTION

Painting by Jean Paul Laurens

—page 397

Maximilian was irreproachable, possessing a generous, refined nature with eminent natural endowments and a polish resulting from his education at court in the midst of accomplished personages of almost every nationality. His intellectual as well as superficial accomplishments were of the very highest order; he was an adept at diplomacy; he spoke fluently half a dozen languages; and his bearing was ever courteous, his personality pleasing in the extreme.

Born in 1832, he was already married, to the Princess Maria Charlotte Amalia, daughter of Leopold I., King of the Belgians, whom he had wedded in 1857. These two were childless, but unusually devoted to each other and in every respect models of virtue and propriety. Maximilian was taller than the average of men, with fine, frank countenance, bright blue eyes and long, flowing beard; while his wife's beauty was of the captivating "sympathetic" type so much appreciated among the Latin peoples. Both were benevolent and kindly disposed toward the masses; but they were not the people's choice, and had they been angels from heaven, says a native historian, they would not have satisfied the Mexicans, holding as they did a false and untenable position on the newly erected throne of Mexico.

The commission sent to Europe to offer the crown of Mexico to Maximilian, and which departed from Vera Cruz in August, 1863, found him amid the delights of his beautiful castle of Miramar, near Trieste. He received the commissioners graciously, but declined entertaining their most flattering offer until a popular vote had been taken in Mexico. Two years before, when addressed with reference to accepting a tentative offer of Mexico's mythical throne, Maximilan had made reply: "My coöperation in favor of the work of governmental reform, or transformation, on which depends, according to your statements, the salvation of Mexico, could not be determined unless a national manifestation should prove to me, in a manner undoubted, the desire of the nation to see me occupy that throne." This was his condition for acceptance: to be called to Mexico by the popular voice; hence, when another deputation, in March, 1864, waited upon him and claimed that this condition had been fulfilled, he was misled into accepting the proffered crown and throne. This act was in accordance, as is well known, with the desire of Napoleon III., who the same day, by the Treaty of Miramar, between the Emperor of France and Maximilian, pledged himself to support the latter on his throne until firmly seated.

At the outset of the expedition by the allied Powers against Mexico each nation had, through its special instructions to the respective commanders of the fleet, disclaimed any intention whatever of interfering with the internal affairs of the country. And yet, within three years of the setting forth of that expedition we find a French army of occupation in the City of Mexico, and the Emperor of France providing by treaty for the imposition of a foreign prince upon a throne supported solely by the bayonets of his soldiers.

Arrived at Vera Cruz, in May, 1864, the new sovereigns were received, both at that seaport and all along the route from the coast to the capital, with a factitious enthusiasm that at first deceived them into believing themselves really the people's choice. But they had not been long in Mexico before the truth became apparent to them that, strive as they might to reach the heart of the Mexicans, they could not do so by any means in their power. What these people had been fighting for (blindly, perhaps, and for many years without guidance) was liberty, and for liberty they were still prepared to sacrifice their possessions and even their lives. It is now known that Maximilian deeply sympathized with the people of Mexico, and it is believed that at heart he was as republican as any of his subjects; yet he must perforce play the part he had assumed, and the Mexicans must support the foreign mercenaries who served as props to his throne, as well as pay for the vast improvements he inaugurated, such as the embellishment of the capital and its suburbs, the construction of the grand Paseo, the great avenue leading to the groves of Chapultepec, and the renovation and beautifying of the castle situated on the hill made memorable by association with Axayacatl and Montezuma, the viceroys and the siege of Mexico by the North Americans. Maximilian's favorite residence was at Chapultepec, with an occasional resort to Cuernavaca, where Cortéz once had an estate, and to Orizaba, the gem of the *tierra templada*. Still associated with the flowers and fountains of the City of Mexico's great central square are the names of Maximilian and Carlota; but less agreeable reminders of their presence in Mexico are the loans they contracted in London for the costly improvements and the payment of the hireling troops of France.

The period of intervention was brief, fortunately for Mexico;

but its effects were disastrous in the extreme, both to the country and to the national *morale*. It protracted that fratricidal strife which had been waged for nearly half a century, it introduced into the politics of the land such elements of distraction as without it would have been unknown. Church and state were at odds, innumerable families were divided, and the prospect for a permanent peace rendered more problematical than ever before. The conservative or reactionary leaders found in Maximilian one more liberal than the most advanced of their party. In fact, it is said that perceiving the masses were overwhelmingly in sympathy with the Republicans, he would have identified himself with them, rather than with the Conservatives, had the leaders of the former not rejected him as impossible to be considered. It was soon apparent that he, like Comonfort and others before him, was to be deserted, perhaps betrayed, by the very party that had invited him to Mexico. Through the instigation of his arch-enemies, he had been induced to sign that revolting measure known as the "Black Decree," of October, 1865, by the provisions of which all persons discovered fighting against the forces of the empire were declared banditti, to be shot as soon as apprehended. This decree was intended to operate mainly against the guerrillas that swarmed the country in every part; but many patriotic Republicans fell victims to this nefarious measure, and the feeling against its putative author was deep and lasting. In fact, it operated against Miximilian after his capture and was the ostensible excuse for his execution. It was urged in its extenuation that the measure was no harsher in its provisions than an anti-imperialist decree issued by Juarez in 1862, in which the death penalty was frequently invoked against the invaders. Again, while the letter of the law was harsh, it was not, doubtless, the emperor's intention to have it enforced in all its severity; and while he was made responsible for its infliction, it was the French soldiery who committed the innumerable outrages against the Mexicans at which humanity shudders.

But whatever the coöperating causes of Maximilian's downfall, the end was swiftly approaching, and, abandoned first by the church, and then by Napoleon III., the unfortunate ruler without a country was henceforth compelled to play his hand mainly alone. Maximilian was at his country retreat in Cuernavaca, when the fatal decision of Louis Napoleon to abandon him to his fate reached Mexico. Though at first stunned, he was not crushed, and the noble Carlota determined to proceed at once to France and implore the emperor to continue his assistance at this most critical juncture. She left Mexico in July, arriving at Paris the following month, and lost no time in securing an interview with Louis Napoleon, who was, however, obdurate, refusing to send another soldier or embark another expedition in support of the tottering dynasty he had been instrumental in establishing. Without aid from him she knew full well there was no hope for the empire in Mexico, and, appalled at the prospect, her reason gave way before the last blow in a series of terrible misfortunes. " Poor Carlota," as the world now knows her, never returned to Mexico, but after a brief visit to Rome, in the vain hope of assistance from the Pope, she was taken to Belgium, where a castle was provided for the unhappy empress, and where she wore the years away subject to fits of insanity with infrequent lucid intervals. The imperial couple never met again on earth, for events swiftly shaped the destiny of both, and Maximilian, after first resolving to abdicate and flee the country, and having already proceeded toward the coast as far as Orizaba, recalled his decision and returned to meet an ignoble death at the hands of his enemies.

The relinquishment by the Emperor of France of his pet scheme—an empire in Mexico under the Archduke Maximilian—was brought about through pressure applied in a masterly manner by the government of the United States, which, ever alert to befriend its nearest neighbor in the south, was at the same time determined that no monarchical government should be established on the American continent. At the outset the French intervention found the United States engaged in suppressing a mighty rebellion on its own soil, and unable to detach even a single regiment for the relief of the hard-pressed Mexicans; but as soon as the Union arms had triumphed in every portion of the disaffected territory, measures were taken for the immediate relief of Mexico. The result was a triumph for diplomacy and the withdrawal of the French army in Mexico, without a single gun having been fired by soldiers of the United States in behalf of the Liberal cause; and for this reason it should be regarded as the greatest of triumphs.

Having in mind that no direct cause for a quarrel existed between the United States and France, which, in fact, were united by the strongest ties of international friendship, yet were the most prominent statesmen of that country firm in the determination that Napoleon should recall his legions and leave the Mexicans to settle their own affairs in the best way possible without foreign intervention. Neither against Napoleon nor Maximilian was there any feeling of personal enmity: but a great principle was at stake—the autonomy of a friendly government, already recognized by the United States, was in peril. Many plans for the accomplishment of Mexican relief were discussed at Washington, where the talented Romero was Mexico's accredited representative, and the great statesman, Seward, was secretary of state, and the decision finally arrived at is fully set forth in a letter, or order, from Lieutenant General Grant to Major General Sheridan, who was then near the Rio Grande with an army of 50,000 men. This force had been massed in that quarter for a very obvious reason; though it consisted mainly of Union volunteers whose terms of enlistment had practically expired at the termination of the Civil War, but who served very well to support the purposes of diplomacy in the matter, and who might readily form the nucleus of an army of invasion.

HEADQUARTERS ARMIES OF THE UNITED STATES,
WEST POINT, N. Y., July 25, 1865.

MAJOR GENERAL P. H. SHERIDAN,
    Commanding Mil. Div. of the Gulf.

GENERAL:
    Major General J. M. Schofield goes to the Rio Grande on an inspection tour, carrying with him leave of absence for one year, with authority to leave the United States. If he avails himself of this leave he will explain to you more fully than I could do in the limits of a letter, and much more fully than I could do now, under any circumstances, because much that will have to be learned to fix his determination, whether to go or not, has yet to be found out in Washington while I shall be away.

    This, however, I can say: General Schofield's leave of absence has been given with the concurrence of the president, he having full knowledge of the object. I have both written my views to the president and had conversations with him on the subject. In all that relates to Mexican affairs he agrees in the duty we owe to ourselves to maintain the Monroe Doctrine, both as a principle and as a security for our future peace.

    On the Rio Grande, or in Texas, convenient to get there, we must have a large amount of surrendered ordnance and ordnance stores, or such articles accumulating from discharging men who leave their stores behind. Without special orders to do so, send none of these articles back, but rather place them convenient to be permitted to go into Mexico, if they can be got into the hands of the defenders of the only government we recognize in that country. I hope General Schofield may go with orders direct to receive these articles, but if he does not I know it will meet with general approbation to let him have them, if contrary orders are not received.

    It is a fixed determination on the part of the people of the United States, and I think myself safe in saying on the part of the president, also, that an empire shall not be established on this continent by the aid of foreign bayonets. A war on the part of the United States is to be avoided, if possible; but it will be better to go to war now when but little aid given to the Mexicans will settle the question, than to have in prospect a greater war, sure to come, if delayed until the empire is established!

We want, then, to aid the Mexicans without giving cause of war between the United States and France. Between the would-be empire of Maximilian and the United States all difficulty can be easily settled by observing the same sort of neutrality that has been observed toward us for the last four years.

This is a little indefinite as a letter of instructions to be governed by. I hope with this you may receive those instructions in much more positive terms. With a knowledge of the fact before you, however, that the greatest desire is felt to see the Liberal government restored in Mexico,—and no doubt exists of the strict justice of our right to demand this, and enforce the demand, with the whole strength of the United States,—your own judgment gives you a basis of action that will aid you.

I will recommend in a few days that you be directed to discharge all the men you think can be spared from the Department of Texas, where they are, giving transportation to their homes to all who desire to return. You are aware that existing orders permit discharged soldiers to retain their arms and accounterments at low rates, fixed in orders.[3]

Very respectfully, your Obt. svt.,

U. S. GRANT,
Lt. Gen.

A careful reading of this letter written by the astute commander-in-chief of the armies of the United States will place one in possession of all the motives actuating the actors in this significant drama of war and diplomacy, as well as the methods to be employed for coercing Napoleon.   Instead of proceeding to the Mexican border, General Schofield went to France for the furtherance of the deep-laid scheme by which the emperor was to be made aware of the imminent risk he incurred in allowing French troops to remain longer in Mexico.   It was a skillfully played game, without a single mismove, for the military diplomat in Paris, assisted by the prestige of the military demonstration on the Mexican frontier, accomplished all that was intended by the statesmen in Washington.   Napoleon's eyes were at last opened to the dangers increasingly menacing, not alone his army in Mexico, but the integrity of his position as a dominant factor in European politics. Hitherto he had been successful in almost every venture he had made; but his prestige received a lasting shock by the failure of his military invasion of Mexico.   It is not by any means an academic

[3] From "The Withdrawal of the French from Mexico; a Chapter of Secret History," by Lieutenant General John M. Schofield, U. S. A. (Retired).— *Century Magazine.*

assumption that but for the Mexican campaign, with its consequent failure of accomplishment, there might have been no crucial battle of Sadowa with its humiliation for Austria, no war with Prussia in 1870, with its terrible consequences to France and Louis Napoleon. The opportunity for Bismarck and Prussia came when Napoleon III. had his hands tied in Mexico, and the surrender at Metz was but a natural sequence to the recall of Bazaine from the country where he held supreme command and committed so many blunders as well as atrocities.

Yielding to the inevitable, then, the Emperor of France recalled Bazaine and his army, the order going into effect in the early part of 1867. Thrown upon his own resources, with the number of his friends constantly decreasing, feeling bound in honor to remain and share the fate of his followers, while the French withdrew from the country, Maximilian realized to the full the dangers and perplexities of his position. It may have been from a quixotic sense of duty that he remained; but the leaders of the Conservatives were now deeply alarmed, and by convincing him that his departure would involve them in certain destruction, and that by uniting with Miramon and Marquez against the Liberals, victory might crown their efforts, he was detained for the fate that met him at Querétaro. He returned to the capital in December, resolved to meet the Liberal army, now advancing southward from the frontier States. The French forces had driven Juarez and the little band that adhered to his fortunes as far north as the frontier town of El Paso on the Rio Grande; but upon the pressure being relaxed these patriots had returned toward the capital of their country. By this time they had reached Zacatecas, where, acting with the energy of despair, the imperialists inflicted a temporary defeat, but retreated upon the city of Querétaro, where Maximilian made his last stand against the now overwhelming forces of his foes.

The Liberal army was rapidly augmented by the patriotic people flocking to it from every direction, so that by the time Miramon had taken position at Querétaro with the imperialist forces, his opponents were estimated at more than 30,000 in number. They were commanded by General Escobedo, a gallant Mexican who had fought all through the war with the United States and held the rank of brigadier general at the time of the French invasion. He had opposed the French at Puebla in 1862, resisted Maximilian in 1864, surprised the garrison of Monterey in 1865, and by the capture of Saltillo, in June, 1866, made it possible for Juarez to establish temporarily his government in that city. By the end of 1866 he was enabled to march upon San Luis Potosi with an army of 15,000 men, and on February 1 he had fallen upon the imperialist army under Miramon and half destroyed it. Escobedo was ever in the van of that refluent wave of Liberals which, gathering force as it swept southward toward the capital, finally became resistless at Querétaro.

Maximilian reached Querétaro on February 19, where he was received with intense enthusiasm, not only by the soldiers of his army, but by the inhabitants of this ancient city, a hotbed of imperialism. Perhaps it was from sentiment more than on account of its situation that Querétaro had been chosen by the emperor as a rendezvous for his debilitated forces, for as a strategic position it had few advantages. Founded in 1531, it is one of the old Spanish cities of Mexico, and delightfully situated in the center of a fertile valley surrounded by mountains. It has, however, an immediate environment of hills, which, commanding the city as they do, rendered it defective as a defensive situation; for soon after the army under Miramon and Marquez had gathered here, to the number of about 9000 men, the surrounding hills were effectually occupied by the swarming Liberals. And here, caught like rats in a trap, the imperialists gathered about their idol, Maximilian, while the enemy so closely invested the city that soon provisions failed and famine threatened both citizens and soldiers. Soon the cavalry were dismounted, owing to the death of their horses from starvation and the necessity of shooting them for food. Three dismal months passed away, at the end of which time it was apparent to all that something desperate must be done. It was resolved to attempt a sortie and escape, if possible, to the sierras, where life might be prolonged, even if eventual escape were impossible. But, though Maximilian had endeared himself to every citizen and soldier in Querétaro by his attentions to the sick and wounded, and had excited their admiration by his bravery and disregard of personal safety, he was to be betrayed by one to whom he had shown many favors, and upon whom he had conferred undeserved distinctions. On the night of May 14, when everything was in readiness for the sortie, a body of Liberals gained access to the city, through the treachery of Colonel Lopez, an officer of Miramon's command, and soon after daylight Querétaro was in possession of Escobedo.

Disdaining to take any advantage of his position in order to escape, Maximilian remained with his soldiers and was captured in the outskirts of the city, at a place known as the Hill of Bells, where he was subsequently shot.   Miramon was wounded, but there was comparatively little bloodshed attendant upon the capture of the city, owing to the treachery of Lopez, by which the Liberals had been able to enter it at night, and the entire force of the besieged was taken after having made but feeble resistance.

A month later a court-martial was convened for the trial of Maximilian, Miramon, and Mejia, the high commanding officers of the imperialist troops, and they were condemned to be shot.   The sentence was confirmed by Escobedo, commander-in-chief of the Liberal forces, who fixed the time of execution for June 16, at three in the afternoon.   On the morning of the day named the condemned were prepared for their end, but a respite was granted till the 19th.   On receiving information of this action the emperor is said to have exclaimed, somewhat impatiently: " What a pity, for I am already prepared to leave the world! "   And having been falsely told that the Empress Carlota had died, he said, resignedly, after some emotion: " Then there is one tie the less to bind me to life."   He looked forward to death as a great relief, and on the morning of June 19, standing on the Hill of Bells, together with Mejia and Miramon, he faced his executioners " with the valor of a gentleman and the dignity of a prince."

Chapter XXXIV

THE RESTORATION OF THE REPUBLIC, AND RECONSTRUCTION. 1867—

THREE of the imperialistic leaders fell before the avenging bullets of the Liberals at the Cerro de las Campanas, Querétaro; but the arch-traitor Marquez, who had been dispatched to the City of Mexico for reinforcements, disobeyed orders, and instead of returning to the succor of Maximilian, marched against General Diaz at Puebla. Defeated by Diaz, he fled first to the capital, and thence by the way of Vera Cruz to Havana, with a vast amount of ill-gotten wealth. During the detention of the Liberal Army of the North at and around Querétaro most desperate fighting had taken place in and southward from the valley of Mexico. The Army of the South was commanded by Don Porfirio Diaz, like Juarez, a native of Oaxaca, and, like him, with Indian blood in his veins. The latter was born a statesman; the former a fighter, a strategist, a commander of men. Having early engaged in opposition to the French invasion and the empire, Diaz had acquired an influence second only to that of the president. He had been twice a captive, but had escaped each time to the hills of Oaxaca and there organized those invincible battalions known as the Serranos, with whom, after the capitulation of Oaxaca, in October, 1866, he marched upon Puebla. This city he took by storm, and then turned upon the recreant Marquez, whom he defeated in a pitched battle, and followed swiftly to the capital, which he immediately invested. Here the imperialists made what was practically their last stand against the Liberal army, and sustained a siege of two months, finally succumbing after being brought to the verge of starvation. Puebla was retaken by Diaz in April, the City of Mexico fell before his triumphant advance on June 20, and Vera Cruz, the last place held by imperialist troops, capitulated on July 4, 1867. On July 15 the Liberal armies were united in the capital, when President Juarez and his loyal cabinet entered the city from which, four years previously, they had been driven by the invaders. Four months later, in November, an Austrian frigate, the *Novara,* the same ship in which Maximilian and Carlota had come to Mexico but a little more than three years previously, bore to Trieste the remains of the unfortunate emperor. This indeed was the end of the empire which Louis Napoleon had endeavored to set up in America, the last act in a tragedy prolonged during more than four years; Maximilian dead, Carlota a maniac, Napoleon a prey to remorse, soon to expiate his crime by the loss of his throne. The war of the intervention had cost Mexico many thousands of lives, not to mention the additional thousands fallen from the ranks of the invaders—a vain sacrifice to Napoleon's ambition. During this war, or from April, 1863, to June or July, 1867, more than a thousand encounters are said to have taken place between the invaders and the patriot forces, including battles and skirmishes, and more than 80,000 soldiers were under arms. Mexico was apparently on the verge of exhaustion at the outset of intervention, and her condition at its ending was lamentable. But this country of fertile soils and inexhaustible mines has a vast recuperative capacity; its sturdy citizens are no less recuperative than its soil. The intervention had accomplished results which ultimately benefited the country—it had eliminated its traitors, stamping them with the mark of Cain; it had united its patriots into an invincible phalanx, for the time being, at least, and it had shown the world of what Mexico was capable when united by a common bond of sympathy and spurred on by common necessity.

President Juarez lost no time in entering upon the great work of reconstruction. He reduced the proportions of the army, causing great discontent thereby among the soldiers, which ultimately resulted in a "revolution"; he instituted changes in the public coinage; issued decrees for the payment of the public debt and for the construction of much-needed railroads; for the organization of public instruction, and for the resumption of external as well as internal commerce, now that the repossession of Vera Cruz and other seaports enabled the former to flow on in unobstructed channels. It seemed at first as if the Mexicans had learned a salutary lesson from their bitter experience during the long years of strife, and for a few months the country was pacific; but soon the old feeling of unrest asserted itself and pronunciamientos became rife in all parts of the republic. The government had been extremely lenient with its recreant citizen-imperialists, following the example set by General Diaz after the capture of Puebla and the capital, in releasing all prisoners on parole. It seems incredible, then, that the first defections were among the Liberals themselves, especially in the brigades of General Diaz and Riva Palacio, both of whom had rendered most distinguished services; but both, unfortunately, were convinced that their services had not met with their deserts, and retired to their homes in a pet.

While the defection of several Liberal chiefs may be regarded as inexplicable, what shall be said of the first of the pronunciamientos, started by no less a personage than the redoubtable Santa Anna? In himself, in fact, Antonio Lopez de Santa Anna presented a living epitome of his country's history for the fifty years then past, for he had been a revolutionist, a pronunciador, for half a century. His first pronouncement, in fact, was against the shortlived empire of Iturbide, in place of which he actually set up the Mexican Republic.

Taking sides with Guerrero in 1828, he turned against him later on in favor of Bustamante, whose overthrow he eventually accomplished in favor of Pedraza, whom he finally succeeded as president. That was in 1833: in 1836 he was defeated and made prisoner by the Texans, but was released the following year and returned to Mexico, in 1838 losing a leg in defense of Vera Cruz, when that city was attacked by the French. Between this period and 1846 Santa Anna slipped in and out the presidential chair with great facility; but at last was banished to Havana, from which place he was called to become commander-in-chief during the war with the United States. Defeated in every encounter with the American generals, he lost prestige for a time and went to Jamaica in 1848, from which island he was recalled in 1853, and made " President for life," which, owing to his harsh and despotic rule, meant for just two years, when he was sent again into retirement, this time taking refuge in Saint Thomas, West Indies. Being permitted to return during the empire, on condition of refraining from politics, he at once began intriguing against the government, and Bazaine sent him back into exile. Again he returned and again he was banished, returning in 1867 and inciting a rebellion in Yucatan, where he was captured, tried by court-martial, and sentenced to be shot. Taking cognizance of his services to Mexico in the past, however, Juarez commuted the sentence to eight years' exile, and after spending five years in New York, the now venerable revolutionist returned to Mexico, under shelter of the amnesty proclamation of 1874, and died two years later, friendless and obscure, in the City of Mexico.

Complications arose with several of the different States forming the confederated republic, the governor and legislature of Zacatecas, for instance, declaring against the Federal authorities, and grave disturbances took place in Jalisco, San Luis Potosi, Hidalgo, Morelia, Puebla, Jalapa, Orizaba, and other sections of the country; but eventually the government defeated all the different bodies of rebels, shot or imprisoned the leaders, and dispersed the rank and file. Juarez was reëlected constitutional president in 1868 without opposition; but more than a year before the expiry of his term there were at least two other candidates in the field and party rancor was strongly developed. His strongest opponent was Señor Sebastian Lerdo de Tejada, a man greatly resembling Juarez himself, whose fortunes he had followed all through the imperial *régime,* having been one of that loyal cabinet that was banished from the capital with the executive, in 1863, and returned with him in triumph in 1867. He was a lawyer by profession and had been a magistrate of the supreme court and a deputy to congress. His sterling qualities endeared him to the patriots, and he was justly reckoned as one of the pillars of the Liberal party. The third candidate was General Porfirio Diaz, who, on account of his prominence in military affairs, was looked upon by his admiring adherents as the logical successor to President Juarez. But the stern old patriot did not consider the necessity for a successor so long as he lived and was competent to administer the affairs of a nation of which he was in a measure sponsor and which he had successfully directed for so long a time. The services of Juarez had been inestimable—that was widely and generally recognized; but many of the people, and especially the Conservatives, the Clericals, their properties having been confiscated and rights overlooked, regarded him as a despot whose arbitrary acts were intolerable. General Diaz combated him on the plea that his continued retention of the presidential chair was "unconstitutional"; yet at a later period he himself clung to that same chair for a much longer time than Juarez, and with no clearer title apparently than his former chief. However, in 1870 there were three distinct parties in the field: the "Juaristas," or adherents of the president; the "Lerdistas," who were opposed to the principle of reëlection (or pre-

tended to be) as non-democratic; and the " Porfiristas," followers
of Don Porfirio Diaz, who claimed to be the real and only " Constitutionalists." Upon the flimsiest of pretexts, which upon close
examination might have been resolved into questions of personal
grievance, the various adherents of the parties in opposition took
the field against the government, the first of the new pronunciamientos occurring in May, 1871, at Tampico, where the Federal
garrison revolted. Troops being sent against the rebels, the re-
sultant casualties amounted to 600 killed or wounded. Eight
hundred dead and wounded resulted from a terrible outbreak in the
City of Mexico when the rebels, having gained possession of the
citadel, with the assistance of convicts from the Belen jail, were
only dislodged at the point of the bayonet.

But these ante-election riots were of no avail, for President
Juarez was declared elected to succeed himself on October 12,
1871, by a majority of votes, the Lerdistas finally throwing their
influence in favor of " Don Benito." Then ensued a battle of the
Dons, for Don Porfirio Diaz, considering himself misused, at once
started a pronunciamiento against his ancient leader and friend,
Don Benito Juarez, while Don Sebastian Lerdo stood aloof and
watched the proceedings with an interest enhanced by the fact that
many of his adherents were joining on one side or the other. More
than a thousand men had lost their lives in the year previous by
taking part in the political strife, and this, too, when Mexico was
supposed to be at peace with all the world. Nearly another thousand perished as a result of encounters directly traceable to the Diaz
manifesto, issued from his hacienda in November, and known as
the " Plan of Noria." The year 1872 is noted in the recent annals
of Mexico for the number of its assassinations and abductions, and
though the rebels were met by the government troops at various
points, and such assassins as were apprehended promptly shot, the
summer of 1872 arrived before peace was in a measure restored to
the distracted country. What would have been the outcome of
the determined opposition of the " Constitutionalists " had Juarez
lived to end his term of office is problematical, but his death, which
occurred from natural causes on July 18, arrested the revolutionary
uprisings by removing their ostensible cause. Then it was seen
and admitted by all, by the revolutionists no less than the Juaristas,
that Don Benito's patriotism was of the incorruptible kind.

Don Sebastian Lerdo de Tejada, president of the Supreme

Court, became the successor of Juarez as provisional president, and the following December he was declared by congress elected to fill his predecessor's unexpired term. President Lerdo followed quietly in the footsteps of Juarez, and being intimately cognizant of the plans entertained by the great statesman, instituted no radical changes in the government. He appealed to the nation for support in the great cause of reform, and proved himself earnestly desirous of peace by proclaiming a general amnesty, under the shelter of which most of those lately in opposition to the government resigned their pretensions and retired from the field. The succeeding three years were mainly peaceful and prosperous, except for the desultory operations of disunited bands of guerrillas and a rebellion in Michoacan and Sinoloa, which dragged itself through a period of eighteen months, when it was extinguished without having involved other States.

The secularization of ecclesiastical properties had gone on during the period of reform, and was forcibly brought to the people's notice in 1873 and 1874, first by the expulsion of some Jesuits, and secondly by an edict of expulsion against three hundred Sisters of Charity, who were accused of secretly undermining the lawful government of Mexico. Border disturbances on the north between Mexico and the United States, and on the south between the former and Guatemala, led to invasions which were crushed in their incipiency, and raised questions which were ultimately settled between the respective governments without serious trouble.

A peaceful invasion of Mexico about this time was that of the Protestant churches, led by the Protestant Episcopal and closely followed by other sects. Though at the beginning the missionaries encountered much opposition from fanatical Mexicans, and several of them fell martyrs to their faith, the government has protected them to the best of its ability. Religion, as well as the press, is free, and great good has resulted from the enlightened efforts of all lovers of liberty and righteousness.

While it would be difficult to determine exactly the date at which Mexico emerged from her condition of insularity and took her place among the nations of the world, it would not come amiss to mention that under the wise administration of Señor Lerdo she certainly laid the foundations for her coming prosperity. That marvel of engineering skill, the Mexican Railroad, which had been in progress of construction sixteen years, was formally opened in

January, 1873, and the coast of Mexico at Vera Cruz was connected with its capital.

By a decree of congress in 1874 a concession was granted for another line northwardly from the City of Mexico, which was the initial step taken in the great movement connecting the capital with the chief cities of the United States. Roads and telegraph lines were now projected in all directions; commerce, both external and internal, developed with great rapidity, and in the fiscal year of 1878 the exports from Vera Cruz alone amounted to more than sixteen million dollars.

It has been claimed, and with reason, that to Lerdo's successor, General Porfirio Diaz, is due the immense progress of Mexico during the last thirty years. At all events no other man has labored so earnestly and continuously for her advancement, and no other one man has done so much for any country on earth, it is believed, as President Porfirio Diaz has done for Mexico. In this connection, then, it will be well to pause a moment and pass in review the salient features of his life.

General Porfirio Diaz, who has been continuously the constitutional President of Mexico for twenty years, and who has been prominently identified with every great political military movement in his country for the last fifty years, was born in Oaxaca, on September 15, 1830, the twentieth anniversary of Hidalgo's war-cry, " Independence." While his ancestry on both sides is Spanish, he is related through his mother, whose grandmother was a Mixteca, to the Mexican aborigines who fought Cortéz so stoutly that they were hardly conquered. The only other Mexican of modern times who ranks with Diaz, Don Benito Juarez, the " Washington of Mexico," was also a native of Oaxaca, of Indian ancestry, but a Zapotecan. The father of Diaz, who died when Porfirio was only three years of age, kept a small tavern in Oaxaca; but the boy early showed his predisposition for the career of a soldier and was always a leader among his youthful companions.

His widowed mother gave him the best educational facilities Oaxaca afforded, and intended him for the church; but he turned to the law and entered the office of Juarez, with whom he was afterward identified in the cause of reform. He took no active part in the war with the United States, his first taste of fighting being at the age of twenty-four, when, proscribed by the tyrant, Santa Anna, he fled to the mountains and joined Herrera's band of guerrillas. Then began the adventures which distinguished him as one who knew no fear and " would rather fight than eat." Three years later he was desperately wounded, and again in 1860, when fighting against the Conservative army, near his home city, Oaxaca.

He won the position of general of brigade by a victory over Marquez in 1861, and in 1862 he took a prominent part in the defeat of the French forces of invasion at Puebla on May 5. The next year he was captured at Puebla, but soon after managed to escape and took the field again. During the Maximilian supremacy Diaz kept up a determined resistance in the south, and Bazaine was sent against him with a large army, finally effecting his capture. He again escaped, and within a few days had assembled a devoted band of Indians from the hill-towns of Oaxaca, and, besides capturing a garrison, routed a force of imperialists. With his " Serranos " as the nucleus of a rapidly gathering army, he recaptured the city of Oaxaca, and, ever active and always indomitable, inspiring confidence by his fearless bearing and superior strategy, he marched northward upon Puebla, to which he laid siege in March, 1867, and stormed and captured it on April 2. He set an example of clemency to all contestants by pardoning the prisoners taken at Puebla, not even excluding the man who had set a price upon his head, dead or alive. Again, after he had followed Marquez to the capital, which he promptly invested, he showed his greatness by refusing to bombard the city, finally capturing it without injury to its buildings or inhabitants, or its inestimable treasures, and on June 20, 1867, became its master and second only to the greatest man in Mexico, in the estimation of its people. General Diaz had already gained the reputation of being Mexico's greatest military genius, and that was more than a quarter of a century ago. Had ambition merely been his spur, he should have been satisfied; but in his subsequent actions there was a certain motive that is only explained by the events of later times. Hitherto he and Juarez had been friends; both these great Oaxacaños had been patriotically fighting for the best interests of their native land; both shared in the ovations of their grateful fellow-countrymen after the capture of the capital and the downfall of the imperialists.

But, as we have seen, when in the October succeeding these important events Juarez was elected president and Diaz defeated at the polls, the latter did not hesitate to " pronounce " against his

former friend and chief, nor did he fail to combat Señor Lerdo, his
successor.   While the United States was celebrating, at Philadelphia, the centennial of its independence by an exposition at which
Mexico, as well as other countries, was represented, the neighboring republic was in the throes of civil war.   When it was seen that
Lerdo's reëlection was inevitable, owing to the fact that he controlled the governmental machinery, and consequently the necessary "votes," General Diaz led a revolt and issued his celebrated
"Plan of Tuxtepec," with "Progress" for its motto.   He attacked
Matamoros and effected a large capture of men and munitions, but
was eventually driven across the Rio Grande, and, after making
another of his miraculous escapes, finally reached Oaxaca by a
roundabout journey via New Orleans and Vera Cruz.   On the
voyage between the two seaports he was recognized by some Lerdistas on board the American steamer in which he had engaged
passage as a "Doctor Torres," of Cuba, and when off Tampico
leaped into the water to swim ashore.   The bay was infested by
sharks, and he was providentially rescued and returned to the ship,
where he was concealed for a week in the purser's room, which
room was the nightly lounging place of vengeful Lerdistas, who
were thoroughly convinced that he ought to be shot on capture.
Smuggled ashore at Vera Cruz, disguised as a stevedore, Diaz
succeeded in reaching Oaxaca, where his loyal Indians gathered
about him in constantly increasing numbers, and marched with him
upon the capital.

At this time there rose to prominence another military leader,
General Manuel Gonzalez, who, on November 16, 1876, being in
command of Porfirista forces at Tecoac, near Puebla, defeated
General Alatorre of the Lerdista army and caused the president to
evacuate the capital and eventually the country.   President Lerdo
left the City of Mexico with his cabinet on November 20, and four
days later General Diaz entered it at the head of his "constitutional" army, the bulk of which was composed of Indians from
the hills of Oaxaca and Puebla, poorly clad and poorly armed.
General Diaz assumed the office of executive, and when called
upon to go forth to quench the aspirations of another presidential
aspirant, Iglesias, at Querétaro, he named Señor Juan Mendez
second general-in-chief of the "constitutional" army and provisional president of the republic.   There were at that time, indeed,
three nominal presidents of Mexico: Diaz, Lerdo, and Iglesias,

besides the so-called provisional President Mendez. Señor Lerdo had been "elected" in the usual manner, which had become well-established by long usage; Diaz had seized the position by force of arms; and the former president of the Supreme Court, Don José Iglesias, claimed to have succeeded to the executive office through the departure of his chief from the country—as provided by law. But the might of General Porfirio Diaz overcame all opposition, for he had now the army behind him, and was, of course, invincible. When he returned from his punitive expedition northward he was "unanimously declared" constitutional president by the convention assembled at the capital on call of Señor Mendez.

Thus General Porfirio Diaz became chief executive of Mexico for the first time. As merely another in the long line of pronunciadors who had vaulted into and over the presidential chair, he was not at first recognized by the United States and foreign governments at large; but it was not long before he made his presence felt as a factor, and an important one, in governmental affairs. Through the efficient service of Señor Romero, who afterward became minister and ambassador at Washington, he reduced order from chaos, especially in the hacienda, or public treasury, and after much difficulty organized his cabinet.

After making vehement but ineffectual protests, Señor Lerdo finally abandoned the field and, escaping to Acapulco, made his way to the United States. The Conservatives took no part in the struggle, having been effectually crushed; but the Liberals were for a while divided among themselves into three parties. There were the Porfiristas, or thick-and-thin adherents of Diaz; the Tuxtepecaños, composed of those who now insisted that Diaz should adhere to the "Plan of Tuxtepec," which, having served as a pretext, he seemed inclined to throw overboard; and the Lerdistas, who claimed that Don Sebastian was the only legally elected executive. This claim of the Lerdistas was, perhaps, just, but as General Diaz had elevated himself to the supreme command, had the army at his back, and moreover seemed disposed to govern according to the constitution of 1857, and was predisposed to progress, it soon came about that Lerdistas and Tuztepecaños were transformed into ardent Porfiristas. A military man, first of all, and above everything else, "Don Porfirio" was universally beloved of his soldiers, whose love and respect he had won in scores of bat-

tles, in every one of which he had acted the hero. He had the
acuteness and ambition of his ancient foe, Santa Anna; but unlike
Santa Anna he had rarely led his soldiers to defeat. And he had
always led them, himself setting an example that any brave man
would be glad to emulate. There is no doubting his magnificent
courage, his integrity, his fine fiber of honor; his personality appeals, commands, dominates. In Santa Anna the Mexicans had a
man of great ambition, but unscrupulous, swayed by selfish and
personal aims; in Juarez they had a man of high and impersonal
aims, a patriot; but a statesman, not a fighter; in "Don Porfirio"
the Mexican people recognized the type they loved, were willing
to fight for, die for: the *Hombre simpatico,* yet the dominant demi-
god of battles.

But "Don Porfirio" had no easy task before him at the
outset. He was known from one end of Mexico to the other for
what he had been—a patriot, yet a pronunciador, indomitable, and
hitherto invincible; but his capacity for governing a nation had
not been tested. There were rebellions and uprisings in various
parts, and in June of 1879 the Mexicans were treated to a novelty
in the annals of pronunciamientos, when the war steamer *Liberty*
"pronounced" against the administration of "Tuxtepec." In
December of that year General Manuel Gonzalez, who for a while
after the decisive battle of Tecoac had resided on his hacienda, and
who during a ministerial crisis was made secretary of war, was
placed in command of a large army for the suppression of the rebellion of Tepic. His success, not only in pacificating the rebels,
but in winning the good will of his soldiers, added to his military
prestige and made him an available candidate for the presidency.
In short, on November 30, 1880, the hero of Tecoac succeeded to
the chief magistracy by the grace of the man he himself had assisted to grasp supreme power four years before.

General Manuel Gonzalez, to whom President Diaz relinquished the reins of government in 1880, was born near Matamoros, Mexico, in 1820, of humble parentage. At first a guerrilla
and a reactionist, he joined with Juarez against the French and
imperialists, from 1861 to 1865; assisted Diaz to overthrow Lerdo
in 1876; became secretary of war in 1878, and President of Mexico in 1880. Without possessing great qualities, he was a man
of invincible determination, equally a fighter and equally brave
with his commander-in-chief. He had been twice desperately

wounded, and had lost an arm in one of his numerous engagements.
A sturdy follower of the fortunes of General Diaz, he at last secured his reward. President Gonzalez was inaugurated December
1, 1881, and General Diaz returned to comparative obscurity as
governor of Oaxaca, though his hand was still seen in the various
schemes of reform and enterprises of magnitude to which the administration was committed. The term of President Gonzalez was
in the main uneventful, but toward the end the people became un-
easy, and it was evident that a stronger than he must assume command of the ship of state. That stronger one, of course, was none
other than Porfirio Diaz, who came again into possession of his
own after an interim of four years, during which Gonzalez served
his country to the best of his capacity. At the time of his re-
accession it was said by an authority: " The great problem of the
hour for Mexico is the execution of her numerous railway projects,
due for the most part to American enterprise, but eagerly accepted
by the Mexican Government as the means for developing her unbounded natural resources and elevating her to the place which
nature designed her to occupy among Western nations." The total
length of the railways in Mexico, in 1881, was about 1000 miles.
The population was about 10,000,000, and the national revenue
had reached $22,000,000. In his message for 1883 President
Gonzalez said: " The country at large is in a prosperous condition, and the financial crises which at times have hampered business will soon leave no trace behind them." The total revenue
for the fiscal year was $33,500,000; the national debt in round
numbers was then $144,653,785. Railway lines had increased to
2800 miles in length, and the telegraph lines aggregated 7000
miles. The Gonzalez administration displayed great activity in
fostering immigration, an impulse was given to manufacturing and
mining, while steps were taken toward abolishing the arbitrary and
burdensome interstate duties, besides making a general reduction
on all other duties of ten per cent.

When General Diaz succeeded a second time to the presidency,
beginning his term on December 1, 1884, the national revenue had
risen to $36,160,000, and the expenditures were $36,325,000. The
grand total of railroads built and in process of construction was
3500 miles, and the exports for the fiscal year amounted to
$41,800,000.

The year 1884 was also memorable, not only for the reacces-

sion of Diaz to the presidency, but on account of the opening of
uninterrupted rail communication with the United States.   And
yet signs were not wanting to indicate that Mexico had proceeded
at too rapid a pace in the development of her trade, especially of
her imports, in the general stagnation of business and the financial
straits to which the government was reduced.   At one time, in the
summer of 1884, Mexico seemed on the brink of a revolution; but
the coming " Don Porfirio " served to calm the public mind, and
trouble was averted.   By the end of 1885 the public debt had been
reduced to $125,000,000; but the financial embarrassment was such
that most drastic measures were taken to tide over the crisis, all
government salaries being reduced, on a scale of ten per cent. on
salaries over $500 per annum to fifty per cent. on those of $15,000
and over, not even the executive being exempt.

After retiring from the presidency General Gonzalez was appointed governor of Guanajuato; but he was no longer a prominent
figure in public life.   He had served Diaz to tide over a certain
period when the latter, according to a clause in the constitution,
could not be eligible for reëlection.   This objectionable clause,
liberally translated, is as follows: " The President will enter upon
his duties on the first of December and will remain in office four
years.   He will not be eligible for reëlection for the period immediately succeeding, neither shall he occupy the presidency for any
reason until four years have passed without his having exercised
executive functions."

The four years had passed, Gonzalez had retired in favor of
his chief, and Diaz was now secure in his supremacy, having had
the constitution changed again to suit his views as to perennial,
or perpetual, presidency, so that for a score of years he has been
able to hold the executive office in a strictly " constitutional "
manner.

In April, 1910, General Porfirio Diaz was again re-elected president.   But for some time previous mutterings of discontent had
been heard from all sections of the country, the general sentiment
being that one man had held power long enough and that Diaz
should at last retire in favor of the younger element.

General Diaz had trained, as his successor, Señor Limantour,
the Minister of Finance, for the time when he would be forced to
retire, but when the outbreak came Diaz's own choice of a successor
was not given a thought.

Señor Francisco Madero placed himself at the head of the malcontents, and open hostilities broke out in November, 1910. Guerrilla fighting spread in almost every state. The United States Government mobilized a large body of troops along the border, but actual intervention was not required.

In May, 1911, the aged President was at last compelled to resign, and on May 30, he, with his family, was expelled from the country.

After General Diaz's departure, a provisional government was set up under the presidency of Señor de la Barra and continued until the election of October, 1911, when Señor Madero was chosen President for a four-year term.

This revolutionary condition still continued after the new government assumed control. President Taft was urged by many of the most important interests to take some steps looking toward intervention by the United States, but to no purpose. Much foreign property was wantonly destroyed and a great deal of foreign capital was driven from the country by the constant fighting and total lack of protection afforded to innocent non-combatants.

The finances of the country, which hitherto had been on a solid basis began to be decidedly impaired. The receipts in 1911 showed a decline of nearly $2,000,000, while the expenditures increased over $8,000,000.

In June and July, 1912, severe earthquakes caused great damage in Mexico City and the Guadalajara district. The first half of the year 1912 saw a continuation of the guerrilla warfare between the new government under President Madero and some of the bands of revolutionists who refused to acknowledge his authority. This guerrilla fighting culminated in open warfare in October, 1912, when General Felix Diaz, a nephew of the deposed President Diaz, was captured, but in February, 1913, escaped and placed himself at the head of a force of over 3,000 men and immediately attacked the National Palace in the City of Mexico, beating back the national troops and holding President Madero a prisoner. In the fighting, General Reyes, once a presidential candidate and an old rival to President Diaz, was killed. General Felix Diaz was soon in virtual command of the city and addressed a peremptory demand to President Madero for his resignation. The fighting through the streets of the city continued until February 18, when the Federal army of President Madero with its commander went over to the side of the leader of the revolutionists, General Felix Diaz. President Madero and his family and chief advisers were made prisoners. General Victoriano Huerta, who had been one of President Madero's chief military commanders, and who had forsaken him for the insurgent leader, General Diaz, was now made Provisional President. Next came the blotting out of all traces and records of the late administration of Madero. The new Provisional President, General Huerta, at once placed under arrest the deposed President, Francisco Madero, his brother Gustave Madero and the former Vice-President, Pino Suarez. They were all at first confined in the National Palace, and charges of malfeasance in office and theft of public funds were brought against them. They were also charged with being implicated in the murder of an army officer. The last dramatic scene in the terrible national tragedy occurred on February 23, 1913. On that day the former President and Vice-President, Madero and Suarez, were transferred under close guard from the National Palace to the penitentiary and were both killed on the way. Provisional President Huerta announced that Madero's and Suarez's friends had attempted to take them from their guards, and in the confusion the two prisoners were shot. The Madero adherents and family, on the other hand, declared that not only had no attempt been made to liberate the prisoners, but that the whole affair was staged by General Huerta to hide the murder of Madero and Suarez. They had been so tortured in the palace, it was claimed, that it was their dead bodies only that were being taken to the prison. It was generally believed both in Europe and America at the time that Madero and Suarez were murdered with the knowledge if not with the complicity of the new government. There existed no proof, however, that the government was a participant in the crime.

After Madero's death General Huerta was acknowledged Provisional President by the Mexican Congress.

American and foreign interests made loud demands for some action by the United States, but President Wilson on March 11, 1913, made a clear statement of the policy of the new administration. This was to be a continuation of the traditional one of strict neutrality and non-intervention in the affairs of any Latin-American republic.

Great Britain, France, and other European nations formally recognized the new government of General Huerta.

Affairs improved under the firm hand of President Huerta, and when Congress met in April, 1913, the President gave assurances that all disorders would be promptly suppressed. He announced that general elections would be held in July. The Chamber of Deputies, however, postponed the date to end of the year when it was thought that peace throughout the country would be established.

The United States delayed acknowledging the new government, which action caused considerable strained relations between the two countries. In August President Wilson of the United States sent a message to Congress that the only condition for the acknowledgment of the Huerta administration would be an immediate cessation of civil insurrection, a definite armistice, and an early election of a new President of the Mexican Republic with the understanding that President Huerta would not stand for reëlection.

These conditions were impossible of acceptance by Mexico and her relations with the United States continued during the year to be strained.

In October the revolutionists defeated General Alvarez near Torreon. In the same month President Huerta raised the duties on imports 50 per cent. In October, 1913, the general elections were held, but the votes were so few that the Congress declared the election void.

Early in 1914 President Huerta began to feel the increasing pressure of financial stringency. He made frantic efforts to stave off coming events, but even by declaring a three months' bank holiday, failed to accomplish it.

The ordering of the United States Atlantic fleet to Tampico and the seizure of Vera Cruz by the American forces were instrumental in the final overthrow of the government. The action of the United States government was hastened by the insult to the American flag by the arrest of the crew of an American launch at Tampico. The South American Republics at once offered their good offices as mediators between the United States and Mexico, which tender President Wilson at once accepted. In May and June, 1914, the arbitrators met in Buffalo and finally came to the following agreement: A provisional government should be agreed upon by delegates of all warring factions in Mexico; that the United States would recognize such a government, and that the United States would not claim an indemnity for the insult to her flag. President

Huerta at last was forced to capitulate and resigned on July 17, 1914. He left the country a few days later. Señor Carbajal was elected provisional President of Mexico. He in turn was succeeded shortly after by General Carranza. In November, 1914, General Carranza was superseded by Señor Gutierrez, and the year closed with little progress having been made to assure a firm and stable government.

Chapter XXXV

COMMERCE AND INDUSTRY—INTERNAL DEVELOPMENT. 1520—

THE foundations for Mexico's commercial and industrial expansion were laid early in its history, soon after its conquest by the Spaniards; but its real progress is a matter of modern times, coinciding very nearly with what the statisticians term the last great period of commercial history. The first ship sailed from New to Old Spain in 1520, bearing gifts from Montezuma to Charles V., and after Cortéz had accomplished the pacification of the country a line of communication was established between Mexico and the Peninsula, consisting first of an annual, and then of a semi-annual fleet of great galleons. Fifteen galleons were commissioned to sail from Seville to Vera Cruz and return, every six months, which, under the immediate successor of Charles V., were increased in number to fifty or sixty. After the Philippines had begun to be exploited, another annual galleon sailed between those islands in the orient and Acapulco on the west coast of Mexico, their cargoes being transported overland to Vera Cruz, and there reshipped to Spain. Annual fairs were held on the west coast at Acapulco, and near the east coast at Jalapa, lasting for forty days or more, at which millions of dollars' worth of merchandise changed hands and to which traders flocked from all parts of the country. The same sort of transactions were also established for South America, the galleons discharging and receiving cargoes at Porto Bello on the Spanish Main.

A chamber of commerce was created in Spain as early as 1503, and some eight years later the Council of the Indies was organized at Madrid, which had supervision over commercial as well as military, and in fact, all colonial, affairs, and was represented in Mexico and Peru by a viceroy in each country. But it became the policy of Spain to hinder rather than develop commerce and industry in her colonies, encouraging only the exploitation of the mineral products, to the total neglect of agriculture and manufactures.

Not only was the entire administration of commercial affairs kept in the hands of Spaniards, to the entire exclusion of foreigners and colonials, but almost prohibitive customs duties were collected on all exports and imports. Manufactures being prohibited in the American colonies, these industries were greatly stimulated in Spain, altogether at the cost of the unfortunate colonial. This monopoly Spain retained for a century and a half, although she experienced interference with her trade before the end of the sixteenth century through the pirates and privateers fitted out in foreign ports and which swarmed in the Caribbean Sea, pouncing upon the clumsy galleons richly freighted with oriental silks, gold and silver ore, and carrying them off as prizes. It was partly the fault of Spain that her commerce with the colonies was so swiftly destroyed, for she had sacrificed both them and herself by concentrating her treasures aboard a few great ships which, when taken, yielded to their captors vast fortunes at a single haul.

But the colonial policy of Spain has already been outlined in the chapters devoted to the viceroyal period, where it has been shown that it was everything for Spain and nothing for the colonies. During the long period of pronunciamientos, wars with the United States and France, and to a great extent through the period of reconstruction, Mexican foreign commerce became paralyzed. Her natural resources, however, were so vast and varied, comprising within her confines, as she does, practically three climatic zones, and with mountains of iron, copper, and silver extending from northern to southern frontier, Mexico soon became full to repletion of crude products for which the world outside was waiting.

Abounding in minerals beyond ordinary comprehension, especially in silver and gold, with glittering threads ramifying the Cordilleras in every direction, Mexico is to-day one of the richest regions of the world. The first silver was found by Europeans in the mines of Tasco in 1522, which had been worked by the Aztecs centuries previously. In 1803 Humboldt estimated the amount of precious metals sent from Mexico to Spain since 1521 at more than $2,000,000,000. The records of the Mexican mint, which date from 1537, show a coinage of $3,500,000,000, nearly all of which is silver. Gold, however, is continually increasing, as new mines are being worked and localities developed. According to Humboldt there were three thousand mines in operation a hundred years ago, and the latest statistics give the number of mineral districts as 1100.

The silver region containing the most famous mines is practically that of the tableland; but most of the gold is found on the slopes toward the *tierra caliente*. The wonderful stories of the yield of Mexican mines are not fabulous, for they can all be verified by statistics. Everybody has heard of the mountain of iron in Durango, Cerro del Mercado, a mass of pure ore estimated at 50,000,000 cubic yards. Precious stones have been found to some extent, some diamonds, emeralds, chalchuitls, opals by millions; and the pearl fisheries of Lower California yield more than a million and a half per annum.

But it is not the writer's intention to pursue this subject (for it demands a volume by itself) further than to indicate the great and original sources of Mexico's wealth. A glance at the statements which follow will convey valuable information respecting the natural resources of the country and its wants as well as its products. In the sixteenth century, as has been indicated, Mexico was "the greatest commercial center of the then known world. During the seventeenth and eighteenth centuries domestic trade began to be developed, and foreign commerce fell off, owing to the constant wars between Spain and the various European states. At the beginning of the nineteenth century the foreign trade of the republic revived, reaching, it is claimed, the sum of 25,000,000 pesos for imports and over 16,000,000 for exports. . . . The domestic trade of the country is made up of the interchange of natural products and the products of native industry for such as are not indigenous to the country, or, if so, are produced on too small a scale to meet the requirements of native consumption; hence the necessity for importing such goods as are required to make up the balance of trade." [1]

The principal articles imported into Mexico are as follows, in their order of importance: Machinery, cotton textiles, iron and steel, wines and liquors, wood textiles, paper, and manufactures. The exports, in the same order, are silver, henequen, or sisal hemp; gold, coffee, cattle, lead, copper, hides, precious woods, broom root, etc.

During the last quarter-century, under the pacific administration of President Diaz, the "increase of public wealth and the general development of the country have been made possible,"

[1] From "Mexico," by the Bureau of the American Republics.

so that the exports and imports have wonderfully augmented. The exports and imports for the year 1875 (just before the beginning of the prosperous period) amounted to a total of little more than $46,000,000 in Mexican coin. Twenty-five years later they amounted to, respectively, imports, $106,285,307; exports, $138,-478,137. The latest statistics available show an increase in imports over those of 1890-1891, which are given as approximately, $130,000,000, of about ten per cent.; and exports, which in the fiscal year 1890-1891 were $148,656,000, nearly the same.

During the year ending June 30, 1908, the value of goods imported from Mexico into the United States amounted to $175,809,123, while on the other hand she purchased from its merchants $146,392,884 worth. According to the latest available Mexican statistics, about sixty per cent. of the total value of goods imported by that country in the fiscal year 1908 came from the United States, as compared with a little over fifty-five per cent. in 1890. Of the goods exported from Mexico, the United States took about seventy per cent. in 1908, and about sixty-eight per cent. in 1890.

Copper and vegetable fibers form the largest individual items of the exports from Mexico, and iron and steel products constitute the largest imports to that country.

Of unmanufactured vegetable fibers (mainly sisal grass) our imports increased from $5,500,000 to over $12,000,000, while of the manufactures of these materials our imports increased from $6,000 to nearly $650,000, and our exports from $58,000 to $228,000. Hides and skins were imported to the value of nearly $3,500,000, while of leather and its manufactures the value of exports increased from $61,000 to $818,000. Our imports of coffee fell off during the decade from over $4,000,000 to less than $3,000,000.

Exports of iron and steel not only constitute the largest item of United States trade with Mexico, but show the largest growth in the last ten years, exports of machinery alone increasing from about $1,500,000 to over $7,000,000. Other items which show large gains are breadstuffs, vehicles, chemicals, coal, and coke, copper ore, vegetable oils, and lumber.

In the fiscal year 1908 Mexico's total imports were $221,535,993, of which the United States furnished more than half, or $146,392,887. Mexico's total exports in the same year amounted to $242,738,000, of which $175,809,123 worth were sold to the

United States. Moreover, Mexico's trade with the United States is growing much faster than with any other country.[2]

The most remarkable development in Mexico has been in railway construction and telegraph extension, about 15,000 miles of railway being now in operation, and 45,000 miles of telegraph lines, besides an extensive system of telephones. When it is considered that the first mile of Mexican railway was completed so late as 1851, and that the first energetic work began in 1857, the present status of transit by steam cannot but be regarded as eminently satisfactory. The first concession was granted as far back as 1837, but it was not until twenty years later that actual construction began, and sixteen years later, or in 1873, that the first Mexican railway was opened to the public. This was the line running from Vera Cruz to the City of Mexico—only 263 miles in length, but presenting engineering difficulties almost insuperable. Completed on January 1, 1873, it was solemnly inaugurated by Señor Lerdo, then president of the republic, and ever since has been an important factor in the upbuilding of Mexico. Three hundred and fifty years had elapsed from the time Cortéz and his companions toilfully marched from the coast to the Aztec capital before the latter was placed in steam communication with the Gulf of Mexico and the Atlantic.

The "railway backbone" of Mexico is the great "Central" system, more than a thousand miles in length, and the first of the international routes to be completed. By its concessions it has branches east and west to the Gulf of Mexico and the Pacific, and its main line northwardly from the City of Mexico to El Paso on the Rio Grande, more than a thousand miles in length, runs through the largest centers of population and penetrates the richest mineral region of the country. The population of the great plateau over which it is mainly built is estimated at four millions, and it passes through many large cities, nine of them being State capitals, with an aggregate population of more than a million inhabitants. The trunk line of the Central, completed fourteen years ago, was swiftly followed by its rival, the Mexican National, which obtains ingress to Mexico from Laredo on the Rio Grande, and passes southward via Monterey and San Luis Potosi. Originally projected as a narrow-gauge line, it adopted the standard gauge later on, and, having secured what is practically an alliance with the

[2] *Cf.* accounts of Department of Commerce and Labor, Bureau of Statistics.

Mexican Government, in 1903, has taken its place as a great trunk line between Mexico and the United States.

The northwestern State of Mexico, Sonora, is crossed by a railroad, from Benson in Arizona to Guyanas on the Gulf of California, about 350 miles in length; in the extreme south the Isthmus of Tehuantepec is spanned by a hundred-mile belt connecting the Pacific with the Gulf of Mexico; southward from the City of Mexico runs a line to and through Oaxaca, which forms an extension of the northern lines which center at the capital; so that it will be seen that Mexico has contributed her share of railway construction toward the great Two-Americas, or Inter-Continental, system that has been projected to eventually connect the Arctic regions with Patagonia. Rail communication, in fact, is afforded southward from the United States systems as far as the Mexico-Guatemala border; important gaps are yet to be filled in Central America and along the Andean tableland in South America, but so much has already been accomplished that the project of connecting the Land of Snow with the Region of Fire is no longer regarded as chimerical.

Nearly all the railway concessions in Mexico carried " subventions " ranging from $5000 to $9500 per kilometer, and years ago it was seen that the government had incurred obligations of this sort that it would never be able to fulfill. All but three of the great railway lines in Mexico are owned by capitalists of the United States, or owe their existence to American capital which has been invested in that country to the extent of $500,000,000 in gold, seventy per cent. of which sum is in railroads. The extent to which Mexico has been aided by capital from across the border may be inferred from the fact that in 1903 there were 1117 American companies, firms, or individuals engaged in various enterprises there which include gas and waterworks, electric light and power plants, telephone systems, manufactures, agriculture, and mining. In mines and mining American capital is interested to the extent of $80,000,000, and in agriculture to the amount of $28,000,000.

" Since the first subsidy was granted to railroads Mexico has paid out more than $100,000,000 for that purpose.

" For public improvements, as harbors, more than $190,-000,000; for the drainage of the valley of Mexico, improvement of streets, sewerage, public buildings, etc., in the capital, less than ten years subsequent to 1903, more than $40,000,000.

" The rehabilitation of Mexico's finances, debts, and revenues, is mainly due to Minister José Yves Limantour, one of the ablest financiers the world has produced, who, though still a comparatively young man, has made a great name for himself and firmly established the reputation of Mexico. He has already served as provisional president of the republic, during an illness of General Diaz, and has been prominently mentioned as his probable successor, dividing this doubtful honor with General Bernardo Reyes, next to Diaz the strongest military man of Mexico.

" Minister Limantour has displayed the highest qualities as a statesman and financier and in a large and growing field. He enjoys the greatest confidence of the world's leading financiers, and the man who can command money to meet the public obligations and for investment is the best fitted to govern Mexico." [3]

In the enumeration of railroads mention should certainly be made of those of Yucatan, Mexico's southern peninsula, which, beginning at Progreso on the coast, have penetrated far into the country in various directions, opening up regions almost unknown to the tourist, reaching the ruins of magnificent cities long since abandoned by their builders, and giving access to other points of interest. The original purpose of their builders was to afford transportation facilities for Yucatan's staple product, the henequen, or native hemp, a vast acreage of which exists there, and the cultivation of which, together with the operation of the roads, has been the means of amassing great fortunes for the Yucateños.

It is only in times comparatively recent that Mexico has engaged in manufacturing articles of any description on an extensive scale. In olden times her Spanish masters forbade manufactures of any kind whatever, and when silk and woolen weaving were attempted their promoters were peremptorily stopped. But to-day, under the stimulus of foreign capital and owing to the example of her nearest neighbors in the north, Mexico has become to some extent a manufacturer of her own special products, and factories and mills, especially for the weaving of cotton and woolens, have sprung up all over the country. The making of cotton cloth, mostly a coarse, unbleached fabric known as " manta," is now carried on extensively, the mills consuming, it is estimated, about from 25,000,000 to 30,000,000 pounds of crude cotton annually. Mexico has soil and climate perfectly adaped to the raising of cotton, yet at least two million dollars' worth is annually imported.

[3] Dr. G. A. Benham, ex-agent of the United States Treasury.

This industry affords employment, direct and indirect, it is said, to more than fifty thousand families, and is steadily growing. The mills are mostly provided with machinery of ancient make and pattern, but of late some have been set up with the best American machinery that could be obtained. There are now more than one hundred cotton mills in the country, the largest and oldest being found at Querétaro, with fourteen in Puebla and thirteen in the Federal District.

The woolen industry ranks next in importance, the principal mills being situated in Aguas Calientes, Durango, Guanajuato, Hidalgo, Puebla, San Luis Potosi, Mexico, Nuevo Leon, and Zacatecas. Wool-spinning as well as silk-weaving are ancient industries in Mexico, although for centuries they were conducted on a small scale. In the making of the gorgeous and unique sarapes and rebozos the weavers of Mexico are unexcelled, some of their hand-loom products bringing more than a hundred dollars each. The hats, or sombreros, worn by the Mexicans are of native manufacture, and their quality may be inferred from the fact that some of them sell at as high prices as the sarapes. The raising of tobacco and the manufacture of cigars and cigarettes are on a large scale; the sugar industry is backward, but has great possibilities; there are not flour mills enough to supply the home demand, though the same cannot be said of the iron foundries, nor of the potteries, which latter produce unique and beautiful examples of the ceramic art.

Observant writers have called attention to what they call the "Americanizing" of Mexico, through the investment in that country of so many million dollars in various enterprises. "American influence and money have caused the sanitary regeneration of the capital and other Mexican cities," says one. "The financial invasion from the United States is in full swing and is sweeping over the country in a tidal-wave of seemingly irresistible power," writes another.

But it has remained for a distinguished native of Mexico, Señor Manuel M. Alegre, to call upon the Mexicans to "Americanize" themselves and abandon their "Latin ideals" in order to escape the threatened perils of "Anglo-Saxon absorption." Alegre is the Spanish synonym for being glad or joyful, and Señor Alegre is fortunately named, for he seems to be an optimist, at least as regards the threatened "absorption." In a pamphlet entitled

" How to Escape the Saxon Peril: By Saxonizing Ourselves," he describes " this phantasm which has became an obsession of the national intellect." . . . " While the peoples of Europe," he says, " are held in continual alarm by the growing industrial development of the United States, in us it produces a kind of patriotic nightmare, in which we see involved the irremediable loss of our nationality. Nobody sets date or occasion for the disaster; but the danger is there, imminent and terrifying, threatening us with its dragon-claws, and at any moment it may swoop down upon us and destroy forever our national existence. This, at any rate, is the belief."

He does not, however, fear those " dragon-claws "; but, on the contrary, he respects and admires the " dragon," or, in other words the great American eagle, which he regards as, on the whole, a beneficent bird. He reminds his countrymen that they have always followed after " the Latin ideal, which is a worn and withered ideal.

" It is the Roman ideal, modified by the theoretical ideal, which is also worn out. Its elements were religion as a temporal, absorbent power; absolute monarchy as a system of government; the preponderance of the state over the masses as a civil condition; the hierarchy of classes as a social condition; the submission and incapacity of woman as a private condition, and the aspiration for art and war as instruments of glory and power.

" But religion is now dethroned, separated from the state; absolute monarchy is a fossil, overwhelmed by the hurricane of revolutions. The preponderance of the state has yielded to the spirit of individual liberty. Privileges have disappeared, and the plain people have reached a state of legal equality. Modern societies are busy with the elevation of woman. War is no longer the chronic condition ot nations, and art is the aspiration of all cultivated societies.

" What remains, then, of the old Latin ideal which has not been destroyed, altered, or accepted by our civilization? "

The much-vaunted " Latin solidarity " he calls another exploded phantasm, what there is of it remaining being " a vague aspiration, an hysterical aspiration to reorganize the past, to engross the future; an aspiration that lives in the brain and heart of some Latin peoples and which produces explosions of eloquence."

But " Saxonization " or " Americanization " is the " stimulation of the national energies by imitating the salient traits of the Anglo-Saxon character which have won for it universal primacy. . . . The Mexican people ought, consequently, to assimilate itself to the American people. Assimilate its character, ideals, and general tendencies. It should not entertain ideals antagonistic to the American people. Rather, let it identify itself with American institutions, with the habit of work of the Americans, with their love of order and liberty, with their generous and ample mentality."

To have produced one such thinker as Señor Alegre—a man capable of rising above the environment of national prejudice and formulating his convictions into a presentment which cannot but be unpalatable to his fellow-countrymen—shows that Mexico has indeed progressed along the path of enlightment.

Chapter XXXVI

YUCATAN. 1502—

WHILE politically a province of Mexico, comprising two States of that republic, the peninsula of Yucatan pertains geographically to Central America, its southern boundary being conterminous with that of Guatemala, and falls naturally into a grouping with the last-named republic and its neighbors. The mass of the peninsula is isolated, while in climate and physical features it is radically different from either Mexico or Guatemala, being hot and dry, low-lying and level in the main.

Yucatan was discovered before Mexico became known to the Spaniards, Columbus sighting its coast in 1502, and Pinzon in 1506, while Hernandez Cordova landed at or near Campeché in 1517, and Grijalva (who actually opened the way to Mexico in 1518) was followed by Cortéz in 1519. The conquistadores were diverted to the more northern Aztec country, fortunately for Yucatan, and not alone Mexico was conquered before the Yucatan peninsula was subjugated, but Central America, and even far-distant Peru.

We have seen, as we followed after Cortéz and his army, that Yucatan was very populous and with evidences of a high state of civilization; but as it gave no promise of gold or mines it was neglected by the Spaniards. According to native tradition, Yucatan was originally populated by the dispersed inhabitants of Xibalba, a powerful theocratic empire of Central America, the capital of which is supposed to have been Palenque, whose ruins may now be found in Tabasco.

Driven from Xibalba by Nahuatl tribes from north of the River Panuco, the survivors of the empire sought refuge in Yucatan, Guatemala, and in Central America generally. Their direct descendants in Yucatan and Guatemala were the Itzaes; and while there are linguistic traces of three different peoples there, the

Itzaes, Mayas, and the Caribs, at the period of the conquest the natives of Yucatan all spoke one dialect, the Maya, which is the prevalent speech of the aborigines to-day.

The Mayas are said to have come into the country about the sixth century; and while they readily allied themselves with the Spaniards after the conquest, the Itzaes, on the contrary, retired to Lake Peten, buried deep in great forests within the limits of Guatemala. Their last place of occupation in Yucatan was Chichen, the city of their ancestors, and it may be remarked in passing that in general features the ruins of Palenque, of Uxmal, Chichen, and other groups in Yucatan, are similar to those of Guatemala and Honduras, or of Central-American type, as distinguished from the Toltec or Nahuatl.

It was not until 1527 that the conquest of Yucatan by the Spaniards was actually undertaken. The previous year Don Francisco Montejo, a cavalier who had voyaged with Grijalva and Cortéz, obtained a royal grant for the conquest and pacification of Cozumel and Yucatan. He was one of the commissioners who sailed from Mexico to Spain in the first vessel that ever performed that voyage, when the Aztec treasures were sent to the king.

With four vessels well equipped Montejo sailed for Cozumel, and landed on the main coast opposite that island four hundred men, who raised the royal standard with loud cries of "*España, españa, vivê españa!*"

They marched inland and first encountered the natives near the aboriginal city of Aké, the site of which is indicated to-day by cyclopean piles of rocks known as "Katunes." Here they fought a terrible battle, for the natives were as fierce as the Aztecs, and by this time had become familiar with the sight and sound of firearms.

After great slaughter on both sides the Yucatacans gave way, but not until the second day of fighting, when the Spaniards were so fatigued that they could not pursue them. Twelve hundred Indians lost their lives, and as many more at another battle the next year near Chichen-Itza, the ancient Itzae capital, where 150 Spaniards were killed and many wounded. One of the caciques of the peninsula sent word that if the Spaniards wanted tribute he would send them fowls on spears and golden grains on arrow-points. In short, the Indians of Yucatan were so numerous and implacable that after eight years of warfare Montejo abandoned for a while the attempt at subjugation and left the peninsula, the last to depart being a cavalier named Nieto, who had first planted the royal banner on the coast amid the *vivas* of the soldiers, most of whom were long since dead.

In 1537, however, the indomitable Montejo returned with another army and landed at Champoton, where, twenty years before, the Indians had beaten off Hernandez Cordova and killed or wounded half his men. A desperate battle was fought here, during which the Spaniards were at one time driven to their boats, but remained and were finally victorious.

In 1540 the city of Campeché was founded, and the next year it was resolved to march upon the Indian capital, Tihoo, upon the site of which the present city of Merida was built, in 1542. At Tihoo, according to the historians, the Spaniards encountered an army of 40,000 Indians, and after an all-day's fight found their march obstructed by the heaps of the slain. This battle at Tihoo, with its thousands of victims, was decisive, and after that all the different caciques dispersed or tendered their allegiance. After fifteen years of fighting Adelantado Montejo found he had won a barren victory, for there was no gold to reward him, and in fact little spoil of any sort. But the peninsula remained peaceful for years after, and was governed as a captain-generalcy, distinct from Mexico and Guatemala. The Indians, however, were never entirely subjugated, and even to-day there are many on the verge of revolt, mainly on the east coast. They are known as " sublevados," and in the past have desolated a vast extent of territory.

There have been revolts in every century since the conquest of the native Indians, those of 1761 and 1847 being especially noteworthy. Yucatan joined the Mexican confederacy in 1824, but in 1840 an independent republic was set up, only to be suppressed in 1843. At the time of the great uprising of the natives, in 1847, Mexican aid was invoked, and Yucatan finally lost her autonomy, in 1861 being divided into the two Federal States of Yucatan and Campeché, as we find her to-day.

It has often been asserted that there is now less land under cultivation in Yucatan than shortly after the Spanish conquest; but at the same time, though most of the vast plantations devoted to the cultivation of the henequen or native hemp are in comparatively few hands, there is a great deal of money in circulation in the country. The natives, who still speak the Maya tongue of their ancestors, get little for their labor, but they are easily satisfied. While their culture is in general superior to that of the Aztecs and most other Mexican Indians, the Mayas are devoid of ambition and seemingly content to exist in a state of peonage. They are collectively a fine-looking people, mild of manners, cleanly, and intelligent up to a certain point; while the half and quarter-breeds, the mestizas and mestizos, are particularly attractive.

HISTORY OF CENTRAL AMERICA

HISTORY OF CENTRAL AMERICA

THE FIVE REPUBLICS. 1522—

AMONG the expeditions sent out by Cortéz from the City of Mexico after its downfall those for the conquest of Guatemala and Honduras were the largest and best equipped. The conqueror had been feeling his way toward either coast of Mexico and also to the southward, in 1522 sending Pedro de Alvarado to accomplish the subjugation of the fierce Zapotecs. Alvarado was so successful in bringing the Zapotecs to terms that he was later dispatched to conquer the country lying to the southward, known as Guatemala. He departed on this mission in December, 1523, with 300 infantry, 135 cavalry, 4 cannon, and 300 Indian allies. Passing beyond Oaxaca, Tehuantepec, and Soconusco, Alvarado encountered desperate resistance from the Indians at or near Quetzaltenango, where he fought three battles in as many days, and met and defeated 15,000 of the enemy. At another native settlement called Utatlan he seized a cacique who had planned an ambuscade of the Spanish army, and whom, after his chaplain had converted him by preaching an entire day in his presence, he hanged to a tree. His summary treatment of the cacique had such an effect that a considerable body of Guatemalans, estimated at more than two thousand, offered their allegiance and assistance, and with them as allies he marched forward toward the city of Guatemala, which he captured without delay. With the assistance of his Indian allies he soon after defeated the warriors of Altitan, who lived on a lake not far distant from the capital of Guatemala, and who wore thick coats of mail and were well armed in the aboriginal fashion. After taking their fortress and garrisoning it with Spanish soldiers, Alvarado next marched against the Ixcuintepecs, almost entirely destroying these barbarous people, and in this manner subjugating Guatemala in a comparatively brief campaign.

Information had come to Cortéz through some sailors that the province of Honduras, which lay beyond Yucatan and Guatemala, was rich in minerals, particularly gold; and, moreover, as he imagined that a strait or passage might exist in that direction leading from the Atlantic to the Pacific, he dispatched another of his captains, Cristóval de Olid, in search of both mines and strait. On January 11, 1524, while Alvarado was engaged in Guatemala, six ships set sail for Honduras, commanded by Olid, with a force of 370 soldiers. The expedition reached its destination after touching at Havana for horses and provisions, and Olid took possession of the country in the name of the King of Spain, and began a settlement, which he named Triumpho de la Cruz. But when he touched at Cuba he had made a compact with the arch-enemy of Cortéz, Velasquez, to cast off his allegiance to Cortéz, and set up an independent government. Eight months passed before intelligence of this defection reached Cortéz in Mexico, who promptly dispatched another fleet to Honduras, under command of his cousin, Francisco de las Casas. The fleet consisted of five ships and carried 100 men, some of whom were the original conquerors of Mexico. Arrived at Olid's settlement, Las Casas hoisted the pennant of peace, but the recreant soldier, one of the bravest and most fearless of the conquerors who had fought with Cortéz, attacked the first landing party with such vigor that he sank one of the ships and killed several sailors, wounding many more. A gale springing up, all the ships were driven ashore and lost, and Las Casas and his men made prisoners by Olid, who released them upon their swearing fealty to him and enmity to Cortéz. He wrote Velasquez of his success, and was so openly vainglorious and confident that he allowed his prisoners to be at large, which circumstances Las Casas took advantage of to conspire with others for his death. The gallant Olid had said he was only too happy to have such a gentleman as Las Casas for a companion, and the other had retorted: "Take care that one of these days I do not kill thee." One night, as they were seated at supper, Las Casas suddenly leaped upon his host and, seizing him by the beard, cut his throat with a penknife, inflicting such wounds that the other conspirators finally overcame the victim of their baseness and cut off his head.

Finding that Las Casas was supported by Cortéz, with the authority of the king behind him, all the garrison joined the new commander and assisted him to form a settlement, which he called Truxillo, and which exists to-day. He then returned to Mexico to acquaint Cortéz with what he had done and to obtain reinforcements.

Cortéz received tidings of the wreck of his ships, but as the months passed away and no other news came, he supposed Las Casas and his command all drowned, and with his accustomed energy at once organized another expedition. There was a lull in his activities in Mexico, and he longed for new fields to conquer, so he resolved to go himself in search of Olid, and, instead of proceeding by sea, to march overland. By the nearest route, as yet unmarked and lying through untracked forests and across deep rivers, the distance to Olid's settlement was all of fifteen hundred miles; but the prospective difficulties did not daunt the intrepid captor of Montezuma. He started out on October 12, 1524, after leaving a strong garrison in the City of Mexico and confidential deputies to act for him in his absence, with a force of about 200 Spaniards and 3000 Mexican warriors. In order to deprive the Aztecs of their leaders, in case they should meditate insurrection, Cortéz also took with him as hostages King Guatemozin and the cacique of Tacuba, besides several other sub-chiefs of importance. He tried to make his retinue impressive, but only succeeded in making it cumbersome by taking along a large number of supernumeraries, such as pages, equerries, grooms, falconers, friars, and priests, and even jugglers, musicians, and puppet-players, besides a chamberlain, surgeon, a majordomo, and a butler.

This march to Honduras was the turning-point in the career of Cortéz, and the beginning of the misfortunes that overtook him after his great work of subjugating Mexico had been accomplished. That his head was turned by his successes seems manifest by the absurdity of his equipment for a march through an unknown country—even in the undertaking itself. Besides maintaining an appearance of state by the assemblage already noted, he took with him his valuable service of plate, and behind the heterogeneous multitude of retainers followed a herd of swine in charge of his chief steward. This grotesque company moved but slowly, as may be imagined, and was a long time in crossing Mexican territory. In the province of Guacacualco (Coatzacoalcos) a number of the old soldiers were settled, as they had hoped, for life, having large estates and encomiendas of Indians, and these veterans, who had already fought and won many battles for Cortéz, were ordered to join him in his wild-goose chase after Olid. One of these old soldiers afterward wrote: "I have already mentioned how this colony was formed out of the most respectable hidalgos and ancient conquerors of the country; and now that we had reason to expect to be left in quiet possession of our hard-earned properties, our houses, and our farms, we were obliged to undertake a hostile expedition to the distance of fifteen hundred miles, and which took up the time of two and a half years; but we dared not say no, neither would it avail us. We therefore armed ourselves, and mounting our horses, joined the expedition, making in the whole above 250 veterans, of whom 130 were cavalry, besides many Spaniards newly arrived from Europe."

In Coatzacoalcos Cortéz finally rid himself of Mariana, his interpreter, who had served him so faithfully in several capacities during the protracted Mexican campaign, by marrying her to a Spaniard of his party, Don Juan Xamarillo, and settling the pair on an estate in this, her native, province. That he would have done better to have kept her by him, at least until the Guatemalan march was over, was soon made manifest by the difficulties he encountered of communicating with the Indians of the southern provinces, and with whose language Mariana was acquainted. Up to this point the conqueror of Mexico had been saluted with bonfires and triumphal arches and many flattering tributes of homage; but beyond the great River Coatzacoalcos he entered a country that knew not Cortéz save by vague report. In place of abundance of provisions and the willing service of burden-bearing Indians ready to transport his luggage and ferry his little army across the numerous streams, he found naught but savages of the wildest kind, who fled at his approach, and who had no provisions to spare or who hid them at the coming of the Spaniards. Days and even weeks were spent in wading marches saddle-girth deep in quaking mud, and in constructing rude bridges across the swift and alligator-infested rivers. At the fording of the River Tabasco the Spaniards found fifty canoes awaiting them laden with provisions provided by the foresight of Cortéz, who had sent messengers ahead to the colony at the river's mouth; but a few days farther on they came to a river so wide and deep that they could not bridge it, but were detained four days while making canoes in which to cross. Three days more were passed floundering in an immense morass through which there was no trail. Impeded by tropical vines that entangled both men and horses, and stung by innumerable insects, the army was entirely exhausted when it finally emerged upon solid land. The provisions were gone, so foraging parties sought out food in the Indian villages, an abundance of maize being found, which sufficed for several days. Another river, however, which took three days to cross, depleted the supply so that the company was brought to the verge of starvation. Another Indian settlement was fortunately discovered just in time, from the granaries of which all received sufficient for their needs; but during the halt for rest and refreshment here Cortéz learned that some of the Mexicans had perished of hunger and fatigue; more than this, that his caciques had seized several natives whom they had encountered by the way and had eaten their flesh after baking their bodies over coals and heated stones. By way of example, Cortéz caused one of the caciques to be burned alive, and about ten days after he committed another crime of the sort by hanging Guatemozin and the Prince of Tacuba to a tree in the forest. They were accused of plotting the destruction of the Spaniards, who, now reduced in strength and numbers, would have fallen an easy prey to the Mexicans had they really intended to destroy them.

In the gloom of the trackless forest the now morose Mexicans and indignant Spaniards stumbled on, guided only by a compass that Cortéz had with him and a rude map made by an Indian. One night, close following upon the execution of Guatemozin and his cousin, Cortéz received several injuries by falling amid the ruins of an Indian temple, in which he was wandering, weak from hunger and tortured, perchance, by the upbraidings of his conscience. He concealed his injuries as well as he could, but a desperate wound in his head was visible to all.

Emerging finally from the vast forest, in which they had wandered for weeks, the miserable adventurers came to a plain, where the sun shone with tropical intensity and wilted them with its heat. But plenty again greeted them in the shape of numerous deer, which the cavaliers ran down on their horses; and again they came to a lake in which were small fish, which they netted by the thousand. Thus abundance alternated with famine, but dread hunger threatened soon after the lake was left behind, when, the rainy season having commenced and the rivers being in flood, it became necessary to delay the march for days in order to throw bridges across the raging torrents. It was after they had penetrated finally to within the confines of Guatemala that the most toilsome work was encountered, in crossing a rocky region were the flint-stones were so sharp that all the horses and most of the men were lamed, eight of the former perishing by the way.

But at last, after enduring incredible privations, after losing hundreds of his men from famine and fatigue, after his own intrepid spirit had been brought to the verge of despair, Cortéz arrived upon the banks of a river which led to the sea, and at the mouth of which, he learned, Olid had established his settlement. Four days later the famished and exhausted army reached the sea —only to discover (what the reader already knows) that Olid had been assassinated, that the colony was in perfect accord with and subjected to Cortéz; that, in fact, his terrible journey, of more than fifteen hundred miles, with its consequent dangers, deaths, and toils, had been altogether needless, and far worse than useless.

The colony was already at starvation's point, and the advent of this famishing company necessitated foraging parties for the plunder of the natives. Confronted with this new danger, Cortéz acted with his wonted energy, and himself went on an exploring tour of nearly a month, in which he was severely wounded in the face by hostile Indians. Leaving Naco, where the unfortunate Olid had been executed, Cortéz sailed for Truxillo, the colony established by Las Casas, from which place he sent a long dispatch to the King of Spain and a valuable present of gold, which, according to Bernal Diaz, was taken from what remained of his valuable service of plate. In point of fact, little gold was discovered at that time on this coast, and no news arriving from Mexico, Cortéz was in deep dejection. When it did arrive, however, his friends, assembled outside the apartment to which he had retired, heard him groan in anguish, for the tidings were to the effect that not only had his whole party been given up as lost, but his own funeral services had been celebrated and his property sold to defray the expense of masses for his soul's salvation. The deputies whom he had left to act in his absence had arrested his own friends, the natives were encouraged to revolt, and the colony, in fact, was on the verge of civil war.

Little wonder that Cortéz was reduced to despair, and that

he "had gotten a Franciscan habit to be buried in." As soon as he had read the letters he "was overwhelmed with sorrow and distress," says Bernal Diaz del Castillo in his history. He "retired to his private apartment, where we could hear that he was suffering under the greatest agitation. He did not stir out for the entire day; at night he confessed, and ordered a mass for the ensuing morning, after which he called us together and read to us the intelligence he had received, and whereby we learned that it had been universally reported and believed in New Spain that we were all dead, and our properties had in consequence been sold by public auction."

Overwhelmed by the appalling tidings, Cortéz at first resolved to remain in Central America and apply himself to the colonization of the country; but at last, after he had listened to the arguments of his companions, he consented to return to Mexico. A vessel was made ready, and after several false starts he finally made the voyage without further mishap, though sick nigh unto death, landing near Vera Cruz on May 16, and making his triumphal entry into the City of Mexico on June 19, 1526.

The survivors of the expedition to Honduras, who had many a time cursed Cortéz as the author of their misfortunes, returned to Mexico overland and by the way of Guatemala. "I recollect," says blunt and faithful Bernal Diaz, "that we threw stones at the country we left behind us." They were met by one of Alvarado's captains, who conducted them to Old Guatemala, and thence to Olintepeque, where Alvarado's main force was quartered. By this time Alvarado had nearly accomplished the subjugation of the Guatemalan Indians, and after a few fights, in which the former companions of Cortéz joined very cheerfully, they all arrived at the frontiers of Mexico and Guatemala, whence they made their way to the City of Mexico, arriving there after an absence of two years and three months. Cortéz received them with tears of joy, and the inhabitants of the capital went forth to meet them; but after the novelty of their appearance was over, these faithful followers of the great captain were allowed to fall into neglect.

Alvarado "went to his residence in the fortress, of which he had been appointed alcalde," and later to Spain, where he was received with great favor by the emperor, and appointed governor of Guatemala. Returning to the scene of his conquest, he there ruled as might be expected of the man who had massacred the

Mexican nobles in 1520. His reign was a cruel and oppressive one; he devoted himself to gaining the gold of the country rather than to its advancement, and as many adventurers had followed him to Guatemala and Honduras, he had no difficulty in organizing various expeditions to Peru, where he came in conflict with Pizarro and obtained some of the Inca's treasure; and to northern Mexico, later on, where he received a wound that caused his death, in 1541, six years before the demise of his great commander, Cortéz.

In the preceding narrative of events that led up to the conquest and colonization of Guatemala and Honduras it is clearly shown that the impulse came from Mexico, to the northward. But that country itself had been brought to the attention of Europe through explorations sent out from Cuba, which was colonized by settlers from San Domingo. There were, then, several centers of conquest and colonization: first, San Domingo, from which had resulted Cuba; then Mexico, then Guatemala-Honduras; second, Darien, crossing which Vasco Nuñez de Balboa had discovered the Pacific Ocean in 1513; and, following after him, Pizarro accomplished the conquest of Peru in 1531-1532.

Balboa, it will hardly be necessary to remind the reader, was beheaded by Pedro Arias de Avila in 1517. After his death Avila continued his explorations along the Caribbean coast of Central America, attempting settlements at various points, and one of his agents, " whom he had sent to make conquests in Nicaragua and Leon," came in contact with Las Casas and Cortéz. Thus the explorers from two different centers of colonization met, the one party coming down from the north and the other from the south. Avila's agent, Captain Francisco Hernandez, had reduced the natives to obedience and established a colony. Having been warned that Avila would do to him as he had done to Balboa—whom he had decapitated, notwithstanding he was then married to his daughter—Hernandez desired to sever connection with that monster and establish relations with his sovereign in Spain through Cortéz. Called back to Mexico, Cortéz could not assist him, and Hernandez was soon after arrested by Avila's emissaries and beheaded. His fate is aside from the main current of this narrative; but these facts are related in order to show the trend of exploration, and to outline the chain of discoveries by which the country now known as Central America, and comprising the republics of Guatemala,

Honduras, Nicaragua, Salvador, and Costa Rica, was made known to the world.

On his fourth voyage, in 1502, Columbus first sighted the north coast of Honduras, sailing along which he finally doubled its eastern cape, which he called Gracias à Dios, or " Thanks to God," and thence coasted the Caribbean shores of Nicaragua, as well as of Costa Rica, which last he named the " Rich Coast," from the abundance of gold he found in possession of the natives. He was so impressed, in fact, that he attempted a settlement on the River Belen, which he was obliged to abandon the following year on account of the hostility of the Indians.

Twenty years later, as already related, Avila established settlements on this coast, and after the two groups of conquistadores had finally met and divided the territory between them the colonization of the central continent went on apace. It was from the first, and remained for three hundred years, a Spanish possession. The natives were allied to the Mayas of Yucatan, with an Aztec intrusion in Nicaragua, and the remains of a remote civilization are found in every republic, the monuments of Guatemala and Honduras being especially noteworthy. The Indians found in possession by the Spaniards fought fiercely and obstinately in defense of their native land, but in vain. They were finally overwhelmed by the invading Spaniards, but their valor and their virility are shown by their preponderance in the population of to-day. Like the Aztecs, and unlike the more effeminate natives of the West Indies, the aborigines of Central America survived the cruelties of the conquest, and their descendants occupy the greater portion of the land at the present time.

When, after three hundred years of occupation, the Spaniards were driven from the country, no such sanguinary scenes were enacted as attended the birth of freedom in Mexico. The Spanish yoke was thrown off easily, in some cases reluctantly, and the fighting began after 1821, in which year independence was declared. During Spanish supremacy Guatemala was governed as a captain-generalcy, which included fifteen provinces of Chiapas, Suchitepeque, Escuintla, Sonsonate, Salvador, Vera Paz, Petten, Chiquimula, Honduras, Costa Rica, Tontonicapan, Quesaltenango, Solola, Chimaltenango, and Sacatepeque, covering the entire territory now known as Central America, and since split up into five republics.

The reign of the viceroys in Guatemala, which during the Spanish régime included all of what is now known as Central America, was like that of the viceroyal period in Mexico, and presents few salient points of interest for the reader of to-day. It was cruel and extortionate, yet the common people, through long endurance of political ills, had become so accustomed to it that they were apathetic as to a change. When, however, they had a taste of freedom, all their warlike energies were aroused and the land was vexed with innumerable uprisings similar to those which disturbed Mexico during its period of discontent.

Shortly after the expulsion of the Spaniards a Central American federation was formed, which maintained a precarious existence until 1839, when it was overthrown by an ignorant Indian, Rafael Carrera, who practically founded the present Republic of Guatemala, over which he ruled with a rod of iron until his death in 1865. Soon after his demise rose to eminence Justo Rufino Barrios, who in 1867 led a band of revolutionary volunteers against the government and gained a final triumph in 1871. Two years later he became president and issued decrees proclaiming the freedom of the press and suppression of the religious orders. In 1876 he combated the reactionary party, which was assisted by Salvador and Honduras; a liberal constitution was proclaimed in 1879 and the next year Barrios was reëlected president for a term of six years. In February, 1885, he published a proclamation " intended to effect the union of all the Central American republics under one central government; but cabals on the part of the presidents of Honduras and Salvador frustrated this purpose and led to renewed warfare." Barrios was fatally wounded in an attack upon the forces of Salvador, when he had a son killed at his side, and died in Chalchuapa, April 2, 1885.

In 1887 a treaty was concluded at Guatemala between the five republics of Central America for " establishing an intimate relationship between them, and, by making the continuance of peace certain, to provide for their future fusion into one country." This desirable consummation has not yet been attained, but the mere fact of a convention with this aim in view was a long step in the direction of political union and permanent peace.

A further violation of the general peace conditions in Central America occurred when, on June 22, 1906, Guatemalan troops invaded Salvador, and on July 14, war was declared between Guatemala and Honduras. Three days later, however, the three countries thus interested, Guatemala, Honduras and Salvador agreed upon an armistice. This resulted in the signing of a treaty on July 20, on board the United States cruiser *Marblehead*. The present conditions of the country are excellent, the population being, in 1908, 1,882,992, with exports of $10,174,486, and imports of $7,316,574.

The political development and governmental status of all the Central American republics partook of the same general character. Honduras, as we have seen, was discovered by Columbus in 1502, settled by Cortéz and Avila twenty to thirty years later, and, like Guatemala, was held by Spain three hundred years, when, in 1823, it revolted and joined the Central American Union the same year, becoming independent in 1839. Nearly thirty years of strife followed the declaration of independence, and it is only within the last part of the nineteenth century that the country has enjoyed anything like a settled condition of affairs.

In spite of this, however, troubles arose with the other Central American States, and Honduras has been at war with Guatemala and Salvador within the past couple of years. As yet a general peace has not been secured, through which these five States can work together in harmony, to the advancement of all. It is the hope of the diplomatists of them all, as well as the policy of the United States, to secure such a treaty that will be equally binding. Honduras is one of the smallest numerically, containing only 500,136 population. Its exports during 1908 were $1,834,060, while its imports during the same time were $2,829,979.

Salvador, the smallest, but the most thickly populated, of the five republics, was originally known as Cuscatlan, and was conquered by Pedro de Alvarado after a prolonged contest in the year 1525-1526. Throwing off the Spanish fetters in 1821, and joining the confederacy in 1823, since 1839 it has been practically independent, maintaining itself as a republic since 1853. It has taken an active part in the internecine strife which for so long a period prevented progress in the central continent, seeming to desire a "finger in every pie," and in 1890 resenting with arms the proposed union between the different states by a brief war with Guatemala. The republic has participated in the various disturbances of Central America, but in spite of this, with a population of 1,116,253, it has a revenue of $18,131,400, and its expenditures for 1908 were

$18,308,564. The exports for 1908 were $15,163,460, while the imports for that same year were $3,440,721.

Nicaragua early felt the impulse of Spanish exploration northward from the Isthmus, its city of Granada having been founded in 1524, and various settlements made on both its coasts. Occupying a commanding position, with its territory extending from the Caribbean to the Pacific, Nicaragua had a peculiar value in the eyes

CENTRAL AMERICA

of the Spaniards; but they were finally expelled in 1821, after three centuries of dominance, and from 1823 to 1839 the country was a member of the federation of States. Revolutions convulsed the republic for a long time after its assertion of independence, and war was carried on, not only with Guatemala and Costa Rica, but with Great Britain; with the last named on account of its protectorate over the Mosquito Coast, which it held during two centuries and then relinquished to Nicaragua in 1860. Between 1855 and

THE FIVE REPUBLICS 441

1860 Walker, the American filibuster, took part in the contest in Nicaragua between two parties in dissension, and created a strange rôle which he played to the end.

Nicaragua was of special interest to the United States in connection with the construction of an inter-oceanic canal, presenting as it did an alternative project to that of Panama. Several cuts across the continent were proposed when the United States began its surveys, as at Tehuantepec, Nicaragua, Panama, and Darien; but it was at last brought down to a question of feasibility between Nicaragua and Panama, the many advantages in favor of the latter resulting in its selection in 1902.

Nicaragua, like all its sister republics in the central continent, possesses a mountainous country, but with a deeper depression between the Caribbean and Pacific than any of the others. It also has every variety of climate, with consequent abundance of vegetable productions, its climatic changes ranging from the heat of the coast country or *tierra caliente,* through the templada, to the fria, or cold region of the mountains.

It is in the main a healthful country; but, being the home of volcanoes (as indeed all Central America may be called), there is always danger to be apprehended from terrestrial disturbances; aside from the possibility of which, however, the Nicaragua project had many indisputable advantages. These advantages may be summed up as climatic, hydrographic, topographic; the large and deep lake of Nicaragua, at an elevation of over one hundred feet above sea-level, affords a perpetual supply of water, easily controlled.

During the past few years Nicaragua has been before the public on more than one occasion. During the latter part of 1906 it had trouble with Honduras, but the Powers insisted upon a settlement by arbitration, and matters continued in abeyance until February 19, 1907, when Honduras sent troops against the Nicaraguan forces on the frontier, and was defeated. Nicaragua pressed the vantage gained, taking the Honduras capital on March 26. The United States then intervened, pursuing its policy of urging peace between the Central American countries, and on September 17 a protocol was finally signed at Washington to prepare a peace treaty. This brought about such amicable relations between Nicaragua and Honduras that on July 8, 1908, troops were ordered from the former country to aid Honduras in putting down a rebellion. In the meanwhile, affairs between Nicaragua and Salvador had reached such a pitch that April 16, 1909, preparations were begun for war against Salvador. Nicaragua also became involved in other directions, finally having trouble within its own borders with insurrectionists. It was in connection with the latter that Nicaragua incurred the displeasure of the United States. Two Americans, Leroy Cannon and Leonard Groce were executed by the Nicaraguan government November 18. The United States government immediately demanded an explanation, ordering two warships to Nicaraguan ports. On December 1 Secretary Knox dismissed the representative of Nicaragua from Washington, notifying that government it would be held responsible for the death of the two American citizens. The Nicaraguan government claimed that these two men were numbered among the insurgents, were captured and executed according to the rules of warfare. The feeling against President Zelaya, however, was so great that he resigned, and on December 20, José Madriz was elected president by the Nicaraguan Congress. This was not accepted by General Estrada, and the United States did not favor the selection. Former President Zelaya left Nicaragua on Christmas day, and after going to Mexico, made his way to Paris, where he is now engaged in trying to formulate a defense for his actions, particularly those in connection with the execution of the two Americans. In the meanwhile the new government of Nicaragua exonerated the members of the court martial that executed Cannon and Groce, upon the grounds that they acted according to Zelaya's orders. Matters were still, in the spring of 1910, in an unsettled state. The claims of the United States had not been satisfied. Civil War was raging in Nicaragua, and until that was settled, little satisfaction could be obtained. While all this internal trouble was convulsing the country, the Central American Peace Conference had been in session at San Salvador. Among other measures, it had adopted the gold standard, a system of tariff reciprocity for all five of the countries, the unification of the consular services abroad, and the compulsory use of the metric system.

Costa Rica, like Nicaragua, occupies the entire breadth of the continent between sea and ocean. Its history is practically that of the others, with only local variations on the word "pronunciamiento." During its brief existence it has enjoyed nearly a dozen different "constitutions."

It was named the "Rich Coast" by Columbus, but it was not until three hundred years later that its mines were really developed and revealed their wonderful riches. The same may be said of all the republics, which are similar in their natural resources, with a tropical vegetation in the main, with vast mineral wealth being increasingly exploited, with a vigorous population chiefly devoted to agriculture (when not in revolution) and comprising more Indians and mixed peoples than whites. This population, in 1908, was 311,176; the revenue for that year was $7,916,475, but the expenditures were $9,191,450. The exports for 1908 were $1,870,-820, while the imports were $1,511,627.

Costa Rica suffered a most serious disaster in May, 1910, when Cartago, for the second time in its history, was destroyed by an earthquake. The dispute between Costa Rica and Panama regarding their boundary claims was at last referred in October, 1912, to a commission to settle.

In Nicaragua in 1910 President Madriz was finally defeated by the revolutionists and compelled to retire to Costa Rica, where he shortly afterward died. General Estrada succeeded as Provisional President and was himself succeeded in October, 1911, by Senor Diaz as President for the full term.

In August, 1912, another revolution broke out. This was headed by General Mena, who seized the forts at Managua and took possession of the city of Granada. On August 6, 1912, the United States gunboat *Annapolis* landed 100 marines at Corinto and sent them to the capital, Managua. On August 24, 2,000 additional American troops were sent to Corinto. Peace was reestablished on October 9, 1912.

The internal and economic conditions of Nicaragua suffered severely from the constant revolutions. By an arrangement with American banking firms Nicaragua was able to resume payments in October, 1912, on her national debts. A further payment was made in the early months of 1913.

In Salvador General Fernando Figuero, who had been elected president in 1907, was succeeded by Dr. Manuel Enrique Araujo on March 1, 1911. Not only had general trade conditions improved under the Figuero administration, but substantial advancement was made along many different lines. On November 5, 1911, the Centennial Anniversary of the State's independence was celebrated.

The finances at the end of 1912 were in a most satisfactory

state. Large payments have been made on the public debt. All
pay accounts of the army and navy were made to date and have
been regularly maintained ever since. All diplomatic and consular salaries too were paid in full as well as all arrearages of whatever class of governmental salaries and accounts were paid to date.
By 1913 the revenue of the State had increased over sixteen per
cent while the national debt had been reduced by nine per cent.

In Guatemala Señor Manuel Estrada Cabrera at the end of
his second term was reëlected President for a further term of six
years from March 15, 1911. On December 8, 1911, the convention
concluded between Guatemala and Honduras on the boundary question was further extended until March 1, 1914.

Renewed efforts were made in November, 1912, to compel
Guatemala to make some settlement on its foreign debt. A parcel
post was inaugurated early in 1912. The new national military
academy was opened on June 30, 1912, and the establishment of
a school of aviation was authorized.

The Guatemalan railways were consolidated with certain ones
of Salvador and merged into the International Railways of Central
America by a group of American bankers. The Pan-American
railroad was completed as far as Mariscal on the Guatemalan
border from the Mexican side and on the Guatemalan side to
Las Cruces.

Honduras in 1911 was again in a state of political unrest.
President Miguel Davila was forced to resign and was succeeded
by Provisional President Dr. Francisco Bonilla, a former president.
Bonilla, who had been a refugee in the United States for four years,
was chosen President on November 3, 1911, for a term of four
years. He assumed office February 1, 1912.

The year 1912 was a more prosperous one for the republic
than many former ones. The customs receipts from all sources,
especially at Puerto Cortez, showed a good increase.

The government established a school for girls and a school
for teaching the manufacture of straw hats at Tegucigalpa. Congress also helped education by founding thirteen additional scholar-
ships for Honduran students abroad. Six of these will be sent
to study engineering in the United States.

The foreign trade of Nicaragua during 1913 was very good,
the imports being $5,770,000, while exports were $7,700,000, the
highest amount reached in ten years. In 1914 the foreign trade fell

off greatly, the imports being $4,100,000, and exports $5,000,000, coffee and dyewoods being the largest items of export.

In Guatemala the imports during 1913 amounted to $10,000,-000 with exports of $14,449,000. In 1914 the imports reached $9,331,000 with exports of $12,750,000. Coffee is Guatemala's chief export.

In Salvador the foreign trade during 1913 and 1914 was good. The great products of the country, silver and gold, coffee, indigo, sugar, rubber, and hides, all showed increasing production.

Costa Rica also saw two prosperous years in 1913 and 1914. The total foreign trade amounted in 1913 to $19,211,049, while in 1914 it increased slightly. Bananas and coffee continue to head the exports, but the products of the mines as well as the valuable woods form a substantial part of the total foreign trade.

Honduras had in 1913 a total foreign trade of $8,432,000, while in 1914 it amounted to over $9,000,000. Bananas are the principal source of the exports, but coffee, cocoanuts, rubber, and sarsaparilla are growing in importance.

HISTORY OF
THE WEST INDIES

HISTORY OF
THE WEST INDIES

Chapter I

EXPLORATION AND SETTLEMENT. 1492-1793

IN that vast territory comprising the West Indies, Mexico, and
Central America, the United States should be particularly interested, if merely on account of relative contiguity and possible
commercial supremacy. In all those countries combined there is
an approximate total population of sixty million, with exports and
imports aggregating more than a billion dollars annually.

With but few exceptions, throughout the whole extent of that
vast area covered by the two continents and the Caribbean islands
the language generally spoken is Spanish, or structurally Latin, like
the French of Haiti and the Portuguese of Brazil. Hence this
region has well been termed "Latin America," the Latin-Ameri-
cans and their numerous relations of mixed bloods being everywhere predominant. And yet, strange as it may appear, there is
now little sympathy with Spain among these peoples having racial
and linguistic affinities with her. She is regarded as the mother
country of the greater portion, it is true, but the prevailing indifference may be attributed to the fact that anciently she treated
her American colonials more as if she stood to them in the relation
of the proverbial step-mother. At all events history shows that
she was a most unnatural parent, treating her children with great
inhumanity, and carrying on, through three hundred years and
more, a policy of oppression that resulted in nearly all Spaniards
becoming objects of aversion, even of detestation.

The "Gachupines," or peninsular Spanish, left behind them a
legacy of hatred that has survived to the present time, and no attempt on the part of Spain to rehabilitate herself or to establish
an *entente cordiale* with the peoples of her long-lost territories can
ever succeed.

The nineteenth century was a sad one for Spain. At its opening her sway practically extended over nearly all the territory (except that occupied by Brazil) lying beyond the southern boundary line of the United States. At its ending she found herself reduced to the ownership of but a beggarly portion of her colonial empire, having lost by the war of 1898 alone possessions in America and Asia of an aggregate area of 165,000 miles and a population of more than 10,000,000.

The first quarter of that century witnessed the severance from Spain of all her Mexican, Central American, and South American colonies, besides Florida and the Louisiana Territory. During the reign of weak and vicious Ferdinand VII. she lost all that remained of the Americas save Cuba and Puerto Rico. Mexico raised the standard of revolt in 1808, Venezuela in 1810, Chile, Peru, and the rest following swiftly after, until nothing remained except the islands from which she was expelled by the Americans in 1898.

Of the nine independent republics and twenty dependencies comprised in Mexico, Central America, and the West Indies, with aggregate areas of a million square miles and a population approximating twenty-four million, there is no more interesting country than Cuba, the largest and most populous island in the West Indies.

Discovered in October, 1492, on the 28th of that month, by the renowned navigator Christopher Columbus, while pursuing his first voyage to the New World, it was first named by him after Princess Juana. It was also called Fernandina; but its aboriginal name has persisted, and finally survives, most fortunately, for as Cuba the island is universally known to-day.

Generously endowed by nature, this "Pearl of the Antilles" early attracted the attention of the Spaniards; but it was not until 1508 that Cuba was circumnavigated (by Sebastian de Ocampo), Columbus having died in the belief that it was a continent.

Through the discovery of gold in Hispaniola (now known as Haiti—San Domingo) the settlements in that island took precedence of those in Cuba by nearly twenty years. But as soon as the colonists settled in the latter island they took a firm hold on the soil and in a few years were far more prosperous than those in the sister isle (where the quality of permanency was lacking), and which soon went into decadence.

The first expeditions for the exploration and colonization of

Mexico started from Cuba, and when the great natural advantages of this island became known, and especially its fine port of Havana, the upbuilding of the colony went on rapidly and uninterruptedly. It was actually colonized by Diego Velasquez, who was sent from Hispaniola for that purpose by Don Diego Columbus, son of the great admiral and then viceroy of the Indies. His expedition landed on the south coast of Cuba in 1511, not far from the entrance to Guantanamo Bay; but his first actual settlement was at Baracoa, the next year, 1512, where an old castle is still pointed out as one of his forts.

Santiago and Trinidad were founded respectively in 1514 and 1515, and a settlement was begun, also on the south coast, at or near the present site of Batabano, which was called San Cristobal de la Habana. The present city Havana, however (the since famous and yet flourishing capital of Cuba), had no existence previous to the year (1519) in which Cortéz set sail from its harbor for Mexico, though that harbor had been discovered by Ocampo in 1508.

With Diego Velasquez sailed Hernando Cortéz and Bartolomé de las Casas, both of whom afterward loomed largely in the history of America, the former as the conqueror of Mexico, or New Spain, and the latter as the first "defender" of the Indians. Not far from Santiago (from whose port Cortéz first set forth Mexicoward) Las Casas at one time held possession of an encomienda of Indians, and there had his eyes opened to the atrocities perpetrated by his countrymen upon the innocent natives.

Thus Cuba had much to do with the conquest of the continent, after the decline of Hispaniola, for not only were all the Mexican expeditions sent from that island—under Grijalva, Cordova, Cortéz, Narvaez—but also those for the conquest of Florida, most noteworthy among which was the expedition commanded by Hernando de Soto in 1539.

The aborigines suffered the fate of those in Hispaniola and the Bahamas—that is, they were soon exterminated. In Mexico and Central America, as well as in Florida and some of the smaller isles of the West Indies, the Indians were either too virile or too numerous to succumb altogether to Spanish cruelties, barbarous and long-continued as they were; but in Cuba, also in Jamaica, Hispaniola, and Puerto Rico, they became practically extinct with the century.

The Siboneys, as the Cuban aborigines were called, were a remarkably fine people, with few faults and many virtues. They occupied the greater portion of the island, dwelling particularly along the coasts, and subsisted by means of fishing and agriculture of a rude sort. Columbus found them on the north coast, near the port of Gibara, the hills back of which are supposed to have been his first Cuban landfall. He first obtained from them tobacco, hammocks, and yucca, or cassava, it is believed, and in Cuba first looked upon vast fields of maize or Indian corn. Sailing around the east end of Cuba, departing from Cape Maisi for Hispaniola or Haiti, he returned to Spain from the Bay of Samana in San Domingo.

Some of his crew subsequently came over with Velasquez in 1511, and were among the first colonists; though the attempt at colonization was made long after the island was discovered. Their pursuits (after having harried the natives out of existence) were at first chiefly pastoral, nearly or quite seventy years elapsing before the cultivation was undertaken of those since great staples of Cuba, sugar-cane and tobacco. In place of the natives (who were entirely extinct in Cuba before the sixteenth century had ended) negro slaves imported from Africa proved more enduring and tenacious of life. They thrived under Spanish cruelties, in fact, and to-day their descendants comprise a large proportion of the Cuban population.

Cuba's history after its conquest by the Spaniards may be found, as it were, in epitome, in that of Havana and Santiago, which have been thriving cities from the first, each possessing a magnificent harbor. Each city, also, was a favorite object of attack by the buccaneers who infested the Caribbean Sea and Gulf of Mexico. Thrice during the sixteenth century Havana was at the mercy of foreign invaders, French and Dutch, and was threatened by Sir Francis Drake, whose favorite coasting-ground was between Cuba and the Spanish Main. In 1624 Havana was attacked by the Dutch, and in 1762 was taken by the English, assisted by colonials from New York and New England.

The depredations of the buccaneers, who made their rendezvous at Tortuga, on the north coast of Haiti, and later in Jamaica, during the seventeenth century, were exceeded only by the devastations by hurricanes and fires. But, possessing the finest harbor opening to the Gulf of Mexico, Havana easily acquired and maintained supremacy as the " Key of the New World." It took the title of " city " in 1592, and steadily gained in wealth and population, until to-day it is the largest and most flourishing place in the West Indies. It was a walled city for more than two hundred years, or from 1655 to 1880, but has long since overleaped its restrictive bounds of stone and mortar and spread out into the open country.

Its chief fortification, Moro Castle, whose construction was begun more than three hundred years ago, was first reduced by the British in 1762, just one hundred years after the Moro of Santiago had been blown up by Lord Winsor, who took and sacked the latter city in 1662, carrying off its church bells and vast treasure.

Santiago, like Havana, was the object of frequent attacks by buccaneers and pirates, and as early as 1537 its land-locked harbor was the scene of a desperate but chivalrous battle between a French and a Spanish privateer. Beneath the waters of that harbor, according to tradition, lie the ribs of a galleon which once sailed with the ill-fated Spanish armada; and, as already stated, a great captain who assisted at the defeat of the armada, Sir Francis Drake, was often seen in Caribbean waters.

Sufficient has been noted to bring to mind the fact that the history of Cuba was for centuries a troublous one, even before the Cubans themselves found voice and proclaimed to the world their long-endured and terrible wrongs. During those centuries, and until within a comparatively recent period, Cuban soil was cultivated by the labor of slaves, and Cuban revenues were plundered by rapacious Spanish officials. All that time, and under the most outrageous oppressions, even, a native population (the " Creoles ") was growing up that eventually became entirely distinct from the ruling people.

These " Creoles " spoke the same language as their masters, the " Peninsular Spaniards "; they possessed the same characteristics, but most of them were of mixed blood, in their veins that of the negro, in some instances of the Indian, mingling with the Spanish. By the " Peninsulars " they were looked down upon and treated as inferiors, and for more than three centuries they submitted, as a people, to oppression and extortion in every shape. They were patient, long-suffering, and even during the period of political disquietude in Spain, when Charles IV., Ferdinand, and

Godoy were squabbling among themselves, the islanders remained loyal to the mother-land.

Though Spain lost Mexico, Venezuela, Chile, Peru—all Central and South America, in fact—Cuba and Puerto Rico kept faith with the Spaniards and remained true to the Peninsula. The " ever-faithful isles," they were called by the Spaniards, who also regarded them fondly as the ever-prolific and ever-to-be-oppressed as well!

Chapter II

CONSPIRACIES AND REVOLUTIONS IN CUBA
1793-1896

THE first disturbances may have had their incitement in the great immigration from Haiti, when the settlers of that island, mainly French—such as were not massacred by the Haitians—sought refuge in Cuba, to the number of 30,000. This was in 1793-1804, when, in the latter year, the total immigration was swelled, it is estimated, to nearly or quite 200,000 by French and Spanish settlers from Louisiana and San Domingo. Through these accessions the island received a great impetus by the introduction of expert coffee and sugar-cane planters, most of the latter coming from Louisiana.

During the latter part of the eighteenth century there were occasional sporadic uprisings in Cuba, the number increasing after the opening of the nineteenth, induced by the severity of the government, as administered by Captains-General Someruelos and Apodaca. One of these outbursts, that instigated by José Antonio Aponte in 1812, and directly traceable to the example and influence of Haiti, was repressed with relentless severity, the leader and eight accomplices meeting death by hanging.

The very first Cubans " sacrificed in the sacred cause of independence," as the native historian relates,[1] were Francisco Aguero y Velasco and Andrés Manuel Sanchez, who, while fomenting an agitation in the country districts, were captured and hanged, in 1826. That same year one of the principal questions before the famous Panama Congress initiated by the great liberator, Simon Bolivar, related to the emancipation of Cuba and Puerto Rico from Spanish bondage, but owing to the tacit opposition of the United States (as understood by the representatives of such Latin-American States as were gathered there) nothing was done.

In 1830 occurred the insurrection of the " Black Eagle " (Aquila negra), but there was no greater disturbance of a revolu-

[1] "*Nociones de Historia de Cuba*," Havana, 1904.

tionary character until 1844, when a conspiracy was unearthed in which hundreds of natives, both white and colored, were involved. Many were imprisoned, others were banished, and the list of Cuban martyrs was augmented by the shooting of the poet, " Placido," Santiago Pimienta, Andrés Dodge, and several less prominent insurrectionists at Matanzas.

Having submitted for centuries to Spanish oppression, the natives of Cuba were long in making up their minds to fight for freedom, and it must be admitted that the first great aggressive movements looking to that end were initiated by strangers, who entered the island, or made attempts to do so, and took up arms for a people too supine to battle for themselves. The first of the great " filibusteros " who landed an insurrectionary expedition on the Cuban coast was a naturalized American named Narciso Lopez a Venezuelan who had risen to high rank in the Spanish army, having fought the colonists in South America and the Carlists in Spain. His first expedition was a failure, for, after landing at Cardenas on May 19, 1850, he was compelled to retreat, was arrested, and tried on his return to the United States; but, being acquitted, he organized another expedition, which had a measure of success. On August 12, 1851, Lopez landed this second expedition, consisting of nearly 500 men, at Playitas, near Bahia Honda, where he committed the error of dividing his forces, and was defeated in the battle that ensued with the Spaniards, captured, taken to Havana, and publicly garroted on September 1.

There were only five Cubans in the first Lopez expedition, not twice as many in the second, and the latter was blotted out by the Spaniards without a native hand having been raised in behalf of the gallant Americans who had come to free the Cubanos from oppression. In the castle of Atarés, which still guards Havana's inner harbor, fifty " filibusteros " (including brave young Critten-den, son of an American senator) were summarily shot on August 16, 1851. Twelve at a time, two ranks deep, the foremost kneeling to receive the bullets sped by Spanish soldiers, they were foully murdered and then mutilated.

Twenty-two years later, in 1873, a similar fate befell the captain of the *Virginius,* who was shot, together with fifty of his men, at the slaughter-house in Santiago. And the United States bore with insult and Spanish contumely almost without a protest. Verbal protests were uttered, it is true, but the Spaniards cared no whit for these. The only protests they could understand, and the only ones they were capable of heeding, were such as came from the cannon's mouth in the summer of 1898. They were then compelled, though much against their wills, and they have ever since understood, for they were thoroughly whipped and cowed. Since then, indeed, has Spain changed for the better.

The Cubans began to think for themselves, and to think about fighting for themselves, about forty years ago, and the protracted conflict known as the "Ten Years' War," beginning in 1868, was the result. A truce was concluded in 1878, and for the next seventeen years the Cubans were comparatively quiet, but by no means content, for they had been basely betrayed by the Spaniards. They were in a continually increasing state of ferment, and their disaffection culminated in February, 1895, in the proclamation of the republic.

When in 1878 the Cuban congress had signed the treaty of peace with Spain, there were several active leaders who would not accept the situation and who entered their most energetic protests, among them being those intrepid fighters, the Maceos. Of the Maceo brothers (survivors of eleven sons of a patriot-father) two won imperishable fame in Cuba; and the same may be said of that courageous, humane, and discreet old fighter, Maximo Gomez, who received the acclaim of all patriotic Cubans at the end of the war. Gomez, however, is not a Cuban, though the greatest man in the island for whose liberties he fought during so many years.

What the outcome of the rebellion of 1895 would have been had not the United States intervened no one may say with certainty; but while such "bush fighting" as the patriots carried on served to keep the Spaniards in a state of constant irritation, and might have been maintained indefinitely, still it never could have been efficacious in ridding the island of the tyrants, for the forts and coast cities were impregnable to Cuban attacks.

Proclaimed in September, 1895, the Cuban constitution, modeled mainly after that of the United States, was maintained in the interior of Puerto Principe province. At first the rebellion was confined to the eastern end of Cuba and certain isolated sections of the interior, where the patriots found secure hiding-places among the hills and mountains; but at two or three different times Gomez and Maceo made wonderful marches between the hills of

Puerto Principe and those of Pinar del Rio, the western province of the island.

Up to the time of their first grand sweep over two-thirds the length of the island, performed by Gomez and his men (when they traversed five of Cuba's six provinces and covered about six hundred miles, all the way burning and plundering, not only sugar plantations but towns and villages) the Spaniards claimed that the insurgent outbreak was only " local"; but after that this claim was no longer advanced.

It is true that in the main the insurgents hid themselves in the forests and mountains, emerging only to plunder and destroy, and precipitately retreating to their strongholds at the first appearance of the enemy; but in January, 1896, the half-clad, imperfectly armed commands of Gomez and Maceo performed their astounding feat of sweeping the island almost from end to end and driving the surprised Spaniards to their retreats in the fortified cities.

Expectation was then all agog, and almost anything might have been believed of the insurgent Cubans. On the one hand, it was asserted that they would compel the surrender of the capital itself; on the other, that when the Spaniards got them in the right place they would sally forth and drive them into the sea. Neither calamity eventuated, however, for cautious old Gomez knew better than to attack impregnable Havana, and he also avoided all other strong Spanish places, confining his attentions to the vast fields of sugar-cane, which he set on fire, with a view to removing a profitable source of Spanish revenue. His real object was only disclosed when, having gained possession of a small but deep harbor in Pinar del Rio province, he held it long enough to receive expected supplies from the United States by the famous *Bermuda* expedition.

By this means, capturing and holding for a time a weakly defended or unfrequented harbor until supplies could reach them from the north, the insurgents received greatly needed arms, medicines, and ammunition, and then effected their retreat without seeming to have been in the least impeded by the Spaniards. The latter had tried to pen their foes in the eastern part of the island by constructing trochas across the island from north to south, at one place, between Jucaro and San Fernando, a distance of more than fifty miles, having built a line of block-houses, two hundred in number, connected by means of barbed wire entanglements and furnished not only with garrisons, but with electric search-lights and telephones, besides a parallel railway. Notwithstanding this " invincible barrier "—as the Spaniards considered it—the insurgents " made no bones " of crossing from one side of the island to the other whenever they felt disposed to do so.

It was from the clamor that ensued from this achievement, and from an engagement in which the then Captain-General Campos was worsted, that the latter was recalled, and in his place the ineffable Weyler sent to Cuba, arriving at Havana in February, 1896. This bloodthirsty Spaniard with a German name, General Valeriano Weyler, had already achieved unenviable fame in Cuba by his atrocities, and it was a most unfortunate move on the part of the Spanish Government, this sending out to govern the Cubans one whom they cordially detested. The insurgents thereby gained the accession of many extremists, who would otherwise have been only lukewarm in their adhesion to the patriotic cause.

The immediate acts of " Butcher " Weyler, the new captain-general and practically the viceroy in Cuba, did not belie his record, for his edicts partook of that barbarous character which his worst enemies had ascribed to him. He was a braggart as well as a butcher, for he boasted that the rebels would be swept from the island forthwith, and that the grinding of cane would commence within a month after he landed at Havana; but neither was the grinding of cane permitted by the insurgents, nor were they decimated to any appreciable extent.

All the world now knows what Weyler did: that he waged war upon defenseless youth and woman, that he starved to death the non-combatants, tortured the reconcentrados, desolated the fairest spots in Cuba. His atrocities roused the people, and swiftly after his arrival followed the concurrent resolution of the United States Senate and House, recognizing the belligerency of the Cuban insurgents. This resolution was promptly transmitted to President Cleveland; but by his non-action was made of value only as an expression of popular feeling in the United States at that time, which was that the sympathies of the American people were with the insurgent Cubans.

Chapter III

THE AMERICAN INTERVENTION IN CUBA. 1896-1898

THE Spaniards made their most important capture, which was in fact the first of the kind, when they took the American schooner *Competitor* in the act of landing arms and reinforcements for the insurgents on the coast of Pinar del Rio. The harbor in which she was taken is one of the numerous indentations on the north coast of that province, and very near to that in which the *Bermuda* made her successful landing. This incident threatened to lead to international complications, owing to the fact that two American citizens aboard the vessel were condemned to death by the court-martial convened by Weyler immediately on the arrival of the prize in Havana harbor. The decision of the court was sent to Madrid for revision, however, and all difficulties for the time averted.

The same month of April, 1896, Antonio Maceo gained a brilliant victory over the Spanish battalion " Alfonso XIII.," which had been sent out from Havana for the express purpose of punishing the bold insurgent. But for the opportune arrival of a Spanish war vessel off the point on the coast where the insurgents had compelled the battalion to take refuge, the Spanish force would have been annihilated. Maceo had been left in command of Pinar del Rio, while Gomez had broken through the much-vaunted trocha a second time, and countermarched to his favorite stronghold in Puerto Principe province. Thus early in the campaign these skilled commanders, Gomez and Maceo, showed that they had determined to play the " waiting game," by much marching and little fighting wearing out the enemy, and saving their precious ammunition, which was difficult to obtain.

In this summary of the first actions of the war but scant justice can be done to individual acts of heroism, though they were relatively numerous. What was rather unusual among the Latin peoples, some women were occasionally actively engaged in the field, while many of the patriots played the part of heroes.

Though the Spaniards rarely succeeded in bringing the Cubans to an engagement, they cannot be accused of cowardice or an inclination to shirk their arduous duties. Spain sent thither the flower of her troops; but most of the soldiers were very young and even immature. At the opening of the war Spain's military force in the West Indies, including 6000 men in Puerto Rico, was estimated at more than 100,000 strong. The Spanish soldiers fought well, but with an intuitive perception that they were opposing a righteous cause, which would in the end prevail. On the other hand, the insurgents had staked their all for hearth and home, autonomy, liberty!

In a swift review of the relative performances of the contestants, many anomalies present themselves, the greatest anomaly, perhaps, being the Spaniard himself, who, though personally the " pink of courtesy," had been for years aiding and abetting governmental practices which were the outcome and expression of tyrannical bureaucracy, like an " Old Man of the Sea " fastened upon a naturally high-minded and generous people. It was to this governmental Moloch that the common people of Spain offered the best blood of their youth and manhood.

What were the real feelings and animating sentiments of the Spanish soldiers appear in the testimonial they addressed to their American opponents after the surrender of Santiago: " You have fought us as men, face to face, and with great courage—a quality which we had not met with during the three years we have carried on this war against a people without religion, without morals, without conscience, and of doubtful origin, who could not confront an enemy, but, in concealment, shot their noble victims from ambush and then immediately fled! "

One of the inexplicable things of this war was that, though the Spaniards had, long before its commencement, announced a complete system of blockade, to be enforced by ninety gunboats and steam launches, they could not effectually prevent the filibusters from landing reinforcements and supplies almost at will.

Another was that, while the insurgents ranged throughout the interior of the island, reaching out to the coast on either side whenever they considered it necessary to establish communication with the outside world, the Spaniards confined their efforts to the guarding of the trochas and fortified cities of the coast, such as Havana, Matanzas, and Santiago.

The time had come when the cause of Cuba attracted world-wide attention, and when the oppressions of Spain bore so hard upon the unfortunate islanders that armed intervention seemed imperative. Still, Spain might yet have escaped the immediate penalty of her many sins (having recalled Weyler and substituted Blanco, and endeavored to placate the United States with specious promises) had not that crowning horror, the treacherous destruction of the battle-ship *Maine* in Havana harbor, swept away all thought of compromise.

It was on February 15, 1898, that the *Maine* was blown up, while lying at the buoy in Havana harbor to which she was assigned by the Spanish captain of the port. Although Spanish authorities declared the disaster due to the negligence of her sailors, subsequent investigation conclusively proved that the battle-ship was blown up from the outside, and few Americans ever believed that Spain was not, at least indirectly, culpable for the terrible catastrophe which caused the death of 260 American sailors. More than two months elapsed, however, before President McKinley, after " exhausting every effort to relieve the intolerable condition of affairs at our doors," finally sent the ultimatum to Spain. War was virtually declared on April 21, but nearly every day between the date of the sinking of the *Maine* and the demanding by the Spanish minister at Washington of his passports was fraught with important events.

During the month of March naval preparations had been pushed with energy; the "national defense bill" appropriating $50,000,000 was passed by the House on the 7th; on the 28th the official *Maine* inquiry report was sent to Congress; on April 9 Consul General Lee was recalled from Havana; on the 21st Minister Woodford at Madrid was given his passports, and Admiral Sampson's fleet was ordered to blockade the Cuban ports. On the 23d President McKinley issued his first call for volunteers (125,-000), and on the 24th England declared her neutrality, followed four days later by the chief governments of Europe and America. On the 25th Commodore Dewey sailed from Hong Kong to his glorious victory seven days later in Manila Bay, May 1.

The first shot of the war is said to have been fired from the U. S. gunboat *Nashville,* while effecting the capture of a Spanish merchantman, near Key West, on April 22; but the first action was off Matanzas, on the 27th. The first Americans killed were Ensign

Bagley and four companions, in an engagement off Cardenas, May 11; while the first land engagement occurred the next day, when the *Gussie* expedition, commanded by Captain J. H. Dorst, of the Fourth Cavalry, landed the first detachment of United States troops on Cuban soil. This landing was effected near Cabanas, about forty miles west of Havana, and "within fifteen minutes after disembarkation our force met and repulsed a Spanish regiment (1200 strong) and killed the colonel and several of his men." [1] This expedition, however, failed in its purpose and returned to Key West. On the 18th the transport *Florida* sailed from Tampa with soldiers to aid the Cubans, and a million dollars' worth of ammunition and supplies; from this time forth munitions of war being supplied to the insurgents in accordance with the Senate bill of May 5.

It was on May 19 that Admiral Cervera's squadron was definitely located at Santiago, after its will-of-the-wisp wanderings across the Atlantic, and henceforth, until near the end of the war, the port and city of Santiago figured most prominently as the theater of great events.

On May 31 the steamer *Florida* arrived at Key West, after having delivered to the insurgents 310 men, 33,000 rifles, and a large quantity of ammunition. On June I Admiral Sampson took command of the fleet blockading Santiago, and on the 3d Lieutenant Hobson and seven companions sank the collier *Merrimac* at the mouth of the harbor, themselves being taken prisoners immediately afterward. The bombardment of Santiago's outer fortifications began the first week in June, and was continued intermittently during the siege, but without any appreciable result. On June 8 over 16,000 men left Tampa under General Shafter, with Santiago as the objective, and on the 10th 600 American marines landed near the entrance to Guantanamo Bay, where, two days later, they repelled an attack by Spaniards, with some loss.

The landing of troops under General Shafter began on June 21, at Daiquiri, about seventeen miles eastward from Santiago harbor, and was completed on the 23d, an engagement between the cavalry and Spanish troops taking place on the 24th, at Las Guasimas, or Siboney.

The heights of San Juan and the fort at El Caney were stormed and taken one week later, on July 1, and attempts of the Spaniards to retake these positions were repulsed. Shafter's

[1] R. A. Alger, "Spanish-American War."

army landed in Cuba June 22-24. The surrender of the Spanish garrison at Santiago was procured July 16 (the formal capitulation next day). From June 24 to July 16 represents the length of time covered by the siege and actual hostilities. The losses in battle during the entire period, including the engagements of Las Guasimas, El Caney, and San Juan Ridge, amounted to a total of but 243 killed, officers and men, and 1445 wounded.[2]

July 3 was made memorable by the attempted escape of Cervera's squadron from Santiago harbor, and its total destruction by Admiral Sampson's blockading fleet. On this occasion the Spaniards lost all their ships, more than 600 men were killed, and 1700 taken prisoners by the victors, whose loss was only one man killed and a few wounded. The total American losses in the various naval engagements amounted to but 17 killed, with less than 100 wounded; while the Spanish losses (in Cuba and the Philippines) reached 2000 killed and quite as many wounded.

On July 9 General Toral, in command at Santiago, offered a conditional surrender of that city, and, being refused by General Shafter, finally and formally surrendered on the 17th. Generous terms were accorded by the Americans, and eventually all Spanish prisoners, including those from Cervera's squadron, were repatriated at the expense of the United States. It is a noteworthy fact that there were no American prisoners (save the gallant Hobson and his comrades) for the Spaniards to offer in exchange. It is also noteworthy that while the Spaniards professed great admiration for the invading Americans (whom they had fought bravely, though vainly, in defense of Santiago) they had nothing but contempt for the Cubans.

In point of fact, all the evidence goes to show that while the Cubans are entitled to great credit for protracting the war to the extent of gaining the coöperation of the United States, after armed intervention was assured active coöperation on their part failed to materialize.

"The only Cuban who took part, and fearlessly exposed himself, in the assault of San Juan Hill, was killed on its crest. He bravely hewed down a portion of a barbed-wire entanglement with his machete in the face of a severe Spanish fire." The same authority for this statement (former Secretary of War R. A. Alger), in defending the Americans from the aspersions of their enemies (that they owed their hardships at San Juan Hill and later while

[2] R. A. Alger, "Spanish-American War."

in the trenches to their own folly, in throwing away their haver-
sacks and surplus provisions), remarks: "The usual way is to
stack everything but guns and ammunition, and the least clothing
possible. Americans, however, had never before campaigned
where everything left behind was stolen!"

Contemporary letters indicate the ill-feeling existing between
the Cubans and the American soldiers, owing to the reluctance of
the former to perform any duty whatever of a military character—
except that of foraging for themselves—at which they were active
and expert. General Garcia's ragged "patriots," who were wel-

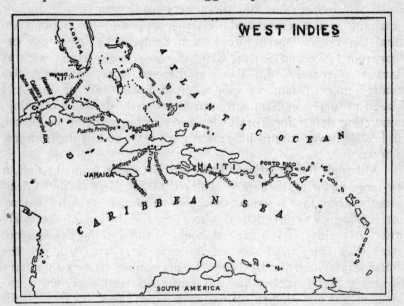

comed effusively by the Americans as they burst out of the woods
at Guantanamo, Las Guasimas, and around Santiago, who were
clothed and fed from the scant stores that General Shafter was
struggling to get to the front, before and after the surrender of
Santiago—these ungrateful Cubans would not turn a hand to help
the invaders, though the latter had shed their blood and poured
forth their treasure in freeing Cuba from oppression.

The Cubans would not fight, neither would they work, even
refusing to assist at bearing the wounded Americans from the
field, though the latter were fighting their battles and braving
death in defense of Cuban liberty, in behalf of Cuban autonomy.

The ingratitude of Cuba is now notorious; at that time it came as a surprise and shock to those who had so enthusiastically offered their lives in defense of a principle which in the abstract its beneficiaries hardly understood!

With the surrender of Santiago Spanish dominion also ceased over the entire eastern end of Cuba; but the island was by no means in the hands of the Americans. Its coast was invested, its chief ports blockaded; but there still remained the rich and populous city of Havana, with its defensive forts and castles, and their swarming garrisons. Twenty-four thousand Spanish prisoners went with Santiago province; but still there were many thousand Spaniards remaining in the central and western portions of the island. Admiral Cervera had been forced from Santiago by imperative orders from Governor-General Blanco, whose headquarters were at Havana. General Toral also was directed from that point, five hundred miles distant, as well as from Spain, and at first had refused to surrender Santiago until so ordered. It was a crushing, humiliating defeat for Toral, who never recovered from its effects, but brooded over it until his reason gave way, and he died, insane, in 1904.

Although the Americans had been victorious from the first, a few more victories of the sort achieved at Santiago would so decimate the army that it would soon become incapacitated by disease. For Santiago was invested, captured at the height of the sickly season of rains, and American soldiers suffered far more from fevers than from the bullets of the enemy. Hence, though the United States had hardly begun to draw upon its vast military resources, and though American arms had been everywhere triumphant, the government cordially welcomed overtures from Spain looking toward the establishment of peace.

Spain formally sued for peace on July 26, virtually accepted the terms offered by the United States on August 2, and a protocol suspending hostilities was signed at Washington on the 12th. Meantime, until the signing of the protocol, active operations had been going forward in Puerto Rico (the main military expedition for the invasion of which had sailed from Guantanamo Bay under General Miles), though for a time suspended in Cuba. On August 14 Generals Blanco and Macias acknowledged the receipt of orders from Madrid for the suspension of hostilities, and on the 16th the former resigned his office as governor-general. On August 17

President McKinley named a commission consisting of Major General James F. Wade, Major General M. C. Butler, and Rear Admiral William T. Sampson, to arrange with a similar Spanish commission for the evacuation of the island. Spain had practically relinquished all claims of sovereignty over Cuba, with a provision for its occupation by the United States, pending its complete pacification, the details to be arranged by the commission.

Two months later, or on October 18, Puerto Rico was in exclusive possession of the United States; but on account of the vast army of Spanish troops still remaining in Cuba (estimated at more than 100,000) at the time of the surrender, a longer period was necessary for its complete evacuation. This was not actually accomplished until January 1, 1899, when, for the first time in nearly four hundred years, the Spanish flag ceased to float above the harbor of Havana, and the Stars and Stripes took its place.

Thus, by the evacuation of Havana and the eastern part of the island Cuba came under the military control of the United States, and by its provisional occupation the government became responsible for the preservation of order and the protection of life and property. Notwithstanding the friction at first existing between the "patriot" armies of Cubans and the American troops, the change from Spanish to American control was accomplished with little disturbance.

The island was divided into military districts, each one in charge of a military governor, with a governor-general at Havana. The first American governor-general, or military governor, of Cuba was Major General John R. Brooke, who was appointed by President McKinley in December, 1898, and held office a little more than a year. He had at this time about 34,000 troops in the island, or only about one-third the number of Spanish soldiers that had been repatriated during the three months previously; yet he grasped the government with a firm hand and maintained perfect order throughout the length and breadth of his domain.

Chapter IV

MILITARY GOVERNMENT IN CUBA. 1898-1902

ONE-THIRD the native population of Cuba had been exterminated by war and famine; the pacificos, the reconcentrados, were still huddled together in the filthy camps so vividly described by Senators Proctor, Gallinger, and Thurston after their visit to Cuba in 1897, or roaming disconsolately around the towns and cities. On every side appeared the effects of disease, desolation, and crimes committed in the name of war's necessities.

It was General Brooke's mission—in which he eminently succeeded—to render the military character of the new government as inconspicuous as possible, while at the same time maintaining a firm grasp on the people and their affairs, regarding them as being under the tutelage of the United States until "such time as they should be declared capable of organizing a stable government, maintaining internal order, and fulfilling international obligations."

"This temporary government under the authority of and representing the United States assisted the Cubans in constructing their constitution, in organizing their own government in all its branches, and in arranging their new tariff and customs regulations; it took early and decisive measures for stamping out the yellow fever and improving the sanitary conditions of the island generally; it reformed the system of public education and corrected the abuses which had become connected with the administration of the schools, hospitals, prisons, and railroads; it initiated measures for the proper sewering, paving, lighting, policing, and adornment of the cities, and for the improvement of the roads and lands in the rural districts; it settled strikes, improved harbors, railways, telegraph and telephone systems, and introduced accuracy and efficiency into all ramifications of the public service."

After remaining a year in office General Brooke was succeeded by Brigadier General Leonard Wood, formerly colonel of the famed "Rough Riders," whose rapid rise in rank has had no parallel in American military annals. As a result of his brief but

brilliant campaign before Santiago he was promoted to be brigadier general of volunteers, and shortly after was appointed military
governor of Santiago province. In his gubernatorial capacity he
displayed superb executive ability as an organizer, and made his
medical knowledge efficacious in the cleansing of Santiago and the
virtual stamping out of smallpox and yellow fever.

He suppressed the mountain bandits, he created work for such
Cubans as were given to industry by opening country roads, sewers,
aqueducts, city streets, building hospitals; in fact, renovating and
actually regenerating that picturesque and ancient city which,
during centuries of Spanish misrule, had been festering in filth
unspeakable.

The example of men like Brooke and Wood was a tower of
strength to the American Government, when it was laboring with
all its might to bring about a settled condition of affairs in distracted Cuba. The eastern provinces almost immediately became
peaceful and prosperous, the vagrant soldiers of the erstwhile
patriot army finally gave up their weapons and settled down to
labor on the plantations, while the revenues from this rich region
soon exceeded the expenditures for all purposes, vast as they were.

Having shown his capacities as military governor of Santiago, General Wood was appointed to succeed General Brooke,
when, in the process of pacification and reorganization, it became
necessary to appoint a man of tact and executive force. Political
complications had arisen which demanded a diplomat at the helm
as well as an able military leader or commander, and General
Wood exerted all his energies to soothe the excited Cubanos. He
steered them through the turbulent seas of their constitutional
convention, and dexterously avoided the rocks upon which, perhaps, another less discriminative might have run the newly launched
Cuban " ship of state."

His tact was admirable, his courage equal to every emergency,
and his administrative faculties of a high order. In no position in
which he was placed had he failed to more than realize expectations. And all this may be said without the disparagement of any
other official, civil or military, who was called to the front in those
troublous times. His peculiar adaptability to the exigences of the
occasion in Cuba is but another instance of the men for the emergency always appearing at the right time in different crises of a
country's history.

Having reviewed the long series of outbreaks and revolutions that finally culminated in the crucial events of 1898, which resulted in the expulsion of the Spaniards, through the armed intervention of the United States, it will now be necessary for the purposes of this history only to take cognizance of Cuba as she exists to-day—an independent republic firmly based upon the principles of freedom.

In pursuance of the declared intention of the United States as expressed by the joint resolution of Congress, April 28, 1898, and approved by President McKinley—that "the people of Cuba are, and of right ought to be, free and independent"—an intention that had been ever in view and consistently adhered to by the government, President Roosevelt, on July 25, 1900, directed that a call be issued for the election in Cuba for members of a Constitutional Convention, "to frame a constitution as a basis for a stable and independent government in the island."

In accordance therewith the military governor, General Wood, issued the following proclamation:

"Therefore, it is ordered that a general election be held in the Island of Cuba on the third Saturday of September, in the year 1900, to elect delegates to a convention to meet in the city of Havana at twelve o'clock noon on the first Monday of November, in the year 1900, to frame and adopt a constitution for the people of Cuba, and as a part thereof to provide for and agree with the Government of the United States upon the relations to exist between that government and the Government of Cuba, and to provide for the election by the people of officers under such constitution and the transfer of government to the officers so elected.

"The election will be held in the several voting precincts of the island under and pursuant to the provisions of the Electoral law of April 18, 1900, and the amendments thereof."

In calling the convention to order the military governor of Cuba made the following statement:

"As military governor of the island, representing the President of the United States, I call this convention to order.

"It will be your duty, first, to frame and adopt a constitution for Cuba, and when that has been done to formulate what in your opinion ought to be the relations between Cuba and the United States.

" The constitution must be adequate to secure a stable, orderly, and free government.

" When you have formulated the relations which in your opinion ought to exist between Cuba and the United States, the Government of the United States will doubtless take such action on its part as shall lead to a final and authoritative agreement between the people of the two countries to the promotion of their common interests. . . .

" When the convention concludes its labors I will transmit to the Congress the constitution as framed by the convention for its consideration and for such action as it may deem advisable."

The convention was duly held in Havana, and after desultory discussions protracted through many months the constitution was completed, accepted, and signed by the delegates in February, 1901. In its original form, however, it was not consonant with what the President and Congress of the United States had desired, and a commission was sent to Washington in order to discuss the question with the United States Government. On the return of this commission to Cuba, the conditions indicated in the so-called " Platt Amendment " were incorporated in the constitution as an " appendix," and the instrument promulgated and put in force by proclamation of President Roosevelt.[1]

These conditions, which were, though reluctantly, admitted, are: " Cuba shall not make any foreign treaty which may tend toward placing the island or any portion thereof in jeopardy; no loans can be issued unless a surplus of revenue is available for the service of such obligations; the United States can intervene to preserve the independence of Cuba, or to insure protection for life and property; the acts of the United States military administration in Cuba since 1898 are recognized as valid; proper hygienic precautions must be taken to protect public health on the island; ownership of the Isle of Pines is left for future consideration; coaling

[1] " El 5 de noviembre de 1900 se reunió la *Convencion Constituyente,* y comenzó sus trabajos, quedando aprobada el 21 de febrero de 1901, la Constitución, que juntamente con el Apendice acordado por la misma Convencion el 13 de junio, 1901, fue promulgada como Constitución de la Republia de Cuba, y pueste en vigor por orden del Presidente de los Estados Unidos, Mr. Theodore Roosevelt."—*Nociones de Historia de Cuba.*

stations shall be sold or leased to the United States in localities to be hereafter decided; and these conditions shall be embodied in the Cuban law of Constitution."

By the treaty of peace between the United States and Spain, signed at Paris December 10, 1898, the latter relinquished sovereignty of Cuba and the United States assumed all obligations for the protection of life and property; United States troops, already in occupation of parts of the island, replaced the Spanish garrisons when they were withdrawn in 1898; and three years later, Cuba having assumed the obligations imposed upon the United States by the Treaty of Paris, preparations were made by the secretary of war of the United States to terminate the military occupation, and permit the installation of the Government of Cuba.

All conditions imposed by the United States having been complied with and fulfilled by Cuba—viz.: for "leaving the government and control of Cuba to its people so soon as a government shall have been established under a constitution which, either as a part thereof, or in ordinance appended, defines the future relations of the United States with Cuba in substantial agreement with the ' Platt Amendment ' "—President Roosevelt recommended, in a message to Congress dated March 27, 1902, measures for diplomatic and consular representation in Cuba.

Previously, however, a national election had been held in Cuba, and in February, 1902, Señor Tomas Estrada Palma had been declared president of the new republic by the electors chosen in January of that year. The new government was as follows: President of the Republic, Tomas Estrada Palma; Vice-President, Luis Estevezy Romero. The cabinet: Secretary of State and Justice, Carlos de Zaldo; Secretary of the Interior, Luis Yero Buduen; Secretary of Public Instruction, Leopoldo Cancio; Secretary of Public Works and Acting Secretary of Agriculture, Luciano Diaz; Secretary of the Treasury, José M. Garcia Montes. Governors of provinces: Havana, General Emilio Nuñez; Pinar del Rio, Colonel Luis Perez; Santiago de Cuba, General Francisco Echavarria; Santa Clara, General José Miguel Gomez; Puerto Principe, General Lope Recio; Matanzas, Colonel Domingo Lecuona; Chief of the Rural Guard, General Alejandro Rodriguez.

The Republic of Cuba was actually inaugurated on May 20, 1902, when the transfer of sovereignty took place, after nearly three years and a half of "intervention." At noon of that memorable day for Cuba the flag of the United States was hauled down at the government palace in Havana by General Wood, and that of the new republic hoisted in its place.

The official announcement by the military governor of the transfer of authority, by which Cuba entered upon her career of independence and home rule under President Palma, follows herewith:

" HEADQUARTERS DEPARTMENT OF CUBA,

" HAVANA, May 20, 1902.

" To THE PRESIDENT AND CONGRESS OF THE REPUBLIC OF CUBA:

" *Sirs:* Under the direction of the President of the United States I now transfer to you as the duly elected representatives of the people of Cuba the government and control of the island, to be held and exercised by you, under the provisions of the Constitution of the Republic of Cuba, heretofore adopted by the Constitutional Convention, and this day promulgated; and I hereby declare the occupation of Cuba by the United States and the military government of the island to be ended.

" This transfer of the government and control is upon the express condition, and the Government of the United States will understand that, by the acceptance thereof, you do now, pursuant to the provisions of the said Constitution, assume and undertake all and several the obligations assumed by the United States with respect to Cuba by the treaty between the United States of America and Her Majesty the Queen Regent of Spain, signed at Paris on the 10th day of December, 1898.

" All money obligations of the military government down to this date have been paid as far as practicable. The public civil funds derived from the revenues of Cuba transferred to you this day, are transferred subject to such claims and obligations, properly payable out of the revenues of the island, as may remain. The sum of $100,000 has been reserved from the transfer of funds to defray anticipated expenses of accounting, reporting, and winding up the affairs of the military government, after which any unexpended balance of said sum will be paid into the treasury of the island.

" The plans already devised for the sanitation of the cities of the island and to prevent a recurrence of epidemic and infectious diseases, to which the Government of the United States understands that the provision of the Constitution contained in the fifth article of the appendix applies, are as follows:

"First.—A plan for the paving and sewering of the city of Havana, for which a contract has been awarded by the municipality of that city to McGivney, Rockeby & Co.

"Second.—A plan for waterworks to supply the city of Santiago de Cuba, prepared by Captain S. E. Reckenbach, in charge of the district of Santiago, and approved by the military governor, providing for taking water from the wells of the San Juan Canyon, and pumping the same to reservoirs located on the heights to the east of the city.

"Third.—A plan for the sewering of the city of Santiago de Cuba, a contract for which was awarded to Michael J. Dady & Co. by the military governor of Cuba, and now under construction.

"Fourth.—The rules and regulations established by the President of the United States on January 17, 1899, for the maintenance of quarantine against epidemic diseases at the ports of Havana, Matanzas, Cienfuegos, and Santiago de Cuba, and thereafter at the other ports of the island, as extended and amended and made applicable to future conditions by the order of the military governor dated April, 1902.

"Fifth.—The sanitary rules and regulations in force in the city of Havana (and in any other city having official rules, etc.).

"It is understood by the United States that the present government of the Isle of Pines will continue as a *de facto* government, pending the settlement of the title to said island by treaty pursuant to the Cuban Constitution and the Act of Congress of the United States approved March 2, 1901.

"I am further charged by the President of the United States to deliver to you the letter which I now hand you.

"LEONARD WOOD, Military Governor."

The Secretary of State issued the following official notification to the ambassadors and ministers of the United States accredited to foreign governments:

"DEPARTMENT OF STATE,
"WASHINGTON, May 20, 1902.
"*Sir:* I am directed by the President to inform you that the military occupation of the Island of Cuba by the United States has

this day ceased, and that an independent government, republican in form, has been inaugurated there, under the Presidency of His Excellency Señor Don Tomas Estrada Palma.

"You are instructed to convey this information through the appropriate channel to the government to which you are accredited.

"I am, sir, your obedient servant,

"JOHN HAY, Secretary."

"The present government of Cuba is republican in form and in actuality. It is a government 'of the people, by the people, for the people.' Its constitution, regularly adopted on February 21, 1901, and afterward modified satisfactorily to the United States by the adoption of the so-called 'Platt Amendment,' is similar to the constitution of the United States. The president serves four years and appoints his own cabinet. The congress consists of a senate and a house of representatives, one representative being chosen for every 25,000 inhabitants, as nearly as possible. Each province elects it own governor and controls it own internal affairs. The rules governing citizenship correspond in general to those in force in the United States. The financial and commercial conditions have been greatly improved. Although the old Spanish money is still in circulation, the Cuban currency system has been placed on a stable gold basis, adjusted to United States standards. This important transformation was effected during the United States occupation, but so wisely and gradually that local industries, which had been previously adjusted to the old Spanish standards, were not damaged. The tariff was changed in several particulars for the advantage of Cuban agricultural interests, reductions being made in favor of the importation of foods, agricultural machinery, locomotives, steel rails, and other commodities."

The independency of Cuba began under more favorable auspices than its most ardent friends had anticipated, for the people of Cuba, though perhaps hardly appreciative of what the United States had done for them during their period of tutelage, yet were overjoyed at the prospect of finally "coming into their own"—a condition which had been long promised, long deferred, yet ever believed in by the faithful fighters for *Cuba libre*.

With liberty and autonomy in a greater measure than had ever been expected, the Cubans had greater cause for rejoicing than any other people on earth. The island having been most thoroughly regenerated by the outgoing Americans, its resources were developed to a great extent, its cities cleansed and made free from that scourge of centuries, yellow fever, and salutary lessons were inculcated respecting sanitation. Public schools were established, its finances firmly based, and its treasury left with a surplus, unheard of in Spanish times.

There were threats of disturbance from some of the politicians and "patriots," as there were not offices enough for all the former, nor funds enough (despite the generous gift of $3,000,000 from the United States) for placating the latter. But the real fighters and patriots, like General Gomez and a few others, who had shed their blood and given their fortunes for the cause, nobly upheld the government and protected Cuba's credit.

It is doubtful if any other great nation ever did for another and weaker one what the United States did for Cuba without direct recompense or hope of reward. The full measure of Cuba's obligation to the United States may never be known; but the concrete results of the intervention period are forcibly presented and correctly summarized in General Wood's final Report of 1902:

"The government was transferred as a 'going concern'; all the public offices were filled with competent, well-trained employes; the island was free from debt, other than such obligations as were of a current character, and had a surplus of over a million and a half dollars available for allotment; was possessed of a thoroughly trained and efficient personnel in all departments and completely equipped buildings for the transaction of public business; the administration of justice was free; habeas corpus had been put in force; old prison abuses had been stopped; police courts had been established; a new marriage law on lines proposed by the Roman Catholic bishop of Havana, giving equal rights to all denominations, was in operation; a general electoral law embodying the most enlightened principles of modern electoral laws had been put in force, and the people were governed in all municipalities throughout the island by officials of their own choice elected under this law; trials in Cuban courts were as prompt as in any State in the Union, and life and property were absolutely safe; sanitary conditions were better than those existing in most parts of the United States; yellow fever had been eradicated from the island; a modern system of public education, including a reorganized university, high schools, and nearly

3700 public schools, and laws for its government, was in successful operation; well organized departments of charities and public works operating under laws framed by the military government had been established; a new railroad law had been promulgated; the customs service had been thoroughly equipped; the great question of church property had been settled; a basis of settlement between mortgage creditors and debtors had been agreed upon and in successful operation for a year; municipalities had been reduced from 138 to 82 in number; public order was excellent; the island possessed a highly organized and efficient rural guard; an enormous amount of public works had been undertaken and completed; ports and harbors had been much improved; old lighthouses had been thoroughly renovated and new ones built; Cubans and Spaniards were living in harmony; in short, the government as transformed was in excellent running order; the people were making rapid progress; beggars were practically unknown; the courts had the confidence and respect of the people. . . .

"The work called for and accomplished was the building up of a republic by Anglo-Saxons in a Latin country where approximately seventy per cent. of the people were illiterate; where they had lived always as a military colony; where general elections, as we understand them, were unknown; in fact, it was a work which called for practically a rewriting of the administrative law of the land, including the law of charities and hospitals, public works, sanitary law, school law, and railway law; meeting and controlling the worst possible sanitary conditions; putting the people to school; writing an electoral law and training the people in the use of it; establishing an entirely new system of accounting and auditing; the election and assembling of representatives of the people to draw up and adopt a constitution for the proposed new republic; in short, the establishment in a little over three years, in a Latin military colony in one of the most unhealthful countries in the world, of a republic modeled closely upon lines of our great republic, and the transfer to the Cuban people of the republic so established, free from debt, healthy, orderly, well equipped, and with a good balance in the treasury. All this work was accomplished without serious friction. The Island of Cuba was transferred to its people as promised, and was started on its career in excellent condition and under favorable circumstances."

Chapter V

THE REPUBLIC OF CUBA TO-DAY. 1902—

THE first President of the Cuban Republic, Señor Tomas Estrada Palma—familiarly known in the island as " Don Tomas "—was born in the little town of Bayamo, Santiago province, in 1835. His father, a wealthy planter, educated him for the bar, and he achieved some success in his profession. At the age of thirty-three, however, he joined the insurgents at the beginning of the Ten Years' War, rose to the rank of general, and afterward filled the presidential chair of the provisional (insurrectionist) government.

Owing to the prominent part he took in the insurrection, his family estates were confiscated, his mother was murdered by Spanish troops, and in 1877 he was captured and taken as a prisoner to Spain. There he was retained for nearly two years in prison, persistently refusing to take the oath of allegiance to Spain; and when finally released he vowed never to return to Cuba until she should have achieved her independence. In pursuance of this resolve he went to Honduras after his release, where he married the daughter of that republic's president and was made postmaster-general. After a short residence in Honduras he came to the United States, settling finally at Central Valley, New York, where he opened a school for boys, as a means of gaining a livelihood. He is best remembered in the United States, of course, as the head and front of the insurrectionist junta which had its headquarters in New York, and but for which Cuban independence might never have been won.

His career as a soldier is so far in the past that most people now living have forgotten it, as he fought for *Cuba libre* nearly thirty-five years prior to his being elected president of the newly formed republic. He is best known in Cuba and elsewhere as a statesman of elevated aims, pure morals, and integrity of purpose. Although he had resided many years abroad, he was, next to General Maximo Gomez, the most popular man in Cuba. It was owing, doubtless, to the persuasion and personal influence of that redoubtable old warrior, the idol of the people, that Palma was chosen by the electoral college, as General Gomez himself would have been elevated to the high position had he consented to receive the nomination. Instead of allowing his name to be presented, General Gomez chose rather the quietude of retirement, and resides unostentiously in Havana, surrounded by his attractive family.

Events have shown that in choosing Señor Palma as their first executive the Cubans acted well and wisely, since he has displayed a serene, judicial temper superior to all annoyances, and has held in a firm grasp such of his unstable constituents as were prone to create disturbances. The same week that witnessed the coronation of Spain's youthful sovereign, when he had been declared of age, saw the city of Havana in the throes of preparation for the inauguration of Cuba's first executive. Her streets, like those of Madrid, resounded with enthusiastic "*vivas*"; and they were also in the Spanish tongue; but not for Spain or for Spain's young ruler. They were all for a plain old gentleman then but recently from the United States—where he had resided for a score of years, and once claimed citizenship—Señor Don Tomas Estrada Palma, Cuba's president-elect. There may have been more of magnificence attendant upon the coronation ceremonies at Madrid, but not nearly so much enthusiasm, so much real cause for rejoicing, nor such unaffected simplicity and true patriotism.

President (then President-elect) Palma landed in Cuba at Gibara, on the north coast, April 20, just a month previous to the date set for his inauguration, and thence proceeded across country to the little town of Bayamo, his birthplace, by the old insurgent route, which he had trodden many times in pain and peril in the Ten Years' War. He was first elected President of the Cuban Republic (then a thing hoped for, but not realized) twenty-five years before he made this triumphal journey, when he returned as the chosen executive of the free and independent republic then existing as an actuality. Though a tour of triumph in a certain sense, his trip to his birthplace and to the grave of his murdered mother was saddened by these painful memories that thronged upon him, as he recalled the events that had taken place since he left the island, a captive of the Spaniards.

President Palma brought to the executive chair the ripe experience of an active life and a sagacity acquired through trials and tribulation. He indulged in no roseate dreams of enthusiastic youth, but declared, with the sane judgment of old age, that the course for the Cubans to pursue had been marked out for them by their liberators, and that it was incumbent upon them, at least, not to stray from that path of liberty and progress.

Addressing his countrymen just prior to his inauguration, President Palma said: " None of us may hope to fully express the joy we feel at the approach of May 20, that date destined to be so great a one in our history, which marks the birth of a new republic on the American continent. This date will forever mean to us of Cuba that one of the greatest and most powerful nations of modern times, not content with helping us to win our liberty, not satisfied with having spent the blood of her loyal sons in torrents in our behalf, has justly and wisely stood between us and the rest of the world, has shown us how to govern the young republic, has continued to extend to us her guiding hand and her wise counsels, and now, having done so, she fulfills her pledges to us and to the world, and generously turns over to our government the island she has helped us to wrest from our enemies! "

Actuated by sentiments of gratitude and loyalty to the great government that had made possible the aspirations of Cuban patriots, Señor Palma took as his model the constitution and workings of the more powerful republic, and aimed, if anything, at going beyond the United States in the integrity of his intentions to live simply, rule wisely, and establish an economical form of government, despite the tremendous pressure that was brought to bear upon him from every side. The cabinet positions, those most craved by aspiring Cubans, were few, and the departmental positions were already filled with men trained by the departing Americans to perform their tasks conscientiously and well.

He declared himself, at the outset, in favor of free and better education; disposed to develop to the utmost Cuba's vast resources; for the maintenance of the closest and friendliest relations with the United States, and of uniting the various and diverse political elements, so that they should work harmoniously in the best interests of the newly established government.

He then gave out that he considered the most important offices within his gift to be the secretaryships of education and agriculture, and in this announcement he struck the keynotes of progress and prosperity. He has adhered to his plans with commendable tenacity, has resisted the pressure brought against him by place and fortune-hunters, and in every important measure has verified the confidence placed in him by the Cubans, and the wisdom of their choice. The enemies of Cuba have been disappointed in her constant and cumulative successes, diplomatic and material, for peace has prevailed throughout the republic from the very first moment of its foundation, and the promise for the future is very bright indeed.

That President Palma's sentiments remained unchanged after his accession to power came out strongly in his remarks on the occasion of the departure from Cuba of the last American soldiers then quartered at Cabañas barracks, Havana, on February 4, 1904.

"On this momentous occasion," he said, "the sincerity and depth of my feelings overcome me, and my heart must supply the deficiency of words. We now see leave our shores the last troops the United States left in Cuba after helping us to secure our independence and the blessings of freedom.

"They could stay longer under some pretext, or they could impose upon us an unjust demand. But, on the contrary, the Government of the United States willingly proves its disinterestedness and the sincerity of the aid it rendered us by taking those troops away, and shows us that we have, as an independent people, the confidence of one of the most powerful nations on earth.

"This act of the United States, in withdrawing its troops from Cuban territory, reflects upon them everlasting glory and makes us proud of ourselves, for it means that nobody doubts our competence to govern ourselves, or our ability to maintain peace and order and guarantee the rights of all the inhabitants of this island.

"This new consideration shown us, together with the services we have previously received at their hands, will bind the Cuban people to the American people forever in a strong tie of sincere gratitude!"

That President Palma should have adhered so consistently to the ideals set forth by the retiring Americans, that he should still be animated by feelings of gratitude toward the great republic that made his aspirations possible, and have expressed those feelings, two years after he had taken into his grasp the reins of power, makes for the stability of the government over which he was placed by the votes of the people.

New conditions in Cuba opened most auspiciously for the island and its inhabitants, and to equal or surpass those prevailing during the period of American occupancy it was incumbent upon the Cuban officials that their efforts should never be relaxed. The United States did more than its duty by Cuba; it is to the lasting credit of the Cubans that when they had opportunity they nobly rose to the occasion and showed the world what they could do for themselves. When the Stars and Stripes was withdrawn from the palace in Havana and the forts across the harbor, and in its place the flag of free and independent Cuba run aloft, there was an end to the old régime of Spanish misrule and barbarities, and an inauguration of the new.

The predictions of Cuba's enemies have not been fulfilled, for, instead of "lapsing into barbarism, like Haiti," the new republic has progressed along the lines her friends indicated during the period of military occupation and forged into the fabric of their enlightened policy.

When General Wood was first installed as military governor of Cuba he found, he said, prisons enough to accommodate all the Cuban children, but an entire absence of schools and provisions for even their primary instruction. That was in accord with the Spanish policy throughout its colonies. But after two years of American rule more than 75,000 children found accommodation for their educational needs, and in President Palma's message to the Cuban congress in November, 1902, he stated that more than 3000 schools were then maintained, with a regular attendance of 163,400 scholars of both sexes.

By the Cuban constitution primary education is declared compulsory, "and shall be gratuitous, as also that of arts and trades. The expenses thereof shall be defrayed by the state, during such time as the provinces and municipalities may lack means therefor"; and as a result the first year of the Cuban budget showed an expenditure of $3,700,000 for public instruction. More than $3,000,000 of this large sum was expended for the primary schools, or twenty per cent. of total public expenditures.

Several questions relating to mutual intercourse between Cuba and the United States were left for settlement under what might be termed "unfinished business." These related to the ownership of the Isle of Pines, coaling and naval stations for the United States, the Cuban loan, and a treaty of reciprocity.

Under the treaty negotiated and ratified with Spain the status of the Isle of Pines was to be the same as that of Puerto Rico, and, though only sixty miles from the southern coast of Cuba, its ownership passed to the United States. There has been a very determined opposition to the ratification of a treaty by which the sovereignty of Cuba over this island should be recognized, but in 1906 the question was definitely settled in favor of Cuba retaining the island. While contiguity, merely, might seem to have weight in the settlement of this vexed question, there also arose the rights of American settlers, who had invested to the amount of more than a million dollars, and who removed thither with their families, and resisted the Cuban administration, insisting that the island should continue to remain an American possession.

The island contains about 800,000 acres of land, though much of it is low and marshy, with varied scenery, mineral springs, and a climate that is perfectly adapted to the raising of tropical fruits and vegetables. In some respects it is a desirable acquisition to the insular possessions of the United States, but, though occupying an advantageous position, strategically considered, it has no harbors which could be made available for naval or coaling stations by the United States.

According to the provisions to that effect in the constitution of Cuba, sites for naval stations were granted the United States in July, 1903, at Bahia Honda, on the north coast, and at Guantanamo, on the south, not far distant from the harbor of Santiago. The latter station was transferred to the United States in November, 1903, and four hundred marines were sent out to take possession, after participating in the formal transfer. Active operations have since been going on at Guantanamo looking to the establishment there of a great naval base and coaling station for United States war vessels, which will be of inestimable value, in view of the expanding interests of the American Government at Panama and in the Caribbean Sea.

Three magnificent strategic positions are now commanded and controlled by the United States, sufficing for the assembling of its fleets, and enhancing the prestige of its naval power in southern waters. These are Bahia Honda, less than fifty miles to the westward of Havana, commanding the Gulf of Mexico and the Straits of Florida; Guantanamo, nearest to the Windward Passage, Jamaica, Panama, the east coast of Central America, and the Spanish Main; and Culebra, between Puerto Rico and Saint Thomas, dominating the Lesser Antilles and the northeast coast of South America.

Within a year after the establishment of Cuban independence it was authoritatively said of Cuba: " Events have clearly indicated a growing prosperity on the part of the new republic. The public receipts from customs, etc., have proved ample for meeting the public expenditures, and these have been wisely and economically managed in a manner conducive to the best interests of the commonwealth. The productive capacity and energy of the people have greatly increased, as shown by the statistics of production and trade. The balance of trade, which for several years prior to 1902 was against Cuba, is now again in its favor. There is no public debt, except for current and temporary obligations, and the treasury contained (on September 1, 1903,) more than $3,000,000, after paying all obligations."

It had been provided, by the " Platt Amendment " clause of the Cuban constitution, that Cuba should " not assume to contract any debt, to pay the interest on which and make reasonable provision for the ultimate discharge of which, the ordinary expenses of the island, after defraying the expenses of the government, shall be inadequate."

At the beginning of 1903, however, it was perfectly apparent that this disability had been removed, owing to the vast resources of the island having provided an income more than adequate for complying with the conditions laid down in the amendment. As a consequence, a loan of $35,000,000 was " floated " in February, 1904, bonds having been issued to run forty years, with annual interest at five per cent. These bonds were taken by a financial company of New York, at 90½, and payment therefor was sent to Cuba in three installments, during June, September, and December, 1904.

Cuba had already become indebted to the amount of $2,195,350 gold-bearing bonds at six per cent., and she still owed her veterans (in whose interests, ostensibly, the large loan was negotiated) the sum of $60,000,000, " for fighting her battles with Spain." In order to discharge this obligation fully, bonds or scrip have been issued to the veterans themselves, to the total amount of the deficit, though the " patriots " who " fought and bled for their country " have almost universally hypothecated their scrip for about twenty-five per cent. of the face value to the Spanish-Cuban bankers. Thus Spain benefits by the necessities of Cuba, and not only in the matter of the loans and scrip issues, but also, more or less indirectly, through the generosity of the United States toward Cuba in the larger concession as to reciprocity.

Although Spain formerly controlled the trade of the island, in a great measure she will not have lost much in the end, for through her long-established commercial houses, with their branches in Cuba, Cuban trade is mainly controlled. But even with the ever-present incubus of Spanish trade supremacy, Cuba will continue to prosper, and will have a surplus for the discharge of her national obligations.

"From 1893 to 1898 the revenues of Cuba, under excessive taxation, high duties, and the Havana lottery," according to the Cuban census report of 1890, "averaged about $25,000,000 per annum . . . Of this amount $10,500,000 went to Spain to pay the interest on the Cuban debt, $12,000,000 were allotted for the support of the Spanish-Cuban army and navy and the maintenance of the Cuban Government in all its branches, including the church, and the remainder, less than $2,500,000, was allowed for public works, education, and the general improvement of Cuba, independent of municipal expenditures. As the amounts appropriated annually in the Cuban budget were not sufficient to cover the expenditures and there was a failure to collect the taxes, deficits were inevitable. These were charged to the Cuban debt, until, by 1897, through this and other causes, it aggregated about $400,000,000, or an amount *per capita* of $283.54—more than three times as large as the *per capita* debt of Spain and much larger than the *per capita* debt of any other European country!"

Without discussing the political, moral, or social aspects of the matter, it is apparent that these great and radical alterations have resulted and will continue to result in material advantage to the Cubans and to the nations having commercial dealings with Cuba, with the possible exception of Spain, which had formerly a monopoly of the Cuban market in many important details. Cuba can now invite trade and immigration on fair terms. Its public expenditures are no longer devoted to the support of foreign officials and a foreign army, but are in the interest of the public welfare and progress. Taxes are now low, and ninety per cent. of the revenue comes from the customs duties. The old millstone of the enormous Spanish-Cuban debt has been cast off. The community is solvent, independent, and progressive. Those who now sell to Cuba know they will be paid and what kind of money they will get. Those who emigrate to Cuba know they are safe in settling there.

Chapter VI

RECIPROCITY BETWEEN CUBA AND THE UNITED STATES. 1902—

THE subject of reciprocity between Cuba and the United States appeared prominently as a subject of discussion almost coincidentally with the establishment of the Cuban Republic, and was a fruitful source of dissension and recrimination. Having obtained everything she had fought for, and through the armed intervention and subsequent military occupation of her territory by the United States advanced to a position among the nations which she never could have attained unaided, yet Cuba expected, and even demanded, continued support from the hand that had freed her from the fetters of centuries.

Most fortunately for her the sentiment also existed in the United States that, having shed the blood of American soldiers in accomplishing her freedom, and having poured out American treasure without stint in establishing the island's position of independence, the obligation was one of honor to provide for her "material well-being" for all future time.

Without pausing to discuss the objections to this proposition from the American view-point—as to the necessity for further assisting a nation which, owing to that aid, had started in the race free from debt and international obligations, which had absorbed already millions of American money without thought of recompense, which possessed natural climatic advantages far superior to the United States, and a trade position (together with unique products, such as sugar and tobacco) peculiarly advantageous and unsurpassed—it is enough to state that the sentiment of "reciprocity" prevailed.

After a systematic and exhaustive study of the subject had been made by committees, and prolonged debate in the House, a bill was formulated and passed which, when sent to the Senate, was referred to the Committee on Relations with Cuba, and, never having been reported back, "died with the expiration of the Fifty-seventh Congress."

The United States Congress having failed to pass any measure authorizing tariff concessions on Cuban products in return for " similar concessions " offered by Cuba on imports, President Roosevelt authorized the negotiation of a commercial treaty with Cuba, which was signed in Havana on December 11, 1902. No action was taken on this convention by the Fifty-seventh Congress, but at a special session of the Senate, called for March 5, 1903, it was considered, and, together with amendments, was ratified March 19. The Cuban Government ratified the amended instrument nine days later; it received the " approval " of Congress at a special session called by President Roosevelt, the House, November 19, 1903, and the Senate, on December 16, passing a bill affirming this treaty.

President Roosevelt affixed his signature to the treaty December 19, and issued his proclamation, in conformity with the Act of Congress, proclaiming the convention between the United States and Cuba to be in effect on the tenth day of its issuance.

President Roosevelt's broad and statesmanlike presentation of the subject, and his continued insistence that full justice (even more than full justice) should be done to Cuba, won the country to his way of thinking and gave Cuba the measure she so ardently desired. His views are set forth in his message to the Senate and House of Representatives, as follows:

" I deem it important before the adjournment of the present session of Congress to call attention to the following expressions in the message which, in the discharge of the duty imposed upon me by the Constitution, I sent to Congress on the first Tuesday of December last:

" Elsewhere I have discussed the question of reciprocity. In the case of Cuba, however, there are weighty reasons of morality and of national interest why the policy should be held to have a peculiar application, and I most earnestly ask your attention to the wisdom, indeed to the vital need, of providing for a substantial reduction in the tariff duties on Cuban imports into the United States. Cuba has in her constitution affirmed what we desired, that she should stand, in international matters, in closer and more friendly relations with us than with any other power; and we are bound by every consideration of honor and expediency to pass commercial measures in the interest of her material well-being."

This recommendation was merely giving practical effect to

President McKinley's words when, in his messages of December 5, 1898, and December 5, 1899, he wrote:

"It is important that our relations with this people [of Cuba] shall be of the most friendly character and our commercial relations close and reciprocal. . . . We have accepted a trust, the fulfillment of which calls for the sternest integrity of purpose and the exercise of the highest wisdom. The new Cuba yet to arise from the ashes of the past must needs be bound to us by ties of singular intimacy and strength, if its enduring welfare is to be assured. . . . The greatest blessing which can come to Cuba is the restoration of her agricultural and industrial prosperity.

"Yesterday, June 12, I received by cable from the American minister in Cuba a most earnest appeal from President Palma for 'legislative relief before it is too late and [his] country financially ruined.'

"The granting of reciprocity with Cuba is a proposition which stands entirely alone. The reasons for it far outweigh those for granting reciprocity with any other nation, and are entirely consistent with preserving intact the protective system under which this country has thriven so marvelously. The present tariff law was designed to promote the adoption of such a reciprocity treaty, and expressly provided for a reduction not to exceed twenty per cent. upon goods coming from a particular country, leaving the tariff rates on the same articles unchanged as regards all other countries. Objection has been made to the granting of the reduction on the ground that the substantial benefit would not go to the agricultural producer of sugar, but would inure to the American sugar refiners. In my judgment provision can and should be made which will guarantee us against this possibility without having recourse to a measure of doubtful policy, such as a bounty in the form of a rebate.

"The question as to which, if any, of the different schedules of the tariff ought most properly to be revised does not enter into this matter in any way or shape. We are concerned with getting a friendly reciprocal arrangement with Cuba. This arrangement applies to all the articles that Cuba grows or produces. It is not in our power to determine what these articles shall be, and any discussion of the tariff as it affects special schedules or countries other than Cuba is wholly aside from the subject-matter to which I call your attention.

" Some of our citizens oppose the lowering of the tariff on
Cuban products, just as three years ago they opposed the admission
of the Hawaiian Islands, lest free trade with them might ruin certain of our interests here. In the actual event their fears proved
baseless as regards Hawaii, and their apprehensions as to the damage to any industry of our own because of the proposed measure
of reciprocity with Cuba seems to me equally baseless. In my judgment no American industry will be hurt, and many American industries will be benefited by the proposed action. It is to our advantage,
as a nation, that the growing Cuban market should be controlled
by American producers.

" The events following the war with Spain and the prospective
building of the isthmian canal render it certain that we must take,
in the future, a far greater interest than hitherto in what happens
throughout the West Indies, Central America, and the adjacent
coasts and waters. We expect Cuba to treat us on an exceptional
footing politically, and we should put her in the same exceptional
position economically. The proposed action is in line with the
course we have pursued as regards all the islands with which we
have been brought into relations of varying intimacy by the Spanish
war. Puerto Rico and Hawaii have been included within our tariff
lines, to their great benefit as well as ours, and without any of the
feared detriment to our own industries. The Philippines, which
stand in a different relation, have been given substantial tariff concessions.

" Cuba is an independent republic, but a republic which has
assumed certain special obligations as regards her international position in compliance with our request. I ask for her certain special
economic concessions in return; these economic concessions to benefit us as well as her. There are few brighter pages in American
history than the page which tells of our dealings with Cuba during
the past four years. On her behalf we waged a war of which the
mainspring was generous indignation against oppression, and we
have kept faith absolutely. It is earnestly to be hoped that we will
complete, in the same spirit, the record so well begun, and show in
our dealings with Cuba that steady continuity of policy which it is
essential for our nation to establish in foreign affairs if we desire to
play well our part as a world-power.

" We are a wealthy and powerful nation; Cuba is a young
republic, still weak, who owes to us her birth, whose whole future

whose very life, must depend on our attitude toward her. I ask that we help her as she struggles upward along the painful and difficult road of self-governing independence. I ask this aid for her because she is weak, because she needs it, because we have already aided her. I ask that open-handed help of a kind which a self-respecting people can accept be given to Cuba, for the very reason that we have given her such help in the past. Our soldiers fought to give her freedom, and for three years our representatives, civil and military, have toiled unceasingly, facing disease of a peculiarly sinister and fatal type with patient and uncomplaining fortitude, to teach her how to use aright her new freedom. Never in history has any alien country been thus administered with such high integrity of purpose, such wise judgment, and such single-minded devotion to the country's interests. Now I ask that the Cubans be given all possible chance to use to the best advantage the freedom of which Americans have such right to be proud and for which so many American lives have been sacrificed.

"THEODORE ROOSEVELT.

"White House, June 13, 1902."

In his proclamation reciting the details of the convention entered into between the United States and Cuba, President Roosevelt announced that the said convention was " to facilitate their commercial intercourse by improving the conditions of trade between the two countries," and added that satisfactory evidence had been received that the Republic of Cuba had " made provision to give full effect to the articles of said convention."

"Wherefore, I have caused the said convention, as amended by the Senate of the United States, to be made public, to the end that the same, and every clause thereof, as amended may be observed and fulfilled with good faith by the United States and the citizens thereof."

In anticipation of the proclamation of this treaty (which was framed especially for the relief of Cuba's sugar and tobacco producers, who, without its aid, could not dispose of their crops to advantage), the Cuban congress enacted a new tariff, " placing higher duties on all imports, especially with a view of reciprocity arrangements with the United States."

Whatever may have been the incentives on either side, it is a satisfaction to note that President Roosevelt's noble and disinterested motives have brought forth good fruit, for since the treaty went into effect Cuba has enjoyed a prosperity unparalleled in her annals. Every agricultural industry has benefited by the impetus to Cuban commerce, which has increased even beyond the most sanguine expectations of her friends and the most ardent advocates of reciprocity.

Sugar-grinding began all over the island under the most auspicious circumstances, " and the planters, elated over the passage of the long-delayed reciprocity measure, are looking to the future with optimistic eyes," reported the United States consul at Cienfuegos, in December, 1903. The crop then on hand, he stated, exceeds that of any former year, and his prediction that the sugar crop of 1904-1905 would be phenomenal in the history of Cuba, and that much land which had been untilled for several seasons, as well as many acres of absolutely virgin soil, would be brought under cultivation, was abundantly verified by the vast output of that season.

President Palma, in his annual message to the Cuban congress, in November, 1904, congratulated the island that she was in the most prosperous condition known to her history. The imports for the fiscal year ending June 30, 1904, reached a total of $74,492,000, which was an increase of $11,872,000 over those of the year previous; while the exports amounted to $94,399,000, or an increase of more than $16,000,000 over the previous year. And, in the exports, sugar came first, to the amount of $57,000,000!

Incidentally, it may be noted that, as pointed out by President Palma, Cuba's finances were in a very prosperous condition. The total army debt, he explained, would not be more than $57,000,000, of which one-half, or $28,500,000, was then being paid. For the payment of her loans Cuba's internal tax yielded $3,360,000 annually, and furnished a surplus above the amount actually needed of $1,270,000.

Reciprocity has bestowed vast and enduring benefits upon the Cubans, but that there is no sentiment in trade, and that commerce will persist in flowing through channels arbitrarily marked out by those in control, regardless of real or implied obligations, the latest commercial statistics seem to show. According to the report of the United States minister to Cuba, indicating the trade between that island and the United States for the first quarter of the fiscal year 1904, it appears that while the imports into the United States from

Cuba were greatly augmented, exports from that country to Cuba increased only three per cent.

The United States took vast quantities of Cuba's sugar and tobacco, the bulk of her output, in fact; but while her imports from this country increased only three per cent., those from France showed an increase of eight per cent., from Spain sixteen, from England twenty, and from Germany twenty-one per cent!

This condition was predicted, as well as clearly explained, by General Tasker H. Bliss, former chief of the Cuban customs service during the intervention, in his valuable report of July, 1902. On " the practical working of the tariff " he says:

" It will be seen that the course of the world's trade with Cuba, having once entered into free and unobstructed channels, with the abolition of the former restrictive tariff, has shown little tendency to variation during the three and one-half years of American administration.

" With the loss of her favoring differentials, Spain lost such part of the trade as she could not keep in open competition, and other nations gained it. The United States, of course, retained its trade in flour and certain other foodstuffs, and in machinery, which it had won in spite of the hostile discrimination of the Spanish tariff, and in the general readjustment of commercial relations which followed the withdrawal of Spanish sovereignty it gained some trade which it did not have before.

" But almost from the beginning the natural trade channels became well defined, and it now appears evident that the volume coming from any given direction, as from the United States, for example, cannot be swelled without some artificial obstruction hindering the flow in other channels.

" With a return of better agricultural conditions in Cuba and the corresponding increase in her purchasing power, there will, of course, be an absolute increase of trade in all directions; but the relative proportions from the different sources of supply will probably show no material change.

" This condition is perfectly natural; is, in fact, the only one that could result from unrestricted trade. The position which the United States occupies with respect to Cuban trade is precisely that which it occupies with respect to all Central and South American countries. In fact, its trade relations with Cuba are more favorable than with the latter countries, because the value, *per capita,* of merchandise imported into the island from the United States is greater than the value of similar importations into other countries of Latin America. This relative advantage which the United States has secured in this direction is due, probably, to the important factor of ' direct ' trade. There are several lines of vessels trading direct between Cuba and ports of the United States. If there is anything in the United States which the inhabitants of Cuba want they can get it by the most direct route in the shortest time, with delivery guaranteed on an exact date. But if the planter or manufacturer in Cuba had to obtain his machinery from the United States in the way that the planter or manufacturer in South America would have to obtain it, if it had to be shipped from New York to England, or France or Germany, and then reshipped, he would undoubtedly do as the South American does, viz., place his order in the country with which he has direct steamer connection.

" So, as a result of greater facilities for direct trade, the United States has a larger proportion of Cuba's foreign trade than it has in the case of other countries similarly situated. But why should it not have all of it instead of only the 45.9 per cent. which it actually has? It has been said and often repeated that the cause is to be found in a deep-rooted prejudice against American goods. But there is no prejudice in Cuba against American flour, or American hams, lard, and pickled meats, or American machinery, or American furniture, or, in fact, against anything from the United States which can be supplied at a lower cost for the same quality or of better quality for the same cost.

" To other causes than prejudice we must look for the real explanation of the fact that the United States has failed to control the foreign trade of Cuba.

" The first of these is the indifference shown by American manufacturers to the essential requisites for securing this foreign market. They manufacture immense quantities of various articles for the home trade, consulting in every possible way as to the material, quality, style, and price; the tastes and preferences of the local consumers. And the surplus stock they expect to sell in Cuba, where they have consulted the tastes and preferences of no one. The result is what might have been anticipated. They fail to sell, and they charge it to local prejudice. They make every effort to consult the local prejudices at home and to manufacture accordingly, and as a result they hold the home trade, even when the tariff puts up no bars to competition. English, French, Spanish, and German manufacturers consult the local prejudices of Cuba, and as a result they capture the trade."

This accurate forecast of trade conditions in Cuba following upon the bestowal of reciprocity, and the suggestions of one who had made an exhaustive study of the subject, are worthy of being pondered by those who would enter into trade relations with the rich and prospering little republic that lies at the gateway of the vaster country of South and Central America. All the Latin-American countries are alike in respect to their trade prejudices and preferences, and to successfully cater to and control the commerce of one is to obtain an " open-sesame " to all the others.

In 1905 President Palma was reëlected after an exciting campaign. Corruption was openly charged against the administration, and the opposing party—the Liberals, with General José Miguel Gomez at their head—refused to acquiesce. Disturbances occurred early in the new year, and by August feeling had developed to the point of insurrection. There were demands in the island for American intervention for the protection of property and the settlement of the governmental dispute. A few United States marines were temporarily landed at Havana, but President Roosevelt ordered their withdrawal in order to give the Cuban factions opportunity to settle their differences by themselves. It was very evident, however, that American intervention was eagerly looked to by both parties, as well as by the American business interests in the islands.

The resignation of President Palma and a new election under the auspices of a commissioner of the United States were proposed. It was thought that this plan would in all probability bring about a return to peace, for the attitude of the United States was firm in demanding the permanent pacification of the island. Palma resigned, and on September 29, 1906, Secretary of War Taft of the United States issued a proclamation taking possession of the island for the purpose of restoring order, protecting life and property, and establishing permanent peace. A disarmament commission under General Funston was formed to oversee the dispersal of the insurgent bands. This assumption of authority was purely provisional and in accordance with the original pledge of the United States to intervene whenever necessary " for the preservation of Cuban independence, and the maintenance of a government adequate for the protection of life, property, and individual liberty."

On October 9, Governor Taft declared a general amnesty to the rebels, and having placed affairs in excellent shape, he left Cuba, with Charles E. Magoon in charge as Provisional Governor. The latter issued a decree giving amnesty to members of the armed forces in Cuba, April 20, 1907. For some months commissioners worked upon a treaty that would settle for all time the Cuban disturbances, and finally it was signed at Washington, December 20. In the following August, General Menocal received the Conservative National nomination for president, while on September 3, José Miguel Gomez was nominated by the Cuban Liberals. September 14 was set aside for the presidential elections, which resulted in the success of Gomez. The latter was proclaimed president-elect on January 20, 1909. After his inauguration, one of the first acts of the new president was the signing of a general amnesty bill. Since then, Cuban affairs have been under his wise control, and the country is in the highest state of prosperity, outside capital finding ready and profitable investment here.

The population in 1908, was estimated to be 2,048,980. The exports were $116,592,648, while the imports were $105,218,206.

During 1909-10, the first year of General Gomez's administration, the finances of Cuba were put in a better condition, and public order was well preserved. In 1911 the trade and commerce continued to improve, and at the beginning of the year the balance of trade was considerably in favor of Cuba.

Beginning with the fall of 1911 there began to be much talk of corruption under the new Gomez administration, in granting concessions and in the multiplication of public offices. Havana seemed to be the hotbed of these rumors while the country districts remained quiet and content.

The factions of the "ins" and the "outs" began to show strong party feeling in politics. The feeling of the veterans of the War of Cuban Independence was especially bitter against those office holders who had not fought for Cuban liberty. There were even some holding positions who had been in open sympathy with Spain. Congress was forced at last to suspend the Civil Service laws. To avert a crisis the United States Government at Washington issued a stern note of warning in January, 1912.

President Gomez finally restored a semblance of order by giving way to the veterans, and dismissed a number of objectionable office holders. One of these dismissed officials added to the ferment by obtaining a judgment from the courts declaring his dismissal was unconstitutional, since the suspension of the Civil Service laws was an unconstitutional act.

The political unrest started by the outbreak of the veterans soon caused a like state of revolt among the army and the negroes. In the spring of 1911 this was especially pronounced. In the eastern provinces the negroes broke out in open revolt, with resulting labor troubles in the provinces. The lives and property of the inhabitants, many of whom were Americans and foreigners, were threatened. Mr. Knox, the American Secretary of State, visited Havana in April, 1911, and it was felt that nothing short of American intervention would bring lasting peace to the island. An American battleship squadron was concentrated at Key West. These preparations caused great excitement in the Cuban capital, and the government succeeded in overawing the insurgents to some extent. In September, 1911, the United States Government was forced to peremptorily demand the monthly payment of $400,000 due American contractors for work on sewers and paving in the city of Havana. This was paid on September 25.

A new source of controversy arose from the presidential decree giving a railway concession for a new road between Caibarien and Nuevitas, and between Camaguey and Santa Cruz del Sur. This was bitterly fought by the Cuban Central Railway, which claimed exclusive rights in the territory.

The presidential elections of November, 1912, were quiet notwithstanding the height of public feeling. The election proved a victory for the conservative party by a majority of about 13,000. General Mario G. Menocal was elected President. The new government came into power on May 20, 1913, when General Menocal was inaugurated. The new president has been the manager for a number of years of a large sugar plantation. His program, as announced, was to cultivate closer relations with the United States and to push agricultural and industrial development throughout the island.

Chapter VII

HAYTI AND SAN DOMINGO. 1802—

EDITED BY PHILIP PATTERSON WELLS, PH. D.

FEW colonies have been the scene of changes so surprising as the Island of Hayti, or San Domingo. It was here that Columbus planted the first American colony; and its flourishing capital, long after the mineral wealth of the island had become of little account, remained one of the principal glories of the Spanish Indies. Westward of this Spanish settlement the buccaneers established the French colony, which, as we have already seen, grew into importance as the Spanish settlement declined. We have traced in another volume the strange history of the rise and progress of the Western settlement; of its share in the revolutionary struggles of France; of the union of the blacks and mulattoes, and their terrible struggle with the whites. There is nothing so interesting to be said about the Eastern settlement. At the treaty of Basle it was ceded by the Spanish minister Godoy to France. The Haytians, under Toussaint, entered upon it as the representatives of the French; but they were expelled by the French generals who were sent by Bonaparte in 1802 to reduce the whole island, and it remained in possession of the French until 1809, when they were driven out by the help of the English as the allies of Spain; and the capital town of San Domingo remained in possession of the English until the peace of 1814, when it was resigned to Spain. In a few years, however, there was a revolution; the colony then, as we shall presently see, put itself into the hands of Boyer, the President of Hayti, and the whole island was thus during his presidency reduced under a single government. After his fall the Spaniards again made themselves independent, and the island was divided, as it still remains, into the Haytian and Dominican republics. The fortunes of the western part of the island, which on its independence assumed the old name of Hayti, form one of the most curious chapters in modern history. It almost seems to us like a philosophical romance written by Swift or Voltaire; and it is certain that if any satirist had written such a story it would have been censured as too improbable. That the negroes of a West India island should succeed in defeating not only their white masters, but the wealthy and intelligent race of mulattoes who shared the island with them, might have seemed unlikely enough; but that they should be able to defy and destroy the best of the French armies, the heroes of Marengo and the Pyramids, and to make themselves independent of Bonaparte when all Europe was crouching at his feet, must have seemed impossible. At every subsequent stage the history of Hayti reveals fresh surprises. Negro adventurers making themselves emperors and kings; creating their swarthy princes, dukes, and counts; practicing all the stale devices of despotism; their subtlety, avarice, and cruelty; the ruin and degeneration of the poor negro people, and their sudden awaking into fierce activity; the strange aspect of negro society, with its debased French dialect, its Christianity mingled with fetichism, and its general travesty of European life; in the midst of all this the revival of republican ideas, derived from France, and their occasional triumph, followed by an inevitable relapse; all this done by an African race only half Europeanized through serfdom on a foreign soil, and launched into political existence by the convulsions of the French Revolution, certainly make up a picture without a parallel.

When the destruction of the French forces in San Domingo fell like a thunderbolt upon the European world, it came to be seen that of all facts in history the establishment of the Haytian nation was not only one of the most curious, but also one of the most portentous. It was the composite result of many separate movements; of the extermination of the natives, of many years of French enterprise in the plantations, of the African slave-trade, of intercourse with Europe, and of the spirit of political independence culminating in the shock of the French Revolution. Seldom in history had so swift, so complete, and so terrible a vengeance overtaken oppression and cruelty; and the warning note, as we have seen, was not heard in vain by the statesmen of England. The independence of Hayti rapidly precipitated the abolition of the slave-trade, and ultimately of slavery in the English colonies. It did far more than anything else to establish for the negro and colored races a place in the civilized world; and the feeling of wonder and abhorrence which it at first excited was gradually exchanged for one of interest, and even sympathy. But it was long enough before this change took place. One of the richest regions of the world was now in possession of the despised race who had been imported as slaves to cultivate it; and we can hardly credit the awful retribution which they exacted from the race of oppressors. In the beginning of 1804 the independence of the negroes under Dessalines was sufficiently assured; but they were not satisfied until they had completed a general massacre of nearly the whole of the whites, including aged men, women, and children, who remained in the island, numbering, according to the lowest estimate, 2500 souls. Thus did Dessalines, in his own savage words, render war for war, crime for crime, and outrage for outrage, to the European cannibals who had so long preyed upon his unhappy race.

The negroes declared Dessalines emperor; and in October, 1804, he was crowned at Port-au-Prince by the title of James I. Dessalines was at once a brave man and a cruel and avaricious tryant. He acquired great influence over the negroes, who long remembered him with affectionate regret; but he was not warmly supported by the mulattoes, who were by far the most intelligent of the Haytians. He abolished the militia, and set up a standing army of 40,000 men, whom he found himself unable to pay, from the universal ruin which had overtaken the island. The plantation laborers refused to work, as they always do in the absence of an over-ruling necessity; Dessalines authorized the landowners to flog them. Dessalines was himself a large planter; he had thirty-two large plantations of his own to work, and he forced his laborers to work on them at the point of the bayonet. Both he and his successor Christophe, like Mohammed Ali in Egypt, grew rich by being the chief merchants in their own dominions. With the view of encouraging planting, he burned down whole plantations of valuable dyeing woods, thereby destroying the best export trade of the island. He failed in an expedition against San Domingo, the Spanish part of the island, whence the French General Ferrand still threatened him; and at length some sanguinary acts of tyranny roused against him an insurrection headed by his old comrade Christophe. The insurgents marched on Port-au-Prince, and the first black emperor was shot by an ambuscade at the Pont Rouge, outside the town. The death of Dessalines delivered up

Hayti once more to the horrors of civil war. The negroes and mulattoes, who had joined cordially enough to exterminate their common enemies, would no longer hold together; and ever since the death of Dessalines their jealousies and differences have been a source of weakness in the black republic.

In the old times, Hayti, as the French part of the island of Española was henceforth called, had been divided into three provinces: South, East, and North. After the death of Dessalines each of these provinces became for a time a separate state. Christophe wished to maintain the unlimited imperialism which Dessalines had set up; but the constituent assembly, which he summoned at Port-au-Prince in 1806, had other views. They resolved upon a republican constitution, consisting of a senate of twenty-four members, who were to have the real government in their hands, Christophe retaining the title of president. Christophe, who was like Dessalines, a mere military leader, and knew nothing of the mysteries of statesmanship, collected an army with the view of dispersing the constituent assembly; but they collected one of their own, under Pétion, and forced him to retire from the capital. Christophe maintained himself in Cap François, or as it is now called, Cap Haytien: and here he ruled for fourteen years. In 1811, despising the imperial title which Dessalines had desecrated, he took the royal style by the name of Henry I. Christophe, as a man, was nearly as great a monster as Dessalines. He was the slave of furious passions. His chief amusements were to cane his generals and degrade them to the ranks; to pump cold water on the heads of his judges, and to send his ministers of state to hard labor on the terrible fortifications of La Ferrière, where each stone is reckoned to have cost the life of a human being. He drank himself into a semi-paralysis; and from this time a revolution became inevitable. Yet Christophe at his best was a man capable of great aims, and a sagacious and energetic ruler. He raised education, industry, and commerce to a position from which they steadily lapsed under the republic. He greatly improved the condition and discipline of his troops; there was, indeed, no department of state in which he did not display judgment and ability. Believing that it was for the benefit of Hayti to discard everything French as soon as possible, Christophe tried to introduce the English language, but without success. Resolving to surround himself with all the proper belongings of his position, he procured costly robes and jewels from England for the solemn coronation of himself and his black queen. He inquired diligently how George III., to whom, though a negro of almost pure descent, he bore a near resemblance, usually dressed and comported himself; and his common dress was made in imitation of King George's well-known Windsor uniform. He built his palace of Sans Souci, a few miles from Cap François, in imitation of the country seats of the great European monarchs. He established a new order of chivalry, that of St. Henry; he had his grand almoner, and grand cupbearer, and all the usual append- ages of feudal royalty. He made bishops and archbishops, and created an aristocracy of black barons, counts, and dukes, so that his court was full of Royal Highnesses, Serene Highnesses, Graces, and Excellencies. One of the best things that Christophe did was to reverse the absurd exclusive policy of Dessalines, and to throw open his ports to the ships of foreign nations. In imitation of Napoleon he also compiled a new statute-book, which he called the *Code-Henri*. In 1820, after a cruel massacre of some women of their race, the mulattoes arose in arms to dethrone him; and Henry I., finding himself deserted by his own negro generals, shot him- self in his own palace. With Christophe the monarchy of the North ceased. His intended successor was an ancient negro whom he had made Grand Marshal of Hayti and Prince of Limbé, called Paul Romain. Romain pretended to side with the revolution; but being detected in a conspiracy with the Duke of Marmalade, both were shot by the soldiers. In a month or two after Christophe's suicide the whole island was united under the rule of President Boyer.

While Christophe was making himself independent in the North, Alexander Pétion, a man of far greater worth and capacity, was elected president, with the right of nominating his successor, in the Western Province, where the mulattoes predominated. Pétion was a mulatto of the best type; he had been educated at the military academy of Paris, and was full of European ideas; in 1802 he had been the leader of both Dessalines and Christophe, and during the eleven years of his rule the Western Province recovered some share of its old prosperity. He organized the revenue, threw open commerce, made provision for the education of the people and for enabling them to become owners of land, but his liberal policy did not win him the confidence of the negroes. Pétion discontinued the system of forced labor which had been rigorously maintained by Dessalines and Christophe; and hence, though the produce supplied from Port-au-Prince was perhaps greater than that from Cap François, the prosperity of the rural districts in his part of the island quickly diminished. He was deceived in supposing that the negroes in their uncivilized condition would become active and industrious as soon as they became owners of land. He secured Hayti against the intrigues of the French politicians after the Restoration; and his constitution, which took its final shape in 1816, was afterward adopted by Boyer, thus exercising an important influence on the future of the republic. It had many defects, one of which was that the president was to be chosen for life, with the power of nominating his successor, thus becoming a sovereign in everything but the name. The house of representatives was to be chosen for five years, and the senate, which was elected by the president and the lower house, for nine. Pétion employed Rigaud, the old rival of Toussaint, who, unlike Toussaint, had succeeded in escaping from his French prison, to subdue the turbulent South Province; but this man made himself independent, and got the provincial assembly to declare him governor with absolute power. Thus, besides the Spanish part of the island, Hayti was now divided into three hostile provinces under the rule respectively of Christophe, Pétion, and Rigaud. Christophe made war upon Rigaud, and the latter, unable to defend himself, and deserted by his own people, starved himself to death in 1811. Pétion, disgusted by the ill success of his efforts to make Hayti a homogeneous nation, and dreading the advancing power of Christophe, committed suicide in the same way in 1818, having nominated as his successor in the presidency his lieutenant, Jean Pierre Boyer, another of the mulatto race who had distinguished himself in the war of liberty.

Boyer began his presidency by a successful campaign against Christophe, and in a short time he had besides this reunited the South to the West Province. Still greater successes awaited him. On the suicide of Christophe, the army of the Northern Province, weary of the tyranny of one of their own race, declared for Boyer. The French part of the island was now once more under a single government; and Boyer turned his attention to the much larger Spanish territory, with the old capital of San Domingo, where a Spaniard named Muñez de Caceres, with the aid of the negroes, had now followed the example in the West, and proclaimed an independent government. The Dominicans, however, were still afraid of Spain, and were glad to put themselves under the wing of Hayti; Boyer was not unwilling to take possession of the Spanish colony, and thus it happened that in 1822 he united the whole island under his presidency. In the same year he was elected president for life under the constitution of Pétion, whose general policy he maintained; but his government, especially in his later years, was almost as despotic as that of Christophe. Boyer was the first Haytian who united the blacks and mulattoes under his rule. It was mainly through confidence in him that the government of Hayti won the recognition of the European powers. Hitherto even the new free state of Colombia, to the establishment of which Hayti had lent material aid, had hesitated to recognize it; but in 1825 its independence was formally recognized by France, on a compensation of 150,000,000 of francs being guaranteed to the exiled planters and to the home government. This vast sum was afterward reduced, but it still weighed heavily on the impoverished state, and the discontents which the necessary taxation produced led to Boyer's downfall. He attempted in vain to revive agriculture by renewing the policy of Toussaint and Christophe. His *Code Rural,* which was voted 'in 1826, was very much like some famous old laws in the English Statute book, which enable the magistrates to apprehend vagrant and idle people and set them to work, whether they will or no. The *Code Rural* was perhaps a good measure, but legislation will not always undo the misfortunes which have come of bad government. Boyer also introduced a paper currency, which in after times proved most ruinous to the island by disturbing its credit. It also facilitated revolutions; for money is necessary to a new government, and by the help of the printing press a successful insurgent can always coin what money he pleases. Boyer's paper money soon fell in value, and by 1842 it passed for little more than a third of its nominal worth. The credit and prosperity of the island could not be reëstablished, and his government grew weaker and weaker. The large and unmanageable army which had become necessary had at last to be reduced, because Boyer could no longer pay for its maintenance; and this led at once to the break-up of the government. The Spanish part of the island revolted; and in 1842 an ambitious man of letters named Dumesles, and a major of artillery named Rivière-Hérard, set on foot a conspiracy to seize the government.

Boyer, though he could scarcely have thought himself secure in his position, was slack in repressing it. In 1843 he was beaten successively at Pestal and Léogone, and fled to Jamaica in an English vessel. The revolution of 1848 attracted him to Paris, where he died in 1850. Decayed as was the prosperity of Hayti toward the end of Boyer's presidency, it still had a foreign trade in proportion to its population not much below those of Great Britain and of the United States. We thus see that, in spite of everything, Hayti had much to lose by misgovernment, and cannot wonder at the fall of the government of Boyer.

The word gerontocracy, signifying government by old men, has been framed to express the system by which the Haytian Government was during several years carried on. The Haytian nation, as we have seen, consisted of two irreconcilable races; and was besides divided into three provinces which maintained a perpetual rivalry. The independence of Hayti had been won originally by the valor of the negroes; but the constitution, with all its belongings, was the work of the mulattoes, and since the time of Pétion the government practically had been in the hands of a few of this race. But under Boyer the constitution had been undermined, and the government had become almost as arbitrary as in the time of Dessalines. Boyer was succeeded by the insurgent general Hérard, whose policy, as he pretended, was to restore the constitution. He proclaimed the responsibility of ministers to the assembly, abolition of the military commissions by which the government had been carried on by his predecessor, and a term of years instead of the presidency for life. But the negroes, profiting by the divisions among the mulattoes, now rose in arms. The mulattoes were chiefly inhabitants of the towns; the negroes mostly a poor, idle, and fast-multiplying peasantry. They were by far the most numerous race; they had lost all confidence in mulatto government, and indeed in government of any sort, for such ideas as they had on the subject mostly tended to socialism; and large numbers of them, under the names of *piquets* and *zinglins,* now formed themselves into armed bands, and sought to obtain a general division of property under some communistic monarch of their own race. The mulatto officials now cajoled the poor negroes by bribing some old negro, whose name was well known to the mass of his people as one of the heroes of the war of liberty, to allow himself to be set up as president.

The Boyerists, as the mulatto oligarchy were called, thus succeeded
in reëstablishing their power at the very moment when the negroes
believed it to be completely crushed. Hérard, who was ill-qualified
for his office, soon had to abdicate the presidency, and the Boyerists elected in his place a veteran negro general named Guerrier.
They now completed their ascendency by abolishing the constitution and forming themselves into a council of state. Guerrier,
who was an incapable old drunkard, died in the next year, and the
council replaced him by another old negro soldier called Pierrot.
Pierrot, however, showed himself unwilling to remain a mere tool
of the mulattoes. He thought of the glory of negro royalty under
Dessalines and Christophe, and he knew that by the aid of the
negroes he might easily renew it. But the mulattoes were too
quick for his intended *coup d'état*: and in 1846 he was replaced
by General Riché, an old negro lieutenant of Christophe's. The
negroes had, of course, found out by this time the system by which
they had been thus cajoled. They rose in several places against the
government, and an army of *piquets,* under a ferocious negro called
Aca-au, gave General Riché much trouble. Riché died under mysterious circumstances in less than a year, and the ruling oligarchy
were now divided between two other imbecile old negroes, named
Souffran and Paul. After eight scrutinies they could not decide
which was duly elected, and the president of the senate suddenly
brought forward as a candidate one whom they thought only a
third military puppet. This was General Solouque, and he was
elected president in 1847. No one was more astonished at his elevation than Solouque himself; but he showed himself, as we shall
see, quite equal to his position. Solouque was an illiterate negro
whose recommendations to power were that he was old enough
to have taken part in the War of Independence, having been a
lieutenant under Pétion, and that he was popular with the negroes,
being devotedly attached to the strange mixture of freemasonry
and fetish worship by which the Haytian blacks maintain their political organization. The history of Pierrot and Riché was not
lost upon Solouque. He at once got rid of the mulattoes to whom
he owed his elevation, and surrounded himself with a new body
of adherents. The devices of the Boyerists were by this time
worn out, and everyone knew that a fresh despotism was impending.

Solouque was apprehensive of being deprived of his position

by the same hands that had elevated him, and he sought by every possible means to secure the support of all belonging to his own race. He imprisoned a general who had shown himself too eager to repress the *piquets;* and on some demonstrations being made in this officer's favor, he prepared a *coup d'état.* He caused a general massacre to be made of the mulattoes at Port-au-Prince, after which he marched into the south, put himself at the head of the *piquets,* and established military commissions in all the towns. A negro reign of terror was now established all over the country; the mulatto party was crushed, and Solouque caused himself to be proclaimed emperor, by the title of Faustinus I. (1840). The bold action taken by Solouque was well adapted to win the admiration of the negroes, and he was crowned in 1852, with all the imperial pomp and circumstance which negro imagination could suggest. He reigned nine years; and the story of his reign is one of massacre and confiscation, varied only by disastrous expeditions against the Spanish republic in the eastern part of the island. Nothing could be weaker than Solouque's state policy. He declared sugar and coffee, the staple products of the island, as well as most of the other products of the soil, to be imperial monopolies. Believing that his empire chiefly needed for its consolidation a well-ordered system of social grades, he created a black nobility out of his adherents, including four princes of the empire and fifty-two dukes. Solouque's rule, however, was not really strengthened by such dignitaries as the Duke de Lemonade, the Duke de Trou-Bonbon, and the Prince Tape-à-l'œil; and his real resource was a standing army of *piquets,* whom he obliged to cultivate his own sugar plantations. His military discipline was as cruel as his greed was insatiable, and at length, as in the case of Christophe, his own soldiers turned against him. When his misgovernment could be borne no longer, and a leader was sought to dethrone him, all eyes were fixed on Geffrard, a mulatto general who had served under Rivière-Hérard, and who had long represented the party of fusion. In December, 1858, Solouque attempted to arrest Geffrard; but he escaped from the capital, and the tyrant contented himself with imprisoning his wife and daughters. The prisons were soon crowded with mulattoes: and Geffrard having put himself at the head of the remains of the republican party, reëntered Port-au-Prince and dethroned Solouque, just in time to prevent an atrocious massacre. Solouque was allowed to retreat to Jamaica, carrying with him his black empress, the imperial jewels, and a considerable amount of treasure.

In 1859 General Geffrard was elected president of the Haytian Republic. The constitution of 1816 was reëstablished; a truce of five years was made with the Dominicans, and Geffrard applied himself with some success to the restoration of the national prosperity. The negroes, as usual, were the chief obstacles. They can never remain contented with a mulatto government; while experience shows that tranquillity may be to some extent preserved by placing a negro at the head of the government, and keeping him as far as possible subject to constitutional checks. Geffrard held the presidency for eight years; at the end of which, unable to carry on the government any longer, he resigned, and was succeeded by the insurgent negro General Salnave. Salnave's policy was, of course, to restore the empire, and he attempted to make himself dictator on pretense of introducing reforms in the constitution. The senate, however, was beforehand with an impeachment; the whole people were by this time weary of imperialism; independent generals soon established themselves both in the north and the south, and Salnave was shot as a traitor to the nation in 1869. His *piquet* partisans were still strong in the south; and the succeeding mulatto president, Nissage-Saget, was unable to hold his ground. All the negroes, even the most intelligent, are impatient of mulatto rule, and suspicious of the means used to secure it; and as they are the great majority of the people, there can be no doubt that if they had fair play in the elections the island would generally be under a negro president. To obviate another military revolution, there was a new election: and the negro general, Domingue, who had been a candidate for the presidency against Nissage-Saget in 1869, was elected president in 1874. But in 1876 Domingue was displaced by a mulatto revolution, which gave the presidency to General Boisrond-Canal, who was now elected for a term of four years. He was, however, forced to resign and flee the country in 1879, and was succeeded by the negro leader Saloman. Saloman was in turn deposed in 1888, and was followed, after an interval of civil war, by General Hippolyte, who ruled until his death in 1896. His successor, General Simon Sam, was driven from power in 1902, and another period of civil war resulted in the proclamation by the army of General Nord as president. Thus the first century of Haytian independence has been marked by fre-

quent and bloody civil wars, resulting in the setting up of one inefficient and corrupt government after another. Competent observers have declared that the people are relapsing into savagery,
and that paganism and cannibalism are common among them. The
constant disorder and the arbitrary acts of the government have
more than once involved the country in difficulties with foreign
nations. A notable case occurred in 1897, when one Lueders, a
Haytian-born German, who had secured German citizenship, was
illegally arrested. Germany demanded his release, with indemnity of $1000 for each day of his imprisonment. Upon the
refusal of these terms the German consul hauled down his flag.
Thereupon the good offices of the American minister secured the
release of Lueders. Two German warships appeared at Port-au-
Prince on December 6 and threatened to bombard the town within
twenty-four hours unless the indemnity was paid. The Haytian
government yielded and paid the money. Action of this character
in the western hemisphere by a European nation always excites
the jealous suspicion of the American people, and might lead to a
serious disturbance of the world's peace. The United States is
therefore interested in behalf of stable government in Hayti.
Therefore, when, on January 16, 1908, a revolution was begun
under Jean Juneau, the United States was concerned. This rebel
was soon captured, however, and executed on January 25. More
trouble was experienced that same year, and on November 20, troops
were sent to the southern part to suppress the revolt which had
broken out. Affairs became so turbulent that General Antoine F.
C. Simon assumed temporary charge, December 8. His recognition on December 17, by the United States, decided him to take
full charge, and on December 20, he took the oath of office. At
present he is the incumbent of the presidency, and under his rule,
with a population of 1,500,000, Hayti exported during 1908, products to the amount of $3,478,848, with an import trade during
that same year of $4,701,160.

The history of the Spanish part of San Domingo, since its independence, has but little to do with that of the Haytian Republic.
The instinct of independence here proceeded from quite other
causes. The first outbreak, as we have seen, was simultaneous
with the revolt against Spanish rule on the American continent;
and the acquisition of the colony by Hayti under Boyer no doubt
preserved it from being retaken by a Spanish fleet. We have seen

that its revolt from the Haytian domination had commenced before
the fall of Boyer in 1843. The Haytian Republicans had treated
it as a conquered country, and endeavored to efface every trace of
Spanish nationality; and the white inhabitants, who were a large
majority, naturally revolted against the government of the western
mulattoes. The revolt was led by the landowners, but all classes
joined heartily in the movement, which was soon successfully accomplished. Since its independence the history of San Domingo
belongs rather to that of Spanish America than to that of Hayti.
A conservative constitution, in imitation of that of Venezuela, was
proclaimed in 1844, the first president of the new state being Pedro
Santana. For fourteen years the Dominican Republic maintained
a precarious existence against the attacks of its Haytian neighbors, which were invited by the continual struggles of the democratic party to modernize the community. As the liberal party
gained ground, the patriotism of the conservatives decayed. Some
of them were for reunion with Hayti, others for submission to
Spain; and at length, in 1858, Santana, who had been obliged to
quit the island, suddenly invaded it and established a despotic provisional government, which in 1861 ceded the island to Spain.
This event is connected with the revival of European intervention
in America in the time of Napoleon III. of France, who took advantage of the Civil War in the United States to forward his
schemes. Spanish troops once more took possession of the colony;
but the democratic party, which was now greatly increased in
numbers, rose against the occupation, and in three years' time San
Domingo was again left to the devices of its native politicians.
The liberal President Baez was now placed at the head of the
government, but being unable to make head against an insurrection, he decided on trying to secure progress for San Domingo by
incorporating it with the United States.

After the close of the American Civil War this project formed
a part of the expansion policy of Seward, Secretary of State
under Presidents Lincoln and Johnson. His efforts in this direction were continued by the following administration. In July,
1869, President Grant sent General O. E. Babcock to inquire into
conditions in the island. This mission resulted in the negotiation
of a treaty of annexation and a convention for the acquisition of
the town and bay of Samana for a naval station. The treaty was
acceptable to the Dominicans, but aroused strong opposition in

the United States, and failed of ratification in the Senate. Annexation was approved by a congressional commission in 1871, and brought forward again by the Dominican Government in 1874, but the opposition in the United States was too strong to be overcome. The political history of the Dominican Republic during the sixty years of its independence is a monotonous record of civil strife and revolution. One successful revolutionist after another has seized the presidency by force, only to be driven from power by a new rebellion. A fortunate few retained the office for the full term. Some degree of stability was attained under the absolute despotism of President D. Ulysses Hereux, whose rule of fifteen years was ended by his assassination July 26, 1899, since which time the island has suffered from chronic revolution, military chieftains seizing power in rapid succession and driving opponents into exile. These struggles have been accompanied by injuries to foreigners residing or trading in the republic, by the granting of valuable concessions for little or no consideration, and by the accumulation of large claims against the republic in the hands of foreigners. In these circumstances President Morales sought the aid of the United States, and on January 22, 1905, it was announced that a protocol had been signed providing for the administration of the customs revenue by the United States, forty-five per cent. to be used for the expenses of the Dominican Government, and the balance, less the cost of administration, for the payment or adjustment of foreign creditors. Subject to these conditions the United States is to guarantee the political and territorial integrity of San Domingo. A treaty formally embodying the agreement was submitted to the United States Senate but failed to be ratified. The population shows a healthy increase, it being estimated at 610,000 in 1908. During that same year the exports were $7,638,536, while the imports were $5,156,121.

The Dominican states have done little to demonstrate their capacity for self-government. Their independence has been protected first by geographical isolation and climatic conditions, and second by the policy of the United States in regard to European interference in the western hemisphere. But swift steamships have put an end to isolation, and the scientific treatment of disease has made possible successful campaigning in the tropics by an army of white men. The United States has acquired the neighboring island of Porto Rico, and is beginning to see that if European intervention is to be prohibited American intervention may become necessary, unless the island governments attain sufficient stability to give reasonable protection to life and property, and to fulfill international obligations.

In Hayti General Antoine F. C. Simon brought no reforms, and his government was as inefficient as those that preceded him. A revolution broke out on July 20, 1911, and the United States gunboats *Petrol* and *Peoria* were despatched to Port-au-Prince to protect American and foreign citizens. The Simon government was overthrown and General Firmin, the leader of the revolutionists, captured the city of Port-au-Prince.

On July 23, 1911, General Leconte, who had been exiled to Jamaica, landed once more on his native soil. He at once collected a large force, made triumphal entry into the capital, and was elected Provisional President of the republic. Another revolution broke out under General Fouchard, but it failed to overthrow Leconte's government. General Leconte was then recognized by the United States and ruled until August 8, 1912, when he perished in the burning of the presidential palace caused by the explosion of a large quantity of ammunition that had been stored in the cellar of the palace. Over three hundred soldiers and citizens lost their lives by this accident.

General Augusto Tancred succeeded to the presidency. In 1913 the finances of the country were still greatly involved although the general receiver of customs is an American citizen, and the whole custom finances are administered through him by a special convention signed with the United States.

The year 1909 marked an epoch in the history of the republic of San Domingo, as it was one of unusual prosperity and progress. Two railroads were completed, connecting Santiago and Moca and Salcedo with Puerto de Sanchez. In 1910 the National Bank of San Domingo was established mainly through Cuban financiers.

In November, 1910, trouble broke out with Hayti on the subject of the boundary between the two republics, the dispute finally being submitted to the Hague tribunal for settlement.

President Ramon Caceres was assassinated in November, 1911, and Señor Eladio Victoria assumed control of the government as Provisional President, and was regularly elected to that office on December 6, 1911.

On February 5, 1912, the Chamber confirmed the election of Señor Victoria for the regular term of six years.

The finances of the republic were placed under the supervision of an American citizen who was appointed receiver of customs.

On June 5, 1912, another revolution broke out, this time under the leadership of one D'Orcilien, and the struggle between the government troops and insurgents continued during the months of July, August, and September. In September, 1912, the United States intervened to restore order. Marines from the *Wheeling* landed to protect American interests. They also seized the custom house and restored order.

In November a compromise was reached between the followers of President Victoria and the revolutionists by which the President resigned office on November 26, 1912. Archbishop Nouel was elected Provisional President and installed on December 1, 1912.

During 1913 the Dominican Republic suffered greatly from revolutionary disturbances. The country in 1914 continued to be in a great state of unrest. In August, 1914, President Wilson sent a commission to endeavor to bring about a betterment in the republic's condition and, if possible, to establish peace. Finally an armistice was agreed upon. President Bordas Valdes was induced to resign, and Dr. Ramon Baez became Provisional President with the understanding that he was not to be a candidate for election as permanent President. The election took place on October 25, 1914, and resulted in the selection of Juan I. Jiminez, who took office on December 4, 1914. In Hayti, General Tancrède Auguste died on May 2, 1913. Michel Oreste was elected to succeed him on May 4, but great disturbances followed. Hayti accepted a peace plan of Secretary Bryan on June 10, and the country gradually began to become settled again.

But in 1914 the series of revolutions so common to the country began again. A revolution broke out against President Oreste. The rebels soon grew strong enough to capture Cape Haytien and Gonaïves. President Oreste fled to Colombia. Senatu Theodore and General Zamor both proclaimed themselves President. Zamor entered Port-au-Prince on February 7, 1914, and was at once acclaimed as President. He was subsequently recognized by the United States. In October, Theodore, however, repulsed the government troops and forced the surrender of President Zamor, who was exiled, and Theodore assumed the reigns of government. In December, 1914, affairs became so disorganized that the United States made overtures to secure supervising control over Haytian finances with a view to reorganizing the various branches of the government.

APPENDIX

APPENDIX -

THE RULERS OF MEXICO

NATIVE KINGS

THE HUE HUE TLA PALLAN DYNASTY

CHICHIMEC KINGS

(*More or less mythical*)

1. Nequameth.—2. Namocuix.—3. Miscohuatl.—4. Huitzilopochtli.—5. Huetmuc.
6. Nauyotl.—7. Quauhtepetla.—8. Nonohualca.—9. Huetzin.—10. Quauhtonal.—
11. Masatzin.—12. Quetzal.—13. Icoatzin.

REIGN OF THE TOLLAN DYNASTY

		A. D.
1.	Chalchiuhtlanctzin, son of Icoatzin (Chichimec)	720
2.	Ixtlilcuechahuac	771
3.	Huetzin	823
4.	Totepehu	875
5.	Nacaxoc	927
6.	Mitlen	979
7.	The Queen Xiutlaltzin	1038
8.	Tepencaltzin (Discoverer of Pulque)	1042
9.	Topiltzin	1094
10.	Death of Tepencaltzin and Queen Xochitl, and destruction of the nation	1103

KINGS OF THE TENAYUCAN, OR TEZCOCAN DYNASTY

1.	Xolotl the Great	1120
2.	Nopaltzin	1232
3.	Huetzin Pochotl	1263
4.	Quinantzin	1298
5.	Techotlalatzin	1357
6.	Ixtlilxochitl	1409
7.	Tetzotzomoc, } Usurpers {	1419
8.	Maxtla	1427
9.	Netzahualcoyotl	1430
10.	Netzahualpili	1470
11.	Cacamatzin. (Spanish invasion during his reign)	1516
12.	Cuicuitzcatzin	1520
13.	Coanocotzin	1521
14.	Ixtlilxochitl	1521

508   APPENDIX

REIGN OF THE AZTEC KINGS

A. D.

1. Huitzihuitl (Guide to the Valley of Mexico) . . . . . —
2. Xiuhtemoc (Chief) 1318
3. Acamapichil 1352
4. Huitzilihuitl 1403
5. Chimalpopoca 1414
6. Izcoatl 1427
7. Montezuma I 1436
8. Axayacatl 1464
9. Tizoc 1477
10. Ahuizotl 1486
11. Montezuma II (Spanish invasion in his reign) 1502
12. Citlahuatzin 1520
13. Quauhtemoc or Guatimotzin 1520

THE CULHUACANS

(Tribes contemporary with the Aztecs)

1. Xiutemoc 1109
2. Nauhyotl 1124
3. Achitometl 1141
4. Xohualalorac 1241
5. Calquiyautzin 1241
6. Cocox 1241
7. Acamapictli I 1301
8. Xiutemoc 1303
9. Acamapictli II 1355
10. Chimalpopoca 1402
    After death of this monarch, tributary to Tezcoco

KINGDOM OF AZCAPOTZALCO

(Tribes contemporary with the Aztecs)

1. Acolhua I 1168
2. Acolhua II 1239
3. Tetzotzomoc 1343
4. Maxtla 1427

THE TECPANECAS OF TLACOPAN

(Tribes contemporary with the Aztecs)

1. Totoquiyauhtzin I 1430
2. Chimalpopoca 1469
3. Totoquiyauhtzin II 1487
4. Tetlepanquetzal 1503
    This monarchy terminated with the last king, who was hanged by
    Cortéz.

CONQUERORS AND AUDIENCIAS

1. Hernando Cortéz 1521
2. Luis Ponce 1526

A. D.

3. D. Márcos Aguilar . . . . —
4. Alonzo Estrada and Gonzalo Sandoval 1527
5. Gonzalo de Sandoval . . . . —

6. { Nuño de Guzman
   { Juan Ortiz Matienzo } First Audiencia 1528
   { Diego Delgadillo

7. { Sebastian Ramirez de Fuenleal
   { Juan Salmeron
   { Alonzo Maldonado } Second Audiencia . . . 1529
   { Francisco Ceynos
   { Vasco de Quiroga

VICEROYS

1. Antonio de Mendoza 1535
2. Luis de Velasco 1550
3. Gaston de Peralta 1566
4. Martin Enriquez de Almanza 1568
5. Lorenzo de Mendoza 1580
6. Pedro Moya de Conteras 1584
7. Alvaro Manrique de Zúñiga 1585
8. Luis de Velasco (the second) 1590
9. Gaspar de Zúñiga 1595
10. Juan de Mendoza 1603
11. Luis de Velasco (second time) 1607
12. Fr. Garcia Guerra 1611
13. Diego Fernandez de Córdova 1612
14. Diego Carrillo Mendoza, Marques de Gelves 1621
15. Rodrigo Pacheco Osorio, Marques de Cerralvo . . . 1624
16. Lope Diaz de Armendariz, Marques de Cadereita . . . 1635
17. Diego López Pacheco, Duke of Escalona 1640
18. Juan de Palafox y Mendoza 1642
19. García Sarmiento, Conde de Salvatierra . . . . —
20. Márcos Torres y Rueda 1648
21. Luis Henriquez de Guzman 1650
22. Francisco Fernandez de la Cueva, Duke of Albuquerque . . 1653
23. Juan de la Cerda 1660
24. Diego Osorio Escobar 1664
25. Antonio Sebastian de Toledo . . . . . . —
26. Pedro Nuño de Colon 1673
27. Fr. Payo de Rivera . . . . —
28. Tomás Antonio de la Cerda 1680
29. Melchor Portocarrero 1686
30. Gaspar de la Sandoval 1688
31. Juan Ortega Montañez 1696
32. José Sarmiento y Valladares, Conde de Montezuma . . . —
33. Juan Ortega Montañez (second time) 1701
34. Francisco Fernandez de la Cueva . . . . . . —
35. Fernando de Alencastre, Duke of Linares 1711
36. Baltasar de Zúñiga, Duke of Arion 1716
37. Juan de Acuña, Marques de Casa-Fuerte 1722
38. Antonio Vizarron 1734
39. Pedro de Castro y Figueroa 1740
40. Pedro Cebrian y Agustin, Count de Fuen-Clara . . . 1742
41. Francisco Güemes y Horcasitas, Conde de Revilla-Gigedo . 1746
42. Agustin Ahumada, Marques de las Amarillas 1755
43. Francisco Cajigal de la Vega 1760

A. D.

44. Joaquin de Monserrat . . . . —
45. Cárlos Francisco de Croix 1766
46. Antonio María de Bucareli 1771
47. Martin de Mayorga 1779
48. Matías de Galvez 1783
49. Bernardo de Galvez 1785
50. Alonso Núñez de Haro 1787
51. Manuel Antonio Flores 1787
52. Juan Vicente Guemes Pacheco, Conde de Revilla-Gigedo . . . 1789
53. Miguel de la Grua Talamanca 1794
54. Miguel José de Azanza 1798
55. Félix Berenguer de Marquina 1800
56. José de Iturrigaray 1803
57. Pedro Garibay 1808
58. Francisco Xavier Lizana 1809
59. Pedro Catani, President of the Audiencia. (Revolution) . . . 1810
60. Francisco Xavier Venegas . . . . —
61. Félix Calleja 1813
62. Juan Ruiz de Apodaca 1816
63. Francisco Novella 1821
64. Juan O'Donojú. (Independence) . . . . —

SOVEREIGN PROVISIONAL JUNTA

65 { Antonio, Bishop of Puebla . . }
    { Juan José Espinosa de los Monteros, } 1821
    { José Rafael Suarez Pereda, Secretary, }

REGENCIES

66. { Agustin Iturbide . . }
    { O'Donojú . . }
    { Manuel de la Bárcena . } 1822
    { Isidro Yanez . . }
    { Manuel Velazquez de Leon }
67. Agustin I. (Iturbide), Emperor 1822

EXECUTIVE POWER

68. { General Bravo, }
    { " Victoria, }
    { " Negrete, } 1823
    { " Guerrero, }

PRESIDENTS AND DICTATORS

1. General Guadalupe Victoria 1824
2. " Vicente Guerrero 1829
3. José María Bocanegra 1829
4. { Pedro Velez . . }
   { General Luis Quintanar, } 1829
   { Lúcas Alaman . . }
5. General Anastasio Bustamante (first time) 1830
6. " Melchor Muzquiz 1832

A. D.

7. Manuel Gómez Pedraza . . . . —
8. Valentin Gómez Farías (first time) 1833
9. General Antonio López de Santa-Anna (first time) . . . —
10. "   Miguel Barragan 1835
11. José Justo Corro . . . . —
12. General Anastasio Bustamante (second time) 1837
13. Xavier Echeverría 1841
14. General Antonio López de Santa-Anna (second time) . . . —
15. General Nicolás Bravo . } from 1841 to
16. "   Valentin Canalizo, } 1843
17. "   José Joaquin Herrera (first time) 1844
18. Mariano Paredes y Arrillaga 1846
19. General Nicolás Bravo, *ad interim* (second time) . . . 1846
20. "   Mariano Salas . . . . —
21. Antonio López de Santa-Anna (third time) . . . . —
22. Valentin Gómez Farías (second time). (American War) . . 1847
23. General Antonio López de Santa-Anna (fourth time) . . . —
24. "   Pedro María Anaya (first time) . . . . . —
25. "   Antonio López de Santa-Anna (fifth time) . . . —
26. Manuel de la Peña y Peña (first time) . . . . . —
27. General Pedro María Anaya (second time) . . . . —
28. Manuel de la Peña y Peña (second time) 1848
29. General José Joaquin Herrera (second time) . . . . —
30. "   Mariano Arista 1851
31. "   Juan B. Ceballos 1853
32. Juan Múgica y Osorio . . . . —
33. General Manuel María Lombardini . . . . . . —
34. "   Antonio López de Santa-Anna (sixth time) . . . —
35. "   Rómulo Diaz de la Vega, General-in-chief (first time) . 1855
36. "   Martin Carrera . . . . —
37. "   Rómulo Diaz de la Vega (second time) . . . —
38. "   Juan Alvarez . . . . —
39. "Proprietor" Ignacio Comonfort, as substitute for Alvarez . . —
40. Comonfort, as Constitutional President 1857

REVOLUTIONARY CHIEFS

41. General Félix Zuloaga (first time) 1858
42. "   Manuel Robles Pezuela . . . . —
43. José Ignacio Pavon . . . . —
44. General Miguel Miramon (first time) . . . . . . —
45. "   Félix Zuloaga (second time) 1859
46. "   Miguel Miramon (second time) . . . . . —

REGENCY IMPOSED BY THE INTERVENTION

{ Bishop Juan B. Ormaechea . }
{ General Juan N. Almonte . }
47. { "   Mariano Salas . } 1864
{ Archbishop Pelagio A. Labastida }
48. Archduke of Austria, Maximilian, with title of Emperor . . 1864

CONSTITUTIONAL PRESIDENTS AND MILITARY CHIEFS

                                                   A. D.

49. Benito Juarez, at San Luis and Vera Cruz 1858
50. General Jesus Gonzalez Ortega 1860
51. Benito Juarez, at Mexico City 1861
52. The same, in the Interior, and at Paso del Norte, 1863 to . . . 1867
53. General Porfirio Diaz (in chief) . . . . —
54. Benito Juarez, at Mexico City . . . . —
55.   As Constitutional President, from 1868 to 1871
56.   As Constitutional President 1871
57. Sebastian Lerdo de Tejada, as President of the Court of Justice, by the death of Juarez, from July 19 to December 1872
58. Sebastian Lerdo de Tejada, Constitutional President from January 1, 1873, to 1876
59. General Don Juan N. Mendez (provisional), December 6, 1876, to May 4 1877
60. General Porfirio Diaz, May 5, 1877, to November 30 1880
61. General Manuel Gonzales, December 1 1880
62.   "   Porfirio Diaz, December 1 1884

BIBLIOGRAPHY

BIBLIOGRAPHY

This Bibliography does not represent all the authorities referred to in this volume or consulted in its preparation. It does aim to supply a list of the important readable or reference books which may be appealed to by the general reader interested in pursuing further the study of the Isthmian countries and the islands of the West Indies. The list is purposely made to include many works on the romantic phase of the history of these Spanish-American countries, as well as recent volumes of travel and description.

MEXICO AND CENTRAL AMERICA

Bancroft, Hubert H.—" The Native Races of the Pacific States of North America." 5 vols. New York, 1875-1876.
> Bancroft was familiar with a vast number of early Spanish works on the early inhabitants of Mexico and the Pacific country. In arrangement the volumes successively take up: " The Wild Tribes "; " Civilized Nations "; " Myths and Languages "; " Antiquities "; and, finally, " Primitive History."

——" Resources and Development of Mexico." San Francisco, 1894.
> A standard work.

——" A Popular History of the Mexican People."

Bandelier, A. F.—" On the Social Organization and Mode of Government of the Ancient Mexicans." Cambridge, 1880.
> In the Twelfth Annual Report of the Peabody Museum of American Archæology and Ethnology.

Baxter, S.—" Spanish-Colonial Architecture in Mexico." Boston, 1903.
> A most sumptuous work, not ordinarily accessible in libraries, but very valuable for reference on the interesting subject of architecture in Mexico.

Beebe, C. W.—" Two Bird-Lovers in Mexico." Boston, 1905.
> Will be especially appreciated by the nature enthusiast.

Bell, C. N.—" Tangweera." London, 1899.
> Deals with the Indians of the Mosquito Coast.

Belt, T.—" The Naturalist in Nicaragua." London, 1874.

Bonaparte, Prince Roland—" Le Mexique au Début XXe Siècle." Paris, 1904.

Bowditch, C. P. (ed.).—" Mexican and Central American Antiquities, Calendar Systems, and History." Smithsonian Institute, 1904.

Brigham, T.—" Guatemala, the Land of the Quetzal." London, 1887.

Brocklehurst, T. U.—" Mexico To-day." London, 1883.
> With an account of the prehistoric remains.

Burke, U. R.—" Life of Benito Juarez." London, 1894.
> The life of Juarez constitutes a part of the history of Mexico in its most critical period.

Butler, Wm.—" Mexico in Transition." New York, 1892.

Campbell, Rean.—" Complete Guide and Descriptive Book of Mexico." Chicago, 1904.

Charnay, Désiré.—" Ancient Cities of the New World." London, 1887.
An account of the author's travels in Mexico and Central America during
the years 1857-1882.

Chevalier, Michel.—" *Le Mexique ancien et moderne.*" Paris, 1886.
A translation by Alpass appeared in London, 1864.

Colquhoun, A. R.—" The Key of the Pacific—the Nicaragua Canal." London,
1896.
Like all of this author's works, this volume is an interesting presentation.

Conkling, A. R.—" Appleton's Guide to Mexico." New York.

Conkling, Howard.—" Mexico and the Mexicans." New York, 1883.

" Coronado's Letter to Mendoza, 1540." Published by the Directors of the Old
South Work. Boston, 1903.

" Cortes's Account of the City of Mexico." Published by the Directors of the
Old South Work. Boston, 1903.
Two extremely interesting little pamphlets; source material in miniature.

Croffut, W. A.—" Folks Next Door." 3d ed. Washington, D. C., 1904.
The " log-book of a rambler," and excellently descriptive of travels in Mexico.

Cubas.—" Mexico: Its Trade, Industries, and Resources." Mexico, 1893.
An English translation by Thompson and Cleveland.

El economista Mejicana, published weekly. Mexico.

Enriquez, R. de Zayas.—" *Las Estados Unidos Mejicanos, 1877-1897.*" New
York, 1899.

Flint, H. M.—" Mexico under Maximilian." Philadelphia, 1867.

Gibbs, J. R.—" British Honduras." London, 1883.

Gooch, F. C.—" Face to Face with the Mexicans." London, 1890.

Gonzales, D.—" *Geografia de Centró America.*" San Salvador, 1877.

Hale, Susan.—" The Story of Mexico." New York, 1891.

Helps, A.—" Spanish Conquest in Mexico." 4 vols. New York, 1903.

Howell.—" Mexico: Its Progress and Commercial Possibilities." New York,
1892.
Mexico to-day furnishes one of the most important industrial studies, and
it is regrettable that so few books deal with the country from the important
material standpoint.

Icazbalceta.—" *Documentos para la historia de Méjico.*" 20 vols. Mexico, 1853-
1857.

——" *Colección nueva de documentos para la historia de Méjico.*" 5 vols. Mexico, 1892.
Important to the historical student.

Keane, A. H.—" Central and South America and West Indies." (" Stanford's
Compendium of Geography " series.) London, 1901.
The standard English work of geographical reference.

Kozhevar, E.—" Report on the Republic of Mexico." London, 1886.

La Bédolliere, Emile G. de.—" *Histoire de la guerre du Mexique.*" Paris, 1866.

Lumholtz, C.—" Unknown Mexico." New York, 1903.
Descriptive volumes of absorbing interest and real value, vividly portraying
the country and its people.

Lummis, C. F.—" The Awakening of a Nation." New York, 1898.

McGary, E.—" American Girl in Mexico." New York, 1904.

Mallen, B.—" Mexico Yesterday and To-day, 1876-1904." Mexico, 1904.

Noel, J. V.—" History of the Second Pan-American Congress." Baltimore, Md.,
1903.

Noll, A. H.—" From Empire to Republic." Chicago, 1903.

——" Short History of Mexico." Chicago, 1903.

Ober, Frederick A.—" Hernando Cortés, Conqueror of Mexico." New York, 1905.
——" Travels in Mexico." Boston, 1884.
——" Mexican Resources." New York, 1884.
Palacio, Vincente Riva (ed.).—" *Mexico al través de los siglos.*" 5 vols. Mexico, 1887-1889.
   The standard work on Mexican history, published under the editorial supervision of Vincente Riva Palacio: Vol. I, Chavero, " *Historia antigua y de la conquista;*" Vol. II. Palacio, " *Historia de la dominación española en Mexico desde 1521 á 1808;*" Vol. III, Zarate, " *La guerre de independencia;*" Vol. IV, Olavarria y Ferrari, " *Mexico independiente, 1821-1855;*" Vol. V, Vigil, " *La reforma.*"
Pimentel, F.—" *Obras Completas.*" 5 vols. Mexico, 1903-1904.
   On the peoples, languages, literatures, etc., of Mexico.
Prescott, W. H.—" History of the Conquest of Mexico." London.
Ratzel, Fried.—" *Aus Mexico, Reiseskizzen aus den Jahren 1874-1875.*" Breslau, 1878.
   Still ranks as a standard work.
Romero, M.—" Mexico and the United States." New York, 1898.
   A study of their relations.
——" Geographical and Statistical Notes on Mexico." New York, 1898.
   Valuable for reference.
Routier, G.—" *Le Mexique de nos Jour.*" Paris, 1895.
Sapper, C.—" *Das Nordliche Mittel-Amerika.*" Brunswick, 1897.
——" *Mittelamerikanische Reisen und Studien aus den Jahren 1888 bis 1900.*" Brunswick, 1902.
Schiess, W.—" *Quer durch Mexico.*" Berlin, 1902.
Schroeder, O.—" Republic of Mexico." Denver, Col., 1903.
Seler, E.—" *Auf alten Wegen in Mexiko und Guatemala.*" Berlin, 1900.
Short, John T.—" The North Americans of Antiquity. Their Original Migrations and Type of Civilization Considered." New York, 1880.
   A careful study of material gathered from the Smithsonian reports and the work of specialists in this field, with the Spanish and Mexican sources especially considered.
Smith, A. D.—" *Historia de la Revolución de Mexico contra la dictadura del General Santa Anna.*" Alice, Texas, 1904.
Southworth, J. R.—" The Mines of Mexico." Mexico, 1905.
Starr, Frederick.—" Readings from Modern Mexican Authors." Chicago, 1904.
——" Physical Characters of the Indians of Southern Mexico." Chicago, 1903.
Stevenson, S. Y.—" Maximilian in Mexico." New York, 1899.
Surra, J.—" Mexico: Its Social Evolution." 3 vols. Mexico, 1905.
Tweedie, Mrs. A.—" Mexico as I Saw It." London, 1901.
——" Porfirio Diaz." London, 1906.
Wells, D. A.—" A Study of Mexico." New York, 1886.
Winton, G. B.—" New Era in Old Mexico." Nashville, Tenn., 1905.
Wright, Marie R.—" Picturesque Mexico." Philadelphia, 1898.

WEST INDIES

Canini, I. E.—" Four Centuries of Spanish Rule in Cuba." Chicago, 1898.
Clark, Wm. J.—" Commercial Cuba." New York, 1898.
   The commercial and industrial conditions in Cuba are a living and growing

topic of interest to Americans to-day, who recognize the possibilities of development for all the islands of the Greater Antilles.

Davey, R.—"Cuba, Past and Present." London, 1898.

Davis, R. H.—"The Cuban and Porto Rican Campaigns." New York, 1898.
Written in this author's well-known readable, narrative style.

Dinwiddie, Wm.—"Porto Rico, Its Conditions and Possibilities." New York, 1899.
Another study, from the material standpoint, of one of the greater islands of the archipelago.

Fiske, A. K.—"History of the Islands of the West Indian Archipelago." New York, 1899.

Flack, H. E.—"Spanish-American Diplomatic Relations Preceding the War of 1898." Baltimore, 1906.
One of the Johns Hopkins' publications and an important contribution to political history.

Froude, J. A.—"The English in the West Indies." London, 1888.

Hamm, M. A.—"Porto Rico and the West Indies." New York, 1899.

Hill, R. T.—"Cuba and Porto Rico with the other Islands of the West Indies." New York, 1898.

Hooper,—"The Forests of the West Indies." 1888.

Matthews, F.—"The New-Born Cuba." New York, 1899.

Musson, G. P., and Roxburgh, T. L.—"The Handbook of Jamaica." London, 1896.

Porter, R. P.—"Industrial Cuba." New York, 1899.

Pritchard, Hesketh.—"Where Black Rules White: A Journey Across and About Hayti." New York, 1900.
A good description of the present political and social conditions. The author believes the Haytians to be incapable of self-government.

Quisenberry, A. C.—"Lopez's Expeditions to Cuba, 1850, 1851." New York, 1906.
An interesting account of the Spanish-American general and filibuster.

Rainsford, Marcus.—"Historical Account of the Black Empire of Hayti, Comprising a View of the Principal Transactions in the Revolution of St. Domingo with its Antient and Modern State." London, 1805.
This is a valuable source for the beginnings of the Haytian republic. The appendix includes important documents of the revolution. The author visited the island in 1790.

"Report of the West India Royal Commission, 1897." 4 vols. London, 1897.

St. John, Sir Spenser.—"Hayti: or the Black Republic." London, 1884. New revised edition, New York, 1890.
A depressing picture of political and social degeneracy in Hayti, exposing the corruption and inefficiency of the government and the prevalence of voodooism, cannibalism and other barbaric vices. The author resided for many years in the country as the representative of the British government.

Tippenhauer, L. G.—"Die Insel Haïti." Leipzig, 1893.

INDEX

INDEX

A

Abascal, Marques de la Concordia: honored, 228

Acapulco: captured by the Dutch, 162; importance of, 192; siege of (1813), 244

Aculco: battle of (1810), 238

Agramont, Nicholas: captures Vera Cruz, 178

Aguayo, Marques San Miguel de: appointed governor of Florida and Texas, 189

Aguero y Velasco, Francisco: death of, 451

Aguilar, Marcos de: joins Cortéz, 13

Agustin I, Emperor of Mexico: see Iturbide

Aké: battle of (1527), 424

Alarcon, ——: founds Bejar, 189

Alarcon, Francisco: explorations of, 112

Alatorre: at the battle of Tecoac, 406

Albuquerque, Francisco Fernandez de la Cueva, Duke of: made viceroy of New Spain, 170; his administration as viceroy of New Spain, 186

Alegre, Manuel M.: sketch of, 420

Alexander, Barton S.: in the Mexican War, 349

Allende (San Miguel el Grande): founded, 117

Allende, Ignacio: in the rebellion of Hidalgo, 238

Almanza, Martin Enriquez de: his administration as viceroy of New Spain, 128; made viceroy of Peru, 131

Almonte, Juan Nepomuceno: member of provisional government, 387

Alvarado, Pedro de: returns to Cuba with report of Mexican discoveries, 5; joins Cortéz, 10; commands in the City of Mexico, 31; at the siege of Mexico, 52; his expeditions against the Zapotecs and against Guatemala, 66, 429; conquers Salvador, 439

Alvarez, Juan: elected president, 382

Alvear, Gaspar: crushes Indian insurrection, 152

Amozoque: battle of (1847), 327

Ampudia, Pedro de: his campaign against the United States, 284

Anaya, Pedro María: elected provisional president of Mexico, 320; elected president of Mexico, 374

Angostura: battle of (1847), 306

Anne, Queen of England: concludes treaty with Spain, 187

Anson, George: attempts to intercept Spanish treasure ship, 195

Apodaca, Juan Ruiz de, Conde del Venadito: his administration as viceroy, 251

Aponte, José Antonio: leads revolt, 451

Aranjo, Buenaventura: at the battle of Cerro Gordo, 325

Aréché, José: investigates the executive conduct of the Marques de Cruillas, 203

Arion, Baltasar de Zúñiga, Duke of: his administration as viceroy of New Spain, 188

Arizona: bought by the United States, 381

Armendariz, Miguel Diaz de: commissioned to enforce the aborigine laws in the West Indies, 110

Arrangoiz, General: concludes an armistice with General Scott, 352

Arroyo Hondo: massacre of (1847), 305

Arteaga: in the Reform War, 383

Atristain, Miguel: signs Treaty of Guadalupe Hidalgo, 377

Austin, Moses: contracts for colonization of Texas, 279

C

Q, R

S

V, W